CATHOLICISM

CATHOLICISM

VOLUME ONE

by Richard P. McBrien

WINSTON PRESS

Book design: Maria Mazzara·Schade

Except for citations within citations, all Scripture texts used in this work are taken from the *New American Bible*, copyright © 1970, by the Confraternity of Christian Doctrine, Washington, D.C. Used by permission of the copyright owner. All rights reserved.

Quotations from the documents of Vatican II are reprinted with permission of America Press, Inc., 106 W. 56 Street, New York NY 10019. © 1966. All rights reserved.

The chart entitled "Twentieth-Century Views on the Christology of the New Testament," which originally appeared in *Horizons* (vol. 1, 1974, p. 38), is reprinted with permission.

Library of Congress Catalog Card Number: 79-55963
ISBN (volume I): 0-03-056668-1
ISBN (volume II): 0-03-056906-0
ISBN (entire work): 0-03-056907-9

Printed in the United States of America

5 4 3 2

Winston Press, Inc., 430 Oak Grove, Minneapolis, MN 55403

CONTENTS

Volume One

PART TWO: GOD 179

Volume Two

PART FOUR: THE CHURCH 565

CONCLUSION 1167

PREFACE

This book is not written with the specialist in mind, although I should hope that specialists will find it useful. The reader of this book needs only two resources: intelligence, and a basic interest in Catholicism. A formal theological background is not needed, however helpful it might be. Accordingly, words and concepts whose meaning theologians take for granted are defined and explained. All topics are presented in a clearly organized, easy-to-follow pattern. Each problem is stated and explained in itself, in relation to other questions, and then in its full historical development, beginning with the Bible. Detailed summaries are provided after each chapter (indeed these might profitably be read *before* each chapter). The Table of Contents, the Glossary, and the double Index provide additional help.

Those who wish to go more deeply into the subject-matter of this book, however, can easily do so. The brief but meaty list of Suggested Readings at the end of each chapter provides further assistance, as does the following list of basic reference tools to which the serious reader should have access.

The Christian Faith in the Doctrinal Documents of the Catholic Church. Joseph Neuner and James Dupuis, eds. Westminster, Md.: Christian Classics, 1975.

Dictionary of the Bible. John L. McKenzie. Milwaukee: Bruce, 1965 (republished in paperback, New York: Macmillan, 1967).

The Documents of Vatican II. Walter Abbott and Joseph Gallagher, eds. New York: America Press, 1966.

Encyclopedia of Theology: The Concise Sacramentum Mundi. Karl Rahner, ed. New York: Seabury Press, 1975.

The New Catholic Encyclopedia. 17 vols. New York: McGraw-Hill, 1967—.

The Oxford Dictionary of the Christian Church. 2d ed. F. L. Cross and E. A. Livingston, eds. London: Oxford University Press, 1974.

WHY THIS BOOK?

This book is written out of the conviction that there is a pressing—I should like to say even urgent—need for it, or at least for some book very much like it. More than two decades have already passed since the election of Pope John XXIII in 1958. Four years later he convoked the Second Vatican Council, and everyone agrees that the Catholic Church has not been the same since. Catholicism has been torn by conflict between those who have embraced the new with a barely concealed indifference, if not contempt, toward the old, and those who have obstinately resisted change, so disillusioned were they with the apparent character and direction of change. Most other Catholics fell somewhere in the middle—distressed by the turmoil but uncertain of the Church's future course. Meanwhile, another generation has come along which has not been party to the debate at all. It is a generation which too often has looked in vain for those who can bridge the widening gap between the past and the present, the old and the new, the traditional and the contemporary. And therein lies the story, the driving force, and the purpose of this book.

I am convinced that healing and reconciliation are possible because there *is* a fundamental unity between the pre-Vatican II Church and the post-Vatican II Church, the many significant differences notwithstanding. I intend this book, therefore, as a bridge between the Church of yesterday and the Church of today, and between conservative, traditionally minded Catholics, on the one hand, and progressive, renewal-minded Catholics, on the other. A knowledge of history provides that bridge, and that is why this book adopts an historical method and approach. The more history we know the less likely we are to distort the reality of Catholicism by shaping it to our own predispositions and by trimming it to fit our own limited vision and range of experience.

I have in mind, for example, the attitude of those younger, progressive Catholics who, through no particular fault of their own, do not know very much about pre-Vatican II Catholicism. They suspect that Catholicism's past would somehow contradict its present course. And since they are satisfied with that present course—its ecumenical openness, its spirit of freedom, its concern for justice and human rights, its readiness to change—they prefer to let the past rest in peace, or at least to leave themselves in "good faith" about it.

I have in mind also the attitude of those older, progressive Catholics who once learned a detailed history of Catholicism but who now remember how narrowly conceived that history was. It was too often an account of consecutive institutional triumphs, of the vanquishing of patently absurd heresies, of relentless and remarkably smooth doctrinal movements from truth to greater truth. Events and theological developments surrounding Vatican II discredited that history in their eyes, and they have not seriously taken it up since.

I have in mind, too, the attitude of those more conservative Catholics, old and young, who are satisfied that they know that history well enough, and believe that the Church's present course is, at worst, a betrayal of Catholicism's past, or, at best, an unenlightened dilution of its genius and grandeur.

History is not fully honored by either the progressive or the conservative side, for history both *roots* and *relativizes*. Catholicism did not begin with Vatican II, nor was it set in theological and pastoral cement with the Council of Trent. When taken whole and unrevised, history teaches us that Christian faith and its Catholic expression have assumed many different forms. The tendency of the conservative is to freeze certain forms and equate them with the essence of Catholicism. A criticism of the form becomes an attack upon the Catholic faith itself. The tendency of the progressive is to keep every form so radically open to change that no abiding core or center can ever be discerned. The progressive tends to believe that there are no enduring Catholic principles by which to reappropriate old forms, modify existing forms, or construct new forms.

I have tried in this book to do justice to the true values and legitimate concerns of both sides: the conservative's regard for continuity and stability, and the progressive's regard for development and growth. History provides the major link between the two because it is a reality that is at once absolute and relative. It is *absolute*—and therefore a principle of *permanence*—because it comes from the creative hand of God, is sustained by the providential care of God, and is destined for fulfillment in the final Kingdom of God. But history is *relative*—and therefore a principle of *change*—because it is also the history of humankind, of an unprogramed interaction between grace and freedom.

Insofar as history is absolute and permanent, we have to come to terms with it. It is there. We cannot ignore it or erase it. It defines us. We are who we are because of it. We are historical beings, which means that we do not create ourselves anew, from ground zero, each day. We begin at a point we did not choose and in the midst of a process we did not originate.

On the other hand, history is also relative and changeable. It is even now in process. It is still to be. We are called to become something greater than we are. Tomorrow can be different from today or yesterday. We are to "fill the earth and subdue it" (Genesis 1:28).

CONTROVERSIAL THEOLOGY VERSUS CONSTRUCTIVE THEOLOGY

Finally, this book is not an exercise in *controversial* theology. I am not arguing a point of view peculiar to myself or to a small school of Catholic theologians. As far as possible, this is a work of *constructive* theology, one that tries to see the whole in terms of the interrelationship of all its parts, and the parts always in terms of their relationship to one another and to the whole. Accordingly, this is not only a book *about* Catholicism but a book written in the *spirit* of Catholicism as well, i.e., of openness to all truth wherever it is found. At least that has been my explicit intention from beginning to end. My deepest hope is that I have succeeded, however modestly, in that purpose.

October 1979   Richard P. McBrien

ACKNOWLEDGMENTS

Although this book was undertaken and completed without benefit of the usual foundation grants, academic sabbatical, or corps of graduate assistants, there are many people who have provided both encouragement and assistance. I wish I could identify each one here, but that is precluded by limitations of space. This book is already very large! I can acknowledge, therefore, only a representative sampling of the contributions which have helped to bring this project to what I hope is a successful conclusion.

J. Frank Devine, S. J., of the Weston School of Theology in Cambridge, Massachusetts, stands in the front rank. He was consistently generous not only with theological and editorial suggestions but with personal support born of long friendship. Frank read the entire manuscript as it was being written, and he was one of the very few persons who really appreciated from the beginning the scope, magnitude, and promise of this enterprise.

John Kirvan, an author, editor, and publisher in his own right, was the one who first invited me to do a book for Winston Press, but he got far more than he expected. John was an effective and often reassuring liaison between myself and the publishers. I am, of course, indebted also to the entire administrative, editorial, and promotional staff at Winston for their strong commitment to this book at every stage of development. A particular word of appreciation, however, goes to Cyril A. Reilly, who did such excellent editorial work.

Pope John XXIII National Seminary in Weston, Massachusetts, provided the facilities: a room to work in, a splendidly useful library, exceedingly helpful staff, and the warmest of hospitality. The rector, James W. DeAdder, and the entire faculty took an active interest in the book as it progressed through the academic year 1978-1979. I owe a special word of gratitude to Ann Kidney, assistant librarian. I shall never forget her readiness to drop everything to help me locate a book, an article, or just a fact. Her spirit and efficiency are a credit to the seminary librarian, James L. Fahey. Gerald Donovan was also a constant source of encouragement.

My colleagues at Boston College, both in the Institute of Religious Education and Pastoral Ministry which I directed and the department of Theology where I served as a Professor of Systematic Theology, provided yet another base of assistance and support. I would not have had the necessary time away from the regular routine of the Institute office had the staff not taken up the slack in commendably competent and cheerful fashion: Padraic O'Hare, associate director; James O'Neill, former administrative officer; Mary Boys, S.N.J.M., Thomas Groome, and Claire Lowery, R.S.C.J., faculty members; and Audrey Mudarri, secretary, who also typed the Glossary. But a very special word of thanks must go to my personal secretary of many happy years, Mildred Meyer, who typed about ninety-five percent of the book and, what is more remarkable, managed to keep all of my other activities, projects, and commitments in some measure of order.

Certain members of the department of Theology gave specific assistance: Robert Daly, S.J. (chairman), James Hennesey, S.J. (Church History), Frans Jozef van Beeck, S.J. (Christology), and, in substantial ways, James O'Donohoe (Moral Theology) and Philip King (Old Testament). Ernest Fortin, A.A., also maintained a welcome interest in the project.

Valuable assistance from theologians and other scholars outside of Boston College was forthcoming from John Connelly, of St. John Seminary, Brighton, Massachusetts, who was an important consultant for the theology of human existence and the philosophical distinctiveness of Catholicism, and J. Bryan Hehir, of the United States Catholic Conference, who supplied both material and advice in the area of social ethics. John T. Finnegan, past president of the Canon Law Society of America, provided important assistance in canonical matters, especially those related to the sacrament of Matrimony. I am also indebted to Dermot Lane, past president of the Irish Theological Association, for assistance in the area of Christology, and to Robert J. Wister, of the Archdiocese of Newark, for assistance in the area of Church history.

The book, of course, shows the influence of many other scholars who were not personally consulted but whose writings were of immense value: Karl Rahner, S.J., Avery Dulles, S.J., Raymond Brown, S.S., John L. McKenzie, Edward Schillebeeckx, O.P., Rudolf Schnackenburg, René Latourelle, S.J., Bernard Lonergan, S.J., Peter Berger, Andrew Greeley, and others whose books and articles are mentioned in the Suggested Readings at the end of each chapter.

Pastors, religious educators, and various persons involved in other pastoral ministries were also generous with their reactions and advice: especially Francis J. O'Keefe, pastor of St. Matthew's Church, Tolland, Connecticut, and Beverly Brazauskas, S.S.J., director of religious education at St. Matthew's; Peter Rosazza, auxiliary bishop of Hartford, Connecticut; James and Pauline Ludwig of Webster, Massachusetts; Carla Rutter, H.M., of Warren, Ohio, and Susan Jenkinson, R.S.M., of Providence, Rhode Island.

I am grateful to my friend James Flynn, C.S.S., provincial of the Stigmatine Fathers, Newton, Massachusetts, who read most of the manuscript as it was being written and gave me moral and material support, including the donation of his own secretary's services as a deadline approached. I, therefore, thank Ann Cincotta for her assistance.

Although I assumed responsibility for the preparation of both Indexes, I received technical advice from Richard O'Keeffe, of George Mason University, Fairfax, Virginia. Carol Klein and Mary Costea of Boston College did the typing.

Convention dictates that I insist that I must bear final responsibility for the book. I do so proudly. I have never enjoyed a project as much as I have enjoyed this one. I only hope it will make the kind of contribution to the Church and to theological and religious education which I have intended from the outset.

CATHOLICISM

INTRODUCTION

These first two chapters form an introductory unit to the whole book. Chapter 1 situates the book in its *ecclesiastical* context: What is the state of the Catholic Church today? How does the present crisis of Catholicism relate to previous crises in the Church's history? What choices are open to it as it looks toward the future? (A later chapter—Part I, chapter 3—will situate the book in its larger *human* context.)

Chapter 2 identifies and explains the ground rules for the whole study. If we are engaged here in an interpretation of faith, what does faith mean? What are its dimensions? Its characteristics? Its sources? Its effects? By what principles do we "interpret" that faith? Are there authoritative sources? If so, what makes those sources "authoritative"? What connection is there, if any, between the faith of an individual before God and the faith of a community, namely the Church? What role, if any, does the Church have in the clarification or even the definition of faith? To what extent is an individual member of the Church bound by those official interpretations?

Although other parts of the book—on God, on Jesus Christ, on the Church, and on Christian existence—will bear far more directly and more substantively on the content and practice of Catholic and Christian faith, no chapter will be so fundamental to the entire exploration of Catholicism as chapter 2.

· I ·

CATHOLICISM IN CRISIS

THE MEANING OF *CRISIS*

This chapter is about the present state of the Catholic Church. No matter what position one might take on various controversial issues facing Catholicism today, everyone would agree that the Catholic Church has changed significantly over the last few decades and especially since the Second Vatican Council (1962–1965). Many have described this process of change as a crisis. But do we correctly understand what a crisis is? What difference would it make if we did not?

To appreciate the importance of knowing precisely what a crisis is, it might be helpful to remind ourselves that language is not simply an instrument of communication. It also defines reality. But the definition is not always accurate, nor even just. Language, as a defining mechanism, can be and has been placed in the service of racism and sexism. An adult black man is addressed as "boy." Women are referred to as "girls." Language would make us all a race of "men" seeking "brotherhood" under the "fatherhood" of God. The social, cultural, political, and economic implications of such language have become increasingly apparent.

Words are rarely neutral. Sometimes their misuse is very serious, as in the cases cited above. Sometimes our errors evoke only amusement, not outrage, as television commentator Edwin Newman engagingly disclosed several years ago in his *Strictly Speaking: Will America Be the Death of English?* (Indianapolis: Bobbs-Merrill, 1974). And sometimes the effect falls somewhere in between, as in the case of our word *crisis.*

· 3 ·

The word *crisis* is frequently misused. For many it has a consistently negative ring. Thus, an international crisis may mean that hostile troops are massing on the border of some innocent country. Heads of state and other government officials are summoned to emergency meetings. Appeals for restraint and humaneness are heard from the United Nations, the Vatican, and whichever superpower happens to be allied with the threatened nation.

A medical crisis means that a patient is close to death. Teams of doctors, nurses, and aides are rushed to the bedside. The family is alerted and advised to expect the worst.

An economic crisis means an impending collapse of one of the world's major currencies or the bankruptcy of a key financial institution perceived to be essential to the well-being of a city, state, or country.

The crisis, of course, might be much less dramatic and much less severe in its effects. But in the popular mind the negative overtones remain, as in "We've got a crisis on our hands. They'll all be here in fifteen minutes and the coffee pot's just given out."

Because so many of us are conditioned to picture a crisis as bleak and forbidding, a threat not only to our personal comfort and convenience but to our survival as well, the title of this chapter might seem to suggest that the Catholic Church is at the brink of disintegration. It is a time for emergency meetings and transfusions. Meanwhile, theologians and sociologists have the unhappy task of notifying the family and preparing them for the worst.

The Catholic Church, and all of Christianity for that matter, *is* in crisis. It has been for at least two decades. But this is not to say that the present crisis is its first or, what is more significant, its last. Nor is it necessarily to impute some radical deficiency or failure somewhere along the line. A crisis can, to be sure, emerge from carelessness, imprudence, and/or incompetence. An indolent, overweight smoker may be largely responsible for the medical crisis generated by his massive heart attack. But a crisis may just as likely occur in the relatively normal course of human events, through a complicated confluence of historical, social, political, economic, cultural, demographic, intellectual, and biological factors. A crisis, therefore, may not be only a time for worry in the face of perceived peril, but a time for exhilaration in the face of perceived opportunity.

The word *crisis* belongs to a larger family of words: *critic, critical, criticism, criterion,* and the like. Each of these words is derived ultimately from the Greek verb *krinein,* which means "to separate" or "to decide." Accordingly, a "critic" is one who, like the Lord of the parable of the Sheep and the Goats in the twenty-fifth chapter of St. Matthew's Gospel, separates the worthy from the unworthy. In doing so he or she exercises a "critical" function and manifests "critical" skills, that is, the ability to discern real quality in the midst of mediocrity or sham. Such "criticism" is based on "criteria." A "criterion" is a standard, a means of judging, of discerning and separating good from bad.

It is within this modest network of terms that the word *crisis* fits. A crisis is, literally, a turning point, a moment or stage at which a process of whatever kind can go in two or more different directions. It is a time of separating out, of deciding (*krinein*). To be in crisis—whether political, medical, or indeed religious—is to be at the threshold of decisive change, usually, but not always, attended by considerable risk and suspense.

THE CHURCH IN CRISIS: YESTERDAY AND TODAY

Crisis is as much a part of human experience as birth, growth, and death. In fact, there can be no growth without crisis, as recent psychological explorations into the stages of human development by Jean Piaget, Erik Erikson, and Lawrence Kohlberg have shown. The findings of such researchers have, in turn, been applied to an understanding of Christian faith and its moral implications by Methodist theologian James Fowler and many Catholic religious educators whom he has influenced. Consequently, to acknowledge that the Catholic Church is in crisis is to say only that it has reached another turning point in its long two-thousand-year history. The Church is confronted with new opportunities for growth, new temptations to repress and regress. And this is the way it has always been. Only those without any sense of history at all assume that the Church is passing through its baptism of fire, its initiation into crisis. The fire of crisis was ignited in the foundational period of the New Testament and has been reignited many times since then. Only the height and fury of the flames have varied from crisis to crisis.

New Testament Crises

Two major turning points confronted the Church in its foundational stage. The *first* had to do with the scope of its mission. Was it to be a Church for the Jews alone, or for the Gentiles as well? And if the latter, were the Gentiles to be subject to the traditional laws and customs of Judaism? The *second* turning point, or crisis, had to do with the apparent delay of the Second Coming of Jesus Christ. Many had expected the end of this world and the inauguration of the new age to occur within their own lifetimes. Indeed, one of the principal controversies of modern New Testament scholarship has centered upon the expectations of Jesus himself. Did he expect the coming of the Kingdom within his own lifetime? Was he then compelled to revise his expectation and conclude that his own death was a precondition for the coming of the Kingdom? And if so, did his disciples share this assumption? Should the community of Christian faith prepare itself for a long historical life, replete with sacraments, doctrines, moral codes, and the like, or should it pursue a course similar to one adopted early in Thessalonia, of eschewing meaningful labor, abiding structures and institutions, and contenting itself instead with a period of passive waiting for the imminent end of the world (2 Thessalonians 3:6-15)?

The *first* crisis was resolved once and for all in the year 50 at the Council of Jerusalem (Acts of the Apostles 15:1-35). The mission to the Gentiles, already initiated at Antioch (Acts of the Apostles 11:19-26) and dramatized by Peter's Baptism of the Roman centurion Cornelius and several of his friends (Acts of the Apostles 10), was formally approved, with the remarkable, even revolutionary, stipulation that circumcision would not be required of converts to the faith (see chapter 18 for a fuller discussion of this important decision). As in the resolution of most crises in the history of the Church, the losing side was granted a face-saving concession. Certain Jewish laws would nonetheless have to be observed, such as the prohibition against eating meat with blood still in it or the meat of animals not killed according to Jewish ritual.

The *second* major crisis was not so decisively resolved, although the balance clearly shifted against those who preferred the Thessalonian option. The *parousia*, or Second Coming, could no longer be regarded as imminent. The Church would have to dig in, as it were, for the long course. It would have to be attentive to the building of a full and rich liturgical life as a way of keeping alive not only the memory of what God had accomplished in Jesus Christ but also the hope of future glory, "until he comes" (1 Corinthians 11:26). It would have to see to it that there were competent ministers to carry forward the pastoral work of the Apostles and other disciples, and creeds and codes to specify and clarify the demands of Christian existence in a world of competing possibilities and even of open hostility. (We shall, of course, examine these issues in greater detail in Part IV, on the Church.)

Some Post-biblical Crises

Similar turning points have marked the history of the Church just as surely as have the regular celebration of the Eucharist, the preaching of the Gospel, the administration of the sacraments, and the like.

Gnosticism

Gnosticism forced the New Testament Church to come to terms with its understanding of authority and its proper exercise. The Gnostics argued, among other things, that salvation comes through the possession of special knowledge (*gnosis*) and that such knowledge is available only to a select few by a process that is at once narrow and secret. Over against this view such major figures as St. John the Evangelist and St. Irenaeus (d. ca. 200) argued that salvation comes through the work of the incarnate Word of God and that the knowledge of this saving work is in principle available to everyone. They also argued that its meaning is attested to and confirmed by those special ministers of the Gospel (bishops, *episcopoi*) who are entrusted with the responsibility of preserving the continuity of faith with the apostolic tradition (*paradosis*).

The Edict of Constantine

The Edict of Constantine in 313 marked another major turning point in the Church's history. Throughout the third century the Roman government waged a severe and relentless campaign of repression and persecution against the Church. The relatively new religion was adjudged dangerous to the state because of Christianity's fundamental conviction that God's authority alone is absolute and that human authority is to be obeyed only when it is in conformity with God's. The Church's agony ended with the ascendancy of Constantine in 312; he attributed his final victory over Maxentius, his chief rival to the throne, to assistance from the Christian God. As a result, he agreed early the following year to grant complete religious toleration to Christians and even to restore all their property rights. Eventually, the new emperor pursued a vigorous campaign against pagan practices as Christianity became the official religion of the state. At the same time he lavished money and monuments upon the Church, including St. Peter's in Rome, constructed over the presumed site of Peter's grave. The clergy were accorded preferred status and were exempted from military service and forced labor. Roman law was modified to accommodate Christian values, and Sunday was established as a day of rest. Sexual offenses were punished, and more humane policies toward slaves, orphans, widows, and children were adopted.

The newly privileged condition of the Church carried with it, however, some exceedingly unsatisfactory implications. Civil authorities exploited the relationship for political purposes. Conversions to the faith often had as much to do with social status as with religious conviction. The clergy grew apart from the laity as class lines sharpened.

The Church had been faced with a decisive choice in 313, and it selected a particular course. Some have argued that it is still suffering the consequences.

Christological Controversies

The great Christological controversies of the fifth century presented a twofold crisis for the Church, the one doctrinal, the other jurisdictional. First, it was faced with widely divergent understandings of the humanity and divinity of Jesus Christ. How much diversity could the Church sustain without disrupting its bonds with the apostolic faith itself? Secondly, the Church was faced with concomitant challenges to the authority of its chief officer, the bishop of Rome and the successor of St. Peter in the primacy of authority. How much freedom from papal authority could it tolerate without disrupting the bonds of Christian unity? We shall be returning to these issues in Part III, on Christ, but for the moment it is sufficient to note that the dual crisis *was* resolved at the Council of Chalcedon in 451: Jesus is one divine person with two unconfused and unmixed natures, the one human and the other divine. That formula has held ever since—an extraordinary achievement indeed. And the papacy, in the person of Pope Leo the Great (d. 461), enhanced its prerogatives and prestige. But as in the resolution of other crises, negative forces were also set loose. Tensions between Rome and Constantinople were to intensify, and a major schism between West and East would be sealed by the beginning of the thirteenth century. That schism perdures even to this day, the remarkable improvement in ecumenical relations notwithstanding.

Aristotelianism

The emergence of Aristotelianism in the twelfth and thirteenth centuries presented the Church with yet another crisis, this time of an exclusively intellectual nature. Should the Church expose its historic faith to the rational speculations of a pagan philosopher? Its initial response was characteristically guarded. A temporary ban was imposed in 1215, but by the middle of the century the study of Aristotle (d. 322 B.C.) was widely accepted and pursued. St.

Albert the Great (d. 1280) and St. Thomas Aquinas (d. 1274) were his two principal disciples. Although his achievement has been celebrated generously by popes and bishops alike since then, Aquinas was attacked in his own day as a dangerous innovator and a rationalist. Over against his approach were ranged such imposing figures as St. Bonaventure (d. 1274), John Duns Scotus (d. 1308), and William of Ockham (d. 1347). The tension between those emphasizing reason and the intellect, as Aquinas did, and those stressing the will, as Bonaventure did, has continued to the present day. Yet another important crisis was faced but never fully resolved.

Conciliarism; Protestant Reformation

Conciliarism in the fifteenth century and the Protestant Reformation of the sixteenth century posed two separate, but obviously closely related, crises for the Church. Although there were several different theological issues at stake in the Reformation, the common thread running through both the Conciliar and Protestant movements was the question of, and challenge to, ecclesiastical authority, and specifically the authority of the pope. The first challenge was at least temporarily resolved: Conciliarism was overcome and the unity of the Church preserved. The story of the Reformation, of course, is more familiar. It would not have so organizationally tranquil an ending. How much reform in head and members, in creed and code, in liturgy and devotion, could the Church endure without breaking faith with the apostolic community? How much freedom of conscience and of action could the authorities of the Church, and the pope in particular, allow without compromising or even abdicating responsibility for the integrity of faith and morals? These were the kinds of questions that constituted the crisis, or turning point, which immediately preceded the Protestant Reformation. Did the Church separate out the choices intelligently? Did it make the right choices? Did it follow the correct course? Was the Catholic Counter-Reformation too little, too late? Or indeed did it only make matters worse?

The Enlightenment; Catholic Modernism

Perhaps no crisis in the entire post-biblical history of the Church has proved more significant than the crisis precipitated by *the Enlightenment* of the seventeenth and eighteenth centuries. In essence, this was a philosophical movement which progressively rejected extrinsic authority in the determination of truth in favor of the authority of reason. One accepts something as true not because some officeholder in the Church says it is true but because there are good and sound reasons for believing it to be true. And, of course, the reverse is also the case. What cannot be established clearly by reason can make no claim upon our belief. The necessary condition for the exercise of reason is freedom. The Enlightenment, therefore, sounded a call for freedom of inquiry, freedom of decision, and freedom of action. Left to himself or herself, without the artificial constraints of religion and supernatural principles, the human person could reach the fullest extent of his or her potential.

How would the Church respond to the new challenge of modernity? Could it simply hold fast to its traditional values and convictions? Could it pretend to ignore the findings of science? Would an appeal to the sacred texts, whether of the Bible or of the ecumenical councils or of the popes, provide a persuasive rebuttal to the arguments advanced by reason and empirical observation? As often before, the Church's initial response was negative and strongly condemnatory. That spirit is unmistakably operative in the official pronouncements of such figures as Pope Gregory XVI (d. 1846) and Pope Pius IX (d. 1878), who ruled the Church for the greater part of the nineteenth century (1831-1878), and particularly in the latter's *Syllabus of Errors* (1864). The decisive rejection of modernity by these two popes notwithstanding, the issues continued to fester under the surface, breaking out for a time in the early part of the twentieth century in the form of *Catholic Modernism*, sharply condemned by yet another pope, St. Pius X, in 1907. It reemerged in other forms in the late 1930s and into the 1940s, where again it suffered condemnation by Pope Pius XII (d. 1958) in his encyclical letter *Humani Generis* (1950) before enjoying some measure of official acceptance at the Second Vatican Council (1962-1965).

The Present Crisis

Symptoms

It seems reasonably simple to sketch the contours of Catholicism's present crisis because it has been part of our personal experience for nearly two decades and is still with us. But we should be restrained in our confidence. As the history of the Church amply demonstrates, important crises are slow in developing and sometimes just as slow in being resolved. Even after the crises have been resolved, the longer-term implications cannot be assessed until decades or centuries have passed.

Nevertheless, the symptoms of this present crisis do seem clear enough: the sharp decline in Mass attendance and in vocations to the priesthood and the religious life; the higher incidence of divorce and remarriage; the widening of theological dissent; diversity and pluralism to the point of confusion and doubt in theology, catechetics, and religious education generally; the rejection of papal authority in the matter of birth control, and resistance to that authority on other issues such as the ordination of women and priestly celibacy; the ecumenical movement's challenge to Catholic identity and distinctiveness; the alienation of young people from the Church; the abiding social and cultural dominance of science and technology, with its correlative impact upon traditional spiritual values and motivation; the continuing and inevitable involvement of the Church on both sides of the historic struggle between rich and poor, oppressor and oppressed; the raised consciousness of women in the Church.

Remote Causes

The remote causes of the present crisis are theological and philosophical. We are wrestling anew with age-old questions which have since been filtered through, and therefore transformed by, the Enlightenment and post-Enlightenment movements: What does it mean to be human? Is there really more to life than meets the eye? Is the answer knowable, in any case? Is there, in other words, an ultimate or transcendental dimension to secular experience, and is it available through reason alone, through faith alone, or through "reason illumined by faith" (Vatican I)? Is there any person or story which focuses this ultimate meaning for us? If so, what impact does such a person or story have upon our consciousness and our moral behavior? At what point and under what circumstances is such impact made?

Before Immanuel Kant (d. 1804) and the Enlightenment, the questions were usually answered straightforwardly and with much assurance. The answers, it was asserted, are available in the sacred texts (Bible and doctrinal compendia alike) and, what is more significant, in the living voice of the Church expressed in the office of pope and bishops (the latter completely dependent upon the former). Such a view, it must be acknowledged, is not without support in the Church today. For many traditional Catholics, the Enlightenment simply never happened.

On the other hand, there are progressively oriented Catholics who, since the Enlightenment, act as if the post-Enlightenment had never happened, as if reason and freedom reign together in unchallenged dual supremacy. But there are social, political, cultural, and even economic forces which compromise our precious intellectual objectivity, and there are profound and often hidden psychic forces which substantially modify, and even sharply diminish, our equally cherished personal freedom. This is not to say, of course, that reason now yields to socially determined forces and that freedom yields to psychically determined forces, but only that neither reason nor freedom can be celebrated uncritically, almost blindly, in ironic denial of the Enlightenment's own highest principles.

Proximate Causes

There is some difference of opinion regarding the proximate causes of the present crisis. Sociologist Andrew M. Greeley assigns principal blame to Pope Paul VI's encyclical on birth control, *Humanae Vitae* (1968). On the basis of scientific research, he concludes that American Catholicism "has suffered a severe trauma brought on not by 'enlightenment' or secularization or acculturation or even by the revolt against authoritarianism. The

disaster for American Catholicism was the result of a single decision made because of the decrepit and archaic institutional structure of the church, a structure in which effective upward
communication practically does not exist" (*The American Catholic*, pp. 126-151).

Others like political commentator Garry Wills, novelist Wil-
frid Sheed, and social scientist Daniel Callahan—Catholics
all—have argued that Catholicism just could not survive the twin
modernizing pressures of the Second Vatican Council and the
acculturation of the immigrants. They maintain that as Catholics
became better educated, they began thinking for themselves, and
then the council came along and destroyed what remained of the
old Catholic culture.

A third explanation has been advanced by Protestant theologian Langdon Gilkey. The causes of the present crisis go deeper
than either the acculturation or the encyclical hypotheses.
Neither development would have had the effects they had upon
Catholicism if something more basic had not already occurred at a
more profound level of Catholic consciousness. It is the "dissolution of (the) understanding of the supernatural as the central
religious category" (*Catholicism Confronts Modernity*, p. 52).

"In the span of a generation," Gilkey notes, "the absolute
authority of the church regarding truth, law, and rules of life, has
suddenly vanished. . . . The collapse of this authority has not
occurred because certain church doctrines, papal decrees, bishops'
rulings and so on were at last found to be in error, or . . . obviously
'wrong' or 'old-fashioned' in relation to the modern mind" (pp.
52–53). Such explanations, he maintains, miss the heart of the
issue and fail to get at the deeper source of the present crisis,
which is the loss of the traditional Catholic sense of the supernatural. Catholics feel free to reject official Church teachings not
simply because they perceive them to be in error but because they
no longer perceive them to be propounded with the authority of
God. There has been, in Gilkey's terms, a "geological shift" in
values, away from the supernatural and to the natural, and he
calls this a modernizing of the Catholic mind.

One can readily perceive value in all three attempts to identify the proximate causes of the present crisis. There has been an

acculturation process at work—at the levels of education, socialization, occupation, and the like—which has had some effect on
contemporary Catholic consciousness and behavior. And some
data seem to support the Greeley hypothesis regarding the devas-
tatingly negative effect of the birth-control encyclical. But would
either of these factors actually have provoked a crisis of this
apparent magnitude if there had not also occurred what Gilkey
has called a "geological shift" in values, a new perception of the
meaning of the supernatural order and a new appreciation for the
human and natural order?

If "the collapse of the supernaturalistic forms of Catholicism. . . is the key to understanding both the effect of modernity on
traditional Catholicism and the current crisis in Catholic life. . .,
(then) the task for twentieth-century Catholicism calls for the
reinterpretation of the transcendent, the sacred, and the
divine—the presence of God to men—into worldly or naturalistic
forms of modern experience rather than in the supernaturalistic
forms of Hellenic and medieval experience" (pp. 58-59). Among
the symbols to be reinterpreted, says Gilkey, are God, revelation,
authority, salvation, law, and hope for the future. The reinterpretation must be done in such a way that the historic Catholic values
of community, tradition, grace, and sacrament are not only preserved but given powerful new expression "so that a new birth can
take place. For on the creative resolution of this contemporary
challenge to Catholicism depends the health of the whole church
in the immediate future" (p. 60).

THE PRESENT CRISIS AND THIS BOOK

The crisis facing Roman Catholicism today has largely shaped this
book's purpose, method, and organization and has helped to give
the book its distinctive qualities.

Purpose

The *principal purpose* of this book is, at the same time, its principal challenge: to identify, explain, and explore the traditional
doctrinal, moral, ritual, and structural symbols and components of

Catholicism without prejudice to the twin values italicized, but not patented, by the Enlightenment, namely, freedom of inquiry and freedom of decision. Or, conversely, its purpose is to encourage and assist Catholics and others to explore, understand, and exercise their faith in freedom without prejudice to our abiding responsiblity to reconcile our understanding, our judgments, and our decisions with the theological criteria embodied in Sacred Scripture, the writings of the great Fathers and doctors of the Church, the official teachings of the ecumenical councils and the popes, the liturgy, and the *sensus fidelium*, or "consensus of the faithful" maintained through the centuries, everywhere and at every time.

The Catholic faith, and the Catholic tradition by which that faith is transmitted from generation to generation, is a given. That is, it is a reality which existed before us and exists apart from us. Catholicism is not created anew, from the start, in every decade. It is there already as an historical fact. It is a reality to be known and assimilated.

But that faith, and the tradition by which it is communicated, is not static or lifeless. In a sense, it *does* have to be rediscovered and reappropriated in every succeeding generation. The Gospel means, after all, "good news." It is the Gospel not only because it is "good" but also because it is "news."

This book will serve its primary purpose, therefore, if it provides those who do not know the tradition well with a comprehensive view and grasp of that tradition; and, secondly, if it persuades those others who *do* know the tradition that the task of appropriation and assimilation is never finished, that the tradition is best preserved, not by repetition and routine, but by freshly rethinking and reapplying it in every new age and circumstance, and indeed in the face of every new crisis of growth or decline.

Method

The method is, therefore, at once traditional and contemporary. It is *traditional* in that the presentation considers every major element of Christian and Catholic faith from the point of view of its place in Sacred Scripture, in the written reflections of the great Fathers and doctors of the Church, the official declarations of the councils and popes, and the living interpretation of the community itself as embodied in the community's worship, devotional practices, and moral action. The method is *contemporary*, on the other hand, in that it proceeds inductively rather than deductively. It begins not from the given of the sacred texts, whether of the Bible or of doctrine, but from the given of human existence and of present Christian experience. However, the deductive is certainly not excluded. Biblical, patristic, and doctrinal sources remain always at the core of each theological argument and conclusion.

Organization

Although the book is about the content and moral implications of Christian and Catholic faith, it insists that one cannot understand the meaning and demands of Christian existence (Part V) unless one also understands the nature and mission of the Church itself (Part IV). And one cannot understand the nature and mission of the Church unless one also understands the person and ministry of Jesus Christ (Part III), whose Body the Church is. And one cannot understand the person and ministry of Jesus Christ unless one also understands, or at least begins to understand, what we mean by "God," whose Son and agent Jesus claimed to be (Part II). And, finally, one cannot understand the reality of God unless one also understands what it means to be human, for God is perceived as the source of humankind's perfection, the ultimate fulfillment of human potential (Part I). To say, in other words, that something enhances our humanity while something else diminishes it is to make a judgment in the light of certain explicit or implicit criteria. The construction of such criteria is a work not only of philosophy, sociology, psychology, or anthropology. At its deepest level, the task is theological. (In the next chapter we shall define what we mean by theology, indicating how it relates to other intellectual disciplines in their common pursuit of truth.) To propose the final meaning of human existence is to propose a "doctrine" of God. In the end, anthropology and theology converge.

Distinctiveness

It goes without saying that this is not the first attempt, nor will it be the last, at constructing a comprehensive theological statement about Catholic faith and practice. We have witnessed in recent years the reemergence of the catechism as an expression of theological synthesis and as an instrument of religious education: the so-called "German Catechism," with its emphasis on the glories and joys of being a Christian (*A Catholic Catechism*, New York: Herder and Herder, 1957); the so-called "Dutch Catechism," with its existentialist starting-point and its narrative, rather than question-and-answer format (*A New Catechism*, New York: Herder and Herder, 1967, rev. ed., 1969); *The Common Catechism*, the first ecumenical effort (involving German Catholics and Protestants) to range over the entire terrain of Christian belief and life (New York: Seabury Press, 1975); *An American Catholic Catechism*, a collaborative enterprise by North American Catholic theologians, originally written for a theological journal for clergy, *Chicago Studies*, and drafted in question-and-answer form (New York: Seabury Press, 1975); John A. Hardon's *The Catholic Catechism*, which follows the basic structure of the old *Baltimore Catechism*—creed, commandments, sacraments—and some measure of its theological orientation as well (New York: Doubleday, 1975); and another corporate effort, this time by theologians and non-theologians alike, entitled *The Teaching of Christ*, but with an immediate emphasis on the teaching of the Church's hierarchy (Huntington, Ind.: Our Sunday Visitor Press, 1976).

This book is not a catechism, although in structure and content it may appear similar to one. A catechism, as Father Hardon himself acknowledges, "makes no claim to explain what it contains, except insofar as words need clarification or the terms that are often technical need to be simplified. . . . It presumes that what is here described is already believed. . ."(pp. 24-25). (For a fuller discussion of the relationship between theology and catechesis, see the next chapter.)

But neither is this book a personal theological brief, as is, for example, Karl Rahner's imposing *Foundations of Christian Faith* (New York: Seabury Press, 1978). It is intended, as the Preface pointed out, for the intellectual enrichment of anyone who is seriously interested in studying the treasures of the Catholic theological tradition. But its contents, language, and organization make it easily usable at the university and college levels, for adult education and inquiry classes, for the continuing education of clergy, religious, and all ecclesiastical ministers, ordained and non-ordained alike, for very advanced high school groups. The book does not seek to present and argue a point of view peculiar to the author or to a relatively limited, even marginal, school of theological opinion. As far as possible, every representative position on each major doctrinal question will be identified, explained, and compared with other pertinent positions. If a theological consensus has been reached, it will enjoy the benefit of the doubt.

The final product, therefore, is slightly more akin to Anglican theologian John Macquarrie's *Principles of Christian Theology* (New York: Charles Scribner's Sons, 1977, 2nd ed.) than to Catholic theologian Hans Küng's *On Being a Christian* (New York: Doubleday, 1976). The latter work, although comprehensive and systematic, advances a particular Christological point of view (one difficult to describe as yet as a consensus position) and in a style that is often exhortatory, albeit sometimes eloquently so. Macquarrie's work, on the other hand, deliberately seeks a balance between what Macquarrie calls the existentialist and the ontological approaches to Christian theology: the one emphasizing the personal and the subjective, the other emphasizing the essential and the objective. But Macquarries's leaning is clearly toward existentialism, in the tradition of Martin Heidegger (d. 1976).

Unlike Macquarrie's book, however, the present work depends completely on no single philosophical world view. And it is written with a more explicit sense of responsiblity to the Church of the past and to the specific biblical, theological, doctrinal, and pastoral emphases which have always characterized the Catholic tradition.

This book, then, has been written in the midst of yet another major crisis in the history of Roman Catholicism and as a response to that crisis. It has been written with the conviction that at such turning points as these the Church needs to be in touch with its own roots, needs to see with clear, unbiased vision the whole sweep of Catholic tradition, needs to see the interrelationships among all the elements of its doctrine and practice. Only by understanding its own past can it understand what it is now. Then, and only then, can it press forward with confidence and hope.

SUMMARY

1. The word *crisis*, frequently misused, means a *turning point*. The Catholic Church is "in crisis" today in that it finds itself at yet another turning point, where it is called upon "to decide" (*krinein*) upon the direction it will take for the future.

2. As history shows, a crisis is an opportunity for growth at least as often as it is a prelude to decline or even disaster.

3. The Church faced crises from the very beginning. In the *New Testament* alone we discover such major crises or turning points as the controversy over extending the mission to the Gentiles without requiring them to accept the complete Jewish law, and the state of perplexity created by the apparent delay of the Second Coming of Christ.

4. *Post-biblical crises* have had to do with the interpretation of revelation (Gnosticism), the political standing of the Church (the Edict of Constantine), the content of faith (the Christological controversies), the legitimate activities of theology (the emergence of Aristotelianism), the meaning and exercise of authority (Conciliarism and the Protestant Reformation), and the perception and appropriation of truth itself (the Enlightenment and Modernism).

5. *Today's crisis* is better known by its symptoms than in its causes, whether proximate or remote. Its *symptoms* are clear: declining Mass attendance, decrease in vocations to the priesthood and religious life, alienation of the young, resistance to the teaching authority of the pope and bishops, and so forth. Its *causes* are somewhat less obvious: cultural changes, the encyclical on birth control, the "geological shift" away from traditional notions of the supernatural order.

6. In light of the present crisis, this book has a twofold purpose: to disclose the Catholic tradition (its doctrines, its rituals, its institutions, its spirituality) to those who do not know it sufficiently well, but to expound it in a way that is consistent with the theological and doctrinal developments of recent decades.

7. Although the book is about the content and moral implications of Christian and Catholic faith, it recognizes that one cannot understand the meaning of Christian existence apart from an understanding of the

mystery of the Church, and the Church apart from an understanding of Jesus Christ, and Christ apart from an understanding of God, and God apart from an understanding of what it means to be human.

8.   The book is neither a catechism, designed principally for new or potential members of the Church, nor a personal theological brief, arguing a particular point of view which as yet has failed to achieve a consensus within the Church. It is rather an exposition of the Catholic tradition that is at once conservative and critical, looking at the same time to the past and to the future, hoping all the while that the present is thereby faithfully served.

SUGGESTED READINGS

Bokenkotter, Thomas. *A Concise History of the Catholic Church*. Rev. ed. New York: Doubleday, 1979.

Dolan, John P. *Catholicism: An Historical Survey*. Woodbury, New York: Barron's Educational Series, 1968.

Gilkey, Langdon. *Catholicism Confronts Modernity: A Protestant View*. New York: Seabury Press, 1975, chapter 1.

Greeley, Andrew. *The American Catholic: A Social Portrait*. New York: Basic Books, 1977.

Marty, Martin. *A Short History of Christianity*. New York: New American Library, Meridian, 1959.

· II ·

FAITH, THEOLOGY, AND BELIEF

THE PROBLEM

If the Catholic Church is in crisis today, it can be explained, at least in part, by the persistent failure of many Catholics to discern and understand the differences among *faith*, *theology*, and *belief*. Some bishops, pastors, and educational administrators assure nervous audiences of parents that the task of the religious educator is not to teach the latest views of modern theologians but to teach "the faith." Although there is some truth to this assertion, beneath it often lies the assumption that faith is available in some non-theological state—that it is possible, in other words, to isolate the former from the latter as one might separate two chemicals in a laboratory experiment. It is the burden of this chapter to show why this is not the case.

What we are examining here are the ground rules for thinking, speaking, writing, preaching, and teaching about God, about Jesus Christ, and about the supernatural order in general. What is the source of our knowledge of such realities? What principles govern our interpretation and communication of that knowledge? How do we know if our interpretations are accurate? Are there protective and/or corrective devices by which to recognize and to overcome error and distortion?

This chapter, therefore, is about faith, theology, and belief. It is also about the many expressions of belief: Sacred Scripture, doctrines and dogmas, and the liturgy. And, finally, it is about the process by which such beliefs are critically assimilated and transmitted to others: religious education and its several forms, such as catechesis, the teaching of theology, and Christian *praxis*. Each of these topics will be defined, explained, and interrelated in logical sequence. For many readers, this may be the most practical, perhaps even the most important, chapter in the entire book.

ELEMENTS OF THE PROBLEM
Faith

How do we come to the knowledge of God, of Jesus Christ, of salvation, of the Holy Spirit, or of any other religious or supernatural reality? Is it by empirically and scientifically verifiable methods alone, or is such knowledge also derived from some other level of experience?

A crucial distinction is immediately in order. Our knowledge of God, Christ, salvation, or similar topics, may be the knowledge of an uninvolved, dispassionate observer such as a sociologist, an anthropologist, or a psychologist, or it may be the knowledge of a highly involved, committed believer in God, Christ, salvation, and related realities.

An atheistic sociologist could spend a lifetime examining the effects of theism on the institutions and cultural expressions of a given national or ethnic group. He or she may produce hundreds of articles and several books which carefully examine the control-group's belief system. He or she may indeed become an expert on the meaning of God, *as perceived by* this particular community of believers. But those are the key words: "as perceived by." We are not speaking here of the sociologist's own knowledge of God, but of his or her knowledge of other people's knowledge of God. So it is possible for someone to know much *about* God, Christ, the Holy Spirit, grace, and redemption, without at the same time *believing in* any one of these realities.

On the other hand, there are people (presumably most of those using this book) who are convinced that they know at least something about God because of God's own self-disclosure through Christ, the prophets, the Apostles, the Church, the created order, and even direct mystical experience. Without doubt, it is *this* kind of knowledge, not that of the sociologist, which is at the heart of our problem. "No one," the author of the Fourth Gospel reminded us, "has ever seen God" (John 1:18).

A believer's knowledge of God is of a necessarily different order from that of the uncommitted observer. The believer's knowledge does not originate in laboratory tests, scientific observation, nor computer technology. And it certainly does not originate in common sense or everyday human experiences. Insofar as a believer insists that he or she knows something about God, that knowledge is attributed, in one way or another, to faith.

For the moment, it is enough to say that *faith is personal knowledge of God.* (*Christian* faith, therefore, is personal knowledge of God *in Christ.*) But already we can see that our emphasis is on the personal rather than on the cognitive or the propositional. Faith is not primarily belief in truths (propositions) which have been revealed to us by God through the Bible and the Church; rather, it is the way we come to the knowledge of God as God. The object of faith, in other words, is not a doctrine or a sacred text, but God, our Creator, Judge, and Savior.

We might also usefully distinguish "faith" from "the faith." The latter expression refers to the whole composite of beliefs held by Christians in general or by Catholics in particular. That expression is closer to what we mean by "doctrines" (see below) than it is to what we have been saying about "faith" itself.

Theology

Faith is personal knowledge of God. It is our perception of God in the midst of life. Unalloyed faith does not exist. Nowhere can we discover and isolate "pure faith." Real faith, living faith, if you will, exists always and only in a cognitive, (more or less) reflective, (more or less) scientific state. Every thought about the meaning of faith is precisely that: a thought about the meaning of faith. Every word of interpretation designed to articulate and illuminate the meaning and implications of faith is again precisely that: a word of interpretation, not faith itself. When some Catholics warn against the contamination of "the faith" by theology, they reveal a fundamental confusion about the relationship between faith and theology.

Faith is not theology, to be sure, but neither does faith exist apart from, or independently of, theology. Theology comes into play at that very moment when the person of faith becomes intellectually conscious of his or her faith. From the very beginning, faith exists in a theologically interpreted state. Indeed, it is a redundancy to put it that way: "theologically interpreted." For the interpretation of one's faith is theology itself.

Theology is, as St. Anselm of Canterbury (d. 1109) defined it nine centuries ago, "faith seeking understanding" (*fides quaerens intellectum*). More specifically, *theology is that process by which we bring our knowledge and understanding of God to the level of expression.* Theology is the articulation, in a more or less systematic manner, of the experience of God within human experience.

Theology, in the broad sense of the word, may emerge in many forms: a painting, a piece of music, a dance, a cathedral, a bodily posture, or, in its more recognizable form, in spoken or written words. These forms, of course, never do justice to the perception which they hope to express. Not all theology is good theology. We can ineptly or incorrectly translate our experience or knowledge of God. We might even have a thoroughly distorted or false experience of God in the first place, which no form, however cleverly constructed, can ever redeem.

When all is said and done, religious educators, bishops, preachers, parents, and the Church at large do not transmit or hand on faith apart from theology. They hand on faith in and through the theology they are using. In other words, they transmit particular interpretations or understandings of faith in their various and multiple forms. It is entirely beside the point, therefore, to warn religious educators against teaching theology instead of handing on the faith. *Faith exists always and only in some theological form.* The question before the Church today and in every age is not *whether* that faith will be transmitted according to some theological interpretation, but rather *which* theological interpretation is best suited to the task at a particular moment.

What is so unacceptable about appeals to "the faith" over against the "private views of theologians" is that a particular theology is implicitly equated with faith itself. Consequently, any criticism of that theology is automatically perceived as an undermining of faith. In effect, what is proposed is that "the faith," which must not be confined and corrupted by *any* theology, can only be understood properly in terms of *one* theology, often the neo-scholastic theology popular in Catholic colleges and seminaries just prior to the Second Vatican Council.

Belief

If theology is faith brought to the level of self-consciousness, then belief is theology in a kind of snapshot or frozen state. Theology is a *process*: belief is one of its several *products*. In the general sense of the word, a belief is something accepted as true even in the absence of clear and convincing evidence. In the theological sense of the word, *a belief is a formulation of the knowledge we have of God through faith.*

Belief has many forms. At the one end of the spectrum, these beliefs are widely shared and officially approved (doctrines, dogmas). At the other end, they are held by select groups or individuals and are not officially proposed for universal acceptance (for example, the presumed appearances of the Blessed Mother at Fatima and Lourdes).

There are many Christian beliefs, even though there is only one Christian faith. Christian faith, as defined above, is knowledge of God in Christ, who is the key and focal point of all human experience. Over the centuries of Christian history there have been literally thousands of beliefs held and transmitted at one time or another—i.e., interpretations of faith which significant segments of the Christian community have found useful for expressing and articulating their own knowledge of God in Christ. Some of these beliefs endured the test of time (e.g., the great Christological dogmas), while others have receded beyond the range of vision or even of collective memory (e.g., the Two Swords theory of papal authority, proposed in the Middle Ages).

What has been true in Christian history is true also in the
contemporary Church. Hundreds of different beliefs vie with one
another for attention and acceptance. Some of these beliefs are
grounded firmly and deeply in the tradition of the Church, e.g.,
belief in the Real Presence of Christ in the Eucharist, while others
have shorter and/or more tender roots, e.g., belief in the infallibility of the pope. The sorting-out process, however, is never finished.
We are faced constantly with the problem of evaluating and
reevaluating our beliefs in the light of our ongoing experience and
of our subsequent theological interpretations of that experience.
These, in turn, are judged against that "instinct of faith" which
somehow gives the whole Church its inner coherence and its
radical identity and continuity in the midst of change. It is at the
point of the "somehow" in the preceding sentence that our rich
poetry about the Holy Spirit inserts itself.

At key historical moments in that sorting-out process
(moments of "crisis," as we saw in chapter 1), the Church, acting
through members set apart by the inspiration of God, by theological competence, and/or by episcopal ordination, is compelled to
make decisions and to bring those decisions to the level of formal
expression. These expressions may take different forms: letters,
liturgical documents, narratives, and theological reflections
which the Church itself recognizes to be fundamental, normative,
constitutive expressions of its faith (*Sacred Scripture*); official
teachings based on Sacred Scripture and the ongoing experience of
the Church (*doctrines*); official teachings proposed with such
solemnity that their rejection is tantamount to *heresy*, which is a
denial of some truth of faith deemed by the teaching Church to be
essential to that faith (*dogmas*); or officially approved and/or mandated cultic acts and sacramental celebrations through which the
community ritualizes in word and action what it believes in the
depths of its heart and consciousness (*liturgy*). Indeed, there is a
Latin axiom, "*Lex orandi, lex credendi*," which means literally
that the law of praying is the law of believing. We express our
belief in our worship.

In stop-action language: Theology ("faith seeking understanding") follows faith, and belief follows theology. In fact, however, faith and theology do not really exist apart from one another,

whereas belief and theology can and do exist apart. The theologian can express all sorts of judgments about the reality of God as he or she presumably experiences God, without at the same time resorting to formulae or propositions which have already attracted wider attention and acceptance, whether officially (as in the case of a doctrine) or unofficially (as in the case of a belief about the healing effects of Lourdes water).

Religious Education

Although religious education has more to do with communication than it does with speculation, it would be a grave oversimplification to suggest that religious education is merely the delivery system for a faith-community's beliefs. Religious education is more than the process of communicating what has been grasped by theology and officially adopted by the Church. The religious educator is at once theologian and educator, for *the field of religious education is located at the point where theology/belief and education intersect.* On the one hand, the religious educator must himself or herself critically investigate and understand what is to be communicated and, on the other hand, must attend to the methods, context, and effects of the communicative process.

The aim of religious education is to help people discern, respond to, and be transformed by the presence of God in their lives, and to work for the continuing transformation of the world in the light of this perception of God. *Christian* religious education focuses on Jesus Christ as the great sign or sacrament of God's presence in human history and, more specifically, in the Church which is the People of God and the Body of Christ. Christian religious education, or simply "Christian education," is concerned, therefore, not only with the transformation of the individual and of the world in the light of Christ, but with the transformation of the Church, which is the primary context for our experience of God as Creator, as Redeemer, and as Reconciler.

Just as there are many different forms of belief, so there are several different forms of religious education or of Christian education. Religious education, first of all, is as divisible as religion itself. There are at least as many different kinds of religious education as there are religions. Christian education, too, can be divided along denominational lines: Lutheran education, Baptist education, Catholic education, etc. And Christian education can also be divided according to specific purposes. *Catechesis*, for example, introduces the new or potential member of the Church, whether a child or an adult, to the whole of the Christian proclamation. The purpose of catechesis is, as the Greek word from which it is derived suggests, the "echoing" of the Christian Gospel in a way that is at once pastoral and systematic. Catechesis, therefore, is not the same as *preaching*, which is yet another form of religious or Christian education. Catechesis is systematic in intent and method (whether it employs the question-and-answer format or not). Preaching is not. Catechesis seeks to echo the Christian message in a way that provides the new or potential member of the Church with a sense of the interrelatedness of Christian mysteries or doctrines and of their relative centrality and importance. All catechists and preachers, however, are Christian educators, but not all Christian educators are catechists and preachers.

Much the same can be said of still other forms of religious or Christian education. The *teaching of theology* is clearly a form of religious education, but it differs from catechesis in that it is directed primarily at those who are already mature members of the Church, and it differs from preaching in that it is scientific, appealing immediately to critical reason rather than to a conversion of the mind and heart. So, too, Christian *praxis* is a form of religious education. It is at the same time critical reflection on action already taken, and action that is taken after critical reflection. *Praxis* is not related to theory as practice is related to theology. *Praxis* involves the coming together of theory and practice to produce something different from each. It is, in any case, a way of doing religious education, one of its several forms.

This chapter began with a brief description of the problem created by our failure to understand the differences among faith, theology, and belief. We identified these as the "elements of the problem," emphasizing their relationships one with another.

What follows is a fuller, more detailed discussion of these elements, taking note of their historical evolution and their deeper theological meaning.

FAITH

Old Testament Notions of Faith

The Hebrew verb 'āman (meaning "to be firm" or "to be solid," and therefore "to be true") is the Old Testament equivalent of the New Testament Greek word pisteuein. The Hiphil (or causative stem) of the Hebrew 'āman, meaning "to accept something as true," always indicates a personal relationship. Thus, our acceptance of something as true is really the acceptance of the person who proposes it for belief. The Israelites accepted Moses as their leader on the basis of their trust in him personally. They accepted him as one designated by God.

The Hebrew noun ᵉmûnah means "solidity" or "firmness" (see Exodus 17:12) and this solidity or firmness, in turn, offers security (Isaiah 33:6). God offers security because of God's own fidelity (Psalm 36:6) to the divine promises and the Covenant with Israel. God's fidelity is, in turn, grounded in love and mercy (hesed). Because God is faithful (neᵉmān), one must believe God's word and accept God's commands (Deuteronomy 9:23; Psalm 119:66). Thus, Abraham believed Yahweh when the Lord promised him numerous descendants.

The book of Isaiah offers certain peculiar features regarding the reality of faith. The notion of faith implies an acceptance of the power and will of God to deliver Judah from political crisis, and the acceptance is demonstrated by abstinence from all political and military action. To do otherwise is to fail to trust Yahweh. One who believes has no worry (Isaiah 28:16). The scope of faith is unlimited; it demands total commitment to Yahweh.

The intellectual quality of faith is more prominent in chapters 40-66 of Second, or Deutero, Isaiah (so called because modern biblical scholars hold that this part of the book did not have the same authorship as the first thirty-nine chapters). The Israelites are the witnesses of the true God to the extent that they draw other nations to know, believe, and understand that Yahweh is their Lord (Isaiah 43:10). But even this faith is not purely intellectual. "Knowing" God, in this sense, is not speculative knowledge. Rather it is the experience of God through God's revealed word and saving deeds. The more common way of describing the faith relationship with Yahweh in the Old Testament is through the notion of hearing rather than believing, and the hearing must lead to acceptance and obedience.

The foundation stone of Old Testament faith is God, the One to whom the world and all living things owe their created existence and upon whom everything depends for survival and well-being (see Genesis 1-2, Exodus 3, e.g.). Old Testament faith expresses itself in repentance, obedience, and trust. (See, for example, the story of Noah in Genesis 6:9,22; 7:5, and that of Abraham in Genesis 22:1-18.) In the Old Testament the response of faith is, therefore, primarily a moral response, i.e., one of trust and obedience rather than of belief.

Old Testament faith is essentially related to the Covenant (see Deuteronomy 6:17; 7:11), and humankind's response entails the keeping of the Commandments. Consequently, Old Testament faith is also basically corporate rather than individual (see the Psalms). It is related to the fear of the Lord, but not fear in the commonsense meaning of the word. Fear of the Lord means rather a willingness and a readiness to do the will of God, and this, in turn, generates a genuine feeling of security and trust (Job 4:6). But there can be no compromises. Old Testament faith makes an exclusive demand upon Israel (Exodus 20:3; Deuteronomy 5:7). God tolerates no idolatry.

Finally, in the period after the Exile, i.e., after the Edict of Cyrus in 538 B.C., faithfulness to the Law is the expression of faith (see especially Daniel and Judith).

New Testament Notions of Faith

Synoptics

In the Synoptics (the Gospels of Matthew, Mark, and Luke, called Synoptics because, when they are looked at side by side, similarities of structure and content immediately appear), Jesus demanded faith (Matthew 9:28; Mark 4:40; Luke 8:25), praised faith when he discovered it (Matthew 8:10; Luke 7:9), and declared its saving power (Matthew 9:22; Mark 5:34; Luke 8:48). In the Synoptic Gospels the act of faith is directed to God the Father and to Jesus himself. Faith is, first of all, trust in God (Mark 5:34,36; 9:23; 11:22-23; Luke 17:6), but it is also directed toward Jesus; i.e., it is the acceptance of Jesus as the one he claimed himself to be (Mark 8:27-30,38). Behind all of Jesus' utterances about faith there lies that sense of his special relationship to God as Father (Mark 8:38; 9:37 = Matthew 10:40; Mark 12:1-11, 35-37; Matthew 10:32-33; 11:27-30; 16:17-19).

Primitive Christianity—Acts of the Apostles

Faith is the acceptance of the message of the Gospel (Acts of the Apostles 8:13-14), and the "believers" are those who accept the preaching of the Apostles and join the Christian community. The object of belief is the apostolic preaching, and this belief is centered on Jesus as the Risen Lord (5:14; 9:42; 11:17; 15:11). "Therefore let the whole house of Israel know beyond any doubt that God has made both Lord and Messiah this Jesus whom you crucified" (Acts of Apostles 2:36). Belief in the Lordship of Christ is at the core of the apostolic preaching and, therefore, at the heart of faith itself. Acceptance of Jesus as Lord is expressed through repentance, and this is sacramentally demonstrated in Baptism, to which there is attached the guarantee of forgiveness and the renewal by the Holy Spirit: "Peter answered: 'You must reform and be baptized, each one of you, in the name of Jesus Christ, that your sins may be forgiven; then you will receive the gift of the Holy Spirit" (2:38). (For the relationship between faith and Baptism, a point to which we shall return in the discussion of the Church and the sacraments in Part IV, see also Acts of the Apostles 10:43; 18:8; 20:21.)

In primitive Christianity faith requires a break from the past and from other religious allegiances. But it is especially a break from sin. It is belief in God's word as personified in Christ, and so faith necessarily involves a personal relationship with Christ. In the Acts of the Apostles faith is not simply a subjective attitude but also embodies objective content ("The word of God continued to spread . . . There were many priests among those who embraced the faith"—6:7; elsewhere in the New Testament, see Jude 3:20; Romans 1:5; 4:14; 10:8; Galatians 1:23; Ephesians 4:5; 1 Timothy 1:19; 3:9; 4:6). Finally, the faith of primitive Christianity is directed not only toward the saving events of the past but also toward the future and toward the saving power of the Risen Lord even now (Acts of the Apostles 2:17-21; 3:18-21).

The Pauline Literature

For Paul justification is achieved through faith and Baptism. The connection between justice and faith was taken over by Paul from Genesis 15:6 ("Abraham believed God, and it was credited to him as justice"—Romans 4:3). Faith, then, is the key to reconciliation with God and liberation from sin. One must simply confess one's own helplessness and make oneself open to divine grace (Ephesians 2:8-9). Faith is the principle of life for the righteous (Romans 1:17; Galatians 3:11), and, in conjunction with Baptism, effects a new creation (2 Corinthians 5:17; Philippians 3:9-10). The central object of faith is Christ (Galatians 2:20), but for Paul it is not only a matter of faith in Christ but more especially of faith in the preached word (Romans 10:8). Indeed, faith comes through preaching (Romans 10:13-15).

Paul summarizes the content of the preaching in various ways. Essentially the preaching proclaims that God was in Christ reconciling the world to himself (2 Corinthians 5:19; Colossians 1:12-20), that Jesus is Lord, and that God has raised him from the dead so that through his resurrection he might communicate new life to those who believe and are baptized: ". . . if you confess with your lips that Jesus is Lord, and believe in your heart that God raised him from the dead, you will be saved" (Romans 10:9). And this same text indicates that faith is not simply interior but must be expressed and confessed. There is, in fact, a good summary of the confession of faith in 1 Timothy 3:16: "Wonderful, indeed, is the mystery of our faith, as we say in professing it: 'He was manifested in the flesh, vindicated in the Spirit; seen by the angels; preached among the Gentiles, believed in throughout the world, taken up into glory.'" So with Paul, as with the Acts of Apostles, faith looks not only to the past but also to the future (1 Thessalonians 4:14), and even though faith grants a measure of assurance and confidence, it still retains a degree of obscurity (2 Corinthians 5:7).

Faith, according to Paul, is also obedience (Romans 1:5; 16:26), demanding total surrender to Christ. And it is not accomplished in a single act. Faith must grow (2 Corinthians 10:15). So, too, it can become weak and die (1 Thessalonians 3:10; Romans 14:1). And the principle of growth is always *love*. "In Christ Jesus neither circumcision nor the lack of it counts for anything; only faith, which expresses itself through love" (Galatians 5:6). But for Paul only the interior illumination of the Holy Spirit enables us to grasp through faith the mystery of Christ's death and resurrection (1 Corinthians 2:2-16; 12:3; Ephesians 1:17-18; 3:14-17; Colossians 2:2). The believer passes from ignorance of God to the knowledge and love of God through the action of the Spirit (Galatians 4:8-9; Ephesians 4:18; 5:8; 2 Corinthians 4:6). Everything is oriented toward union with God through Christ and in the Holy Spirit (Romans 8:11,19-23,29; 1 Corinthians 6:15-20; 2 Corinthians 5:8; Philippians 1:19-23; 3:19-21; 1 Thessalonians 4:17).

The Johannine Literature

The Johannine theology of faith is basically similar to the Pauline, except that John places greater stress on the knowledge aspect of faith. To believe in Christ is to know him. The object of faith is more explicit in John: that Jesus came from God (John 16:30), that he is the Holy One of God (6:69), that he is the Messiah (11:27). Jesus is the object of faith, and since Jesus is one with the Father, faith in Jesus is faith in the Father (5:19-27; 12:44,49; 14:1,6-11; 16:27-30; 1 John 2:23).

This knowledge, however, is not assimilated independently of the power and presence of the Holy Spirit. Faith is impossible without the interior "attraction" of grace, by which we are taught to know Christ (John 14:15-23; 15:15,26; 16:13), and by which we share in Christ's own filial knowledge of God (John 6:44-46,57). The believer, therefore, already possesses eternal life (John 3:16-17,36; 5:24; 1 John 3:15; 5:12-13), which consists of knowing

Christ (John 17:3) and which tends ultimately to the vision of God (John 17:24,26; 1 John 3:1-2).

What is perhaps unique in the Johannine writings is that faith is placed in the words of Jesus (John 2:22; 5:47; 8:45) as well as in the words of the Apostles or in the apostolic preaching (17:20). In fact, throughout the Fourth Gospel and the First Epistle, the role of the witnesses of faith is emphasized: John the Baptist (1:29-35), God's own witness as guarantor of the faith (1 John 5:7-12), Christ and the Holy Spirit, and even the Christian saints (John 14:12-14). Faith involves the acceptance of the witness, and this, in turn, raises the question of the sign that accompanies the witness. For according to the Johannine presentation, faith arises under the impact of signs (John 1:14; 4:50-54; 8:30; 10:42; 11:45-47; 12:9-11). In the Synoptics, for example, Jesus performs a miracle in response to faith. In John, miracles are employed to evoke faith (17:6-8).

Faith brings life (3:36); unbelief brings condemnation (3:18-20). For John, the greatest tragedy is the sin of unbelief (1:10-11; 16:9). And like Paul, John insists that the work of faith is love of neighbor (1 John 3:23).

Other New Testament Sources

In the Epistle to the Hebrews (especially chapter 11) faith is the solid reality of *hope*, the conviction about the invisible world. It is Jesus who initiates and consummates faith (Hebrews 12:2). One must believe in God, and believe that God creates and rewards the just (11:6). The Letter of James speaks of faith in terms which undeniably are far different from Paul's. It seems that James thought that Paul's views on freedom from the law needed further clarification, if not correction. James insists that faith does not exempt one from all of the obligations of the law. Faith without works is dead. But the works proposed by James are not the works of the law. They are charity to the needy (James 2:15-17), assistance to those in danger (2:25), and so forth. The works of the law mentioned in 2:8-11 are love of one's neighbor and the prohibition of adultery and murder. In the Pastoral Epistles (First and Second Timothy, and Titus), Jude, and the Book of Revelation (Apocalypse), the notion of belief becomes more concrete as the Church itself gradually develops. Faith is a mystery imparted to Christians (1 Timothy 3:9) and is something to be preserved (2 Timothy 4:7; Revelation 14:12).

Patristic Notions of Faith

The term "Fathers of the Church" embraces all ancient Christian writers down to Gregory the Great (d. 604) or Isidore of Seville (d. 636) in the West, and John of Damascus (d. 749) in the East.

The earliest of the writers, the Apostolic Fathers, identified faith with the acceptance of the Christian message or with the knowledge of God and of Christ. The first step toward a certain formulation of faith as assent given to revealed truths was made by St. Justin (d. 165). The believer is one who assents to certain truths and who knows them as truths. St. Irenaeus (d. ca. 200) spoke more of the object of faith than of the act itself. For Irenaeus, the Church proposes the object of faith and the believer accepts it as true and thus comes to a knowledge of the truth. It was Clement of Alexandria (d. 215) who referred to faith as a passing from darkness to the light of knowledge, whose object is God revealed to us in Christ. The knowledge of faith suffices for salvation, but there is given an even higher form of knowledge (*gnosis*) which one can achieve through faith. It was the heresy of *Gnosticism* which distorted this concept of faith as knowledge, making it accessible only to an elite few.

Later Fathers, such as Origen (d. 254), St. Cyril of Jerusalem (d. 386), St. Athanasius (d. 373), St. John Chrysostom (d. 407), St. Cyril of Alexandria (d. 444), St. John of Damascus, and others also wrote of faith in this vein, as assent to doctrines proposed for our belief by the Church. None of these Fathers, however, developed so impressive a theology of faith as St. Augustine (d. 430). For him the act of faith is essentially the assent given to the revelation (see especially his *Commentary on St. John's Gospel*). The knowledge of faith progresses toward the wise understanding of mysteries, but this knowledge remains obscure in comparison with the fullness of the Beatific Vision (i.e., the final, unobstructed, unmediated, "face-to-face" experience of God in heaven, to which Paul refers in 1 Corinthians 13:12).

The Fathers of the Church insisted that faith involves knowledge and assent, and they were always clear about the authority underlying both. From the beginning they employed the simple biblical formula, "Believe in God." Thus, God is the motive or ground of belief, according to the writings of Irenaeus, Clement of Alexandria, Ambrose (d. 397), John Chrysostom, Cyprian (d. 549), and others. Augustine taught that faith cannot be supported by internal evidence. Faith is not the product of reasoning but is founded upon the authority of a witness. Finally, the divine testimony is always worthy of faith because God is infallibly all-knowing and truthful.

The object of such faith is the mystery of Christ. For Augustine the whole mystery proclaimed by Sacred Scripture is the mystery of Christ. All of revelation has its central unity in Christ, to whom it is ordered and in whom it is consummated once and for all.

But faith is not something we merit. According to Augustine, it is always a free gift of God. By the same token, we are free to accept or reject it. This was the consensus of theological opinion among the Fathers at least until the outbreak of the semi-Pelagian controversy in the fifth century. *Semi-Pelagianism*, a variation of Pelagianism, to which we shall refer again in chapter 5, held that grace is not necessary for the beginning of faith (*initium fidei*). Only after we have freely chosen to pursue a life of faith does the grace of God enter in to support our journey to salvation. Against this heresy Augustine insisted on the complete gratuity of the entire process of justification and salvation. The initial act of faith which is the foundation of the whole supernatural life and the beginning of justification is itself a free gift of God and something totally unmerited by us.

The heart of the Augustinian position is this: We are freely saved, but salvation is ultimately the effect of God's own goodness and mercy (*ḥesed*); therefore, salvation is gratuitous and so is the beginning of salvation, which is faith. Subsequent patristic writings, influenced so much by Augustine's works, concentrated their attention on such key New Testament texts as John 6:44-46,65 ("No one can come to me unless the Father who sent me draws him...") and Ephesians 2:8 ("...salvation is yours through faith. This is not your own doing, it is God's gift...").

But even if faith is entirely the gift of God, the Fathers taught that it also involved some element of human cooperation. Accordingly, one can only believe if there seems to be some basis or reason for believing. Some of the earliest Fathers (e.g., Justin) tried to show the truth of the Christian message by pointing out the various ways in which Christ fulfilled the prophecies of the Old Testament. The Greek Fathers (Origen, Basil, d. 379, John Chrysostom, and others) and Latin Fathers (Ambrose, Jerome, d. 420, and especially Augustine) pointed as well to miracles and prophecies. It is important to note, however, that these Fathers—and Augustine in particular—were not arguing that one could establish the credibility of faith on the basis of reason or evidence. On the contrary, for Augustine the internal truth of the mysteries of faith can never be demonstrated. But the availability of such signs as miracles and prophecies does show that our faith is not without some support and credibility, even within the created and visible order of reality.

Second Council of Orange (529)

This is the first of many references in this book to official teachings of the Catholic Church, whether of councils or of popes. Unlike many seminary and college textbooks in use before and even during the Second Vatican Council, this book will present conciliar and papal teaching within the historical context in which it was formulated and promulgated. We readily acknowledge today that we can no longer adopt a fundamentalistic approach to the interpretation of Sacred Scripture by reading the sacred texts apart from their setting within the particular biblical book and the particular situation in which and for which they were written (the so-called *Sitz im Leben*, "situation in life")—and this is clear from such official documents as Pope Pius XII's 1943 encyclical *Divino Afflante Spiritu*, the 1964 Instruction of the Pontifical Biblical Commission, and the 1965 *Dogmatic Constitution on Divine Revelation* of Vatican II. Neither, then, can we adopt what has been called a "non-historical orthodoxy" in our approach to the official texts of Church documents.

The Second Council of Orange, a local council held in southern France and acting under the direct influence of Augustine's theology, condemned semi-Pelagianism. Two year later Pope Boniface II (d. 532) confirmed the council's decision. "He is an adversary of the apostolic teaching," the central decree reads, "who says that the increase of faith as well as the beginning of faith and the very desire of faith . . . inheres in us naturally and not by a gift of grace" (the council cites Philippians 1:6,29 and Ephesians 2:8).

This may be one of the most important, and least known, teachings of the Catholic Church, one more frequently acknowledged in the breach than in the observance. Through much of our own century Catholic *apologetics* (i.e., the systematic attempt to show the reasonableness of faith and to refute, at the same time, the principal objections raised against Christian belief) has proceeded on the unstated assumption that reason alone can show the truth of Christian faith, and that grace is necessary only to make such reasoned "faith" a saving faith. The argument was constructed in this way: (1) The Bible is a historical document. Those who are purported to be its authors can be shown to be such. The events and persons about whom they write can be shown to be real events and persons, on the basis of independent historical evidence. (2) The Bible tells the story of Jesus Christ, who claimed to be divine and who proved his claim by his miracles and especially by the primary miracle of the resurrection. (3) The Bible also tells how Jesus founded a Church and invested it with full authority to teach, rule, and sanctify. (4) The Catholic Church alone can trace its history back to the time of the apostles and to the Lord himself. *Therefore . . .*

If the truth of Catholic faith is so clear, why do so many continue to reject it or remain indifferent to it? Because (so the argument goes) they are either too lazy to examine the evidence fully and carefully, or because, having the evidence and recognizing its truth, they find it too difficult to change their lives in conformity with the truth they now perceive.

It is as if the non-believer were completely free, even without God's grace, to begin the process of examining the evidence and then to accept or reject it. But the Second Council of Orange (and Augustine before that) insisted that even the beginning of faith (*initium fidei*) is a gift of God. Thus, God calls some, but apparently not all, to Christian faith. On the other hand, God calls all to salvation (1 Timothy 2:1-6, the classical text). But salvation is impossible without faith (a Pauline teaching later officially ratified by the Council of Trent in the sixteenth century). Therefore, there must be saving faith that is not explicitly centered on Christ. But even that faith must be a free gift of God. Accordingly, God calls some people to salvation through communities, institutions, and agencies other than the Church. We shall return to this point in our consideration of Christ and the Church in Parts III and IV.

St. Thomas Aquinas

No theologian in the entire history of the Church has had such a decisive impact on Catholic thought and the shaping of the Catholic tradition as St. Thomas Aquinas (d. 1274). His *Summa Theologica* is the most comprehensive synthesis (that is what the word *summa* means) of the biblical, patristic, and medieval understandings of the Christian faith, and has guided, for good or for ill, the interpretation and articulation of that faith ever since, recent fluctuations in its "popularity" notwithstanding. Aquinas was accorded special theological status by Pope Leo XIII's (d. 1903) encyclical *Aeterni Patris* (1879).

For Aquinas the act of faith is essentially an act of the intellect, but not just any act of the intellect. It is *thinking with assent*. What do we believe? God. Why do we believe? On the authority of God revealing. For what purpose do we believe? That we might be united forever with God in the Kingdom of heaven (*Summa Theologica*, II-II, qq. 1-7).

Our grasp of God, however, is never the end-product of scientific reasoning and demonstration. Whatever arguments we employ either show only that faith is at least not impossible or absurd, or else they are arguments which are themselves drawn from sources (especially Sacred Scripture) whose divine authority is, in turn, accepted on faith.

Thus, even though Aquinas emphasized the intellectual dimension of faith, he never lost sight of faith's close relationship with hope and charity, and therefore with the will as well as the intellect. Faith is directed to the good as well as to the true: "Faith is the substance of things to be hoped for" (Hebrews 11:1). Without hope, faith has no direction or goal. Without charity, faith is simply dead (II-II, q. 4).

For Aquinas, faith is essentially and absolutely supernatural. Its source is God; its motive is God; its goal is God. If there are certain external signs of the truth of faith (e.g., miracles and prophecies), they are without force in the absence of the internal cause of belief, which is the Holy Spirit (II-II, q. 6). Unless the grace of the Spirit is present, elevating the intellect above its own limited natural capacities, we cannot truly believe in God.

Council of Trent (1545-1563)

Just as Augustine influenced the decrees of the Second Council of Orange, so did Aquinas influence those of Trent, a major ecumenical council held in northern Italy in the immediate aftermath of the Protestant Reformation and for the purpose of confronting, however belatedly, the crisis created by the Reformation.

The Council of Trent's decrees on faith were formulated against the Protestant, and especially Lutheran, notion of trusting faith (*fides fiducialis*). Recently, Catholic theologians such as Karl Rahner and Hans Küng have argued that the differences between Trent and the Reformers on this question were more verbal than substantive, but they were not perceived that way at the time, nor for centuries thereafter.

The council's teachings on faith are to be found in the *Decree on Justification* which was formulated during one of the most important sessions of the council, the sixth, which lasted from June 21, 1546, until January 13, 1547. It described justification as "a passing from the state in which man is born a son of the first Adam, to the state of grace and adoption as sons of God through the second Adam, Jesus Christ our Savior." The process of justification begins with God's grace through Jesus Christ. This call to justification is completely unmerited. We remain free to reject it, but apart from divine grace we could not take one step toward justification and salvation (a clear echo of the teaching of the Second Council of Orange).

Trent also insisted on the objective content of faith. Faith is not exclusively fiducial, as Luther implied, but includes also some assent to revealed truths. Furthermore, in the spirit of the Epistle of James, faith without works is dead. Faith is not a saving faith apart from hope and charity.

Finally, Trent clarified the meaning of the statement: The sinner is gratuitously justified by faith. "We may be said to be justified freely, in the sense that nothing that precedes justification, neither faith nor works, merits the grace of justification; . . . otherwise . . . grace is no longer grace."

In summary: Without furnishing a formal definition of faith, the Council of Trent taught that faith is *strictly supernatural* and at the same time a *free* act; taught that faith is *necessary for justification and salvation*, and not simply a matter of intellectual acceptance of truths; and taught that faith *can coexist with sin*, contrary to the position of some sixteenth-century Protestants.

First Vatican Council (1869-1870)

Whereas Protestantism had posed the primary challenge at Trent, it was *Rationalism* (the belief that nothing can be accepted as true unless reason can perceive it to be true) and, to a lesser extent, *Fideism* (the belief that reason is of no value at all in the understanding of Christian truth), and *Traditionalism* (the belief that one must rely upon faith alone as communicated in the traditions of the Church) which provided the stimulus for Vatican I's additional official teachings on this question.

On April 24, 1870, Vatican I promulgated its doctrine on faith in the Dogmatic Constitution *Dei Filius* (the first two Latin words of the document, which mean literally "the Son of God"). *Against Rationalism*, the council taught that our belief in revealed truth is "not because its intrinsic truth is seen with the light of reason, but because of the authority of God who reveals them," and that saving faith is impossible without "the enlightenment and inspiration of the Holy Spirit. . . ." *Against Fideism and*

Traditionalism, the council taught that the "submission of faith" must be "consonant with reason" and that that is why God provided various signs, especially miracles and prophecies, whereby the revelation itself might be recognized as being of divine origin. The assent of faith, therefore, is "by no means a blind impulse."

Beyond that, the council also widened the Scholastic notion of faith, which focused so much on its intellectual aspect. Vatican I spoke of the act of faith as one by which we offer ourselves to God in "free obedience." The council also repeated the teaching of Trent on the essential link between faith and justification and on the priority of faith in the supernatural order.

The force of the council's arguments, therefore, was more strongly placed against Rationalism than against Fideism—so much so, in fact, that one bishop suggested that the council add a note to canon 6 to the effect that the council did not intend to deter the faithful from at least examining the motives of credibility. It is perhaps all the more surprising that Catholic apologetics after Vatican I continued on a somewhat rationalistic course, leaving Catholics with the impression that good arguments make conversion to the Church inevitable, except for those persons too indifferent to consider them or too perverse to accept their moral consequences. Nothing could be farther from the teaching of Vatican I, or indeed of the entire Catholic tradition.

Second Vatican Council (1962-1965)

Despite what is occasionally said uncritically and without historical perspective, the Second Vatican Council did not revolutionize or set aside the Catholic tradition as we knew it before 1962. Vatican II's teaching on faith, for example, is entirely consistent with the record we have been tracing and examining thus far. Faith is essentially supernatural: ". . .the grace of God and the interior help of the Holy Spirit must precede and assist. . ." (*Dogmatic Constitution on Divine Revelation*, n. 5). It requires assent to revealed truth but also a giving of oneself to God as well in an "obedience of faith." Its supernatural character notwithstanding, there are signs and wonders which can lead us to faith under the impulse always of divine grace.

Nevertheless, there are at least two new emphases in Vatican II's teaching on faith. Both were prompted by the modern discovery of, and appreciation for, pluralism. *First*, there is a recognition that the freedom of the act of faith means just that. Faith is a free gift of God, and ours is a free response to that gift. Neither God's hand nor ours can be forced. In a world of increasingly diverse religious and non-religious convictions, we must learn to respect the consciences and the motives of those who do not, or cannot, accept Christian faith (*Declaration on Religious Freedom*, n. 2). *No one is to be penalized, socially or politically, for his or her convictions about religious matters.*

The *second* new emphasis is similar to the first. Just as the Church has grown to respect diversity in the human community at large, so has it grown to respect diversity within the Body of Christ itself. The *Dogmatic Constitution on the Church* (n. 15) and the *Decree on Ecumenism* (n. 3) both acknowledge that *Christian faith exists outside the Catholic Church*, that it is a justifying faith, and that it relates one not only to Christ but to the Church as well.

Faith: A Synthesis

Earlier in the chapter we were satisfied, "for the moment," to define faith as personal knowledge of God, and Christian faith as personal knowledge of God in Christ. In the light of the preceding historical and theological discussion, it is clear that faith is indeed personal knowledge of God, but there is much more to it than that.

1. Although faith is personal knowledge of God, that knowledge is always achieved and activated within a given community of faith, whether the Church as we know it or some other religious body, and beyond that within the whole human family.

2. This knowledge of God is not merely knowledge in the cognitive or intellectual sense, although it *is* that, too. It is a knowledge which implies trust and a total commitment of the self to God, a commitment of heart as well as of mind.

3. Faith is not just the knowledge of God in general, but the knowledge of God which comes through the reception and acceptance of God's word. In the Christian sense, faith is the acceptance

of God's Word-made-flesh in Jesus Christ, and then of the preaching of that Word by the Apostles and the Church.

4. The acceptance of God's word in Christ and in the Church demands not only intellectual assent but also obedience—obedience to the Commandments and to the New Law of the Gospel, which calls us to work for social and political liberation as well as personal transformation of the individual.

5. If there is to be genuine obedience, there must be some acknowledgement of past failures, a conversion (*metanoia*, or change of mind), and repentance.

6. Faith always remains free. The "evidence" for faith is never overwhelming. There are signs and witnesses. But these are always external and never finally persuasive in themselves. The only motive of faith that ultimately counts is internal: the presence of the Holy Spirit.

7. On the other hand, faith and reason are not absolutely separate. Even if one does not "reason to" faith, faith must always be "consonant with reason." Thus, St. Paul urges us to worship God "in a way that is worthy of thinking beings" (Romans 12:1). A fuller statement of this relationship will be developed in chapter 5, where the problem of nature and grace is taken up.

8. Faith is a matter of the highest human importance, because without it we cannot be justified or saved. But since God wishes the salvation of all persons, faith must be available in principle even to those outside the Church.

THEOLOGY
Theology and Faith

There can be no theology without faith. By definition, theology is "faith seeking understanding" (Anselm). It is, as we defined it earlier in this chapter, "the interpretation of one's faith." Theology is not the interpretation of someone else's faith, but of one's own, or of one's own community of faith. It is possible, in other words, to subject the Bible to very careful literary scrutiny and to come to the highest appreciation of its style, content, and message, without at the same time accepting it as the very Word of God. So, too, it is possible to write and speak of Jesus of Nazareth in the most admiring terms without at the same time accepting him as Lord and Savior, the very Son of God in our midst. None of this is theology.

Theology is not simply talk *about* God, or *about* Christ, or *about* the Bible, or even *about* faith. Theology happens only when someone is trying, in a more or less systematic and critical manner, to come to a better, clearer, more refined understanding of his or her own faith *in* God and *in* Christ, as it has become available to us *in* the Bible, *in* the Church, or wherever else.

When "theology" is done without faith, it is really a *philosophy of religion*. The theologian reflects on his or her own faith-commitment; the philosopher of religion reflects on the faith-commitment of others. The injunction of Augustine, *"Crede ut intelligas"* ("Believe that you might understand") makes no sense to the non-believer. We do not go to theology for our faith. Theology is there to give us a greater understanding of what we already believe.

Theology and Belief

On the other hand, theology has an important critical function to perform. It does not simply take what is believed and try to put the best face possible on it. Theology has the responsibility of measuring what is believed against established *criteria.*

1. Is the belief rooted in, or at least consistent with, the Bible?

2. Has the belief been expressed and defended, at least in substance, by the Fathers and doctors of the Church?

3. Has the Church officially proposed this belief in council or through some other magisterial forum?

4. Conversely, has the official Church ever rejected this belief in whole or in part, indirectly or by implication?

5. Is the belief consistent with the official teachings of the Church on other related matters of faith?

6. Is the belief consistent with the present consensus of theologians on this or related matters of faith?

7. Is the belief consistent with scientific knowledge?

8.   Is the belief consistent with our corporate experience of faith?

What happens, however, when those beliefs become official? Theology retains its critical function even in the face of official beliefs, such as doctrines and dogmas, not to mention disciplinary decrees of Vatican congregations. Theology still must ask if the official belief is consistent with the Bible, the teaching of the Fathers and doctors of the Church, previous official pronouncements, other recent or contemporary official pronouncements, the present consensus of theologians, the findings of other sciences, and finally the experience of Christians themselves.

This critical process occurs not only after a belief has been made official, but also and always before. *The very formulation of a doctrine is a work of theology.* Before a belief is officially adopted and proposed for wider acceptance in the Church, a decision has to be made about its truth and the appropriateness of commending it to the larger community at this time and in this manner. The decision about its truth cannot be made apart from the theological criteria outlined above. Insofar as a particular belief is elevated to the level of a doctrine, it is regarded, rightly or wrongly, as consistent with the biblical message, the writings of the Fathers and doctors of the Church, and other ecclesiastical pronouncements of past and present, and it presumably represents the best fruits of contemporary theology and related sciences. Finally, it is not only consistent with the present experiences of Christians, but its promulgation will in fact enhance and enrich that experience.

Accordingly, the question is not *whether* theology will exercise a critical function in the formulation and subsequent reflection upon doctrine, but rather *which* theology will. Sometimes it is not clear for decades, even centuries, if the Church has employed the best theology in its doctrinal pronouncements.

Origin and Development of Theology

Self-Conscious Faith in God

Theology is as old as self-conscious faith in God. As soon as human beings began thinking about the ultimate meaning of life, about their relationship to the whole cosmos, about the direction of history (although the notion of "history" as such is a relatively modern development), about the experience of the holy and the sacred, they were beginning to do theology. Theology precedes not only Christianity but even Judaism as well.

The Apostles

Christian theology begins with the Apostles. It developed for two reasons: (1) because the Apostles had to reconcile for themselves the message of Jesus Christ with their own religious experience as Jews; and (2) because the Apostles had to preach the "Good News" that Jesus had bequeathed to them, and this meant interpreting and translating the Gospel for diverse communities and cultures.

Why are there, for example, *four* Gospels in the New Testament? If the Gospels are nothing more than objective accounts of what Jesus said and did, why the need for four? Why not only one? The answer is that the Gospels are more than historical narratives or biographies. They are, first and foremost, *testimonies of faith*: the faith of the evangelist himself and the faith of the community to which he belonged. Each Gospel is an interpretation of the significance of Jesus Christ, directed to different audiences (e.g., Luke's is Gentile, Matthew's is Jewish). As such, each is a work of *theology*. Indeed, the whole of the New Testament is theological to one degree or another.

But *New Testament theology* is more *catechetical* than speculative (with the obvious exceptions of the Fourth Gospel and some of the Pauline letters). Theology became more deliberately *systematic* as the first serious intellectual challenges were raised against Christian faith. There developed in the second and third centuries an *apologetical* theology. The Apologists (e.g., Justin, Clement of Alexandria, Origen, Irenaeus) tried to speak to the cultured in their own language. Technical theological terms were created. Specific theological problems were defined. In the struggle against Gnosticism, for example, the continuity between Old Testament and New Testament had to be established and clarified. In the controversy over the necessity of rebaptizing those who had left the Church and later returned, a theology of the Church (ecclesiology) began to take shape. The need to distinguish inspired from noninspired literature forced the question of the canon of Sacred Scripture ("canon" = the list of books accepted by the Church as inspired and, therefore, as part of the Bible).

Neo-Platonism; Roman Juridical Thought

With the Edict of Constantine in 313 the Church acquired legal status, and its theology began to show the marks of the Church's new situation: It was strongly influenced by neo-Platonism, the last of the great Graeco-Roman philosophies, and by Roman juridical thought. Given this combination, reality was increasingly perceived in hierarchical terms, with God as the remote, otherworldly, "supreme Being." It was within this intellectual framework that some of the great theological issues of the times were faced: the inner life of the Trinity, the divine-human status of Christ, and the necessity and effects of grace. Terms and concepts taken over from contemporary Greek culture were employed against *Arianism* in the formulation of the doctrine that in Christ there is one divine person (*hypostasis*), with two natures (*physis*), the one human and the other divine. Those natures are united, without confusion or division, in the one divine person, i.e., hypostatically. (Arianism had taught that Christ was more than a man but less than God.) Similar concepts were applied to the Trinity: circumincession, procession, generation, spiration. And these, in turn, were incorporated into official teachings and creeds of the Church of the fifth century: the *Council of Chalcedon* (451) and the *Athanasian Creed*.

Monasteries

As circumstances changed, so, too, did the character of Catholic theology. With the dissolution of the Roman Empire in 476 and the breakdown of traditional social and political institutions, intellectual and cultural leadership within the Church passed from the great bishop-theologians (Augustine, Athanasius, Basil, Gregory of Nyssa, d. 394, Gregory Nazianzen, d. 390) to the monasteries and to such monastic theologians as Anselm of Canterbury, who began as an abbot and later became an archbishop,

Bernard of Clairvaux (d. 1153), Hugh of St. Victor (d. 1141), Bonaventure (d. 1274), and others. Theology assumed a *devotional* character consistent with its new monastic environment.

Universities

Indeed, those who had been formed in the spiritual theology of the monasteries found it most difficult to accept, much less adapt to, the new theology coming out of the universities, as represented by Albert the Great, Thomas Aquinas, and their intellectual disciples who were known as the Schoolmen, or Scholastics (thus, the term *Scholasticism*). It was Anselm who provided the bridge between the two approaches: the one emphasizing the sufficiency of faith as expressed in Sacred Scripture, and the other insisting on the need for critical reflection on that faith, using not only Sacred Scripture, but the writings of the Fathers, theologians, and philosophers, even non-Christian philosophers such as Aristotle. Theology, Anselm argued, is "faith seeking understanding."

Although there were clear differences among the Schoolmen, one could also distinguish a certain common mentality in their approach to theology. All agreed on the power of reason to come to some basic, albeit imperfect, understanding of the mysteries of faith and to construct some overarching synthesis of the whole Christian doctrinal system (thus, Thomas' own *Summa Theologica*). The pessimism of Augustinianism, with its emphasis on the depravity of the human condition and the corresponding weakness of human powers, such as reason, gave way to a new intellectual optimism. Things were seen to have natures of their own which do not consist simply of their reference to God. We come to a knowledge of God and of our faith, therefore, not only through direct spiritual illumination but more usually through our sense experience of the visible and the concrete. To this end we are aided by the use of *analogy*, a way of explaining the meaning of one reality by showing its similarity to another (e.g., God is not a "father" in the strict sense of the word, but God's relationship to us is *like* that of a father to his children). But the Schoolmen also agreed on the authority of the Bible as a kind of textbook from which proofs could legitimately and necessarily be drawn. Reason, in other words, was not without guides and limits.

The Scholastic position was embraced neither immediately nor universally. Resistance continued from those still suspicious of the powers of reason (Bonaventure, in particular). Parallel approaches were also developed, e.g., by John Duns Scotus (d. 1308). And inevitably others took the new emphasis on reason to apparent extremes, as may have been the case with Nominalism, which tended to reduce theology to a kind of word-game. The theologian is a manipulator of terms and concepts, none of which can lead us to, much less put us in touch with, the reality of God. The movement, identified in large part with William of Ockham (d. 1347), is regarded as the forerunner of such modern philosophical schools as Logical Positivism, which also denies the possibility of getting beyond words to the reality of things in themselves.

Scholastic theology had certain inherent *weaknesses* as well as strengths. *First*, it relied too heavily on reason and logic. The Bible and the writings of the Fathers very often took second place to Aristotle and Scholastic colleagues. *Secondly*, theological questions were regularly studied apart from their historical context. The Bible was read not, as we insist today, according to its original setting and literary meaning, but rather as if it were primarily a collection of independent sayings or principles which could be used independently of one another to support particular theological and even philosophical arguments. *Thirdly*, Scholastic theology tended to invent distinctions and sub-distinctions unnecessarily ("How many angels can dance on the head of a pin?" is a caricature, of course, but it suggests the kind of useless subtlety that occasionally emerged at the time). *Finally*, Scholastic theology too quickly constructed systems of thought and then elevated these systems to the status of self-contained authorities. Theology became for many a matter of competition between or among systems.

Seminaries; Religious Orders

As controversy followed controversy and subtlety piled upon subtlety, the role of the universities as centers of theological thought declined, and they were replaced by the seminaries and the schools of religious orders. Manuals of theology bore the words "dogmatic-scholastic" in their title, thus expressing the intention to wed the positive, historical element with the speculative, rational element. The format and structure of these new seminary textbooks was the same as of those used by future priests in Catholic seminaries up to, and in some cases beyond, the Second Vatican Council. First, the thesis was given (e.g., "The Church is the Body of Christ"). This was followed by the *status quaestionis* ("state of the question"), in which various current opinions on the thesis were presented. Next came the proofs: from the Bible, the Fathers and doctors of the Church, and the teachings of the Church. There were additional arguments of much less weight, drawn from theological reason and from "convenience" (e.g., "It is *fitting* that God should have done such-and-such; but God is all powerful and *could have done* such-and-such; therefore, God *did* such-and-such.") The defense of the thesis concluded with various corollaries, or *scholia*, which applied the thesis to some related minor questions.

Episcopal theology of the earliest Christian centuries had been concerned with a defense of the faith against non-believers and heretics; *monastic* theology, with its spiritual and devotional implications; and *university* theology, with giving the whole body of Christian faith some coherent, logical unity and structure. *Seminary* theology, on the other hand, was concerned primarily with preparing future priests for the service of the Church as preachers, teachers, and confessors. From the end of the seventeenth century until the first half of the twentieth century, Catholic theology focused its attention on questions that would likely confront the priest in the course of his ministry. And because the priest is an official of the Church, it was important that he should have access to, and communicate, the official teaching of the Church rather than his own private opinions. Accordingly, the emphasis was always on the authoritative sources by which a given thesis was shown to be true. Reverence for the Bible notwithstanding, the primary authority was always the teaching of the official Church, i.e., papal statements, conciliar declarations, and Vatican decrees.

Möhler, Newman, Scheeben

The seeds of yet another major theological transformation (indeed, the one in which we now find ourselves) were already being sown in the late eighteenth and nineteenth centuries. The outstanding theologian of this period was Johann Adam Möhler (d. 1838), who recovered a sense of theological development, a sense of history, and a sense of viewing the Christian message as an organic whole rather than as a collection of theses. He rejected the rationalistic spirit of much contemporary Catholic thought and reunited dogmatic and moral theology. In 1879 Pope Leo XIII's encyclical *Aeterni Patris* sounded the call to reconnect Catholic theology with its own best tradition: Thomas Aquinas in particular, but also Augustine, Bonaventure, and others. Unfortunately, much of the restoration assumed a diffident, defensive, and frequently hostile attitude to the new intellectual trends of its own time. But the idea of genuine historical development continued to gain strength. Cardinal John Henry Newman (d. 1890) constructed his own celebrated theory of doctrinal development, linking it with the faith of the community itself down through the centuries. Another major contributor to the new historical and wholistic approach to Catholic faith was Matthias Scheeben (d. 1888).

Modernist Crisis

The Modernist Crisis of the late nineteenth and early twentieth centuries, however, interrupted the course of this new historical and integrated approach to Catholic theology. From today's perspective the interruption was only temporary, but "temporary" meant that it spanned the entire theological careers of many twentieth-century scholars and the entire intellectual formation period of the overwhelming majority of priests ordained in this century. Like most movements and systems in the history of the Church, Modernism is more nuanced and more complex than first appears, either to its devoted defenders or to its tenacious critics. One might suggest, at the risk of oversimplification, that the Modernists (Alfred Loisy, d. 1940, and others) took the new nineteenth-century emphasis on history and opposition to abstractionism too far to the left. Like the Nominalism of the post-Scholastic era, Modernism held that there can be no real continuity between dogmas and the reality they presume to describe. Dogmas have a negative function at best. They warn against false notions. They are above all practical. A dogma is a rule of conduct more than a rule of truth. Thus, to say that "Jesus is risen" means that we must regard him as we would have done before his death, or as we would a contemporary.

It is fair to say that the Modernists, in their commendable effort to bring some historical realism to the interpretation of Christian faith, adopted too uncritically certain common notions of history abroad during the nineteenth century, along with that century's "dogmatic" and ideological rejection of values (including the supernatural) that cannot readily be observed and tested apart from a study of concrete persons and events. Modernism, therefore, began, as all heresies do, with a partial truth and inflated it into a comprehensive, and therefore radically flawed, system of thought which denied the capacity of the human mind to grasp and express the supernatural in ways that are open to objective examination, in accord with objective criteria of truth and appropriateness.

Because it was so vehemently condemned by Pope Pius X (d. 1914) in his encyclical *Pascendi* (1907) and then made the subject of a negative oath that every future priest, bishop, and professor of religious sciences had to take from 1910 until 1967, Modernism stalled the progress which Catholic theology had been making under the impact of such scholars as Möhler, Scheeben, and Newman. It would not be until the Second Vatican Council (1962-1965) that Catholic theologians would feel free once again to depart from the traditional textbook approach and study theological questions in their wider historical and even ecumenical contexts. In the meantime, there were several fits and starts.

Twentieth-Century Renewal

Even as the atmosphere in all Catholic seminaries and religious houses remained tense and their intellectual spirit exceedingly cautious, there were all the while signs of extraordinary renewal:

the biblical work of Marie-Joseph LaGrange (d. 1938), later endorsed, for all practical purposes, by Pope Pius XII's encyclical on biblical studies, *Divino Afflante Spiritu* (1943); the ecumenical and ecclesiological work of Yves Congar, later confirmed by Vatican II's *Dogmatic Constitution on the Church* and its *Decree on Ecumenism*; and the philosophical and systematic work of Karl Rahner, recognized generally today as this century's leading Catholic theologian.

Each of these scholars and many others had been condemned, or at least severely restricted, at some point in their careers by Vatican authorities who appealed to guidelines laid down in Pope Pius XII's encyclical *Humani Generis* (1950). This document rejected what it called "the new theology" as it had been developing on the Continent just after the Second World War. This "new theology" was linked with Modernism because of its presumed downplaying of the supernatural order and of the teaching authority of the official Church. But the practitioners of the "new theology," unlike their putative predecessors in the Modernist movement, have come to enjoy the approval even of the official Church itself. They served as experts (*periti*) at the Second Vatican Council, or as members of the new Theological Commission established by Pope Paul VI (d. 1978), and some continue to fill important and influential positions in seminaries and universities, on editorial boards of theological journals, and as consultants to diocesan, regional, national, and even international bodies.

Divisions of Theology

Faith-Community

There are different kinds of theology. The interpretation of faith differs on the basis of the faith-community in which, and for which, that interpretation occurs. Thus, there is Christian theology, and within that, Catholic theology, Protestant theology, Anglican theology, Orthodox theology, and so forth. Then, of course, there are Jewish theology, Moslem theology, and as many other kinds of theology as there are religions. Every self-conscious attempt to come to a better understanding of what one believes about God, about the ultimate meaning of life, about our hopes for the future, and so forth, is a work of theology at one level or another.

Content

There are differences even *within* Christian and Catholic theology. Theology differs according to content. There is *dogmatic theology*, which interprets faith as it has been expressed in official teachings of the Church (since not every official teaching is a dogma, this theology should more accurately be called *doctrinal* rather than dogmatic). There is *moral theology*, which interprets the impact of faith on our attitudes, motives, values, and behavior. The division between doctrinal and moral theology is not a happy one. The latter was separated from the former in the sixteenth century for the convenience of priest-confessors, as we shall see in chapter 25.

There is also *spiritual* or *ascetical theology*, which focuses on the inner transformation effected by the presence of faith and grace in the human mind and heart. There is *pastoral theology*, which seeks to understand the implications of faith for the actual situation of the Church, specifically for preaching, ministry of various kinds, counseling, and the like. There is *liturgical theology*, which interprets the meaning of faith as expressed in the rituals and devotions of the Church. And some have spoken recently of a *structural theology*, which seeks to understand the faith in its various institutional expressions within the Church, thus combining the insights of the Church's canon law with its theological self-understanding, or ecclesiology.

Methods

Catholic theology also differs according to its various methods. There is *positive* or *historical theology*, which seeks to understand and interpret the faith as that faith has been articulated already in some principal historical source, such as the Bible, the writings of the Fathers and doctors of the Church, the ecumenical councils, or the great theological controversies of past centuries. *Biblical theology*, therefore, is a subdivision of historical theology. It attempts to come to an understanding of the faith as expressed and communicated in the pages of Sacred Scripture. Until the twelfth century Catholic theology was, for the most part, biblical theology. *Patristic theology*, too, is a kind of historical theology. It attempts the same task as biblical theology, but in reference to the writings of the Fathers of the Church rather than the Bible. *Doctrinal theology* can also be viewed as a subdivision of historical theology insofar as the quest for understanding is limited to an examination of official teachings of the Church.

On the other hand, theology may be *speculative* rather than historical; such theology seeks an understanding of the faith in light of the best of contemporary knowledge and experience and without limiting the historical inquiry to any given source, such as the Bible or doctrines.

Finally, there is *systematic theology*, which embraces every kind of theology mentioned thus far. It is comprehensive in its method. It seeks to understand and articulate the Christian whole by examining each of its parts in relation to one another and to the whole. Anglican theologian John Macquarrie has called it a work of "architectonic reason." Some schools of theology refer to it as *constructive theology*. This book, in fact, is an attempt at a systematic theology.

Catholics have often confused *doctrinal* or *dogmatic theology* with the whole of Christian theology, as if theology were always and only our critical (and sometimes not so critical) reflection on, explanation, and defense of the official teachings of the Church. Protestants, on the other hand, have sometimes confused *biblical theology* with the whole of Christian theology, as if theology were always and only our critical (and sometimes not so critical) reflection on the biblical message.

But if all theology were biblical theology, then there could not have been any theology at all before the Bible was written. But if there were no theology before the Bible, how did the Bible get written? The very process by which the Bible came into being is itself a theological process. For the same reason, if all theology were doctrinal or dogmatic, so that there can be no real theology without doctrines to understand, explain, and defend, how could there have been any theology at all before the first doctrinal pronouncement was issued? And if there was no theology before doctrine, how did doctrine even begin to exist? For doctrines are beliefs that have received official approval. And beliefs, in turn, are expressions of faith. But expressions of faith emerge from a process known as theology, which is the interpretation of faith.

Perspective

One final division: Theology may also be distinguished according to its perspective. These various perspectives, however, are not scientific divisions, as are those based on content or method. But it may be helpful to the reader to be advised of the differences among theologies as they are likely to be reported in the press and other popular media. *Liberal theology* (with the capital *L*) is not the same as *liberal theology* (with the lower-case *l*). The former refers to a specific movement in Protestant theology, beginning in the nineteenth century and continuing, with considerably diminished force, to the present. Like Catholic Modernism, Protestant Liberal theology "reduces" the supernatural content of faith to its least common denominator and, for all practical purposes, eliminates that supernatural content entirely from consideration. Lower-case liberal theology refers to a progressive *style* of theology. The adjective *liberal* is entirely relative in its meaning. Thus, it may be regarded as "liberal" to favor the ordination of women. Others may consider support for the ordination of *anyone* as "reactionary."

There is also *orthodox theology* and *conservative theology*. Orthodox theology is the interpretation of faith which confines the process of interpretation to sources generated by the Church itself: the Bible, or the Fathers and doctors of the Church, or doctrinal pronouncements and creeds. Orthodox theology may also be known as *confessional theology* (more of a Protestant term, since it refers to the confessions of faith adopted by the Church not only outside but also inside the Protestant Reformation). Conservative theology, on the other hand, refers to a *style* of doing theology, a style that is cautious in the face of proposed change. Again, it is a highly relative term. There are also variations on the orthodox theme. Within Protestantism there is *neo-orthodoxy*, associated with the names of Karl Barth (d. 1968) and Reinhold Niebuhr (d. 1971), which challenged Liberalism to reconnect itself with the long-standing themes of Reformation thought on the sinfulness of humankind and the need for the redemptive grace of God.

Other approaches to theology include *radical theology*, which usually refers to the "death-of-God" movement of the mid-1960s; *secular theology*, another mid-1960s movement, which emphasized the this-worldly character of Christian existence and the Church's abiding responsibility to transform the world; *liberation theology* (whether Latin American, black, or feminist), which stresses the motif of liberation from economic, racial, and cultural oppression and reinterprets the sources of Christianity in accordance with that motif; *political theology*, which insists on the connection between theory and practice and, therefore, suggests that every statement about God and salvation must be translatable into a statement about the human condition in its total social and political situation; *existential theology*, at the other side of the spectrum from political theology, which emphasizes the individual believer as the *locus* for God's saving activity so that all theological reflection is reflection about one's own personhood and the meaning of one's own human existence; and *process theology*, developed against the presumably static traditional theology of the mainstream churches, which understands God and all reality as in a constant "process" of change and movement forward—nothing is fixed or immutable; and hence, process thought bears some family resemblance to Liberalism and Modernism.

Theology: A Synthesis

We defined theology earlier in the chapter as the interpretation of one's faith or, with Anselm, as faith seeking understanding. In the light of the preceding historical and systematic discussion, it is clear that theology is indeed the interpretation of faith, but that it is also much more complex than that.

1. *Not all interpretations of faith are theological.* Theology happens when there is *an interpretation of one's own faith.* Apart

from that faith, the exploration of faith is a philosophy of religion rather than a theology.

2.   On the other hand, theology has an important *critical function* to perform. It must ask if the various expressions of faith (beliefs) are *true*, or at least *appropriate*, to the Christian tradition. Do they conform with Sacred Scripture, the writings of the Fathers and doctors of the Church, the Church's official creeds and teachings, the consensus of the faithful, and scientific knowledge?

3.   *Theology is as old as self-conscious faith in God.* Christian theology began with the awareness that God was present in Christ, reconciling the world to himself (2 Corinthians 5:19). The *Apostles* and *Evangelists* were the first Christian theologians. The *Apologists* were the first to systematize theology.

4.   Almost from the beginning Christian theology has drawn from *contemporary thought-forms and culture* to express, explain, and even to defend the faith: from contemporary Greek philosophy during the controversies of the fourth and fifth centuries, from Aristotelianism during the Middle Ages, and from modern philosophy in the present age.

5.   Theology also changed its character as it has moved from one *pastoral need* to another and from one *environment* to another: The theology done by the great bishops of the fourth and fifth centuries was different from the theology of the monasteries around the end of the first Christian millennium, and that theology differed, in turn, from the medieval theology of the universities, and that from the seminary theology of the seventeenth and eighteenth centuries, and that from the historical and ecumenical theology of today, done again in universities, but more distinctively in the public forum, i.e., through books, articles, and lectures.

6.   *There are as many kinds of theology as there are religious faiths.* Theology also differs according to *content* (doctrinal, liturgical, etc.), *method* (historical, speculative, etc.), and *perspective* (Liberal, liberational, etc.).

7.   In the end, *Christian theology is a more or less systematic effort to come to terms with, and to express, our experience (knowledge) of God in Christ.*

BELIEF
Dimensions of the Question

When there has been a movement from faith to understanding, and from understanding to expression, we are in the realm of belief. It may be the belief of a single person or of many persons. It may be a belief that is manifestly in error or at least not yet accepted by the community at large, or it may be a belief that the Church proposes to the whole community for acceptance, even under pain of excommunication from the group. We shall be speaking in this last section of the chapter about official belief, i.e., about expressions of faith which have been accepted by the community at large as having authoritative, even normative and binding, force for every member of the Church. At one level of belief, we have the Bible. At another level, we have doctrines and dogmas. At a third, we have liturgies. At a fourth, we have catechisms and other instruments of Christian education.

The Bible

Canonicity

The word *bible* is derived from Latin and Greek words (*biblia*) which mean "books." The Bible is a *collection of books* rather than a single literary composition. The books of the Bible are called "sacred" because they are regarded as inspired by God and are not simply the product of ordinary human creativity and effort, although they are that as well. They are considered "canonical" because they are on the list, or *canon*, of books which the Church officially regards as inspired. The canon was definitively and solemnly determined by the Council of Trent in 1546.

Old Testament, New Testament

The Bible is also divided into Old Testament and New Testament. The former is centered on the old covenant of Sinai; the latter is centered on the new covenant of Jesus Christ. One of the earliest heresies, *Marcionism*, denied the revelatory character of the Old Testament. In its rejection of Marcionism, the Church has insisted from the earliest days on the essential continuity between the two testaments. There is no basis at all, in other words, for the once-common belief that the Old Testament is the law of fear and the New Testament, the law of love. The call to mercy and love (*hesed*) is at the core of Jewish faith as it is of Christian faith. The two testaments have a common theological focus: the *Kingdom of God*, i.e., the reign or rule of God that is already present in the world and is destined to be realized in all of its perfection at the end of human history when God will be "all in all" (1 Corinthians 15:28).

Inspiration

Because the Bible is believed to be inspired by God, it has an authority equaled by no other written source. It is, in the theological sense, the *norma normans non normata* ("the norm which is the standard for all other norms but is not itself subject to a higher norm"). The understanding of the Bible's authority is rooted, as we have said, in its inspired character.

Inspiration signifies in general the divine origin of the Bible. Already in the Old Testament there was the conviction that certain books are sacred because they are inspired by God. This belief was carried over into the New Testament, where the Old Testament is cited some 350 times in such a way as to show that Jesus and the New Testament writers shared the conviction that the Old Testament was indeed inspired by God. "All Scripture is inspired by God and is useful for teaching..." (2 Timothy 3:16). The New Testament itself does not claim inspiration, but the Fathers of the Church from the very beginning included the New Testament with the Old Testament in the inspired corpus of books.

The question of inspiration did not become a theological issue until the nineteenth century, after the First Vatican Council's formal definition. Subsequently, a vigorous debate developed, not over the *fact* of inspiration but over its *manner*. In 1893 Pope Leo XIII issued an encyclical, *Providentissimus Deus*, in which he declared that "God so moved the inspired writers by His supernatural operation that he incited them to write, and assisted them in their writing so that they correctly conceived, accurately wrote down and truthfully expressed all that He intended and only what He intended; and only thus can God be the author of the Bible." The teaching of Vatican I and Leo XIII is reaffirmed at Vatican II in its *Dogmatic Constitution on Divine Revelation:* "...Sacred Scripture is the word of God inasmuch as it is consigned to writing under the inspiration of the divine Spirit" (n. 9).

Inerrancy

Closely linked with the belief about inspiration is the belief about inerrancy. If the Bible is of God, it cannot be in error since God is the author of truth, not lies. A consensus of biblical and theological scholars favors the following principles: (1) The words of the Bible are true only in the sense in which the human authors conveyed them. Therefore, we must determine how they thought, what influenced them, and so forth. (2) The human author himself was not necessarily without error. Many of his personal opinions and even convictions may have been wrong. But inerrancy means that these opinions and convictions did not affect the message itself. (3) Inerrancy does not rule out the use of common literary devices, such as poetry, figures of speech, paradox, approximation, compressed narratives, inexact quotations, folklore, legend, song. (4) The human authors were Oriental, not Western. They did not think metaphysically or according to the rules of Scholastic logic. (5) Insofar as the principle of inerrancy applies, it applies to those essential religious affirmations which are made for the sake of salvation. "The Books of Scripture must be acknowledged as teaching firmly, faithfully, and without error that truth which God wanted put into the Sacred Writings for the sake of our salvation" (Vatican II, *Dogmatic Constitution on Divine Revelation*, n. 11).

Tradition as Criterion

But how do we know that the Bible is inspired and immune from error in those matters which pertain to our salvation? This is not an easy question to answer. As we mentioned earlier, the New Testament makes no claim about itself. The Catholic Church has always maintained that *there is no other criterion except its own traditions*, and that these, in turn, are vehicles of divine revelation. The inspiration of the Bible has been believed from the beginning and, beyond that, has been the subject of an official definition by the Church. Even as we try to understand its meaning in the light of modern notions of authorship, of history, and of psychology and sociology of knowledge, we recognize that the fact of inspiration is a given. One cannot be true to the Catholic and Christian faith without affirming at the same time the inspired, and therefore finally normative and authoritative, character of the Bible.

But what about the authority of *tradition*? Does not the Catholic Church teach that there are two separate *sources of divine revelation*, Sacred Scripture and Tradition, and that the latter is more authoritative than the former? The simplest answer is "No." It is true, on the other hand, that the Council of Trent did speak of two sources of revelation, the one written and the other unwritten. And it is also true that many Catholic theologians interpreted the Council of Trent to mean that Scripture and Tradition are two separate streams of revelation and that the one (Tradition) is the final measure of the other (Scripture). It seemed for a time that this position was about to be endorsed at the Second Vatican Council, but Pope John XXIII (d. 1963) in November 1962 sent the draft of the *Dogmatic Constitution on Divine Revelation* back to the Theological Committee of the council. When the document returned, it spoke not of two separate and independent sources of divine revelation but of a single divine revelation expressed and available in different forms: "It is clear that sacred tradition, sacred Scripture, and the teaching authority of the Church, in accord with God's most wise design, are so linked and joined together that one cannot stand without the others, and that all together and each in its own way under the action of the one Holy Spirit contribute effectively to the salvation of souls" (n. 10).

A more accurate formulation of the Scripture/Tradition relationship than the usual explanation offered before Vatican II would underscore the principle that *Scripture is itself a product of Tradition*. It is not as if you first have Scripture and then you have Tradition which is, among other things, the Church's reflection on Scripture. Tradition comes before and during, and not just after, the writing of Sacred Scripture. In fact, careful study of the various books of the Bible, including the Gospels themselves, discloses several layers of tradition from which the individual books have emerged and taken final form. Those traditions may be oral (preaching), liturgical (prayer formulae), narrative (recollection of important events, especially Jesus' passion), and so forth.

In the *wider meaning* of the word, tradition refers to *the whole process by which the Church "hands on"* (the literal meaning of the word *tradition*) *its faith to each new generation*. This handing on occurs through preaching, catechesis, teaching, devotions, gestures (e.g., the sign of the cross), doctrines, and indeed the Bible itself. In the *narrow meaning* of the term, tradition refers to *the content of the Church's post-apostolic teaching*. The Second Vatican Council opts for the *wider meaning* of the term: "The Church, in her teaching, life and worship, perpetuates and hands on to all generations all that she herself is, all that she believes" (*Dogmatic Constitution on Divine Revelation*, n. 8). The Church's tradition is its lived and living faith.

One final distinction: There is Tradition (upper case) and tradition(s) (lower case). Tradition (capitalized) is the living and lived faith of the Church; traditions are customary ways of doing or expressing matters related to faith. If a tradition cannot be rejected or lost without essential distortion of the Gospel, it is part of Tradition itself. If a tradition is not essential (i.e., if it does not appear, for example, in the New Testament, or if it is not clearly taught as essential to Christian faith), then it is subject to change or even to elimination. It is not part of the Tradition of the Church. It is a perennial temptation for Catholics to confuse traditions (e.g., obligatory priestly celibacy) with Tradition: on the one side of the spectrum, to make a non-essential tradition a matter of orthodoxy; or, on the other side, to treat a matter essential to faith (e.g., the Real Presence of Christ in the Eucharist) as if it were non-essential and therefore dispensable. The process of sorting out Tradition and traditions is ongoing, and involves the teaching authority of the official Church, the scholarly authority of theologians, and the lived experience of the Christian community itself.

Doctrine/Dogma

Meaning of Terms; Promulgation

A belief that receives the official approval of the Church, whether through a pronouncement of an *ecumenical* council (literally, a council drawn from "the whole wide world"), a pope, or a body of bishops in union with the pope (as at an international *synod* or at a *general* council, i.e., representative of segments of the Church universal), is called a *doctrine*. A doctrine that is taught with the fullest solemnity, i.e., so that its rejection is heresy, is called a *dogma* (literally, "what seems right"). The promulgation of doctrines and dogmas is the prerogative and responsibility of the pope alone, acting as head of the Church; the pope and bishops acting together in ecumenical council or international synod; or a body of bishops, subject to the (at least implicit) ratification of the pope—e.g., as in the case of the publication of a national catechism.

New Testament

One finds official beliefs already in the New Testament. Paul, for example, uses the word *tradition* in 1 Corinthians 11:23 (the words of Eucharistic institution) and 1 Corinthians 15:3-5: "I handed on to you first of all what I myself received, that Christ died for our sins in accordance with the Scriptures; that he was buried and, in accordance with the Scriptures, rose on the third day; that he was seen by Cephas, then by the Twelve...." The clear suggestion is that Paul is using fixed formulae for these recitals, i.e., expressions of belief which had received the official approval of the Church and were widely accepted as normative statements of Christian faith.

Present Meaning

It was not until the eighteenth century, however, that the term *dogma* acquired its present meaning, namely, a teaching (doctrine) which the Church explicitly propounds as revealed by God. The notion was formally adopted by the First Vatican Council and in the Church's *Code of Canon Law* (see canons 1323, #2; 1325, #2; and 2314, #1). According to Vatican I, *a dogma must meet the following conditions*: (1) It must be contained in Sacred Scripture or in the post-biblical Tradition of the Church, and as such considered part of God's revelation. (2) It must be explicitly proposed by the Church as a divinely revealed object of belief. (3) This must be done either in a solemn decree or in the Church's ordinary, universal teaching. Such teachings are "irreformable," i.e., they are not subject to review by a higher authority in the Church.

Magisterium

A *solemn decree* could have only one of two sources: an ecumenical council whose head is always the pope, or the pope speaking as head of the universal Church but apart from a council. *Ordinary, universal teaching* may be communicated in a papal encyclical, a synodal declaration, a decree of a Vatican congregation with the approval of the pope, or an ecumenical council. In the *widest sense* of the term, *teaching authority belongs to the whole Church*. The Second Vatican Council taught that the whole People of God participates through Baptism in the threefold mission of Christ as Prophet, Priest, and King (*Dogmatic Constitution on the Church*, n. 30). In the *more restricted sense, magisterium* applies to *particular groups of teachers whose authority is grounded in their office* (as in the case of the pope and the bishops) *or in their scholarly competence* (as in the case of the theologians). The charism of teaching, after all, is not linked exclusively with the office of bishop or superior in the New Testament (see Romans 12:6-8 and 1 Corinthians 12:28-31). In the Middle Ages Thomas Aquinas distinguished between the magisterium of the cathedral chair, i.e., the teaching authority of the bishop, and the magisterium of the professorial chair, i.e., the teaching authority of the theologian. In the *strictest sense* of all, however, the term *magisterium* has been *applied exclusively to the teaching authority of the pope and the bishops.*

Historical Summary

Without a *historical perspective*, Catholics will continue to understand the concept of *magisterium* according to its early twentieth-century meaning. In apostolic times there were many different charisms and ministries involved in the teaching process: Those of apostles, prophets, evangelists, teachers (*didaskaloi* = theologians), and administrators. Already in the days of the Fathers of the Church there were tensions among prophets, teachers, and pastors. From early in the third century the prophets receded as a recognized group within the Church, and teachers were increasingly subordinated to the bishops. Irenaeus, in his fight against Gnosticism, insisted on the primacy of the bishops' teaching as a sure guide to Christian truth, while Clement of Alexandria and Origen argued that the teachers are, in a way, part of the apostolic succession and that the Church need not look only to the hierarchical magisterium for pure apostolic doctrine. Tertullian (d. 225), in fact, tended to reduce the role of bishops to a purely disciplinary function. But in the third and fourth centuries the onslaught of new heresies solidified the magisterial standing of the bishops. Indeed, most of the principal theologians were themselves bishops. Juridical authority and intellectual competence resided in the same person.

The bishops lost ground in the Middle Ages when laymen, especially political rulers, came to the fore. From the tenth to the thirteenth centuries, the papacy in combination with religious orders assumed magisterial leadership. In the later Middle Ages, ecumenical councils such as Constance (1414-1418) and general councils such as Basle (1431-1439) included theologians in their ranks, but with the Protestant Reformation the juridical and clerical character of councils and of the *magisterium* generally was underscored. Teaching became less a matter of insight and enlightenment and more a matter of the imposition of approved formulae. The Church divided according to those who taught (and presumably no longer had to learn) and those who learned (and presumably had nothing to do with teaching). That hard and fast distinction between the teaching Church (*ecclesia docens*) and the learning Church (*ecclesia discens*) has only recently begun to disappear.

Recent Practice

The change in thinking is reflected in the *different style of teaching* recently adopted by the hierarchy. It tends to be less authoritarian, less absolutist, and less closed to other points of view. The change in thinking is also reflected in the more sophisticated process by which such teaching is formulated. Collegiality has introduced a spirit of collaboration or cooperation which is the antithesis of unilateral decision-making.

There is also a greater respect for the *historical context* of doctrinal or dogmatic pronouncements. Fundamentalism in the interpretation of dogma is no less objectionable than fundamentalism in the interpretation of Sacred Scripture. *Mysterium Ecclesiae*, a 1973 declaration of the Congregation for the Doctrine of the Faith (formerly the Holy Office, and, before that, the Inquisition), acknowledged in principle the historical conditioning of dogma. Not only do the mysteries of faith transcend the powers of the human intellect, it said, but the very expressions of revelation are historically conditioned and therefore their meaning is not always self-evident to those in some other historical setting. The meaning of dogmatic language may change from one historical period to another. The truth itself may be expressed incompletely (even if not falsely). The original dogmatic teaching may have been directed at specific questions or certain errors, and these may not be the same questions or errors at issue in some later period of the Church's history. And the dogmatic formulae themselves inevitably bear the marks of the philosophical and theological universe in which they were first constructed. The formulae may not always be the most suitable for every time and place. Indeed, they must sometimes give way to new expressions which present the same meaning more clearly and more completely. At the same time, of course, *Mysterium Ecclesiae* rejects the Modernist notion that a dogma can never express Christian truth in a determinate way (see the Appendix of this book for excerpts from this document).

Recognizing a Dogma; Dissent

Two major questions remain: (1) How do we know the difference between a dogma and a doctrine? and (2) Under what circumstances, if any, is dissent against a doctrine or a dogma possible and even legitimate?

The determination of what constitutes a dogma is always a theological problem. Surprising though it may seem to many, *there is no list of dogmas to which all Catholic theologians or even pastoral leaders would agree.* Some criteria for determining what constitutes a dogma are: (1) The teaching is explicitly identified with the essence of Christian faith. (2) It is the clear intent of the teaching Church to bind the whole Church on the matter. (3) The teaching is contained in Sacred Scripture and/or is unmistakably present in the various doctrinal pronouncements of the Church through the centuries.

Beyond that, the actual formulation must be scrutinized to see to what degree the dogma *as expressed* is authoritative. The following criteria may be helpful: (1) The argument supporting the teaching must be internally coherent and persuasive to those competent to judge. (2) There must be evidence that various legitimate schools of thought on the matter were taken into account in the drafting of the dogmatic statement and that their arguments, even if rejected, were evidently understood. (3) The dogmatic teaching must be received by the Church at large and accepted as an accurate, appropriate, and unerring expression of its faith. (This last criterion, "reception," has only recently been recovered as part of authentic Catholic tradition.)

Dissent is never possible against a dogma, assuming that the preceding criteria have been taken into account—in other words, if there is no question that it is a dogma, and if its meaning is clear to all. *To reject such a dogma,* however sincere or well-intentioned the act, *places one outside the Catholic Church and technically makes one a heretic.* Dissent against a formulation which is *purported* to be a dogma or against a particular *interpretation* of a given dogma is allowed to those who have competence to register such dissent, especially theologians and other scholars of the Church. This is not to say, however, that the authority of dogmas finally depends upon their acceptance by theologians and other scholars.

Dissent against a non-dogmatic teaching (doctrine) is always a possibility, although the less competent one is to understand the issue at hand, the less responsible is the dissent he or she might render against the teaching. The first instinct of the faithful member of the Church is to accept the teaching (internal or religious assent) and to express that acceptance (external assent). One may legitimately withhold external assent if sufficient doubt remains. This would be the case if (1) the teaching did not seem to make sense (even if one is wrong, one cannot pretend to see truth where none seems present); (2) the teaching seems to conflict with other, clearly established truths of faith; (3) the teaching conflicts with one's own Christian experience regarding the matter in question; or (4) the teaching generates dissent from other members of the Church who merit respect by reason of their scholarly competence, pastoral experience, or personal integrity and prudence.

A theologian, on the other hand, unlike the ordinary faithful, has a responsibility to subject every doctrinal pronouncement to critical scrutiny, for that is an essential part of the theologian's ministry to the Church. If the theologian concludes that a particular teaching is in error or at least significantly defective, he or she not only may withhold internal and external assent but even has the right and duty to *express* dissent in the public forum: first, among his or her professional peers to test this original reaction; and then, to the extent necessary, among a wider audience whose Christian lives may be directly affected by the teaching. The recognition of this right and duty is also a relatively new development in Catholic thinking and practice.

In the days before the revolution in communications, the public expression of dissent was almost moot except in the most unusual cases. Today official teachings are immediately available to everyone, and those competent to evaluate them are almost immediately asked for their opinion. Many such matters become the subject of public controversy. Public disagreement with official teachings is inevitable. The challenge, therefore, is to formulate and express that disagreement according to objective and recognizable criteria and in a pastorally sensitive way.

Liturgy and Christian Education

Basically the same principles apply here as were applicable above. Creeds, prayers, and other formulae of worship are expressions of belief that are officially approved and proposed for general acceptance and use. They, too, are always subject to theological scrutiny according to the criteria already enumerated. The same is true of catechisms and other instruments of Christian education. Insofar as they reproduce dogmatic formulae, they assume the authority of the formulae. Insofar as they express doctrine, the doctrine is no more and no less authoritative in the catechism than it is in its original setting. Insofar as the catechism or educational instrument expresses theological opinions, those opinions are as strong or as weak as the arguments which support them. And that applies, of course, to this book as well.

It is precisely through our eucharistic and sacramental celebrations, on the one hand, and through the religious instruction process, on the other, that the vast majority of Catholics come into contact with the beliefs of the Church.

Belief: A Synthesis

1. A *belief* is any *expression of faith* and, more immediately, of theology. The belief, however, may be accurate or inaccurate, appropriate or inappropriate, in accordance with the authoritative sources of Christian Tradition (Bible, ecumenical councils, writings of the Fathers and doctors of the Church, papal encyclicals, general councils, synods of bishops) or with the actual experience of the community of faith.

2. The *Bible* (as well as the other "authoritative sources" mentioned above) is itself an expression of belief. It has an eminence among all other sources because it alone is inspired by God. As such, it is protected from fundamental error in matters pertaining to salvation.

3. The process of formulating authoritative beliefs continued after the biblical period, and in a much more systematic

fashion in order to meet the challenges of non-believers and believers alike. The assorted post-biblical expressions of belief have been called *Tradition*.

4. It is inexact to speak of *Tradition* as if it were simply opposed to Sacred Scripture as a separate and independent source of divine revelation. *The Bible is itself the product of Tradition—of many traditions, in fact.*

5. In the *wider meaning* of the term, Tradition refers to *the whole process of "handing on" the faith* from Christian generation to Christian generation, through preaching, catechesis, teaching, devotions, gestures, doctrines, and the Bible itself.

6. In the *strict sense* of the term, Tradition refers to *the content of the Church's post-apostolic teaching*, written and unwritten alike.

7. There is also a distinction to be made between Tradition and tradition(s). Tradition (with a capital *T*) is the living and lived faith of the Church; traditions are customary ways of acting or expressing matters related to faith which may or may not be essential to that faith. (Benediction of the Blessed Sacrament is a non-essential tradition; the celebration of the Eucharist is an essential tradition.)

8. *A doctrine* is *a belief that is officially taught by the Church*; a *dogma* is *a doctrine taught with the highest solemnity and is immune from fundamental error.* One might reject a doctrine, but not a dogma, and remain within the communion of Catholic faith.

9. The distinction between a dogma and a non-dogmatic doctrine, however, is not completely helpful because *there is no list of dogmas to which all Catholic theologians or even pastoral leaders would agree.*

10. Insofar as *dogmas* are human expressions of belief, they are *subject to the same limitations of language, style, structure, and even appropriateness as any human expression.* To say, therefore, that dogmas are *irreformable* (as the First Vatican Council taught) is to say that they are *not subject to review by some higher authority in the Church.*

11. The *official beliefs* of the Church are communicated by an authoritative teaching body known as the *magisterium.* The

term *magisterium* also applies to the teaching authority residing in that body of teachers.

12.   In the *widest sense* of the term, *magisterium* may also apply to *the whole People of God*, whose authority is rooted in Baptism; in the *narrower sense*, to *the hierarchy and the theologians,* whose authority is rooted in office and competence respectively; and in the *narrowest sense*, to *the hierarchy alone.*

13.   Dissent against an official teaching is possible, perhaps at times even mandatory. *In principle, dissent against a dogma is impossible for a Catholic.* It is an act of heresy, and as such separates one from communion with the Church. *In practice, it is often difficult to decide when, in fact, a doctrine has acquired dogmatic status.*

14.   *Dissent against a doctrine presupposes some competence* on the part of the dissenter, whether a competence of *scholarship* or a competence of *intelligent experience.*

15.   *Liturgy* and *Christian education* embody and communicate beliefs. Indeed, *it is through these two channels that most Catholics come into immediate contact with the beliefs of their faith-tradition.*

SUMMARY

1.   If Catholicism is in *crisis* today, it can be explained in part by the persistent failure of many Catholics to understand the differences among faith, theology, and belief: *Faith is not theology; theology is not belief; faith is not belief.*

2.   *Faith* is personal knowledge of God gained through the experience of God (revelation). *Theology* is the interpretation of one's own faith. *Belief* is an expression of faith and, as such, is a work of theology.

3.   Beliefs take many different *forms*: the Bible, doctrines and dogmas, writings of the Fathers and doctors of the Church, decrees of ecumenical councils, general councils, synods of bishops, papal encyclicals, creeds, liturgies, catechisms, and other instruments of Christian education.

Thus:

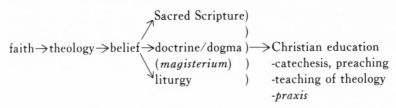

4. *Faith* is at the same time individual and communal, of the mind and of the heart, free and certain, reasonable and supernatural.

5. *Theology* is the interpretation of one's own faith in God; *Christian* theology is the interpretation of one's own Christian faith—that is, of one's own perception of God in Jesus Christ.

6. *Belief* is an expression of faith and a work of theology. The most authoritative expression of faith (because it is inspired by God) is the *Bible*. After that, there is *dogma* (a teaching proposed by the official Church with the highest degree of solemnity). After that, there is *doctrine* (or any official teaching of the Church proposed by the pope alone, an ecumenical council, a general council, or a synod of bishops). After that, there are the *writings of the Fathers and doctors of the Church*. Each of these expressions of belief is a work of *magisterium*, i.e., of teaching authority (whether of office or of competence or of both).

7. Other forms of belief are contained in creeds, the liturgy, catechisms, and other instruments of Christian education. Each is as authoritative as the source or sources from which it is drawn or which now sanction and commend it to the Church at large.

8. The whole process of handing on the faith (as outlined in the schema above) is called Tradition. Theology begins at the point where a person begins to reflect on his or her faith. Tradition begins at the point where such reflections are communicated to others.

9. Fidelity to Tradition (capitalized to exclude all non-essential and non-binding customs and opinions) is not inconsistent with dissent, so long as that dissent is formulated and expressed in a responsible manner, i.e., derived from one's area of competence.

SUGGESTED READINGS

Congar, Yves. *A History of Theology.* New York: Doubleday, 1968.
Dulles, Avery. *Apologetics and the Biblical Christ.* Westminster, Md.: Newman Press, 1963.
_____. *The Survival of Dogma.* New York: Doubleday, 1971.

Moran, Gabriel. *Scripture and Tradition: A Survey of the Controversy.* New York: Herder & Herder, 1963.

Moroux, Jean. *I Believe: The Personal Structure of Faith.* New York: Sheed & Ward, 1959.

Rahner, Karl. "The Development of Dogma." *Theological Investigations.* Baltimore: Helicon, 1961, vol. 1, pp. 40-77; "Considerations of the Development of Dogma." 1966, vol. 3, pp. 3-35.

Schillebeeckx, Edward. *The Understanding of Faith: Interpretation and Criticism.* New York: Seabury Press, 1974.

PART ONE

HUMAN EXISTENCE

HUMAN EXISTENCE

INTRODUCTION

The first theological question we ask ourselves is "Who am I?" or "Who are we?" It is precisely in our attempt to come to terms with the meaning of our own lives that we raise the question of God, of Christ, of Church, and of Christian moral behavior.

We raise the question of *God* because we seek the deepest and surest foundation of meaning that we can find.

We raise the question of *Christ* because we seek some concrete, personal, historical expression of that foundation of meaning. Christ is our way of getting in touch with God.

We raise the question of the *Church* because we seek some institutional and communitarian expression of Christ as the personification of ultimate meaning. The Church is our way of getting in touch with Christ.

And we raise the question of *Christian existence* because we seek some experiential verification of the meaning we embrace. Christian living is the way we express our relationship with the Church, with Christ, and ultimately with God.

But we start with the question of ourselves, with the question of *human existence*. It is, after all, *we* who have come to a belief in God, in Christ as the Word of God, and in the Church as the Body of Christ. It is *we* who seek to find meaning and order in our lives and in our world. Since all theological questions *begin* with us, as the ones who raise them in the first place, theology cannot afford to take for granted the *questioner* if it really hopes to understand both the questions we ask and the answers we have been fashioning in response.

Accordingly, chapter 3 offers a *description* of the human situation today, a situation which poses particular kinds of questions and demands particular kinds of answers. We live in a so-called *modern world*. In what does *modernity* consist, and how does it affect our self-understanding?

Chapter 4 explores the range of answers which have emerged in the modern world. Under the umbrella term of *anthropology*, the chapter considers in sequence the understandings of human existence which have been developed in the natural and social sciences, in modern literature, in philosophy, in theology, and in the official teachings of the Catholic Church.

Chapter 5 actually attempts a coherent *theology of human existence* (or theological anthropology) by examining the biblical, doctrinal, and theological meaning of the human person, and specifically an understanding of *nature, grace,* and *Original Sin.*

A theological anthropology sums up the whole of theology, for in our understanding of human existence we progressively articulate our understanding of God, of Christ, of redemption, of Church, of the moral life. No aspect of theology is untouched by our anthropology. Therefore, no theology can begin without immediate attention to the question of human existence.

·III·

THE HUMAN CONDITION
TODAY

"THE SIGNS OF THE TIMES"

Like most ecclesiastical declarations emanating from the Vatican (the tiny political entity which houses the Catholic Church's central administrative offices), the documents of the Second Vatican Council are known by the first two words in the original Latin text. Thus, the *Dogmatic Constitution on the Church* is called *Lumen gentium* ("Light of Nations") and the *Dogmatic Constitution on Divine Revelation* is called *Dei verbum* ("The Word of God"). But the conciliar documents are also identified by their general titles (the other designation given in the preceding examples).

The general title for the council's only "pastoral" constitution is of particular significance. Known on the one hand as *Gaudium et spes* ("Joy and Hope"), it is also commonly cited as the *Pastoral Constitution on the Church in the Modern World.* The preposition *in* is exceedingly important. The constitution is not about the Church *and* the modern world, but about the Church *in* the modern world. The former construction would have emphasized the over-againstness of the Church in relation to the world, as if the Church were somehow different from, and even at odds with, the human community at large. The latter construction emphasizes the integration of Church and world. The Church is not the non-world. The Church is not something completely apart from the world. Rather, the Church is in the world and the world is in the Church.

Even here, in so seemingly a trivial matter, one can perhaps appreciate a basic difference in the traditional theological approaches of Catholicism and Protestantism. Protestantism emphasizes the *dialectical*. Affirmation is set against negation, "Yes" against "No"; e.g., in society individuals are set against the larger community. Catholicism, on the other hand, emphasizes the *analogical*. Realities are more similar than different; e.g., society is like a human body; the parts are not at odds with the whole nor the whole with the parts.

The *Pastoral Constitution* itself emerged from the deliberate collaboration of two of the most important Catholic leaders in the twentieth century, Pope John XXIII and Cardinal Leo–Jozef Suenens, Archbishop of Malines-Brussels in Belgium. On Christmas day, 1961, Pope John formally convoked the council in a constitution entitled *Humanae Salutis* ("Of Human Salvation"). The document used the phrase "signs of the times" (previously limited, by reason of its biblical origins, to the frightening events that are to precede the end of the world) in an entirely optimistic sense. Pope John would employ the term in the same positive manner more than a year later in his encyclical letter *Pacem in Terris* ("Peace on Earth"). Developments are occurring in human history, it said, which the Christian ought not necessarily shrink from, fear, or resist. They are perhaps instruments of divine revelation. God may be summoning us to recognize new challenges and to devise new ways of meeting these challenges. God may be calling us to conversion in its deepest meaning, a "change of mind" (Mark 1:15).

"Indeed," the pope wrote, "we make ours the recommendation of Jesus that one should know how to distinguish the 'signs of the times' (Matthew 16:4), and we seem to see now, in the midst of so much darkness, a few indications which augur well for the fate of the Church and of humanity."

Soon after the pope's official convocation of Vatican II, Cardinal Suenens issued a pastoral letter for the Catholics of his archdiocese on the state of the Church and the opportunities open to it. Pope John saw the letter and advised Suenens that it represented his own views exactly. The influence of the Suenens letter on the pope's opening speech to the council on October 11, 1962, was pronounced. Pope John dismissed the worries of those "prophets of gloom, who are always forecasting disaster, as if the end of the world were at hand." Divine Providence, he declared, is "leading us to a new order of human relations" in accordance with "God's superior and inscrutable designs." This new order is one founded on unity: the unity of the entire Church and of all humankind The council, therefore, must be attentive to both kinds of un.ty. Its focus cannot be exclusively on the Church.

Less than two months later, on December 4, Cardinal Suenens addressed the council as its first (of four) sessions moved toward adjournment. We need to do more, he urged, than examine the mystery of the Church as it is in itself (*ad intra*). We must also reflect on its relationship with the world at large (*ad extra*). Commentators have interpreted this speech by Cardinal Suenens to have been a crucial moment in the history of the council, and certainly for the genesis of the *Pastoral Constitution on the Church in the Modern World*. They also suggest that the cardinal made his speech with the knowledge and approval of the pope.

And so a unique kind of ecclesiastical document was produced, a "pastoral constitution," in which the Church is said to have the "duty of scrutinizing the signs of the times and of interpreting them in the light of the Gospel .... We must therefore recognize and understand the world in which we live, its expectations, its longings, and its often dramatic characteristics"(n. 4).

What is that world like? What is the state of the human community today? What is the present human condition, of which the Church is an integral part and for which it has an abiding missionary responsibility?

THE MODERN WORLD
A World of Change

It has been observed that if the last fifty thousand years of human existence were divided into lifetimes of approximately sixty-two years each, there have been about eight hundred lifetimes. Of these eight hundred, six hundred and fifty were spent in caves. Only during the last seventy lifetimes has it been possible to communicate through the written word, and only during the last six lifetimes has the human community had access to the printed word. Only during the last four lifetimes have we been able to measure time precisely, and only in the last two have we had the use of an electric motor. And within the same lifetime, our own, we have seen part of the world pass successively from agriculture as the primary form of human labor, to the manual labor of factories, and then to the so-called white-collar labor of salespersons, administrators, educators, communicators, and so forth.

In the meantime the world's population has experienced explosive, almost incomprehensible, growth in this century. More than one hundred years ago only four cities had a population of a million or more. By 1900 there were nineteen; by 1960, one hundred and forty-one. Just over ten years later the urban population had doubled again.

The same kind of accelerated change has occurred in the area of transportation. In the year 6000 B.C. the camel caravan provided the fastest transportation over long distances: about eight miles per hour (what a moderately quick jogger covers in about the same time). It was not until about 1600 B.C. that, with the invention of the chariot, the speed of travel increased from eight to twenty miles per hour. This "record" was to stand for several thousand years. The first steam locomotive, introduced in 1825, reached a speed of only thirteen miles per hour, and the great sailing ships of the same period were half again as slow. Not until the nineteenth century, with improvements in the steam engine, did we attain speeds of one hundred miles per hour. And it had taken the human race thousands upon thousands, even millions, of years to do it. What is perhaps more remarkable is that it then took only fifty-eight years to quadruple that limit, so that by 1938 planes were breaking the four-hundred-miles-per-hour figure. In another twenty-five years even that seemed modest, as the new jets doubled the mark. And then by the 1960s rockets approached speeds of four thousand miles per hour, and astronauts in space capsules were circling the earth at eighteen thousand miles per hour. The next frontier was the moon, and who knows where after that?

The whole dizzying process has generated what social commentator Alvin Toffler calls "future shock...the shattering stress and disorientation that we induce in individuals by subjecting them to too much change in too short a time"(*Future Shock*, p. 4). Sociologists differ among themselves on the interpretation of this phenomenon. Many agree that such rapid changes as these have led inevitably and inexorably to a breakdown of traditional values and traditional human relationships. Others have argued, with just as much conviction, that the human effects have been much less radical than is supposed.

The Elements of Change

That the world has undergone major change is a fact beyond reasonable debate. And the process of change continues. That, too, is clear. The causes and elements of change are less obvious, if only because many people, even those with some special responsibility for the quality of human life on our planet, have not attended to them in any coherent, systematic way. What follows represents just such an attempt. Its limited and schematic character should be readily apparent. The outline may serve, nonetheless, as a useful framework for our subsequent studies on what it means to be human, how we experience God in the midst of life, the role of Jesus Christ in making sense of existence, and the place and function of the Church in and for the world.

Science and Technology—Mobility and Communications

It is generally agreed that the so-called *modern period* of world history begins around 1500. Not coincidentally, it is just about the time of the *disintegration of Christian unity* in the West and of the rise of *critical reasoning* and *skepticism*. For whatever social, economic, political, cultural, or philosophical and religious reasons, our world has been decisively shaped by the development of science and technology. *Science* understands the way things work; *technology* applies science to practical problems. Both together have generated the kinds of extraordinary (and extraordinarily rapid) changes to which we referred earlier in this chapter. The two most significant developments have been in the areas of *transportation* and *communication*.

The automobile and the jet airplane have given the average person in economically advanced countries a *mobility* of the most unprecedented kind. The world of direct human experience is no longer geographically confined. We can meet people, talk with them, hear their points of view, argue with them, learn from them, teach them, influence them, be influenced by them on a scale unthinkable for those whose means of transportion were limited to the horse, the sailing ship, or one's own two legs.

But neither are our human contacts limited any longer to the direct and the immediately tactile. Because of the correlative revolution in *communications* we have access to one another through television, radio, telephone, films, newspapers, magazines, paperback books, and tapes. Ideas and opinions have countless outlets, and they circulate more freely than ever before in human history. The modern person is a person in constant *dialogue* with others. And through that dialogue he or she is conscious more than ever before of human *interdependence* and of the importance, even the urgency, of human *unity*.

Material and Educational Growth

If increased mobility and communications are the most significant effects of the scientific and technological revolutions, those effects have become, in turn, instruments of the same scientific and technological revolutions which produced them. They are two of the principal factors in *material and educational growth*.

Unlike those who lived before us—fifty years ago or fifty *thousand* years ago—most people in the economically advanced and politically liberal countries of the world can take for granted those *material goods* that were once the constant preoccupation and anxious concern of every man, woman, and child: adequate food, comfortable housing, sufficient clothing, necessary medicines, productive work, and opportunities for leisure. We have created what some philosophers have called a "meta-cosmos"—something over and above the natural order of things given ultimately by God. We have taken the raw material of the world (*cosmos*) and given it an order and a shape beyond (*meta*) what was there.

To summarize: *Communications* make it possible for us to know where and how our material needs can be met, and *mobility* makes it possible either to gain access to material goods or to have others deliver them to us.

Educational progress is another major by-product of the scientific and technological revolutions. We are no longer limited in our choice of beliefs, because we are exposed to a whole range of them. We are no longer limited in our choice of life-styles and values, because we are brought in touch with a whole spectrum of expressions and convictions. We are no longer limited to our own commonsense wisdom or that of our relatively small circle of family, relatives, and friends to make sense of the meaning of human existence, because we are linked with the greatest minds and greatest discoveries of present and past alike.

Education is indeed liberating in that it frees us from illusions, from decision-making based on insufficient or erroneous information, from boredom, from dependence on the sensate and the tangible, from limited choice of occupation and recreation, and especially from the dark suspicion that things cannot be other than they are.

To summarize again: *Communications* make it possible to expand our narrow individual universe of human experience by putting us in touch with persons, institutions, and scientific findings that widen our range of choice and our opportunities for growth; *mobility* makes it possible for us to reach people and institutions, and to be reached by them in turn, for our mutual enrichment.

Ambivalence of Progress

But material and educational progress is not without ambiguity, even ambivalence. As a minority of the world's population is lifted to the heights of material satisfaction, the view from the top can be sobering. The gap between rich and poor is sharpened. (That is not to say, however, that material progress in itself creates the gap, as if the poor did not exist before the scientific and technological revolutions of the last century.) We see, too, how many problems are not only left unattended by this rapid progress, but also how many problems are themselves the product of that material growth: the nuclear arms race and the stockpiling of nuclear weapons, international conflicts, civil wars, economic crises, inflation, pollution, traffic congestion, health hazards in our food, water, air, and manufactured products, crime of all varieties, and the rejection of spiritual values.

Educational growth discloses the same kind of gaps and contradictions. On the one hand, education helps the individual to understand his or her dignity as a person, his or her uniqueness, and the meaning and opportunities of freedom and personal responsibility. Moreover, education not only broadens but sharpens one's *vision of reality*. Even as it expands the range of possibilities open to personal choice, it also exposes the countlessly subtle and sometimes blatant assaults upon that freedom through the manipulation by certain kinds of advertising, through outright deception by those in government, business, or even religion, and through psychic and social conditioning. The recent popularity of books which summon the individual to greater assertiveness (looking out for Number One, playing a power game, monitoring your erroneous zones, pulling your own strings, being your own best friend) is itself an indication that many people feel themselves to be less and less in control of their own lives.

Education also expands our *social horizons*, disclosing that economic, cultural, and societal structures and patterns need not be as they are or have been. The whole affirmative action movement for women and minorities is a direct outgrowth of this discovery.

But there have been *counter-trends* as well. Even as we perceive anew the reality of our interdependence, we find ourselves living in an age of increasingly bitter racial and international conflicts, of the proliferation of the most heinous sorts of crimes, especially against the elderly, and of increasing pressures against the integrity and cohesiveness of families and of neighborhood communities.

Education, finally, expands our *political vision*, yielding for many a much greater measure of sophistication in the use (and abuse) of power: whether on the left (in various liberation movements, some of which are dedicated to violence as a normal means of effecting change), on the right (in various resistance movements, expressed either in civil repression by totalitarian governments or bloodlessly in the Proposition 13-type tax revolts of the late 1970s), or in the center (where many adopt a so-called "moderate" position, not out of philosophical conviction but simply to gain time and see which way the wind is blowing).

Religion and Change

We live in a time of accelerated change. The moving forces behind that change have been science and technology; their primary products have been material and educational growth. And mobility and communications have made those products widely available.

Religion has not escaped the effects of such change, both good and bad. The Second Vatican Council's *Pastoral Constitution on the Church in the Modern World* acknowledged this. There has been an extraordinarily significant change in attitudes and in human structures in our time and, as frequently happens, many accepted values have been called into question. This is especially true of the young, who often feel less responsible to the past because they have had little, if anything, to do with its shaping and direction. Consequently, they grow impatient with, even rebellious toward, traditional norms and customs. They want a more direct and effective hand in the development of policies for the present and for the future, and particularly of those decisions which have an immediate impact on their own lives.

These new conditions in the world today have had an effect, therefore, on religion as well, and on a scale not limited to the experience of the young: "On the one hand a more critical ability to distinguish religion from a magical view of the world and from the superstitions which still circulate purifies religion and exacts day by day a more personal and explicit adherence to faith. As a result many persons are achieving a more vivid sense of God.

"On the other hand, growing numbers of people are abandoning religion in practice. Unlike former days, the denial of God or of religion, or the abandonment of them, are no longer unusual and individual occurrences" (*Pastoral Constitution*, n. 11).

At first, therefore, the scientific and technological revolutions of this century and the major changes they produced seemed to move religion, including Christianity, off its accustomed foundations. Belief in a supernatural order of reality was shaken. Many Christians in the mid-1960s shifted from a sacred to a secular perspective in the hope of saving the credibility of the Gospel. Some were influenced in this new course by the prison writing of a young German theologian.

The world has "come of age," Dietrich Bonhoeffer (executed by the Nazis in 1945) asserted in his now-celebrated *Letters and Papers from Prison*. The world no longer takes the religious premise for granted, he said. It no longer assumes that God is "up there," ready at every moment to intervene in our human affairs, to rescue or to punish. We must learn today that only a "suffering God" can help us, one who allows us to share the pain and agony and risk of creation and to be, like the Son of God, a "man for others."

The challenge for the Church, Bonhoeffer argued, is to find a way to preach the Lordship of Jesus Christ to a world without religion, to present a kind of "religionless Christianity" that not only makes sense but may even be persuasive. By "religionless Christianity" he did not mean a religion without prayer, without worship, without doctrine, without formal institutional structures. He meant rather a Christianity that does not *confuse* the faith itself with these institutions and structures. They are embodiments, expressions, and even carriers of faith, but they are not themselves identical with faith. To be Christian, in other words, is not to perform certain devotional or ascetical practices, but to live in a fully human way, in the service of others, as Jesus lived and served.

The second challenge for the Church, Bonhoeffer maintained, is to find a way to be a servant community in the spirit of Jesus, the Suffering Servant of God (a discussion of this and other Christological titles will be taken up in chapter 12). What is to be the place of the Church (literally, "those who are called forth") in a world without religion? Can the Church continue to appeal to humankind as if the world were in some perpetual foxhole, the bullets and mortar shells whizzing overhead? Science and technology have changed the human situation. We no longer ascribe every bolt of lightning and every burst of thunder to the anger of God. As we continue to gain a certain amount of mastery over the material world, we are less and less inclined to accept a supernatural explanation of events when a purely scientific explanation will do.

But that traditional apologetic, Bonhoeffer insisted, was ignoble in any case. The Church cannot rest its preaching of the Gospel and its invitation to Christian faith on the premise that humankind is incapable of governing its daily affairs without constant attention to, and direct assistance from, the God of the heavens above. God, on the contrary, is to be found not on the borders of our life where human powers give out, but at its center. God is indeed the "the beyond in the midst of life." That is the Church's peculiar task and challenge in this age: to model itself on the servant presence of God in the midst of life, to use whatever resources it has in the service of those most in need.

Bonhoeffer's fundamentally straightforward insights were taken up by Anglican bishop-theologian John A. T. Robinson, Baptist theologian Harvey Cox, and various Protestants who became known as "death-of-God" theologians. In each instance (although with substantially different conclusions) these younger theologians accepted Bonhoeffer's remarkable starting-point —that the world has changed dramatically, that it no longer takes the reality of God and the supernatural order for granted (if it ever fully did anyway), and that it sees no necessary connection in any case between religious faith and formal affiliation with a religious community. Bishop Robinson's analysis appeared in a best-selling book, *Honest to God*, published in 1963; Harvey Cox's in a similarly successful work, *The Secular City*, published in 1965; and the "death-of-God" theologians in various articles and books, the most important of which was Thomas Altizer's *The Gospel of Christian Atheism* in 1966.

All these writers agreed that theology now had to be done according to a secular motif. (The word *secular* is from the Latin *saeculum*, meaning "world.") The Church is in and for the *world*, not above or apart from it. And Christ is a "man for others," not simply God in human form, remote from us and our human concerns. For Robinson and Cox this did not mean the denial of God or of spiritual realities (although the latter were not very strongly underscored in Cox until some of his later writings). It meant rather a new way of thinking and speaking about God, a new way of understanding the mission of the Church, and a new style of Christian existence. For the "death-of-God" group, however, it *did* mean the denial of God, the rejection of the Church, and the development of humanism without belief in the Lordship of Christ.

The Robinson-Cox approach prevailed over the "death-of-God" approach. The theology of Christ, of the Church, and of Christian morality was recast by many writers in the light of the changed human condition. The "human face" of Jesus, the servanthood of the Church, and the freedom and social responsibility of Christian existence were all emphasized, but without denying the abiding importance and religious value of each in itself.

But the Robinson-Cox approach did not prevail over *all* other approaches. With the social and political dislocations of the latter part of the decade, typified by the anti-Vietnam war protests and the dissolution of President Lyndon Johnson's "Great Society" program for domestic economic reform, Christian activism yielded in some quarters to a new Christian asceticism. There was a withdrawal from social and political involvement into new forms of spirituality represented in the Catholic Charismatic renewal, a movement begun in the aftermath of Vatican II as a way of better expressing and experiencing the Church as a community of prayer, rooted in the Bible and motivated by the power of the Holy Spirit.

By the mid-1970s the pendulum swung again, this time closer to the center. The response to the apparent eclipse of God and the supernatural, so abruptly perceived after the Second World War, was increasingly formulated on a "both/and" rather than an "either/or" basis. Jesus Christ is indeed fully human and totally sensitive to, and involved in, our personal concerns, but his sensitivity and involvement are of significance to us only because he is in the first instance the Son of God and the Lord of history. The Church is indeed called to be a servant community, but its service is of significance because it is in the first instance the Body of

Christ. And Christian existence is indeed a life of freedom and social responsibility, but it is a freedom given by the Holy Spirit and a responsibility for the Kingdom of God, or the realization of unity through the transforming presence of God's love and justice.

Chapter 6 will be devoted entirely to the problem of belief and unbelief. The preceding exposition and analysis, therefore, has been deliberately brief.

THE CHURCH IN THE MODERN WORLD

Sociologists describe the modernization process in different ways. Many insist that it has happened in spite of, or even over against, the Church; others, far fewer in number, insist just as strongly that Christian faith has made the scientific and technological revolutions possible in the first place. The former interpretation is offered by Talcott Parsons and his school of disciples; the latter view, by Andrew Greeley and, to some extent, Harvey Cox.

Parsons notes the growth of competing institutions alongside the Church and the family (governmental bureaucracies, business organizations, universities). Productive and economic functions shifted away from the family unit to the new corporations, while the Church yielded many of its legal, economic, and welfare roles to the new state bureaucracies. Greeley has argued, over against this view, that certain uniquely Christian notions led to the conclusion that science is not merely for knowledge but also for action: History is a process rather than a cycle; the universe is purposeful and therefore understandable; the world is a sacrament of God's presence, and we are called by God to collaborate with the divine plan by vigorous action in and for the world.

Harvey Cox had made a similar point in *The Secular City*. Secularization (i.e., the process of moving away from a religious answer to *every* human problem and toward the acceptance of substantial responsibility for the quality of human life) is not the enemy of the Gospel. On the contrary, the Bible's own sense of history requires it, starting with the Lord's command to Adam and Eve to name the animals in the Garden of Eden (Genesis 2:19-20). Unfortunately, humankind has frequently shrunk from the responsibility, starting with the moment in the same Garden of Eden when Adam and Eve allowed a serpent to dictate their action (Genesis 3:1-7).

Whatever the sociological explanation of the modernization process, it is clear that the world has changed markedly over the past few centuries, and has changed even more rapidly over the past several decades. We have already reviewed those changes. It is evident that science and technology have contributed mightily, not to say decisively, to them. Whether science and technology have developed in reaction to the Church and its faith, or whether science and technology have developed because of, and under the inspiration of, the Church and the Church's faith is a matter of sociological debate. From a purely theological point of view, however, the Greeley/Cox position is readily sustained, as we shall argue in the next two chapters.

The principal products of the scientific and technological revolutions, as we have seen, have been material and educational progress. These, in turn, have been supported by advances in transportation and communications. And these, in turn, have accentuated an essential aspect of human existence which was perhaps not sufficiently understood before the so-called modern period—namely, that men and women are persons in *dialogue*, that we grow by dialogue, that through dialogue we become increasingly aware of our interdependence, and that through our new awareness of interdependence we become increasingly sensitive to our responsibility for *the unity of the human race*.

The Church, therefore, need not be threatened by modernization. On the contrary, the modernization process only confirms what Christ and the Church have consistently taught: We are brothers and sisters, children of one Father in heaven, and we are to love one another as the Father has first loved us (John 15:9-17; 1 John 4:7-21). Modernization has disclosed that we cannot live isolated lives, that we can be fully human only insofar as we are open to the other in dialogue and in mutual support. Unfortunately, the principle is too often honored in the breach.

The Second Vatican Council, in the same *Pastoral Constitution*, correctly saw the crisis of modernization as a special opportunity for the Church. In the face of such developments, it said, more and more people are raising the most basic questions about the meaning of life or raising those questions with a new sharpness: "What is man? What is this sense of sorrow, of evil, of death, which continues to exist despite so much progress? What is the purpose of these victories, purchased at so high a cost? What can man offer to society, what can he expect from it? What follows this earthly life?" (n. 10).

These are the kinds of questions which are addressed in the next chapter.

SUMMARY

1.   The Catholic Church's first official *positive* acknowledgement of modernization (as opposed to the vehemently negative assessments of Pope Pius IX in his *Syllabus of Errors,* for example) came in the Second Vatican Council's *Pastoral Constitution on the Church in the Modern World*, known also by its Latin title, *Gaudium et spes* ("Joy and Hope"), drawn from the first words of the Latin text.

2.   The document is significant for its title: the Church *"in"* rather than *"and"* the modern world. The Church is not over against the world or apart from it. *The Church is in the world, and the world is in the Church.*

3.   The document is also significant for its positive emphasis on the "signs of the times," i.e., *those events of history through which God continues to speak to us and summon us to respond for the sake of the Kingdom*, which is the reign of God's love and justice throughout the whole of creation.

4.   The world in which the Church lives and for which the Church exists is *a world of change* at once profound and rapid. The change is evident in the growth of the world's population and in the improvement in the means of transportation and communication.

5.   Improvements in *transportation and communication* have been made possible by *science* (understanding how things work) and *technology* (applying science to practical problems). Their principal products have been *material growth* and *educational progress*. And these, in turn, have been enhanced by the aforementioned improvements in transportation and communication.

6.   But material and educational progess have *not* been *unmixed blessings*. The former has also produced a nuclear arms race, wars, pollution, health hazards in food, crime of all kinds. The latter has made more people aware of, and therefore troubled by, the gaps between

appearance and reality on a whole range of important human issues: personal freedom, sexual and racial identity, the use of power.

7. *Modernization* has also had a strong impact on religion in general and on Christianity in particular. *Positively,* religion has been increasingly purified of magical and superstitious overtones; *negatively,* many have abandoned the practice of religion as they have embraced rational and scientific explanations for problems once resolved by formally religious principles.

8. Christian theology responded to the "world come of age" (Bonhoeffer) in the mid-1960s by stressing the *secular or worldly aspects of Christian faith*: Jesus is a "man for others," the Church is a servant community, and Christian existence is one of freedom and social responsibility.

9. A *swing away from Christian activism* developed in the late 1960s and early 1970s. This new mood (represented, for example, in the Catholic Charismatic movement) emphasized spontaneity of prayer rooted in the Bible and in an unshakable confidence in the Holy Spirit.

10. The pendulum, however, swung again back toward the *center* by the mid-1970s. Christian activists increasingly recognized the need for prayer and other traditional spiritual values and practices, while charismatics and others acknowledged the abiding importance of social justice in the life and mission of the Church.

11. Whether the modernization process happened in spite of, or over against, the Church and its faith (Parsons and others), or whether it happened because of the Church and its faith (Greeley and others) is primarily a matter of *sociological debate.* On the basis of theological principles alone, however, the argument seems weighted in favor of the latter position.

12. In any case, modernization has italicized the necessity of dialogue for human growth and the fact of interdependence within the entire human community. The Church, therefore, need not be threatened by modernization. *It is a process which confirms, rather than undermines, the Church's historic message: that we are all brothers and sisters under God in Christ and that we must love one another and work unceasingly for the unity of the world.*

SUGGESTED READINGS

Berger, Peter. *The Heretical Imperative: Contemporary Possibilities of Religious Affirmation.* New York: Doubleday, Anchor, 1979.
Cox, Harvey. *The Secular City.* New York: Macmillan, 1965.

Geertz, Clifford. *The Interpretation of Cultures*. New York: Basic Books, 1973.

Greeley, Andrew. "Modernization." *No Bigger Than Necessary*. New York: New American Library, Meridian, 1977, pp. 29-43.

Robinson, John A. T. *Honest to God*. Philadelphia: Westminster Press, 1963.

Toffler, Alvin. *Future Shock*. New York: Random House, 1970.

Vatican Council II. "The Church in the Modern World" (*Gaudium et spes*). *The Documents of Vatican II*. Ed. Walter M. Abbott. New York: America Press, 1966, pp. 199-308.

·IV·

UNDERSTANDINGS OF HUMAN EXISTENCE

THE QUESTION: WHO ARE WE?

There can be no reasonable doubt that we live in an age of rapid and substantial change. However, some will argue that the changes have been, for the most part, beneficial to the human community. Others will insist that they have been harmful, even destructive. Each side takes its stand on the basis of some (often unstated) understanding of what it means to be human. One cannot, after all, have an opinion about what contributes to human progress unless one first has an opinion about what human beings need and identifies such needs in the light of one's perception of the fundamental structure and purpose of the human person and of the larger human community in which the person lives. Similarly, one cannot have an opinion about what impedes human progress unless one also has some antecedent opinion about what makes us "human" in the first place, and about what might threaten the "human" in all of us.

Anthropology is the umbrella term we use to embrace all of the scientific and disciplinary ways in which we raise and try to answer the question, "Who are we?" *Anthropology is our explanation of ourselves.* It means etymologically "the study of human-kind" (*logos* and *anthropos*). What makes the anthropological question unique is that we are at once the questioner and the questioned. Consequently, our answers are always inadequate. They can only lead to further questions and further attempts at answers.

Indeed, if we could really get to the bottom of the matter and answer the question of ourselves without remainder, we would at that moment cease to be human. But even to draw that conclusion one has to have some prior understanding of human existence. Implied in that judgment (i.e., that we would cease to be human if we were to answer the question of ourselves finally and forever) is the conviction that freedom and openness to the future are intrinsic to the human condition. If we knew exactly what makes us what we are, what makes us act the way we act and think the way we think, every human thought and action would be programmable to achieve the precisely desired and/or intended effect.

We would marry only those whom our calculations revealed to be completely compatible with us. We would choose as friends only those with similar computerized clearance. We would associate ourselves professionally or occupationally only with those who could work with us most efficiently and effectively and who could best enhance the development of our careers. There would be no more risks, no more taking of chances. Everything and everyone would be plotted on a grid.

Life would no longer be a mystery to be faced and experienced with love, trust, hope, wonder, and not a little anxiety and fear. Decisions would no longer be provoked by crises of any kind. We would not have to choose between compelling alternatives. Motives would be unmistakably clear. Projections would be mathematically established.

Our freedom would be the freedom to bow to the evidence, or the freedom to be irrational and deny the undeniable (but even that display of irrationality would have been calculated and anticipated). As for the future, it would no longer be open. We would know it as we know the present and the past. Only physical and natural disorders (disease, famine, earthquakes, hurricanes, and the like) could disrupt our calculations, and even those would come increasingly under human control to the extent that human weakness, error, or lack of foresight was responsible for them in the first instance.

Even humor would disappear, for it essentially rests on our capacity to see discrepancies (things are not what they seem). The pompous general, in full uniform, slips on a banana peel in the midst of a military parade. The neighborhood bully is discovered to be terrified of spiders. An overbearing tightwad loses a ten-dollar bet after boasting loudly that he would be a sure winner. Indeed, there could be no real discrepancies at all. Things would always be as they seemed, for the motives and inner psychic forces governing the action of others would be apparent to all. Nothing would, or could, catch us off guard or by surprise. Laughter, which according to some philosophers is our way of defying the darkness of doubt and ignorance about the future, would be reduced to the sardonic chuckle of one "in the know."

Some, at first glance, might find the prospect of a totally calculable society positively exciting. Most others, it can fairly be assumed, would be frightened and appalled by the thought. In any case, the point remains moot for the time being. The emergence of test-tube babies, computer dating services, and various forms of behavior modification notwithstanding, we are still a long way from that kind of world. In the meantime, all of us continue to "make do" with what we have, to make decisions laden with risks, and to place our trust in people we are never fully and finally sure of.

We are, as the German philosopher Friedrich Nietzsche (d. 1900) put it, an "as yet undetermined animal." We can look back in history at the way we have used our freedom and then draw inferences about who we really are, about our motives and our actions. And since that history is *not yet finished*, our understanding of ourselves is always tentative, subject to revision. Since that history is also *multi-faceted*, our understanding of ourselves is possible only if we use a variety of approaches: biology, ethology, sociology, economics, politics, psychology, literature, philosophy, and theology.

The rest of this chapter will be taken up with the views on human existence of such disciplines as these. Given the nature of this book, major emphasis will be placed on philosophical and theological positions.

A SPECTRUM OF ANSWERS
The Natural Sciences:
Biology, Ethology, and Anthropology

For centuries our self-understanding as human beings had been expressed in terms of the *Ptolemaic world view:* The earth is the center of the whole universe, and we are the center of the earth by the design and will of God. With the *Copernican revolution* the sun displaced the earth as the center, and so we, too, were pushed closer to the margin of the cosmic order. But there endured a tenacious confidence in the powers of reason and in the intellectual faculty as the great line of demarcation between human beings and the rest of life. This conviction, too, would be put to the test in the middle of the nineteenth century.

Darwin

Charles Darwin (d. 1882) was a *biologist* who, in his early years, was at the same time a believing Christian. He accepted the fixity of species and their special creation as depicted in the book of Genesis. But doubts began to emerge in 1835 when he visited the Galápagos Archipelago, where he noticed that very small differences were present in the so-called species inhabiting separate islands. His original doubts were only reinforced by additional observations of flora, fauna, and geological formations at widely separated points of the globe. All living things, he tentatively concluded, have developed from a few extremely simple forms, through a gradual process of descent with modification. He developed a theory of natural selection to account for the process, and especially for the adaptations of living things to their often hostile environments. His findings were published in *The Origin of the Species* (1859).

At first there was strong opposition to his views from biologists themselves. They insisted that directly observed phenomena must somehow be brought under general laws. But before long all scientific opposition collapsed under the weight of arguments of the kind and force marshaled in a later work, *The Descent of Man*, published in 1871. The field of battle was left entirely to his newly aroused enemies in the ranks of Christianity. Darwin himself was a modest man, not given to polemics. His public image as an enemy of the Bible and the Church was as much caused by the activities of T. H. Huxley ("Darwin's bulldog"), who delighted in crossing swords with theologians, as by his own scientific hypotheses. But Darwin himself eventually grew away from his traditional faith. He concluded that "the whole subject is beyond the scope of man's intellect . . . . The mystery of the beginning of all things is insoluble for us; and I for one must be content to remain an Agnostic."

We cannot easily overestimate the importance of Darwin's work. No longer can any serious person reflect on the meaning of human existence as if each one of us lived in an environmental or cosmic vacuum. We are not disembodied spirits. We are bodily creatures, materially linked with the rest of creation, and especially with other living beings. Reason may indeed set us on a qualitatively different level of reality, but so, too, do our will, our emotions, our sexuality, our esthetic sense, and our total bodiliness.

Other natural scientists carried Darwin's insights forward. Harvard University *sociobiologist* Edward O. Wilson suggests that "the genes hold culture on a leash. The leash is very long, but inevitably values will be constrained in accordance with their effects on the human gene pool." Nature's first commandment, Wilson argues, is to do what is genetically advantageous. In two of his principal works, *Sociobiology: The New Synthesis* (1975) and *On Human Nature* (1978), he advances the thesis that aggression, sexual differences, religious impulses, and even altruism are biologically based products of natural selection. But unlike other sociobiologists he does not go so far as to justify either war or male dominance as the inevitable outcome of our biological destiny. On the contrary, we have seen only a small portion of the human behavior that is possible. The cultures which enhance or impede this genetic potential represent only a fraction of what is possible.

Lorenz

Konrad Lorenz, an Austrian *ethologist* (ethology is that branch of biology which focuses primarily on behavior), also pursued a path similar to Darwin's. From early childhood he recorded his observations of waterfowl and noted the impact of environment on their behavior. The essence of his thought is contained in his book *The Evolution and Modification of Behavior* (1953), but he is perhaps best known for his later work, *On Aggression*, published in 1966. Although he concedes that some behavior is environmentally conditioned (the extreme form of this view is proposed by the psychologist B. F. Skinner), he holds that other behavior is genetically programmed or "imprinted." Environmental factors, of course, develop what is innately present. But it is never sufficient to change the environment if one is to change behavior. In this he strongly opposes those who seem to argue that society, not the criminal, is responsible for crime.

Every person has what Lorenz calls a *nonrational sense of values*. This alone, he says, can prevent a retrograde evolution of civilized society because we have managed to eliminate in the meantime all other selective factors in human evolution. Included among these nonrational senses of values is *human love*. Lorenz argues that the abuse of sex through gross commercialization may be at least as harmful as excessive violence in the media. The destruction of the higher emotions, the disappearance of love (falling in love, being in love), may present more of a danger to the survival of culture than violence as such. Accordingly, Lorenz has relatively little enthusiasm for the popularization efforts of such writers as Robert Ardrey (d. 1980), *The Territorial Imperative* (1966), and even less for Desmond Morris, *The Naked Ape* (1967). The latter, he insists, treats culture as if it were biologically irrelevant. If one is to call human beings apes, then let them at least be culture-apes or the "ideal conception of all apes." That human beings are naked is irrelevant. We might just as well be furry.

Eiseley

Still other natural scientists interpret human existence in grim and pessimistic terms. *Anthropologist* Loren Eiseley's *The Firmament of Time* (1962) speaks of the evolution of the human being as if it were some kind of natural disaster drowning out the ancient sounds of nature "in the cacophony of something which is no longer nature, something instead which is loose and knocking at the world's heart, something demonic and no longer planned —escaped, it may be—spewed out of nature, contending in a final giant's game against its master."

The Social Sciences: Psychology, Sociology, Economics, Politics

Freud, Jung, Fromm

Whereas natural scientists have been interested in the interaction of human behavior and the world outside the person, *psychologists* have been concerned with the interaction of human behavior and the world *inside* the person. But even this statement has to be qualified. It may apply in large measure to the founder of modern psychology, Sigmund Freud (d. 1939), but to a much less extent to those who have followed in his path and/or developed courses of their own, such as Carl Jung (d. 1961) and Erich Fromm (d. 1980).

Freud, like Darwin, made his discoveries about human existence through direct observation. Darwin examined non-human life; Freud examined the human. He concluded that human behavior is shaped by unconscious drives and motivations and that these, in turn, have some sexual correlation. Our psychic lives consist in the inner struggle of conflicting drives for power and sexual gratification, on the one hand, and the psychic and social inhibitions against the fulfillment of those drives, on the other. One of his earliest works is also perhaps his most original, *The Interpretation of Dreams* (1900). Therein, he proposed the principle of wish fulfillment, the Oedipal complex, and the influence of infantile life in conditioning the human adult.

Strongly influenced by the *mechanical materialism* of his day, Freud's basic theories were highly quantitative. Even culture he regarded as a quantitative activity in which civilization is more or less determined by the degree or intensity of the *repression of instincts*. But Freud was no biological determinist. He saw that in history the only alternative to having no culture at all and no neuroses is having civilization with the repression and neuroses it necessarily entails. He looked upon the whole process of repression as a result of the social development of humankind. Unfortunately, he was innocent of the major sociological writings of the late nineteenth and early twentieth centuries: those of Marx, Durkheim, and Weber. He remained primarily interested in the psychological and physiological, even though he was considerably shaken by the events of the First World War and became noticeably less optimistic and rationalistic about human nature.

Nor was Freud a psychological determinist. On the contrary, he was trying to liberate us from those hidden psychic forces which direct our actions. If he had been a determinist, he would not have vested any hope in *therapy* as a means of changing motivation and behavior by making the person aware of the unconscious forces at work in his or her psychic life.

Freud, of course, will always have a cloud over his head in religious circles. Religion, for him, is the product of *wish-fulfillment*. God in heaven replaces the fallible and weak human father. By becoming and remaining religious, a person can prolong the status of a child into adult life. Religion, therefore, perpetuates infantile behavior patterns, especially those having to do with guilt and forgiveness. For that reason, religion is a particularly damaging species of illusion because it militates against our necessary efforts to distinguish always between what is and what we want reality to be.

One of Freud's colleagues, Carl Jung, tempered this harsh attitude toward religion. It was Jung who introduced the distinction between the individual and the *collective unconscious*. The latter originates in those patterns of behavior (archetypes) which are determined by the human race itself and which show themselves in dreams, visions, and fantasies, and are expressed in myths, religious stories, fairy tales, and works of art. Consequently, the many images which abound in human history are more than primitive expressions. They are a necessary and profound expression of a communal experience. And this is especially true of Christianity and its rich symbol system.

Erich Fromm, a German psychoanalyst, is in the tradition of Freud (in fact is often referred to as a "neo-Freudian") but, by his own account, wishes to liberate Freud's most important discoveries from his somewhat narrow libido theory. Unlike Freud, Erich

Fromm insists that much human behavior is *culturally* rather than biologically conditioned. Culture structures persons to conform to the social mold. We are what we have to be, in accordance with the requirements of the society in which we find ourselves. Depending upon our response to these social exigencies, we can be either productive persons or automatons.

Productive persons, Fromm says, are individuals who are relatively independent of others in producing what they need for themselves as they function in society, not just economically but emotionally and intellectually as well. A productive person has a sense of his or her own authority, and the courage of his or her convictions. This is what authenticity means. Automaton conformists, on the other hand, yield to the dictates of others, faithfully obeying every signal designed to control human behavior.

Clearly, Fromm holds, the second kind of individual is the one closer to the norm of humanity. We are indeed freaks of nature in that we represent "the only case of a living organism having awareness of itself." We are beings, therefore, who seek an answer to the question of why we were born and why we are living. But we can progress or regress. We progress by increasing our powers of reason, love, and relatedness to others. We regress by seeking only security. In Fromm's judgment, we seem to be losing the battle, although compelling human figures like Pope John XXIII are encouraging reminders of the deep reservoir of strength still present within the human community.

Marx

Karl Marx (d. 1883) is, of course, *sociologist, economist,* and *political theorist* wrapped up in one. Best known for his *Communist Manifesto* (1847) and *Capital* (1867), Marx, like Darwin, argued that human beings are definable only in relation to other realities. For Darwin, human beings are part of the larger natural order. For Marx, they are part of the larger *social* order. "The essence of man is no abstraction inherent in each separate individual," he wrote. "In its reality it is the ensemble of social relations." And Marx, like Freud, insisted that human problems are traceable to conflicts produced by *alienation*. For Freud, the alienation is from one's true self; for Marx, the alienation is from the fruits of one's labors and thus from the industrialized world and from other people. We are distinguished from the rest of the animal kingdom by the way we express our lives: by our work, by our various activities, by our changing of the environment, and especially by our producing our own means of subsistence.

But no individual human being, Marx holds, can sufficiently express himself or herself without benefit of society. Only in society, by joint effort, can we express ourselves in the complex way we do. Human beings, therefore, do not really appear on the historical scene until there is society, for *it is only in and through society, the collective, that we are who and what we are.* It is already there when we are born, and it conditions the kind and quality of lives we lead. The individual is derived from society and, therefore, is secondary and subordinate to it.

However, Marx maintains, if each person is essentially social, then each person should enjoy and share in all of the fruits of social collaboration. But because of the structure of capitalist societies, we are divided into the haves and the have-nots, masters and slaves, capitalists and proletarians. The great mass of humankind is alienated or separated from the products of its labors. Instead of expressing themselves through their labor (as in a work of art), most human beings are forced to sell their products to some entrepreneur in order to survive. Moreover, instead of expressing themselves fully through a variety of activities, they are forced to perform only one monotonous task all day long while someone else performs another (a process Marx called the "division of labor").

The solution to this unhappy state of affairs lies in changing the economic base on which society is built, Marx argues. It is not enough, in other words, to *interpret* the world (as Marx accused Feuerbach (d. 1872) of doing), but we must also struggle to *change* it. The way to free human beings from alienation is to destroy its causes: private property and the division of labor. We shall once again enjoy the fruits of our own labors and the labors of our fellow human beings in a society he called "communist." In such a society, *each contributes according to ability and receives according to need.* When we have all we need, there will be no envy, theft, or other crimes against our fellow human beings. The world, one might suggest, awaits the evidence.

Important elements of Marxist theory have, of course, been adopted generally, even in the West. There is a greater recognition of the need to change social and economic structures to achieve justice. We have become more fully aware of the impact of economic factors in the history of ideas and on our accumulation of knowledge. And *laissez-faire* liberalism, of the sort Marx himself faced, has been rejected as an unacceptable and ultimately unjust expression of economic values. On the other hand, there is an unmistakable conflict between Marxist theory and human freedom: freedom of expression, freedom of worship, freedom of movement, freedom of communication, freedom of thought. The crude and cruel suppression of the uprisings in Hungary (1956) and Czechoslovakia (1968), the harassment of Alexander Solzhenitsyn and other Soviet dissidents, and the human slaughter that followed the Communist "liberation" of Cambodia in 1975 are only a few cases in point.

There have been recent efforts to extricate Marxism from its almost obsessive preoccupation with economics and use it instead as an all-embracing critical social theory, with some emphasis on cultural criticism and even psychoanalysis. A noteworthy example is the so-called Frankfurt School of social criticism, composed of such figures as Herbert Marcuse (d. 1979), Jürgen Habermas, and others. They have tended to explain very well what has to be changed in human society to maximize freedom but less well what has to be preserved. The objectives of the change also remain vague. From its very beginning, in fact, this group of theorists has resisted the temptation to develop a coherent philosophical system. It has always functioned instead as a kind of gadfly of other existing systems and points of view.

The Humanities: Literature

The implications of the Marxist image of human beings were explored by Arthur Koestler in *Darkness at Noon* (1961). The novel's subject is the great Soviet purges of the 1930s and the imprisoning, interrogation, and trial of Rubashov, one of the old guard of the Russian revolution. Rubashov now feels a sense of guilt for some of his actions on behalf of the Party, including even the sacrifice of his own secretary. He had done it unquestioningly. The Party was clearly supreme over every individual need or want. But looking back over his behavior, Rubashov now sees how inhuman it was. In his fidelity to an abstract idea, he had effectively denied the reality of human beings.

John Steinbeck's *Grapes of Wrath* (1962) offers a different approach. Tom Joad, whose family has been uprooted from Oklahoma to work in the fields of California, devotes himself to the fight for social justice through the organization of the workers and the strikes. His response to alienation is not filtered through an abstract philosophical system but through personal dedication to real people caught in inhuman conditions. Yet even Tom Joad is not free of further torment. He kills the man who has killed his friend, Jim Casy, and has to leave his family.

Both novels show how socialized we are. The sources of alienation are in society itself, and our common challenge is their removal.

T. S. Eliot (d. 1965) begins with life as it is experienced today: empty and inauthentic. In the *Love Song of J. Alfred Prufrock* (1917) we find social consciousness almost completely inverted. Prufrock thinks only of what others think of him (Fromm's "automaton conformity"). For Prufrock as for Sartre, hell is other people. It is the world of the *Waste Land* (1922), dry and lifeless, a kind of death in life. In the latter part of *Waste Land* the thunder brings rain, but it signifies the rebirth of an individual, not the salvation of humankind. The landscape remains desolate. In his later writings, however, Eliot draws from Christian mysticism, which requires prayer, silence, and ritual. But that mysticism is also for a community, not just for an individual. The community he describes is hierarchically structured, and so Eliot's image of the human race is of one that is divided into classes. Meaningfulness is derived from one's sense of place within the hierarchy. There is a kind of "high Church" elitism here that is barely concealed.

Georges Bernanos' (d. 1948) *Diary of a Country Priest* (1936) poses a contrast with Eliot's Becket in *Murder in the Cathedral*

(1935). The country priest is young, inexperienced, and pastorally awkward. Beset by a lack of self-confidence and illness, the priest nonetheless assumes the burdens of his people, identifying readily with their suffering and pain. His clumsiness and ineptitude remain with him to the end. But unlike too many of our contemporaries torn by inner conflicts, self-hate, and insecurity, the country priest deals with life in a manner that is at once honest, humble, and self-accepting. And so he dies at peace.

We have, to be sure, only lightly touched the surface in this brief exploration of the meaning of human existence in literature. A more thorough investigation would take us through Shakespeare, Milton, Dostoevsky, Tolstoy, and countless other recent and modern works.

Philosophy

The distinction between philosophy and theology is not easily discerned. The old explanation will simply not do, namely, that philosophy proceeds from reason, while theology proceeds from revelation and faith. On the other hand, it is almost impossible to define philosophy. Any attempted definition proves to be itself one of the many philosophies which now exist. The question of the distinction between philosophy and theology is further complicated by the fact that theology and at least some philosophies claim to be concerned with the whole of reality and, therefore, universal in scope. The solution offered by the First Vatican Council—that truth comes from the same God and cannot be contradictory—is not sufficient. It is not clear, for example, whether one can be both a philosopher and a theologian at the same time, or whether such a choice has to be made at all.

Why, then, will the traditional explanation not do, namely, that philosophy proceeds from reason, and theology from revelation and faith? Because reason itself enters into the process of understanding faith and of identifying criteria and signs of revelation. On the other hand, revelation and grace are universally available, even to the philosopher. No matter how hard he or she might try, the philosopher is inevitably influenced by the faith (Christian or not) which he or she brings to the investigation of a

PART I HUMAN EXISTENCE

problem. Indeed, the problems themselves are often as much theological as they are philosophical: What does it mean to be human? How are we free? What does happiness consist in? What is justice? What is the measure of truth? How and why are we propelled in the pursuit of truth? Philosophy clearly points itself and its practitioners in the direction of God, and so onto the course marked out by theology itself.

But there is no single philosophy nor only one point of view on the ultimate meaning of life. "Philosophical" understandings of human existence cover a wide range on the spectrum: existentialist, phenomenological, processive, positivist, and pragmatic.

Existentialism

The Danish Lutheran Sören Kierkegaard (d. 1855) is perhaps the founder of modern *existentialist* thought. He was the first to emphasize the *subject* as a responsible person who must always be ready to stand alone before God without benefit of some social, even ecclesiastical, shield. By thus stressing individuality and authenticity, Kierkegaard challenged the Hegelian emphasis on the abstract and the universal. Our individuality, Kierkegaard argued, is bound up with the awareness of our limitations and especially our awareness of impending death. Therefore, it is our relationship with the Absolute that finally counts, not our relationships with one another. "Sickness unto death" and "dread" are characteristic of "existential man." But Kierkegaard does not interpret them as Freud had. In his *Fear and Trembling* (1843) Kierkegaard contrasts the "ethical man" with the "religious man." The former is one who subordinates himself to universal moral imperatives (as Kant would have it); the latter obeys divine commands made directly to him as a person, as Abraham did when he was commanded to slay his son Isaac. For Kierkegaard, Abraham is a model of the responsible individual, who obeys the call of faith without seeking to be justified before anything less than the presence of God. His responsible bond with God is maintained, not by means of the categorical imperative, but by reason of his personal, inward dedication of self to God.

Friedrich Nietzsche, in the same spirit but with far different results, also wanted to do away with externally imposed values. We can recover our lost freedom only through internally created values, he held. Like Kierkegaard, Nietzsche rejected Hegel's system of universals and abstractions. In *Thus Spake Zarathustra* (1883) the transcendent no longer has any effective power and is submerged in the evils of the times. Under the circumstances man has to deify himself (Nietzsche's superman), but is aware of his own impotence in the face of a hostile world. Meaning is not out there, waiting to be perceived and appropriated. It is something we have to create by ourselves. And since this process is carried on by many men and women, the real image of the human person will emerge only through the struggle of various groups in value-creating acts. But, of course, Nietzsche had to assume some of the values that he insisted had to be created.

Unlike Jean Paul Sartre (d. 1980), for whom human existence is hell, Albert Camus (d. 1960) eventually finds meaning in life, especially in such later works as *The Rebel* (1952). Although we must rebel against the absurd, against tyranny, and even against God, our rebellion must be controlled or it can lead to disaster. We can never justify the harming of other human beings. There must, in fact, be *dialogue* among us. It is only through dialogue that we discover values together. Such values come not from abstract principles but from reflection on concrete life-situations. Modern persons must struggle against those forces in the world which war against dialogue: oppression, injustice, fear, and the like.

Martin Buber (d. 1965), the Jewish theologian and philosopher, took dialogue a step beyond Camus. He wrote of the paradox inherent in every dialogue, where each party remains himself or herself even as he or she draws very close to the other. The principal expression of his view is contained in his *I and Thou* (1958). Our relationships are of two kinds: I-thou and I-it. There is nothing wrong with the latter unless they dominate and eventually suppress the former. The opposite of I-thou dialogue is monologue, which implies selfishness and manipulation. Buber is clearly more positive than Kierkegaard about the value of interpersonal relations with other human beings. We accept God precisely insofar as we accept God's creation.

The existentialist philosopher who has exercised the greatest influence on modern theology is Martin Heidegger (d. 1976). His *Being and Time* (1927) may be the most significant philosophical book published in this century. He provides, in fact, a bridge between existentialist thought and *phenomenology*. If we are to come to an understanding of what it means to be human, Heidegger argues, then we must reflect on what it is that we are and do. This requires some preliminary descriptive steps.

We must first of all look to see what shows itself (*phenomenon*) or lets itself be seen in human existence. The test of such description is to compare it with what we ourselves actually know of existence through our own firsthand participation in it. But it is not a simple matter. Existence is not an object we can set before us and describe from the outside. We ourselves are the existents that are to be described, and self-knowledge is exceedingly difficult. Indeed we all have a tendency to conceal the truth not only from others but even from ourselves. We have to strip away the cover. When we do, we find that selfhood is not ready-made but rather is always on the way and always incomplete at any given moment. We can either attain to authentic selfhood by realizing the possibilities open to us, or we can fall below the standard of authentic existence.

An analysis of human existence discloses certain tensions or polarities. First, there is the polarity between *existence and facticity,* that is, between freedom and finitude. We exist in a world. Our possibilities, therefore, are not unrestricted. They are limited by the concrete situation in which we find ourselves, including all the "givens" of human existence such as intelligence, race, temperament, environment, heredity.

A second polarity exists between *rationality and irrationality.* Our minds move toward truth, and at the same time toward untruth, error, and deception. Freud, as we have already noted, helped us see the frightening extent to which our lives are governed by dark and irrational forces.

A third polarity exists between *responsibility and impotence.* We recognize what we "ought" to be doing and yet cannot bring ourselves to do what is demanded. In the words of the Epistle to the Romans: "What happens is that I do, not the good that I will to do, but the evil I do not intend. This means that even though I want to do what is right, a law that leads to wrongdoing is always ready at hand. My inner self agrees with the law of God, but I see in my body's members another law at war with the law of my mind; this makes me the prisoner of the law of sin in my members" (7:19–23).

A fourth polarity exists between *anxiety and hope*. In a sense, this polarity sums up all the rest. A life lived in the midst of tensions generated by such polarities as these can never be free from anxiety, i.e., from a sense of the threat of absurdity and negativity. On the other hand, such a life can be lived only on the basis of the hope that life is somehow worthwhile. Anxiety springs from the sense of the radical difference that separates us from the totality of reality, while hope springs from the sense of belonging to that totality and having some affinity with it.

A fifth polarity exists between the *individual and society*. Human beings realize themselves and their varied possibilities only in and through interaction with other human beings. *Sexuality* and *language* make this unmistakably clear. Every human being is incomplete insofar as the reproductive function is concerned, and the existence of language shows that we are essentially beings in need of communication with one another.

But it is *death* that sets the framework of human existence. When one becomes aware of the boundary or limit of human existence, then one also has recognized that this is one's *own* existence. If there is no thought of death and if the future is regarded as stretching out indefinitely, then there is no great sense of urgency or responsibility. In the inauthentic mode of existence, death is covered up. We employ euphemisms and treat the whole matter impersonally. We acknowledge that everyone must die, but we somehow manage to put our own death off into the indefinite future.

Authentic existence, however, requires that we come to terms with our own death and recognize it for what it is: the boundary and limit of our own personal existence. We are thus compelled to think of all the possibilities that are open to us this side of death and to try and bring these possibilities into some kind of overarching unity. (Recent discussions of the stages of human development—mid-life crisis, etc.—are consistent with Heidegger's perspective.) Death, therefore, is not simply the end of life, but the force that introduces a wholeness and unity into life.

Phenomenology

If existentialism is primarily concerned with the human person as a source of freedom and spontaneous activity, *phenomenology is concerned chiefly with the person as knower.* The connection, however, between knowing and deciding is very close, and so, too, is the connection between these two philosophical movements.

Edmund Husserl (d. 1938) is the founder of modern phenomenology, and the publication of his *Logical Investigations* in 1900 and 1901 marks the beginning of this movement. This work attacked what Husserl called "psychologism," which in its extreme forms is found in behaviorism. Consciousness, Husserl argued, is not materially explainable. It has a structure and rules proper to itself. Consciousness is never closed in upon itself, however. It has an intentionality; i.e., it is always conscious of something, of *phenomena.*

Phenomenology studies such phenomena, not as things in themselves (as other sciences do) but as objects of intentionality. But it does not revert to psychologism because phenomenology maintains that there is a fundamental and irreducible duality between consciousness and the world. The two are correlated as the eye is correlated with the field of vision. There can be no field of vision without the eye, and yet the two remain distinct. For the same reason there can be no reality without consciousness. The task of phenomenology is to describe the various regions of reality in the way they appear to consciousness, and to show what activity consciousness must carry out in order to allow such regions of reality to appear.

For Husserl, as for Heidegger, we are beings in time. Our past experiences enter into our present consciousness and personality. A material thing like a stone can pass through innumerable events and not be changed at all by them. A human person, on the other hand, is changed by what happens. The past is borne within the person because present consciousness retains what is past. And yet we are never imprisoned by the past. We never entirely lose the possibility of changing or redeeming the past, because the present is also open upon the future.

And what applies to the person as individual applies to the human community as a whole. Human temporality, therefore, is not a passive reality. We are not simply caught up in the flow of time. Through our consciousness we look forward to the future and retain the past. We are thereby empowered to engage in a process of inquiry into who and what we really are.

Maurice Merleau-Ponty (d. 1961) is in the same philosophical tradition as Husserl. He differs from him, however, by reducing consciousness to the lived corporeal experience. We are *embodied* spirits.

Process Thought

Alfred North Whitehead (d. 1947) began as a mathematician but turned to philosophy. His mathematical penchant for order, generalization, and systematization, however, never left him. He insisted on the interrelatedness of all reality and on human knowledge's exclusive concern with relatedness. The perceiver is a natural organism reacting to the world around him. But our experience of that world is of durations (events), not of point-instants. Change is otherwise unintelligible. In change the past flows into the present, as durations can but instants cannot. The past remains fixed and determined, however, while the future is open and indeterminate. Because of freedom we can "clutch at novelty" and alter the course of events. Religion, in the meantime, helps us maintain some sense of the importance of our individual experience within the social relationships and flowing experience of life.

One commentator has suggested that no one will ever succeed in writing a short account of Whitehead's work. That is undoubtedly true. It is a very complicated system of thought. On the other hand, the recent, almost inordinate, popularity of "process thought" in Catholic educational circles suggests that complexity is no obstacle. If the truth be told, it is only the *general notion* of process rather than the actual body of process philosophy which has been appropriated and applied.

Positivism

The starting-point of positivism is that *the only possible source of knowledge is our sense experience.* If we have no tangible data, we can make no judgments and reach no conclusions. We can deal only with what is there. The sociological counterpart of philosophical positivism is August Comte (d. 1857), who argued that science can be concerned only with facts, not values. Ludwig Wittgenstein (d. 1951) is the principal exponent of philosophical positivism. The task of philosophy, for him, is not the investigation of facts (which is the task of the exact sciences) but the logical analysis of language-units (words, propositions, speech as a whole) by which we speak of the world. There are only two kinds of meaningful propositions: those about factual relationships stemming from experience and verifiable by experience, and those about purely logical relationships which provide no factual knowledge and hence are valid independently of experience.

Positivism provides little in the way of a philosophy of human existence. Positively, it underlines our responsibility to reality as it is, not as we would like it to be. Negatively, it lacks openness to experience in all its dimensions including the religious and metaphysical, which means that positivism, in spite of its humane intentions, is silent in the face of the great human problems. "And so it is impossible," Wittgenstein writes in his *Tractatus Logico-Philosophicus* (1921) "for there to be propositions of ethics."

Pragmatism

John Dewey (d. 1952) is in the tradition of Darwin and process philosophy. The leading characteristic of his thought is its evolutionary emphasis. Many of Dewey's criticisms, in fact, are directed against the older traditional metaphysics which stressed the unchanging essence of humankind and of the universe. Human thought, therefore, is not for constructing great cosmic systems of reality but for solving problems in an intelligent and reflective way. Experience is something to be reconstituted. There is nothing beyond experience. We have to take reality as we find it and reconstruct our goals in keeping with our situation and our environment.

There is, of course, a strong similarity not only between Dewey and Darwin but also between Dewey and Marx. All three hold that it is not enough to theorize about reality; we are called upon to change it. A concept without practical consequences has no real meaning. Thus, the term *pragmatism* describes this school of thought. Dewey also used the term *instrumentalism*. Ideas, hypotheses, and theories are only so many tools for attaining concrete goals in life. But if there are no metaphysical principles independent of practical content, there can be no absolute moral norms by which one can determine the good. An ethical relativism follows.

Philosophies of Human Existence: A Synthesis

Modern philosophy is essentially a reaction against classical philosophy (Aristotle, Plato, Aquinas) on the one hand, and Idealism (Hegel) on the other. In modern philosophy there is an emphasis on the *subject*, on the *changeable*, on the *particular*, and on the *practical*, as opposed to the objective, the unchanging, the universal, and the theoretical. Thus, *Existentialism* stresses the individual's obligation to take responsibility for his or her life, and, along with *Phenomenology, Positivism, Process thought*, and *Pragmatism*, it stresses the individual's obligation to attend to reality and to history as they are, not as we would wish them to be or as we would abstractly conceive them to be. Neither reality nor the history within which human reality is framed is static and unchanging; they are in process, from a past that is fixed because complete to a future that is as yet open, undetermined. We are called upon to shape that future by reconstructing our experience and reforming our environment to the extent that consciousness and practicality allow. Human existence, therefore, is not a given to be examined, but a potential in process of realization.

Theology

Existentialism

The major existentialist theologian of this century is Rudolf Bultmann (d. 1976), a German Lutheran. It was he who applied the philosophy of Heidegger to the interpretation of the New Testament. And it was he who initiated on the Continent and in the United States a whole school of theological reflection characterized by an emphasis on the faith and consciousness of the individual believer. Nowhere is his approach expressed more simply or more succinctly than in his *Jesus Christ and Mythology* (1958).

"The question of God and the question of myself," he wrote, "are identical." Accordingly, when the Bible tells me about God, he says, it really is addressing me about myself, about the meaning of human existence. For Bultmann, existentialist philosophy offers the most adequate perspective and conceptions for understanding human existence. It does not say to me "In such and such a way you must exist." It says only "You must exist" or at least says what it means to exist.

Every person has his or her own history, Bultmann goes on. Always the present comes out of the past and leads to the future. We realize our existence if we are aware that each "now" is the moment of free decision: What is the element in the past to be retained? What is our responsibility toward the future? No one can take another's place, since every one of us must die his or her own death. In our loneliness we realize our existence.

Christian existence (or "eschatological existence") is not a worldly phenomenon but is realized in our new *self-understanding*. I encounter God not in the other nor even in myself but in the divine Word. So focused, in fact, is Bultmann's thought on the individual believer that some critics (e.g., Johannes Metz) have described his theology as "privatized." The socio-political dimension is all but lost.

Paul Tillich (d. 1965), another German Lutheran existentialist theologian who spent many years lecturing in the United States, stressed the anxiety *(Angst)* of moderns, not as something neurotic or pathological, but as something intrinsic to the human condition. Such anxiety has several sources. First, every person must have *meaning* in life, or the power of self-affirmation and integration is lost. Secondly, each has to struggle constantly with the burden of *guilt*, whether from specific actions or as a vague, general backdrop. Without some means to deal with guilt, we are led into moral confusion and aimlessness. Finally, there is the underlying *fear of death*, which poses the greatest threat of all to the self. Only by coming to terms with the world can we deal with this anxiety about death.

It is by our participation in God, who is the infinite power to resist the threat of nonbeing, that we acquire the "courage to be" fully, even in the face of these three forms of anxiety. Similarly, when we become deeply aware of historical existence as full of ambiguities, we become filled with perplexities and despair. The Christian answer is the notion of the *Kingdom of God*, which is the meaning, fulfillment, and unity of history.

Reinhold Niebuhr (d. 1971), an American Protestant theologian, also centered his attention upon the category of *anxiety*. Anxiety arises from our recognition of the limitations and contingencies of our existence and from our imagining a life infinitely better than this one. Such anxiety generates sin because we seek to bring anxiety under control by pretending to have power or knowledge or virtues or special favors from God, and this pretense leads, in turn, to pride, cruelty, and injustice. Or else we seek to escape our anxieties by turning inward and pursuing a life of sensuality.

Though not inevitable, sin is universal and existed even before we became sinners. The condition of sin and anxiety, however, leaves us in a state of despair. We sense ourselves as being at once bound and free. We are bound insofar as we are involved in the flux of time; we are free insofar as we stand outside of time. We are aware of this capacity to stand apart because we know ourselves as object, we can judge ourselves as sinners, and we can survey the past and the future. We also know that nothing actually operating in history can ever sufficiently deliver us from despair, despite our optimistic illusions to the contrary. Only a divine, forgiving, timeless love beyond history, such as has been revealed in Jesus Christ, gives meaning to human life.

Phenomenology

A Dutch Catholic theologian, Edward Schillebeeckx, adopts a phenomenological approach to the meaning of existence, consistent with the basic approach he followed earlier in his treatment of the sacraments, in *Christ the Sacrament of Encounter with God* (1960). Rejecting both positivism on the one hand and the classical definition of human nature on the other, Schillebeeckx proposes a theology of human existence based on what he calls "anthropological constants" (see his "Questions on Christian Salvation of and for Man," in *Toward Vatican III: The Work That Needs to Be Done*, David Tracy, ed. New York: Seabury Press, 1978, pp. 27-44). These constants point in a general way toward lasting human impulses, orientations, and values. Among these constants are the following: (1) the relation of the human person to his or her own bodiliness (a human being *is* and *has* a body); (2) our coexistence with other persons (the human face is an image of oneself *for others*); (3) our relation to social and institutional structures (they are not something added but are intrinsic to our existence); (4) our relation to space and time; (5) our capacity, even our drive, to imagine an ideal state (*Utopia*) which becomes the impulse of hope for the future.

Since the human condition is inevitably characterized by suffering, all action which seeks to conquer suffering presupposes at least an implicit and vague anticipation of a possible, future universal meaning (Kingdom of God). We refuse, therefore, to submit to the absolute reign of technocracy (which is itself one of the causes of suffering). Schillebeeckx's phenomenological approach is akin to, and certainly highly sympathetic with, the liberation approach summarized below in the subsection on theological pragmatism.

Process Thought

The most celebrated theological exponent of process thought is Teilhard de Chardin (d. 1955). His influence on recent and contemporary Catholic thinking is difficult to calculate but impossible to deny. Some have suggested, in fact, that his spirit hovers over the Second Vatican Council's *Pastoral Constitution on the*

Church in the Modern World, particularly its assertion that "the human race has passed from a rather static concept of reality to a more dynamic, evolutionary one" (n. 5).

Teilhard's basic premise is that all of reality, the whole of the cosmic order, is moving toward a goal (the *Omega Point*), gradually progressing from one state of development to another, each one more unified than the preceding. The highest stage of material development is life. The highest stage in the development of life is human life. With human life, consciousness achieves a level of self-reflection. We not only *know*; we *know that we know.* Human existence, therefore, represents a new and unique order of being.

Although it may appear that the "cosmic involution" (the movement toward unity) has been halted, this is not true. *Hominization,* or the progressive development of human life to higher and higher levels, continues with even greater vigor than before. We can observe this in the increasingly powerful thrust toward *socialization.* As a result of socialization, humankind is continuing to advance towards the supreme degree of consciousness. The conclusions of physics, biology, and psychology confirm this judgment, Teilhard insists. As a result of humankind's standing on its own feet, life is here and now entering a new era of autonomous control and self-orientation. We are beginning to take over the biological forces which heretofore have determined our growth. The whole evolutionary process is moving constantly toward unification and spiritualization, with the whole cosmic system rising unmistakably toward a critical point of final convergence. We shall have reached such a level of self-consciousness that no further growth will be possible. This he calls the Omega Point.

As a Christian, Teilhard equates the Omega Point with Christ. *History, therefore, is in movement toward Christ.* But Christ is already present in the world. There is even now a Christic dimension to the cosmic order. The Church, in this schema, is the "reflexively Christified portion of the world," the focal point at which human socialization based on charity occurs. Indeed, this is the whole impulse of creation. "To create is to unite," Teilhard declares. The whole of history is the story of the progressive unification of reality and of the human community in particular.

But an inevitable consequence of creation is *sin* (here, of course, Teilhard's thought runs counter to traditional Catholic doctrine on Original Sin, to which we shall return in the next chapter). Because created reality is multiple, it is essentially subject in its arrangements to the operation of chance, and therefore is "absolutely barred from progressing towards unity without sporadically engendering evil, and that as a matter of statistical necessity."

Just as sin is inevitable, so, too, is *incarnation*. There can be no creation without union of Creator with the created. For in order to create, God must be immersed in the multiple, and is even forced into war with the evil element in the multiple. The coming of Christ—another inevitable requirement and effect of the evolutionary process—maintains the evolutionary effort toward hominization by providing a focus of biological involution (involution meaning here again the movement toward unification). In Christ-Omega the universal comes into exact focus and assumes a personal form.

For the person who sees what is happening, who perceives the whole evolutionary process in the light of Christ, everything becomes animate and a fit object for love and worship. *Christian charity*, far from being simply a soothing lotion poured over the world's suffering, *is the most complete and the most active agent of hominization.*

Theological Positivism

For anyone who has been following the argument very closely thus far, this may seem a curious, if not a dubious, category. How can there be a *positivism* that is at the same time *theological?* Is not positivism a denial of what is not directly observable? And does that not include God above all else? The answer is, "Yes, of course. But ...." We are referring here not to positivism in its technical philosophical sense (such as we described in the brief section on Wittgenstein) but to positivism as a general method or approach.

Positivism limits the study of a reality to that reality's appearance in a given source or sources. A *theological* positivist is one who equates theology with the study of a given source or sources. Thus, theology is not (as we defined it in the second chapter) the process of giving expression to our experience of God, but rather the study of *documents* in which the experience of God has been recorded and interpreted (especially the Bible or the official teachings of the Church). The theological positivist understands theology as the study of the Bible (which is really equating all of theology with biblical theology) or with the study of doctrines and dogmas (which is to equate all of theology with dogmatic theology). Theology is either "the testing of Church doctrine and proclamation . . . by the standard of the Holy Scriptures" (Karl Barth, d. 1968) or is the transmission of the teaching of the Church (the methodological assumption of many Catholic theology textbooks in use prior to Vatican II).

The similarity between Wittgenstein and Barth, for example, is at least superficially apparent in the latter's definition of theology with which he begins his massive, multi-volume *Church Dogmatics*: Theology is "the scientific test to which the Christian Church puts herself regarding the language about God which is peculiar to her." For Wittgenstein, the task of philosophy is the logical analysis of language-units (words, propositions, etc.) by which we speak of the world. It does not get beyond the language to deal with the reality so described or talked about.

In theological terms, the Word of God in Sacred Scripture is taken as a given. It is simply there. One does not question it or challenge it. One comes to terms with it. For some Catholics, the same attitude prevails regarding the pronouncements of the official magisterium. Our understanding of human existence, therefore, is to be derived totally from the Bible or from the official teachings of the Church. Philosophy, or anthropology in the widest sense, is of no significant account in the inquiry.

Pragmatism: Liberation Theology

The parallel between philosophical and theological pragmatism is the same as the parallel between philosophical and theological positivism. In the strict sense of the terms, there is no theological pragmatism, just as there is no theological positivism. But there are similarities in method and approach. It is those similarities which engage our attention here.

The closest approximation of philosophical pragmatism in contemporary Christian theology is in the *Latin American liberation school*. We have already referred briefly to liberation theology in the second chapter. Its principal exponents are, on the Catholic side, Gustavo Gutierrez of Peru and Juan Luis Segundo of Uruguay, and, on the Protestant side, Hugo Assmann of Brazil. They reject both the traditional Catholic and traditional Protestant approaches to theology, the one emphasizing doctrine and intellectual assent, and the other emphasizing the Bible and trusting faith. Theology is faith seeking understanding, the liberation theologians admit, but faith is "the historical *praxis* of liberation."

The Word of God is mediated, they insist, through the cries of the poor and the oppressed. Theology, therefore, can only be a form of *praxis*; i.e., it must always be directed toward the changing of the existing social order. It cannot simply interpret it without reference to the practical consequences of the theory of interpretation. Only by participating in the struggles of the poor and the oppressed, Gutierrez argues, can we understand the implications of the Gospel message and make it have an impact on history. This, in turn, imposes a specific method on theology, which Juan Luis Segundo calls a "hermeneutic circle." This requires that our interpretation of the Bible change continually with the continual changes in our present-day reality, both individual and social.

The similarity not only to pragmatism but to positivism as well should be apparent. For the liberation school, theology's reflection on *praxis* is grounded in the Bible. Theology is essentially the study of the Bible insofar as it can be interpreted according to a liberation motif. That motif is, in turn, communicated through actual participation in the struggle for liberation. The affinity, finally, with the Marxist view of human existence is too obvious to draw out here.

Transcendental Thomism

For Karl Rahner the problem of human existence is not simply one theological question among many others. The "question of man," he insists, "must be looked upon, rather, as the whole of dogmatic theology." He argues that such a view is entirely consistent with Thomas Aquinas' teaching that God is the formal object of theology. As soon as it is understood that the human person stands alone in the whole of creation as the one being who is absolutely oriented toward God and whose very essence is determined by this orientation, then it becomes clear that a thorough study of the human person necessarily involves the study of God, and vice versa. Whatever we might say about the ultimate meaning of human existence is something said at the same time about God, who is the author, support, and destiny of human existence. And whatever we might say about God, therefore, is something said also about human existence.

Such an anthropology, Rahner suggests, must be a *transcendental* anthropology. The word *transcendental* is not easily defined. It means literally that which is capable of going beyond or above or over something else. The "transcendent," therefore, is that which is actually above, beyond, and over the tangible, the visible, the immediately available. God is *the* Transcendent, in that God is above, beyond, and over everything else. God is the one to whom all reality is oriented. Anthropology is transcendental, therefore, when the human person is seen, not simply as a collection of biological and behavioral responses, but as a being whose meaning is to be found beyond the purely corporeal and beyond the satisfaction of physical, social, psychological, political, economic, and cultural needs. The person is transcendental insofar as the person is oriented beyond himself or herself toward God as the source, sustainer, and final perfection of the person's existence.

If you wish to understand human existence, you must seek to discover the conditions in the human person which make it possible for the person to arrive at knowledge of God, to whom the person is oriented. For Rahner the *a priori* condition (i.e., the condition that must be present before any other if there is to be any knowledge of God at all) is *grace*, which is the presence of God in the knowing subject. In other words, *the human person is capable of transcending himself or herself in the knowledge of God, to whom his or her whole life is oriented because God is already present in the person as the transcendent force or condition which makes such knowledge possible.*

This *transcendental method* has been at work in theology, Rahner notes, at least since Thomas Aquinas, but it has been given a new and stronger impulse by modern philosophy, i.e., the philosophy which has developed *after* Descartes (d. 1650), Kant (d. 1804), and the existentialist movement. Much of this philosophy is deeply un-Christian, insofar as it begins *and ends* with the autonomous personal subject which has closed itself to the experience of God. But this philosophy is also most deeply Christian (more, in fact, than its traditional critics in the Catholic Scholastic philosophy of recent decades have understood) because in the Christian understanding of human existence the human person is not one element in a cosmos of things, subordinated to some abstract, impersonal system of reality based on *things.* On the contrary, the human being is the personal subject upon whose freedom as a subject the fate of the entire cosmos depends.

And indeed this has been the direction modern philosophy has been taking us in recent years. The human person is seen not simply as part of a larger cosmic mosaic, but as the most active agent, under God, in the forward movement of history itself. That is why the principal themes of today's philosophy (and correspondingly of much of today's theology) include hope, society, the critique of ideology, freedom, and planning for the future.

And that is why there is also so much emphasis today, in theology as well as in philosophy, on the anthropological dimension of all statements about the ultimate meaning and direction of life and of history. We cannot accept teachings as "truths revealed by God" if they have no apparent connection with our own understanding of ourselves, an understanding derived from our experience as human beings. A proper understanding of the relation between nature and grace would make this clear (a point to which we shall be returning in the next chapter).

To put the matter more simply (assuming at the same time the obvious risk of *over*simplifying): God is not "a" Being separate from the human person. God is Being itself, permeating the person but transcending the person as well. Because God permeates as well as transcends us, there is no standpoint from which we can "look at" God objectively, in a detached manner, as it were. God is always present within us, even before we begin the process, however tentatively and hesitatingly, of trying to come to terms with God's reality and our knowledge of God.

Accordingly, everything we say about God can be translated into a declaration about our own existence. God is a constitutive dimension of our existence. To talk about God is to talk about ourselves as well. The Word of God is not some message given from some heavenly perch, but rather it *is* God. And this is the distinctiveness of Jesus' preaching, namely, that God is present to us, not as some abstract power, but as the very core of our being (what the Scholastics called "uncreated grace"). God, therefore, enters into the very definition of human existence.

We are alive by a principle that transcends us, over which we have no power, and which summons us to surpass ourselves and frees us to be creative in the shaping and redirection of history. History is not determined by inanimate forces or by causes which already exist. Tomorrow can be different from today because God is present to history through the free human persons who are at history's center. Nowhere is this principle more sharply focused or more effectively realized than in Jesus Christ, who is the Word of God-made-flesh, the point at which the human community becomes fully conscious of itself as human and assumes full responsibility for the shaping of its future under God.

Another way of expressing this in a manner consistent with the basic lines of Transcendental Thomism has been proposed by Bernard Lonergan, author of the widely influential *Insight* (1957) and *Method in Theology* (1972). Lonergan, too, breaks away from the classical philosophical doctrine that the human person is static, unchanging, unaffected by the movement of history and variations in the environment. The human person is, on the contrary, "constituted by meaning."

Take the example of a family. On the one hand, we are convinced that families exist. We talk about them. We think we see them. We feel ourselves part of one or more. And yet no one can really touch a family or even see a family, for that matter. A family is a reality "constituted by meaning." We *interpret* a particular collectivity of human beings (a man, a woman, children) to be something *more than* what appears on the purely physical level.

We are living at a time, furthermore, when the family is under severe stress. Scientists and other social commentators distinguish among the so-called traditional family, the nuclear family, the single-parent family, the extended family, the communal family, and so forth. The reality itself changes as the meaning changes. And because meanings change, so, too, can the reality of human existence change.

We human beings, insofar as we are constituted by meaning, are, like the family, not directly available to scientific investigation or to "seeing" and "touching" in the usual sense of those words. We see and touch ourselves and other bodies that have specific characteristics and modes of behavior. But our judgment that we and they are "human" is exactly that, a *judgment*. It is a judgment that follows *understanding*, and that understanding, in turn, follows *insight*.

Such an understanding of the human person as "constituted by meaning" stands in striking contrast to the traditional classical and Scholastic definitions of the human as "rational animal." The "constituted-by-meaning" view is a *dynamic* understanding of the human, seeing the human as open to development and change, whereas the classical definition assumes a *static*, once-and-for-all given nature. Furthermore, the "constituted-by-meaning" view takes the concrete and the historical seriously, whereas the classical view is abstract. Indeed, according to Lonergan, it is precisely our new *historical-mindedness* (the distinctive feature of the modern, as opposed to the classical, mentality) which has allowed us to move beyond the earlier formulation of human existence without rejecting its own measure of truth.

But the newer view also provides a firmer philosophical, and also theological, basis for the notion of *responsible* human existence. The human person as "subject" is one who is conscious, oriented toward interrelationship with others, and capable of becoming something other than he or she presently happens to be (i.e., is capable of becoming "self-constituting"). Through increasing degrees of consciousness—from unconscious sleep to dreaming consciousness to experiential consciousness to intelligent consciousness to rational consciousness and finally to rational self-consciousness—the human person as "subject" arrives at the level of deliberating, evaluating, choosing, and finally acting. The subject is a *doer*, not just a thinker. As a doer, the subject has the potential for self-formation, for effecting changes in others or in the environment.

All the while, the subject is conditioned by the fact that one *is* a human subject: in particular places and times, in particular circumstances shaped by tradition and culture, under the impact of specific historical events, and shaped by one's own free decisions and the free decisions of others. One develops a biography which discloses the self. It is as a "subject," therefore, with all of these historical contingencies, that one *becomes* what one is.

Theologies of Human Existence: A Synthesis

The emphasis on the subject, the changeable, the particular, and the practical that we see in modern philosophy is carried over into theology. The theological *existentialism* of Bultmann, Tillich, and Reinhold Niebuhr focuses on the anxiety which characterizes human existence: anxiety in the face of meaninglessness, sin, and death. God alone allows us to overcome the contingency of human existence.

The theological *phenomenology* of Schillebeeckx explores the dimensions of that contingency and suggests that we experience transcendence in the struggle to conquer the suffering which characterizes the human condition. In this regard, Schillebeeckx's position is akin to that of the *liberation theologians* (whom I have placed in parallel with the philosophical pragmatists), in that human existence is marked by economic conflict, disparity, and oppression—and the suffering this generates. Theology, therefore, is not reflection on God or human existence as such; it is a form of *praxis*, i.e., it is a form of participation in the struggle on behalf of the poor and the oppressed. It is reflection on the human condition as an oppressor-oppressed condition of human relationships and is a formulation of ways in which that condition can be transformed by justice. There is a sense, therefore, in which existentialism and liberation theology are at cross purposes, although there are also important points of convergence: particularly their common rejection of the principle that things are necessarily the way they are and we must accept them and deal with them as they are.

Process theology is not necessarily inconsistent with either of these two approaches. It stresses the dynamic movement of history and the changeability of all reality, including God. Conservative process thinkers might stress the inevitability of the process, whereas left-of-center process thinkers would stress the responsibility of human agents in the direction and construction of history. The latter are, of course, in tune with the concerns of the liberation school.

Transcendental Thomism would seem, at first glance, to be closer to existentialism than to the more politically conscious liberation approach. But Rahner's insistence on the intimate connection between nature and grace, and between theology and anthropology, provides a foundation for an essential link between the two approaches: the emphasis on the subject (as in Bultmann) and the emphasis on the socio-political order (as in liberation theology). Indeed, even within existentialism itself (especially with Reinhold Niebuhr) we have a politically refined sense of social justice. History, for the Transcendental Thomist, is not something to be taken for granted, something inevitable, but something to be shaped and directed by free human persons in whom God, the author of creation, is present as the One who makes the new ever possible, and whose Word, in fact, provides the critique by which the old can be corrected and changed. It is in the context of history, in fact, that we *become* who we are.

Insofar as Transcendental Thomism comprehends and preserves the best that is present in the aforementioned philosophical and theological approaches, it will serve as the integrating principle of our own theology of human existence, developed in the next chapter.

Official Teachings of the Church

Official pronouncements (i.e. by popes, ecumenical councils, and general councils) have advanced the following points on the meaning and context of human existence:

1.   God is the Creator of the whole world, material as well as spiritual, and remains present to it through Providence.

2.   All created things, therefore, are good because they come from the creative hand of God. But human persons are the crown of divine creation.

3.   The dignity of the human person resides in the person's intimate relationship with God. The human person has a soul. (This is the transcendental dimension of human existence.)

4.   We are, at the same time, essentially oriented to other people. Human existence is social existence.

5.   The human condition is also characterized by a split. We are plagued by weakness and sin. We experience ourselves as limited creatures, and this generates a sense of anxiety.

6.   Nonetheless, we are called by God to master ourselves and our environment, and we are empowered to do so by grace and especially by the grace of Jesus Christ.

7.   Death is not the end of human existence. Life is changed, not taken away (to use a line from the Preface of the Mass for the Deceased). We are destined for glory.

These teachings are synthesized from the following sources:

1.   The provincial Council of Constantinople (543), which condemned certain positions associated with followers of Origen, namely, that the human body is a degrading place of exile to which preexisting souls have been consigned.

2.   The provincial Council of Braga, in Portugal (561), which also rejected the anti-matter, anti-body teaching borrowed the Origenists.

3.   Pope Innocent III's "Profession of Faith" (1208), prescribed for all those returning to the Church from the heresy of *Albigensianism*, a French offshoot of the ancient heresy of *Manichaeism*, which taught that matter is evil, and from *Waldensianism*, another French-based movement which assumed the same

dualistic notion of spirit and matter but which had as well an anti-clerical dimension directed against the display of worldliness and power in the Church.

4.   The Fourth Lateran General Council (1215), which spoke the final word against the Albigensian and Waldensian errors. Its teaching was later adopted by the First Vatican Council (1869-1870).

5.   Similar condemnations can be found in the Council of Vienna (1311-1312), the Council of Florence (1442) in its *Decree for the Jacobites*, the Fifth Lateran Council (1513), the *Syllabus of Errors* promulgated by Pope Pius IX (1864), the First Vatican Council, as mentioned above, and Pope Pius XII's encyclical letter, *Humani Generis* (1950).

6.   Nowhere is the official teaching more succinctly expressed—and without the intrusion of polemical intent—than in the *Pastoral Constitution on the Church in the Modern World* of Vatican II (1965). The principal elements of that teaching follow:

a.   We are created in the image of God, capable of knowing and loving God and appointed by God to master all of the earth for the sake of God's glory (n. 12; see also Genesis 1:26; Wisdom 2:23; Sirach 17:3-10; Psalm 8:5-6).

b.   But God did not create us as solitary creatures. We are created male and female, and, therefore, as essentially social beings (n. 12).

c.   "The call to grandeur and the depths of misery are both a part of human experience" (n. 13).

d.   We cannot, however, despise our bodies nor the created world in which we find ourselves, even though both may be the source of pain and anxiety. For by our interior qualities we outstrip the rest of creation. God is present to our hearts, awaiting our discovery (n. 14).

e.   "In fidelity to conscience, Christians are joined with the rest of men in the search for truth, and for the genuine solution to the numerous problems which arise in the life of individuals and from social relationships" (n. 16).

f.   Only in freedom—not from blind internal impulse nor from mere external pressure—can we direct ourselves toward goodness. But since our freedom has been damaged by sin, only with the help of God's grace can we bring our relationship with God and thereby with the whole of creation to full flower (n. 17).

g.   In the face of death the riddle of human existence becomes most acute. Technology cannot calm our anxiety about death, for the prolongation of biological life cannot satisfy that desire for a higher life which is inescapably lodged in the human heart (n. 18).

h.   "Although the mystery of death utterly beggars the imagination, the Church has been taught by divine revelation, and herself firmly teaches, that man has been created by God for a blissful purpose beyond the reach of earthly misery" (n. 18).

7.   A similarly positive statement on human dignity and freedom in light of the redemption is set forth in Pope John Paul II's first encyclical, *Redemptor Hominis* (1979).

SUMMARY

1.   In a time of rapid and substantial change, the meaning of human existence assumes new and urgent force. Various attempts have been made to answer the question "Who are we?" These efforts can be subsumed under the generic term *anthropology*.

2.   Answers have been proposed by the *natural sciences* and by *Charles Darwin*, in particular. We are creatures linked biologically with the rest of creation. Human existence is not simply given. It is something to be worked out through the process of evolution and adaptation to the environment.

3.   If the natural scientists have been concerned with the interaction of human behavior and the world outside the person, one of the *social sciences, psychology,* has been concerned as well with the interaction of human behavior and the world *inside* the person. This is the special contribution of *Freud*. Human existence is not simply a matter of knowing what to do (intellect) and then deciding to do it (will). There are unconscious drives, forces, and motives that influence, probably even determine, our choices and our behavior.

4.   Other social sciences, i.e., *sociology* and *economics*, focus on the social, economic, and political context in which human persons find themselves. *Karl Marx*, like Freud, insisted that human problems are

traceable to conflicts produced by alienation. For Freud, the alienation is from one's true self; for Marx, the alienation is from the fruits of one's labors and thus from the industrialized world and from other people. It is only in and through society that persons can live as human beings. The collective defines who and what we are.

5. The *humanities*, too, and especially *literature*, disclose an understanding of human existence, but one that is inevitably broad and diverse. Persons are seen as people at odds with themselves and with others, struggling to work out their identity in the resolution of conflicts.

6. *Philosophical* understandings of human existence similarly cover a wide range of approaches: the *existentialist*, the *phenomenological*, the *processive*, the *positivistic*, and the *pragmatic*. There is a *common emphasis* on the *subjective*, the *changeable*, the *particular*, and the *practical*, over against the objective, the unchanging, the universal, and the abstract. Human existence is not a given to be examined, but a potential in process of realization.

7. There are similar emphases in contemporary *theology*, although one can detect two apparently opposed orientations: the one (*existentialist*) which focuses on the subject and the importance of achieving sufficient self-understanding, and the other (*liberationist*) which focuses on the subject's responsibility to criticize and to change an unjust social order. *Transcendental Thomism*, at first glance closer to existentialism than to the liberation approach, may provide a bridge between the two.

8. For the *Transcendental Thomist* history is not something to be taken for granted, something inevitable, but something to be shaped and directed by free human persons in whom God is present as the One who makes the new ever possible, and whose Word provides the critique by which the old can be corrected and changed.

9. The *Church* over the centuries has *officially taught* that God is the Creator of the whole world, material as well as spiritual, and that all reality, including the bodily, is good. Our dignity resides in our intimate relationship with God, in spite of which we experience anxiety about the meaning of life, sin, and death. We are called, nonetheless, to master ourselves and our environment and are empowered to do so by grace. Death is not the end of life but the beginning of a new phase of life. We are destined for glory.

SUGGESTED READINGS

Baum, Gregory. *Man Becoming.* New York: Herder & Herder, 1970.

Ferkiss, Victor. *Technological Man: The Myth and the Reality.* New York: New American Library, 1969.

Moltmann, Jürgen. *Man.* Philadelphia: Fortress Press, 1974.

O'Grady, John F. *Christian Anthropology.* New York: Paulist Press, 1975.

Pannenberg, Wolfhart. *What is Man?* Philadelphia: Fortress Press, 1970.

Rahner, Karl. "Theology and Anthropology." In *The Word in History.* Ed. T.P. Burke. New York: Sheed & Ward, 1966, pp. 1-23.

Rousseau, Richard W. "Secular and Christian Images of Man," *Thought* 47 (Summer 1972), 165-200.

·V·

TOWARD A THEOLOGY OF HUMAN EXISTENCE

THE QUESTION

The preceding chapter surveyed a relatively wide range of scientific and disciplinary areas—e.g., biology, psychology, sociology, philosophy. This chapter is explicitly theological. It offers an actual position on the question of human existence, one that strives to be consistent with the Catholic tradition which provides the focus for this entire book.

This question, it must be reasserted here, is as fundamental for Christian theology and for Christian faith as is the question of God. Indeed, the question of human existence and the question of God, as we pointed out in the preceding chapter, are two sides of the same coin. Our statements about God and Jesus Christ, about creation and salvation history, about life and death, about sin and judgment, about the Church and Christian morality, are always in some important measure a reflection of our understanding of human existence and of the human condition.

For example, if I think of myself as utterly without worth, I am saying something about the divine estimation of God's own handiwork, about the effectiveness of Jesus Christ's redemptive work on my behalf, about the power and impact of Original Sin, about the value of being a member of the Church and of having access to its sacraments, about the meaningfulness of my life as a Christian, and about the basis of our common hope in the coming of God's Kingdom.

Correspondingly, if I think of myself and others as nothing more than a collection of neurological responses to be conditioned and programmed at will, then that, too, says something about my understanding of a whole schema of theological questions, not least of which are the questions of sin and redemption.

THE HUMAN PERSON
Biblical Views

Old Testament

In the Old Testament the human person is, before all else, a *creature* of God, formed out of the clay of the ground (Genesis 2:7). The word which designates "man/woman" in the concrete sense is *adam*. The word for "clay" is *adamah*. This etymological connection is crucial. We are not composite beings, made of body and soul as two separate parts (as the medieval Scholastic philosophers had it). Soul and flesh are not contrasted in the Old Testament. Unlike the Greeks, who look upon a human being as an incarnated spirit, the Hebrews regarded the human person as an animated body. We do not *have* a soul and a body; we *are* soul and body.

The hope of salvation, therefore, is expressed in terms of the *resurrection of the body* ("But your dead shall live, their corpses shall rise . . . "—Isaiah 26:19; see also Daniel 12:2-3, and 2 Maccabees 7:14), and this is taken up and developed in the New Testament (" . . . if the dead are not raised, then Christ was not raised; and if Christ was not raised, your faith is worthless" — 1 Corinthians 15:16-17; see the entire fifteenth chapter as well as Mark 12:18-25; John 6:39-40; and Acts 24:15). The idea of the *immortality of the soul*, on the other hand, is *not* developed in the writings of the later Old Testament period nor in the New Testament. The notion of immortality reflects a world view fundamentally different from the Bible's anthropology. Indeed, it is more akin to Greek philosophy (i.e., the human person as incarnated spirit) than to the Hebrew mentality (i.e., the human person as animated body).

Bodiliness is also the basis of our relationship with one another. Human existence, in the Old Testament, is *coexistence with other persons*. That coexistence is, in turn, founded on our primary relationship with God. Each of us is equally powerless in the face of God's transcendence, and at the same time of equal value before God. We are commanded by God to love our neighbor (yes, even in the *Old* Testament!): "You shall love your neighbor as yourself" (Leviticus 19:18; see also 19:9-18,34; and 25:35-38). Our responsibility for one another is underlined by the prophets as well: "But if you would offer me holocausts, then let justice surge like water, and goodness like an unfailing stream" (Amos 5:23-24; see also 8:4-6, and Isaiah 3:13-15).

Coexistence with, and even interdependence upon, one another is highlighted in a special way in the *sexual relationship*. Created male and female, human persons are most deeply themselves in a relationship of intimate mutual love (Genesis 1:27). "The Lord God said: 'It is not good for the man to be alone' . . . . That is why a man leaves his father and mother and clings to his wife, and the two of them become one body" (Genesis 2:18,24).

Human existence—at once dependent upon God and interdependent in relationship with others—is, therefore, *responsible existence*. The Lord gave Adam an order, not to eat from the tree of knowledge (Genesis 2:16). Human existence is a life of responsibility to the will of God. Fulfilling that responsibility need not be a matter of fear and drudgery; it can be one of merriment and joy (1 Kings 4:20; Psalm 43:4). Unfortunately, we are not always faithful to God's will.

The Old Testament also sees human existence as *sinful existence*. Although there is no fully developed notion of Original Sin, we are presented as sinners whose hearts are filled with pride and are thereby closed to the call of God and the cry of our neighbor (e.g., Genesis 8:21; Psalm 143, Psalm 2). Sin is portrayed as something breaking out in the world and harming not only the individual but history itself (Genesis 3-11). And that consciousness of sin deepens as the history of salvation unfolds. "Can the Ethiopian change his skin? The leopard his spots? As easily would you be able to do good, accustomed to evil as you are" (Jeremiah 13:23). But the same prophet assures us of the Lord's forgiving spirit: "The days are coming, says the Lord, when I will make a new covenant with the house of Israel and the house of Judah . . . . I will be their

God, and they shall be my people ... for I will forgive their evildoing and remember their sin no more" (Jeremiah 31:31-34).

Human existence, therefore, is or can be *hope-filled existence*: hopes for a savior and a time of salvation, for resurrection of the body and new life, for the fulfillment of the promises of the new covenant.

New Testament

The New Testament's understanding of human existence is consistent with, and develops from, the Old Testament's. Thus, we find no abstract or speculative "philosophy" of human existence, with elaborate divisions of soul and body, or of intellect and will. As in the Old Testament, human existence is *historical existence*, life emerging from, and shaped by, the concrete experiences of everyday happenings.

Accordingly, *Jesus* does not formulate some universal doctrine of fraternal charity, replete with criteria and conditions. Instead he tells the story of the Good Samaritan and asks, "Which ... was neighbor to the man who fell in with the robbers?" (Luke 10:25-37). All of us, he insists, are sinners, in need of *conversion* or of a fundamental change of mind and of heart: "This is the time of fulfillment. The reign of God is at hand! Reform your lives and believe in the gospel!" (Mark 1:15). The reform must be, in fact, so radical that we are required even to love our enemies: "My command to you is: love your enemies, pray for your persecutors ... If you love those who love you, what merit is there in that? ... In a word, you must be made perfect as your heavenly Father is perfect" (Matthew 5:43-48).

In the end, we shall be judged by the quality of our response to those in need, friend and enemy alike: " ... as often as you did it for one of my least brothers, you did it for me ... as often as you neglected to do it to one of these least ones, you neglected to do it to me" (Matthew 25:31-46). Just as Jesus' own existence is an existence in the service of others (Mark 10:45), so must every person's be *a coexistence of service*.

Paul's understanding of human existence is developed in the light of the death and resurrection of Christ. As such, it draws out some of the anthropological implications of Jesus' own preaching. Paul, like Jesus and the Old Testament before him, refuses to speculate about the philosophical nature and properties of the human person. He, too, rejects the body-soul dualism of contemporary Greek thought. For him the resurrection in which we all hope will be a *resurrection of the body* (1 Corinthians 15), because the body (*soma*) is intrinsic to the being of the human person (1 Corinthians 15:15-19). "Body" is not just that through which the spirit acts; it is the whole person. The human person is body (Romans 12:1; 1 Corinthians 7:4; Philippians 1:20).

But we find ourselves *sinners* in the world, in the hands of alien forces, i.e., the domain of the "flesh" (*sarx*) which is in rebellion against God (Romans 8:6-8, 10:3; 2 Corinthians 10:5). When Paul considers the human person as alienated from himself and from God, he speaks of the person as flesh, as sinner. Flesh must be "put off" at Baptism (Romans 8:9-13), while body, i.e., the person as a whole, is to be transformed at the resurrection (1 Corinthians 15:44; Philippians 3:21). The "old man" is to yield to the "new man" in Christ (Ephesians 2:5; 2 Corinthians 4:16; Galatians 1:11-12; 1 Corinthians 3:3).

But even the "new man" in Christ lives in a state of tension, between the "already" of Christ's saving work on our behalf and the "not yet" of its final perfection in the Kingdom of God. By *faith*, and through a life based on faith, we work out our salvation in the midst of this tension: "But now that faith is here, we are no longer in the monitor's charge [i.e., the law's]" (Galatians 3:25; see also Romans 3:14; Colossians 2:12,20). In this faith there is no longer any fear of death ("O death, where is your victory? O death, where is your sting?"—1 Corinthians 15:55), but rather *hope* for the appearance of Christ when we "shall appear with him in glory" (Colossians 3:4). But over all these virtues, including even faith and hope, we put on *love*, "which binds the rest together and makes them perfect" (Colossians 3:14).

For *John*, as well as for Paul, the "world" is prone to evil, not because God created it evil, but because it is populated by men and women who are sinners. Indeed, the world would be lost if it were not for Jesus Christ; by sending the Son, God brings the world to a crisis or turning point, but out of a motive of love (John 3:16-17).

God sends the Son not to judge the world but to save it (1 John 4:9,14). Without an act of liberation from on high (John 3), we are imprisoned within a domain of evil. By having faith in Jesus Christ, we receive a fresh possibility of life from a new source. This *new life* is an eschatological existence, i.e., an existence between our situation as it is—imperfect, limited, prone to sin—and the Kingdom of God as it has been promised to us. In the meantime, we find a new home in the community of the faithful and in the *love of the brethren* by which we prove our sinlessness (1 John 3:14-18; 4:19-21).

It is not for us to decide whether or not we shall be "born again." On the contrary, no one comes to the Father unless the Father draw that person (John 6:44). But as a believer, the person must abide in Jesus' word and act according to his command (1 John 1:6-7; 2:3-6). The hope that is in all of us for a life completely fulfilled is, for John, to be directed to the *present* rather than to the future. We find the "new life" here and now by faith (1 John 1:2-3; John 17:3). To be human is, in the deepest sense, to live by grace, i.e., by the presence of God in our hearts and in our midst.

Patristic Views

There are no real breakthroughs in the writings of the Fathers of the Church beyond the anthropological perspective of the Bible. What the patristic period contributes is an element of systematization (Tertullian's *De Anima* is the beginning) around certain fundamental principles—e.g., the human person as the *image of God*, and the history of the universe as *the history of divinization and salvation*. These themes are expressed nowhere more clearly or more forcefully than in Irenaeus's *Adversus Haereses* (literally, "Against the Heresies" of Gnosticism and other related errors).

At the heart of Irenaeus' theology is his theory of *recapitulation*, borrowed from Paul but expanded considerably. Recapitulation, for Irenaeus, is taking up in Christ of all that is or has been from the beginning. God gathers up everything which had been sidetracked by the fall of Adam and renews, restores, and reorganizes it in Jesus Christ, who becomes the Second Adam. Since the whole human race was lost through the sin of the First Adam, the Son of God had to become a human being in order to bring about the re-creation of humankind. "When he became incarnate and was made man," Irenaeus wrote, "he recapitulated in himself the long history of man, summing up and giving us salvation in order that we might receive again in Christ Jesus what we had lost in Adam, that is, the image and likeness of God" (III,18,1).

But the tendency to dichotomize remained. In the writings of the Eastern, Greek Fathers (e.g., Gregory of Nyssa) the tension between matter and spirit endured. Human fulfillment is possible because on one side of human nature, the spiritual, the human person stands already on God's side. Our goal is the vision of God after death. This vision comes only after purification and restoration to our original purity. For Western, Latin theology (e.g., Augustine) the tension is between the person as sinner and the merciful God. "Every man is Adam, every man is Christ" (cited by Henri Rondet, *The Grace of Christ*, p. 136). The history of the world, therefore, is seen essentially as the history of reuniting what was divided rather than "the free history of God himself in the world" (Rahner).

The Medieval Period

That there is still no decisive breakthrough even after the passage of many centuries should not be too surprising. As we pointed out in the preceding chapter, the most significant scientific, philosophical, and eventually theological advances in our understanding of human existence did not occur until the eighteenth and especially the nineteenth centuries, with the discoveries of Darwin and Freud, the new social analysis of Marx, and the new focus on the human person as subject in the philosophy of Kant, in existentialism, and in Transcendental Thomism.

There is no independent theological anthropology in any of the medieval treatises in theology. "Man" is simply listed among the various creatures: lower than the angels but higher than the animal kingdom. (Darwin, of course, would later undermine the assumption that some inviolable gap exists between human beings and the animal world.) This "objective" view of human existence could not, and did not, do justice to the special character of the person. Little or no attention at all was given to the history of salvation. Human beings do not grow and develop; they simply are, with an unchanging essence.

The medieval distinction between mortal and venial sin, for example, did not even set contemporary theologians to wondering about the basis for such a distinction in human action itself. There was still no real theological analysis of such fundamental human experiences as anguish, joy, and death. The world and its history were merely the ready-made scene for the unfolding of each individual human drama. Would the person finally save his or her soul, or not? There was nothing new to be added to the world and its history. If the world and history were not in process, neither were human beings.

And yet there were also some counter-indications in medieval theology—evidence of some initial movement toward a genuine anthropology. If reflections on salvation had a non-historical cast to them, their strongly individual focus also prepared the way, however unwittingly, for the modern period's subsequent emphasis on the person as subject. Medieval theology stressed the importance of the *Beatific Vision,* i.e., the direct, unobstructed experience of God after death by the saved individual. It provided also for non-sacramental possibilities of salvation, i.e., the so-called *votum sacramenti* (desire for the sacrament). If an individual's basic good will could, under some circumstances, replace the need for Baptism, then there must be something of fundamental and enduring importance about the activities and processes of the human mind, will, and subjective consciousness. This assumption was also reflected in medieval theology's remarkably provident teaching on the inviolability of conscience, even when it is in opposition to ecclesiastical law.

Scholastic philosophy, and the theology which flowed from it, provided what proved to be a true basis for the later recognition of genuine subjectivity, in that it noted, as Rahner says, that "anything is or has being in proportion to the degree in which it is subjectivity in possession of itself." Or, in the spirit of Teilhard de Chardin, life moves to higher and higher levels of self-reflection. The highest forms of life not only "know"; we "know that we know." The more conscious we are of ourselves, of our knowing powers, of our powers of decision, of the implications of our thoughts, our judgments, and our actions, the more we are in possession of ourselves. And the more we are in possession of ourselves, the greater is the level of "genuine subjectivity." The point, therefore, is that although medieval theology was not particularly attentive to the subjective side of human existence (on the contrary), there were elements and orientations in medieval thought which already anticipated the modern movement in the direction of subjectivity.

The Modern Period

Because of the scientific, philosophical, and theological developments outlined in the preceding chapter, the time for an anthropological recasting of all the traditional doctrines is at hand. But the task is as yet uncompleted. Early indications of a trend, however, are evident in the emergence of historical theology, in the recognition of religious pluralism and of the universality of God's saving grace, in the new regard for the world as something to be transformed by, or into, the Church, and in the recent renewal of interest in spirituality for the individual in his or her personal relationship with God.

The Second Vatican Council, to which reference was made also in the preceding chapter, also fails to construct a theological anthropology, but there are elements present therein which are consistent with the trends just noted: (1) the insistence on conscience as the guide to truth and to genuine solutions to current problems; (2) the declaration that "only in freedom ... can we direct ourselves toward goodness"; and (3) the reference to our desire for a higher life, a desire which is "inescapably lodged in the human heart" and which makes it possible for us to transcend our anxiety about death (*Pastoral Constitution on the Church in the Modern World*, nn. 16-18).

Theology of the Human Person: A Synthesis

The *Bible* views the human person as a creature of God, as animated body. Our *bodiliness* is the basis of our relationship with one another. *Human existence is coexistence.* But such existence is also fraught with as many risks as opportunities. Human existence is at once responsible, sinful, and hope-filled. The focus of its hope is the resurrection of the body, and the ground of that hope is the preaching, ministry, and saving death and resurrection of Jesus Christ, whom we accept in faith and to whom we manifest our fidelity in love. To live according to this dynamic of faith, hope, and love is to enter a new life, to become *a new creature in Christ.* This new life and new creaturehood is, as always, shared with others, in accordance with our social nature and the coexistent character of human existence. The immediate context of the sharing is the community of the faithful, which is the Church.

Until modern times, there was little or no significant development of a theology of human existence beyond that already expressed in the Bible. The *Fathers of the Church*, especially Irenaeus, spoke of the human person as the image of God, and of human history as the history of salvation—a process in which all things are being recapitulated in Christ. The *medieval period*, consistently with the prevailing philosophy of the times, viewed human existence "objectively," i.e., as an unchanging form of created life essentially unaffected by the process and vicissitudes of history. There were, however, some elements in medieval theology which anticipated, to some extent, the modern turn toward the "subjective." Medieval theology's emphasis on the inviolability of conscience is one example to which we earlier referred.

Under the impact of scientific and philosophical developments, *modern theology* focuses its attention on the consciousness of the human person, on the person's freedom and responsibility, not only to co-create himself or herself but to co-create the world and its history under God. The *Second Vatican Council's* insistence on the importance of conscience, freedom, and the innate desire for a higher life reflects this modern shift to the subject.

NATURE AND GRACE
Nature

Until this century, the formal concept of "nature" served only as a basis of contrast with "grace" in Catholic theology. "Nature" is a concept, however, which is still almost totally absent from the Eastern Orthodox theology of grace and has generally been resisted by Protestant theology.

The Catholic tradition has always been insistent that *the grace of God is given to us, not to make up for something lacking to us as human persons, but as a free gift that elevates us to a new and unmerited level of existence.* Hypothetically, we could have a *natural end.* This would be something akin to *Limbo,* a state of "natural happiness" reserved for those who die in infancy without the grace of Baptism and without, of course, the possibility of having ever expressed even an implicit desire for Baptism (*votum sacramenti,* again) through free choices which happen to be consistent with the will of God. The real, historical order, however, is already permeated with grace, so that a state of "pure nature" does not exist. In other words, if grace supposes nature, nature in its own way supposes grace, insofar as the grace of Christ sustains us in our actual existence and orients us toward a supernatural end, the Kingdom of God. This emphasis on the importance of the natural and of the natural order is historically and theologically characteristic of Catholicism.

Eastern Orthodoxy, on the other hand, stresses the spiritual side of human existence to such an extent that the natural foundation is sometimes all but lost. *Much of Protestantism,* meantime, has so emphasized the depravity of the natural human condition apart from the grace of God that the natural order can only be viewed in thoroughly negative terms.

"Nature," to be sure, is not directly a biblical concept but arises from subsequent theological reflection on the New Testament's (especially John's and Paul's) proclamation of "the grace of God through Christ." *We infer who we are as creatures of God by reflecting on who we have become through Christ.* By the grace of Christ we enter into a new relationship of communion with God, and we are transformed interiorly by the Spirit of Christ. As we have already suggested, the Fathers of the Church, from Irenaeus on, understood this participation in the life of God through Christ as a true *divinization*. The Latin Fathers, especially Augustine and Pope Leo the Great (d. 461), adopted this concept and made it the foundation of the whole theology of grace in the medieval period, as is particularly evident in Thomas Aquinas.

But the emphasis is not upon divinization alone, but upon its *gratuitous* character as well. We neither deserved nor needed grace. We would not have been less than human without it. Although, in fact, God created us and the world in and through Christ, God could have created us without including the communication of grace (or better: God's *self*-communication.)

Hence, the theological concept of "nature" means that we are bodily creatures who are intelligible (i.e., whose existence makes sense) and who would have been open to full human growth apart from the grace of divinization. The creation of humankind and of the world is theoretically possible without the incarnation of the Son of God in Jesus Christ. The whole self-communication of God—in creation and in the incarnation—is free. Human existence non-divinized by grace is a possible hypothesis.

"Nature," therefore, is neither a purely positive nor a purely negative concept. It is *not purely positive* because it is a concept one *derives* from reflecting on something higher, namely, grace. It is *not a purely negative* concept because it implies the rationality of the human person and the person's fundamental relationship to God, to other persons, to the world, and to its history apart from grace.

The theological concept of nature is, of course, very different from the philosophical or the naturally and socially scientific (as we have already seen in the preceding chapter), because theology views the human person as having *a radical capacity (potentia obedientialis) for the divinizing grace of Christ*. This fundamental aspect of the theological concept of nature is not derived from Darwinian or Freudian experimentation, nor from Marxist analysis, nor even from philosophical reflection, but from inferences drawn from the revelation that we are, in fact, called to a participation in the very life of God through Jesus Christ. (The notion of "revelation," which is so obviously crucial in the preceding sentence, will be explained in chapter 7.)

It is important to add here, by way of conclusion, that the traditional Catholic emphasis on "nature" is not without its dangers—dangers of which Protestants and Orthodox have been mindful. One might easily be led to the exaggerated view that the purely natural person does, in fact, exist and that grace is something merely "added" to, or superimposed upon, nature. It cannot be denied that the introduction of the concept of nature in the explanation of grace can lead, and has led, to a dualistic vision of human existence in relation to God. God is, on the one hand, our creator, and, on the other hand, our Savior through Christ—with a different relationship to the human person in each case. Hence the importance of the problem of "nature and grace" to which we are now attending in this section of the present chapter.

Grace

Old Testament

In the Old Testament the Hebrew noun *ḥēn* designates a quality which arouses *favor*. The word appears most frequently in the phrase "to find favor in the eyes of" God or other persons. One who seeks favors throws himself or herself completely on the good will of the one from whom the favor is sought. The verb *ḥānan*, "to show favor," designates an attitude which is proper toward the needy, the poor, the widow, the orphan, and so forth. One shows favor by gifts, by assistance, and by refraining from punishment. Yahweh shows favor by giving prosperity (Genesis 33:11), by giving children (Genesis 33:5), by accepting sacrifice (Malachi 1:9). Most frequently Yahweh shows favor by delivering from distress (e.g., Psalms 4:2; 6:3; 9:14; 25:16; 26:11; 27:7). Yahweh delivers Israel from its enemies (2 Kings 13:23; Isaiah 30:18-19; 33:2), even when Israel deserves punishment for its sins. Such favor is also forgiveness (Psalms 41:5,11; 51:3; Isaiah 27:11; Amos 5:15). Yahweh's favor is shown *freely*. It can be given or withheld (Exodus 33:19).

New Testament

In the New Testament the corresponding noun for *grace* is the Greek *charis*. It becomes a key word in the Christian message. The word occurs frequently in the introductory and final greetings of the various epistles, usually accompanied by the word *peace*. Thus: "To all in Rome, beloved of God and called to holiness, grace and peace from God our Father and the Lord Jesus Christ" (Romans 1:7). The word designates the *good will of God*, sometimes in a general sense (e.g., Acts of the Apostles 14:26; 15:40) and most frequently in reference to the saving will of God executed in Jesus Christ and communicated to humankind through Christ. Such grace makes us *righteous* (Romans 3:24; Titus 3:7). By grace Paul (and others) are called (Galatians 1:15). Grace appears in Christ for our salvation (Titus 2:11). By it Jesus suffered death for all (Hebrews 2:9). Faith and love are fruits of grace (1 Timothy 1:14).

Elsewhere in the New Testament the emphasis is less on the saving will of God and more on *that which is given* (James 4:6; 1 Peter 5:5). The Word is full of grace (John 1:14,16). It is a store to which we have full access through Christ (Romans 5:2). It abounds more than sin (Romans 5:15,20; 6:1). It is given us in Christ (1 Corinthians 1:4). It is within the Christian (2 Corinthians 9:14), and extends to more and more people (2 Corinthians 4:15). The prophets foretold it (1 Peter 1:10). Christians are its heirs (1 Peter 3:7), called to grow in the grace and knowledge of Jesus Christ (2 Peter 3:18).

Grace stands in opposition to *works*, which lack the power to save (Romans 11:5-6; Ephesians 2:5,8-9; 2 Timothy 1:9). Grace stands also in opposition to the *law* (Acts of the Apostles 15:11; Galatians 2:21; 5:4). The Christian is not under the law but under grace (Romans 6:14-18). Grace is a gift, not something owed (Romans 4:4).

The *Gospel* itself can be called grace, in which the Christian should stand and remain steadfast (1 Peter 5:12; Acts of the Apostles 13:43). It is indeed the Gospel of the grace of God (Acts of the Apostles 20:24), or the word of God's grace (Acts of the Apostles 14:3; 20:32).

Grace is also *the principle of Christian life, action, and mission.* The first martyr, St. Stephen, was full of grace and power (Acts of the Apostles 6:8). Paul's apostolate was an apostleship of grace (Romans 1:5, and other passages). His hearers partake of it (Philippians 1:7). It is the *power* by which the apostle performs his apostolic functions (Romans 12:3; 1 Corinthians 3:10, 15:10; Ephesians 3:7-11). It produces good works (2 Corinthians 8:1). The grace of God, not earthly wisdom, guides our conduct (2 Corinthians 1:12).

Its only appearance in the Synoptic Gospels is in Luke. It refers to the heavenly reward, hence to a *salvation that is to come* (6:32-34). In 1:30 and 1:52 the Old Testament use of the word survives. But when Luke employs the term to express his own theological insights, he identifies it with the salvation wrought by God in Christ and since Christ, particularly through the words of the Gospel and the preaching thereof (4:22). On the whole, the terminology which Luke uses is not derived from Paul but reflects a wider tradition which may be pre-Pauline.

One final note regarding the meaning of the word *grace* in the New Testament: The Greek noun *charis* is to be distinguished from the noun *charisma* (a term popular today in the so-called charismatic renewal as well as in popular political terminology, as in "charismatic candidate"). The *charismata* (plural of *charisma*) are a particular type of spiritual gift which enable the recipient to perform some office or function in the Church. Such offices or functions are enumerated in Romans 12, 1 Corinthians 12, and Ephesians 4.

Apostolic Fathers

The Apostolic Fathers (Irenaeus and others) and the theologians of the *first two centuries* repeat the doctrine of Sacred Scripture, initially stressing its moral demands and then focusing more sharply on the effect of divinization, as we saw earlier in the chapter. The first theological reflections are made on the possibility of losing and then recovering the grace of Baptism (*The Shepherd of Hermas* and Tertullian). *The first major controversy* erupted in the second and third centuries under the impact of

Gnosticism, a heresy which made salvation both non-universal and non-historical. Salvation was given instead to a select few, and it consisted of a special knowledge (thus, the term *gnosis*). Its principal opponents were Irenaeus, Tertullian, and Hippolytus (d. 235).

"We need not mention how necessary it is to do again the work that Saint Augustine and Saint Thomas once did," Henri Rondet has written. "It is most probable that the genius who could attempt such an enterprise has not yet been born" (*The Grace of Christ*, p. 384).

Greek Fathers; Western Fathers

The Greek Fathers (from Origen on) developed a doctrine of grace in keeping with the Trinitarian questions of the period. Because the Spirit is truly God, we are truly *divinized* by the presence of the Spirit; and because we are truly divinized, the Spirit must be divine. It is through the incarnation of the divine *Logos* (word) that the Spirit enters the world. Therefore, the Greek doctrine of grace is optimistic about salvation.

The Western Fathers (Augustine, and others) were less interested in the intellectual and cosmic aspects of divinization and more *moralistic* in tendency. They also oriented their theology of grace toward the history of salvation and of the individual because of their struggle against *Pelagianism* (the fifth-century heresy which held that human beings can, without the grace of God, achieve supernatural salvation). Grace is a free gift of God and, because of sin, is necessary for salvation. But there is some trace, even in Augustine, of a denial of the universal salvific will of God. Some are *predestined* to salvation, others to damnation.

Later Patristic Period; Early Middle Ages

The later Patristic period and the early Middle Ages overcame the tendency toward predestinationism. The great age of Scholasticism gave precise formulation by means of Aristotelian categories and terminology (*habitus*, "disposition," "accidents") to the nature and effects of grace. The concept of the strictly supernatural character of salvific grace was slowly elaborated. It was a free, unmerited gift of God, for saint and sinner alike.

Reformation

With the Reformation in the sixteenth century and the emergence of new heresies within the Catholic Church (e.g., Jansenism), it was necessary for theologians—and eventually the Council of Trent—to defend the freedom of the human person under grace, the truly inward new creation of the human person by habitual grace, the strictly supernatural character of grace, and the universality of God's saving will. The controversy over precisely *how* we can reconcile human freedom with divine power (the debates between the Molinists and the Banezians, for example) was left undecided in 1607 and remains so even today.

Official Church Teachings

The major formulations of official Church teachings were drafted in response to the two principal distortions of the nature and effects of grace: *Pelagianism* on the left (because it was too optimistic about human freedom) and *Protestantism* on the right (because it was too pessimistic about human freedom). Against the first tendency toward complete self-reliance, the Church officially affirmed at the Second Council of Orange (529) the necessity of grace in every person's life, from beginning to end. Against Protestantism, the Council of Trent (1547) asserted that we are interiorly transformed by the grace of Christ.

During the post-Tridentine period, attention was centered on the relationship between human freedom and divine help (*actual* grace), but, as we have just noted, the issue was never resolved. In the meantime, the biblical and patristic perspective tended to be pushed to the background. Catholic theology (and Catholic spirituality, too) was so much influenced and shaped by existing controversies, on the one hand, and by the response of the official teaching authority, on the other, that we had, in effect, begun to lose sight of the inner renewal all of us experience through the indwelling of the Holy Spirit and through our concomitant personal union with Christ. The return to biblical and patristic emphases began under Pope Leo XIII and reached new levels of emphasis in the Second Vatican Council.

Principal examples of this official teaching follow.

1. Second Council of Orange (529): "If anyone asserts that by his natural strength he is able to think as is required or choose anything good pertaining to his eternal salvation, or to assent to the saving message of the Gospel without the illumination and inspiration of the Holy Spirit . . . , he is deceived by the heretical spirit . . . " (canon 7; see also canons 3-6,8).

2. Council of Trent (1547): "Thus, not only are we considered just, but we are truly called just and we are just, each one receiving within himself his own justice, according to the measure which 'the Holy Spirit apportions to each one individually as He wills' (1 Corinthians 12:11), and according to each one's personal disposition and cooperation" (chapter VII; see the entire "Decree on Justification").

3. Pope Leo XIII, encyclical letter *Divinum Illud* (1897): ". . . by grace God abides in the just soul as in a temple, in a most intimate and singular manner . . . . Now this wonderful union, which is properly called indwelling . . . is most certainly produced by the divine presence of the whole Trinity: 'We will come to him and make our home with him' (John 14:23); nevertheless it is attributed in a particular manner to the Holy Spirit."

4. Second Vatican Council, *Dogmatic Constitution on the Church* (1964): "The Spirit dwells in the Church and in the hearts of the faithful as in a temple . . . " (n. 4).

The Problem of Nature and Grace

"Grace" is essentially God's *self-communication to us men and women, and, secondarily, the effect(s) of that self-communication.* "Nature" refers to *human existence apart from God's self-communication and the divinizing effect of that self-communication.* Theology, however, carries the concept of "nature" one step beyond philosophy or anthropology, namely, to mean human existence without grace but at the same time as radically open to, and capable of receiving, grace (*potentia obedientialis*).

What is the *relationship* between the two realities of nature and grace? *The problem of the relationship between nature and grace is as fundamental a problem as one will ever come upon in all of Christian theology.* The nature-grace issue underlies the following relationships: creation and incarnation, reason and faith, law and Gospel, human freedom and divine sovereignty, the history of the world and the history of salvation, human progress and the Kingdom of God, natural law and the law of Christ, humanity and the Church, and so forth.

The problem of nature and grace is focused in the questions: *Does grace really change human nature, and if so, how is human freedom preserved? How is the human person able to accept freely the self-communication of God in grace?*

The Catholic theological tradition works its way through two extreme positions, to which reference has just been made: the extreme left of *Pelagianism*, which emphasizes so much the superiority of nature over grace that it effectively submerges the transcendental, supernatural dimension of salvation; and the extreme right of *Protestantism* (at least Protestantism as perceived and condemned by Trent), which emphasizes so much the superiority of grace over nature that it effectively submerges the dimension of human freedom and cooperation in salvation. The parenthetical qualification is necessary because subsequent historical studies have shown that the positions of Luther, Calvin, and Melanchthon were more nuanced than first appeared.

The Catholic theological tradition is grounded, first of all, in the New Testament's perspective of a Christocentric universe (1 Corinthians 8:6; 15:24-28,44-49; Romans 8:19-23,29,30; Ephesians 1:9-10,19-23; 3:11; Colossians 1:15-20; 3:4; Philippians 3:21; Hebrews 1:2-3; John 1:3; 12:32). All *creation* is oriented toward the *Covenant* between God and the People of God, and the Covenant, in turn, toward the *New Covenant* grounded in the incarnation of the Son of God in Jesus Christ. The human community and the entire world in which the human community exists is oriented toward Christ and is sustained by him. Although hypothetically it could have been otherwise, it in fact has not been otherwise. There is no creation except in view of Christ. There is no Covenant except in view of Christ. There is no human existence, therefore, except in view of Christ and of our New Covenant in Christ.

This intrinsic orientation of the human person and of the entire human community in Christ radically excludes any dualism, or sharp separation, between nature and grace. Although *in principle* we could know God apart from revelation and apart specifically from the revelation of God in Christ, *in fact* we cannot and do not know God apart from this revelation (Romans 1:18-28; Acts of the Apostles 17:24-27).

Sin is an exercise of human freedom *against* the relationship. Grace, however, is not destroyed by sin. The sinner remains radically open to the possibility of conversion and of forgiveness. If grace were not still available to the sinner, conversion and forgiveness would be impossible. The call of God to conversion and repentance (1 Corinthians 1:9; Galatians 2:20; Romans 8:28-30) would be meaningless unless there were some basis in the human person for responding to the call. Grace supposes even in the sinner the capacity to receive it. This capacity is what Karl Rahner and other Transcendental Thomists call our "limitless openness to being and ultimately to the Absolute," which openness constitutes the human person as "spirit in the world" (the title of one of Rahner's earliest works).

Grace supposes the nature of the human person. Theologically, nature includes the radical capacity for grace. That radical capacity is called, more technically, a *"supernatural existential."* This "supernatural existential" is *a permanent modification of the human spirit which transforms it from within and orients it toward the God of grace and glory.* This "supernatural existential" is not grace itself but only *God's offer of grace* which, by so modifying the human spirit, enables it freely to accept or to reject grace. *Every human person has this radical capacity* and many, perhaps most, have actualized it by receiving grace. That does not mean that they are conscious of grace as grace. On the contrary, Rahner argues," . . . the possibility of experiencing grace and the possibility of experiencing grace *as* grace are not the same thing" (*A Rahner Reader*, p. 185).

If grace supposes nature, so, too, does *nature suppose grace*, to the extent that the grace of Christ orients and sustains us in our very human existence. Catholic theology, from Augustine through Aquinas to the Transcendental Thomists of the present century, has argued, in fact, for a "natural desire" for direct union with God. It is only in the vision of God that the human mind can satisfy fully and definitively its desire to know. No finite reality can satisfy that desire. It is only in the encounter with God, the Absolute, that its deepest spiritual aspirations are fulfilled.

By ourselves, however, we could never go beyond the knowledge of the limited and the created. Such knowledge, on the other hand, is consonant with human existence. We would not thereby be less than human because we could know only the limited and the created. In fact, however, God gives us the radical capacity to transcend the limited and the created. There is now a radical capacity in nature itself, and not merely superadded to nature, by which we are ordained to the knowledge of God. Thus, all dualism between nature and grace is eliminated. There are not in the human person two separate finalities, the one oriented toward the vision of God, and the other oriented toward human fulfillment apart from the vision of God. *Human existence is already graced existence.* There is no merely natural end of human existence. *Human existence in its natural condition is radically oriented toward God.*

This means, too, that the whole universe is oriented to the glory of God (Romans 8:19-23). *The history of the world is, at the same time, the history of salvation.* It means also that authentic human progress in the struggle for justice, peace, freedom, human rights, and so forth, is part of the movement of, and toward, the Kingdom of God (Vatican II, *Pastoral Constitution on the Church in the Modern World*, n. 39). It means as well that human freedom is never to be conceived totally apart from grace, because it is always modified and qualified by grace; so, too, the grace of God is operative only insofar as it interacts with, and radically transforms, the natural order of the human person. The movement and dynamism of human freedom, on the one hand, and divine sovereignty, on the other, will converge perfectly at the end, in the vision of God and the final realization of the Kingdom. Each person and all of history will then achieve their definitive meaning.

ORIGINAL SIN
The Problem

There are three common misunderstandings of Original Sin. The *first* assumes that the doctrine denies human freedom and therefore exempts us from responsibility for the condition of the world and of human relationships. This first school of thought rejects such a doctrine and insists instead that with the right technology, politics, and education, we can and must strive to overcome social and individual evils.

The *second* identifies Original Sin with the absurdity of human existence. We can do nothing about our situation. We are radically and thoroughly flawed. This is the view of pessimistic existentialism, e.g., Sartre.

The *third* misunderstanding equates Original Sin with personal sin—a personal sin which somehow is imposed on our otherwise innocent shoulders. Such a view of Original Sin forces us to accept it, or write it off, simply as a "mystery" or to reject the doctrine as an intrinsic contradiction. How can one be really guilty of something that someone else committed?

Accordingly, the doctrine of Original Sin does not play a very large part in contemporary Catholic theology and even less in liberal Protestant theology. It no longer enters into our theology of human existence. We assume, for example, that Baptism annuls it in any case, so that it remains a vital problem only for unbaptized babies.

Biblical Notion

Old Testament

Contrary to a popular belief within the Church, the Old Testament has no formal concept of Original Sin. Clearly it is aware of sin and especially of its corrupting effects (Genesis 6:12). But Genesis 2:8-3:24 (the account of the first sin of Adam and Eve) should not be read apart from chapters 4-11. Genesis 3 is only an introduction to what amounts to a series of anecdotes intended to show how sin, once admitted into the world, spreads everywhere, bringing death and destruction in its wake.

New Testament

In the New Testament, and especially in *Paul*, we find the substance of a doctrine of Original Sin (1 Corinthians 15:21-23, and Romans 5:12-21). In the latter passage Paul speaks of Original Sin by first drawing a parallel (verse 18) between Adam and Christ. Because of Adam we are sinners without the Spirit (verse 19), but because of Christ we are sought by God's saving will and are, therefore, in a state of objective redemption. And both these effects—the one from Adam's sin and the other from Christ's saving work—are antecedent to human freedom and personal decision. What *we* do is to ratify the deed of Adam by personal sin (verse 12) or the deed of Christ by faith.

Paul, of course, does not, nor can he, explain *how* this is so, how it is that we are affected by the sin of Adam without any personal decision. He insists only *that* it is so, and he argues from the universality of *death*. Because we all die, we are all implicated in sin, since death is the effect of sin. This sense of our corporate involvement in sin cannot be separated from the biblical belief in the solidarity of the human community and in its notion of corporate personality, sometimes linked with the Suffering Servant of God in Isaiah 40-55.

But since death is the effect of sin, death (the death of Christ) can also be the instrument of its destruction. It is by dying to sin with Christ that we are liberated from it (Romans 6:1-23). Through Christ's death comes new life. In dying with Christ we rise also with him (1 Corinthians 15:3,17; Galatians 1:4). Our dying and rising with Christ does not eliminate the enduring conflict between the spirit and the flesh, but we can achieve the final victory through Christ and the Spirit (Romans 8:1-17).

Post-biblical Theological Developments

Augustine

The biblical teaching on Original Sin, which as we have noted is exceedingly brief, was not developed until Augustine. The Greek Fathers (Irenaeus, Basil, Gregory of Nyssa, *et al.*) were too much involved against the heresies of Gnosticism and Manichaeism (both of which insisted that all matter is evil) to lay stress on such a doctrine. They were trying to show, on the contrary, how the incarnation elevated and transformed the whole created order. But the situation was just the opposite for Augustine. He faced not those who rejected the goodness of nature but those who glorified nature to excess, i.e., the Pelagians. Unfortunately, Augustine portrayed Original Sin as a situation in which every human being finds himself or herself, but from which only some are rescued. Although God desired the salvation of all in Christ, only those who are justified by faith and Baptism are actually saved.

Furthermore, Augustine linked Original Sin with *concupiscence* (i.e., the human person's *spontaneous desire* for material or sensual satisfaction). It is an effect of Original Sin and is transmitted by the libido in the parents' love by which a person first comes into existence. To the extent that concupiscence infects every human act, all of our deeds are in some sense sinful. Augustine did not suggest that every such deed is a *new* sin, but he never worked out the intrinsic difference between Original and personal sin because, for him, the consequences of both kinds of sin are the same in the next world.

Middle Ages; Trent; Post-Trent

In the Middle Ages, from Anselm of Canterbury onward, the essence of Original Sin was increasingly equated with the *lack of sanctifying grace* (medieval theology's new term for the divine indwelling) brought about by Adam's actual sin. Concupiscence now appeared simply as a consequence of Original Sin (Aquinas). Thus, it became possible to explain how Baptism blotted out Original Sin without at the same time canceling all of its effects, including concupiscence.

The Council of Trent (to which greater attention will be devoted below) agreed with the Protestant Reformers that Original Sin, caused by Adam's sin, affects all (except Mary) and that it is really overcome by justification. But *against* the Reformers, Trent insisted that Original Sin does not consist in concupiscence itself, since this remains even in the justified. Rather, Original Sin is the lack of original righteousness (justice) and holiness. Post-

Tridentine theology tried to answer the obvious difficulties associated with the traditional doctrine of Original Sin—e.g., How is it possible to translate blame from Adam to ourselves?

Contemporary Theologians

Contemporary theologians (especially Rahner) reject the notion that Original Sin is simply the sinful act of the first man or is a matter of collective guilt, since both of these views lead to contradictions and are not required by the dogma of Original Sin in any case. It is a mystery because grace itself is a mystery. The self-communication of God is antecedent to our free decision or proof of our worthiness (*ante praevisa merita*). Just as there is a state of holiness which is antecedent to our personal decision and which nonetheless qualifies and conditions our moral lives, so there is a lack of holiness which ought not to be, and that lack posits a state of unholiness which is also antecedent to our personal decision and which qualifies and conditions our moral lives. The fact that the mystery of Original Sin is subordinate to the mystery of grace explains why the actual doctrine of Original Sin appears in the Bible only when our divinization by the Spirit is explicitly grasped (as in Paul).

Contemporary theologians also reject the notion (suggested by Augustine and others) that Original Sin is more pervasive and more universal than is redemption, since everyone is affected by Original Sin but some are not effectively touched by the cross and resurrection of Christ. On the contrary, Original Sin and being redeemed are two constitutive components of the human situation in regard to salvation, which at all times determine human existence. "It may be assumed that sin was only permitted by God within the domain of his unconditional and stronger salvific will, which from the beginning was directed towards God's self-communication in Christ" (K. Rahner,"Original Sin," *The Concise Sacramentum Mundi*, p. 1151).

A *positive* statement of contemporary theology (especially Rahner) comprises the following principles:

1. All human beings are offered grace and, therefore, redemption *through Christ*, and not simply insofar as they are

human beings or members of the human community. This grace is given us as the *forgiveness of sins*. Indeed, Jesus himself thought of his own death on the cross as an expiatory death "for all." (More on this, of course, in Part III on Christ, especially chapter 12.)

2.   The human person lacks God's grace precisely because he or she *is* a person and a member of the human community. At the same time God wills that we should have grace. Thus, if it is not present, this must be because of some guilt freely incurred (otherwise it contradicts God's will). Yet the absence of grace (a condition incurred freely by sin) is also against God's will, even when the individual is not at all responsible for its absence. This lack of grace, which ought not to be, has in an *analogous* sense the character of sin: It is very much *like* sin, in that it is contrary to the will of God, but it is at the same time *unlike* sin, in that it does not involve a free decision against God's will. But God remains attached to us in spite of the sin of Adam. God bestows grace freely now, not in view of Adam, but in view of Christ. As children of Adam, we do not have grace. As sons and daughters of God in Christ, we do.

3.   The lack of grace is an inner condition of each one of us in that we are all human, but it is also *situational*. We are born into a "situation" in which, because of Adam's sin, grace is not at our disposal in the manner and measure which God intended. Accordingly, we now have to make our decision about salvation under the impact of both *concupiscence* and *death*, each of which is an effect of Original Sin. For that reason, and in spite of the work of Christ on our behalf, all of us are still directly concerned with Original Sin in our daily lives. We are, to that extent, "wounded" or weakened in our natural powers.

4.   On the other hand, this does *not* mean that death and concupiscence are totally unnatural, that we would not have experienced them were it not for Adam's sin. It means, rather, that both are in contradiction to what we are in the concrete. They are indications of the as-yet-incomplete victory of grace. The process of history begins at the point where neither death nor concupiscence has been eliminated.

5.   Our human situation in the face of a free moral decision is always *dialectically* determined: We are in Original Sin through

Adam and at the same time are oriented toward Christ and the God of glory. Either we freely ratify our state of Original Sin by personal sin, or we freely ratify our redeemed condition by faith, hope, and love. Our situation is one in which our decision to ratify is always qualified by concupiscence and death, on the one hand, and by the fact of our having been redeemed, on the other. Our moral standing before God, however, is always and finally determined by our free choice, weakened though it be.

6.   The doctrine of Original Sin remains always pertinent to our lives as Christians and to Christian theology. It indicates (a) that grace is given historically, and not as a necessity of human existence; (b) that it comes from Christ, not from Adam at the beginning of history; (c) that the goal of history is greater than it was at the beginning of history; (d) that our situation of death, concupiscence, and other experiences of human limitation cannot simply be abolished in history, because they were there from the beginning; and (e) that our efforts, therefore, to overcome the effects of Original Sin (injustice, war, etc.) constitute a duty that cannot be completed in this world and, therefore, a duty that is never done.

Official Teachings of the Church

Sixteenth Council of Carthage

The Sixteenth Council of Carthage (418), a gathering of two hundred bishops, condemned the errors of the British monk *Pelagius*, who reduced Adam's sin to one of bad example and insisted that grace is not absolutely necessary for salvation. The canons (or principal doctrinal formulations) of the council were later approved by Pope Zosimus (d. 418).

Indiculus

The *Indiculus* (between 435 and 442), a summary of the doctrine of grace, was composed probably by Prosper of Aquitaine (d. 460), a disciple of Augustine and the strongest opponent of *semi-Pelagianism*, which held that none of us requires grace at the beginning but that God grants it as needed later. This document subsequently received papal approval and was used as the standard exposition on grace by the end of the fifth century.

Second Council of Orange

The Second Council of Orange (529) finally settled the matter against the *semi-Pelagians*. This local council accepted the teachings of Caesarius of Arles (d. 542), another of Augustine's disciples, plus material from Prosper of Aquitaine. Pope Boniface II (d. 532) approved Orange's action.

Council of Trent

The Council of Trent (sixth session, 1547), "Decree on Justification," said: We have lost innocence through the sin of Adam, and have inherited not only death but also sin. Nevertheless, we are redeemed by Christ interiorly and not just by a divine decree which leaves us unchanged within. Although we still suffer from the effects of Original Sin, God's justice inheres in us (see especially chapter 16 of the decree).

Humani Generis

Pope Pius XII's encyclical letter *Humani Generis* (1950) insisted on the truly gratuitous character of the supernatural order (i.e., God was not *required* to create us for glory) and on the importance of our common descent from one pair of parents. This latter position is not regarded by most Catholic theologians today as necessary to the doctrine of Original Sin.

SYNTHESIS: TOWARD A THEOLOGY OF HUMAN EXISTENCE

It is obvious by now that theology does not follow the same clear lines of direction that one might find in such disciplines as accounting, law, chemistry, or the statistical sides of political science and economics. Like all of the humanities, theology is concerned with the question of human existence. But human existence can only be studied by human beings. We ourselves raise the question *about* ourselves. We have already noted in the preceding chapter that there is no standpoint from which we can "look at" God objectively, in a detached manner, as it were. This is so because God permeates as well as transcends us. For the same reason, there is no standpoint from which we can "look at" ourselves objectively, in a detached manner. We are at once the subject and the object of the inquiry. Consequently, our answers are always inadequate. They lead to further questions and to further attempts at newer answers.

The Christian "standpoint" is inevitably qualified by the conviction that God is real, that the real God is available to us, and that the real, available God is a principle of consciousness, knowledge, and moral action within each one of us, even within those who do not explicitly advert to God's presence as well as within those who explicitly reject the possibility of a divine principle of human existence.

We are persons who are self-aware (i.e., we not only *know*; we *know that we know*, and we know ourselves *as knowers*). *We are beings in possession of ourselves as subjects.* And this is the case even before we have had an opportunity to reflect on our existence from various disciplinary points of view (all of which we have placed under the umbrella of *anthropology*).

The knowledge that we have of ourselves before any of us has had an opportunity for systematic investigation and reflection is called *a priori* knowledge (as opposed to *a posteriori* knowledge, i.e., the knowledge of objects which is disclosed to us through study and examination). For the Christian, and indeed for every religious person, our *a priori* knowledge of ourselves as persons includes the light of faith as a "supernatural existential." In other words, *God is present in us from the beginning as the principle and the power of self-knowledge.* We are, "from the very circumstance of (our) origin, . . . already invited to converse with God" (*Pastoral Constitution on the Church in the Modern World*, n. 19). We do not come to the knowledge of God by a step-by-step investigation of data, arguments, and evidence. Rather, *our knowledge of God begins at the very moment when we become really conscious of ourselves as personal subjects,* as human beings, with all that this implies.

The Christian knows himself or herself as a creature, and a limited, flawed creature at that. But *the Christian also knows himself or herself as a person addressed by God in history, as a person touched by God's presence (grace).* What the Christian hears about himself or herself from the corpus of religious doctrines, especially in Sacred Scripture, the Christian recognizes as something of what he or she already knows about himself or herself in faith. *In the presence of some authentic statement about the meaning of human existence, the human person recognizes its truth almost spontaneously.* Aquinas called this "knowledge by connaturality." It "rings true," as it were. What is proposed is seen as consonant with what is immediately experienced *a priori,* in the act of self-consciousness.

Grace makes possible human nature's capacity for the connatural reception of God's self-communication in the Word (biblical, preached, theological, personal, and especially incarnate). *Hypothetically,* human nature could exist without the capacity for God. *Historically,* human nature has the capacity and cannot be without it. However, because of what is hypothetically true about human nature, one can explicitly reject God's presence without, at the same time, denying or destroying oneself *as human.*

Human nature is open to, but cannot absolutely demand, God's self-communication in grace. Grace remains always *grace* ("gift"). We have no title to it, and yet, given the present historical order and the intention of God, we are not fully human without it. But within that set of principles governing human existence there is an extraordinarily wide range of possibilities for the realization of our humanity. *Our historicity* (or situation in the world and within the process of human events) *means that we are significantly affected, and changed, by our environment, our bodiliness, our race, our sexuality, our social institutions, our interpersonal relationships, and so forth.* We discussed these and other factors in the preceding chapter.

But even though theological anthropology includes in principle all of the rest of theology, each of the other major doctrinal elements of Christian theology, and especially the question of

God, requires separate (though not unconnected) treatment. We are not retreating from our previous assertion that reflection on human existence is inevitably reflection on God, and vice versa. But because we are beings who by our very nature have the center of our existence outside ourselves, in God, our statements *about* God are more properly made outside of theological anthropology as such.

For the same reason we must keep theological anthropology and Christology apart, not absolutely, but for purposes of study and reflection. This does not mean that our theological statements about human existence can prescind from what we have come to know about Jesus Christ. On the contrary, a number of such statements (e.g., about the resurrection of the body) are possible only because of Christology. In that sense, Christ does not fit himself into some preexisting notion of human existence, but human existence itself is qualified and illuminated by God's grasp of it in Christ. *Christology is the recapitulation of theological anthropology.*

On the other hand, we do already know something about ourselves before Christ and apart from Christ, so that when we encounter Christ in history, we recognize him as human. Theological anthropology, therefore, cannot be pursued solely from within Christology, but must always be pursued in relation to it.

SUMMARY

1.   The *Old Testament* understands the *human person* primarily as a *creature* who *is* a *body* (and does not simply *have* a body) and whose hope of salvation is expressed in terms of the *resurrection of the body.* Bodiliness implies *coexistence* with other "bodies," especially in *sexual* relationships. That coexistence must be *responsible,* but because human freedom can be abused, human existence is also *sinful.* In spite of the spread of sin, human existence is *hope*-filled.

2.   The *New Testament* also understands human existence as *historical.* It is limited existence, qualified by sin. *Jesus* calls us all to *conversion* and *repentance,* to a working out of our salvation through a change in our relationships with others. *Paul,* too, speaks of the *bodily* condition of human existence and of our common hope in the resurrection of the body, a hope based on the saving work of Christ and the power

of the Holy Spirit. For *John*, to be human is to live by *grace*, i.e., by the presence of God in our hearts and in our midst. Our sinful selves and our sinful world would be lost if it were not for Christ and the *new life* that he brought us and that we enjoy even now.

3. The *Fathers of the Church* made no real breakthroughs in our understanding of human existence. There was some strong emphasis on the human person as the *image of God* and on human history as the *history of divinization and salvation* (Irenaeus, and others). It is Christ who *recapitulates* within himself all that is human in the individual and in history. But a tendency to *dichotomize* between matter and spirit perdures.

4. The *medieval period* focused principally on the person as *object*, a creature among creatures: lower than the angels, higher than the animal kingdom. "Man" was an unchanging essence, unchanged by environment and by history. But at least the beginnings of a turn to the *subject* can be found here, e.g., in medieval theology's concession that one could receive the grace of Baptism by *desire*, a subjective rather than objective principle.

5. Under the impact of scientific, philosophical, and theological developments outlined in the preceding chapter, a fundamental shift in our understanding of human existence has occurred in the so-called *modern period*. Emphasis is placed on our self-awareness as persons, and on our freedom and responsibility. This new direction in thought is reflected to some discernible extent in the *Second Vatican Council's Pastoral Constitution on the Church in the Modern World*.

6. *"Nature"* refers to the human condition apart from grace, but with the radical capacity to receive grace. *"Pure nature"* is a *hypothetical* concept. It refers not only to human existence apart from grace, but to human existence without the radical capacity to receive grace as well (known as the *potentia obedientialis* in medieval Scholastic theology, and as the "supernatural existential" in modern Transcendental Thomist theology).

7. Until this century, "nature" served only as a point of contrast with *"grace"*, i.e., God's self-communication. *Grace supposes nature*, but *nature* in its own way *also supposes grace*, insofar as the grace of Christ sustains us in our actual, historical existence and orients us toward our one supernatural end, the Kingdom of God.

8. Nature is not directly a biblical concept. It is one that is inferred from subsequent reflection on the New Testament's proclamation of the new order of grace in Christ. We infer who we are as *creatures* of God by reflecting on who we have become through the grace of Christ.

9.   The concept of "nature" also underlines the essentially *gratuitous* character of God's self-communication. We are bodily creatures who are fully intelligible and fully open to human growth apart from grace. *In historical fact*, however, we have been given the radical capacity for grace, and therefore *the fullness of our growth is linked inextricably with our growth in the grace of Christ as well.*

10.   The concept of "nature" is not without dangers. Its use easily leads one to a *dualistic* understanding of human existence, as if grace were something merely *added* to, or superimposed upon, nature.

11.   The reality of *grace*, on the other hand, is fully and deliberately expressed in the Bible. In the *Old Testament* it means literally a "favor." It has to do with our attitude toward the needy, with the experience of liberation from distress and from sin. As a "favor," it is always given, or withheld, *freely.*

12.   In the *New Testament* the word for grace, *charis*, becomes a key word in the Christian message, designating the *good will of God*, expressed in Christ and producing such *effects* as righteousness, faith, love, and new life. Grace stands in opposition to *works* and *law*; not that works and law are of no account, but only that they do not of themselves save us. *Salvation* is from *grace*. It is a free gift, something not owed us because of our performance of works or our observance of laws.

13.   The *doctrine of* grace developed systematically under the impact of certain major heresies: *Gnosticism*, which challenged the *universality* of grace and of salvation; *Pelagianism*, which challenged the *necessity* of grace for salvation; and historic *Protestantism*, which challenged the *effectiveness* of grace in transforming us interiorly. Major opposition to each of these views was mounted by *Irenaeus, Augustine*, and the *Council of Trent.*

14.   The *relationship between nature and grace* is a fundamental issue for theology because it underlies so many other important relationships: creation and incarnation, reason and faith, law and Gospel, human freedom and divine sovereignty, the human community and the Church, and so forth. How does grace change nature without destroying human freedom and responsibility? How is the person able to accept freely the self-communication of God in grace?

15.   The *Catholic theological tradition* avoids two extreme positions: the one which emphasizes nature so strongly that it effectively diminishes the significance of grace, and the other which emphasizes grace so much that it effectively suppresses nature. Thus, on the question of the Kingdom of God, the extreme left would make of it the work of human effort alone, with subsequent divine approval, and the extreme

right would make of it the work of divine power alone, accepted in trusting faith by God's people.

16. The Catholic theological tradition is rooted in a *Christological* and, therefore, *incarnational* and *sacramental* perspective. There is no creation except in view of Christ. And whatever there is in the visible, created order is itself, at least in principle, the expression of the invisible presence and power of God. Although, *hypothetically*, we could know God apart from the "supernatural existential" (i.e., the radical capacity which God gives us from the beginning), *in fact* we do not know God apart from that *a priori* condition.

17. This *"supernatural existential"* is not grace itself, but only God's offer of grace. It is an offer given to every person. *Grace, therefore, supposes nature, i.e., the radical capacity to receive grace. But nature also supposes grace. There is a kind of "natural desire" for direct union with God.* It is only in that union that we can finally and fully satisfy our desire to know and to become what we sense we are called to become.

18. The *whole universe, too, is oriented by grace to the Kingdom of God. The history of the world is, at the same time, the history of salvation.* Therefore, the struggle for justice, for example, is part of the movement of, and toward, the Kingdom (*Pastoral Constitution on the Church in the Modern World*, n. 39). *Grace transforms not only persons but the whole created order* (Romans 8:19-23).

19. Our understanding of the relationship between nature and grace, however, must also contend with the reality of *sin*, both *personal* and *Original*. Sin does not destroy the relationship of communion with God once and for all, but it modifies it once and for all.

20. The *Old Testament* has no formal concept of Original Sin. It is aware of sin and of its widespread corrupting effects.

21. The *New Testament*, and especially *Paul*, develops the notion of "original" sin by drawing a parallel between the sin of Adam and the saving work of Christ (Romans 5:12-21). *We either ratify the sin of Adam and make it our own by personal sin, or we ratify the work of Christ and make it our own by faith.* Just exactly *how* we are affected by the sin of Adam, Paul cannot say. *That* we are affected by the sin of Adam is clear from the fact that we all *die*, and death, he perceives, is a consequence of sin. Only by dying with Christ can we overcome the destructive effects of sin.

22. This biblical teaching remained undeveloped until *Augustine*. Faced with those who exaggerated the goodness of nature (Pelagianism),

he stressed the sinful and wounded condition of every person. Unfortunately, he also insisted that while everyone is affected by sin, not everyone is rescued from it in fact. A certain theological disposition toward *predestinationism* followed from such an emphasis. Furthermore, Augustine linked Original Sin with *concupiscence* so strongly that he suggested that the sin (and one of its principal effects, concupiscence) was transmitted in the sexual union of our parents.

23.   By the *Middle Ages*, and especially with *Aquinas*, concupiscence was viewed simply as a consequence of Original Sin, and the sin itself as simply *the lack of sanctifying grace*. Thus, by Baptism the sin is completely blotted out (sanctifying grace is bestowed), although the effects of sin remain.

24.   *Contemporary theologians*, especially *Rahner*, reject the notion that Original Sin is simply the sin of the first human being or is a matter of collective guilt. These views, they hold, cannot be sustained biblically nor theologically. They also reject the Augustinian notion that Original Sin is more pervasive and universal than is redemption.

25.   Positively, contemporary theologians argue that (1) every human person is *offered* grace; (2) the *absence* of grace follows from some *guilt* freely incurred by the *person*; (3) the absence of grace also follows from the human *situation* itself; i.e., because of Adam's sin we are born into a situation in which grace is not at our disposal in the manner and measure that God first intended; it is a situation, too, in which the *effects* of that sin weaken our capacity to decide in favor of salvation; (4) death and concupiscence, however, are not totally unnatural, since history begins at the point where neither is absent; (5) our human situation, therefore, is *dialectically* determined; i.e., we are, at the same time, wounded by the effects of sin and oriented toward Christ and the God of glory; and (6) all of our efforts to overcome the effects of Original Sin (injustice, war, etc.) constitute a duty that cannot be completed in this world, and, therefore, a duty that is never done.

26.   The *official teachings of the Church* insist on the reality of Original Sin, on the absolute necessity of grace for salvation, and on the interior effects of such grace: the Sixteenth Council of Carthage (418), the *Indiculus* (435-442), the Second Council of Orange (529), the Council of Trent (1547), and Pope Pius XII's encyclical *Humani Generis* (1950).

27.   The difficulty in constructing a theological anthropology is rooted in the inescapable fact that we are at once the investigators and the ones investigated. *We cannot achieve a standpoint from which a pure, unobstructed, completely objective understanding of human existence is possible.*

28.   *Neither can we Christians reach a standpoint from which we can prescind from the effects of God's grace on our consciousness and on the very process of inquiry and self-reflection.* God is available from the beginning. There is in every one of us a radical capacity to know ourselves as persons in the light of the reality of God, and to know God as the ultimate object of our every striving toward human growth and fulfillment. This is an *a priori* knowledge of God. *Hypothetically,* human nature could exist without it; *in fact,* however, we do not exist without it.

29.   *Our theological statements about human existence cannot prescind from Christology, since much of what we know about ourselves we know because of what we know about Christ. On the other hand, we already know something about ourselves before Christ and apart from Christ,* in that our existence is *historical* existence and the reality of God is disclosed therein.

30.   When we encounter Christ in history, we recognize him as human because we already have some understanding of what it means to be human. This is not to say, on the other hand, that the humanity we encounter in Christ does not far surpass our previous expectations and assumptions.

SUGGESTED READINGS

Barth, Karl. *Church Dogmatics.* III/2. New York: Scribner, 1960.

Baum, Gregory. *Man Becoming: God in Secular Experience.* New York: Herder & Herder, 1970.

Fichtner, Joseph. *Man the Image of God: A Christian Anthropology.* New York: Alba House, 1978.

Haight, Robert. *The Experience and Language of Grace.* New York: Paulist Press, 1979.

Macquarrie, John. *Principles of Christian Theology.* 2d rev. ed. New York: Scribner, 1977, chapter 3.

Rahner, Karl. *Foundations of Christian Faith.* New York: Seabury Press, 1978, chapters 1-5.

——————. *Hominisation: The Evolutionary Origin of Man as a Theological Problem.* New York: Herder & Herder, 1965.

——————. *A Rahner Reader.* Ed. Gerald A. McCool. New York: Seabury Press, 1975, chapters 1-4,9.

Rondet, Henri. *Original Sin: The Patristic and Theological Background.* New York: Alba House, 1972.

—————————. *The Grace of Christ: A Brief History of the Theology of Grace*. Westminster, Md.: Newman Press, 1967.

Tavard, George. *Woman in Christian Tradition*. Notre Dame, Ind.: University of Notre Dame Press, 1973.

PART TWO

GOD

GOD

INTRODUCTION

We move now from the question of human existence to the question of God because the reality of God enters into the very definition of what it means to be human.

But if God is so fundamental and so central to human existence, why is it that many of us reject or practically ignore the reality of God? Why is it so difficult to *believe* in God? Why do any of us, Christian or non-Christian, believe in God at all (chapter 6)?

Belief in God must arise from some experience of God, clear or obscure. How, when, where, and under what circumstances is the reality of God made available to us? Are there recognizable signs of God's self-communication, or *revelation*? What is it that is communicated in the first place (chapter 7)?

To whom is God revealed? What are the effects of revelation on the individual, on society, and on institutions (the question of *religion*)? How do the religions of the world differ, one from another? To what extent are they similar? To what extent are non-Christian religions signs and instruments of God's saving love toward the whole human family? Does Christianity have a special place in salvation history nonetheless (chapter 8)?

Our understanding of God enters into our understanding of ourselves. We believe that God has somehow been made available to us in Jesus Christ. As a particular people with a particular history, we have developed a highly structured response to the revelation of God in Jesus Christ. At the core of the Christian religion, as of any other religion, is our doctrine of God. Who is *the Christian God*, and how is that God related to us and to human history at large (chapter 9)?

How has the Christian doctrine of the *triune* God developed, from its biblical origins to the present day? What are the principal elements of the Christian doctrine of the Trinity? What place and importance does it hold in the total exposition and practice of the Christian faith, and in the comprehensive statement of Christian theology (chapter 10)?

In addressing the question of God, Part II comes to the heart of the matter, both of this book and of theology itself. All else converges here. Our understanding of God is the foundation and context for our understanding of creation, redemption, incarnation, grace, the Church, moral responsibility, eternal life, and each of the other great mysteries and doctrines of Christian faith.

Every theological question is a variation on the *one* theological question: the God-question. But the invisible reality of God is mediated through the visible created order. The gracious and merciful God is at work in Jesus Christ. The Church is, as the late Pope Paul VI expressed it, "a reality imbued with the hidden presence of God." In the end God will be "all in all" (1 Corinthians 15:28).

This notion of God-in-all is closely linked with the distinctively Catholic emphasis on *sacramentality* (a notion that will be developed more fully in Part IV and recapitulated in chapter 30). The Catholic tradition has always insisted on the principle of mediation: The invisible depths of reality are manifested in visible ways. God, the foundation of all that is, is disclosed through signs: the cosmos, history, persons, mystical experience. Jesus Christ is the great sign or sacrament of God's presence and saving activity among us. The Church is, in turn, the sign or sacrament of Christ's and the Holy Spirit's healing and reconciling presence in the world.

But from beginning to end, it is God who is mediated through each and all of these signs: not the God of philosophy, not an abstract God, but the triune God.

The mystery and doctrine of the Trinity means that the God who created us, who sustains us, who will judge us, and who will give us eternal life is not a God infinitely removed from us. Our God is a God of absolute closeness, a God who is communicated truly in the flesh, in history, within our human family, and a God who is present in the spiritual depths of our being and in the core of our unfolding human history as the source of enlightenment and of community.

The doctrine of the triune God is what Christian faith is all about.

·VI·

BELIEF AND UNBELIEF
TODAY

THE PROBLEM

The reality of God enters into the very definition of what is means to be human. Human existence is qualified from the beginning by the God-given radical capacity ("supernatural existential," *potentia obedientialis*) to get beyond ourselves and to reach out toward that which transcends us, the Absolute, and toward that which raises us to a new level of existence, a sharing in the life of the Absolute (grace). The question of God, in other words, is implied in the question of human existence. And the opposite holds true as well. As soon as we address the problem of God, we are confronted with the problem of human existence.

But if the divine is so central to the existence of human persons, why do so many of us reject or ignore the reality of God? How is it that our radical capacity for grace is not universally actualized? In short, why are there unbelievers as well as believers?

The problem of unbelief is complicated by the fact that *unbelief is always relative*. Unbelief is a negative concept. It presupposes something positive which it negates. From the point of view of religious faith (whether Christian, Jewish, or Moslem, for example), unbelief is a denial of or at least an avoidance of God. But from another point of view, these religious traditions themselves may be forms of unbelief. To the ideological Marxist, religious faith may be a refusal to believe in the dialectical historical process or the classless society. To the positivist, religious faith may represent a stubborn refusal to believe in the conclusions of scientific experimentation. To the unecumenical Catholic, unbelief may include the rejection of the pope as supreme head of the Church.

The term unbelief is being used in this chapter to mean *the denial or at least disregard of the reality of God* (whether God is named "ultimate concern," the Transcendent, the Absolute, the "beyond in our midst," the ultimate dimension of secular experience, the other dimension, Being, or whatever else). There are, of course, different *kinds* and different *degrees* of unbelief. There are also different *sources*. (We treated the question of belief more technically, of course, in chapter 2.)

According to the Second Vatican Council, *atheism* (which we are equating here with unbelief) has many forms. The *Pastoral Constitution on the Church in the Modern World* summarizes these: *classical atheism*, or the outright denial of God; *agnosticism*, or the refusal to decide whether to believe in God or not (a decision wherein one effectively decides *not* to believe in God); *positivism* (which rejects all reality which cannot be verified by scientific testing); an excessive *humanism* (which exaggerates the human capacity to control the universe through technology and which emphasizes freedom to the detriment of order); the rejection of *false notions* of God which the atheist assumes to be official doctrine; the transfer of ultimate concern from God (the Transcendent) to material things (the totally immanent); and the transfer of blame for social evil from individual, institutional, environmental forces to God as the One who thwarts the struggle for *liberation* by shifting our attention from this world to the next.

"Undeniably," the *Pastoral Constitution* declares, "those who willfully shut out God from their hearts and try to dodge religious questions are not following the dictates of their consciences. Hence they are not free of blame." But then the council proceeds to an extraordinary admission: "Yet believers themselves frequently bear some responsibility for this situation . . . .To the extent that they neglect their own training in the faith, or teach erroneous doctrine, or are deficient in their religious, moral, or social life, they must be said to conceal rather than reveal the authentic face of God and religion"(n. 19).

Some major *sociologists of religion* would agree with the main lines of the council's explanation, but their analyses are more broadly based. Thus, at a 1969 symposium in Rome, cosponsored by the Vatican's Secretariat for Non-Believers, University of California sociologist Robert Bellah noted that the phenomenon of unbelief was limited to relatively small groups of intellectuals and cultural elites until the eighteenth century. With the expansion of these classes (especially through education and the concomitant rise in literacy) in the nineteenth century, a new spirit spread to a larger public: a fuller appreciation for the dignity of the individual and the importance of free inquiry, on the one hand, and a reaction against authority (or at least authoritarianism), on the other. This was accompanied, as we already saw in the two previous chapters, by a shift in *philosophical* emphasis from the objective to the *subjective* orders. Belief became less an imposed system than a matter of personal decision.

So widespread was this change that many nineteenth-century rationalists and positivists predicted the demise of religion. But that never happened. Why not? Because the anti-religious forces made the same mistake that many religious people have committed: they confused religious belief with *cognitive* belief. Thus, with the collapse of cognitive belief, religious belief as such was sure to follow.

But this assumption about the collapse of religious belief was never verified by the facts. The large portion of religious people had never regarded cognitive, intellectualized belief as essential to their religious lives. What they embraced instead was an *embodied* truth, transmitted not through definitions and logical demonstrations, but through narratives, images, and rituals. This insight is fully consistent with the *Pastoral Constitution's* insistence that "the witness of a living and mature faith ... penetrating the believer's entire life ... activating him toward justice and love ... " is even more important in overcoming unbelief than is "a proper presentation of the Church's teaching" (n. 21).

Faith, according to Bellah and other sociologists, is deeply embedded in our existential situation and is part of the very structure of human experience—an insight which Bellah correctly attributes to Pascal (d. 1662) and Kierkegaard (d. 1855), and which we might also link with Rahner and Lonergan as well. Religion, therefore, is not "a matter of objective-cognitive assertion which might conflict with science, but a symbolic form within which one comes to terms with one's fate" (see *The Culture of Unbelief*, p. 46). Faith, consequently, is an *inner* reality, and the belief which follows from faith is inner-directed. But that does not mean that faith and belief are purely private. Such faith and such belief relate us to others, to the total human community, and indeed to the whole universe—bringing us even to the point of sacrificing our lives for others.

How widespread is the opposite, unbelief? Again, it depends on how you define it. In one sense at least, everyone is a believer; everyone believes in something important. And insofar as people express their belief, they are "religious." In the context of the United States, for example, such beliefs may issue forth in what Bellah has called "civil religion." It is the linking of one's search for personal authenticity with a sense of national identity and national purpose. The Peace Corps would be one major instance of it. It had something of the character of a secular monastic order, complete with a vow of poverty and a heroic devotion to the service of others.

But if you take belief to mean some *explicit* affirmation of the reality of God, then unbelief is considerably more prevalent, and certainly more in evidence than in previous centuries—again, because of advances in education generally, in literacy particularly, and because of the modern philosophical shift to the "subject."

And that is why the obverse side of the problem of God is the problem of the unbelieving person. Indeed, the problem of God—of belief and unbelief—becomes a problem only when it is concretely stated in such terms. According to the Bible and to the kind of philosophical theology represented by Transcendental Thomism, the presence of God is integral to the very structure of our historical existence. Therefore, the person who does not "fear God" (in the biblical sense of responding obediently to the presence and call of God) somehow does not exist, and that person's nature is somehow less than, or other than, human. On the other hand, the unbeliever *does* exist. He or she is there. And that is the problem.

We shall not, in this chapter or anywhere else in this relatively ambitious book, solve that problem. There are some things that we can do no more than accept as part of our historical situation (a "given" of reality) and deal with as intelligently and as constructively as possible.

The problem of belief and unbelief, therefore, is not primarily the problem of communicating the correct information about God so that everyone will be able to know it, and in knowing it perceive at once its truth. Nor is it simply a problem of laziness or bad will on the part of those to whom the information is directed. Rather, *the problem of belief and unbelief is,* once again, *the problem of human existence.* Is human existence finally and ultimately worthwhile? Is it meaningful? Is it purposeful? Is it intelligible? Is it directed to some end beyond itself? Or is it simply "full of sound and fury, signifying nothing"? And the problem of human existence is but the other side of the *problem of God.* For the question of the intelligibility, purposefulness, and worthwhileness of human existence is always answered, positively or negatively, in terms of God or some verbal surrogate for God.

SOME CONTEMPORARY VIEWS OF THE PROBLEM

Hans Küng

Swiss theologian Hans Küng, professor at the University of Tübingen in West Germany and author of many influential and controversial books on the Church, has perhaps made his deepest impression thus far with his massive volume *On Being a Christian.* He discusses the problem of belief and unbelief early on in the book, in the section on God.

His approach is consistent with the one adopted in this book. "In order to answer the question of God," he insists, "it must be assumed that man accepts in principle his own existence and reality as a whole ... " (p. 70). Our attitude to reality, if we are ever to reach God, has to be one of fundamental trust and confidence. Not that such trust automatically eliminates uncertainty of every kind. Reality is there as a fact, and yet it remains always engimatic, without any clearly visible support or purpose. The challenge is to find some kind of satisfactory answer, and in this quest the believer is in competition with the unbeliever. Which one can more convincingly interpret the basic human experiences?

Even someone who does not think that God exists could at least agree with the hypothesis that *if* God existed, a fundamental solution to the problem of human existence would be provided. God would be seen as the ultimate reason for all that is, as reality's ultimate support, ultimate goal, and ultimate core. Threats of death, meaninglessness, rejection, and nothingness would be overcome. But we cannot proceed from the *hypothesis* of God to the *reality* of God.

Besides, it is also possible to formulate the *opposite* hypothesis: If God does *not* exist. One must concede that it is indeed possible to deny the reality of God. Atheism (or unbelief in its most explicit form) cannot be refuted on the face of it. There is more than enough *uncertainty* about reality to justify, or at least explain, why someone might decide to deny the reality of God. On the other hand, atheism is also incapable of positively excluding the alternative. If it is possible to deny God, it is also possible to affirm God. Just as atheism rests on a *decision* about the ultimate meaning (or meaninglessness) of reality, so, too, does belief. Just as there is enough *uncertainty* about reality to explain, and perhaps even justify, unbelief, so, too, there is enough *clarity* in reality to explain, and perhaps even justify, belief.

And so the terms of the problems become clear. *If* God is, God is the answer to our most fundamental questions about reality and about human existence. *That* God is cannot be proved or demonstrated or otherwise established beyond all reasonable doubt. It can ultimately be accepted only in a confidence founded on reality itself. Since the "evidence" is so uncertain, it cannot be imposed upon us conclusively. There remains room for human freedom. We are free to decide: to affirm the fundamental worthwhileness of reality and of human existence, or to deny it. Each path is fraught with risks. The decision not to decide (agnosticism) is itself a decision against the intelligibility and purposefulness of reality. It is a vote of no confidence, and *confidence* is what belief and unbelief are really all about.

Michael Novak

The American philosopher Michael Novak, a disciple of Bernard Lonergan, has written several popular books on an extraordinarily diverse range of subjects (fiction, sports, Vatican II, politics, as well as philosophy and theology). None is more pertinent to our discussion here than his *Belief and Unbelief: A Philosophy of Self-Knowledge*.

Although Novak would not disagree with Küng's analysis of the problem, Novak proceeds from a more explicitly philosophical starting point than Küng does. That starting point is Lonergan's approach to human understanding and the structures of consciousness. Religion is based on the drive to understand. Even when all the goods of health, education, security, and wealth are in our possession, we still hunger to know who we are. And we infer from this hunger to know that there is some intelligent source of this hunger. "Belief in God based on fidelity to understanding is based upon fidelity to oneself. In discovering one's own identity, one discovers God" (p. 182).

How, then, does belief differ from unbelief? The believer is attentive to the data of his or her own consciousness, and the unbeliever is not, or at least interprets the data differently. Since no one has ever seen God (John 1:18), one stands always before a silent and invisible God. One "sees," and another does not "see." Being irreligious is like being tone-deaf or color-blind. At least that is how the believer looks at it. But perhaps the believer perceives what is not there. The believer, therefore, can never be certain that his or her belief is accurate and true. "He is held in darkness by a hidden God" (p. 23).

On the other hand, it is in believing that reality assumes intelligibility. If one believes in God, one understands why one is inclined to pay respect to other persons and why one is inclined to be faithful to understanding, to friendship, and to creativity. In the end, however, "The serious nonbeliever and the serious believer ... share a hidden unity of spirit. When both do all they can to be faithful to their understanding and to love, and to the immediate task of diminishing the amount of suffering in the world, the intention of their lives is similar, even though their conceptions of what they are doing are different" (p. 191).

Gregory Baum

Following not Lonergan but the French philosopher and theologian Maurice Blondel (d. 1949), Gregory Baum pursues a similar line of analysis. Belief is not a matter of accepting as true certain elements of some unlikely story about God, but a matter of interpreting human experience in a particular way. Blondel named his approach "the method of immanence." The Christian message reveals the hidden (supernatural) dynamism present in human life everywhere. The message is not foreign to life; it explains what has been going on in life and where it is leading us.

In his book *Faith and Doctrine*, Baum carries Blondel's apologetical approach one step further. He identifies the elements of ordinary human experience which contribute to a believing as opposed to an unbelieving response. He calls them "depth experiences," i.e., ordinary human experiences that are memorable, that are the source of many decisions, and that tend to unify human life. Those depth experiences may be specifically religious, or they may be secular. In the final accounting, however, they are all religious in that they ultimately put us in touch with God.

The specifically *religious* experiences are the experience of the holy and the experience of contingency. The so-called *secular* depth experiences are the experience of friendship, encounter, conscience, truth, human solidarity, and compassionate protest.

The religious literature of the world abounds in testimonies to the experience of the *holy*. It is what William James (d. 1910) described in his *The Varieties of Religious Experience* (1902) as a "sense of reality, a feeling of objective presence, a perception of what we may call 'something there,' more deep and more general than any of the special and particular 'senses' by which the current psychology supposes existent realities to be originally revealed."

Rudolf Otto (d. 1937), another major analyst of religious experience, insisted in fact that the sense of the sacred or of the transcendent is a purely *a priori* category. It is not something derived from sense experience, he argued in his classic work, *The Idea of the Holy* (1917). The experience of the sacred is rooted instead in "an original and underivable capacity of the mind implanted in the 'pure reason' independently of all perception." (The similarity to Rahner's notion of the "supernatural existential" is difficult to miss.)

The experience of *contingency* is our feeling of radical dependency, our sense of limitation, even of insignificance, and our concomitant sense of insecurity. At the same time we are profoundly aware that we belong to another who is vast, strong, caring, eternally reliable, that we are part of a larger unity which has meaning and in the context of which we find the strength to face life. It is an experience alluded to many times by Jesus himself (the parables of the lilies of the field and the birds of the air, for example) and systematically developed in the works of the great nineteenth-century Protestant theologian Friedrich Schleiermacher (d. 1834).

The experience of *friendship* gives us a new kind of self-possession. We become reconciled with ourselves as we are accepted by another. And since we become more ourselves, we have more energy available for the mission of life. Closely related to the experience of friendship is the experience of *encounter* (as in a teacher–student relationship) that profoundly changes and shapes our lives. The Jewish philosopher and theologian Martin Buber (d. 1965) is one of the principal systematizers of encounter experiences.

Conscience, too, is a depth experience. It is the experience of moral responsibility. We realize the call to transcend ourselves and our own self-interest and to act on behalf of others. In so doing we sense that we are acting in accordance with what is deepest in us and thus opening ourselves to reality and to life as it is and as it is meant to be. A thinker who has assigned to conscience a central place in Christian theology is Cardinal John Henry Newman (d. 1890).

Truth is another depth experience. At certain moments in our lives, whether in conversation, research, or reading, our resistance to truth is overcome and we experience a conversion of the mind to a higher level of consciousness. We suddenly see the picture. And because we see, we are able to plan and redirect our lives differently, make decisions in a new way, and enter more deeply into personal unity. St. Augustine stands out among those who have understood life as a series of conversions to truth. Bernard Lonergan's notion of conversion is also pertinent here, as we shall see in chapter 26.

The experience of *human solidarity* makes us aware of the unity of the human family and its common destination to growth and reconciliation. The experience transcends our ideologies and even shatters them. We realize our interdependence. We share in the joys and sufferings of people everywhere. We recognize the deathly, inhuman character of prejudice, hatred, and discrimination. Baum names Pope John XXIII as one in whom this experience bore astounding fruits. One could add the work of Methodist theologian James Fowler, who, building on the psychological theories of Harvard professor Lawrence Kohlberg, speaks of the sixth stage of faith-development as "universalizing faith."

Connected with the sense of human solidarity is yet another depth experience, that of *compassionate protest*. It is the experience of those who become deeply disturbed by the misery in life, who are burdened by the presence of injustice, exploitation, and war. They identify with those who have no hope in this world. Such persons speak out as prophets, as accusers, as critics, even at the risk of their reputations, their physical safety, and their lives. Martin Luther King, Jr. (d. 1968), personifies this experience. And so, too, perhaps do some of the *theologians of liberation* in Latin America.

Depth experiences such as these bring us in touch with reality at its deepest level, and in so doing they bring us in touch with ourselves. Or to put the matter differently, as we reflect on the content and meaning of our human experiences, we begin to see that there is more to life than meets the eye, that there is an intelligibility (to use the Lonerganian term) which grounds, explains, and directs all that is. *To believe means to affirm the intelligibility of reality.* Or, in Baum's terms, *to believe means to recognize the significance of our depth experiences.* They put us in touch with the God who is immanent to human life. They explain our lives and give them direction.

Peter Berger

A sociologist of religion in the Lutheran tradition, Peter Berger has developed an apologetic similar to Baum's. He, too, argues for an anthropological starting point in his *A Rumor of Angels.* What is there, if anything, in ordinary human experience which gives rise to belief in transcendental reality? What Baum called "depth experiences" Berger calls "signals of transcendence." He defines them as "phenomena that are to be found within the domain of our 'natural' reality but that appear to point beyond that reality" (pp. 65-66). As such, they express essential aspects of our being. They are not the same as Jung's archetypes, because they are not unconscious and do not have to be excavated from the depths of the mind. They belong to ordinary, everyday experience.

Berger identifies five: our propensity for order, our engagement in play, our unquenchable spirit of hope, our sense of outrage at what is thoroughly evil, and our sense of humor.

Our propensity for *order*, Berger argues on the side of philosopher of history Eric Voegelin, is grounded in a faith or trust that ultimately all reality is "in order." This transcendent order is of such a character that we can trust ourselves and our destiny to it. Human love—parent for child, man for woman—defies death. Death cannot annihilate the reality and fruits of love. There is an order which banishes chaos and which will bring everything to a unity at the end. And belief in God vindicates that order.

Play also mediates transcendence. When one is playing, one is on a different time, no longer measured by the standard units of the larger society but by the peculiar ones of the game itself. In the "serious" world it may be Tuesday, 11:00 A.M., March 5, 1981. But in the universe of play it may be the second inning, the fourth round, the fifth match, or two minutes before the half. The time structure of the playful universe takes on its own specific quality, a kind of eternity. Religion—belief in God—is the final vindication of childhood and of joy, and of all the playful gestures that replicate these.

Even the Marxist philosopher Ernst Bloch (d. 1978) has argued that our being cannot be understood adequately except in connection with our unquenchable propensity to *hope* for the future. We realize ourselves in projects, as we seek to overcome the difficulties and the limitations of the here and now. The artist, in failing health, strives to finish her creative work. A man risks his life to save another. Herein, we have a kind of depreciation or even denial of the reality of death. And it is precisely in the face of the death of others, and especially of those we love, that our rejection of death asserts itself most loudly. It is here, above all, that everything we are calls out for a hope that will refute the empirical fact. So deeply rooted is this attitude that one might conclude it is part of the very essence of human existence. Belief in God vindicates the gestures in which hope and courage are embodied.

The argument from *damnation* or *outrage* is the other side of the argument from hope. Some evils (e.g., the Nazi war crimes) are so obscene that we are convinced they cry to heaven for vengeance. And we are equally convinced they *will* be condemned and punished. Belief in God validates our deeply rooted conviction in a retribution that is more than human.

Finally, there is the argument from *humor*. By laughing, we transcend the present, the given, what is. We see discrepancies. The neighborhood bully is in deathly fear of spiders. A fastidious writer makes an egregious mistake in grammar. So we see that our imprisonment in the conditions of the present is not final. Things are not always what they seem. They can be other. Belief in God vindicates our laughter.

OFFICIAL TEACHINGS OF THE CHURCH

The preceding apologetical approaches do not seem to be inconsistent with the official teachings of the First Vatican Council and are certainly not inconsistent with those of the Second Vatican Council. The former council declared that "God, the beginning and end of all things, can be known with certainty from the things that were created through the natural light of human reason, for 'ever since the creation of the world His invisible nature has been clearly perceived in the things that have been made' (Romans 1:20) . . . " (*Dogmatic Constitution on the Catholic Faith*, chapter 2).

Nor is the First Vatican Council's teaching a denial of the necessity of grace. The same council insists on the necessity of faith for salvation, and faith is always the work of grace (chapter 3 of the *Constitution*). Furthermore, we have already argued, with Rahner and others, that human reason does not exist in an historical vacuum. Our history is the history of salvation. Our reason, indeed our whole consciousness, has been radically modified by God's offer of grace. There is no such order of reality as a purely natural order. Likewise there is no such reason as a purely natural reason. Hypothetically, that could have been the case. But in fact it is not. Thus, when Vatican I argues that we can know God through the power of human reason alone, that teaching is not necessarily inconsistent with the view that all of our knowledge of God is, in the first instance, made possible by God, by the offer of grace, by the "supernatural existential."

The Second Vatican Council, we pointed out earlier in this chapter, acknowledges that there are many reasons for unbelief, at least one of which is the failure of the Church to live up to its own teaching. If we are to persuade the world of the reality of God, it will not be done simply through a more effective communication of doctrine. It will happen chiefly through our putting the Gospel into practice (*Pastoral Constitution on the Church in the Modern World*, n. 21).

The council also seems to be pursuing the same theological course outlined above. The Church knows "that her message is in harmony with the most secret desires of the human heart . . . .Far from diminishing man, her message brings to his development light, life, and freedom . . . .'Thou has made us for Thyself, O Lord, and our hearts are restless till they rest in Thee' (*Confessions* of St. Augustine)" (n. 21). For that reason we must be prepared always to enter into dialogue with one another, believers and unbelievers alike, in order to learn from one another's human experiences and to assist one another in the interpretation of those experiences (nn. 21 and 23).

What is to be said, finally, of the abiding presence of *unbelief* in the world? According to Vatican II (the *Pastoral Constitution*, nn. 19-22; the *Dogmatic Constitution on the Church*, n. 16; and the *Decree on the Church's Missionary Activity*, n. 7), not every instance of positive atheism, i.e., explicit rejection of God, is to be regarded as the result and the expression of personal sin. Even the atheist can be justified and receive salvation if he or she acts in accordance with his or her conscience. Over against the earlier teaching of the textbooks, the council assumes that it is possible for a normal adult to hold an explicit atheism for a long period of time, even to life's end, without this implying moral blame on the part of the unbeliever.

The council also seems to rule out the notion that those who die without explicit faith in God but who live good lives are destined for some form of natural happiness alone. The council, in the *Decree on the Church's Missionary Activity*, implicitly affirms our thesis that the natural order is already graced and that there can be no purely and distinctly natural end of human existence. Even the so-called nonbelievers can reach a saving faith without having accepted the explicit preaching of the Gospel.

CONCLUSION

Belief and unbelief are two sides of the same human coin. They represent different interpretations of the mystery of human existence. *The believer interprets reality and human existence as finally worthwhile, intelligible, and purposeful.* The unbeliever interprets reality and human existence as finally without intelligibility or purpose and, therefore, without ultimate worth. *Neither belief nor unbelief can be established or disproved by arguments alone.* The believer sees what the unbeliever does not see. Still, the believer's perception is not arbitrary. There are dimensions of human experience which cannot be explained fully apart from the God-hypothesis—call them "depth experiences," "signals of transcendence," or whatever else. This does not mean that the case for belief is clearly the stronger of the two, but only that *the case for belief is not without warrants.*

Michael Novak expresses the problem movingly in his *Belief and Unbelief* (p. 24):

> The believer need not forgive God for the suffering of this world; like Job, he may accuse God to his face. But he does not cease to remain faithful to the conscience which cautions him not, finally, to be dismayed. Belief in God, he knows, could be an empty illusion, even a crime against his own humanity. He knows the stakes. If he is faithful to his conscience and thinks clearly concerning what he is about, he has no place in his heart for complacency or that sweet pseudoreligious 'peace' that sickens honest men. His belief is not unsteady—quite the contrary—though he knows that the thread supporting it, however firmly, is so slender that in the night it cannot by any means be seen. This commitment to conscience keeps him faithful, and his daily experience may make his commitment as plausible as Sartre's experience made his, but there is no final way short of death of proving who is right. Each man has but a single life, during which his choice may go either way. That choice affects many things in his life, but one thing it does not affect: his reliance on his own conscience (formed, no doubt, in friendship with other men) as his sole concern and comfort.
>
> No one has seen God.

SUMMARY

1. The *"problem"* of belief and unbelief is focused in these questions: If God is so central to human existence, why do so many apparently reject or ignore God? How is it that their radical capacity for grace is not actualized? Moreover, "unbelief" is a relative concept. "Unbelief" in relation to whom or what? In this chapter the term refers to the denial or at least the disregard of the reality of God.

2.   There are different *sources* or reasons for unbelief: a refusal to decide (*agnosticism*), a rejection of all scientifically unverifiable reality (*positivism*), an exaggeration of the human capacity to control the universe (excessive *humanism*), *false notions* of God, substitution of material goods for God (*materialism*), transfer of blame for social evil from human and institutional failure to the stunting effects of religious faith.

3.   The *Second Vatican Council* acknowledged that the failure of believers to live up to their beliefs is one of the chief causes of unbelief.

4.   *Sociologists of religion* attribute the growth of unbelief to the expansion of the naturally critical intellectual classes through *education*, the rise in *literacy*, and a *philosophical shift* to the *subject*. Belief becomes more a matter of personal decision and less a matter of socially imposed doctrine.

5.   The collapse of belief in the nineteenth century, however, did not bring with it the collapse of religion because the sort of belief that collapsed was *cognitive* belief, not religious belief (in God). That noncognitive belief is deeply embedded in our existential situation and is part of the very structure of human experience.

6.   For that reason, some would argue that pure unbelief does not exist. Everyone believes in something important insofar as everyone is in quest of personal authenticity. If, on the other hand, belief is understood to mean explicit acknowledgment of the reality of God, then there is as much unbelief around as there are people and institutions which say, or imply, that they prescind completely from the reality of God.

7.   In the end, the problem of belief and unbelief is at once the problem of God and the problem of human existence, for reasons which we have already spelled out in Part I. Belief in God is belief in the worthwhileness, the intelligibility, and the purposefulness of human existence.

8.   This approach which unifies belief in God and the affirmation of human existence is adopted widely in contemporary Christian theology. *Hans Küng* admits that neither belief nor unbelief can be finally proved, but the hypothesis of God answers more questions about the meaning and purpose of reality and of human existence than does unbelief. To believe is to approach reality with *confidence*. *Michael Novak*, following Bernard Lonergan, argues that belief follows from reflection on the structures of our own consciousness and the process of human understanding. Our unrestricted desire to know implies some intelligent source of this hunger for understanding. *Gregory Baum*, following Maurice Blondel, adopts a method of immanence. Belief in God explains and gives direction to our deepest human experiences: of the holy, of our

contingency, of friendship, of conscience, of human solidarity, and so forth. We begin to see that there is more to life than meets the eye, that God is present to life as the source of life's meaning and as the principle of life's movement. *Peter Berger* has a similar approach. He calls the "depth experiences" of Baum "signals of transcendence" —namely, our propensity for order, our engagement in play, our unquenchable spirit of hope, our sense of outrage at what is thoroughly evil, and our sense of humor. Belief in God vindicates each of these universal human experiences.

9. The *First Vatican Council* taught that we can come to the knowledge of God through natural reason alone. This teaching is not inconsistent with our present understanding of the relationship of nature and grace (see the previous chapter). Since this is already a graced order of existence, reason does not operate in a historical vacuum. God is already present to it, elevating it to a higher order of existence. It is *graced reason* which, according to Vatican I, can know God as the beginning and end of all things.

10. The *Second Vatican Council* insists, furthermore, that the Church's message is in harmony with the most secret desires of the human heart. There is a correlation, in other words, between belief in God and self-knowledge, which is exactly the point contemporary theologians are making. It is erroneous, therefore, to assume, as our earlier textbooks did, that all those who explicitly reject or ignore God are culpable and subject to damnation. Even the unbeliever can attain a saving faith implied in his or her commitment in conscience to those values and activities which are reflections of divine reality.

SUGGESTED READINGS

Baum, Gregory. "A Modern Apologetics." *Faith and Doctrine: A Contemporary View*. New York: Newman Press, 1969, pp. 51-90.

Berger, Peter. "Theological Possibilities: Starting with Man." *A Rumor of Angels: Modern Society and the Rediscovery of the Supernatural*. New York: Doubleday, 1969, pp. 61-94.

Caporale, Rocco, and Grumelli, Antonio, eds. *The Culture of Unbelief*. Berkeley: University of California Press, 1971.

Küng, Hans. "The Other Dimension." *On Being a Christian*. New York: Doubleday, 1976, pp. 57-88.

Marty, Martin. *Varieties of Unbelief*. New York: Doubleday, Anchor Books, 1966.

Novak, Michael. *Belief and Unbelief: A Philosophy of Self-Knowledge.* New York: Macmillan, 1965.

Shea, John. *Stories of God: An Unauthorized Biography.* Chicago: Thomas More, 1978.

Whelan, Joseph, ed. *The God Experience: Essays in Hope.* New York: Newman Press, 1971.

·VII·

REVELATION

THE PROBLEM

The Bible itself admits that "no one has ever seen God" (John 1:18). And yet we talk *about* God and *in the name* of God all the time. Where do we derive our "information" about God? How does God communicate with us? Under what conditions and circumstances does such communication occur? How can we be sure that we have, in fact, been "in touch with" God rather than with our own wish-projections and imaginings? Does God communicate with others besides ourselves? Or is God hidden, almost as a matter of principle, from great segments of the human family? Is the *form* of communication verbal, pictorial, dramatic, mystical, historical, social, political, natural, or what? *What* is communicated or disclosed? Is it facts about God and the "other world"? Is it God's own self-communication? Would we have "known" that which is revealed even if it were not revealed? If God does indeed reveal, why is it that so many creatures of God seem either indifferent to, or ignorant of, God's revelation? Or is it perhaps very difficult to pick up God's signals?

The "problem" of revelation, therefore, is the same as the "problem" of belief and unbelief. In this chapter we are addressing ourselves to the question once again, but this time from a more deliberately biblical, historical, doctrinal, and theological point of view.

BIBLICAL NOTIONS OF REVELATION
Old Testament

At the heart of the faith of Israel is the conviction and affirmation that God has intervened in history, modifying the course of Israel's historical experience and the lives of individuals within Israel. Although the Old Testament does not use the technical term *revelation* to describe this process, the expression "word of Yahweh" seems to come closest in meaning. Even in the case of the *theophanies* (e.g., Yahweh's appearance in human form to Abraham to announce the birth of Isaac and the destruction of Sodom, Genesis 18:1-33), it is not the fact of seeing God that is primary in importance but rather the fact of hearing God's word. This is particularly evident in the call of Abraham (Genesis 12:1-3) and in God's dealings with Moses (Exodus 33:11,21-23).

Theophanies and Oracles

The earliest stage of revelation in the Old Testament is characterized by the predominance of theophanies and oracles. Yahweh appears in order to conclude an alliance and changes the name of Abram to Abraham (Genesis 17:1-22; for other appearances to Isaac and Jacob see Genesis 26:2, 32:25-31; 35:9). It is impossible, however, to determine precisely the nature of such manifestations. At times they are presented as if they were external visions, and at other times as internal ones. In general, the Old Testament reflected its own Oriental milieu. The Bible, therefore, employs techniques that were characteristic of its cultural environment: e.g., divination, dreams, omens. They were, of course, purified of their polytheistic or magical connotations. Before a war or the conclusion of a treaty, Israel would "consult" God through its seers and especially its priests (1 Samuel 14:36; 22:15). Israel acknowledged that God could be revealed in dreams (Genesis 20:3; 28:12-15; 37:5-10; 1 Samuel 28:6; 1 Kings 3:5-14). Joseph excelled in the interpretation of dreams (Genesis 40-41). Gradually Israel began to distinguish between dreams by which God truly communicated with the prophets (Numbers 12:6; Deuteronomy 13:2) and those of the professional seers (Jeremiah 23:25-32; Isaiah 28:7-13).

Sinai Covenant

The Sinai Covenant is a decisive movement in the history of revelation, but it can be appreciated only in the light of the entire history of salvation. Through the Covenant, Yahweh became head of the nation and delivered Israel from Egypt. In return, Yahweh exacted a pledge of fidelity to the Law (Exodus 20:1-17) or to the "ten commandments" (Exodus 34:28). The Law discloses the divine will. Obedience brings blessings; transgression brings malediction. The whole destiny and subsequent history of Israel was now tied inextricably to the will of God as manifested in the event by which Israel was liberated from the bondage of Egypt. The prophets never ceased to apply to the events of their own day the implications of the Sinai Covenant. Whatever legislation followed was considered a prolongation of the Decalogue, or Ten Commandments.

Prophecy

The phenomenon of prophecy also enters into the Old Testament's basic notion of revelation. Moses is the prototype of the prophets (Deuteronomy 34:10-12; 18:15,18), but it is only with Samuel that prophecy becomes a frequent occurrence in the history of Israel (1 Samuel 3:1-21). Amos, Hosea, Micah, Isaiah, the prophets who preceded the Exile (which lasts from the destruction of Jerusalem by the Babylonians in 587 B.C. to the Edict of Cyrus in 538 B.C.), conceived themselves as guardians and defenders of the moral order prescribed by the Covenant. Their preaching is always a call to justice, to fidelity, to the service of the all-powerful God. But because of Israel's frequent infidelity to the Covenant, the divine word uttered by the prophets more often than not brought condemnations and warnings of punishment (Amos 4:1; 5:1; 7:10-11; Hosea 8:7,14; 13:15; Micah 6-7; Isaiah 1:10-20; 16:13-14; 28:13; 30:12-13; 37:22; 39:5,7).

Jeremiah occupies a particularly important place here because he attempted, as the others did not, to determine the criteria by which the authentic word of God could be recognized: (1) the fulfillment of the word of the prophet, i.e., what the prophet says will happen, happens (Jeremiah 28:9; 32:6-8; Deuteronomy 18:21-22); (2) the prophecy's fidelity to Yahweh and to the traditional religion (Jeremiah 23:13-32); and (3) the often heroic witness of the prophet himself (Jeremiah 1:4-6; 26:12-15). For Jeremiah the word of Yahweh is always superior to himself and to everything else. Yahweh places the word in his mouth as if it were a material object (Jeremiah 1:9). At times it provides delicious nourishment (15:16); at other times, it is a source of torment (20:9,14). Through the word, Israel is summoned to fidelity to the Law and the Covenant. It is a word of independent and irresistible dynamism and force: "Is not my word like fire, says the Lord, like a hammer shattering rocks?" (23:29).

Deuteronomy

With the book of Deuteronomy the two currents, legal and prophetic, converge. The connection between *Law and Covenant* is emphasized more than ever. The history of Israel is the history of its fidelities and infidelities to both. If Israel wishes to live, it must put into practice every word of the Law (Deuteronomy 29:28), for this Law from God is the source of all life (32:47). Deuteronomy also enlarged upon the meaning of the "word of Yahweh" already given in Exodus. It no longer applies only to the Ten Commandments but to every clause of the Covenant (28:69), i.e., to the whole corpus of moral, civil, religious, and criminal laws. It placed everything under the heading of the Mosaic Law (28:69; 30:14; 32:47). The word of the Law is something to be interiorized: "No, it is something very near to you, already in your mouths and in your hearts; you have only to carry it out" (30:14). The Law consists precisely in this: " . . . you shall seek the Lord, your God; and you shall indeed find him when you search after him with your whole heart and your whole soul" (4:29).

Historical Literature

Parallel to the prophetic and deuteronomic currents is the historical literature (Joshua, Judges, Samuel, Kings), which places the word of God in an even more thoroughly historical context. Hereafter, Israel would never think of its religion apart from the category of history. It is the word of God which makes history and renders it intelligible. Throughout the long history of the kings, the words of Yahweh penetrate the course of events and express their religious significance (e.g., 1 Kings 2:41; 3:11-14; 6:11-13; 2 Kings 9:7-10; 21:10-15). A particularly significant text is the prophecy of Nathan (2 Samuel 7) which provides the foundation for royal messianism. By reason of this prophecy the dynasty of David became directly and forever allied to Yahweh (2 Samuel 7:16; 23:5). This prophecy, furthermore, is the point of departure for a theology, elaborated by the prophets, which is eminently one of promise, turned always toward the future, in contrast to the theology built on the Sinai Covenant, whose demands are meant to apply to the present moment.

Exile

At the time of the *Exile*, the prophetic word, without ceasing to be a living word, became increasingly a *written* word. The word confided to Ezekiel is inscribed on a scroll which the prophet had to assimilate before he could preach its contents (Ezekiel 3:1-3). It remains always a word of *judgment*. Ezekiel repeats the refrain that Yahweh does acts of judgment in order that Israel might know that he is Yahweh, that it is Yahweh who acts, and that Yahweh is holy (6:14; 7:9,27; 11:12; 12:20; 13:23). Ezekiel meantime attempts to form a new Israel during its period of Exile. His word is also a word of comfort and hope (33:1-9). But it is never enough simply to hear the word; one must live it (33:32). In Deutero-Isaiah (Isaiah 40-55) the word is boldly personified as a dynamic reality which creates history itself. It dominates history (45:19; 48:16). "So shall my word be that goes forth from my mouth; It shall not return to me void, but shall do my will, achieving the end for which I sent it" (55:11).

Wise Conduct of Israelites; Creation

Yahweh is revealed, finally, in the wise conduct of the faithful of Israel. The wise person is the one who fulfills the Law of God (Sirach 15:1; 19:20; 24:23; Ecclesiastes 12:13), for all *wisdom* comes from God (Proverbs 2:6). The wisdom of God is manifested in the works of God and is communicated to those who love God (Sirach 1:8-10; Wisdom 9:2; Job 28:12-27). Wisdom comes forth from the mouth of God from the very beginning of the world (Sirach 24:3-31). Thus, wisdom is itself identified with the word of God. It is at once creative and revealing (Wisdom 7-9).

Indeed, *creation* itself discloses the reality of God. The whole created order gives echo to the word of the One who named its creatures, and these created beings manifest the divine presence, majesty, and wisdom (Psalm 19:2-5; Job 26:7-13; Proverbs 8:23-31; Sirach 42:15-25,43; Wisdom 13:1-9).

New Testament

The major themes of the Old Testament—creation, history, prophecy, law, wisdom—are recapitulated in the New Testament in the person of Jesus Christ: "In times past, God spoke in fragmentary and varied ways to our fathers through the prophets; in this, the final age, he has spoken to us through his Son, whom he has made heir of all things and through whom he first created the universe. This Son is the reflection of the Father's glory, the exact representation of the Father's being, and he sustains all things by his powerful word" (Hebrews 1:1-3). *Christ is the summit and fullness of revelation.*

Synoptics

In the Synoptic tradition (Matthew, Mark, and Luke) Christ is the one who reveals insofar as he proclaims the Good News of the Kingdom of God and teaches the word of God with authority (Mark 1:14-15; Matthew 23:10, 5:21—7:29; 24:35). *His authority to reveal is based on his sonship.* As Son, he knows the secrets of his Father: "No one knows the Son but the Father, and no one knows the Father but the Son—and anyone to whom the Son wishes to reveal him" (Matthew 11:27; see also Luke 10:22). The Apostles, in turn, have been commissioned by Christ to pass on what they have heard from him and what they have seen in him (Mark 3:14). They are to preach the Gospel and invite men and women to accept it in faith (Mark 16:15-16). The essential *content* of the revelation is the salvation that is being offered to humankind under the form of the Kingdom of God, which is announced and definitively realized by Christ (Mark 1:15). The time is fulfilled. The reconciling power of God (which is what the symbol "Kingdom of God" means) is in our midst. Be open to it. Let it transform your consciousness and your behavior. Christ reveals the Kingdom, therefore, in his word, in his works, and in his presence.

Acts of the Apostles

The Acts of the Apostles describe the apostolic activity as in continuity with the action of Christ. The Apostles have heard Christ speak, preach, and teach, and they have received a commission to give witness to his resurrection and his work (1:1,22; 10:39), to preach and to teach what he prescribed and taught (2:42). Their function, therefore, is that of *witnesses* and *heralds*. They preach and teach what they have seen and received (e.g., 8:5; 9:20), namely, the word of God (15:35; 18:11), the word of Christ (18:25), and the word about Christ (28:31). More specifically, they proclaim the Good News of salvation through Christ (10:36; 13:26; 20:21), that Jesus is risen (2:32), and that he is the Messiah, the Lord, and the Savior.

Paul

For Paul revelation is the *free and gracious action of God by which he offers us salvation in and through Christ* (Romans 16:25-27; Colossians 1:26). The mystery that revelation communicates is God's plan of recapitulating all things in Christ (Ephesians 1:8-10). Because it *is* a mystery (i.e., because the invisible is manifested through the visible but remains all the while invisible), what is disclosed or unveiled (the root meaning of the word *revelation*) remains all the while hidden (1 Corinthians 2:7). Nonetheless, certain witnesses have "seen" it—namely, the Apostles and the prophets (Ephesians 3:5), and it is concretely realized in the Church (Ephesians 3:8-11).

But nowhere is revelation more fully personified or embodied than in Jesus Christ (Romans 8:3; Galatians 4:4; Philippians 2:7). The Epistles look forward as well to an *eschatological revelation,* i.e., the final and complete outpouring of God. When Jesus comes again, God will be revealed more clearly than in the incarnation itself (1 Corinthians 1:7; 2 Thessalonians 1:7; 1 Peter 1:7,13). So, too, will the glory of the Christian be revealed (Romans 8:18-21; 1 Peter 1:5; 4:13; 5:1).

Paul also seems to speak of what theologians once called "natural revelation" (although, in light of our earlier reflections on nature and grace and on the historical impossibility of a state of pure nature, "natural revelation" must be a hypothetical concept, if not entirely meaningless). In the Old Testament, Yahweh is manifested through *nature* (Wisdom 13:1-9, e.g.); so also for Paul: "Since the creation of the world, invisible realities, God's eternal power and divinity, have become visible, recognized through the things he has made" (Romans 1:20).

And he speaks, finally, of "private" revelations to himself (2 Corinthians 12:1-7; Galatians 2:2) and expects that other Christians will experience revelations which will give them a deeper understanding of the Gospel (Ephesians 1:17; Philippians 3:15). These personal revelations are *mystical insights* which are given to the individual alone.

John

John conceives revelation as the *Word of God-made-flesh* (John 1:1-18). This Word is manifested in creation itself (1:3), through the Law and the prophets (1:11), and finally through the incarnation. The whole life of Christ gives testimony to the Father, and this testimony is perfect in its content and in its expression (17:4,6,26). He is the Word of God (1:1-2) and the Son of the Father (1:18). What he has seen and heard of the Father he communicates to us (8:38; 8:26,40). The Word is acceptable to us because the Father gives testimony regarding the Son: in the works of Christ by which he is acknowledged as the Son, sent by the Father (5:36; 10:25) and through the interior action of the Father by which he draws us to Christ (6:44-46). In the Johannine theology of revelation, *Christ is both God revealing* (1:18; 4:23) *and God revealed* (1:1; 14:5-6). For John, the Word of God appears in the flesh (3:6; 1 John 1:1-2). It is both light and life (John 9:5; 8:12; 12:46; 17:3).

Whoever sees Jesus Christ, therefore, sees the Father (14:10-11). The Holy Spirit will complete the revelation of Jesus and insure the accuracy of the apostolic teaching (14:26; 16:13)—an emphasis no doubt prompted by the rise of pseudo-revelation and pseudo-prophecy in the primitive Church.

Theological Note

We cannot forget here what we acknowledged in the preceding chapter. Belief cannot be demonstrated beyond all reasonable doubt, nor can unbelief be positively disproved. And the same limitations hold true for unbelief. What, then, are we to say about the biblical views of revelation just summarized? *First,* the Bible does not prove the *fact* of revelation. The Bible only testifies to its own belief that God is a living God and that the living God has been disclosed to us in various ways at various times and nowhere more fully than in Jesus Christ. *Secondly,* the Bible presents an *interpretation* of history. It *infers* from the experience of Israel and the early Church that God was active in our corporate and individual lives through the Law, the prophets, the wisdom of Israel, and supremely through Christ. But such a view is always an inference. The presence and saving action of God in Christ, or anywhere else, was not self-evident. It was possible for someone to "look" and yet not "see." What we have in the Bible, therefore, is an understanding of revelation which follows from certain presumed experiences of God but is not necessarily revelation itself. The Bible reports various revelatory experiences along with its interpretation of those experiences. To return to the schema in chapter 2: (1) our experience of God is recognized as an experience of the divine reality (*faith*); (2) we reflect on the nature and meaning of that experience (*theology*); (3) we articulate what we have reflected (*belief*); and (4) we reflect further on the ways in which that original experience of God occurred in our lives (*theology of revelation*). What we have been doing thus far in this chapter is working at that fourth level, namely, trying to identify and synthesize the Bible's understanding not of revelation as such but of the meaning of the very *notion* of revelation.

What we have to remember at the same time is that revelation does not emerge as a major theological question until after the Enlightenment. What follows immediately in this chapter, therefore, is very schematically presented because there is relatively little historical data with which to work.

PATRISTIC NOTIONS OF REVELATION
Apostolic Fathers

For the Apostolic Fathers (Clement of Rome, d. ca. 96; Polycarp, d. ca. 155; Ignatius of Antioch, d. ca. 107), revelation is the "Good News" of salvation. Christ is its supreme herald and embodiment. The Apostles are its messengers, just as were the prophets before them, and the Church receives and transmits their teaching. Ignatius of Antioch, following John and Paul, insisted that the Word of God was manifested first of all in creation (*Epistle to the Ephesians* 15:1) and then in the Old Testament through the prophets (*Epistle to the Magnesians* 9:1-2; *Epistle to the Philadelphians* 5:2). All of these earlier manifestations of the Word pointed to, and culminated in, the supreme manifestation of the Word in Christ. Jesus Christ is the one and only Master, and he alone can provide the knowledge of the Father (*Epistle to the Ephesians* 15:1; 17:2; *Epistle to the Magnesians* 9:1). Ignatius' writings frequently lashed out against heretics and false doctrines (Judaism, Gnosticism, Marcionism). The triple criteria of true doctrine for him were Christ, the Apostles, and the Church as represented in the bishop and his presbyterate (or group of priests). Fidelity to the Church in the person of the bishop insures fidelity to Christ (*Epistle to the Smyrneans* 8:1).

Apologists

The Apologists (Justin, and others) shared the same understanding of revelation, but they were inclined to focus more sharply on its philosophical aspects. Because they wrote for, and in dialogue with, the contemporary intellectual community, they wanted to show that the *Logos* (truth) which all philosophers lovingly pursued was embodied in the *Logos*-made-flesh, Jesus Christ. Christians are his pupils and disciples, members of his school. Irenaeus' view is especially significant. Irenaeus stressed the dynamic and historical character of revelation, underlining its movement, its progress, and its profound unity. He saw the Word of God in creation, in the theophanies of the patriarchal period, in the Law, the prophets, Christ, the Apostles, and the Church. Revelation is a movement from God to God: from Trinity to the Beatific Vision (our unobstructed experience of God in heaven). Christ is at the center of the movement. *Revelation is the epiphany or manifestation of God in Christ.* And, over against Marcionism, Irenaeus argued that it is in Christ that the two Testaments are joined: The Old Testament proclaims Christ-announced; the New Testament proclaims Christ-in-fact. Revelation is the teaching of the Son of God, the Gospel message, the apostolic tradition, the faith of the Church, the Christian mystery, the truth, the rule of salvation, the norm of life, Christ himself. Revelation, therefore, is not a human doctrine but a gift of love, which invites the response of faith and leads to eternal life.

Greek Fathers

Among the Greek Fathers there were two major schools: the *Alexandrians* and the *Cappadocians*. The *Alexandrians* (Clement, Origen, Athanasius, Cyril) developed an understanding of revelation very similar to the Apologists'. For Clement, Christ is the answer to our quest for truth. But true knowledge can be obtained only through charity, the life to which the *Logos*-made-flesh calls us. Christ reveals the Father and the mysteries of eternal life. The Apostles share in his teaching authority and are commissioned to preach the Gospel to the whole world. They have transmitted to the Church the deposit of faith which they have received and preserved intact.

The *Cappadocians* (Basil, Gregory of Nyssa, Gregory Nazianzen) were engaged primarily in repelling the Trinitarian and Christological heresies (especially *Arianism*), but in the process they also indirectly developed a theology of revelation. We have two means of access to the Father: visible creation and the teaching of faith. Understanding of the divine mysteries comes only through Christ, under the illuminating force of the Holy Spirit. Christ is the Word-in-person who witnesses to, and instructs us in, the divine mysteries. The Apostles have the mission to proclaim the mystery as the Good News.

Latin Fathers

The Latin Fathers (Tertullian, Cyprian, Augustine) were on the whole less speculative than the Greek Fathers in their treatment of revelation. Augustine's theology of revelation, developed in his commentary on the Fourth Gospel and in his *De Gratia Christi* (*On the Grace of Christ*), is closely linked with his doctrine of *illumination*, which centers on God as the light of truth. Revelation is understood, therefore, more as *an inner light by which we are able to believe than as that which is proposed for belief.* The one Word of God is at once invisible (the illumination and inspiration of the Spirit) and visible (Christ). In Christ we have God revealing and God revealed. The prophets and the Apostles participate in the light of Christ and give witness to what they have seen and heard. That apostolic witness and word are contained in Sacred Scripture and in the proclamation of the Church. Here below we walk in faith, but our faith aspires to the vision of God.

Augustine's teaching dominated the remainder of the Patristic period in the West. Revelation continues to be understood as any kind of divine illumination. Only in the high Scholasticism of the thirteenth century does the term *revelation* become restricted to "supernatural knowledge" and eventually to the content of Church doctrine.

MEDIEVAL NOTIONS OF REVELATION

The Augustinian tradition is especially strong in the theology of Bonaventure, who also identified revelation with the illuminative action of God or with the subjective illumination which results from God's action. Bonaventure did not clearly distinguish between the notion of revelation and that of inspiration, often confusing the two. On the other hand, Bonaventure did understand the mystery of revelation in its larger historical and processive context: relating it first to the Trinity, to the history of salvation, to the disclosure of God in the natural order, to contemplation, and finally to the Beatific Vision.

The cognitive emphasis emerges particularly in Thomas Aquinas. *Revelation is that saving act by which God furnishes us with the truths which are necessary for our salvation.* Revelation occurs in history, moving us toward a greater and greater understanding of the revealed truths. The sacred deposit of these truths is built up gradually from the time of the patriarchs and prophets in the Old Testament to the time of the Apostles. The incarnation marks the fullness and consummation of revelation. Although Aquinas acknowledged that revelation had no other purpose than to proclaim the Good News of salvation, he was interested primarily in the process by which the recipient and bearer of revelation (especially the prophet) assimilated the revelation and handed it on. He portrayed such a process as essentially *cognitive.* Thanks to a special illumination from God, the prophet judges with certitude and without error the various objects presented and seizes the truth which God intends to communicate. The majority of humankind does not have such direct access to revelation. It is always mediated through preaching, and this preaching, in turn, has been authenticated by the miracles and other signs which God provides (*Summa Contra Gentiles,* book 3, ch. 154). Revelation, however, does not achieve its perfection until the Beatific Vision (*Summa Contra Gentiles,* book 4, ch. 1).

The opening of Part II-II of his *Summa Theologica* is where Aquinas provides his fullest discussion of the *content* of revelation. What is it that we discover in and through revelation? It is "the First Truth insofar as it is manifested in Sacred Scripture and in the doctrine of the Church" (q. 5, a. 3). How is the *First Truth* made known? Through statements or propositions which are presented to the human mind for acceptance or rejection (q. 1, a. 2). The principal expressions of revelation are contained in the articles of the Church's creeds (q. 1, aa. 6-9).

Aquinas follows Augustine to the extent that, like Augustine, he insists on the absolute necessity of an interior illumination from

God which elevates the mind to perceive and accept what God reveals. But unlike Augustine, he does not identify this interior divine illumination with revelation itself. For Aquinas and his school, revelation assumes a more *objective* character.

It is always important, of course, to view Aquinas' theology of revelation in the context of his whole system of philosophical and theological thought. For Aquinas, all knowledge is achieved only in the act of *judgment*. Revelation, which is *the highest type of knowledge*, implies the reception of some data and a light by which to pronounce judgment on the data's truth or falsity. This is the case with "natural knowledge"; so, too, is it the case with "supernatural knowledge." Truths are proposed to the mind, and we *assent* to those truths. In revelation, divine truths are proposed through preaching and are authenticated by miracles. We give supernatural assent to those truths under the light of faith (q. 173, a. 2).

And, thus, for Aquinas reason is an ascending movement of the mind from creatures to God, while revelation is a descending action by which the divine truth enters the human mind by a free communication. Revelation, in turn, has two stages: In this life we accept the divine truth on God's word in faith; in the next life we see God face to face, without the need for faith.

For many centuries this was to be the standard Catholic view on the relation between faith and reason.

THE COUNCIL OF TRENT

The Council of Trent has no explicit teaching on revelation as such. It develops its position indirectly, by what it says about the *sources* of revelation and by what it says about *faith*. The Gospel, which is "the source of all saving truth and rule of conduct," is contained "in the written and unwritten traditions which have come down to us, having been received by the Apostles from the mouth of Christ himself, or from the Apostles by the dictation of the Holy Spirit, and have been transmitted as it were from hand to hand ... and preserved in continuous succession in the Catholic Church" (*Decree on Sacred Books and on Traditions to Be Received*, Session IV, 1546).

This teaching was set against the newly emerging *Protestant* view that the Word of God is available in Sacred Scripture alone, and that the Bible is self-authenticating and self-interpreting by the power of the Holy Spirit.

We saw already in the chapter on faith (chapter 2) that this council opposed also the Protestant, and especially Lutheran, emphasis on *trusting* (fiducial) faith. "Adults are awakened for that justice," the council declares in its *Decree on Justification* (Session VI, 1547), "when, awakened and assisted by divine grace, they conceive faith from hearing (cf. Romans 10:17) and are freely led to God, *believing to be true what has been divinely revealed and promised . . .* " (my italics).

FROM TRENT TO VATICAN I

Influenced by the new rationalistic climate of the day, both Catholic and Protestant theologians moved in the sixteenth and seventeenth centuries in the direction of a new and more rigid Scholasticism. The post-Tridentine Scholastics (Suarez, d. 1617, and de Lugo, d. 1660) stressed the objective character of revelation. God reveals through legates or intermediaries. Revelation is some static reality which one receives from others. And with increasing attacks on the whole concept of revelation, the defenders of traditional Christian faith became more, not less, inflexible on the issue.

The names of the opposition include some of the most important figures in the history of philosophy: Benedict Spinoza (d. 1677), who argued that revelation can add nothing to our knowledge that has not already been attained by reason; John Locke (d. 1704), for whom revelation makes available truths which are knowable to reason alone but which the great bulk of humankind is nonetheless ignorant about; Immanuel Kant (d. 1804), for whom the knowledge of God is impossible for speculative or theoretical reason but is accessible to practical reason alone, i.e., the voice of conscience; Georg Hegel (d. 1831), for whom revelation is the necessary self-generation of Absolute Spirit through the dialectic of historical process rather than the free intervention of a personal and gracious God in history; and Ludwig Feuerbach (d. 1872), for whom the idea of God is nothing more than a human projection.

Under the impact of both Rationalism (Spinoza, Locke, *et al.*) and Idealism (Kant, Hegel, *et al.*), Catholic theology began to grapple anew with the problem of revelation. Some of the early efforts failed because they imbibed too much of the errors they hoped to correct.

Thus, we had Catholic *semi-Rationalists* (Georg Hermes, d. 1831; Anton Günther, d. 1863; and Jacob Frohschammer, d. 1893), who accepted revelation as valid but who maintained at the same time that reason could also independently establish all the truths of revelation. At the other extreme, we had Catholic *Fideism* (Louis Bautain, d. 1867), which underrated the powers of reason, and Catholic *Traditionalism* (Louis de Bonald, d. 1840; Félicité de Lammenais, d. 1854; and Augustin Bonnetty, d. 1879), a particular form of Fideism which held that God made a general revelation at the beginning of time and that the human race has been "living off" this general revelation ever since.

Mainstream Catholic attempts at coming to terms with the new spirit of Rationalism and Idealism, but without falling into semi-Rationalism on the left or Fideism and Traditionalism on the right, were fashioned by certain Jesuit theologians at the Roman College (now the Pontifical Gregorian University), Giovanni Perrone (d. 1876) and Johannes Franzelin (d. 1886), the Tübingen theologian Johannes Adam Möhler (d. 1838), England's John Henry Newman (d. 1890), and the German scholar Matthias Scheeben (d. 1888).

Scheeben, with commendable theological balance, emphasized both the external (historical) and internal (supernatural) dimensions of revelation, which culminates in Christ as the fullness of all revelation. Christ is at once the sign and reality of God's revealing presence. Scheeben also distinguished among three different levels or forms of revelation: revelation of *nature* (*revelatio naturae*): God is manifested through the works of creation; revelation of *grace* (*revelatio gratiae*): God is manifested through the divine word expressed by the prophets, Christ, the Apostles, and the Church; and revelation of *glory* (*revelatio gloriae*): God is fully manifested in direct vision at the end. Revelation in all three senses is destined for the totality of humankind.

THE FIRST VATICAN COUNCIL

The teaching of Vatican I had both a negative and a positive side. *Negatively*, the council's teaching was formulated against *Rationalism* (which proclaimed the complete autonomy of human reason), *Materialism* (which denied immaterial and spiritual reality), *Pantheism* (which spoke of everything as being not only a manifestation of God but identical with God), *semi-Rationalism* (which accepted the fact of revelation but affirmed the power of reason to apprehend the truths of revelation without divine assistance), *Fideism* (which accorded no significant role at all to reason), and *Traditionalism* (a form of Fideism).

Positively, the council taught that revelation can include truths of the *natural order* and that there are *mysteries* (truths of faith which are entirely beyond the natural powers of reason to apprehend) which can and have been revealed. Revelation comes implicity through the natural order of created things, and explicitly through the teachings of Christ, the prophets, the Apostles, and the Church. What is revealed is God and the eternal decrees of the divine will. The content is accepted on the authority of God, with the help of divine grace, not on the basis of rational argument. The whole human race is the recipient of revelation. There are some truths we could have grasped apart from revelation, but only with the greatest difficulty. There are others which we could never have grasped apart from revelation. Accordingly, revelation is *morally necessary* for the majority of humankind to come to a knowledge of religious truths of the natural order (e.g., the immortality of the soul); and it is *absolutely necessary* for all with regard to truths of the supernatural order (e.g., the Trinity). The Church's task is faithfully to guard and officially—and sometimes infallibly—interpret the revelation entrusted to it by Christ and the Apostles. On the other hand, the assent of faith is not blind or arbitrary. It must be "consonant with reason."

The doctrine of Vatican I must be understood, of course, against the background of the period. The *Dogmatic Constitution on the Catholic Faith* was intended not as a full statement on the meaning of revelation but as an answer to the various philosophical and theological systems which were threatening the integrity of the faith. Vatican I's teaching on revelation is less concrete and less historical than was Trent's, and certainly more abstract. What it lacks in biblical and personalist tones (something to be contributed by Vatican II) it compensates for in its remarkable conceptual clarity.

MODERNISM AND EARLY TWENTIETH-CENTURY CATHOLIC THOUGHT

But the Vatican Council's clarity did not hold for a group of theologians within the Catholic Church who were still trying to meet the Liberal enemy halfway. The movement was called *Modernism* because its adherents sought to adapt Catholicism to what was valid in modern thought, even at the risk of introducing some discontinuity between new forms of belief and the Church's past teachings. The principal Modernists were Alfred Loisy (d. 1940), George Tyrrell (d. 1909), and Edouard Le Roy (d. 1954). Drawing from the Liberal Protestant writings of the late nineteenth century, they identified revelation with a universal human experience—an ever-evolving personal knowledge of God attained in the ordinary course of life. Accordingly, they downplayed both the dogmatic content of revelation and its supernatural origin and process of communication.

Modernism was condemned in three separate ecclesiastical documents: the decree *Lamentabili* of the Holy Office (1907), the encyclical letter *Pascendi* of Pope Pius X (1907), and the *Oath Against Modernism* (1910). Over against Modernism, these documents declared that (1) revelation has a transcendental as well as immanent character; (2) it proceeds from a special intervention on the part of God; (3) it has a doctrinal aspect; and (4) it is a free gift of God, and not something demanded by, or already present in, the human person.

By present standards, these anti-Modernist documents seem excessively narrow in their own theological perspective. They tended to settle the issues on a purely disciplinary basis (removing Modernists from teaching positions, censoring writings, etc.) instead of trying to provide some good, solid answers to the various difficulties with which the Modernists were struggling. It is clear today that the Church could concede many points to the Modernists without at the same time undermining the traditional notion of revelation or indeed of the whole supernatural order.

The most constructive Catholic response to Modernism was formulated by Maurice Blondel (d. 1949), who, as we have already seen, anticipated the work of such theologians as Karl Rahner and Gregory Baum. He rejected both the excessive immanentism of Modernism (which excluded any transcendental dimension) and the excessive extrinsicism of the anti-Modernist documents (which tended to portray revelation as something coming totally from outside). Blondel called his mediating position the "method of immanence." An analysis of human action, he suggested, shows a dynamism which moves us toward a goal lying beyond our power to achieve it, but which, if it were offered as a supernatural gift, would be a genuine fulfillment of the human. The Transcendental Thomist movement of the early twentieth century was itself directly indebted to Blondel: Joseph Marechal (d. 1944), Henri Bouillard, and others.

THE SECOND VATICAN COUNCIL

The Second Vatican Council, in its *Dogmatic Constitution on Divine Revelation* (1965), reaffirms the various elements of the doctrine of revelation as proposed by earlier councils and in earlier official papal documents. It is Vatican II's *perspective* which differs from that of these other teachings. (1) It places the problem and mystery of revelation in the context of the history of salvation. (2) It views revelation not simply as divine speech, or as the communication of specific truths, but as something comprising both word and deed: "This plan of revelation is realized by deeds and words having an inner unity: the deeds wrought by God in the history of salvation manifest and confirm the teaching and realities signified by the words, while the words proclaim the deeds and clarify the mystery contained in them" (n. 2). (3) The "word" (*dabar*, the Hebrew root) is dynamic, and not merely conceptual: "God ... through the word creates all things and keeps them in existence" (n. 3). (4) Revelation is both cosmic and historical; i.e., it is communicated through the works of creation and in the course of the history of Israel, of Christ, and of the early Church. (5) Christ reveals, not only through his words and teachings, but also through his redemptive work itself and especially through his passion, death, resurrection, and glorification. (6) The deposit of faith is not simply a static entity. There is true growth of understanding on the part of the Church: "For, as the centuries succeed one another, the Church constantly moves forward toward the fullness of divine truth until the words of God reach their complete fulfillment in her" (n. 8). (7) Although the Church authentically interprets the word of God, the teaching office is "not above the word of God, but serves it, teaching only what has been handed on, listening to it devoutly, guarding it scrupulously and explaining it faithfully in accord with a divine commission and with the help of the Holy Spirit ... " (n. 10). (8) Finally, there is a much stronger and more general emphasis on the place of Sacred Scripture in the Church (" ... all the preaching of the Church must be nourished and ruled by (it)" (n. 21).

While Vatican II subtracts nothing from the earlier official teachings, it does add a new and fuller theological dimension more in keeping with advances in biblical studies and in Catholic theology accomplished in this century alone. We turn now to an outline of that contemporary Catholic theological terrain.

CONTEMPORARY THEOLOGICAL VIEWS OF REVELATION

Contemporary theological positions fall into three general categories: (1) those which continue to emphasize the *objective* and/or *cognitive* aspect of revelation; (2) those which work primarily out of *subjective* and/or *personalist* categories; and (3) those which *combine* elements of both.

Revelation as Objective and/or Cognitive

Although the purely *cognitive* understanding of revelation was the common notion of revelation in textbooks of Catholic theology throughout most of this century, it is no longer seriously proposed. Even relatively conservative approaches such as John Hardon's *The Catholic Catechism* (1975) and the joint effort known as *The Teaching of Christ* (1976), edited by Ronald Lawler, Donald Wuerl, and Thomas Lawler, reflect the broader biblical, historical, and personalist perspective of the Second Vatican Council, even as they continue to underline the objective character of revelation and the assent aspect of faith.

The so-called objective emphasis continues today in more surprising places: in Wolfhart Pannenberg, a German Lutheran theologian, in particular. God is made known indirectly, through those mighty acts by which divine sovereignty over history is exhibited and exercised. Indeed, one of Pannenberg's principal works is entitled simply *Revelation as History* (1968). Pannenberg contends that revelation in history can be recognized by anyone, even without faith. In effect, he falls back into Rationalism or at least semi-Rationalism.

A modification of the revelation-as-history approach is offered by Catholic theologian Edward Schillebeeckx in his *Revelation and Theology*, vol. 1 (1967). God is revealed in history, but the word of God in both Old and New Testaments is necessary to illuminate and clarify the revelatory character of those historical events. This is a compromise position which bears striking resemblance to Vatican II's *Dogmatic Constitution on Divine Revelation*, summarized above.

Another variation is advanced by those in the so-called *liberation theology* school. God is disclosed in the historical *praxis* of liberation. It is the situation, and our passionate and reflective involvement in it, which mediates the Word of God. Today that Word is mediated through the cries of the poor and the oppressed. According to Gustavo Gutierrez, the liberation school's principal exponent, "History is the scene of the revelation God makes of the mystery of his person. His word reaches us in the measure of our involvement in the evolution of history" ("Faith As Freedom,"

Horizons 2/1, Spring 1975, p. 32). The Word of God is distorted and alienating unless one is committed to change for the sake of the Kingdom. Such a commitment to liberation gives rise to a new way of being human and of believing, of living and thinking the faith, of being called together as Church. Revelation, therefore, happens when we recognize and accept God's summons to us to participate in the historical struggle for liberation.

Revelation as Subjective and/or Personal

If the preceding theories of revelation define revelation almost entirely from the viewpoint of God, others focus on the believing subject—in keeping with the fundamental orientation of modern philosophy. It is an approach strongly proposed on the Protestant side by Rudolf Bultmann. Revelation happens when our eyes are opened to the possibilities of authentic human existence and when we begin to respond to the transforming power of the Word of God. Preaching summons us to decision. *In the dynamic of the preaching and of the decision which the preaching evokes we have the event of revelation.*

A similarly subjective emphasis is given on the Catholic side by Karl Rahner, following in the philosophical tradition of Transcendental Thomism and, at least partially, in that of Heideggerian existentialism. The call of grace (the "supernatural existential" to which we referred in chapters 4 and 5) renders us restless for God. God is present to everyone of us and is offered in grace to whoever is freely open to the divine presence. For Rahner, revelation is either transcendental or predicamental.

Transcendental revelation is the change of horizon or world view which the presence of God effects in the person. *Predicamental* revelation is what is given in historical events and formal teachings (Bible, doctrines, etc.). But predicamental revelation is always secondary to transcendental revelation. Once grace has been given and accepted into the inner life of the person (transcendental revelation), it inevitably tends toward expression in the believer's ideas, beliefs, and moral action (predicamental revelation). Christ is the high point of both kinds of revelation. He is one in whom God is fully present, and he is at the same time the fullest expression of that presence in history. In Rahner's words, Christ is *"at once God himself as communicated, the human acceptance of this communication and the final historical manifestation of this offer and acceptance"* ("Revelation," *The Concise Sacramentum Mundi*, p. 1462; italics are Rahner's).

Variations on the subjective/personalist approach to revelation from within the Catholic tradition are provided by Gregory Baum in *Man Becoming* (1970) and Gabriel Moran in *The Present Revelation* (1972).

"Mediating" Views of Revelation

Without denying that theologians like Rahner embrace both sides of the objective/subjective dialectic, one might also note other efforts in contemporary theology to achieve a self-described mediating position between the two poles. It is a position characteristically adopted by Catholic theologian Avery Dulles. Revelation and faith dialogically interact so that the believer responds creatively to the self-manifestation of God, not simply in the depths of his or her own subjectivity, but in the cosmos and in history. Revelation, therefore, is neither an external datum that imposes itself on any alert and open-minded observer (Pannenberg) nor a free expression of one's own subjectivity (Bultmann), but a disciplined response that unfolds under the aegis of faith within a community and a tradition.

Dulles and others who seem to follow this "mediating" position are themselves in the tradition of Rahner, but they assert that they place greater emphasis on Rahner's concept of predicamental revelation (revelation as externally expressed) than Rahner himself does. Transcendental revelation, Dulles insists, never exists except in dialectical combination with its predicamental counterpart. There is no such thing as revelation in general, just as there is no faith in general, nor religion in general. Revelation occurs, and is expressed, within a given historical situation, community, and tradition. In that sense, there is a Christian revelation, a Moslem revelation, an Islamic revelation, a Hindu revelation.

TOWARD A THEOLOGY OF REVELATION
Some Theological Elements:
Creation, History, Prophecy, Mystery

Like every major part of the Christian theological network of doctrines, revelation can only be comprehended in terms of its relationship with other doctrines and symbols of Christian faith. Thus, our notion of revelation is impacted by our understanding of God, of human existence, of Christ, of Church, of grace, of nature, of history. Indeed, one can point to any major component of the Christian doctrinal system and legitimately suggest that all of theology is embodied and/or implied therein, whether it be the theology of human existence, of history, of Jesus Christ, or indeed of revelation itself.

A complete synthesis of the theology of revelation, therefore, would demand some substantive reference to each and all of the other major doctrines. This is impractical, and unnecessary in any case, since this whole book is itself an attempt at a comprehensive and systematic statement of the whole Catholic tradition. What is included in the synthesis which follows, therefore, is only those important doctrinal elements which are not formally treated elsewhere in this book. *Human existence* has already been examined in Part I. We are at this point about the task of developing a theology of *God*. Our attention will soon turn to the questions of *Jesus Christ* and the *Church*. Accordingly, we shall limit ourselves here to a consideration of the relationship between revelation and *creation, history, prophecy,* and *mystery*.

Creation

It must be said, first of all, that creation has to do with more than the beginning of all reality. Even if we were to assume that the world has always existed co-eternally with God, the question of creation would still present itself. Creation, in other words, has to do also with the *lasting relationship between God and reality*, and between God and us in particular. (There will, of course, be a further discussion of this relationship in chapter 9 in connection with the question of *Providence*.)

The doctrine of God, and the doctrine of revelation as well, presupposes a doctrine of creation. How would we know that there *is* a God unless God were somehow available to us? And how can God be available to us except through the created order? And how can we even begin to express our understanding of God except in terms of our perceived relationship with God? That relationship is a creaturely relationship. God is the source and sustainer of our very being.

The doctrine of creation is also intimately allied with the question of *nature*, to which we have already addressed ourselves in chapter 5. "Nature" is that which is. The nature of a being is what it is, as distinguished from other beings. In terms of human existence, "pure nature" is what we are apart from our call to divinization, apart even from our radical capacity to hear and to respond to that call (the "supernatural existential" or *potentia obedientialis*, again). But pure human nature does not exist. We are, from the beginning, open to divine grace.

In terms of the whole created order, "nature" means "being" (our word *nature* is derived from the Greek *physis*, which means not only "being" but also "becoming"). Thus, in the Heideggerian sense, nature is "the process of arising, of emerging from the hidden" (*An Introduction to Metaphysics*, pp. 13-15,17). Every created being stands between nothing and being and is at various degrees of proximity to the one or to the other. There is, in other words, a hierarchy of beings. Those are higher which display a wider range of being and a greater unity: increasing complexity without fragmentation.

We humans are at the highest level of created material/spiritual being. We are both distinct from nature (we alone know that we know) and at one with nature in that we, too, are part of the whole created order. Matter is not evil, as some of the earliest heresies (Gnosticism, Manichaeism) insisted. It comes from the creative hand of God, in one and the same creative act by which God brought forth spiritual realities: "God looked at everything he had made, and he found it very good" (Genesis 1:31).

Among those spiritual realities are *angels*. The word itself is derived from the Greek *angelos*, which, in turn, is the translation of the Hebrew *mal'ak*, which means "messenger." The existence of angels is of theological relevance here for two reasons: (1) angels remind us that there is more to the created order than what we actually see, feel, hear, and taste; and (2) all such spiritual forces other than God are less than God; i.e., they, like us, are part of the *created* order and are not themselves rivals of God in the production of good or the insertion of evil into the world. (The official teaching *that* angels exist as *creatures* of God is given by the Fourth Lateran Council in 1215 and by the First Vatican Council in 1869-1870.) In the Bible, angels function as their name suggests—as messengers of God (2 Samuel 14:17; 2 Kings 19:35; Exodus 14:19; and in the Book of Revelation generally).

Since they are intelligent creatures with freedom, angels have the capacity to reject God, as we do. Those angels which have rejected God are portrayed as demons in league with Satan (1 Corinthians 15:24; Ephesians 2:2). In other words, not every "signal" from the world of the numinous necessarily bears a "message" *from God.* The world of the numinous is as ambiguous and as fraught with sin as is the world of the tangible. Occasional bizarre happenings and behavior associated with various religious cults only reinforce that principle (e.g., the murder of a United States Congressman, other members of his investigative party, and nearly a thousand members of the People's Temple religious group in Guyana, South America, in 1978 is only one of many such cases).

Creation, we must repeat, is already an *act of grace.* It is *an act of divine self-giving.* The being of God is poured out so that there might be beings who can share in the being of God. The supreme act of self-giving occurs in the incarnation when God is so identified with a created reality (the humanity of Christ) that God and the created reality are uniquely one. (We shall return to the theology of the incarnation in Part III.) Indeed, the whole of the creative process is directed toward, and therefore culminates in, the union of the divine and the human in Jesus Christ.

If there were no creation, we could not know God, because there would be no one there to know God. If there were no creation, there would be no *nature*, for nature is the product of creation. Nature arises from the creative act which itself moves from nothing to being. *Creation also makes history possible*, not just in the sense that there must be reality before there can be history, but in the deeper sense that reality must be in movement before there can be history. And creation is a continuous process of movement toward higher and higher levels of being. It is within that progressive movement of history that God "speaks" to us.

Creation, in fact, is considered to be the first chapter in the history of salvation. Creation as ongoing reality underlies the whole of the saving process. God is disclosed not only by the emerging of reality from nothing, but by its continuation and dynamic movement "before our eyes," as it were. We take a look at reality as it is and see how marvelously structured and ordered it is (natural scientists should appreciate this even more than theologians and philosophers do). That does not in itself "prove" the existence of God, but it certainly makes it easier to attribute purposeful intelligence to reality than to ascribe its structure and order to chance. "For from the greatness and the beauty of created things their original author, by analogy, is seen" (Wisdom 13:5).

It is the *Church's official teaching* that God created the whole world, spiritual as well as material realities (against all forms of dualism, Gnosticism and Manichaeism especially); that the world is distinct from God (against Pantheism); that God created the world in freedom, to manifest divine goodness and glory. All created things, therefore, are good. Indeed, they have their own rightful autonomy and are not simply means to some spiritual end.

This teaching is contained in the documents of the Fourth Lateran Council (1215), the Council of Florence's *Decree for the Jacobites* (1442), the First Vatican Council's *Dogmatic Constitution on the Catholic Faith* (1870), the encyclical letter of Pope Pius XII, *Humani Generis* (1950), and the Second Vatican Council's *Pastoral Constitution on the Church in the Modern World* (1965). The latter document is especially important because it underscores the autonomy of the created order and draws out the principal practical implication of such autonomy, namely, ". . .if methodical research in any branch of learning is carried out in a truly scientific manner. . ., it will never really conflict with the faith, because both secular things and the realities of faith derive from the same God. . ." (n. 36).

For the same reason, we might add here, if we discover God through the created order, we need not underestimate the revelatory character of that discovery by referring to it as "natural" revelation (and, therefore, not truly revelation in the strict theological or doctrinal sense). On the contrary, there is only one Creator, who is available to us in a variety of ways and under a variety of forms. Just as there is no such reality as "pure nature," neither is there any such reality as "natural revelation." All revelation, whether through created things or through the prophets, Christ, the Apostles, and the Church, is derived from the same God.

History

For the Christian, history is not simply the place or context wherein God communicates eternal truths to humankind. History is itself the creative act of God through which God is manifested and continues to be manifested to us. The climactic moment of history is always the event of Jesus Christ.

Because God is disclosed in and through creative acts, and because these creative acts (to which we respond and with which we cooperate) constitute history, *we come to a knowledge of God as we reflect on the principal events of our history*. Israel did this before us, fixing its attention constantly on the Exodus in particular (Deuteronomy 6:20-25; Judges 6:8,13; Isaiah 10:26; Jeremiah 2:6; Ezekiel 20:5-6; Psalms 78:12-16; 105:23-38 and other passages too numerous to list). We do so as Christians by reflecting not only on the mighty acts of God in the Old Testament period, but also by reflecting on the supreme creative act of God in Christ, and other "signs of the times" which continue to characterize the world of human experience and history. Nowhere is this perspective more fully developed in the Bible than in the Gospel of Luke and the Acts of the Apostles.

The question whether there are two histories or one, i.e., whether there is a history of salvation alongside of, or even emerging from within, the history of humankind, has been debated since the seeds of a separate theology of *salvation history* were planted in the work of Irenaeus. Irenaeus' basic understanding reappeared in

Augustine's *City of God*. Other formulations were constructed by Joachim of Flora (d. 1202), who spoke of the three ages of history corresponding to the work of each of the Persons of the Blessed Trinity. But not until the seventeenth century did these notions receive explicit development, in the work of Johannes Cocceius (d. 1669), a Calvinist who contrasted the covenant of grace with the covenant of works. The covenant of grace is recounted in Sacred Scripture, with all historical events therein leading up to, and proceeding from, Jesus Christ. Cocceius was the forerunner of the theological movement of the nineteenth century, in which a formal school of salvation history thought (*Heilsgeschichte*) emerged in the writings of a group of scholars at Erlangen University in Germany: Johann Hofmann (d. 1877) and Martin Kahler (d. 1912), in particular. The Erlangen school, in turn, provided a basis for twentieth-century developments in the work of Old Testament scholar Gerhard von Rad (d. 1971) and Lutheran theologian Oscar Cullmann, who is responsible, more than anyone else, for the full-scale construction of a salvation-history perspective, especially in his *Christ and Time* (1946; revised edition, 1964).

The salvation-history perspective is clearly assumed by the Second Vatican Council in its *Dogmatic Constitution on the Church* (nn. 2-4,9) and also in its *Dogmatic Constitution on Divine Revelation* (nn. 2-4).

When it is set over against the dogmatically existentialist views of Rudolf Bultmann, against whom Cullmann waged so many theological battles over this issue, the salvation-history approach is strongly persuasive. Whereas Bultmann and others tend toward the ancient heresy of Marcionism, which denied the revelatory character of the Old Testament (it was completely replaced by the New, they argued), Cullmann, von Rad, and others insisted on the essential connection between the two Testaments and on their coequal status as revelatory documents, linked together by Jesus Christ, toward whom the one leads and from whom the other proceeds.

But to the extent that the salvation-history approach tends to introduce a dualism of nature and grace, of the profane and the sacred, to that same extent is it less acceptable as a theological tool.

History—whatever the adjective placed before the noun—is from the creative hand of God. Insofar as God is knowable through creation and through the creative events which constitute history, God is knowable through history—the whole history of the world, the whole history of humankind, and not simply the history of Israel, of Jesus Christ, and of the Church. For the history of which the Bible speaks will be radically transformed (1 Corinthians 15:35-58) and God will be "all in all" (15:28). Only death remains in history as its "last enemy" (15:26), but history itself is bound for glory, not death. This has been revealed definitively in the incarnation and especially in the resurrection of Jesus Christ (1 Peter 1:3-4; 2 Corinthians 4:14; Philippians 3:10; 2 Timothy 2:11; John 11:25; 6:39-44,54; 1 Corinthians 15).

Prophecy

The prophet is one who, literally, is called to *speak on behalf of another*, in this case on *behalf of God* (Hebrew, *nābi'*). The prophet, as opposed to the institutional figure, stands over against his or her own society, as critic and judge. The prophet proclaims a message which makes demands. Insofar as the prophet claims to speak on behalf of God, the prophet is the bearer of revelation as well as its interpreter. What he or she speaks is the word of God. The word of God comes to the prophet, not for the prophet's own good, but for the community's.

Accordingly, prophecy is not primarily a matter of predicting the future (that is the function of an oracle or clairvoyant). But insofar as the prophet offers an interpretation of events and discusses the consequences of one form of action or another, or of a failure to act, the prophet is indeed concerned with the future.

There are many prophetic voices in the Old Testament: Samuel, Gad, Nathan, Elijah, Elisha, Abraham, Aaron, Miriam, Isaiah, Ezekiel, Jeremiah, Amos, Hosea, Micah, *et al.* None, of course, is greater than Moses. There are also "false prophets" (Isaiah 3:1-3; Jeremiah 5:31; Ezekiel 13:1-23, e.g.). The true prophet is one who speaks on behalf of God in spite of the great difficulty and severe personal risk (Jeremiah 1:7; 6:11; 20:9; Amos 3:8). The New Testament is insistent that God spoke through the prophets (Matthew 1:20; 2:15; Luke 1:70; Acts of the Apostles 3:18,21; Romans 1:2). John the Baptist was accepted as a prophet, but there is some question whether or not Jesus understood himself as a prophet. In one sense, of course, Jesus had to be the supreme prophet, for who could speak on behalf of God more clearly or with more authority? And yet Jesus speaks, unlike the prophets, on *his own* authority. That there were prophets in the early Church is attested to by a number of passages (Acts of the Apostles 11:27; 21:10-11; 13:1-3; 1 Corinthians 13:2; 14:3-5, 24-25; Ephesians 3:5, e.g.). Prophets are listed among the officers of the Church (Romans 12:6; 1 Corinthians 12:10, 28-29; Ephesians 2:20; 3:5; 4:11).

Since revelation is given for all and not for the few, prophecy can be found outside of Israel and the Church. And since revelation is not limited to a particular time in history but occurs within the total historical process itself, prophecy cannot be regarded as if it were completed. God continues to be disclosed through events (the "signs of the times") and through persons who embody the divine presence and who speak boldly on behalf of the God who is present to them.

The signs of true prophecy are never so clear that all persons of good will must agree on who is or is not a prophet. What are some criteria by which to judge one who claims to be, or is regarded as, a prophet? (1) The prophet will claim to speak on behalf of God, particularly on behalf of the Kingdom of God, and will show himself or herself transformed by the word that is communicated to others. (2) The prophetic word will ultimately work for the unity of the Church and for the human family. A prophetic word that destroys unity is automatically suspect. (3) A prophetic word uttered by someone who does not live by that word is almost totally without force. (4) A prophetic word that is so unusual that it bears no visible connection with ordinary life is similarly situated on the borders of credibility. Prophecy is never for display. (5) Prophecy is never so garbled that it cannot be communicated to more than a few. It is always public and community-oriented. Otherwise, we have lapsed into Gnosticism once again.

Formal teachings of the Church on prophecy are exceedingly sparse. The most explicit is given by the First Vatican Council's *Dogmatic Constitution on the Catholic Faith*, in which prophecies

are linked with miracles as "exterior proofs of (God's) revelation
. . . joined to the interior helps of the Holy Spirit." If, for example,
we could accept the late Pope John XXIII as a prophet in the true
sense of the word, then his word, his ministry, and the example of
his whole life would make it easier for us—and indeed for many
outside the Church—to believe that God is real and that the real
God was disclosed to us in this kind, jovial, and pastorally courageous priest.

Mystery

At the opening of the second session of the Second Vatican Council
in 1963, Pope Paul VI spoke of the Church as a mystery, that is, "a
reality imbued with the hidden presence of God." No definition of
the word *mystery* can easily improve upon this one. Because God is
totally other than we are, because God is totally of the spiritual
order, because God, therefore, is not visible to our bodily senses,
our experience of God is always *mediated*. We experience the
reality of God through our experience of created things, or particular persons, or particular events, or through a psychic sense of
divine presence (mysticism). Consequently, every contact with
God is mysterious, or sacramental. The *hidden* God imbues a
visible reality. In grasping that visible reality we grasp the hidden
God.

All revelation, therefore, is mysterious, or *sacramental*, in
character. (*Sacramental* is understood here in its Augustinian
sense, as a "visible sign of an invisible reality.") God is disclosed
mediately, not immediately. We may indeed come to a true knowledge of God, but that knowledge is always mediated. To use
Bernard Lonergan's expression, we know the world as "mediated
by meaning." Thus, Jesus did not primarily bring new truths to us,
new "information" about the other world. He illuminated reality
in new ways, disclosing new meanings.

But God always remains ineffable and beyond comprehen-
sion. The Lord dwells "in unapproachable light, whom no human
being has ever seen or can see" (1 Timothy 6:16). Many of the
Fathers of the Church referred to the darkness on the mountain
into which Moses entered when he went to speak with God. And

Thomas Aquinas had to write that "man's utmost knowledge of God is to know that we do not know him" (*De Potentia*, 7,5, *ad* 14). The Protestant Reformers' theology of the cross (*theologia crucis*) included a protest against our tendency to domesticate God by making God a topic among topics in our theological and philosophical systems.

In the nineteenth century, as we have already seen, the Catholic Church confronted two essentially opposed positions: the one which denied the possibility of any knowledge of God apart from revelation in the narrow sense of the word (some form of direct communication from God), and the other which insisted that everything we know about God we know through reason alone. The First Vatican Council rejected both Fideism on the right and Rationalism on the left. In modern theological terms, Vatican I insisted that God is knowable through the created order (history, events, persons, prophecies) and yet always remains hidden and incomprehensible. Our knowledge of God, therefore, is always sacramental, at the level of mystery.

Since we are persons whose openness to God is without limit because God is without limit, our progress in knowledge and freedom can keep advancing to higher and higher levels, closer and closer to the reality that is God. But it is only because God is already somehow available in the tangible, the visible, the finite, the worldly, the personal, the historical, that we can continue to press for the fullest grasp of God. Indeed, our radical capacity for God (which God has implanted in us as part of our historical nature) makes possible our knowledge and our freedom.

Christ is a mystery insofar as he is the great sacrament of God's presence to us and of our response to that presence (Ephesians 1:9-10). The Church, too, is a mystery, and for similar reasons (Ephesians 5:32). The sacraments and the truths of faith are mysteries of which the Apostles are stewards (1 Corinthians 4:1). The Christian message, therefore, has an all-embracing, comprehensive unity. It is not simply a collection of truths placed side by side, to be believed as they are proposed. The Christian message is about one mystery, the mystery of God, who is revealed sacramentally: in the order of nature, through historical events, through charismatic figures (prophets), through Jesus Christ, who is the great mystery, through the Apostles, through the early Church, and indeed through all those events, objects, and persons which constitute and profoundly shape human experience and human history.

We are never certain, of course, *that* God is present to us in a special way in this or that person or event. We can never be certain either of *what* God calls us to do through particular persons or events. God remains at the same time veiled and unveiled. We cannot escape the realm of ambiguity. The challenge of belief and unbelief confronts us relentlessly. Some "see" and others do not. As we suggested in the preceding chapter, there are no absolute proofs for or against belief, for or against unbelief. On the other hand, belief is not without reason. And therein lies the question of mystery. And therein, too, lies one of the distinguishing characteristics of Catholic theology and of the Catholic tradition: its commitment to the principle of *sacramentality*.

Synthesis: Toward a Theology of Revelation

Revelation is the self-communication of God. It is a process which God initiates and which we recognize and accept because of our radical capacity to be open to the presence and action of God in our history and in our personal lives. *God is disclosed always sacramentally*, mysteriously. Revelation, or the unveiling of God, occurs in nature itself, in historical events, through the words and activities of special individuals (prophets, Apostles, *et al.*), of special communities (the Church in particular), and supremely in and through Jesus Christ, who is at once God-revealing and God-revealed. All of history, and therefore all of revelation, is oriented toward the Christ-event as history's center and core.

But how do we avoid the two extremes of Modernism on the left and a decadent Scholasticism on the right, i.e., the (Modernist) view that God is so thoroughly immanent to the world that revelation constitutes nothing more than ordinary human experience and ordinary human knowledge, and the (Scholastic) view that makes of revelation the transmission of certain truths from one party to another (prophet to Israel, Christ to Apostles, Apostles to Church, Church to members and to the world at large)? To answer this question we must draw again upon our understanding of human existence and of nature-and-grace in particular.

Revelation is God's self-communication, and as self-communication it has a history. The communication is supernatural (i.e., not due to human nature or to human history in its hypothetically "pure" state) and available in principle to every person. Revelation is transcendent (i.e., beyond the material, created order), but it is always and only operative in history. If it were not operative in history, we could not know it, because we are historical beings and the historical is the only context we have for the quest for knowledge and the exercise of freedom. *Revelation, therefore, is always mediated, and always mediated historically.* In other words, we never experience God directly. We only experience God in and through something or someone other than God and other than ourselves.

Revelation has *two aspects*. *First*, it is the *process* by which God is communicated to us. *Secondly*, it is the *product(s)* of this communication, since God's self-communication is always mediated. That product might be a person (thus, Christ is revelation), or it might be a conceptual formulation (the Bible, a dogma of the Church). The mediating product of God's self-communication is revelatory in that it brings about and witnesses to the individual's or community's experience of God. *Christ always remains the supreme moment of revelation, both as process and as product, because in Christ alone God's self-communication totally transforms the mediator, so that the mediator and the mediated are one and the same.* Christ is not only our "go-between" with God. He is also "very God of very God," to cite one of the ancient creeds. Christ is at once the one who mediates for us and the divine reality which is mediated to us.

There is no sharp separation, therefore, between the history of the world and the history of revelation, just as there is no sharp separation between the history of the world and the history of salvation. In other words saving revelation is available within the ordinary fabric of human existence. "Nor does divine Providence deny the help necessary for salvation to those who, without blame on their part, have not yet arrived at an explicit knowledge of God, but who strive to live a good life, thanks to His grace"

(Vatican II, *Dogmatic Constitution on the Church*, n. 16). But salvation is impossible without faith (Hebrews 11:6; Council of Trent; First Vatican Council), and faith is impossible without revelation, since faith is personal knowledge of God, and we can know God only to the extent that God is disclosed to us.

The Church's official teachings and the New Testament's own conviction about the universality of salvation (1 Timothy 2:4; 4:10) assume, but do not formally articulate, a theological position, namely, that every human being is elevated by grace in the very depths of consciousness. Even when grace is not adverted to, it is present and operative as a fundamental orientation to God. *Thus, every human person is already the recipient of divine revelation in the very core of his or her being in that God is present to every person in grace.*

But more than that is given in revelation. The "more than" is what we profess in the articles of the Creed: the saving activities of God in Israel, in Christ, and in the Church. The "more than" is also given in the various persons and events of history as well as in the natural created order itself. Revelation over and above that which is given to every person in the core of the person's consciousness, and apart from Christ himself and the infallible teaching of the Church, is inevitably mixed with error, distortion, misinterpretation, exaggeration, abuse, and the like.

Indeed, those who try to work out a theology of revelation on an extrinsicist basis alone (i.e., revelation is the communication of certain truths from on high) must eventually come to terms with the interior, transcendental side of revelation. Like the proverbial tree falling with no one within earshot, there is no revelation unless there is someone to receive it as such in faith. A person, an event, a natural phenomenon is perceived as mysterious or sacramental, i.e., as bearing and mediating the presence of God, only insofar as it rings true to one's innate sense of God. It is known by what Aquinas called "knowledge by connaturality."

The Modernist, therefore, was wrong to ignore or reject the inevitable historical expressions of God's inner presence to every human being. And the extrinsicist was wrong to limit revelation to what occurs outside the person and outside human consciousness.

It is not enough, however, to say that revelation is always mediated. There are at least *two levels of mediation: the person or the event which mediates, and the interpretation of what is mediated*. Only in Christ do we have what is mediated and an interpretation of what is mediated in one and the same person. The Exodus event, for example, mediates the presence of God. The prophets mediate what has been mediated: They interpret what has happened, and they call it an act of saving revelation. So, too, the dogmas of the Church do not themselves mediate the presence of God. They interpret what has been mediated. In some cases, they interpret the interpretations of what has been mediated. And in still other cases, they may interpret the interpretations of interpretations of what has been mediated (e.g., Vatican II may definitively interpret Trent, which was definitively interpreting Paul, who was trying to interpret Jesus Christ). *Christ remains always the one mediator who definitively interprets all other mediators and mediating events.* The Church, as the continuation of Christ in history, participates in Christ's work of mediation. *The Church is the definitive interpreter of Christ, the Mediator.*

SPECIAL QUESTIONS: PRIVATE REVELATION AND THE CLOSING OF REVELATION

Private revelation is, by exclusion, whatever is not available to the general community, be it the Church or any other segment of the human family. Private revelation is, in principle, possible at all times. Indeed, even public revelation is given to specific individuals such as prophets or Apostles. To speak, therefore, of *"the closing of revelation"* with the death of the last Apostle means only that the Christ-event, which is the definitive and normative self-communication of God by which all other communications are to be measured and tested, has happened in all of its essential parts.

An analogy might be helpful. Christ is like a *master key. In principle*, our knowledge of God in Christ is totally adequate: There is nothing to be discovered about God (about God's mercy, love, fidelity, justice, etc.) which we do not already know through Christ. *In fact*, however, many (indeed most) who know God in

Christ do not know God as fully as they might. Other persons who do not know God in Christ might know God more fully nonetheless. They may not have access to Christ, the master key, but they have keys of their own, some of which open many doors and some of which open a few or only a single door. But these persons do have some measure of access. *In principle*, it is better to have the master key than a key that opens only some doors. *In fact*, however, the revelation of God in Christ does not insure a fuller measure of knowledge of, or love for, God on the part of those who receive it. Others who have access to God's self-communication apart from explicit faith in Christ may exceed their Christian brothers and sisters in both knowledge and love. (The obvious question "Why, then, be a Christian?" will be addressed more directly in chapter 20.)

God continues to be disclosed not only to individuals but also to communities and to the world at large in the same way as before: through natural phenomena, through historical events, through prophetic figures, through the lives of truly holy people. On the other hand, the more private those disclosures, the less subject they are to critical scrutiny and testing and the more prone they are to distortion, illusion, projection, and misinterpretation. Some private revelations have, of course, attracted public interest and some measure of public acceptance: e.g., those to Joan of Arc, Margaret Mary Alacoque (the nine first Fridays), the appearances of the Blessed Virgin Mary at Lourdes and Fatima. Others are clearly bizarre and are quickly condemned even by ordinarily cautious ecclesiastical officials, although such "revelations" often continue to attract a following.

In any case, private revelations have to be tested if they are to influence the Church. What criteria can we apply to the claim that one has received a revelation from God? (1) Is the revelation consistent with the public revelation of Sacred Scripture and of the official interpretations of that revelation by the Church, officially and through the Fathers and theologians? (2) Does the private revelation work toward building up the Body of Christ and the human family, or is it finally divisive? (3) Does the private revelation contribute to our knowledge of God and of our human responsibilities, or is it merely concerned with the unusual and the bizarre ("The Blessed Mother has ordered all nuns to wear their religious habits once again and for all lay women to wear blue berets")? (4) Are the bearers of the private revelation themselves good examples and witnesses of integral Christian and human existence, or are they finally odd, eccentric, difficult to communicate with, and in direct opposition to the Church's social doctrine in their public and political views?

SUMMARY

1. The "problem" of revelation is the same as the "problem" of belief and unbelief. How do we come to "know" God? With whom does God communicate? How does such communication occur? What is communicated? Why do so many apparently miss God's signals?

2. Central to Israel's faith is the conviction that *God has intervened in history*, thereby taking a personal interest in the fortunes of Israel and ultimately of the whole of humankind. God's communications take many forms: created things, theophanies, oracles, dreams, prophecies, laws, wise sayings, historical events, and particularly the Covenant with Moses and the Exodus from Egyptian bondage. It is the *Covenant/Exodus theme* which runs throughout the entire *Old Testament* and which shapes Israel's fundamental understanding of God and of the "word" of God.

3. All of the Old Testament themes are recapitulated in the *New Testament* but are now focused in *Jesus Christ*, through whom God has spoken the final word (Hebrews 1:1-3). It is Jesus who at once reveals the Kingdom of God and is himself the "Word made flesh" (John 1:1-18). The Apostles and the early Church are witnesses and heralds of Christ, and look forward to the day when the "unveiling" of God (the literal meaning of the word *revelation*) will be completed with the Second Coming of the Lord.

4. The Bible—the Old Testament and New Testament taken together—does not *prove* the *fact* of revelation; it only *testifies* to its belief that God is a living God and that the living God has been disclosed to us in various ways at various times and nowhere more fully than in Jesus Christ. Secondly, the Bible offers an *interpretation* of history: its own history and the history of humankind at large. The Bible *infers* from the history of Israel, of Christ, and of the early Church that God is active in our lives, summoning us to lives of fidelity to the divine word of love

and mercy: ". . .only to do the right and to love goodness, and to walk humbly with your God" (Micah 6:8).

5.   For the earliest *Fathers of the Church* revelation is simply the Good News of salvation. Christ is its supreme herald and embodiment, and the prophets, Apostles, and Church are its messengers. Some, such as *Irenaeus*, stressed the historical and developmental character of revelation, culminating always in Christ. Others, such as *Clement of Alexandria*, emphasized the overlapping of the Christian idea of revelation (Christ is the *Logos*) and the notion of truth (*Logos*) in contemporary Greek philosophy. The Latin Fathers, such as *Augustine*, were inclined to be less speculative than their Greek counterparts. Their theology of revelation was closely linked with Augustine's doctrine of *divine illumination; i.e., revelation is something that happens inside rather than outside the person.*

6.   The Augustinian tradition dominates Catholic theology until the thirteenth century, when there is a turn, in the writings of *Thomas Aquinas*, toward the *cognitive* or *intellectual* side of revelation. *Revelation is the truth that God communicates through the prophets, Christ, the Apostles, and the Church.* Revelation, therefore, is the highest form of *knowledge.* Thanks to a special illumination from God, we are capable of *judging* this knowledge to be true.

7.   The *Council of Trent's* teaching on revelation is indirectly formulated; i.e., it has to be inferred from the council's explicit teaching on *faith.* Over against the Protestant notion of trusting faith, the council insisted on the *objective* character of what has been revealed and to what we must assent in faith.

8.   After Trent, i.e., in the *sixteenth and seventeenth centuries,* Catholic theology and contemporary secular thought move in diametrically opposed directions: The former becomes rigidly Scholastic and the latter, rationalistic.

9.   In the *nineteenth century,* Catholic theology finally attempts to come to terms with the Enlightenment. Some were judged to go too far in their efforts to accommodate Catholic theology to modern secular thought. These were the *semi-Rationalists* (Hermes, Günther, Frohschammer). Others resisted modern secular thought to the end. These were the *Fideists* (Bautain and others). Both positions were rejected by *Vatican I.* Middle positions were developed, in the meantime, by Möhler, Scheeben, and Cardinal Newman.

10.   The teaching of *Vatican I* is formulated against various forms of Rationalism on the left and various forms of Fideism on the right. Revelation, the council said, comes through the natural order of created

things (and to that extent is within the range of our rational powers) and also through the mediation of the prophets, Christ, the Apostles, and the Church (and to that extent is beyond the range of unaided reason alone). Revelation is morally necessary for the majority of humankind to know revelation of the first type, and absolutely necessary for all to know revelation of the second type. (*Morally* here has nothing to do with ethics or correct behavior: It is a technical word in theology meaning a little less than absolute, as in "moral certitude.")

11.   The Rationalist spirit reemerges in *Modernism* (Loisy, Tyrrell, LeRoy), which tries to adapt Catholic thought once again to contemporary philosophy. Its emphasis was on the natural rather than the supernatural, and on the subjective rather than the objective. Although Modernism was condemned by *Pope Pius X,* its legitimate concerns and questions were carried forward in a more balanced manner by *Maurice Blondel*, who himself anticipated the development of Transcendental Thomism and the work of such present-day theologians as *Karl Rahner* and *Gregory Baum.*

12.   *The Second Vatican Council* returns to a more biblical, more personalist, more historical understanding of revelation as opposed to the highly conceptual approach of Vatican I. Revelation comprises both word and deed, is not static but dynamic, and communicates not conceptual truths but God and the will of God.

13.   In *contemporary theology* three basic approaches are identifiable: those which continue to emphasize the objective and cognitive aspect of revelation, those which stress the subjective and personalist aspect, and those which try to mediate between the two.

14.   But any *complete theology of revelation* can only be constructed in terms of the whole network of Christian doctrines, so central is revelation to theology. Since this is impossible in a single chapter (and is being attempted, in any case, in the book as a whole), we restricted ourselves to additional discussion of four important theological elements: creation, history, prophecy, and mystery.

15.   Revelation would be impossible without *creation*. The creative act is already revelation, the self-communication of God. *"Nature"* is what arises from the creative act. It is through nature that God continues to be disclosed in a progressive movement through the Christ of history to the Second Coming of Christ. Through an examination of the created order, we infer that all reality emerges from some purposeful intelligence rather than by chance. Accordingly, the discovery of God through creation is not something less than revelation but is a form of revelation itself. All revelation, whether from creation or from the

prophets, Christ, the Apostles, and the Church, is derived from the same Creator-God.

16. Because God is disclosed in and through creative acts, and because these creative acts constitute *history*, we come to a knowledge of God as we reflect on the principal events of our history, as Israel did before us. There are not two histories, the one sacred and the other profane. All history, like all creation, is from the hand of the one God. It is through history—all of history—that God is communicated.

17. *Prophecy* is the act of speaking on behalf of God. Prophecy is related to history as interpretation is related to event. The prophet is less the instrument of revelation than the interpreter of revelation. Insofar as Christ can be considered a prophet, he alone is both revelation and the interpreter of revelation.

18. It is apparent, given the nature of our human condition, that our experience of God is always *mediated*. This means that all revelation, i.e., every form and manner of God's self-communication, is *mysterious* or *sacramental* in character. God, the invisible One, is known always and only through what is visible: e.g., created things, historical events, persons. Insofar as any visible reality contains and communicates the presence of God, it can be called a *mystery*. Christ, therefore, is the great mystery. The Church, too, is a mystery. God remains at the same time hidden and disclosed. The presence of God is never so clear that belief is inevitable, nor ever so obscure that belief is impossible.

19. This commitment to the *principle of sacramentality* is one of the distinguishing characteristics of Catholic theology and of the Catholic tradition generally. Historically, the "Protestant principle" (Paul Tillich) has been wary of identifying God with some finite reality lest such an identification give rise to idolatry. The ecumenical movement of recent decades, however, has seen the Catholic and the Protestant positions come closer together.

20. Revelation is the self-communication of God. It is both the *process* by which God is disclosed and is one or another of the *products* of that process (the Bible, a dogma of the Church, e.g.). In Christ alone do we have the convergence of process and product. He is at once the reality communicated and the sign of the reality.

21. A *balanced theology* of revelation has to avoid the extremes of Modernism on the left and extrinsicism on the right. *Revelation has its origin and foundation outside the human subject, but if it happens at all, it happens within the consciousness of the human subject.*

22. *Revelation*, understood as God's self-communication, is *available in principle to everyone*. All are called to salvation, but salvation is

impossible without faith, and faith, in turn, is impossible without revelation of some kind.

23.   Revelation is *closed* only in the sense that Christ, who is the fullness of revelation, *has already been present to us in history.* Revelation *continues,* on the other hand, in that *God is a living God and remains available to us. But God will not fundamentally alter, and certainly not revoke, the self-communication that has already occurred in Christ.*

SUGGESTED READINGS

Dulles, Avery. *Revelation Theology.* New York: Herder & Herder, 1969.

Jastrow, Robert. *God and the Astronomers.* New York: W. W. Norton, 1978.

Latourelle, René. *Theology of Revelation.* New York: Alba House, 1966.

Moran, Gabriel. *The Present Revelation: In Quest of Religious Foundations.* New York: Herder & Herder, 1972.

Niebuhr, H. Richard. *The Meaning of Revelation.* New York: Macmillan, 1962.

Rahner, Karl. "The History of Salvation and Revelation." *Foundations of Christian Faith.* New York: Seabury Press, 1978, pp. 138-175.

Schlette, Heinz. *Towards a Theology of Religions.* New York: Herder & Herder, 1966.

Schnackenburg, Rudolf. "Biblical Views of Revelation." *Theology Digest* 13 (1965), 129-134.

Vatican Council II. *Dogmatic Constitution on Divine Revelation (Dei verbum),* 1965.

·VIII·

RELIGION AND ITS VARIETIES

THE PROBLEM

There is always a debate about the meaning of the word *religion*. With the growth of many small sects, cults, and movements in the United States, even governmental agencies like the Internal Revenue Service are hard pressed to decide which group can legally be classified as a religion for tax-exemption purposes, and which cannot. Etymology helps us only a little bit.

Religion is derived from the Latin noun *religio*, but it is not clear which of three verbs the noun is most closely allied with: *relegere* ("to turn to constantly" or "to observe conscientiously"); *religari* ("to bind oneself (back)"); and *reeligere* ("to choose again"). Each verb, to be sure, points to three possible religious attitudes, but in the final accounting a purely etymological probe does not resolve the ambiguity.

Let us assume for the moment, however, that religion has something to do with our perception of, and response to, God. Why is it, then, that we have not one religion but many? And of the many, why is it that sociologically marginal, even bizarre, types abound?

And what of the mainstream religions, the so-called major world religions? Does their very existence, not to mention their numerical strength, undermine Christianity's traditional claim to uniqueness and supremacy? If we are to regard them as more or less legitimate signs and instruments of God's saving grace (as does the Second Vatican Council's *Declaration on the Relationship of the Church to non-Christian Religions*), does not that imply they have received divine revelation of some kind and have interpreted it with some measure of clarity? Under what circumstances and through what forms of mediation do the non-Christian religions encounter God in revelation? According to what criteria do they interpret their revelation-experience(s) accurately and adhere to them faithfully?

And what of Judaism? Undoubtedly, the Church's relationship with Judaism is different from its relationship with all other non-Christian religions. Christianity emerges from Judaism. Jesus was himself a Jew. The Church accepts the Old Testament, or Hebrew Scriptures, as just as much the Word of God as the New Testament. Indeed, the Church condemned the heresy of Marcionism early in its history, and has never retreated from that doctrinal insistence on the fundamental unity of the two Testaments. Has Judaism now been superseded completely? Are Jews no longer the People of God? Does Christianity have anything still to learn from Judaism?

And what of the general relationship between religion—*any* religion—and the society in which it finds itself? Is religion, of its very nature, inimical to human interests? Is religion the enemy of freedom, of rationality, of political responsibility? Why have so many regarded religion in this light? Are recent trends in the direction of greater religious involvement in the social and political processes of history consistent with, or opposed to, religion's essential purposes and functions?

And what, finally, of the general relationship between religion and institutionalism? Is religion, of its very nature, so private and so spiritual that it can and must avoid structural expression? Can one be "religious," in other words, without belonging to, and actively participating in, a specific religious group? Can there be such a thing as a "religionless Christianity" (Dietrich Bonhoeffer)?

The subject of religion and its varieties is treated at this point in Part II and in the book as a whole because (1) religion is an immediate product of revelation; and (2) religions embody singly and collectively human understandings of God which are rooted in God's own offer of grace to every person. We cannot fully appreciate the Christian answer to the question of God apart from the spectrum of answers previously or concomitantly provided by others. The same, of course, held true for our exploration of the Christian, and specifically the Catholic, understanding of human existence. That is why the method and content of this chapter bear some modest resemblance to that of chapter 4.

THE NOTION OF RELIGION
Defining Religion

Over the centuries the notion of religion has been defined philosophically, anthropologically, psychologically, sociologically, phenomenologically, culturally, and theologically. It would seem that the best definition would incorporate elements from all rather than from only one or two of these disciplines. But that has not been the case, for the most part.

Some have restricted themselves to an *abstractly philosophical* approach. They have prescinded from all the particularities of the various religions and have tried instead to identify the pure essence of religion as such.

Others have taken a *purely phenomenological* approach, searching for certain visible characteristics common to each of the world's religions.

Others have adopted a *narrowly theological* approach, insisting that there is, and can be, only one true religion, Christianity.

Others have isolated the *psychological* dimension of religious experience (the feeling of absolute dependence; the experience of the holy) and limited the nature and scope of religion accordingly. Some indeed make of religion a mere projection of human wishes, a phenomenon that emerges at the point where human beings can no longer bear their sense of dependence, their anxieties, or even their poverty.

Still others have defined religion *functionally*, locating it at the intersection of *sociology and culture*. Religion is a "given" of the human situation, something to be observed and studied in its total structural composition and defined in terms of its role in meeting social needs and shaping culture.

It is the conviction of this chapter that no definition of religion can ignore any of these methods. Thus, religion requires a *philosophical* analysis if we are to attain any kind of definition at all. Philosophy is concerned with the nature of things, with principles, with theories and laws that transcend the particular and the specific but, at the same time, help to illumine and explain them.

But that philosophical analysis must also be *phenomenologically* developed. Not even in the most narrow medieval philosophies were essences plucked from thin air. All inquiry after truth begins with sense experience. One must first take a look at what is out there before coming to a conclusion about what it is at its core. So, too, with religion. If we hope to define religion as it is and not simply as it might be in one or another philosopher's mind, then we have to take account of religion in all of its varieties.

That very phenomenological exploration will disclose the obviously social and cultural dimensions of religion, its impact on interpersonal relationships, social, political, and economic institutions, art, music, architecture, and the like. No attempt at a definition of religion that is at once philosophical and phenomenological will lack an explicitly *sociological* dimension.

But a closer look at the social aspects of religion will reveal that its varied social expressions are only a reflection of the conversion of mind and heart—for good or for ill—that has occurred in a religion's individual adherents. Religion clearly meets a deeply rooted human need to find meaning in life, as well as the corresponding social need to find a community which shares and sustains that meaning. And so the *psychological* dimension is indispensable to any useful and comprehensive definition of religion.

In the end, however, a definition of religion must be *theological* unless we are to sever all connection between religion and revelation, or between religion and God. Most people, in fact, who would describe themselves as religious or who would be identified as religious according to standard philosophical, sociological, and psychological categories, attest to their own firm conviction that God is on the "other side" of their religious relationship and that somehow God has managed to reach across the "infinitely qualitative distance" (Kierkegaard) between the divine and the human to communicate with them in revelation.

Even if these religious persons' perception of God were in error, and beyond that, even if God did not exist, the psychologist and the sociologist would still have to take the "experience of God" into account, trying to determine its origins, its modes of actuation, and its psychic and social implications.

But for the theologian God *is* real, and so, too, is the corporate experience of God in the world's great religions, however imperfect or even distorted those experiences might be. How, then, is religion to be defined?

As we have noted before, the earliest Fathers of the Church (e.g., Justin, Tertullian, Irenaeus, Clement of Alexandria, Origen) emphasized the link between the *Logos* (truth) of contemporary Greek philosophy and the *Logos*-made-flesh of Christian faith. Whenever human thoughts and actions are determined by, and directed toward, the *Logos*, we are at least at the threshold of religion. But for these Fathers, as for *Augustine* later, there were not many religions, but only one, just as there are not many *Logoi*, but only one *Logos*. And since the Son of God is coeternal with the Father, the *Logos* whom the philosophers and others sought even before the coming of Christ was the same *Logos* who became flesh *in* Christ. The one, true, religion, therefore, "has been expressed outwardly and carried on under one set of names and signs in times past and [under] another set now; it was more secret then and more open now; . . . yet it is one and the same true religion . . . . The saving grace of this religion, the only true one, through which alone true salvation is truly promised, has never been refused to anyone who was worthy of it . . . " (*Letter #102*).

Thomas Aquinas adopted this same positive estimation of the religious orientation of non-Christians. The knowledge of God, through the recognition of the effects of God's action in the world, is possible for every person. Such knowledge is one of the "preambles of faith" (i.e., those truths which can be known apart from the explicit teaching of Christ and the Church and which are a necessary foundation for Christian faith itself).

For Aquinas, religion is one of the "potential parts" of the virtue of *justice*, in that religion bears many of the characteristics of justice but at the same time falls short of the full meaning of the virtue of justice. The essence of justice consists in rendering to another his due. When one has been rendered what is due, equality has been established or restored. But there can be no equality between God and ourselves. Therefore, religion will always be something like the virtue of justice but is not exactly the same.

Thomas agrees that a purely etymological exploration will not finally disclose the meaning of religion. It is simply not clear from which verb the noun is derived. But no matter, because each of the possible sources is consistent with the view that religion "denotes properly a relation to God" (*Summa Theologica*, II-II, q. 81, a. 1).

Is religion for God's benefit or our own? "We pay God honor and reverence, not for His sake (because He is himself full of glory . . .), but for our own sake, because by the very fact that we revere and honor God, our mind is subjected to Him; wherein its perfection consists, since a thing is perfected by being subjected to its superior . . . " (a. 7).

The Thomistic and earlier patristic perspectives were themselves linked together by the *Transcendental Thomists* in this century. Because we are alive by a principle which transcends us, we are not merely *capable* of reaching beyond ourselves to God, which is what an act of religion is all about. We are actually *summoned* to do so. And this is also the position adopted by the *Second Vatican Council*, namely, that we are "at once impelled by nature and also bound by a moral obligation to seek the truth, especially religious truth" (*Declaration on Religious Freedom*, n. 2).

Religion, therefore, has to do with the whole of human existence, and not merely with some special sector of it. God's presence touches the whole person in the totality of the person's relationships not only with God but with all other persons, and with the whole cosmic order as well. *Religion is the whole complexus of attitudes, convictions, emotions, gestures, rituals, beliefs, and institutions by which we come to terms with, and express, our most fundamental relationship with Reality (God and the created order, perceived as coming forth from God's creative hand).* That relationship is disclosed by a process we have called *revelation*. Religion, therefore, is our (more or less) structured response to revelation.

The word *Reality* has been capitalized to insure that religion will not be confused with any "philosophy of life." In the act of religion we deliberately reach out toward God. We perceive God in the persons, events, and things we see, that is to say, sacramentally. Religion presupposes and flows from *faith*. One is not religious who does not think there is more to reality than meets the eye. The religious person believes himself or herself to be in touch with another dimension, with "the beyond in the midst of life" (Bonhoeffer).

This does not mean, however, that every person of faith is also religious. It is possible to have only *implicit* faith in God. Even a person who thinks of himself or herself as an atheist might be a person of faith. Such persons might be rejecting false notions of God, as the Second Vatican Council admitted. In any case, they may be oriented to God through their firm commitment to love, justice, and the like. It is not *explicit* faith in God which saves, but only that faith, explicit *or* implicit, that issues forth in obedience to God's will (Matthew 7:21; see also the Parable of the Sheep and the Goats in Matthew 25:31–46). On the other hand, the actions of a person with *implicit* faith only cannot be called religious except in the widest sense of the word. Religion is an individual, social, and institutional manifestation of some *explicit* faith in God.

Characteristics of Religion

1.   The most basic characteristic of religion is its sense of the *holy* or the *sacred*. For the sociologist Emile Durkheim (d. 1917) the sacred, unlike the secular or the profane, has *no utilitarian purpose* at all. It is something revered for its own sake. It elicits from us what the phenomenologist of religion G. van der Leeuw (d. 1950) has called *awe*. Religious rites are not performed to achieve something so much as to express an attitude. Awe, in other words, develops into *observance*.

Other characteristics of the sacred, for Durkheim, are its being perceived as a *power* or *force*, its *ambiguity*, its *invisible* or *spiritual* quality, its *non-cognitive* dimension, its *supportive* or *strength-giving* nature, and the *demands* it makes upon believers and worshipers. (See *The Elementary Forms of the Religious Life*, 1954.)

Rudolf Otto (d. 1937) has also analyzed what he calls *The Idea of the Holy* (1917), referring to it as the "numinous," i.e., as something beyond rational and ethical conceptions. It embodies a mystery that is above all creatures, something hidden and esoteric, which we can experience in feelings. The holy is the *mysterium tremendum et fascinosum* (a mystery which at the same time overwhelms and fascinates us). It is "wholly other" (which is how the Protestant theologian Karl Barth also referred to God), quite beyond the sphere of the usual, the intelligible, and the familiar. The experience of the holy, according to Otto, arouses a feeling of unworthiness in the believer.

Durkheim and Otto agree, therefore, on the extraordinary character of the phenomenon (the experience of the sacred), its implication of power, its ambiguity in relation to us, its awesome character, and the feeling of dependence it evokes.

2. Religion not only has to do with the impact of the holy upon us but with our *response to the holy* as well. Religion necessarily includes *faith*. The content of that faith may differ from religion to religion, and there will even be sharp differences of interpretation within the same religion, but there can be no religion to begin with unless there is some self-consciousness and reflective awareness of the holy, the sacred, the ultimate, of God. And that is faith, which we defined in chapter 2 as a way of knowing God.

3. Religion inevitably gives rise to *beliefs* of various kinds: some popular, some official (doctrines, creeds). And the more sophisticated the religion, the more likely the emergence of a *theological* tradition, even of *systematic* theology. (We have already outlined, again in chapter 2, the connections among faith, theology, and belief.)

4. Religion is also expressed in various *actions*: *moral behavior* consistent with the beliefs, and *liturgy*, or the ritualization of beliefs.

5. Religion, finally, generates a *community* of shared perceptions, meanings, and values. Each such community has at least some rudimentary *structure*.

It is important to note the connection between the original religious inspiration and the community it eventually generates.

The foundational religious experience is *charismatic* in nature. Max Weber (d. 1920) defines *charisma* as " . . . a certain quality of an individual personality by virtue of which he is set apart from ordinary men and treated as endowed with supernatural, superhuman, or at least specifically exceptional powers or qualities. These are such as are not accessible to the ordinary person, but are regarded as of divine origin or as exemplary, and on the basis of them the individual concerned is treated as a leader" (*The Theory of Social and Economic Organization*, 1947, pp. 358–359). The three chief characteristics of a charisma are that it is unusual, spontaneous, and creative.

A second stage is reached when the charisma is "routinized." Pure charisma can only exist in the act of originating. When the leader dies, his or her disciples face a crisis. Are they to disband, or continue? If they decide to continue, then the charismatic element will somehow have to share the stage with the institutional and the structural. Otherwise, there can be no permanence to the charisma. There has to be stability of thought, of practice, and of organization.

Every religious group that hopes to endure, even those groups which describe themselves today as "charismatic," assumes abiding organizational forms. No group is completely charismatic if it agrees to meet at a certain time, in a certain place, to engage in certain activities, however spontaneous those activities turn out to be. The holding of national meetings, of conventions, the publication of magazines, the circulation of newsletters—all of these represent a routinization of the original charismatic impulse.

The routinization process becomes a serious problem only when the organizational interests overtake the charismatic or even replace them. A religious community must constantly reflect on its original purposes, the values of its founder, the convictions about God and human life which originally set the community apart. It must take care that each of its institutional forms and patterns of behavior facilitates rather than impedes those basic purposes. The challenge to a religious community that would remain faithful to its original charisma is not to find ways to *de*institutionalize itself but to *re*institutionalize itself according to its abiding faith. A religious community without any institutional forms at all, on the other hand, is a religious community which no longer exists, or is on the verge of extinction. By their very nature, charisms die out unless they are somehow routinized, i.e., unless they find adequate institutional expression.

Criticisms of Religion

The very notion of religion can be, and has been, criticized from within as well as from without. *From within,* religion has been characterized as the product of human effort to assert itself over against God. But in revelation it is God who approaches us. We do not approach God. We are simply overtaken by the revelation and accept it as God's word. Anything beyond this, any attempt to "deal with" God from our side, places religion above revelation. This is the view of Karl Barth and, to some similar extent, of Emil Brunner (d. 1966), both of whom insisted on the exclusivity of Christian revelation and, therefore, the intrinsic error of every other kind of "religion."

Religion has also been criticized from within, but with much less negative force, by Paul Tillich ("The divine No to religion is only perceptible where religion exists") and by Dietrich Bonhoeffer, who rejected the Christian tendency to make religion a separate compartment of life. Earlier, of course, we have internal criticisms of *religion-in-practice* by the *prophets* of Israel. Indeed, most of the other major religions (e.g., Islam, Hinduism, and Buddhism) have had reform movements designed to purify the structured manner in which their brothers and sisters in faith had responded to the presence and call of God. The history of the Church is also replete with examples of reformist movements: e.g., the reform of spirituality, of monasteries, of clerical life-styles, of ecclesiastical authority, of canon law, of the liturgy, of seminaries. Significantly, Christianity itself suffered its most severe division in an event known as the Reformation.

Religion is also criticized *from without.* It is perceived as a projection of the human spirit. For Ludwig Feuerbach God is the highest projection of our selves in the objective order. A similar position is taken by John Dewey. For Freud religion is an illusion, a regression to the helplessness and insecurity of childhood, the product of wish-fulfillment. For Marx it is the opiate of the people, numbing their capacity for outrage at the gross inequities of the economic order. Others, like Albert Camus, insist that religion is not the *only* response to a limit-situation, one in which all of our most basic values are put to the test. In his novel *The Stranger* Camus writes of a man condemned to die the next day, achieving a sense of serenity in the face of an impersonal and indifferent cosmos. He displays at the limit-situation the same incapacity for relationships that he had in his daily experiences.

In our earlier chapters on belief and unbelief and on revelation we have already addressed ourselves to such challenges as these from without. The criticisms are not without force. It is not impossible that they are correct. But neither is it obvious that they are correct. On the contrary, there are good and solid reasons for affirming the truth of religion (seen as our structured response to God's revelation), even when in practice religion merits the severest of internal, as well as external, criticisms.

There is, finally, a criticism of religion which defies easy categorization. It is not the criticism of a non-believer, but neither is it the criticism of an internal reformer. It is rather the anti-religious critique of those who insist that they believe in God, perhaps also in Jesus Christ and the Holy Spirit, but who reject the necessity of any ordered, structured, and institutionalized expression of their faith and belief.

One might suggest that there is a subtle pride in this point of view. It assumes a kind of angelic self-understanding. We are not angels but "bodies" in the biblical sense (see chapter 5). We cannot shrug off the facticity of human existence. We are in history. We are constituted by relationships, not only with other persons but with institutions, the natural order, and the whole cosmos. Just as revelation must be embodied somehow if it is to be known, just as God must be sacramentalized if God is to be experienced, so our response to God must find some concrete expression consistent with our nature and our human situation. That expression is religion. It is impossible to respond to God in any way whatsoever without that response being religious. It may be a very primitive, superficial, or simple expression, but if it is expressed at all, it is religious.

This does not deny in the least that religion is abidingly open to distortion, that it can obscure rather than illuminate revelation, that it can crush rather than generate the life of faith in God. Religion is subject to such distortions because it is a response to the invisible God. Since no one has ever seen God, and since no one can ever be absolutely certain (in an empirical or scientific sense) that one has truly experienced God in revelation, we can never be sure that our structured response to the God who reveals accurately reflects, or does justice to, the Object of that experience. But the abuse of religion does not destroy its very use.

Types of Religion

Although the question is not directly addressed until the last section of this chapter, it should be clear by now that a *plurality* of religions is being assumed here. Revelation, saving grace, and the capacity to respond to both are not limited to Israel of old or to Christians from New Testament days to our own. There are as many religions as there are theologically and institutionally distinctive and self-contained responses to the presence of God. On the other hand, because there is but one God, each particular religion participates to one degree or another in the single, universal notion of religion as such. "Religion as such," it must be added, does not exist. There are *religions.* For that reason, the adjective *religious* is helpful in expressing a fundamental attitude or characteristic, but it is insufficiently precise to qualify such nouns as *community, education,* and the like.

Taking as our starting-point the principle that God is at once transcendent and immanent, "the beyond in our midst," religions can be differentiated from one another on the basis of the relative stress they place on the transcendent or the immanent nature of God. The division, of course, is based on our Christian perspective. It is in the central Christian doctrine of the incarnation that God is revealed as *both* transcendent and immanent, the Word made flesh.

We can discern, therefore, two basic types of religions: those which stress the transcendence of God, and those which stress immanence. Within each type there are degrees of emphasis.

Thus, a religion in the transcendence series may stress the otherness of God so much that God's relationship with the world of beings is all but lost, as in *Deism*. A religion in the immanence series, on the other hand, may stress the worldliness of God so much that God's relationship with the world of beings becomes one of complete identity, as in *Pantheism*.

Religions in the *transcendence series* are interested in history and eschatology, their worship tends to be objective and highly verbal, they have a sense of ethical demands following from their faith in God, and they have some measure of rational reflection on that faith (theology). Religions in the *immanence series*, on the other hand, tend toward a timeless, ahistorical understanding, their worship is more elaborately ritualistic, their personal goals are not so much obedience to God's will as absorption into God, and they favor mystical experience over rational reflection.

Among religions in the transcendence series are Judaism, Islam, and Confucianism. Among religions in the immanence series are Buddhism and Hinduism. When pushed to their ultimate extremes, religions in the transcendence series lapse into atheism; religions in the immanence series lapse into fetishism, of which "black magic" is a form. In the first extreme God is pushed so far beyond the reality of this world that the divine disappears altogether. In the second extreme God is so identified with the reality of this world that this world's goods take on the character of the divine itself.

THE NON-CHRISTIAN RELIGIONS
Religions of the Past

Egypt, Canaan

Taking as our starting-point that religion has something to do with our experience of, and response to, God (even if and when our perception of God is faulty and thoroughly distorted), we find that religion has always been part of the human landscape. In ancient Egypt (c. 2778–2263 B.C.) the king was worshiped. Later, when divinity was transferred from the royal throne to the Sun (*Re*), the king was regarded as the son of the Sun-God. Later still, during the period of the Middle Kingdom (2052–1786), monotheism came more fully to the front. *Amon* was the supreme God, not only during the Middle Kingdom but during the New Kingdom as well (1580–1085). Perhaps the most distinctive feature of ancient Egyptian religion was its preoccupation with the afterlife, a belief most visibly manifested in the construction of the pyramids and the laying in of ample provisions for the entombed king to use in the next life.

Another important religion of the ancient East (important because it was part of the religious scene at the time when Israel took possession of the land) was that of the Canaanites. Myth and ritual in Ugarit (present-day northern Syria) centered on the effort to secure the *fertility* of nature. The supreme God, *El*, was nonetheless surpassed in power by *Baal*, who displayed his might in the thunderstorm and the bestowal of fertility.

Ancient Greece

Ancient Greece was another major home of religions. For the Greeks there were many gods (polytheism), "higher powers" possessing all of the Greek ideals of beauty, wisdom, and power. The gods alone are immortal. *Zeus* is the father of the gods and, as such, is supreme. He reigns with the other gods on Mount Olympus, from which point he takes in all reality, including the future. Hence he is a great source of oracles. One of Zeus' two brothers is *Hades*, lord of the underworld; the other is *Poseidon*, whose palace is in the depths of the sea (the "inspiration" also of the American film *The Poseidon Adventure*). *Apollo* is the son of Zeus; he always appears in the prime of youth. He has the power of healing and forgiveness. Among his many functions, he is the source of justice, law, and order in the State, and is as well the god of wisdom. *Dionysius*, on the other hand, inspires wild enthusiasm and frenzy in his followers, and he himself celebrates his feasts among satyrs and beasts. Some Christian theologians in the theology of festivity and fantasy school of recent years have used these two gods as a way of contrasting elements even within the Christian religion. Their argument has been that Christians have been too Apollonian (too orderly, sedate, rational) and insufficiently Dionysian in their religious mentality and practice.

Greek sacrificial rites, centered on the sacrificial meal, had one primary purpose, fellowship. The central place of worship was the temple, where the images of the gods were kept, and the temple was served, in turn, by a priesthood.

Ancient Rome

Ancient Rome was similarly religious. Triads of gods headed the Roman pantheon: first *Jupiter, Mars,* and *Quirinus,* and then Jupiter, *Juno,* and *Minerva.* Jupiter dwelt on mountaintops, was the source of storms, and gave warriors strength in battle. He prized loyalty and justice. Mars was the god of war, and Quirinus was very much like him. Juno, Jupiter's wife, was the guardian of marriage, as Zeus' sister *Hera* had been in Greece, and other parallels with the ancient Greek gods were obvious (Minerva = Athena, Neptune = Poseidon, Venus = Aphrodite, Mercury = Hermes, e.g.). Just as in Greece, the most important religious act was the sacrifice. The gifts were animals or corn, and there were set prayers and rituals. The high priest of the Roman State was called the *Pontifex Maximus,* a title assumed eventually by the pope and only recently disavowed by Popes John Paul I (d. 1978) and John Paul II. The Vestal Virgins were women priests. Piety (reverent devotion) was the key to a correct relationship with the gods, and on the human level it required the honoring of obligations between persons and especially the obligation of love for one's parents. Worship of the emperor was a later development.

Mayans, Aztecs, Incas

Other ancient and now-defunct religions were to be found in the Orient and in certain parts of Europe. In what is present-day Latin America there were the Mayans (focused, it seems, on the rain-god *Chac*), the Aztecs (with their human sacrifices), and the Incas (with their sun and moon gods, *Inti* and *Mama Quilla*). As usual, the temple was the place of worship and contained a golden disc representing the sun; it also contained the mummies of dead kings. There was a well-organized priesthood and, as with the other religions of Central and South America, there was a belief in survival after death.

Religions of the Present

Zoroastrianism

Zoroastrianism, the ancient religion of Iran (Persia), has been preserved to the present in the form of the preaching and teaching of its prophet *Zarathustra* (Hellenized as *Zoroaster*), who lived sometime between 1000 and 600 B.C. It is a religion marked by dualism (the struggle between good and evil) and eschatology (the individual is rewarded or punished after death, depending on his or her behavior in this life). Both principles are said to have influenced Judaism, Islam, and Christianity.

Hinduism

Hinduism, one of India's ancient religions, is obscure in its origins—an obscurity linked undoubtedly with a certain sense of timelessness in Indian history itself. What we do know of its earliest period comes from the sacred book of the *Veda* (meaning *"knowledge"*), which tells of magical cults and priestly powers. The priests (Brahmans) gradually became supreme, and their wisdom is reflected in the *Upanishads* (*Upa* = near; *ni-shad* = sitting down). The title of these texts indicates the position of the pupil in receiving the sacred knowledge imparted by the teacher. Unlike the Veda, the Upanishads are pessimistic in outlook. The sadness of life is reflected in the belief in a cycle of rebirths which is the necessary consequence of each person's *karma* or "work" of good or evil deeds in life. Salvation is possible only through mystical absorption in the knowledge of the one true reality, the Absolute, *Brahma*. Although Hinduism has no doctrine of God, it is an intensely ascetical and meditative religion, as in the practice of *Yoga*. As Hinduism developed, other figures joined Brahma, now perceived as the creator: *Vishnu*, the preserver, and *Shiva*, the destroyer. Of the various forms in which Vishnu appears on earth (*avatāra* = "descent"), that of *Krishna* has great importance. It is as Krishna that Vishnu appears in the *Bhagavad-Gita* (*The Song of the Majestic*). Here he proclaims religious and moral truths. Along with the Sermon on the Mount, the *Bhagavad-Gita* was *Gandhi's* (d. 1948) favorite reading. The persistent influence of Krishna in the United States and other Western countries is evident in the *Hare Krishna* movement, which has proved attractive to many college-age men and women.

Buddhism

Buddhism, also Indian in origin, is derived from the title *Buddha,* which means "enlightened one." *Siddharta Gautama* (d. 480 B.C.) was the first Buddha. He was a member of a princely line who encountered human misery during his frequent trips from his father's palace. He eventually chose to live like a beggar-monk, a homeless ascetic. He is said to have received the *bodhi* ("enlightenment") one night while sitting under a fig tree. He proclaimed the revelation in a sermon. The content is called *dharma,* the doctrine of Buddhism. It teaches that we can break out of the grim cycle of rebirths and attain *Nirvana* ("dissolution") by following the "middle way," avoiding both total, hedonistic absorption in the world and excessive self-torment. *Nirvana* implies the overcoming of all desires and gives salvation according to one's deeds. At first the movement was limited to male monks; then nuns were allowed in, and finally lay persons. There were inevitably strict and less strict observances. *Hinayana* Buddhism allowed entry into *Nirvana* through monasticism alone. *Mahayana* Buddhism, in which lay persons were prominent, holds that salvation is open to all who faithfully revere the many earlier Buddhas and the Buddhas yet to come. It is this latter form of Buddhism which is to be found in *Tibet,* where the *lamas,* and especially the *Dalai Lama* and the *Panchen Lama,* are regarded as reincarnations of a Buddha.

Taoism

Taoism, an ancient Chinese religion, is derived from the term tao, which means "the way." The *tao* comprises a male, active principle (*yang*) and a female, passive principle (*yin*), representing heaven and earth. We must all live in harmony with the order of the universe as determined by the *tao*. Wisdom consists in knowing the will of heaven. One of the principal exponents of *Taoism* was Cung-fu-tse (d. 479 B.C.), whose name was Latinized by the Jesuit missionaries of the seventeenth century as *Confucius*. Confucius collected the ancient writings and added his own interpretations, which had an ethical bent to them. His naturalistic ethics centered on *jen* ("humaneness," "benevolence"). The right order of the *tao* is maintained by the rites (*li*) performed by the emperor, who is the Son of Heaven. Rome strictly forbade the Jesuit missionaries, however, from equating "heaven" or the "supreme ruler" with God.

Shintoism

Shintoism, an ancient Japanese religion, also focuses on the way (*to*) of numinous beings (*shin*). It is essentially a polytheistic religion with a simple worship of nature. Eventually it was amalgamated with Buddhism, which was introduced into Japan in the sixth century A.D. Entrance into paradise is insured for those who trust in the grace of Buddha. Buddhist doctrine is assimilated through meditation on the *Lotus of the Good Religion* (*Hokkekyo*). The practice of meditation, of course, remains central in the many schools of *Zen Buddhism* which reached Japan from China.

Islam

Islam, an ancient Arabic religion, means literally "total surrender to the will of Allah." Its origins lie with its Prophet *Mohammed* (d. 632), who experienced a call from Allah to proclaim monotheism. He began to preach in Mecca, laying emphasis on judgment, the resurrection on the last day, and faith in Allah as the one God. Encountering hostility from the Meccan aristocracy, Mohammed moved to Yathrib. The flight was known as his *hegira* ("abandonment of kindred"), and with it the Moslem era begins. Yathrib's name was changed to Medina, and it was here that Mohammed broke with Judaism, orienting his prayers now to Mecca rather than Jerusalem. He saw his task as reviving the monotheism of Abraham. His early disciples recorded or memorized his teachings, and after his death they were collected into the *Koran*, composed of 114 chapters (*sura*) divided into verses (*ayat*). There is no logical or chronological order to them. There *is* a division between the Meccan and the Medinese *suras*: The Meccan convey the traditional emphases on Allah as creator and judge, on the resurrection, and on hell, while the Medinese contain authoritative directives. Successors of Mohammed are known as *caliphs*, who are responsible for the temporal interests of the community.

In Islam Allah is eternal, simple, omnipotent, supreme over all. There is no distinction between the spiritual and the temporal. Whatever Allah does is completely just. Whatever happens, Allah causes. We freely choose between good and evil, and Allah creates the human act which corresponds with the choice. Allah has sent prophets to speak in his name (Abraham, Moses, Jesus, and lastly Mohammed). He is the creator of angels, devils, and even the *jinn* (genies). There is a future life (paradise and hell). Allah will forgive all sins except apostasy. The faithful are urged to care for the needy, orphans, pilgrims, prisoners, and the like. They are to pray, be loyal to contractual obligations, and be resigned to misfortunes. The "pillars of Islam" are prayer (recited five times each day), profession of faith, alms, fasting, and pilgrimage to Mecca at least once in one's lifetime. *Sari*, the religious law of Islam, is derived from the Koran, the *sunna* (Mohammed's own example), analogy (*qiyas*) and prudent judgments (*ra'y*), and the common opinion of the learned or the customary practice of the people (Islam's principle of flexibility).

In the eighth century Islam suffered a division between the *Ṣufī* and the more orthodox *Sunnites*. The word *ṣūf* means "wool" and refers to the coarse wool garments which the ascetics wore in imitation of the Christian monks. For the Sunnites, to love God is simply to worship and obey him according to established rules. For the Ṣufi, *union* with Allah is possible—a teaching that was detestable to the Sunnites, who insisted there can be no equality and therefore no reciprocity between Allah and ourselves. By the ninth century Ṣufism was flourishing, and it remains at the base of Moslem ethics today.

Christians at first regarded Islam as a heretical movement within Judaism (the view of St. John Damascene, for example). Later, after the Moslem penetration of the West and the West's penetration of the East in the Crusades, extensive dialogue followed contact. Evidence of the dialogue can be found in various writings, especially Thomas Aquinas' *Summa Contra Gentiles*. The dialogue, however, was to cease (and not to reopen until the post-Vatican II period) with the wars against the Turks and the downfall of the Ottoman Empire.

Judaism

Judaism has its origins in the formation of the Twelve Tribes of Israel, which some (especially Martin Noth) identify with the covenant of Shechem described in Joshua 24. Other Old Testament scholars insist that the Israel which worshiped Yahweh existed before Shechem, and that the Shechem covenant enlarged but did not create Israel. More immediately, Judaism emerges from the period when the exiles returned from Babylon in the sixth century B.C. Most of these exiles were recruited from the tribe of Judah (see Ezra 1-2). They saw themselves as the purified "remnant of Israel," i.e., as that portion of the Twelve Tribes which had survived the catastrophe of captivity and submitted to it as the judgment of God upon their guilt (see especially Ezra 6:13-18).

Among the *principal characteristics* of Judaism are its sense of the Covenant, the land, the past, and the Kingdom of God.

The most fundamental conviction of the Jewish people has always been that they are a people of the *Covenant*: Yahweh is the God of Israel, and Israel the people of Yahweh (Exodus 19:4-6; Joshua 24). God is present among the people of Israel as a powerful God (Isaiah 45:14). The promises of descendants to the patriarchs are to be understood in the light of this Covenant (Genesis 13:16; 15:5; 26:4,24; 28:14; 32:13, e.g.). The God of the Covenant, however, is not the object of systematic theological reflection, as in Christianity. The God of Israel is a holy God who calls the people of Israel to be a holy people, faithful to the divine commands linked with the Covenant: the observance of the Sabbath and feast days, the recital of prayers, the keeping of purity laws, circumcision, the maintenance of ancient Jewish tradition, the hope of salvation. The holy God of Israel is ever a God of mercy and justice, concerned with the people, giving them instruction and reproof, inspiring them to right conduct, and inhibiting their impulses to infidelity. As in Islam, even the most ordinary and profane activities of everyday life are to be penetrated by the kingship of God, who is always present and whose presence becomes increasingly effective in its power.

A second major characteristic of Judaism is its *respect and reverence for the past*. Judaism finds courage to live through the hardships of the present by recalling and reflecting upon the glories of the past and God's promises to the patriarchs (Genesis 24:7; 50:24; Exodus 13:5,11; Numbers 14:16; Deuteronomy 4:31; 6:23, e.g.).

There is also Judaism's close relationship to *the land* of Israel as promised by the God of the Covenant. The claim to the promised land has never been abandoned by Israel even to the present day: "Keep all the commandments, then, which I enjoin on you today, that you may be strong enough to enter in and take possession of the land into which you are crossing, and that you may have long life on the land which the Lord swore to your fathers he would give to them and their descendants, a land flowing with milk and honey" (Deuteronomy 11:8-9).

Finally, there is the conviction of faith which sums up and incorporates all of the others, namely, belief in the coming of the *Kingdom of God*. Sometimes, the notion of God's kingship is exceedingly nationalistic, as in the time of the Maccabees (170 B.C.- 70 A.D.) or in the rebellion of Bar Kochba (132-135 A.D.). At other times, the hope of a Messiah to deliver them from captivity into salvation is more universal in outlook. The Book of Ruth, for example, was written to praise a foreign Moabite woman as the ancestress of King David. The Book of Jonah was similarly inspired by universalistic motives. And the Old Testament generally makes clear that Israel was not chosen by God because of its holiness but in spite of its obstinacy and rebelliousness (Deuteronomy 7:6-9; 9:4-9). One should not confuse Judaism's hope in salvation, however, with the traditional Christian hope in eternal life for each person. Judaism's generally optimistic sense of what we can accomplish in this life with God's help (Psalm 8; Zechariah 1:3; Malachi 3:7) has no corresponding sense of any individual call to happiness in some life beyond. It is the people of Israel that will survive and prosper, and not any particular person within it.

The *sources* of Judaism are the *Torah* (literally, divine oracle revealed "by the lot"), which is the most general word for law in Judaism. The Torah has both a written and an oral form. The written Torah is the *Tanak* (Old Testament), consisting of twenty-four books. The oral Torah is to be found above all in rabbinical literature, especially the *Mishnah* (literally, "tradition," "repetition"), which is the official commentary on the Old Testament law and the traditions. The Mishnah is the core of a larger collection of rabbinical opinions known as the *Talmud* ("teaching"). Talmudic interpretation may be literal or practical. The practical interpretations are known as *Midrash* ("searching"), and this, in turn, can be ethical (*halakhah*) or narrative and homiletical (*haggadah*). The former is more important in the religious life of Jews than the latter, which is mostly legend.

Judaism, like all of the great religions of the world, has endured change throughout history. The Old Testament provides a full and rich account of Israel's and of Judaism's historical experiences before the coming of Christ. After the destruction of the Temple at Jerusalem in 70 A.D. Judaism entered a new period of religious life. The *synod of Jamnia* (c. 90) provided a new basis for a religion which now sought to maintain itself without a temple, without political independence, and in a newly pluralistic situation, surrounded by other peoples and other religions, especially Christianity and Gnosticism. It was in the exchange between Judaism and Greek philosophy that the first stirrings of Jewish "systematic theology" occurred, and in the medieval period Jewish thought assumed an Islamic cast, when Jewish Neo-platonism and Aristotelianism appeared on the scene. Among the great philosopher-theologians of the period are Jehudah Halevi (d. 1140), who insisted on the superiority of revelation over reason, and Moses Maimonides (d. 1204), who insisted on the essential conformity between revelation and reason (philosophy) and on the necessity of the latter to apprehend the former. Just as there had been a strong Catholic reaction against Thomas Aquinas for his vigorous use of reason in the understanding of faith, so was there a vehement protest against Maimonides from within contemporary Judaism. It was the Halevian attitude of reserve toward the pretensions of reason that was to dominate until the middle of the eighteenth century, when a sharply rationalistic orientation reasserted itself in the writings of Moses Mendelssohn (d. 1786). Judaism was not to recover its intellectual bearings until the latter part of the nineteenth and the early twentieth centuries with the work of Franz Rosenzweig (d. 1929) and Martin Buber (d. 1965).

CHRISTIANITY AND THE OTHER RELIGIONS

For reasons already summarized in chapter 3 (mobility, communications, e.g.), the modern world is marked in an unprecedented way by the experience of *pluralism*. We are more aware than ever before of the diversity which characterizes the human community. Just as Copernicus helped us see that our earth is not at the center of the universe, and Darwin helped us see that our species did not spring up independently of other life-forms, so our belated recognition of pluralism is helping us see that the world is filled with "heresies", i.e., selective perceptions of reality and selective apprehensions of truth. In such a world, even the Christian faith appears "heretical."

Why, then, are there many religions rather than one? Just as God is in principle available to every person (Rahner's "supernatural existential") and to every people (since we are essentially social), so also religion, as the structured response to the experience of God, is available in principle to every person and people. But since "no one has ever seen God" (John 1:18), we can never be absolutely certain that we have had an actual experience of God or that we have correctly perceived, interpreted, and expressed that experience. Furthermore, God can become available to us only on terms consistent with our bodily existence, i.e., sacramentally. Every experience of God or, from the other side, every self-disclosure of God, is inevitably conditioned by the situation of the person or community to which God has become available in a special way. Those communities are differentiated by time, place, culture, language, temperament, social and economic conditions, etc. Revelation, therefore, is always received according to the mode of the receiver, to cite a central Thomistic principle (*"Quod enim recipitur in aliquo recipitur in eo secundum modum recipientis," Summa Theologica,* I, q. 79, a. 6). Since religion is our structured response to the reception of God in revelation, our response will be shaped by that mode of reception. Indeed, the Son of God became incarnate in a particular time and place, in a particular cultural and religious situation, in a particular man of a particular family, nation, and race.

When one scans the spectrum of religions, past and present, as we have done in outline-form earlier in this chapter, one begins to appreciate the striking similarities between Christianity and the other great religions of the world: their common sense of the supreme majesty of God, their ethical codes, their rites of worship, their priesthoods, their call to judgment, conversion, and reform. Suddenly for many Christians the old skepticism toward the non-Christian religions ("How can anyone seriously believe in them?") is redirected toward Christianity itself ("Why should we think that we're any better than any other religion?"). On the opposite side, some Christians assume a militant posture. They call for renewed efforts at "evangelization" understood not in the broad and comprehensive manner of Pope Paul VI's 1975 Apostolic Exhortation *Evangelii Nuntiandi* ("On the Evangelization of the Modern World")—the proclamation of the word, the celebration of the sacraments, the offering of corporate witness to Christ, and participation in the struggle for justice and peace—but in the narrow sense of "making converts" or of bringing "fallen-away" Catholics back to church.

The first group is victimized by a loss of nerve and/or a lapse of theological balance. It feels that Christianity has lost its intrinsic power to persuade and to convince the non-believer, and so it is better to lift the oars out of the water and let the currents take us where they will. Or this group forgets that the questions of exclusiveness and uniqueness are separate questions. The Christian faith can still be a compellingly *unique* expression of divine revelation in Jesus Christ without at the same time being the *exclusive* sign and instrument of revelation.

The second group seems to be afflicted with historical and sociological naivete. The present state of Christian missions cannot be changed simply through the application of more aggressive techniques or through the commissioning of more dedicated Christian preachers. Decisions were rendered by the Catholic Church some centuries ago which have had the effect of closing off whole countries, indeed whole continents, to the effective presence of Christianity. (For example, the initially successful sixteenth-century mission to China under the leadership of Jesuit Father Matteo Ricci (d. 1610) was aborted when Rome rejected the development of native rites and opposed other cultural adaptations.)

Beyond that, the other great world religions are too intricately enmeshed in the social, political, ethnic, and cultural elements of their geographical settings: Islam with the Arab world, Judaism with a specific people, Hinduism and Buddhism with Asian culture, Taoism and Shintoism with the Oriental experience. There is a relative permanency to the present condition of religious pluralism, it would seem. Less than one percent of the people of China and Japan are Christian, and only two percent of the people of India. We are, in the words of Catholic theologian Yves Congar, "a small church in a large world." This is a fact that we can either wring our hands over or respond to thoughtfully and constructively.

There are at least three thoughtful and constructive responses being fashioned today within the Church. *First,* there is the view that there is still but one true religion and that insofar as other "religions" embody authentic values and even saving grace, they do so as "anonymously Christian" communities. All grace is grace in Christ, who is the one Mediator (1 Timothy 2:5). Therefore, all recipients of grace are at least in principle new creatures in Christ, people whose lives are governed implicitly by the new life in Christ that is at work within them. This is a position which has been identified with Karl Rahner and others.

A *second* position acknowledges the salvific value in each of the non-Christian religions and underscores, as the preceding view does, the universality of revelation and of grace. It does not speak of the other religions as "anonymously Christian," but instead accepts them for what they are: lesser, relative, and extraordinary means of salvation. This is the teaching, for the most part, of the

Second Vatican Council and perhaps of the majority of Catholic theologians today.

Without prejudice to the uniqueness and truth of Christian faith, a *third* view affirms the intrinsic religious value of the other great religions of the world and insists, beyond the preceding position, on the necessity and worthwhileness of dialogue with them. These other religions are not only to be tolerated or even respected; they are to be perceived as having something to teach us, not only about themselves but about God, about life, even about Christ. They are not simply deficient expressions of Christianity. This is the approach of Hans Küng, Heinz Robert Schlette, and others.

It should be evident that these three positions are not mutually exclusive, although the second and the third are closer together than either is to the first. Each respects the uniqueness of Christianity and the salvific value of the other religions. However, each assesses the uniqueness of Christianity and the salvific value of the other religions differently. But the differences are matters more of degree than of kind.

Insistence on the uniqueness of Christianity is not an unimportant matter. There are, after all, significant differences between Christianity and the other religions. Islam is clearly a book religion. Christians, for example, do not have to wash their hands before reading the Bible as Moslems do before reading the Koran. Love of neighbor does not mean the same thing in the teaching of Confucius as it does in the teaching of Jesus. Christianity, far from validating holy wars against its enemies, preaches love of one's enemies. Christianity does not worship sacred cows nor countenance a caste system.

To say, therefore, that other religions are also instruments of salvation is not to say that they are all equally good. On the contrary, there are serious deficiencies in some of them. No religion has as fully developed a theology as Christianity, and some have practically no theology at all. Dialogue, therefore, is exceedingly difficult, if not impossible, in some cases. Because of their lack of any critical component, the other religions are often impotent in the face of modernity. They have no rational weapons against the enemies of the human spirit in our time, and their own world view is frequently naive and unhistorical.

Islam, for example, believes the Koran to have been dictated word for word to Mohammed by an angel. It allows no room at all for an historical understanding of its evolution and composition. Hinduism and Buddhism share a generally cyclical view of reality. Everything is predetermined. Passivity is the favored posture. In Hinduism, a rigid caste system is assumed to be part of the necessary order of things. Confucianism and Taoism are steeped in traditionalism, with ancestor worship and an exceedingly patriarchal notion of society and of the family. Such basic liabilities hamper these religions in their effort to bring meaning into the lives of people and to change the world in accordance with the will of God.

Judaism, of course, poses a special challenge to Christianity. Jesus was himself a Jew, of a Jewish family. His preaching was directed first of all to the Jewish people. The Old Testament was the Bible of the early Christian community. The Gospel presupposed the Law and the prophets: There were common values and common structures in the two religions. And yet from the beginning they were at odds with each other. The anti-Jewish polemic in John's Gospel has been noted by New Testament scholars, and the second-century rabbinical prayer (*Shemoneh 'Esreh*), recited daily, including a curse against "heretics and Nazarenes."

The post-biblical history of Christian-Jewish relations has been, until very recently indeed, a record of hostility, alienation, and atrocities. Jews were slaughtered during the Crusades and exiled from their homes in England, France, Spain, and Portugal in the fourteenth and fifteenth centuries. But, of course, no episode affecting the Jews has had a more profound effect on the Christian conscience than the Nazi extermination of six million Jews at the time of the Second World War. "After Auschwitz there can be no more excuses," Hans Küng has written. "Christendom cannot avoid a clear admission of its guilt" (*On Being A Christian*, p. 169).

Because the persecution of Jews has too often been explained, even defended, on the basis of Jewish involvement in the crucifixion of Jesus, the Second Vatican Council clearly and unequivocally condemned such thinking: " . . . what happened in His passion cannot be blamed upon all the Jews then living, without distinction, nor upon the Jews of today. Although the Church is the new people of God, the Jews should not be presented as repudiated or cursed by God, as if such views followed from the holy Scriptures. ... Moreover, mindful of her common patrimony with the Jews, and motivated by the gospel's spiritual love and by no political considerations, (the Church) deplores the hatred, persecutions, and displays of anti-Semitism directed against the Jews at any time and from any source" (*Declaration on the Relationship of the Church to Non-Christian Religions*, n. 4).

Is there any sense, furthermore, in which the Jews can still be regarded, from the Christian perspective, as part of the People of God? Yes, insofar as they are "the people to whom the covenants and the promises were given and from whom Christ was born according to the flesh (cf. Romans 9:4-5). On account of their fathers, this people remains most dear to God, for God does not repent of the gifts He makes nor of the calls He issues (cf. Romans 11:28-29)" (*Dogmatic Constitution on the Church*, n. 16). And at the end of history the Jewish people will join with us and all others to address the Lord "in a single voice and 'serve him with one accord' (Zephaniah 3:9; cf. Isaiah 66:23; Psalm 65:3; Romans 11:11-32)" (*Declaration on the Relationship of the Church to Non-Christian Religions,* n. 4).

We are left, then, with an agenda for dialogue: to encourage other religions, including Judaism, to bring out what is best and deepest in their own traditions and to encourage them in self-criticism and purification. And since dialogue is by definition a two-way process, it means also that the Church is to be stimulated into appreciating anew its own traditions and into seeing them in a fresher, more critical light. We can learn from the strict simplicity of Islam, the breadth of understanding of the Asian religions, the this-worldliness of Confucianism, the mysticism and commitment to peace of the Oriental religions. We can attempt a Christian theology of Judaism and learn from a Jewish theology of Christianity. Christianity in dialogue will not shrink from emphasizing its own uniqueness, but dialogue will make it increasingly difficult, if not impossible, to claim exclusiveness or unqualified supremacy.

OFFICIAL CATHOLIC TEACHING ON RELIGIOUS PLURALISM

Since the fact of pluralism has struck the consciousness of the Church only recently, especially since the Second World War, the official teachings of the Catholic Church before Vatican II are of a considerably different orientation from those of the council itself and thereafter. There are four historical stages in the development of this teaching. In the first stage the Church's attitude toward other religions was simply negative. It was taken for granted that they cannot lead to salvation. Positively, the Church was teaching that Jesus Christ is the only Mediator between God and humankind, in keeping with 1 Timothy 2:5: "And the truth is this: God is one. One also is the mediator between God and men, the man Christ Jesus, who gave himself as a ransom for all."

The second stage occurred in the medieval period when the Church felt threatened by the continued presence of distinct Jewish communities in the West and by Moslem military aggressiveness. For the first time, the official Church issued pronouncements on the subject, and these were generally negative.

A third stage developed in the nineteenth century when the enemy was no religion in particular but Liberalism and its egalitarian philosophy that one religion is as good (or as bad) as another. Indifferentism is condemned.

A fourth stage has only recently emerged under the impact of the recognition of pluralism. The centerpiece of this stage is the Second Vatican Council's 1965 *Declaration on the Relationship of the Church to Non-Christian Religions (Nostra Aetate)*.

The official doctrine of the Church may be summarized as follows: All religions are related somehow to the Christian economy of salvation; apart from this relationship they have no salvific power; yet their adherents can find salvation, even though their religions are not on an equal footing with Christianity. These other religions contain many authentic values, although they also are mixed with error, and hence need to be purified. But they do contain elements of the supreme truth and seeds of God's word, and divine grace works in them. They deal, therefore, with the one God and with ultimate questions about human existence.

Accordingly, we must support true religious freedom, tolerance, and respect. Our relations with other religious bodies should be characterized by acceptance, collaboration, and dialogue. Christians can learn from the values of other religious traditions. And there should be charity in any case.

Examples of these teachings follow:

The Second General Council of Nicea (787) insists that only those Jews who sincerely wish to convert to Christianity should be received into the Church. Otherwise, they should be allowed to "be Hebrews openly, according to their own religion" (canon 8).

Pope Gregory VII's letter to Anzir, Moslem King of Mauritania (1076), acknowledges that Christians and Moslems worship the same God: " . . . for we believe and confess one God, although in different ways, and praise and worship Him daily as the creator of all ages and the ruler of this world."

The General Council of Florence, *Decree for the Jacobites* (1442), refers for the first time in an official document to non-Christians as "pagans." Earlier that designation had been reserved to schismatics and heretics. On the other hand, the document does not deny the presence of grace beyond the borders of the Church. It also affirms that Christian freedom makes all human customs lawful if the faith is intact and edification attended to. The key negative teaching, however, is contained in this declaration: "(The Holy Roman Church) . . . firmly believes, professes and preaches that 'no one remaining outside the Catholic Church, not only pagans', but Jews, heretics or schismatics, can become partakers of eternal life; but they will go to the 'eternal fire prepared for the devil and his angels' (Matthew 25:41), unless before the end of their life they are received into it."

Religious indifferentism was explicitly condemned in the following: Leo XII's encyclical letter *Ubi Primum* (1824), Gregory XVI's encyclical letter *Mirari Vos Arbitramur* (1832), Pius IX's encyclical letter *Qui Pluribus* (1846), his allocution *Singulari Quadam* (1854), his encyclical letter *Quanto Conficiamur Moerore* (1863), and his *Syllabus of Errors* (1864). On the other hand, *Singulari Quadam* acknowledges that individuals outside the Church may simply be in ignorance of the truth through no fault of their own and so "are not subject to any guilt in this matter before the eyes of the Lord." Furthermore, his *Quanto Conficiamur* reminds us that we should bear no enmity against those outside the Church. "On the contrary, if they are poor or sick or afflicted by any other evils, let the children of the Church endeavor to succour and help them with all the services of Christian love."

Pope Leo XIII marks another shift in the Church's official teaching, a shift which anticipates the later doctrine of Vatican II on religious freedom. In his encyclical letter *Immortale Dei* (1885) he recognizes that a government may, for the sake of a greater good or of avoiding some evil, "tolerate in practice and by custom" various other forms of worship. Furthermore, ". . . nobody (is to) be forced to join the Catholic faith against his will. . . ."

In the First Plenary Council of India (1950), held in Bangalore, convoked by a papal legate, Cardinal Gilroy, and approved by Pope Pius XII in 1951, indifferentism is once again rejected, but for the first time in an official document of the Catholic Church a clearly positive statement is made regarding the spiritual values of the world religions. "We acknowledge indeed that there is truth and goodness outside the Christian religion, for God has not left the nations without a witness to Himself, and the human soul is naturally drawn toward the one true God. . . . But the inadequacy of all non-Christian religions is principally derived from this, that, Christ being constituted the one Mediator between God and men, there is no salvation by any other name."

The teaching of the Second Vatican Council on the subject is contained in the *Dogmatic Constitution on the Church* (1964), the *Declaration on the Relationship of the Church to Non-Christian Religions* (1965), the *Decree on the Church's Missionary Activity* (1965), and the *Pastoral Constitution on the Church in the Modern World* (1965). The council's teaching can be summarized as follows: The council stresses what unites us with other people rather than what divides us (*Declaration*, n. 1). It mentions other religions with respect: Hinduism, Buddhism, Islam, Judaism, and the primitive religions (*Decree*, n. 10; *Declaration*, nn. 2-4; *Dogmatic Constitution*, n. 16). They provide not only human answers to life's problems but also precious religious values (*Pastoral Constitution*, n. 12). They represent goodness intrinsic to the human heart which finds expression in rites and symbols, and are a true preparation for the Gospel (*Dogmatic Constitution*, n. 16; *Decree*, n. 9). They also contain treasures of ascetical and contemplative life (*Decree*, nn. 15,18). Thus, their faith is a response to the voice and self-communication of God (*Pastoral Constitution*, nn. 36, 22).

Indeed, the Holy Spirit was at work in the world even before Christ (*Decree*, n. 4). Religious traditions outside the Church have their place in God's saving design (*Decree*, n. 3), with values that are intimately related to the divine mystery (*Dogmatic Constitution*, n. 16; *Declaration*, n. 2). The Church, therefore, must adopt a wholly new attitude toward non-Christian religions (*Declaration*, nn. 1-5). We are to reject nothing of the truth and holiness we find in them (*Declaration*, n. 2) and should respect even those doctrinal elements which differ from our own because they may also contain a ray of truth (*Declaration*, n. 2; *Pastoral Constitution*, n. 57). We must learn to appreciate the riches of the gifts of God to all the peoples of the world (*Decree*, nn. 11,18).

The right to religious freedom is inviolable (*Declaration on Religious Freedom*, nn. 2-4). We must oppose every form of discrimination based on creed as well as on sex and race (*Declaration on the Relationship of the Church to Non-Christian Religions*, n. 5, hereafter again referred to simply as *Declaration*). We must be open to all forms of dialogue, imbued with the spirit of justice and love, and must engage in a common search for moral and spiritual enrichment (*Pastoral Constitution*, n. 92; *Decree*, nn. 11, 12,16,18,34; *Declaration*, nn. 2,3,5). This will require discernment, but it is part of the Church's task and can be done without compromise of its faith in Christ (*Dogmatic Constitution*, nn. 16,17; *Decree*, n. 9; *Declaration*, nn. 2,5; *Pastoral Constitution*, n. 28).

Pope Paul VI's encyclical letter *Ecclesiam Suam* (1964) insists, on the one hand, that "there is one true religion, the Christian religion, and that we hope that all who seek God and adore Him, will come to acknowledge this. ... Yet we do, nevertheless, acknowledge with respect the spiritual and moral values of various non-Christian religions, for we desire to join with them in promoting and defending common ideals in the spheres of religious liberty, human brotherhood, teaching and education, social welfare and civil order. On these great ideals that we share with them, we can have dialogue, and we shall not fail to offer opportunities for it whenever, in genuine mutual respect, our offer would be received with good will." The same spirit permeates Pope Paul's letter *Africarum Terrarum* (1967) to the hierarchy and the peoples of Africa.

SUMMARY

1. *Religion* is not easy to define. In fact, there is no single definition agreed upon by all, even within the religious sciences themselves. It is not even clear from which word or words the term *religion* is derived.

2. We have *defined religion* here as the whole complexus of attitudes, convictions, emotions, gestures, rituals, beliefs, and institutions by which we come to terms with, and express, our most fundamental relationship with Reality (God and the created order, perceived as coming forth from God's creative hand).

3. That relationship is disclosed by a process we have called *revelation*. Religion, therefore, is our (more or less) structured response to revelation.

4. Other definitions will differ from ours to the extent that they focus more sharply on one or another aspect of religion: the philosophical, the phenomenological, the psychological, the sociological, the anthropological, or finally its peculiarly Christian form.

5. Although the early Christian writers stressed the truth of the Christian religion, they also acknowledged that the saving grace of the Christian faith has never been refused to anyone who was worthy of it (Augustine). It is possible for every person to know God by seeing evidences of God in the created world (Aquinas). Insofar as religion is our response to God's presence, religion is in principle available to every person. And insofar as God *is* present to every person, we are not only capable of reaching beyond ourselves to God; we are actually summoned to do so (Transcendental Thomism, Rahner, Vatican II).

6. But not every person of faith is religious. There is such a thing as *implicit faith*. Implicit faith is sufficient for salvation but insufficient for religion. Religion is an individual, social, and institutional manifestation of some *explicit* faith in God.

7. Every authentic religion has, to some degree, the following *characteristics*: (1) a sense of the *holy* or the sacred (a totally other power or force which at once overwhelms and fascinates us); (2) some self-conscious response to the experience of the holy, i.e., *faith*; (3) the articulation of that response in the form of *beliefs*; (4) *moral behavior* and *ritual* consistent with the perception of the holy; and (5) the emergence of a *community* of shared perceptions, meanings, and values, with at least some rudimentary *structure*.

8. In every religion there is an intrinsic tension between *charism* and *institution*. Charisms are unusual, spontaneous, and creative. But unless they are "routinized," they will have no effect beyond the life and/or presence of the charismatic leader or founder. Routinization is institutionalization. Institutions, however, must also serve the original purposes of the community and reflect the original spirit of the founder's charism.

9. Religion's *critics* are both inside and outside organized religion. *From within*, religion is perceived as the enemy of faith (Barth) or as its false substitute (Bonhoeffer). Religion is also criticized from within by its prophets and reformers who challenge not the very concept of religion but its performance record. *From without,* religion is perceived as a projection of the human spirit, an expression of wish-fulfillment, an illusion, an opiate numbing our capacity for outrage against social injustice (Freud, Marx, and others). Still others criticize religion not because they reject faith but because they reject institutionalization of any kind ("I don't have to go to church; I have a personal relationship with God").

10. The prophetic and reformist criticism is alone acceptable to our understanding of religion. The Barthian critique assumes that Christianity is the exclusive recipient of revelation. The humanistic critique assesses the signals of transcendence differently from people of faith, or ignores those signals entirely. The anti-institutionalists are sociologically naive.

11. For Christianity God is at once transcendent (beyond the world of created reality) and immanent (within the world). Other religions seem to differ from Christianity to the extent that they stress transcendence more than immanence, or vice versa. Religions in the *transcendence series* (emphasizing history, eschatology, objective, verbal worship, ethics, and some measure of rational reflection) include Judaism, Islam, and Confucianism. Religions in the *immanence series* (emphasizing the timeless, the ritualistic, the mystical) include Buddhism and Hinduism. Pushed beyond its outer limits, transcendentalism issues forth in atheism, and immanentism in fetishism.

12. Among the non-Christian religions, there are religions which no longer exist (in ancient Egypt, the ancient East, ancient Greece, ancient Rome, e.g.) and religions which continue to exist. The *ancient religions* have run the gamut from polytheism to monotheism. All have some sense of divinity, some practice of worship, some form of priesthood, and some sense of moral obligation flowing from their relationship to the divinity or divinities. Several believed in life after death.

13. *Religions of the present* include: (1) *Zoroastrianism*, with its emphasis on the struggle between good and evil (dualism); (2) *Hinduism*, which teaches that salvation is possible only through absorption in the knowledge of the one true reality, the Absolute, *Brahma*; (3) *Buddhism*, which teaches that we can break out of the grim cycle of rebirths and attain *Nirvana* (dissolution) by overcoming all desires; (4) *Taoism*, which calls us to live in harmony with the universe as determined by *tao* (the way); (5) *Shintoism*, which is essentially a polytheistic religion with a simple worship of nature; (6) *Islam*, which emphasizes the oneness of God (Allah) and his supremacy over every detail of human existence, and also emphasizes judgment, resurrection, prayer, fasting, and almsgiving; and (7) *Judaism*, which stresses the Covenant, the land, the past, and the coming Kingdom of God.

14. There has always been a plurality of religions in the world, but the recognition of *pluralism* is a peculiar phenomenon of modern times. Why are there many religions rather than one alone? Because God is available to all peoples, widely *differentiated* as they are by time, by geography, by culture, by language, by temperament, by social and economic conditions, etc. Revelation is received according to the mode of the receiver, and the response to revelation (religion) is necessarily shaped by that mode of reception.

15. The *similarities* of religions among themselves pose an opposite question: If religions all have the same source, why are they not all equally valid? Because perceptions of revelation are subject to distortion, and so, too, are the modes of response. Common sense, though not a highly refined philosophy of human values, would tell us that a religion which worships through a communal meal is superior to one which practices human sacrifice.

16. What is to be said, finally, of the "*validity*" of the non-Christian religions? (1) They are "valid" religions insofar as they implicitly share and practice the values inherent in the one true religion of Christianity (the theory of "anonymous Christianity"); (2) they are "valid" religions but are also lesser, relative, and extraordinary means of salvation; (3) they are "valid" in varying degrees, to be sure, but Christianity

has much to learn from them and they from Christianity. Dialogue, therefore, must characterize our relationships with each other. The call to dialogue, however, does not require us to withhold criticism of other religions. The question of truth is always pertinent.

17. *Judaism* always has a special relationship with Christianity for obvious historical and theological reasons. The Jews can still be regarded as part of the People of God insofar as the Covenant and the promises were given them, Christ was born of them, God has not withdrawn his gifts from them, and they, like all of us, are called to the final Kingdom.

18. The *official teaching* of the Catholic Church on the question of non-Christian religions has passed through various stages. In the beginning the attitude was basically negative, since Christ was perceived as the one Mediator between God and us; in the medieval period negative teachings were formulated under the impact of the threat of continued Jewish presence in the West and of Moslem military aggressiveness; in the nineteenth century the enemy was religious indifferentism, and so emphasis had to be placed on the uniqueness and even superiority of Christianity; but with the recognition of pluralism and the changing consciousness of the Church represented by Pope John XXIII and Vatican II, the official teachings moved in a more positive direction.

19. Present official teaching acknowledges the salvific value of non-Christian religions (without prejudice to the unique and central place of Christianity in the economy of salvation) and calls for religious liberty for all and dialogue among all.

SUGGESTED READINGS

James, William. *The Varieties of Religious Experience.* New York: New American Library, Mentor, 1958.

Macquarrie, John. "Religion and Religions." *Principles of Christian Theology.* 2d ed. New York: Scribner, 1977, pp. 149-173.

O'Dea, Thomas F. *The Sociology of Religion.* Englewood Cliffs, N.J.: Prentice-Hall, 1966.

Otto, Rudolf. *The Idea of the Holy.* Baltimore: Penguin Books, 1959.

Rahner, Karl. "History of the World and Salvation-History" and "Christianity and the Non-Christian Religions." *Theological Investigations.* Baltimore: Helicon, 1966, vol. 5, pp. 97-134.

Robertson, Roland, ed. *Sociology of Religion: Selected Readings.* Baltimore: Penguin Books, 1969.

Schlette, Heinz. *Towards a Theology of Religions.* New York: Herder & Herder, 1966.
Smith, Huston. *The Religions of Man.* New York: Harper & Row, 1965.
Smith, William C. *The Meaning and End of Religion.* New York: Harper & Row, 1978.

·IX·

THE CHRISTIAN UNDERSTANDING OF GOD

THE PROBLEM

Nothing in this chapter retracts what has already been noted, namely, that the reality of God can neither be proved nor disproved by rational arguments. The judgment that God has been revealed in a particular person, event, or mystical experience is always precisely that, a judgment, however reasonable and informed it might be. Indeed, as we suggested in the previous chapter, there are many religions rather than one because, among other things, "no human being has ever seen or can see" God (1 Timothy 6:16). We can never be absolutely certain that we have had an experience of God or whether we have correctly perceived, interpreted, and expressed that experience. Since God can become available to us only in some bodily or sacramental way, the self-communication of God will always be conditioned by the historical situation of the person or community to which God is disclosed. Revelation is received, in other words, according to the mode of the receiver. And that is why we must also carry forward here what has already been proposed in the section on human existence, for the God-question is to a very great extent the reverse side of the question of human existence.

What follows in this chapter is a statement and description of the uniquely Christian experience of God. Because Christians are no less human, no less historically situated than others, the Christian perception, interpretation, and expression of God is also, in principle, subject to ambiguity, error, and distortion. On the other hand, it is the *distinctively Christian conviction* that God has been disclosed so clearly and so definitively in Jesus of Nazareth that there is no possibility of *fundamental* error in the perception, interpretation, or formal doctrinal expression of the reality of God. Fundamental distortion is possible only in *secondary* matters of belief. *Ambiguity*, however, is always possible because of the ineffable character of God and the inherent limitations of language.

But this distinctively Christian conviction raises a major problem for theology: If God is one, how is it that Sacred Scripture and the Church's creeds affirm a pluralism within God, that in God there is Father, Son, and Holy Spirit? *The Christian confession of the Lordship of Jesus is inextricably linked with the Christian belief in the Trinity*, for Jesus' place in saving history makes sense only insofar as he has been sent by the Father and, together with the Father, sends the Holy Spirit to heal, to renew, and to reconcile all that has been wounded by sin. The Christian understanding of God, in other words, cannot be expressed fully, let alone explained, apart from the doctrine of the Trinity and the person and work of Jesus Christ.

We shall focus even more sharply on the doctrine of the Trinity in the next chapter (although it is fully integrated into the discussion of God in this chapter), and Part III of the book will be devoted exclusively to Christology.

THE GOD OF THE BIBLE
Old Testament

Given the undeniably intimate relationship between Judaism and Christianity, represented by the unity of the two biblical Testaments, an historical unfolding of the Christian understanding of God must begin with the Old Testament.

It is by now almost an axiom of theology that the People of God in the Old Testament were not interested in philosophical speculation. Their view and grasp of reality tended to be earthy and concrete. This principle applies to their understanding of God. The medieval distinction between essence and existence, for example, was totally foreign to the Hebrew mind. Their God was a living God, known to them through the name *Yahweh* given to Moses and his descendants (Exodus 3:13-15). For the Israelites Yahweh is present and active wherever the name of Yahweh is known, recognized, and invoked. To call upon Yahweh is to summon Yahweh. Yahweh's name is glorious (Psalm 72:19), great (1 Kings 8:42), awful (Deuteronomy 28:58), exalted (Psalm 148:13). The name is also the source of deliverance (Psalm 54:3) and exaltation (Psalms 33:21; 89:25). Yahweh's name is at once supportive (Psalm 124:8) and trustworthy (Psalm 33:21; Isaiah 50:10). To know Yahweh's name is to know Yahweh (Isaiah 52:6; 64:1). And so it was crucial to the success of Moses' mission that he should discover the name of God:

> "But," said Moses to God, "when I go to the Israelites and say to them, 'The God of your fathers has sent me to you,' if they ask me, 'What is his name?' what am I to tell them?" God replied, "I am who am." Then he added, "This is what you shall tell the Israelites: I AM sent me to you."
>
> God spoke further to Moses, "Thus shall you say to the Israelites: The Lord, the God of your fathers, the God of Abraham, the God of Isaac, the God of Jacob, has sent me to you.
>
> "This is my name forever; this is my title for all generations." (Exodus 3:13-15)

What the name *Yahweh* actually means is difficult to determine. There is no unanimity among scholars regarding its derivation. There seems to be general agreement, however, that the name has some etymological connection with the archaic form of the verb *to be* (*hawāh*). The distinguished biblical archaeologist W. F. Albright (d. 1971) links the name with the causative form and suggests that it is only the first word of the entire name, *yahweh-ʾaser-yihweh*, "He who brings into being whatever comes into being." The name would, therefore, signify the creative power of God. Still others have suggested that the name means "I am who I will be," thereby revealing a God in process, one who summons us to collaborate in the building of the future.

Whatever the precise linguistic source, the name *Yahweh* clearly distinguished the God of Israel from every other claimant to the divine title (the other gods, or *Elohim*). Yahweh alone is the creator. Yahweh alone is the revealer. Yahweh alone governs history and humankind. Yahweh alone judges and saves. Yahweh alone possesses the kingdom which is as wide as creation itself. Yahweh alone is a living God (Joshua 3:10; 1 Samuel 17:26,36; 2 Kings 19:4,16; Psalms 42:3; 84:3; Isaiah 37:4,17; Jeremiah 10:10; Hosea 2:1). Yahweh alone gives life (Job 12:10; Deuteronomy 32:39; 1 Samuel 2:6; Psalm 133:3). Indeed, life is given to those who keep the divine commandments (Deuteronomy 30:15-20). One lives by heeding the word of Yahweh (Isaiah 55:3; Ezekiel 20:11,13,21).

New Testament

As we have already seen in the chapter on the religions of the world, monotheism is not peculiar to Judaism alone, nor finally to Christianity. What is *original* about the Christian understanding of God, however, is its *identification of God with Jesus of Nazareth*. The revelation of God in Jesus Christ does not occur merely in the prophetic word he uttered as was the case with the Old Testament prophets. Rather, God is communicated in the very person of Christ. There is an identity between God and Jesus Christ. The Prologue of John's Gospel makes this as clear as does any passage in the New Testament:

There was a man named John sent by God, who came as a witness to testify to the light, so that through him all men might believe, but only to testify to the light, for he himself was not the light. The real light which gives light to every man was coming into the world.

He was in the world, and through him the world was made, yet the world did not know who he was. To his own he came, yet his own did not accept him. Any who did accept him he empowered to become children of God....

The Word became flesh and made his dwelling among us, and we have seen his glory: the glory of an only Son coming from the Father, filled with enduring love. (John 1:6-12,14)

There is a kind of parallel "prologue" in the Epistle to the Hebrews:

In times past, God spoke in fragmentary and varied ways to our fathers through the prophets; in this, the final age, he has spoken to us through his Son, whom he has made heir of all things and through whom he first created the universe. This Son is the reflection of the Father's glory, the exact representation of the Father's being, and he sustains all things by his powerful word. (1:1-3)

In Jesus, therefore, the reality of God is manifested in visible, personal form. And yet the New Testament generally reserves the Greek title *ho theos* ("God") to the Father of Jesus Christ. Jesus is the *Son* of God. We said "generally," because the title "God" *is* bestowed on Jesus here and there, e.g., in the opening verse of John's Gospel ("and the Word was God") and in the Apostle Thomas' confession of faith upon seeing the risen Lord ("My Lord and my God"—John 20:28). Furthermore, the "glory of the great God and of our Savior" which is to appear can be the glory of no other than Jesus (Titus 2:13), and Jesus identifies himself with the Father (John 10:30).

In Jesus Christ not only is the Word made flesh, but all of the saving attributes of Yahweh in the Old Testament are actualized. God pardons through Christ (Ephesians 4:32) and reconciles the world through him (2 Corinthians 5:19). God gives the Spirit through the Son (John 15:26; 16:7). The Christian belongs to Christ, and Christ belongs to God (1 Corinthians 3:23).

The God who acts in and through Jesus Christ and the Holy Spirit is a forgiving God (Matthew 6:14; Mark 11:25; Luke 15:1-32), a merciful God (Luke 1:72,78; 6:36; 2 Corinthians 1:3; Ephesians 2:4; 1 Timothy 1:2; Titus 3:5; 1 Peter 1:3), a kind God (Matthew 19:17; Luke 11:13; 18:19; James 1-5), a loving God

(John 3:16; 16:27; Romans 5:5; 8:37,39; Ephesians 2:4; 2 Thessalonians 2:16; Titus 3:4), a faithful God (1 Corinthians 1:9; 2 Thessalonians 3:3), a patient God (Romans 15:5), the God of all grace (Acts of the Apostles 20:24; Romans 5:15; 1 Corinthians 1:4; 3:10; 15:10; 2 Corinthians 1:12; Ephesians 3:2,7), the God of hope (Romans 15:13), the God of peace (Romans 15:33; 16:20; 1 Corinthians 1:3; 2 Corinthians 1:2; Galatians 1:3; Ephesians 1:2; Philippians 4:9), the God of comfort (Romans 15:5; 2 Corinthians 1:3-4; 2 Thessalonians 2:16), the God of salvation (Luke 1:47; 1 Timothy 1:1; 2:3; 4:10; Titus 2:11; 2 Peter 3:9), a compassionate God who desires the salvation of all (Matthew 18:14; 1 Timothy 2:3,4; 4:10; Titus 2:11; 2 Peter 3:9).

THE GOD OF THE EARLY CHURCH FATHERS
The Apostolic Fathers

The doctrine of *the one God*, the Father and Creator of all things, was a fundamental premise of the Church's faith from the very beginning. Inherited from Judaism, monotheism provided Christianity's first line of defense against pagan polytheism, Marcionite dualism (reality comes from the hands of two opposite but equal forces, the one good, the other evil), and various other contemporary heresies. And yet Christian theology was still in an exceedingly undeveloped state in this earliest of its historical periods. What is to be gleaned from the Fathers of the first century of Christian existence is relatively meagre indeed. The fourth bishop of Rome, Clement of Rome (d. 100), in urging the Christians of Corinth to end their quarrels, divisions, schisms, and other internal hostilities, declared: "Do we not have one God and one Christ and one Spirit of grace, a Spirit that was poured out upon us?" (*Letter to the Corinthians*, 42). The identity of Father, Son, and Spirit with God and their distinctiveness, one from the other, are also suggested by Ignatius of Antioch in his *Letter to the Ephesians*: "You consider yourselves stones of the Father's temple, prepared for the edifice of God the Father, to be taken aloft by the hoisting engine of Jesus Christ, that is, the Cross, while the Holy Spirit serves you as a rope; your faith is your spiritual windlass and your love the road which leads up to God" (par. 9).

The Apologists

Although his writings are not without some ambiguity because of his Platonist philosophical background, Justin insists that "we worship and adore" the Father, the Son, and the prophetic Spirit, and that our faith is fixed on Jesus Christ as "the only proper Son who has been begotten by God, being His Word and first-begotten..." (*First Apology*, chapters 6 and 23). The generation of the Son is conditioned by, and is a product of, the Father's will. But this does not suggest any separation between the Father and the Son. On the contrary, Justin, like the other Apologists, never tired of trying to safeguard the *oneness* of God.

No theologian, however, summed up so authoritatively the thought of the second century as Irenaeus. He approached the mystery of God from two directions: as God exists internally, or immanently, and as God is manifested in the economy of salvation. What is disclosed in history (namely, the trinitarian pluralism of the Godhead) was actually there from all eternity. And over against Marcionite dualism and Gnosticism, Irenaeus declared that "there is only one God, the Creator—He who is above every Principality, and Power, and Dominion, and Virtue; He is Father, He is God, He the Founder, He the Maker, He the Creator.... He is the Father of our Lord Jesus Christ: through His Word, who is His Son, through Him He is revealed and manifested to all to whom He is revealed; for those (only) know Him to whom the Son has revealed Him" (*Against Heresies*, II,30). And not only is God the Creator of all things; God is their provident sustainer as well, ruling with goodness, mercy, patience, wisdom, and justice (III,25).

Third-Century Fathers:
Tertullian, Origen, Dionysius of Rome

The doctrinal preoccupation of the Church's earliest theologians had been, until now, the oneness and unity of God. As challenges to the oneness of God subsided, the Fathers turned their attention to the plural manifestation of God in creation, in redemption, and in reconciliation (known as "economic Trinitarianism"— *economic* because it refers to the measurable "household" activities of God in the world of our experience, i.e., in our "household," as opposed to the unobservable, and therefore unmeasurable, activities within the inner or *immanent* life of God). But this deliberately Trinitarian shift in the understanding of God generated its own set of problems and questions: principally, How is the ancient doctrine of God as *Pantokrator* ("the Almighty") to be maintained if we are to confess that Jesus Christ is equal to the Father as *Pantokrator*?

Tertullian tried to resolve the problem through the use of analogies, the one biological, the other anthropological. First, the Father and the Son are parts of the same organism, but the organism itself is undivided and its power is one. Secondly, the Father and the Son, although distinct from each other, are in complete harmony of mind and will. Neither analogy solved the problem. Both are at the level of imagination, while the problem is at the level of thought. (See his *Apology* and his *Against Praxeus*.)

Origen (d. 254), the greatest of the third-century theologians and certainly one of the most gifted theologians of all time, approached the problem at a higher level. Borrowing from contemporary Platonist philosophy, Origen insisted that there is only one God, but that there is also the Logos which emanates from the One and participates in the One as the image of the divine Goodness. The Father is *the* God (only of the Father does Origen use the definite article). The Logos is not *the* God; he is simply God, and he is God by emanation and participation in a Platonist sense. He is a God "of the second order." As such, he is a diminished deity, since in the Platonist scheme emanation involves some measure of degradation of being. (See his *Principles, Against Celsus*, and *Commentary on John*.) Unfortunately, Origen's solution did not do justice to the actual faith of the Church, namely, that the Logos is God in an undiminished divine sense. The best philosophical instrument at his disposal, Platonism, simply could not supply an answer. Origen's attempt, however, paved the way for the forthright, although finally heretical, solution of Arius (d. 336), a priest of Alexandria, who argued that the Logos is a creature of

God, even though a perfect creature. He came to be out of nothing. "There was when he was not."

Dionysius of Rome (d. 268), twenty-sixth bishop of Rome, provides yet another indication of the mind of leading contemporary theologians on the developing Trinitarian problem. By the time of his pontificate, there were already three clearly distinguishable heresies on the scene: *Sabellianism* (also known as *Modalism*), which taught that God is one person who appears in three different roles according to three different functions: Creator, Redeemer, and Sanctifier; *Subordinationism*, which recognized the trinity of Persons, but made the Son less than the Father and the Spirit less than the Son; and *Tritheism*, which so emphasized the distinction of Persons that there were now three gods instead of one. Dionysius called a synod in Rome and in a letter to the Bishop of Alexandria, also named Dionysius, about whom there had been some rumors of unorthodox teaching, he insisted that all three points of view mentioned above were wrong. Positively, we must hold: (1) there is one *Pantokrator*; (2) Jesus Christ is the Lord; i.e., he is the *Pantokrator;* and (3) Christ, the *Pantokrator*, is the Son, and as such is distinct from the Father who is *the* God, the *Pantokrator*. The bishop of Rome, of course, did not solve the problem, but like most authoritative interventions his at least clarified the limits of the discussion and underlined the principles of orthodoxy which are to be maintained, whatever the proposed explanation or solution.

ARIANISM, THE COUNCIL OF NICEA, AND THE COUNCIL'S AFTERMATH

In every period of the Church's history, theologians have confronted mysteries of faith in one of three ways: first, they in effect eliminate the mystery and reduce everything to what reason can grasp (the Liberal or Rationalist approach); secondly, they throw up their hands and insist that the mystery is so impenetrable that we should ask no further questions of it (the Fideist or anti-intellectual approach); or thirdly, they acknowledge that the mystery never can be resolved, but they press ahead nonetheless, hoping at least to clarify the problem and reach some greater measure of understanding (the mainstream, orthodox approach). Arius pursued the first course. How can we preserve the oneness of God without denying the preeminence of the Son over the entire created universe? Simple enough. The Son, despite his exalted status in the economy of salvation, is a creature like us. He is no more a mystery than you or I.

That is not to say, however, that Arius' attempt at a solution to the mystery of God was simply frivolous in its origins and arbitrary or irresponsible in its conclusions. Given the nature of human intelligence, it was inevitable that someone would eventually ask the questions of how and why. We move always from *description* (the way things look to us) to *definition* (the way things are in themselves). The Bible describes the creative, redemptive, and sanctifying activities of God: Father, Son and Holy Spirit. How are these Persons really related to one another, and in particular the Son to the Father? Can we really safeguard the oneness of God if we insist at the same time on the complete equality of the Son with the Father?

On the other hand, the Arian controversy was more than an intellectual debate. At stake was the very practical matter of our salvation in Christ, to which the same Sacred Scriptures clearly attest. If the Son is not God, fully the *Pantokrator*, wholly situated within the Godhead on an equal footing with the Father, then he is not our Savior and we are not saved. For if the Son is a creature like us, he has no special standing before the Creator against whom we creatures have sinned. His act of reparation on our behalf has no ultimate effect.

It was the Council of Nicea, summoned in 325 by the Emperor Constantine in the hope of restoring unity to the Church, that gave a definitive answer to the Arian question. "We believe in one God the Father, the *Pantokrator* ('the Almighty'), Maker of all things visible and invisible; and in one Lord Jesus Christ, the Son of God, begotten out of the Father, the Only-begotten." Thus far, the affirmation of faith is entirely traditional, fully consistent with earlier creeds and with the biblical formulae as well. But then the council comes to the heart of the Arian controversy: "... the only-begotten generated from the Father, that is, from the being of the Father, God from God, Light from Light, true

God from true God. . . ." Thus, the Son does not emanate from the Father's *will*, as a creature, but out of the Father's *substance*, by a unique mode of origination radically different from the creative act. The Son, therefore, is "begotten, not made." He is not the perfect creature outside the divine order. He is begotten within the divine order and he remains within it. His being is untouched by createdness. Finally, he is "one in being (*homoousios*) with the Father."

The Council of Nicea, therefore, did not simply describe the reality of God; it defined it. It defined what the Son is, in himself and in his relation to the one God the Father. The Son is from the Father in a singular, unshared way, begotten as Son, not made as a creature. The Son is all that the Father is, except for the Name of Father. This is what "one in being," or "consubstantial" (*homoousios*), means. That is what the Son is. "A passage has been made," John Courtney Murray, S. J. (d. 1967), wrote, "from a conception of what the Son is-to-us to a conception of what the Son, Christ, is-in-himself. The transition is from a mode of understanding that is descriptive, relational, interpersonal, historical-existential, to a mode of understanding that is definite, explanatory, absolute, ontological. The alteration in the mode of understanding does not change the sense of the affirmation, but it does make the Nicene affirmation new in its form" (*The Problem of God*, p. 46).

Opposition to the Nicene creed came from both extremes: not only from the Arians on the left but also from the conservative party on the right, those who gathered around Eusebius of Caesarea (d. ca. 340), who is also generally regarded as the first serious Church historian. This party wanted to say no more than Sacred Scripture seemed to be saying, namely, that the Son is "like" (*homoios*) in all things to the Father. The same position appears in the formula of the Synod of Constantinople in 361. *Homoousios*, they insisted, is not a biblical word; therefore, the Nicene formula cannot be a formula of faith. The deeper issue, of course, was the *development of doctrine*. The Eusebians, like many traditionalists down through the centuries, refused to acknowledge the possibility, not to say the appropriateness, of progress in doctrinal understanding. They were at heart fundamentalists, biblical positivists.

The Eusebians' affection for their particular reconstruction of the past (*archaism*) would give rise to the opposite tendency, i.e., the notion that no affirmation of faith can ever be final (*modernism*).

The Nicene formula avoids both extremes. It rejects archaism by transposing the biblical affirmations concerning the Son into a new mode of understanding, but always consistent with the biblical. And it also rejects modernism because the notion "consubstantial" (*homoousios*) sets a final limit in the understanding of faith. There can, and must, be further growth in our understanding of this mystery, but the direction and dimensions of that growth are forever conditioned by the finality of the Nicene formula. And the Nicene formula, in turn, provides a charter and a precedent for the later councils of Ephesus and Chalcedon, which also had to transcend the biblical formulae and attempt an expression of the internal makeup of Christ in the philosophical categories of nature and person. (We shall be returning to the Christological debates and doctrines in greater detail in Part III.)

Through the efforts of Athanasius and Hilary of Poitiers (d. 367), the Eusebians (the so-called *homoiousion* party) were eventually reconciled with the orthodox *homoousions*. Hilary contended in his *On the Councils* that both sides were right and had an obligation to recognize the essentially orthodox concerns of the other side. Since the Nicenes acknowledged the distinction of persons in the Godhead, they could not really deny the *homoiousion* principle. The *homoiousions*, for their part, had to allow unity of substance (*homoousios*) if they believed seriously in the perfect likeness of substance. At the Council of Alexandria in 362 the reconciliation was sealed. With Athanasius in the conciliar chair, the assembly legitimated the "three *hypostases* (persons)" formula of the Eusebian party, provided it merely expresses the separate subsistence of the three Persons in the Trinity. From this emerged a new orthodox formula: "one *ousia* (being, substance), three *hypostases* (persons)."

FOURTH-CENTURY CAPPADOCIAN FATHERS: BASIL, GREGORY OF NYSSA, AND GREGORY OF NAZIANZUS

There remained only the problem of the relationship between the Holy Spirit and the Godhead in general, and between the Holy Spirit and the Son in particular. Since Origen's day theological reflection had not kept pace with the considerable devotional practice centered on the Holy Spirit. Under the impact of denials of the divinity of the Spirit (a group of Egyptian Christians, for example, argued that the Spirit was a creature brought into existence out of nothing), the specifically theological task of articulating the divine equality of the Spirit with the Father and the Son was begun by Athanasius and taken up even more systematically by three major Fathers of the Church, known together as the Cappadocians: Basil (d. 379), his brother Gregory of Nyssa (d. 394), and his friend Gregory of Nazianzus (d. 390). It was Basil who urged that the Spirit must be accorded the same glory, honor, and worship as the Father and the Son; Gregory of Nyssa who emphasized the oneness of nature shared by the three Persons of the Trinity; and Gregory of Nazianzus who insisted that the Spirit, like the Son, is consubstantial, or one in being (*homoousios*), with the Father. (This point would be developed even more fully by Cyril of Alexandria, d. 444, in his *Thesaurus on the Holy and Consubstantial Trinity*.) For Basil the Spirit issues from God not by way of generation (as in the case of the Son) but "as from the breath of his mouth"; for Gregory of Nazianzus the Spirit simply "proceeds" from the Father, as John's Gospel has it; but for Gregory of Nyssa the Spirit is "out of God" and is "of Christ." The Father is uncaused, and the Son and the Spirit are caused. The Son is directly produced by the Father, while the Spirit proceeds from the Father through the Son, but without any trace of subordinationism (i.e., the heresy that the three Persons of the Trinity are somehow unequal).

The essence of the Cappadocian doctrine of God (as expressed in Basil's *On the Holy Spirit*, Gregory of Nyssa's *Letter #38*, *On the Holy Spirit: Against the Followers of Macedonius*, and *On "Not Three Gods,"* and Gregory of Nazianzus' *The Fifth*

Theological Oration) is that the one God exists simultaneously in three ways of being or *hypostases*. Each of the divine *hypostases*, or Persons, is the *ousia* or essence of the Godhead; these Persons are distinguished from one another only by their relationships to one another, and those relationships are determined, in turn, by their origins. Thus, the Father is different from the Son in that the Father is unbegotten, while the Son is begotten by a process of generation; the Son is different from the Spirit in that the Son is generated while the Spirit is spirated by, or proceeds from, the Father and the Son.

Gregory of Nazianzus' expression of the mystery is fully representative of the Cappadocian position:

> But the difference of manifestation, . . . or rather of their mutual relations to one' another, has caused the difference of their Names. For indeed it is not some deficiency in the Son which prevents His being Father (for Sonship is not a deficiency), and yet He is not Father. According to this line of argument there must be some deficiency in the Father, in respect of His not being Son. For the Father is not Son, and yet this is not due to either deficiency or subjection of Essence; but the very fact of being Unbegotten or Begotten or Proceeding has given the name of Father to the First, of the Son to the Second, and of the Third, Him of whom we are speaking, of the Holy Ghost, that the distinction of the Three Persons may be preserved in the one nature and dignity of the Godhead. For neither is the Son Father, for the Father is One, but He is what the Father is; nor is the Spirit Son because He is of God, for the Only-begotten is One, but He is what the Son is. The Three are One in Godhead, and the One Three in properties. . . . (*The Fifth Theological Oration*)

The whole Greek theological approach to the mystery of the triune God would later be summed up by John of Damascus (d. ca. 749) in his *The Source of Knowledge*, part III, "On the Orthodox Faith."

THE COUNCILS OF
CONSTANTINOPLE (381) AND OF ROME (382)

This post-Nicean theology received official endorsement at two councils, the one ecumenical and the other provincial. The First Council of Constantinople (May-July, 381) was called by the Emperors Theodosius (d. 395) and Gratian (d. 383), the one ruling the East, the other the West. The one hundred and fifty bishops attending the council reaffirmed the faith of Nicea. Against the *Macedonians*, who denied the divinity of the Holy Spirit, they held the consubstantiality (oneness-in-being) and the coeternity of the Spirit with the Father and the Son. From this council there emerged the *Nicaeo-Constantinopolitan Creed*, recited in every Sunday Mass throughout the Catholic world (see the Appendix for the full text). The bishops of Constantinople had not themselves composed the creed. They accepted one that was already available and which they deemed entirely consistent with the doctrinal formulations of Nicea.

Pope Damasus (d. 384) did not participate in the Council of Constantinople, and there is no historical evidence that he officially accepted its decisions. The following year, however, he summoned a provincial council in Rome, which issued a set of anathemas or condemnations against those who held false teachings about the Father, Son, and Holy Spirit. The collection of condemnations was subsequently known as the *Tome of Pope Damasus I*. Positively, the council of Rome taught that there is one God of three divine, coequal, coeternal Persons, each distinct from the other, but not so distinct that we have three separate gods.

AUGUSTINE

There was no comparably sophisticated theology in the West (i.e., the Christian world of Latin rather than of Greek) until Augustine, although important contributions had already been made by Irenaeus, Tertullian, Hilary, and others. Influenced by the writings of the neo-Platonist convert to the Church, Victorinus (d. ca. 380), Augustine accepted without question the doctrine that there is one God in whom Father, Son, and Holy Spirit are at once distinct and consubstantial (or "co-essential," as he preferred). Significantly, nowhere does Augustine try to prove this doctrine. He accepts it as a datum of revelation which, in his view, Scripture proclaims almost on every page. His concern is not with proof but with understanding, which is consistent with his fundamental notion of theology as belief seeking understanding. (I believe in order that I might understand.)

Unlike the Greek Fathers, Augustine does not begin with the three Persons as they function in history for our salvation and then work backwards, so to speak, to the unity of the Godhead. He begins rather with the one divine nature itself and tries to understand how the three Persons share in that nature without dividing it. Subordinationism of every kind is rejected. Whatever is affirmed of God is affirmed equally of each of the Persons (*On the Trinity*, Book 5, chapter 9). "Not only is the Father not greater than the Son in respect of divinity, but Father and Son together are not greater than the Holy Spirit, and no single person of the Three is less than the Trinity itself" (8,1). Thus, we are not speaking here of three separate individuals as we would of three separate human beings. There are not three wills, but one. There are not three sources of divine action, but one. Against the obvious objection that Augustine is destroying the several roles of the three Persons (and, therefore, is lapsing into Modalism), he argued that, even though it was the Son and not the Father who was born, suffered, and died, the Father cooperated fully with the Son in bringing about the incarnation, the passion, and the resurrection. It is fitting, however, for the Son to have been manifested and made visible in those events, since each of the divine Persons possesses the divine nature in a particular manner and since, in the external operation of the Godhead, roles which are *appropriate* to a particular Person in view of that Person's origin within the Godhead are fittingly attributed to that Person. And yet all three Persons are always fully involved as one in every external action.

One of Augustine's original contributions to the Christian doctrine of God (and his most effective rebuttal of the charge of Modalism) was his notion of real or *subsistent relations*. Anticipating the teaching of Anselm and then of the Council of Florence that in the Trinity all things are one except what is differentiated by reason of an opposition of relations (e.g., the Father, who is *unbegotten*, is not the Son, who is *begotten*), Augustine opposed the Arian notion that distinctions within the Godhead are either substantial (in which case there are three separate gods) or accidental (in which case God is not purely simple). Whatever the Father, the Son, or the Holy Spirit is, he is in relation to one or both of the others (see *On the Trinity*, Books 5-7). Threeness in God, therefore, is not rooted in threeness of substance or threeness of accidents but in threeness of relations: of begetting, of being begotten, and of proceeding.

What is perhaps Augustine's most original contribution to Trinitarian theology, however, is his use of analogies drawn from human consciousness to explain the inner life of God. (This is not to say that his argument is easy to follow, or in fact can be deemed entirely helpful today.) In every process of perception there are three distinct elements: the external object, the mind's sensible representation of the object, and the act of focusing the mind. When the external object is removed, we rise to an even higher trinitarian level, superior to the first because the process occurs entirely now within the mind and is therefore "of one and the same substance," namely, the memory impression, the internal memory image, and the focusing of the will. In his *On the Trinity* Augustine elaborates the analogy at length in three successive stages, with the following resulting trinities: (1) the mind, its knowledge of itself, and its love of itself, (9, 2-8); (2) memory, or the mind's latent knowledge of itself, understanding, and love of itself (10, 17-19); and (3) the mind as remembering, knowing, and loving God (14, 11-end). Augustine regarded the last of the three analogies as the most satisfactory. It is only when the mind has focused itself on its Creator with all its powers of remembering, understanding, and loving that the image it bears of God can be fully restored. "Since these three, the memory, the understanding, and the will, are, therefore, not three lives but one life, not three minds but one mind, it follows that they are certainly not three substances, but one substance" (10, 11).

Augustine himself was realistic about the limitations of this analogical approach. Analogies, as the saying goes, always limp.

They tell us how things are *like* other things, but they warn us at the same time that the things being compared are also *unlike* one another. Thus, the operations of human consciousness are by no means identical with the inner operations of the Trinity. Remembering, understanding, and loving are three separate faculties of the human mind. In the Godhead there are no distinct faculties. God is absolutely one. Furthermore, in the human mind these three faculties operate independently. In God every act and operation is indivisible (15, 43). Furthermore, why are there only two processions and only three Persons?

We are left, in the end, with the mystery: Scripture and Christian doctrine portray God as acting in three Persons, but Scripture and Christian doctrine also insist firmly and unequivocally on the oneness of God.

Augustine's influence on subsequent Christian belief and theology is, to be sure, enormous. Apart from Boethius (d. ca. 525), who bequeathed the definition of *person* as "an individual substance of a rational nature," no one competes with him for theological impact on later centuries. But the more immediate effect of his approach was also considerable. The so-called *Athanasian Creed (Quicumque)* of the late fifth century clearly bore the stamp of Augustinian thought. Falsely attributed to St. Athanasius, the creedal formula has stood ever since as the Western Church's classical statement of Trinitarian faith. Augustine's influence was also operative in the deliberations of the Eleventh Council of Toledo (675), which drew upon the *Quicumque* creed as well as Augustine's writings for the construction of its own profession of faith, in which it declares that God is both One and Three.

ANSELM OF CANTERBURY

Although no complete history of the Christian understanding of God can ignore the watershed figure of John Scotus Erigena (d. 877), the most famous scholar and teacher of his day and one of the last who tried to reconcile ancient Greek philosophy with the faith (see his *On the Division of Nature*, in which he seems to propose a pantheistic notion of God), our attention turns here to

Anselm, the single most important theologian between Augustine and Aquinas.

Anselm's contribution to the Christian understanding of God is at least threefold: the so-called ontological argument for God's existence; the debt-satisfaction theory of atonement; and the principle that in God everything is one except for the opposition of relationships among the three Persons. Only the last seems to have survived subsequent critical analysis. On the first point, Anselm insisted that God is "a being than which nothing greater can be conceived." But, he said, if such a being exists only in the mind or in the realm of understanding, "the very being, than which nothing greater can be conceived, is one, than which a greater can be conceived. Hence, there is no doubt that there exists a being, than which nothing greater can be conceived, and it exists both in the understanding and in reality" (*Proslogium*, chapter 2). The argument was later rejected by Aquinas and Kant alike. What may be true in the order of the mind is not necessarily real in the order of objective reality. On the second point, Anselm argued that the sin of Adam could be forgiven only if sufficient satisfaction for the sin were offered to the Father. But only a divine person could adequately resolve the debt incurred by human sin. Therefore, God had to become human if we were to be restored to God's friendship. (We shall return to this theory of atonement in Part III on Christology.) On the third point, Anselm argued, following in the tradition of Augustine, that God is absolutely one except for the pluralism of persons created by the opposition of relationships among them. The Father, Son, and Holy Spirit are one God, except insofar as the Father is unbegotten and the Son is begotten, and insofar as the Spirit proceeds whereas the Father and the Son spirate (see his *On the Procession of the Holy Spirit*, chapter 1). This principle is the theological basis for the doctrine of the *mutual indwelling of the three divine Persons*: The Father is always in the Son and the Holy Spirit; the Son is always in the Father and the Spirit; the Spirit is always in the Father and the Son. The mutual indwelling is also known as *circumincession*. The Council of Florence (1442) adopted the principle in its "Decree for the Jacobites": "The Father alone begot the Son out of His substance; the Son alone was begotten from the Father alone; the Holy Spirit alone proceeds from both Father and Son. These three persons are one God and not three gods, for the three are one substance, one essence, one nature, one Godhead, one infinity, one eternity, and everything (in them) is one where there is no opposition of relationship."

In the final accounting, Anselm believed that the mystery of the triune God is "so sublime" that it "transcends all the vision of the human intellect. And for that reason I think it best to refrain from the attempt to explain how this thing is." It is enough for Anselm to be secure in the knowledge *that* God is, and that what we *do* know of God is "without contradiction of any other reason" (*Monologium*, chapter 64). For theology itself is "faith seeking understanding."

THE FOURTH LATERAN GENERAL COUNCIL (1215)

When a new pope is elected to the office of "supreme pastoral ministry" in the Church, one of his first official acts is to take possession of the Lateran Basilica, the cathedral church of the diocese of Rome. It is as bishop of Rome, of course, that the pope serves as head of the Church Universal. The Lateran has also been the scene of five general or ecumenical councils. It was the fourth such council of the Lateran, during the pontificate of Innocent III (d. 1216), which produced a profession of Trinitarian faith as well as a formal doctrinal statement on the reality of the triune God. The council confessed that "there is only one true God. . .Father, Son and Holy Spirit: three persons indeed but one essence, substance or wholly simple nature:. . .the Father generating, the Son being born, the Holy Spirit proceeding; consubstantial, co-equal, co-omnipotent and co-eternal; one origin of all things: the Creator of all things visible and invisible, spiritual and corporal." This creedal affirmation was directed explicitly against *Albigensianism*, one of the most serious heresies in the history of the Church.

Indeed, the late Monsignor Philip Hughes (d. 1967), one of the best known English-speaking Church historians of this century, regarded the seventeen years (1181–1198) that separated Pope Innocent III from Pope Alexander III as "the most critical

CHAPTER IX   THE CHRISTIAN UNDERSTANDING OF GOD

period of the Middle Ages. . . . Of all the dangers that threatened, the greatest of all was the revival of Manicheeism which, beginning a hundred years before this, had by now made its own all the south of France (Provence) and much of northern Italy" (*A Popular History of the Catholic Church*, New York: Doubleday Image, 1949, p. 115). The sect was called Albigenses after the city of Albi, Provence. Its theological position was that matter is evil, that it comes from some source other than the true God. Because matter is evil, we must abstain from food, from marriage, and especially from conception. The sect was well-organized and was extraordinarily successful in gathering adherents from the cultured nobility and from the wealthy merchant class. At first the pope tried to combat the heresy with persuasion and preaching, but when those failed, he adopted more aggressive measures: One was the calling of the Fourth Lateran Council, and another was the establishment of the Inquisition to root out this heresy and others. (For an excellent case-study of how the Church went about this task, see Emmanuel LeRoy Laduries's *Montaillou: The Promised Land of Error*, New York: Braziller, 1978.)

The council taught, therefore, that God is the author of both matter and spirit and that Christ is fully God, with a human as well as a divine nature.

In its second document, the council addressed itself to a bitter dispute between Joachim of Flora (d. 1202) and Peter the Lombard (d. 1160). The dispute was a kind of microcosm of the historic difference between the Eastern and Western approaches to the mystery of the Trinity. The Eastern approach, as noted earlier, was centered on the saving activity of the three Persons in history. The Western approach, with its roots principally in Augustine, was centered on the one divine nature which subsists as Father, Son, and Holy Spirit. Peter the Lombard had systematized this latter approach in his *Sentences*, making the divine essence the center of his speculation. Joachim attacked Peter, accusing him of producing a fourth Person, the "divine essence." The council defended Peter against the accusation that he had produced a quaternity, and sanctioned the doctrine which became the basis of the Trinitarian theology of most Scholastics thereafter: ". . . in God there is only Trinity, not a quaternity, because each of the

Persons is that reality, viz., that divine substance, essence or nature which alone is the beginning of all things, apart from which nothing else can be found. This reality is neither generating nor generated, nor proceeding, but it is the Father who generates, the Son who is generated and the Holy Spirit who proceeds, so that there be distinctions between the persons but unity in nature. Hence, though 'the Father is one person (*alius*), the Son another person, and the Holy Spirit another person, yet there is not another reality (*aliud*),' but what the Father is, this very same reality is also the Son, this the Holy Spirit, so that in orthodox Catholic faith we believe them to be of one substance."

THOMAS AQUINAS

Aquinas' understanding of God is too precise and detailed to summarize in so brief a subsection as this. Its major components, however, are twofold: (1) the identification of essence and existence in God; i.e., God's essence is "to be"; and (2) the participation of the created order in the Being of God, who is the First Cause of all that is.

For the first, he rests his case on the Exodus text (3:14) wherein Yahweh "responds" to Moses' question: "I am He Who Is." For Aquinas, "He Who Is" is the most suitable name for God (*Summa Theologica*, I, q. 13, a. 11). "Every thing," he writes, "exists because it has being. A thing whose essence is not its being, consequently, is not through its essence but by participation in something, namely, being itself. But that which is through participation in something cannot be the first being, because prior to it is the being in which it participates in order to be. But God is the first being, with nothing prior to Him. His essence is, therefore, His being" (*Summa Contra Gentiles*, I, 22).

From this follows the principle that every created reality participates in the Being of God. God is perpetually and immediately present to the world of beings, for God is Being itself, the condition for the existence of any beings at all (*Summa Theologica*, I, q. 8; q. 104). Unlike the God of *Deism*, who creates the world in the beginning and then allows it to work on its own thereafter (much like the clockmaker's relation to the clock), the God of

Aquinas is at once transcendent and immanent to the world (*Summa Contra Gentiles*, II, 21; III, 67–68). But God's intimate involvement in the created universe does not thereby destroy the integrity of free agents. "God works in things in such a manner that things have their proper operation." Otherwise, "the operative powers which are seen to exist in things would be bestowed on things to no purpose, if things produced nothing through them. Indeed, all created things would seem, in a way, to be purposeless, if they lacked an operation proper to them, since the purpose of everything is its operation" (*Summa Theologica*, I, q. 105, a. 5).

Aquinas' understanding of the Being and action of God is consistent with his famous "five ways" to prove the existence of God: the argument from *motion* (there must be a prime mover), the argument from *causality* (every effect must have a cause), the argument from *necessity* (all beings are possible, but one must be necessary if there are to be any beings at all), the argument from gradation or *exemplarity* (our ideas of more or less, of better or worse, presuppose some standard of perfection), and the argument from *design* (the consistent and coherent operation of the whole universe demands some intelligent and purposeful designer). (See *Summa Theologica*, I, q. 3, a. 3). These arguments were not original with Aquinas. He was largely indebted to Plato, Aristotle, Avicenna, Augustine, and especially the Jewish philosopher Moses Maimonides. All of the arguments are reducible to one: the argument from causality. No one argument "proves" the existence of God. They are simply ways in which the believer can begin to "make sense" of his or her belief in God after the fact. (We touched already upon this problem in chapters 5 and 6, with regard to the relationship of nature and grace and the teaching of the First Vatican Council on our knowledge of God.)

Insofar as God ordains all things to their goal, God is *provident*; i.e., God "foresees" and insures what is necessary for the fulfillment of the end of the world and all that is in it (*Summa Theologica*, I, q. 22, a. 1). The human being, as the creature endowed with reason, "is under God's providence in the special sense of sharing in providence inasmuch as he is provident with regard to himself and other things" (I-II, q. 91, a. 2). This sharing of the rational creature in the reason of God (I-II, q. 19, a. 4) is called the "natural law" (q. 91, a. 2). Alongside the natural law is the new law of the Gospel and of the Holy Spirit which is imparted to those who believe in Christ (q. 106, a. 1). There can be only one goal, God, of both the created and the recreated universe, i.e., of the order of nature and the order of grace (I, q. 103, a. 2).

Finally, with regard to the doctrine of the Trinity, Aquinas completed the psychological explanation of the relations of Persons which Augustine initiated and Anselm developed. He was the first to argue that there are two distinct processions (generation and spiration) because a spiritual being has two operations: intellection and volition. These processions produce, in turn, four real relations: paternity, filiation, spiration, and procession, but only three of them are really distinct from one another by reason of their mutual opposition: paternity, filiation, and (passive) spiration (I, q. 28, aa. 1–4). And so there are three Persons, and only three, in God (I, qq. 27–43). Other important medieval theologians, like Duns Scotus (d. 1308), agreed with the conclusion but not with the argument. Anticipating the Greek Orthodox position, Scotus argued that not only opposite relations but also disparate relations (e.g., passive generation and active spiration) distinguished divine persons. Therefore, it was not necessary that the Spirit proceed also from the Son (see *Commentary on the Sentences*, I, d. 11, q. 2).

SECOND COUNCIL OF LYONS (1274); COUNCIL OF FLORENCE (1438–1440)

What these two ecumenical councils had in common was their concern for the split between the Eastern and Western Churches, by now already two centuries old. Both tried to effect some kind of reconciliation, but neither succeeded for very long. Insofar as the schism involved divergent understandings of God, and of the Trinity in particular, the conciliar texts are of interest to us here.

Lyons II adopted as its own a so-called "Profession of Faith of Michael Palaeologus." It was taken from a letter written by the Byzantine Emperor Michael VIII Palaeologus (d. ca. 1282), in which the emperor merely reproduced, without modification, the text of a profession of faith proposed to him by Pope Clement IV (d. 1268) as early as 1267. Clement believed this to be required of the Greeks if reunion was to occur. Insofar as Michael desired reunion, he himself subscribed to it. Not surprisingly, the text reflects the Latin approach to the doctrine of the Trinity: It begins with the oneness of the divine nature and then proceeds to the trinity of Persons, with the Holy Spirit proceeding from the Father *and* the Son (not *through* the Son, as the Greeks would have it). In another document, the *Constitution on the Holy Trinity and the Catholic Faith*, the council explains the Latin doctrine on the origin of the Holy Spirit, insisting, against its Eastern detractors, that the origin of the Holy Spirit from the Father *and* the Son does not imply a double principle in God.

The Council of Florence's teaching on God is contained in two documents: the *Decree for the Greeks* (1439) and the *Decree for the Jacobites* (1442). In the former, the council explains the procession of the Holy Spirit from Father *and* Son, but allows also for the formula cherished by the East, namely, procession from the Father *through* the Son, with the understanding, however, that the Son, just as fully as the Father, is the "cause" or "principle" of the subsistence of the Holy Spirit. The *Decree of Union* was signed by both groups, but when the Greeks returned to Constantinople, public opinion forced them to repudiate it. The Churches remain separated to this day.

Representatives of the Syrian Jacobite Church came to Rome afterwards and engaged in similar negotiations leading to a consensus statement, in this case the *Decree for the Jacobites*, important for its emphasis on the concept of *circumincession* or *perichoresis*, namely, that each Person is always present to the other two Persons: " . . . the Father is wholly in the Son and wholly in the Holy Spirit; the Son is wholly in the Father and wholly in the Holy Spirit; the Holy Spirit is wholly in the Father and wholly in the Son." The Decree is also significant for its articulation of the principle, to which we have already referred in this chapter, that in the Trinity all things are one except what is opposed by the opposition of relations.

PROTESTANTISM AND THE COUNCIL OF TRENT
(1545-1563)

The Council of Trent's doctrinal formulations on God (to which we have already referred in Part I on human existence) cannot be understood apart from the theology of the Reformers. For Martin Luther (d. 1546) the difficulty is not with the immanent Trinity (i.e., the Trinity from the viewpoint of life within the Godhead) but with the economic Trinity (i.e., the Trinity from the viewpoint of the action of God in the world, and specifically in the lives of human beings). Luther believes in, and confesses, the mystery of the Blessed Trinity. But he cannot accept the Catholic principle that God desires the salvation of all, that God is essentially a gracious God, and that God wills us to cooperate freely with divine grace in the working out of our salvation. For Luther, on the contrary, we can do nothing on our own. God has mercy on whomever he wills (Romans 9:18). "He wills that his power should be magnified in man's perdition" (*Lectures on Romans*, chapter 8). But Luther also insisted that the true God says ". . . I take no pleasure in the death of the wicked man, but rather in the wicked man's conversion, that he may live" (see Ezekiel 33:11). "God is the same sort of God to all men that He was to David, namely, one who forgives sins and has mercy upon all who ask for mercy and acknowledge their sins" (*Lectures on Psalms, On Psalm 51:1*). In *Bondage of the Will*, however, Luther stressed God's foreknowledge and omnipotence so much that practically no room is left for our free response. In Christ, of course, we have access to the Father's will and heart. If God be for us in Christ, who or what can be against us (Romans 8:31)? (See his commentary on the First Commandment in *The Large Catechism*.)

John Calvin (d. 1564), the other great Reformer, carries the doctrine of predestination even further. Taking Romans 9:13 very literally, he concludes that God loves some and hates others: "It is just as Scripture says, 'I have loved Jacob and hated Esau'." On the other hand, Calvin acknowledges in his *Institutes of the Christian Religion* that "God has destined all things for our good and salvation. . . nothing that is needful for our welfare will ever be lacking to us" (chapter 14). And yet "By God's bidding. . . salvation is freely offered to some while others are barred from access to it...he does not indiscriminately adopt all into the hope of salvation but gives to some what he denies to others" (Book III, chapter 21). Salvation is owed to no one; therefore, God does no one an injustice by denying it to anyone. Furthermore, if God cannot punish, how is his mercy to be made manifest (chapter 23)?

The Reformers' attitude toward God's salvific intentions underscores again one of the principal historic differences between Protestant and Catholic theology and spirituality. The former tradition, as we suggested in the earlier discussion of the problem of nature and grace in chapters 4 and 5, has tended to emphasize the radical unworthiness of the person, even after God's redemptive activity on our behalf. The Catholic tradition, on the other hand, insists that God not only makes a declaration of our worthiness for salvation, but actually transforms us and makes us new creatures in Christ and the Holy Spirit. God offers this inner transformation to every person, without exception. No one is excluded beforehand. Only a free act of the will, rejecting the divine offer of grace, can impede God's saving designs. The alternate view—predestination to hell as well as to heaven—has been described by the Anglican theologian John Macquarrie as a "fantastic exaggeration of the divine initiative into a fatalism [which] is repugnant not merely because it dehumanizes man but also because it presents us with a God who is not worthy to be worshipped" (*Principles of Christian Theology*, p. 341).

The Council of Trent's *Decree on Justification* teaches that "all men" have been called to the status of adopted sons of God in Christ (chapter 2), but that they can freely reject the grace of adoption (chapter 5). Insofar as we do open ourselves to the divine presence, it is because our hearts have been touched through the illumination of the Holy Spirit (*ibid.*). The process of passing from the condition of sin as a child of the first Adam to a condition of adopted sonship in Christ is called justification (chapter 4). Justification "is not only a remission of sins but also the sanctification and renewal of the inward man through the voluntary reception of the grace and the gifts whereby an unjust man becomes just" (chapter 7). God wills the salvation of all, and God will achieve that purpose "unless men themselves fail in his grace" (chapter

13). Indeed, the council's sixth canon explicitly anathematizes, or condemns, those who say "that it is not in man's power to make his ways evil, but that God produces the evil works just as he produces the good ones, not only by allowing them but properly and directly, so that Judas' betrayal is no less God's work than Paul's vocation."

BLAISE PASCAL (d. 1662)

Pascal, mathematician, scientist, and spiritual writer, is perhaps best known for his unique apologetical argument on behalf of belief in God, namely, the famous wager. First, he says, there is no clear evidence for the existence of God. "What meets our eye denotes neither total absence nor manifest presence of the divine, but the presence of a hidden God" (*Pensées*, #12). God is or is not. Which is it? A game is on. If one gambles that God is not, that person has nothing to gain and everything to lose should God exist. If, on the other hand, one wagers that God is, that person has everything to gain and nothing to lose. For if God exists, faith in God will have its infinite reward. If God does not exist, the person has lost nothing, since there would be no infinite reward in any case. So to "bet on" God is to enter a game weighted in the gambler's favor, for the gambler wagers finite stakes with the possibility of infinite returns.

More significant for our purposes here is Pascal's relatively balanced understanding of the God of faith. Christianity, he declares, teaches us twin truths about this God: "that there is a God whom men can reach, and that there is a corruption in their nature which renders them unworthy of Him." It is crucial that we keep both truths before us. "Knowledge of one alone causes either the pride of philosophers who have known God but not their misery, or the despair of atheists who know their misery but not their Redeemer." It is only in our knowledge of Jesus Christ that we grasp both truths at once, namely, that we have access to God and that we are creatures in need of forgiveness and reconcil-iation. The Christians' God, therefore, is like the God of Abra-ham, of Isaac, and of Jacob, "a God of love and consolation, a God who fills the soul and heart of those whom He hath purchased, a

God who makes them deeply conscious of their misery and of His infinite mercy; who makes His home in their heart, filling it with humility, joy, confidence and love; who renders them incapable of any other object than Himself" (*ibid.*). This God is always a "hidden God," but there is an escape from our blindness through Jesus Christ, "apart from Whom all communication with God has been cut off. . ." (#246).

A fuller statement of Pascal's importance in the history of the Church and of Christian theology generally would require a more complete description of the cultural and ecclesiastical situation in seventeenth-century France, of the development of *Gallicanism* (a movement of French nationalism which, among other things, insisted on the autonomy of the local Church over against Rome and the papacy), of *Jansenism* (with which Pascal was once associated at Port-Royal), and of various other contemporary spiritual movements associated with the names of Fénelon (d. 1715), Bossuet (d. 1704), and others.

FIRST VATICAN COUNCIL (1869–1870) AND ITS ANTECEDENTS
Kant

Immanuel Kant (d. 1804) in his *Critique of Pure Reason* rejected the traditional arguments on behalf of the existence of God, having been awakened from his own "dogmatic slumber" by David Hume's (d. 1776) analysis of causality. Since God is by definition in a totally different order, God's "objective reality cannot indeed be proved, but also cannot be disproved, by merely speculative reasoning" (section 7). Since God operates in the moral order, it is there that God is to be apprehended, if at all. Insofar as we all seek the highest good, we must be able to presuppose that the quest is possible in the first place. "Granted that the pure moral law inexorably binds every man as a command (not as a rule of prudence), the righteous man may say: I will that there be a God, that my existence in this world be also an existence in a pure world of the understanding outside the system of natural connection, and finally that my duration be endless" (*Critique of Practical Reason*, section 8). Since our idea of the highest good in the world leads to the postulation of a higher, moral, most holy, and omnipotent Being which alone can unite our quest for happiness with our obedience to duty, morality thus leads ineluctably to religion. God becomes the powerful moral Lawgiver whose will is the final end of creation and of all human activity (*Religion Within the Limits of Reason Alone*, Preface to the first edition). We feel ourselves at once impelled to seek the highest good, even duty-bound to seek it, but powerless on our own to reach it. We discover ourselves to be living in an ethical commonwealth under the governance of a moral Ruler who is creator, guardian, and administrator. The Lawgiver's beneficence, however, is limited by human cooperation with the holy law. To say that "God is love" means that God approves us insofar as we obey the law. To speak of a *triune* God, however, is to exceed the limits of reason alone, for we cannot grasp God in himself but can only grasp God insofar as he is for us as moral beings (Book III).

Hegel

Georg W. F. Hegel (d. 1831), on the other hand, did posit the reality of the Trinity, but he grounded the reality of the Trinity on a purely philosophical basis. Central to his whole system (expressed most fully in his *Phenomenology of Spirit*) is the insight that all reality develops *dialectically*, moving through contradictions to a resolution thereof; *thesis* (initial knowledge), *antithesis* (contradiction), and *synthesis* (unification). The reality of God proceeds in the same way. The Absolute Spirit, which is God, posits its own opposite other, Matter, and resolves the difference in an eternal return to itself. The Father is Being-in-and-for-itself; the Son is the Other, the finite particularization of the universal; the Spirit is the singleness, the unity of the universal and the particular. The Trinity provides the paradigm for what occurs in all of reality, which moves inexorably through dialectical processes of universality and particularity, and of identity and distinction. Everything is moving finally to the Kingdom of the Spirit, where alone God becomes personal. (See *The Philosophy of Religion, Part III*.)

Once again, only a fuller historical, philosophical, and theological discussion can begin to do justice to the extraordinary impact which both Kant and Hegel have made upon, and continue to make upon, Christian thought, not to say secular thought—e.g., Marxism: Kant in the realms of ethics and fundamental theology, and Hegel in the realm of systematic theology. Indeed, the influence of Hegel upon much of present-day German theology, of both Catholic and Protestant varieties, cannot easily be overestimated. It is particularly strong in Rahner, Metz, Pannenberg, and Moltmann. The impact of Kant on the revision of our traditional notions of our knowledge of God in revelation and faith and of our apprehension of truth generally is also broadly ecumenical. There is no serious theologian working in the area of fundamental theology who has not been affected by the Kantian revolution. On the other hand, Kant's influence in moral theology or Christian ethics has tended to be restricted to Protestantism.

Schleiermacher

Friedrich Schleiermacher (d. 1834) carried forward the now traditional Protestant insistence on the inability of the human mind to grasp the reality of God—a position consistent, of course, with classical Protestantism's understanding of the relationship between nature and grace. Schleiermacher taught that faith is essentially our feeling of absolute dependence. If we find God at all, we find God in our consciousness. Since the Trinity does not emerge from an analysis of human consciousness, it cannot be regarded as a primary datum of Christian faith. (See his *The Christian Faith*, where the Trinity is relegated to an appendix.) It is perhaps fair to say that Schleiermacher is the principal forerunner of Liberal Protestantism of the nineteenth and early twentieth centuries. Together with Adolf von Harnack (d. 1930), who rejected the doctrine of the Trinity as an unacceptable Hellenization of the essential Christian message, he is one of the principal targets of the neo-orthodox revival initiated by Karl Barth around the time of the First World War. For Barth, the Trinity is utterly fundamental and central to God's revelation in Jesus Christ (see the "Prolegomena" of the *Church Dogmatics*).

Kierkegaard

Sören Kierkegaard (d. 1855) constructed a position at odds with both Hegel and Schleiermacher. Against Hegel, Kiekegaard argued that "an infinitely qualitative difference" separates us from God, that we are not in fact absorbed into the universal Spirit but retain our individual selfhood before God. Indeed, so strongly did Kierkegaard insist upon the importance of the individual's responsibility before God that he is generally regarded as the father of modern existentialism. For Kierkegaard God is utterly transcendent, without any need at all for us. On the contrary, it is we who need God if we are to become authentic persons. We are called to an interior conversion of the heart so that we become fixed entirely on the will of God. Against the liberalism represented by Schleiermacher, Kierkegaard argues that "the fundamental error of modern times...lies in the fact that the yawning abyss of quality between God and man has been removed...before God man is nothing (*Journals*, #712). Furthermore, Kierkegaard retains the doctrine of the Trinity as central to Christian faith. Kierkegaard's impact upon Karl Barth, especially in the latter's development of the notion of God as "wholly Other," is exceedingly profound. Through Barth, Kierkegaard would have a part in shaping the direction of neo-orthodox, neo-Reformation Protestant thought in the early and mid-twentieth century, with its emphasis on the transcendence of God and our personal relationship with God, and its corresponding caution regarding the sociopolitical dimensions of the Christian faith.

Feuerbach

Ludwig Feuerbach (d. 1872) regarded God as simply our projection of our own nature into the ethereal world beyond this one. God possesses all of the ideal attributes of humankind (see *The Essence of Christianity*, chapter 2). Feuerbach urged his readers to recognize what we had done and to reclaim our responsibility for the course of the world. Accordingly, he prepared the way not only for Karl Marx but, within the Christian community, for an excessively anthropological method of doing theology in which the study of God is really our own self-study. Within contemporary Catholic theology, Gregory Baum comes as close to that model as any other, without, however, lapsing straightaway into atheism or the complete denial of transcendence. In recent Protestant theology, the so-called "death-of-God" movement associated with Thomas J. J. Altizer and others even more clearly adopted Feuerbach's approach, with a good measure of Hegel and Nietzsche thrown in.

Nietzsche

Friedrich Nietzsche (d. 1900) attributed the development of the idea of God to primitive ancestor worship. As certain ancient tribes prevailed over others, their members credited their ancestors with their victories. While religious beliefs and practices have changed considerably since then, the feeling of owing something to God has continued among human beings. Behind this view, Nietzsche contended, is a will for self-torture. We attribute to God the opposite of the qualities which arouse guilt in ourselves. The presence of a holy God makes us feel sinful, and this tortures us. God also represents the best qualities of a nation. The God of dominant nations is powerful and pitiless. The Christian God, therefore, is despicable because to Christians goodness and mercy are the dominant divine attributes. Indeed, "The Christian concept of God . . . is one of the most corrupt concepts of God that has ever been attained on earth. . . . In God, nonentity is deified, and the will to nonentity is declared holy!" (*The Antichrist*, #18). Nietzsche, with his emphasis on the notion of the "superman," influenced not only the development of "death-of-God" theology in the 1960s but, more menancingly, the emergence of Nazism in the Germany of the 1930s and 1940s.

Vatican I

The First Vatican Council confronted these and other approaches to the question of God: materialism, rationalism, pantheism, and the like. In its *Dogmatic Constitution On the Catholic Faith*, the council taught that "there is one God, true and living, Creator and Lord of heaven and earth, mighty, eternal, immense, incomprehensible, infinite in His intellect and will and in all perfection. As He is one unique and spiritual substance, entirely simple and unchangeable, we must proclaim Him distinct from the world in existence and essence...ineffably exalted above all things that exist or can be conceived besides Him." All contrary positions are explicitly anathematized.

SECOND VATICAN COUNCIL (1962-1965) AND ITS ANTECEDENTS
Twentieth-Century Understandings of God

A complete survey of pre-Vatican II understandings of God within the Christian community would require a comprehensive outline of twentieth-century theology. John Macquarrie has attempted something like this in his *Twentieth-Century Religious Thought* (New York: Harper & Row, 1963), and John Cobb has produced a similar work, although more limited in scope, in *Living Options in Protestant Theology* (Philadelphia: Westminster Press, 1962). The reader already has the barest framework for such an outline in chapters 2 and 4 of this book: In the former chapter there is a descriptive listing of various kinds of contemporary theology, and in the latter chapter there are sketches of various contemporary understandings of human existence. What follows here is a brief survey of the various theological approaches insofar as they embody a particular understanding of God.

First, there are *liberal* and *neo-liberal* theology which tend to reduce the supernatural content of faith to its lowest common denominator. The emphasis in the divine/human relationship is always on the human, particularly in its social and political dimensions. A formal doctrine of the Trinity is marginal to the liberal schema. In this regard, liberal theology draws upon Schleiermacher (from within the Church) and upon Feuerbach and Nietzsche (from outside the Church). Liberalism in theology is primarily, although no longer exclusively, a Protestant phenomenon.

Secondly, there are *orthodox* and *neo-orthodox* theology. Both are also known as *confessional* theology. On the Catholic side, this theology stresses the otherness, the unchangeability, and the providential power of God manifested in and through Jesus Christ and the Holy Spirit. On the Protestant side, this theology stresses divine judgment and the wholly otherness of God. But given the historic emphases on justification-as-transformation in Catholicism and on justification-as-declaration in Protestantism, the otherness of God tends to be more strongly stressed in Protestantism than in Catholicism, while the sacramental availability of God in our ordinary everyday lives tends to be more strongly stressed in Catholicism than in Protestantism.

Thirdly, there is *radical* or *"death-of-God"* theology which, in the spirit of Feuerbach, Hegel, and Nietzsche, insisted that the transcendent God is dead, that transcendence itself has collapsed into total immanence, that what we call divine or supernatural is just another way of describing the human and the natural. This was a mid-1960s exaggeration of the liberal and neo-liberal reductionist understandings of God which have persisted throughout the twentieth century.

Fourthly, there is *secular* theology, another 1960s development, which, like liberal and neo-liberal theology, emphasized the this-worldly character of God and of Christian faith, but without setting aside the content of the Christian tradition. On the contrary, a strong insistence on the social and political dimensions of Christianity is portrayed as consistent with, even demanded by, the principles of the Old and New Testaments and of post-biblical Christian doctrine: God calls us to a life of responsibility in and for the world through the servant Christ ("man for others") and the reconciling Holy Spirit. Indeed, it is in experiencing the "gracious neighbor" that we experience the "gracious God" (John A.T. Robinson).

Fifthly, there is *liberation* theology which also bears a general resemblance to liberal and neo-liberal theology insofar as it stresses the social and political dimensions of the faith, but also resembles orthodox and neo-orthodox theology insofar as it stresses the biblical notion of God as judge and liberator from sin. The God of liberation theology (whether of the Latin American, black, or feminist kind) is a God whose primary, if not sole, passion is the freeing of the oppressed from the bondage of economic, racial, or sexist exploitation. Although rooted in pre-Vatican II insights, liberation theology is in large measure a post-conciliar phenomenon.

Sixthly, there is *political* theology, a more comprehensive category than liberation theology, in which God, and more specifically the Kingdom of God, is seen as the critical principle by which all human, social, and political realities are judged. God is the limit against which all of our notions of justice, humaneness, peace, love, and so forth are finally measured.

Seventhly, there is *existential* theology, which emphasizes the individual believer as the place where God's saving activity occurs in its most concentrated and even in its normative form. Consistent with the position outlined by Kierkegaard in the nineteenth century and subsequently developed by Tillich, Bultmann, and others in the twentieth century, existentialist theology understands God as the source of authentic human personhood. To be exposed to the Word of God is to be open to the principle of conversion and growth. God is not "a" being, but Being itself. God is, more precisely, "holy Being," i.e., Being which *lets be* (Macquarrie). Except for Macquarrie, a formal doctrinal understanding of the Trinity tends to be either obscured or less than central to contemporary existentialist theology.

Eighthly, there is *process* theology, which clearly owes much of its inspiration to the Hegelian understanding of reality but, more immediately, to such twentieth-century theologians and philosophers as Whitehead and Teilhard. God is always in a state of flux, moving forward, co-creating history with us. God is neither static nor fixed. God is a dipolar God, in process of becoming other than what God is now, a process which involves a dialectical relationship between all that is meant by "God" and all that is meant by "world." God is at once absolute (as the one whose *existence* depends on no other being) and relative (as the one whose *actuality* is relative to all other beings). Indeed, God alone is relative to all other beings. God alone affects and is affected by all others (Charles Hartshorne). History is moving inexorably toward the Omega Point, when the Kingdom of God will have been brought to perfection.

Ninthly, there is *Transcendental Thomism*, most notably represented by Karl Rahner, which understands God as *the* Transcendent, above, beyond, and over everything else. God is the one to whom all reality is oriented, by a principle which is itself interior to all of reality. That principle is God. God is the "supernatural existential" which makes possible the knowledge of, and the movement toward, the Absolute. In the completion of that movement, both individually and corporately, we find our human perfection. God, therefore, is not "a" Being separate from the human person, but is Being itself, at once permeating and transcending the person. Because God permeates as well as transcends us, there is no standpoint from which we can get a "look at" God objectively. God is so fully constitutive of our human existence that almost everything we say about God can be translated into a declaration about our own existence as well. This is not to reduce all God-talk to philosophy, but simply to highlight the intimate connection between theology and anthropology in Transcendental Thomism. God is present to history in Jesus Christ and in a special way in the Church, where the human community has become explicitly conscious of itself in its ultimate relationship with God. The similarities with the Hegelian scheme are apparent, but so, too, are the differences.

Tenthly, there are various combinations of the above, some of which possess a measure of internal consistency and coherence while others are arbitrarily or uncritically eclectic.

The Second Vatican Council

The council, it must be noted, did not set out to produce a full-scale theology of God. On the contrary, insofar as it developed a more or less systematic theology of anything, that reality was the Church, as we shall see in Part IV. The council's understanding of God has to be inferred from what it says about other questions: the salvific value of non-Christian religions, the nature of the Church and its mission in the world.

The council's overriding concern was for unity, not only the unity of the Church but of the whole human race. "For all people comprise a single community, and have a single origin, since God made the whole race of men dwell over the entire face of the earth (cf. Acts 17:26). One also is their final goal: God. His providence, His manifestations of goodness, and His saving designs extend to all men (cf. Wis. 8:1; Acts 14:17; Rom. 2:6-7; 1 Tim. 2:4) against the day when the elect will be united in that Holy City ablaze with the splendor of God, where the nations will walk in His light (cf. Apoc. 21:23 f.)" (*Declaration on the Relationship of the Church to Non-Christian Religions*, n. 1).

"The Church knows that only God...meets the deepest longings of the human heart, which is never fully satisfied by what this world has to offer," the *Pastoral Constitution on the Church in the Modern World* declares. Thus, "only God, who created man to His own image and ransomed him from sin, provides a fully adequate answer" to the various questions about human existence. "This He does through what He has revealed in Christ His Son, who became man. Whoever follows after Christ, the perfect man, becomes himself more of a man" (n. 41). The theology of God and the theology of human existence converge at the point of the theology of Christ.

What does most to reveal God's presence in the world is "the brotherly charity of the faithful who are united in spirit as they work together for the faith of the gospel and who prove themselves a sign of unity" (n. 21). This community of faith, the Church, is itself the product of trinitarian action. The Church is called forth by the Father to carry forward the work of the Son with the sanctifying power of the Holy Spirit *(Dogmatic Constitution of the Church,* nn. 2-4). "Thus, the Church shines forth as 'a people made one with the unity of the Father, the Son, and the Holy Spirit' " (n. 4). (The quotation is derived from Saints Cyprian, Augustine, and John of Damascus.)

The call to unity is theologically grounded on the mystery of the Trinity itself. There is "a certain likeness between the union of the divine Persons, and in the union of God's sons in truth and charity" (*Pastoral Constitution on the Church in the Modern World,* n. 24).

GOD AND HISTORY:
SYSTEMATIC REFLECTIONS
Providence

The question of Providence is exceedingly difficult because it is at once comprehensive and complicated. It is comprehensive because it sums up God's relationship to the world and to all of history. It is complicated because it raises the problem of the interaction between divine sovereignty and human freedom. The former can never satisfactorily be described, and the latter can never satisfactorily be explained. With the question of Providence, therefore, we come as close to the heart of the problem of God as we possibly can. And the closer we come, the more deafening the silence.

Providence, first of all, refers to God's "foresight." It has to do with the way God shapes and directs history. Providence is not an exclusively Christian concept, nor even an exclusively religious concept. There are many *secular notions* of "Providence." We find the term first used in the fifth century B.C. and especially in Stoic philosophy. There is a cosmic harmony in the universe insured by some non-personal divinity or divinized rationality. Leibniz invoked a similar notion of a preestablished rational harmony. The Enlightenment's concept of inevitable progress in history is a secular variant of the Christian understanding of Providence, and so, too, are the Hegelian notion of world-reason and the Marxist interpretation of the dialectical movement of history.

The term appears only in the later part of the *Old Testament*, and then under Hellenistic influences (Job 10:12; Wisdom 6:7; 14:3; 17:2). But more important than the term itself is the concept it represents. The Old Testament clearly portrays Yahweh as a powerful, wise, merciful, and caring God. Creation, the election of Israel, the Exodus—all of these and more are manifestations of God's abiding concern for the world and especially for the Chosen People. History is itself the arena of God's saving action (Psalms 9:2; 26:7; 40:6; 71:17; 72:18; Isaiah 9:5; 28:29; 29:14).

The *New Testament* also attests to a basic faith in God's loving regard for the world, but now it is linked explicitly with faith in Christ as the great sign of God's love and concern. Jesus admonishes his listeners for their inordinate anxiety about material needs. "Look at the birds in the sky. . . . Learn a lesson from the way the wild flowers grow. . . . Your heavenly Father knows all that you need" (Matthew 6:26-34; see also 10:29-31). A notion of Providence is also embodied in the New Testament's understanding of *salvation history*. God has a "set purpose and plan," and it has been manifested in the death and resurrection of Christ (Acts of the Apostles 2:22-24). Indeed, even the villains of the piece are seen as instruments of the divine intervention: "They have brought about the very things which in your powerful providence you planned long ago" (Acts of the Apostles 4:28). The salvation-history perspective is more fully developed in Ephesians 1:3-14, where Christ is identified as the center-piece of the divine plan to "bring all things in the heavens and on earth into one under Christ's headship." We were chosen in him by God "who administers everything according to his will and counsel." And all of this has been "sealed with the Holy Spirit" who is "the pledge of our inheritance, the first payment against the full redemption of a people God has made his own, to praise his glory."

The conviction of faith in a provident God has been held consistently within the Church from the beginning. It is central, of course, to Irenaeus' theology of history (e.g., *Against Heresies*, chapter 25), to Augustine's polemic against the Pelagians, who insisted too strongly on the power of unaided human freedom, and to Thomas Aquinas' "sacred doctrine" about God (*Summa Theologica*, I, q. 22). It is as well the straightforward teaching of the First Vatican Council's *Dogmatic Constitution on the Catholic Faith* (chapter 1): "God protects and governs by his Providence all things which he has made. . . ." Finally, the Second Vatican Council urges us to discern in the "signs of the times" evidence of "God's presence and purpose" (*Pastoral Constitution on the Church in the Modern World*, n. 11).

Christian *belief* in the reality of Providence is not in doubt. Christian *understanding* of Providence is another matter entirely. Once again, we are confronted with the relationship of nature and grace (to which we referred in some detail in the preceding Part of the book). Some Catholic solutions have tended to overemphasize divine power at the apparent expense of human responsibility and freedom. We become mere actors in a play written wholly by God, with an ending already precisely determined regardless of our flubbing our lines and missing our cues. We need not trouble ourselves, therefore, about this world's injustices. God will take care of everything in the end. At the other extreme, some solutions have tried so hard to uphold the enduring value of human effort that God becomes little more than a play's producer, backing it with his money and influence but depending utterly upon the ability of the actors for its eventual success. Thus, if we do not overcome injustice by our political efforts, it will simply swallow us up in the end. And still others have attempted a compromise position, assigning divine and human activity on a fifty-fifty basis (we are completely free in our actions, but God must simultaneously *concur* with our free decisions and invest them with efficacy).

The later medieval, post-Tridentine theological debates *de auxiliis* (concerning helps) were not so much about the broad issue of Providence as about the narrower, although related, question of *actual grace*. They were essentially fruitless controversies. The Church never took an official stand on behalf of either party, the Banezians or the Molinists, because both took for granted that every act of free consent was itself from God's grace (anything less than that would have been Pelagian, and thus unorthodox).

Karl Rahner's view is representative of the Catholic theological and doctrinal tradition as it is understood today: We begin from where we are. We profess a faith and practice a religion which comprises prayer for God's intervention, miracles, an understanding of history as saving history, persons invested with authority from on high, an inspired book which comes from God, ritual acts which mediate the presence of God, and so forth. On the other hand, our theological starting point seems to say that "God is everywhere insofar as he grounds everything, and he is nowhere insofar as everything that is grounded is created, and everything which appears in this way within the world of our experience is different from God, separated by an absolute chasm between God and what is not God" (*Foundations of Christian Faith*, p. 82).

Rahner follows the Thomistic principle that God works through secondary causes; i.e., God is the ultimate cause, but not just one cause among many. God-as-cause is in the world as a totality, but not in any particular things within the world. That is, God does not "intervene" in the world in the sense that God acts now here and now there; now in this event, now in that; now in this person, now in that. God "intervenes" in the sense that *God is always there.* The world is fundamentally and radically open to God. "Consequently, every real intervention of God in his world, although it is free and cannot be deduced, is always only the becoming historical and becoming concrete of that 'intervention' in which God as the transcendental ground of the world has from the outset embedded himself in this world as its self-communicating ground" (p. 87).

And so we come back to the fundamental problem for the Christian understanding of God: How can God be God, i.e., totally other, and at the same time in the world, e.g., in Christ, in the Church, in the sacraments? We can exaggerate the first at the expense of the second, and vice versa. With the hope of avoiding both extremes, Rahner offers an example. We get a "good idea." It seems to come "out of the blue." We can interpret it in a purely physiological and psychological way and conclude that it is not in any sense an intervention of God. Or we can experience ourselves as a subject radically open to God (i.e., as a "transcendental subject"). At the moment we accept that experience, the "good idea" becomes a part of that total network of historical and worldly relationships whose meaning and unity are given by God. In that sense, the "good idea" is an "inspiration" from God.

Rahner writes: "Of course it could be objected against this that in this way everything can be regarded as a special providence, as an intervention of God, presupposing only that I accept the concrete constellation of my life and of the world in such a way that it becomes a positive, salvific concretization of my transcendental relationship to God in freedom. But against this objection we can simply ask the counter-question: Why, then, may this not be the case?" (p. 89). He continues: "Because the subject's response in freedom is itself really and truly for the subject himself something given to him, without it losing thereby the character of the subject's own responsible and accountable action, a good decision along with everything which it presupposes as its mediation correctly has the character of an intervention of God, even though this takes place in and through human freedom, and hence can be explained functionally to the degree that the history of freedom can be explained, namely, insofar as it is based on elements objectified in time and space" (*ibid.*).

There is never, therefore, a salvific act of God on our behalf which is not also and always a salvific act of our own. Our actions are truly free, and they are at the same time grounded in the grace or presence of God. We can never even begin to have anything to do with God or to approach God without already being moved by God's grace. On the other hand, this movement toward salvation never takes place without our involvement and our freedom.

To be sure, we have not solved the problem of nature and grace, of divine sovereignty and human freedom, or of Providence as such. But we have at least identified the problem as it is, and taken note of the limits within which all attempted solutions must be developed. No explanation of Providence satisfies the biblical, theological, and doctrinal traditions of the Church if it takes history out of God's hands (Pelagianism, Deism, e.g.). And no explanation suffices which takes history out of human hands (extreme Augustinianism and Calvinism). God is present to every person and to history itself as an inner principle which makes forward movement possible without sacrifice of freedom. Precisely *how* that is done, we do not know. We can, like Rahner and others, propose answers based on specific philosophical premises. But these are always explanations "after the fact," so to speak. And that, after all, is what theology is: faith seeking understanding. Theology does not produce the given, but reflects upon it. Theology does not make "possible" the given, but reflects on the terms of its "possibility." Theology, in the end, is not faith.

Miracles

Few theological questions are treated so unsatisfactorily as the question of miracles. Discussion moves from one extreme to the other: from the extreme right, where miracles are simply accepted in a fundamentalistic sense (they happened in exactly the way they are described in the Bible or by the people in post-biblical times—e.g., the appearances of the Blessed Virgin Mary at Lourdes, France), to the extreme left, where miracles are rejected in principle because they are presumed to be disruptions of the inflexible laws of nature and of physics. In between there are also other sorts of inadequate explanations. We are assured that the *fact* of miracles is not important, only their significance. Or we are reminded, following the Rahnerian approach outlined above, that God is already everywhere as the principle of free action and that, therefore, whatever happens, happens through the grace of God; in that sense everything is a miracle.

All of these explanations fail because they cannot be reconciled with certain clear principles which emerge from the New Testament:

Miracles were as important to the ministry of Jesus as his preaching. They express the saving *power* of God shown in Jesus' healing, feeding the hungry, curing the sick, even raising the dead. Indeed, when the disciples of John the Baptist came out to the desert to ask Jesus if he was the One who was promised, Jesus told them to go back and tell John what they had seen and heard: "The blind recover their sight, cripples walk, lepers are cured, the deaf hear, dead men are raised to life, and the poor have the good news preached to them" (Luke 7:22).

Miracles are linked with faith. "If I do not perform my Father's works," Jesus said, "put no faith in me" (John 10:37; see also 15:24). On the other hand, it is possible to be present at the performance of a miracle and not see it as a miracle at all (notice, e.g., the inability or refusal of many to believe in Jesus even after the multiplication of the loaves and fishes—John 6:26). Indeed, it happened that Jesus could not work miracles in his home country "so much did their lack of faith distress him" (Mark 6:5). Instead he devoted himself to teaching.

The miracle stories are meant to evoke faith, but not all of the stories are on the same plane. The fundamentalist forgets that the biblical accounts are not eyewitness reports, nor scientifically tested documentation, nor historical, medical, or psychological records. They are rather unsophisticated popular narratives, entirely at the service of the proclamation of the Lordship of Jesus. Recent biblical scholarship discloses that there are many different levels at work in the various accounts: Some are patterned after Old Testament models; others follow the narrative styles common to Jewish and Hellenistic stories; others are simply collected accounts (redactional summaries) of the evangelists which give the impression of a continuous and widespread miracle-working activity on the part of Jesus.

But certain events apparently did take place, and they were taken, by friend and foe alike, as marvelous in their own right. The sick were cured, for example. Jesus' enemies did not challenge the fact of the cure but the propriety of curing on the Sabbath.

In the accounts of several of the miracles, too many details are given which have too little interest to have been invented and yet which are so human and true to life that they suggest the presence of an eyewitness. The cure of the possessed boy is a case in point (Mark 9:14-29).

We are left, in the end, with more questions than answers. Did Jesus really walk on water to calm the waves during a sudden storm, or was the story constructed after the fact as a sign that God hears our prayers for help in times of distress? Were those "possessed by the devil" simply suffering from temporary mental illness, or did the impact of Jesus' kindly personality perhaps effect a momentary remission of a more serious emotional problem? Did the story of the coin in the fish's mouth simply answer Jesus' request to catch a fish in order to pay the temple tax? Did other stories, such as the raising of Jairus' daughter from the dead, simply anticipate the resurrection of Christ in order to present Jesus as the Lord of life and death (keeping in mind, all the while, that when the Gospels were written, they were removed from the historical Jesus by a few decades)?

At the very least, something significant and impressive occurred in the life and ministry of Jesus, over and above his preaching and teaching. He had an impact upon people—the sick, the troubled, the bereaved—in a way that clearly set him apart from his contemporaries. Indeed, he himself pointed to his good works as moments in which the power of God operated in him and through him.

That Jesus performed miracles as signs of revelation is certainly the belief of the New Testament Church and of the official

Church of the post-biblical period. The First Vatican Council teaches this in its *Dogmatic Constitution on the Catholic Faith* (chapter 3), and the Second Vatican Council acknowledges their existence at least in passing in its *Dogmatic Constitution on the Church*: "The miracles of Jesus also confirm that the kingdom has already arrived on earth..." (n. 5).

Just *what* those miracles were, from a scientific, empirically verifiable, objective point of view (i.e., apart from faith), is difficult to say. We can at least exclude the too-simple solutions of the extreme left and the extreme right, and reject the practical avoidance of the problem in some of modern theology.

Miracles are manifestations of the power of God and as such are consistent with divine Providence. They were central to Jesus' ministry. They enter into the formation of our own faith. Beyond that, many questions remain open.

Evil

We move from a very difficult problem to a nearly impossible one: *the mystery of evil*. Again, simple answers abound. At the extreme left, God is portrayed as not involved at all in evil because God is not much involved in good either. At the extreme right, God is directly and immediately implicated in evil. God deliberately, almost callously, inflicts suffering and pain upon us in order to teach us a lesson or gain some unknown greater good. And in the middle, we have the usual traditional explanations that God does not cause evil; God only permits it. Or that evil is nothing in itself; it is simply the absence of good. For many, of course, the very existence of evil (natural disasters, the terminal illness of a young child, the sudden death of a father or a mother, a brutal murder, an act of terrorism, Auschwitz) is the single most persuasive argument *against* the existence of God, or at least against the existence of the God of Christianity. They cannot readily explain, on the other hand, how there can also be so much goodness and heroic charity in a world *without God*.

In the preceding discussion, we noted that it is easier to accept the meaning of miracles than it is to accept the fact of their existence. In the case of evil, just the reverse is true: It is easier to accept the fact of evil than it is to understand its meaning.

Evil, like a miracle, is *power*. But unlike a miracle, it is a power against life, not for it. So intense and so focused may this power be that it can be personified as *Satan* (from the Hebrew word *sātān*, which means "adversary"). The New Testament carried over the general Jewish teaching about evil spirits and the devil. He is the evil one (Matthew 13:19), the enemy (Luke 10:19), the father of lies (John 8:44), etc. He is especially opposed to Jesus Christ, and their enmity reaches a fever pitch in the passion (Luke 22:3,31; John 13:27; 1 Corinthians 2:8), but therein the devil is also finally defeated (1 Corinthians 2:8; John 12:31; Revelation 12:7-12). This opposition continues, however, in the history of the Church until it is overcome once and for all at the end (Revelation 20:8,10).

Again, *that* there is evil in the world is obvious. That such evil is often collective and at the same time very personalized is also evident. *What* this evil is in its core is not so clear. To the extent that the Church has addressed itself officially to the question, the official magisterium has affirmed the existence of the devil and of evil spirits, has acknowledged their negative effect on the course of history, and has insisted that they, like all of creation (material and spiritual), come under the sovereignty of God. Contrary to the impression one might gain from some recent novels and films, evil spirits do not control us to the point of suppressing human freedom and responsibility (see, for example, the Council of Trent's *Decree on Original Sin*).

If it is clear *that* evil exists, it is also clear that God wars against it and that we are called to participate with God in the struggle against evil in every form: social injustice, oppression, infidelity, dishonesty, e.g. "Caught in this conflict, man is obliged to wrestle constantly if he is to cling to what is good" (Second Vatican Council, *Pastoral Constitution on the Church in the Modern World*, n. 37). Indeed, God sent his Son to save us from "the power of darkness and of Satan" (*Decree on the Church's Missionary Activity*, n. 3).

The fact of evil is undeniable, but why is there evil at all? If it is any comfort, the reader should be assured that he or she has not missed the definitive explanation somewhere along the line. None of the greatest minds of human history, whether Christian or not, has devised a compelling answer. Nor are we about to do so here, succeeding where all others have failed. We can only identify some of the principal options we have in response to evil, and especially to innocent suffering, and then try to decide which is the most intelligent and which conforms best to Christian faith.

First, we can rebel and revolt, shaking an angry fist if not at the real God then at some conventional idea of God. This is the way of Ivan Karamazov in Dostoevsky's *The Brothers Karamazov* and of Albert Camus in his *Rebel*. Secondly, we can try to bear up stoically, tight-lipped, avoiding the question "Why?" We simply accept what we can neither understand nor change. Or, thirdly, we can stand with *Job*, placing our complete trust in God even in the face of the incomprehensible, and with *Jesus*, from whom we have received the "good news" that God wishes to deliver us from all evil, and indeed that suffering itself can be as redemptive for us individually as it was for all humankind in the passion and death of Christ.

But even Jesus did not *explain* suffering. He endured it, an innocent Lamb in the sight of God (1 Peter 1:19). But in the resurrection his suffering and death acquired meaning beyond themselves. Such meaning is not always, nor even often, apparent. Christ teaches us that suffering *can* have a meaning, or can *acquire* a meaning. We can learn from it. We can be ennobled by it. We can grow through it. For the God who encounters us in suffering is a God who knows suffering from the inside, as it were, in Jesus Christ. God is literally a *sympathetic* ("suffering with") God. The reality of evil and suffering notwithstanding, God is a God of mercy, of forgiveness, of compassion for all. Furthermore, God has promised the Kingdom to those of us who remain steadfast and faithful even in the midst of evil and suffering, a Kingdom where "he shall wipe away every tear from [our] eyes, and there shall be no more death or mourning, crying out or pain, for the former world has passed away" (Revelation 21:4).

In the end, the problem of evil and of innocent suffering reveals as well as conceals the God of love. For if it were not for our faith in God as a God of justice and mercy, of love and peace, of truth and loyalty, we would not recognize the reality of evil in all its depths; nor, what is more important, would we be impelled to do something about it, risking even our lives for the good of others. (Indeed, many who deny God do evil and call it good.) Corruption in government, for example, would not bother us very much, and certainly we would do very little about it, if we did not have at the same time a highly refined sense of moral and political idealism. For some, corruption mocks and negates the ideals (the reaction of the cynic). For others, corruption makes the ideals even more urgently attractive and worthwhile.

But the fact of evil and of innocent suffering remains. We can do nothing about evil in general (i.e., we cannot completely eliminate it from the world) and relatively little about it in the concrete (as our everyday experience attests). But what *is* under our control is the manner in which we respond to what is so frequently inevitable. We are *free*, and our freedom is, in turn, a condition which makes some forms of evil possible. Will our free response be one of rebellion and passivity, or will it be a response of trust and renewed growth? Apart from faith in God, the problem of evil (which presumably *destroys* faith in God!) is unresolvable. And apart from faith in Christ and in the redemptive value of his passion and death, evil and innocent suffering can have no positive meaning at all.

The Church insists on the meaning of miracles, and sometimes stammers a bit regarding their factuality. In the case of evil, however, the Church joins the rest of humankind in acknowledging evil's wretched factuality, but it shares with others the agony of interpretation. Nevertheless, it does not stammer here. The Church's faith and trust are as forthright as Job's, built as they are upon the rock of Christ, and strengthened as they are by the power of the Holy Spirit.

Prayer

Can we change the course of events through prayer? Can we alter God's will and so receive some blessing that otherwise might pass us by? Can we fend off some evil occurrence by specifically imploring God to save us from it?

The problem of prayer is difficult because it is a component of the difficult problems of Providence and of evil. Prayer has to do with the interaction between divine sovereignty and human freedom. Just as we can distort the meaning of Providence by exaggerating the one over the other, so we can distort the meaning of prayer by seeing it, on the one hand, as a method of manipulating the mind and heart of God, or, on the other hand, as a completely useless activity no more sublime or mysterious than autosuggestion or the power of positive thinking.

In accord with the theological position we have already taken, prayer is a conscious, deliberate coming to terms with our actual situation before God. When we explicitly advert to that relationship, we are praying. Every action we perform as a way of expressing our sense of that relationship with God is a prayer. Every act whereby we sacrifice our own personal interests for a higher purpose because of our explicit faith in God is a prayer. Prayer is a *response* to, not an initiation of dialogue with, God. It is an act by which we accept ourselves as subjects radically open to the Transcendent, Who is God. Prayer is, therefore, always an act of faith and of hope, which is fulfilled in our surrender to the love of God.

In prayers of *praise* and *thanksgiving*, we give more explicit and deliberate form to our sense of the majesty and sovereignty of God and of our own place within the total scheme of reality. In prayers of *contrition*, we acknowledge our failure to respect this fundamental relationship with God and deliberately open ourselves anew to God's abiding presence within us, a presence which makes it possible for us to become someone other than we are, someone better than we are. In prayers of *petition*, we explicitly come to terms with our needs and those of other people. We make ourselves ever more sensitive to our obligations to do whatever is possible to fulfill those needs, whether for ourselves or for others. And insofar as those prayers of petition are public (as in the Eucharist), we put other members of the community on notice and draw them into the process of identifying and meeting needs, and they, in turn, enlarge our own horizons and make us more fully aware of the plight of others besides ourselves and our loved ones.

Prayer, in other words, does not effect a change in God but in ourselves. To that extent, prayer affects the course of history indirectly rather than directly.

SPECIAL QUESTIONS:
PERSONHOOD AND FATHERHOOD OF GOD
God As Person

Is God "a person"? We are not asking here the question of the Trinity, whether there are three Persons in the one Godhead. We raise instead the question whether God is a separate Being among beings. Putting the question that way, the answer is "Of course not. God is not *a* person because God is not any one thing or being." But if the noun *person* is taken analogically, the answer has to be different. Does the reality we name "God" have qualities which we also attribute to persons? Yes, insofar as we understand persons as centers of intelligence, love, compassion, graciousness, fidelity, and the like. What we mean by the noun *God* certainly must comprehend such qualities as these. In other words, it is better to attribute "personality" to God than to deny it entirely and to look upon God as some impersonal, unconscious cosmic law. And yet the attribution is always analogical; i.e., God is *like* a person, but God is also very much *unlike* a person. In the end, the revelation of God in the person of Jesus Christ must tip the balance in favor of attributing personality to God than of denying it.

God As Father

If Jesus were still with us in his fleshly, historical existence today, would he be speaking of his relationship to God as one of Son and Father and of our relationship to God as one of children and Father? Or would the raising of our consciousness about sexuality and the oppressive character of sexist language have also affected Jesus' preaching and teaching? This is an entirely speculative question, of course, but it would seem reasonable to suppose that Jesus would have modified substantially his references to God. During his own life-time, Jesus mingled freely with women and emphasized their fundamental human equality before God.

Indeed, even the most vigorous exponents of a feminist point of view exempt Jesus himself from their standard criticisms of institutional religion and of Christianity in particular.

But the facts are that Jesus did live at a certain time, in a certain place, among certain people, within a certain social, cultural, economic, and political context. He was at once a product of, and a prophet to, his own age. But having granted the principle that Jesus' references to the Fatherhood of God are historically conditioned, we must nonetheless come to terms with the transhistorical meaning of those references. Even if Jesus had spoken of God as our Mother, he would still have had the same essential message to communicate about God. What is that message implied in the Fatherhood of God?

God is a loving and caring God (Matthew 6:5-8, 26-34; 7:11; 10:29-31; 18:14; Luke 11:13). God's love must inspire us to love even our enemies (Matthew 5:48). God is likewise a forgiving God, even a model of forgiveness (Matthew 6:14-15; 18:35; Mark 11:25). Nowhere is this more movingly expressed than in the parable of the prodigal son, also known as the parable of the forgiving father (Luke 15:11-32).

Furthermore, Jesus' references to his own relationship with his Father in heaven simply underscore the intimacy of Jesus with God (whether God is spoken of as Father or as Mother, as Husband or Wife, as Son or as Daughter). Jesus' will and God's are one (Matthew 26:39-43; Mark 14:35-39; Luke 22:41-42; 23:34,46). God is the source of Jesus' power and authority (John 1:14,18; 16:15). To know Jesus is to know God (John 14:7-9) because Jesus and God are one (John 10:30). Jesus is in God, and God is in Jesus (John 10:38; 14:10). Whatever Jesus teaches, he has learned from God (John 8:28-38). Whatever Jesus does, he does as the work of God (John 10:32; 14:10). No one comes to God except through Jesus (John 14:6), but God is greater than the historical Jesus (John 14:28). Jesus sends his disciples forth with the same fullness of power with which he was sent (John 20:21).

In each of the preceding texts it is *the Father* and not the more generic noun *God* that is used. But the fact that we can so easily substitute *God* for *Father* suggests that it is not the Fatherhood of God that is important to Jesus but the Godhood of the Father.

SUMMARY

1.   The problem of God is, as we have pointed out before, the other side of the problem of human existence. This chapter, therefore, must be correlated with chapter 5, which outlines a Christian understanding of human existence consistent with Catholicism's perception of the fundamental relationship of nature and grace.

2.   Although Christians are no less conditioned in their understanding of God by history and by factors of various sorts (economic, political, cultural, social, e.g.), it is clear nonetheless that there is a *distinctively Christian conviction about God*, namely, that God has become incarnate in Jesus of Nazareth, and that God is triune. God is Father, Son, and Holy Spirit; i.e., God is creator of all that is, is intimately identified with all that is, and is the principle of life and unity of all that is.

3.   But this distinctively Christian understanding of God raises a major problem: If God is one, how is it that Jesus is also invested with divinity, and how is it, further, that God is also portrayed as triune? These are the questions which largely shaped the history of Christian theology in the first four or five centuries.

4.   Because of the undeniably intimate religious link between Judaism and Christianity, the Christian understanding of God has its roots in the *Old Testament*, where God (Yahweh) is a living God, i.e., is present and active in the history of Israel, is the Lord of all humankind, the giver of all life. One lives by heeding Yahweh's word.

5.   The *New Testament* identifies Jesus with God (especially the Prologue of John's Gospel). All of the saving attributes of the God of the Old Testament are actualized anew in Christ. God pardons and reconciles through Christ. God continues to bestow life through Christ. And God bestows the Spirit through Christ.

6.   Over against pagan polytheism, the earliest *Apostolic Fathers and apologists* stressed the doctrine of the one God, creator and sustainer of all things.

7.   In the *third century*, emphasis shifted from the oneness of God to the triune pluralism of God, when the Church could no longer avoid the difficult questions posed by the apparent discrepancy between its uncompromising monotheism, on the one hand, and the clear testimony of Sacred Scripture and of its liturgical and prayer life that God is Father, Son, and Holy Spirit.

8.   This fundamental confession of faith in the Trinity did not first emerge from philosophical speculation about the inner life of God (the

so-called "immanent Trinity") but from a response to the activity of God in the world (the so-called "economic Trinity").

9. One of the earliest attempts at a solution to the problem of the-one-and-the-three proved unorthodox, namely, the *Arian* solution, which made Christ something more than a man but less than God the Almighty (*Pantokrator*). The implications were serious: If Christ is a creature like us, he has no special standing before God, and we are still in our sins.

10. The *Council of Nicea* (325) gave the definitive answer to Arius. The Son does not "emanate" from the Father's will, as a creature. The Son is "begotten, not made." He is "of the same substance" (*homoousios*) as the Father. For the first time, the Church moved officially from biblical to speculative categories to define its faith.

11. This transition did not occur without opposition. The Eusebians (followers of Eusebius of Caesarea) preferred to say no more than what Scripture seemed to be saying, namely, that the Son is "like" (*homoiousios*) the Father. Through the efforts of Athanasius and Hilary of Poitiers, the *homoousion* and *homoiousion* parties were reconciled. The agreement was sealed at the *Council of Alexandria* (362), from which emerged a new orthodox formula: "one substance, three Persons."

12. Attention shifted in the *fourth century* to the question of the Holy Spirit's relation to the Father and the Son. It was the so-called *Cappadocian* theologians (Basil, Gregory of Nyssa, and Gregory of Nazianzus) who established the coequal divinity of the Spirit with the Father and the Son, without prejudice to the oneness of substance in the Godhead.

13. By the end of the fourth century the Church was in a position to synthesize and officially express its newly systematized trinitarian faith in creedal form. The *First Council of Constantinople* (381) endorsed the so-called *Nicaeo-Constantinopolitan Creed*, which is recited each week in the Catholic Eucharist.

14. *Augustine* approached the mystery of the Trinity from a different starting point. Instead of beginning with the saving activity of the three Persons in salvation history (as the Greek Fathers did) and working back to the unity of the Godhead, Augustine began with the one divine nature and tried to understand how the three Persons share in that nature without dividing it. Threeness in God is not rooted in threeness of substance (essence, being) but in threeness of *relations*: of begetting, of being begotten, and of proceeding. Augustine employed analogies drawn from human consciousness to explain this inner life of the Trinity (remembering, understanding, loving), and this is perhaps his most original contribution to trinitarian theology. He also anticipated the teaching

of the Council of Florence in the Middle Ages that everything in God is one except what is differentiated by the opposition of relations; i.e., the Father and the Son are one God, except insofar as the Father begets and the Son is begotten, and so on.

15. *Anselm*, most famous for his ontological argument for the existence of God (God is an idea than which nothing greater can be thought), carried forward the Augustinian principle that God is absolutely one except for the opposition of relations between and among the three Persons. This, in turn, provided the theological basis for the principle of the mutual indwelling of the three divine Persons: The Father is always in the Son and the Holy Spirit; the Son is always in the Father and the Spirit; and the Spirit is always in the Father and the Son.

16. The *Fourth Lateran Council* (1215) repudiated *Albigensianism*, one of the most dangerous errors ever to attack the Church because of its rejection of the intrinsic goodness of created matter. The council taught that God is the author of both matter and spirit, and that Christ is fully God, with a human as well as a divine nature. The council also produced a doctrinal formulation on the Trinity which became the basis of most of Scholastic theology.

17. *Thomas Aquinas* insisted on the identity of essence and existence in God (God's essence is "to be") and on the participation of the created order in the Being of God, Who is the First Cause of all that is. Insofar as God ordains all things toward their goal, God is a provident God. And insofar as there is only one goal for all reality—created and recreated alike—the order of nature and the order of grace are radically one. Aquinas, too, carried forward the Augustinian approach to the mystery of the Trinity, employing similar psychological explanations of the relations between and among the three Persons.

18. The *Second Council of Lyons* (1274) and the *Council of Florence* (1438-1440) both were concerned with the schism between East and West, and insofar as the split was traceable to the divergent ways in which East and West interpreted the procession of the Holy Spirit in the Trinity, both councils helped clarify the Church's trinitarian faith. *Lyons* reflected the Latin approach in stressing the procession of the Spirit from the Father *and* the Son (*Filioque*). *Florence* reaffirmed the Latin approach, but allowed also for the Greek approach, namely, that the Holy Spirit proceeds from the Father *through* the Son (*per Filium*). For the Greeks the *Filioque* implied a double principle in God; for the Latins the *per Filium* implied a subordination of Son to Father. Neither side intended what the other side thought was implied, and much of the controversy was, in fact, unnecessary.

19. The *Council of Florence* also enshrined the principle, to which reference has already been made, that *in God all things are one except what is differentiated by the opposition of relations between and among the Persons*.

20. Insofar as the *Council of Trent* (1545–1563) addressed itself directly to the problem of God, it did so in reaction against the insistence of the major Reformers (*Luther* and *Calvin* in particular) that God deliberately and explicitly excludes some people from salvation (predestination to reprobation, to use the technical term). The Catholic tradition, articulated at Trent, argues that God not only makes a *declaration* of our worthiness for salvation but actually *transforms* us from within by the indwelling of the Holy Spirit and offers this transformation to every person, without exception. Only a free act of the will on our part can negate God's universal salvific will.

21. The Christian understanding of God tended to zig-zag in the post-Reformation period between Trent and Vatican I (1869–1870). *Blaise Pascal* gave a strongly spiritual or ascetical cast to the theology of God in the seventeenth century, but by the next century serious challenges against traditional theology were mounted by such Protestant philosophers as *Kant, Hegel, Feuerbach,* and *Nietzsche.* The first two proposed new ways of understanding the reality of God (the former, as Supreme Lawgiver; the latter, as historical Process); the other two in effect denied the reality of God altogether. The influence of all four, but especially of Kant and Hegel, on subsequent Christian theology is undeniably strong. Meanwhile, Protestant theologians were also introducing new modes of understanding God. *Schleiermacher*, the forerunner of Liberal Protestantism of the late nineteenth and early twentieth centuries, devalued the doctrine of the Trinity and focused instead on our feeling of absolute dependence on the God of our consciousness. *Kierkegaard*, who anticipated the Barthian neo-orthodox, neo-Reformation reaction of the First World War period, insisted on the "infinitely qualitative difference" between God and ourselves and underlined the individual character of our relationship with God.

22. The *First Vatican Council* (1869–1870) rejected some of these positions (rationalism, pantheism, and the like), insisting on the uniqueness and the difference of God over against the world.

23. The *Second Vatican Council* (1962–1965) taught that God is the origin of all that is; therefore, the human race is called to unity. God also meets our deepest human longings, if only we open ourselves to the divine presence, especially in Christ. The most effective sign of God's presence among us is our fellowship with one another. The Church is

called to be a sacrament of God in the world, a sign of the same unity which is to be found in the Trinity.

24.   *Contemporary Christian understandings of God* are many and varied. Some emphasize the divine side of the God/human relationship; others emphasize the human side. The latter propose more transcendental understandings of God (God as "wholly other"); the former propose more immanentist understandings of God (God is to be met in the needs of the world).

25.   *Transcendental Thomism*, which comes closest to the perspective of this book, understands God as *the* Transcendent—above, beyond, and over everything else—who is at the same time within everything as the principle of life and movement (God as the "supernatural existential"). God is present to history in a particular way in Jesus Christ and in the Church. In the Church the human community has become explicitly conscious of itself in its ultimate relationship with God through Christ and the Holy Spirit.

26.   *Providence* is, literally, God's "foresight" in relation to the created order and to history. Both Old and New Testaments present God as a provident, caring, concerned, powerful God. History is God's history as well as ours. It is salvation history. God's plan and design is centered on Christ, and the sending of the Holy Spirit is the "first payment" against the full redemption offered in Christ.

27.   *Belief* in Providence has been consistent throughout the entire post-biblical history of the Church, but there have been different *understandings* of that belief, some stressing the divine power at the apparent expense of human freedom, and vice versa.

28.   Transcendental Thomism, represented by Karl Rahner, notes with Thomas Aquinas that God works through *secondary causes*. God does not "intervene" in the world in the sense that God interrupts and interferes with the normal course of human events. God "intervenes" in the sense that God is there from the beginning and that the world is radically open to the presence of God from its beginning. Our actions remain completely free, but they are at the same time grounded in the grace or presence of God. Precisely how this is the case we do not know, but we can exclude clearly unsatisfactory solutions which diminish the sovereignty of God or human freedom. We are left, then, with attempted explanations based on specific philosophical premises, such as those identified with Transcendental Thomism.

29.   *Miracles* pose yet another difficult problem, a variation really on the question of Providence. We can come to some understanding of what miracles might mean and what they might signify, but we find it far

more difficult to know what, if anything, actually happened. What is clear, however, is that: (1) miracles were important to the ministry of Jesus; (2) they were challenges to faith; (3) they vary considerably in the way they are "reported" in the New Testament; (4) the factuality of some of them was not challenged, even by the enemies of Jesus; and (5) some "reports" of miracles are too detailed and too true to life simply to be dismissed.

30. *That* Jesus performed miracles is certainly the belief of the New Testament and of the post-biblical Church. Just *what* those miracles were from an objective point of view is difficult to say. We exclude at once, however, two extreme explanations: the one which rejects miracles of any kind as a matter of principle, and the other which accepts the reality of miracles in an uncritical, fundamentalistic way. Miracles, in the end, are manifestations of the presence and power of God and are consistent with the doctrine of Providence. Beyond that, many questions remain open.

31. *Evil*, like a miracle, is power. But unlike a miracle, evil is a power against life, not for it. Sometimes evil is so intense that it can be personalized. The word *Satan* is derived from the Hebrew word which means "adversary." There is a special enmity between Satan and Christ, but Satan is definitively vanquished in the passion and death of Jesus; the triumph of Christ over evil will be made manifest finally and perfectly when the Kingdom of God appears in all its fulness.

32. The problem of evil is the reverse of the problem of miracles. We have a problem with the factuality of miracles, but not at all with the factuality of evil. We find it relatively easy to offer explanations of the meaning of miracles, but we find it very difficult indeed to find meaning in evil.

33. Human response to evil may take three forms: (1) rebellion, (2) resignation, or (3) trust and hope. The third course is that of *Job* in the Old Testament and, of course, of *Jesus Christ* in the New Testament. For the Christian, suffering can have meaning, or at least can acquire meaning. Because of Christ, suffering can be redemptive, even enriching. Furthermore, in Christ God knows what it is to suffer. God is literally a sympathetic ("suffering with") God. God wars against evil and seeks our collaboration in the struggle against the powers of darkness.

34. Indeed, if it were not for our faith in a loving God, the existence of evil would not be so much of a problem. We might not even acknowledge evil as evil (and, in fact, many who do not believe in God do evil and call it good).

35.   *Prayer* is a conscious, deliberate acknowledgment of, and coming to terms with, our actual situation before God. Through prayer we accept our relationship with God and become more fully aware of the implications of that relationship. Our understanding of prayer, however, cannot be prejudicial to the sovereignty of God or to human freedom and responsibility.

36.   Is God "a *person*"? No and yes. No, because God is not *an* anything. God is not even *a* Being. Yes, in an analogical sense. God is *like* a person in that God is loving, caring, compassionate, faithful, forgiving. It is better to attribute personality to God than to deny it to God.

37.   God is also Father, but not in the sexist sense. God has no sex. Our God is not a male. On the other hand, the Fatherhood of God embodies truths about God which transcend sexual identity. God is loving, caring, forgiving, etc. And Jesus' relationship with God is as intimate as the relationship of child with parent, and more! Jesus is the way to God. All his power and authority are derived from God. God is in him, and he in God. It is the Godhood of the Father that counts, not the Fatherhood of God.

SUGGESTED READINGS

Baum, Gregory. *Man Becoming*. New York: Herder & Herder, 1970.

Dupré, Louis. *The Other Dimension*. New York: Doubleday, 1972.

Fortman, Edward J., ed. *The Theology of God: Commentary* . Milwaukee: Bruce, 1968.

——————, ed. *The Triune God: A Historical Study of the Doctrine of the Trinity*. Philadelphia: Westminster Press, 1972.

Gilkey, Langdon. *Naming the Whirlwind: The Renewal of God–Language*. Indianapolis: Bobbs-Merrill, 1969.

——————. *Reaping the Whirlwind: A Christian Interpretation of History*. New York: Seabury Press, 1976.

Kehoe, Kimball, ed. *Theology of God: Sources*. Milwaukee: Bruce, 1971.

Küng, Hans. *On Being a Christian*. New York: Doubleday, 1976. pp. 57–88; 214–65; 295–318.

Lewis, C.S. *The Problem of Pain*. New York: Macmillan, 1945.

Monden, Louis. *Signs and Wonders: A Study of the Miraculous Element in Religion*. New York: Desclee, 1966.

Murray, John Courtney. *The Problem of God: Yesterday and Today*. New Haven: Yale University Press, 1964.

Rahner, Karl. *Foundations of Christian Faith*. New York: Seabury Press, 1978, pp. 44–89.

——————. *A Rahner Reader*. Ed. Gerald A. McCool. New York: Seabury Press, 1975, pp. 23–45; 132–136.

· X ·

THE TRINITY

THE PLACE AND IMPORTANCE
OF THE DOCTRINE

The whole of Christian theology is trinitarian in origin and in content. In terms of *origin*, Christian theology is made possible by the self-communication of God the Father in the Word-made-flesh, and our apprehension of God-in-Christ occurs only because we have been drawn by the Holy Spirit who dwells within our hearts and elevates our whole consciousness. In terms of *content*, Christian theology is concerned with creation, sin, grace, redemption, reconciliation, salvation, and the re-creation of the whole cosmic order in the Kingdom of God. All of these, and more, are component parts of the doctrine of the Trinity. "It is impossible to believe explicitly in the mystery of Christ," Thomas Aquinas wrote, "without faith in the Trinity, for the mystery of Christ includes that the Son of God took flesh, that He renewed the world through the grace of the Holy Spirit, and, again, that He was conceived by the Holy Spirit" (*Summa Theologica*, II-II, q. 2, a. 8).

Because the mystery of the Trinity is at once fundamental and central to Christian theology, the doctrine can be placed either at the beginning or at the end of a comprehensive statement of Christian faith. At the *beginning*, it anticipates the exploration of the whole theological terrain and provides the inquirer with a view of what is to come. At the *end*, it summarizes and synthesizes what has preceded it and provides the inquirer with a substantial review.

A third possibility occurs, however, and it is the one pursued in this book. The doctrine of the Trinity is placed somewhere nearer to the middle, consistent with the process of human discovery operative in the individual consciousness and in history itself. The doctrine of the Trinity presupposes some awareness of God and of God's active and gracious presence in Jesus Christ. That awareness, in turn, presupposes some experience of the Transcendent Other as the generator of this awareness. But the judgment that we have indeed had an experience of God also presupposes some understanding of what it means to be human and of the limits of ordinary human experience (for the experience of God is, by definition, that which carries us to, and beyond, the limits of ordinary, everyday, "objective," empirically verifiable experience).

Accordingly, the doctrine of the Trinity appears in this book as a focal or integrating principle. This doctrine is the way we Christians systematically account for the deepest meaning of human existence and systematically express our experience of the ultimate source of that meaning, which is the triune God, disclosed through Jesus Christ and abidingly active as the instrument of reconciliation and unification in the Holy Spirit.

If the doctrine of the Trinity *presupposes* a theology of human existence and of revelation, and even a Christology, it also *implies* a theology of Christ, as it does a theology of the Church and of Christian existence. Thus, our discussion of the Trinity both sums up what we have been doing from the beginning and sets the agenda for the more explicitly Christological as well as ecclesiological and moral discussions that follow.

Because of the peculiar doctrinal relationship between the mystery of the Trinity and the mystery of Christ, one might persuasively argue that the Trinity ought to be treated systematically *after*, rather than before, Christology. But in a sense, we are doing that. The preceding chapter has, in fact, provided a synthesis of the whole Christian doctrine of God. We have already noted there that the formal doctrine of the Trinity developed under the pressure of confronting the apparent contradiction between the Church's consistent affirmation of monotheism and its simultaneous confession of faith in the Lordship of Jesus. In that sense,

CHAPTER X   THE TRINITY

Christology generates the doctrine of the Trinity and must be presupposed by it.

On the other hand, Christianity has not been immune from a certain *Christomonism*, a kind of "unitarianism" of the Second Person, in which God as Creator and Judge and God as Reconciler and Sanctifier are effectively replaced by the God who is at our side in the service of the neighbor as the "man for others." Christomonism has also diminished our understanding of the Church and of Christian life. How else explain the recent extraordinary rediscovery of the presence and power of the Holy Spirit by the West, if not as an acute reaction to the practical exclusion of the Spirit from Latin Christian consciousness, devotion, and even theology?

There *is* a sense in which our discussion follows rather than precedes Christology, since the basic elements of a Christology have already been presented in the previous chapter. But there is another sense in which a Christology cannot fully be developed except within the larger context of trinitarian doctrine if we are not to lapse into Christomonism. Indeed, the uniqueness of Christ is rooted in his consubstantial union with God the Father. An understanding of that uniqueness must, in turn, presuppose an understanding of God, the one *triune* God.

Furthermore, we have deliberately and intentionally rejected the traditional textbook division between the one God (*De Deo Uno*) and the triune God (*De Deo Trino*), rooted in the medieval syntheses and favored in Catholic theology ever since. *It is theologically impossible to reflect on the mystery of God from the perspective of Christian faith without reflecting at the same time on the mystery of the Trinity.* There is only one God, and that one God is triune. There is no "one God" who is not always and at the same time triune. The only circumstance under which Christians reflect deliberately on the "one God" who is not perceived as triune is in the comparative study of various non-Christian religions, such as we provided in chapter 8, or in a systematic meditation on the God of Abraham, of Isaac, and of Jacob as manifested in the pre-Christian history of Israel. But even in these cases, the trinitarian perspective inevitably shapes the theological process, dictating not only the answers we propose but, what is more important, the questions we raise.

HISTORY OF THE DOCTRINE
Biblical Foundations

Old Testament

The Old Testament is pre-Christian and as such does not provide any trinitarian understanding of God. This is not to say that the Old Testament's understanding of God (summarized briefly in the preceding chapter) is utterly *inconsistent* with the subsequent trinitarian development of the Christian era. The God of the Old Testament is a living God, intimately involved in the history of the people of Israel, sending forth a word through the prophets and the "signs of the times" — a word so identified with its source that it is called the very word of Yahweh. While it would be theologically unjustifiable to suggest some "foreshadowing" of the Trinity in the Old Testament, the personification of certain divine forces (the "word," the "wisdom," and the "spirit" of God) which are distinct from God and yet not simply intermediate powers between God and the world provides a certain prelude to the Christian understanding of God as triune.

New Testament

Even if it is evident that the doctrine of the Trinity is *not* in the Old Testament, it does not follow, by some process of elimination, that the doctrine of the Trinity *is* clearly and unequivocally in the New Testament. As we noted in the preceding chapter, the New Testament speaks simply of "God," the same God who was at work in the Old Testament: the God of Abraham, of Isaac, and of Jacob. The New Testament writers do not even ordinarily speak of Jesus as "God" (except in the rarest of cases, e.g., the Prologue of John's Gospel), since this would be for them an identification of Jesus with the Father. On the other hand, the New Testament recognizes the divinity of the Son. Where the Son appears as pre-existent, he is in the realm of the divine (John 1:1; Philippians 2:6-11). He is the presence of the Kingdom (Matthew 12:28; Luke

11:20), has lordship over the Sabbath (Mark 2:23-28; 3:1-6), and possesses the fullness of the Spirit (Luke 4:18).

But the New Testament does not specify the terms of the relationship between Father and Son, nor among Father and Son and Holy Spirit. It assumes only that there *is* some relationship (Matthew 11:27; John 1:1; 8:38; 10:38; 1 Corinthians 2:10). The Father "sends" the Son and the Spirit (John 14:16,26; 17:3; Galatians 4:6) and gives the Spirit through the Son (John 15:26; 16:7). Many other texts focus more explicitly on the Father-Son relationship (e.g., Mark 12:1-12; John 1:1,14; 2 Corinthians 4:4; Hebrews 1:3). But none of these texts individually, nor all of them together, express a theology of the Trinity as such. They refer to the impact of God upon the primitive Church. They have to do with the actions of God in the world outside of the inner life of God, i.e., with the "economic Trinity" of salvation history as opposed to the "immanent Trinity." It took three or four hundred years before the Church began to make the proper distinctions, to go beyond the formulations of the Bible and the creeds alone, and to see how the "economic Trinity" and the "immanent Trinity" are one and the same.

The God whom we *experience* as triune is, *in fact*, triune. But we cannot read back into the New Testament, much less into the Old Testament, the more sophisticated trinitarian theology and doctrine which slowly and often unevenly developed over the course of some fifteen centuries.

Post-biblical Theological Reflections

The reader is referred again to the historical material outlined in some detail in the preceding chapter. What follows here is a recapitulation and a reshaping of that material.

Patristic Age

The main question facing the Church in the immediately post-biblical period concerned the relationship of the Son to God the Almighty (*Pantokrator*). Statements about the Spirit tended to appear as a consequence of Christological statements. The Spirit was regarded as a synonym for God. But that could be not true of the Son, since the Son had specific roles and was perceived to have a distinctive identity apart from the Almighty. Is the Son subordinate to the Father and, therefore, not "true God of true God" (Nicea), or is he "consubstantial" (*homoousios*) with the Father, "true God of true God" indeed?

Consequently, the trinitarian theology of the Fathers had its starting point in their reflection on the history of salvation, i.e., on soteriology, or the theology of redemption. The coequal divinity of Christ was of the highest urgency, not because doctrinal purity had to be preserved but rather because our salvation was at stake. If Christ is not truly divine, then he is a creature like us and has no special standing before God. We are still in our sins.

The basic unity of the patristic approach notwithstanding, there is also a discernible difference between the theology of the Greek Fathers and the theology of the Latin Fathers. The Greeks were oriented toward the "economic Trinity" (Father, Son, and Holy Spirit as they are experienced in the history of salvation); the Latins, toward the "immanent Trinity" (Father, Son and Holy Spirit as they exist and interrelate within the inner recesses of the Godhead).

Greeks

The Greeks distinguished *hypostasis* (a term close to, but definitely not identical with, the term *person*) from *ousia*, or being. The distinction underscored for them the truth that God (*theos*, the Father, the Almighty) has come to us through the Son and the Spirit. God is revealed through the Son, and through the Son God reaches us in the Holy Spirit. Therefore, our "contact" with God, or more properly God's "contact" with us, is *historically definite* (through the Son) and *immediate* (in the Spirit), contrary to the various heresies of the day—e.g., Modalism, Sabellianism, Arianism.

The Greek Fathers were content, however, to define the relation between the one divine being, or nature, and the three *hypostases* (not quite "persons" in the modern sense of the word) in terms of traditional philosophical categories. The concrete character of these *hypostases* was then deduced from their function in the history of salvation.

Augustine

Augustine fully exemplified the Latin approach, which was to try to explain the nature of the triune God without deriving or inferring the "content" of the Godhead from the way in which the three Persons function for us in the history of salvation. He began not with the three Persons but with the one nature, or substance. Employing a psychological analogy, Augustine argued that the inner life of God is, in effect, necessarily trinitarian. *Ad extra*, i.e., outside of the inner life of God, however, divine activity is common to all three Persons since it proceeds from the one divine nature. Thus, for example, the Father could have become a human being if the Father so willed. (Some Catholic theologians today, such as Karl Rahner, would strongly resist this hypothesis, however, because the significance of the economy of salvation is proportionately diminished.) The importance and usefulness of the Augustinian approach notwithstanding, it obscured the connection between the "immanent Trinity" and the "economic Trinity" and made of the doctrine, at least in much of the Western Church, a matter of abstract speculation alone, of no real pastoral importance, having no place in the pulpit, for example, except perhaps once a year on Trinity Sunday.

Medieval Scholasticism

Augustine's impact on medieval Scholasticism was enormous, and it was only reinforced, not essentially modified, by Thomas Aquinas. Another type of trinitarian theology, more in keeping with the Greek approach and stressing the psychology of love rather than of understanding, was promoted by Richard of St. Victor (d. ca. 1173), Alexander of Hales (d. 1245), and Bonaventure (d. 1274). In his *On the Trinity*, Richard, unlike Augustine, begins with person rather than nature, looking to the unselfish love of human friendship as the reflection of the unselfish love of divine friendship (since we are, after all, made in the image of God). In God there is one infinite love and three infinite lovers: lover produces beloved, and lover and beloved are the productive principle of an equal co-beloved. Alexander of Hales explains the divine processions through the principle that "goodness diffuses itself." The inner life of the Trinity is characterized by perfect charity. In Bonaventure we find this same emphasis on "pure goodness" and "mutual love" as principles underlying the dynamism and plurality of the Godhead (see his *Commentaries on the Four Books of Sentences*). Perhaps because they were less precise than the Augustinian and Thomistic expositions, the so-called Franciscan contributions to trinitarian theology did not succeed in establishing themselves. Attempts at some constructive synthesis of these two approaches are only recently being made, so long has the theology of the Trinity been under the influence of Scholasticism.

Official Teachings on the Trinity

In the preceding chapter we have already presented the principal doctrinal contributions of the official Church to the developing theology of the triune God. Each of the major formulations was placed in its proper historical context. Here we review and summarize those doctrinal pronouncements in a more deliberately *systematic* way. The reader is cautioned, however, not to forget the original historical situation in which the official teaching authority exercised its magisterial duties. Apart from that context, the doctrinal statements become so many "proof texts" of relatively equal importance and authority, their terminology carrying the very same meaning they bear today (e.g., the notion of "person"). Dogmatic and/or doctrinal fundamentalism, we noted in chapter 2, is as much a temptation and a danger for the Church as is biblical fundamentalism.

On the other hand, if we are to have confidence in our theology of the triune God as one that is consistent with, and faithful to, the authentic teachings of the Church, we must take serious account of the doctrinal clarifications and limitations which have accumulated over the centuries.

The Trinity as Absolute Mystery

The Trinity is an *absolute mystery* in the sense that we do not understand it even after it has been revealed. It is a *mystery* in that it is "hidden in God (and) cannot be known unless revealed by God." It is an *absolute* mystery in that it remains forever such. This is the teaching of the First Vatican Council's *Dogmatic Constitution on the Catholic Faith* (1870). The concept of "mystery," however, is left undetermined by the council. A mystery is at least something which clearly transcends the capacity of our ordinary rational and conceptual powers and exceeds, beyond all human imagination, the range and resources of our everyday knowledge. (For a fuller discussion of the notion of "mystery," see again chapter 7.)

God as Triune

That (as opposed to *how*) God is triune is the clear and consistent teaching of the official magisterium of the Church. The Council of Nicea (325) testifies to the Church's official faith in "one God, the Father almighty...and in one Lord Jesus Christ, the Son of God...and in the Holy Spirit." The Council of Constantinople (381) confirmed the faith of Nicea and gave us the so-called Nicaeo-Constantinopolitan Creed which Catholics recite each week at the Eucharist. The teaching of Constantinople was verified the following year at a provincial council in Rome from which appeared *The Tome of Pope Damasus* (d. 384), which declared that there is one God of three, coequal, coeternal Persons, each distinct from the other, but not to the point where we have three separate gods. Against the heretical assault of Albigensianism, which regarded all matter as evil and therefore was led logically to the denial of the incarnation, the Fourth Lateran Council (1215) confessed that "there is only one true God...Father, Son and Holy Spirit: three persons indeed but one essence, substance, or wholly simple nature...." And against certain charges made against Peter the Lombard, the council also taught that "...in God there is only Trinity, not a quaternity...." In response to the great schism of East and West the Second Council of Lyons (1274) and the Council of Florence (1438–1440) both reaffirmed the doctrine of the Trinity, by now almost taking it for granted, and concentrated instead on the ecumenically sensitive matter of the procession of the Holy Spirit from the Father (*and? through?*) the Son. Thereafter the doctrine, indeed the *dogma*, of the Trinity is assumed by official Church sources rather than intrinsically developed and formally restated. A minor exception would be Pope Paul VI's profession of faith, "Credo of the People of God" (1968) which begins with the words "We believe in one God, Father, Son and Holy Spirit. . . ."

God as Father

These same confessions of faith in the Trinity are at once confessions of faith in the divinity of each of the three Persons of the Trinity and, at the same time, in the oneness of the Godhead. From Nicea (325) to Pope Paul VI (1968) professions of faith regularly begin with the words, "We believe in one God. . . ." God the Father is the Lord of salvation history and Creator of all that is. The Father is "unbegotten" but acts, and can only act, in the unity of the Son and the Holy Spirit. The Father generates the Son, and with the Son sends forth the Holy Spirit.

Although not an ecumenical council, the Eleventh Council of Toledo (675) in Spain, attended by only seventeen bishops, gave the Church a profession of trinitarian faith that was cherished and revered for many centuries thereafter. Its profession of faith in God the Father is as succinct and doctrinally precise a formulation as one might discover anywhere in the entire history of the Church:

> And we profess that the Father is not begotten, not created, but unbegotten. For He Himself, from whom the Son has received His birth and the Holy Spirit His procession, has His origin from no one. He is therefore the source and origin of the whole Godhead. He Himself is the Father of His own essence, who in an ineffable way has begotten the Son from His ineffable substance. Yet He did not beget something different from what He Himself is: God has begotten God, light has begotten

light. From Him, therefore, is "all fatherhood in heaven and on earth"(cf. Ephesians 3:15).

God the Son

The Son is begotten by the Father and not made out of nothing, like a creature (as the Arian heresy asserted). The Son is of the same substance with the Father. Thus, the Son is coequal in divinity and coeternal with the Father. It is through the Son as the Word, or *Logos*, of the Father that the Father is expressed in salvation history and within the inner life of the Trinity as well. Because the Son is consubstantial (*homoousios*) with the Father, his Sonship is not simply like that of any other son or daughter of God in the conventional sense of the expression "We're all God's children." Within the human family, of Jesus Christ alone can it be said that he is of the same substance with the Father. In the words of Nicea:

> We believe . . . in one Lord Jesus Christ, the Son of God, the only-begotten generated from the Father, that is, from the being (*ousia*) of the Father, God from God, Light from Light, true God from true God, begotten, not made, one in being (*homoousios*) with the Father, through whom all things were made, those in heaven and those on earth. For us men and for our salvation He came down, and became flesh, was made man, suffered, and rose again on the third day. He ascended to the heavens and shall come again to judge the living and the dead.

God the Holy Spirit

The Holy Spirit is the Father's gift through the Son. It is through the Spirit that the Father is communicated to us with immediacy, and it is through the Spirit that we are able to accept the self-communication of the Father. As the self-communication of God, the Holy Spirit is God given in love and with the reconciling and renewing power of that love. The Spirit has the same essence as the Father, and yet is distinct from the Father and the Son. The

Spirit proceeds from the Father through the Son (despite the bitter East-West dispute on this point, the Council of Florence *did* allow for the preposition *through* as a legitimate alternative to the preferred conjunction *and*). The procession is not a begetting, since this would lead to the supposition that there are two Sons, nor is the Spirit merely a mode in which the Son communicates himself to us. The Spirit originates from the Father and the Son and has a distinct relationship to the Father and the Son which accounts for the Spirit's distinct hypostatic existence within the Godhead and the Spirit's distinct salvific mission in history (without prejudice to the principle of the mutual indwelling of the three Persons, each one in the others). From the First Council of Constantinople:

> We believe...in the Holy Spirit, the Lord and Giver of life, who proceeds from the Father (and the Son), who together with the Father and the Son is worshipped and glorified, who has spoken through the prophets. (And) in one Holy Catholic and apostolic Church. We acknowledge one baptism for the forgiveness of sins. We expect the resurrection of the dead and the life of the world to come.

Two observations: first, the words *and the Son* (*filioque*) were added later in Spain in the sixth century, and from there the usage spread to Gaul and Germany. It was eventually introduced into the Roman liturgy by Pope Benedict VIII (d. 1024). The Greeks ignored the *filioque* and denied the Church's right to make any addition to the ancient creed of Constantinople, as we have already noted. Secondly, the realities of the Church, the forgiveness of sins, the resurrection of the dead, and the life of the world to come are a constitutive part of our affirmation of the Holy Spirit because these are directly attributed to the Spirit's role in salvation history, again without prejudice to the principle of the mutual indwelling of the three Persons (circumincession).

Processions, Relations, Persons, and Nature

From the point of view of our "discovery" of the triune character of God, we first experience the divine *processions*, or missions (we experience the Spirit who has been *sent* by the Father and/through the Son, and we experience the Son as the one *sent* by the Father). The processions, in turn, suggest *relations* between and among *persons* (or distinct *hypostases*) which nonetheless participate coequally, coeternally, and consubstantially in the *nature* of the Godhead, namely, the *divinity*. The official Church provides no final definitions of any of these key doctrinal terms. The magisterium does, however, provide certain fundamental dogmatic principles regarding them:

1. There are two *processions* and only two processions in God: generation and spiration.

2. There are four *relations*, (paternity, filiation, active spiration, passive spiration), but only three *subsistent relations*, i.e., three relations which are mutually opposed and, therefore, distinct from one another (without, however, being distinct from the very Being of God): paternity, filiation, and passive spiration. Active spiration (which involves Father and Son) is not opposed to either paternity or filiation, and, thus, does not constitute a fourth subsistent relation.

3. In God all things are one except what is opposed by the opposition of relations. Those relations which are opposed and, therefore, distinct one from the other are called, as noted above, subsistent relations, or *hypostases*. They give rise, in turn, to the trinity of *Persons* within the Godhead: Father, Son, and Holy Spirit.

4. Because of the unity of the divine essence, of the processions and of the relative oppositions, which constitute the Persons, there is a *mutual indwelling* (circumincession) of the Persons, one in the other two, the other two in the one, so that the Son is for all eternity in the Father, and the Father from all eternity in the Son, and so on.

These teachings are set forth explicitly, but not exclusively, in the Council of Florence's *Decree for the Greeks* (1439) and *Decree for the Jacobites* (1442).

We must take care, however, not to confuse the terminology of the Fathers and of the ecumenical councils of the past with the meanings presently associated with those same words today. This is especially true of the term *person*. It is a notion which for us today is inextricably linked with *consciousness*. A person is an individual center and subject of consciousness. But there exists in God only one power, one will, one self-presence, one activity, one beatitude, and so forth. Insofar as the individual Persons can even be described as "self-conscious" (which at best is an analogical attribution), it is a self-consciousness which derives from the one divine essence and is common to the divine Persons. Our modern psychological and philosophical notions of subjectivity, therefore, must be kept strictly away from the concept of person as applied to the Trinity. The activity of the three Persons is one and the same and can be ascribed to any one of the Persons only by *appropriation*. This axiom, however, deals only with the efficient causality of God. It does not affect the truth that the *Logos* or Son alone became human, or the theory of uncreated grace in which each of the three divine Persons has a special relation to us. To say otherwise would reduce the doctrine of the Trinity to mere words and the Christian understanding of God to an unqualified monotheism.

THEOLOGICAL SYNTHESIS

For too many Christians, the doctrine of the Trinity is only a matter of intellectual curiosity, on the one hand, or a somewhat arbitrary test of faith, on the other. It is as if Jesus at some point in his teaching ministry called the disciples aside and said, "By the way, there *is* just one more thing you should know. In God there are three divine Persons: Father, Son, and Holy Spirit. And yet there is still only one God. It's quite important that you believe what I'm telling you. Your readiness and willingness to believe will be a sign of your faith in me and in my word." Accordingly, the mystery and doctrine of the Trinity is often relegated to an entirely marginal place in the total Christian schema. Even theologians as sober as Karl Rahner have suggested that, as far as many Church members are concerned, the doctrine could be erased completely from the Christian treasury of faith and that many spiritual writings, sermons, pious exercises, and even theological treatises could remain in place with little more than minor verbal adjustments.

A proper theological and pastoral understanding of the Trinity depends upon our perception of *the identity between the so-called "economic Trinity" and the so-called "immanent Trinity."* The two have, in effect, been separated, and the former has been practically forgotten. The doctrine of the Trinity is received as if it were merely an arcane description of the inner life of God—a life that we cannot observe at first hand, in any case. In that view, it has to do with a network of divine relationships which concerns only God and not ourselves, except insofar as Christ asks us to believe his "revelation" about the mystery as a sign of our faith in him and in his total message.

But that, in fact, is not the way the mystery of the Trinity was revealed to us. Nowhere do we find the Lord calling his disciples aside, and "revealing" the Trinity as if it were this week's catechetical lesson. On the contrary, the Church gradually and painstakingly came to certain conclusions about the inner reality of God on the basis of its experience of God within its own human experience. In other words, the Church began to wonder theologically and doctrinally whether there is more to God than traditional monotheism suggests, or whether, at the other extreme, there might be three gods, or two, or perhaps a small community of unequal gods. The Church came to the knowledge of God as triune as it progressively reflected on its experience of the triuneness of God's dealings with us in history. And then the Church concluded that the God whom we experience as triune in history (the "economic Trinity") must also be triune in essence, i.e., within the inner life of the Godhead (the "immanent Trinity").

In traditional categories, the revelation of the economic Trinity *is* the revelation of the immanent Trinity. We did not first "hear about" the immanent Trinity and then search for signs of its activity in our lives. In that case the revelation of the immanent Trinity would have been a merely verbal, highly abstract communication. Rather, our "understanding" of the immanent Trinity came about precisely as a result of our reflection on the very practical, saving activities of the triune God in our lives. Therefore, the doctrine of the Trinity is not a speculative doctrine alone. *It is the way we express our most fundamental relationships with the God of our salvation as well as God's relationships with us.*

We must keep in mind, all the while, that we would not even know about the economic Trinity if its activities on our behalf were not "called to our attention" (the process of *revelation*, already discussed in chapter 2). For those of us living after the biblical, foundational period of the Church, the Bible itself and subsequent creedal statements of the Church serve to "call our attention" to the trinitarian character of God's dealings with us. Those of us reflecting on the mystery of the Trinity today do so because the doctrine is already there, as a given of our Christian experience, consciousness, and faith. In the primitive Christian community—the disciples, the Apostles, the evangelists, the first faithful members of the Church—the seeds of the doctrine were also "given." But not by the Bible, since it did not yet exist. And not by creedal statements, although some of these were already circulating and some few found their way into the New Testament. The earliest Christians were "alerted" to the trinitarian dimension of divine salvation by Christ, first of all, and then by the preaching of the Apostles, and then by attentiveness to their own unusual experience of the triune God (e.g., at Pentecost) in this most unusual period in the history of the Church. But having conceded all of that, the mystery of the Trinity remains precisely that: a mystery, and absolute mystery at that.

If the communication of God in Jesus Christ, the Son, and in the Holy Spirit is really the communication *of God*, then these communications must be attributed to God as God is, immanently, within the Godhead. The divine self-communication, therefore, has two basic modes: of truth (the *Logos*, or Word) and of love (the Spirit). As *truth*, the self-communication takes place in history, through a particular person. As *love*, it brings about the openness of human beings to the presence of God in Christ and makes possible our acceptance of that divine presence. Without being simply identical, these two forms of divine self-communication constitute together the one divine self-communication which manifests itself in truth and love. And yet there is a real distinction between the two forms of self-communication (or processions, or missions): In the one, the Father is expressed as truth; in the other, the Father is received and accepted in love.

One of the most obvious *difficulties* with the doctrine of the Trinity arises from the Church's *use of the word person* to identify the various terms of the divine relationships. We take it to be a theologically non-negotiable matter as well. There is simply no other way of talking about the triune God except in terms of the "one God and the three divine Persons." And yet the New Testament does not use the term *person*. Indeed, it was introduced only very gradually into ecclesiastical language. And even when the Church passed beyond the biblical formulations, its theologians and official magisterium did not immediately fasten upon the term *person (prosopon)*. The initial preference was for *hypostasis*. *Hypostasis* can be predicated of any being, not merely of rational beings. It applies to whatever exists in itself. *Persona* always means the *intellectual* subsistent. Moreover, our modern notion of "person" further complicates the problem, since the modern notion is so much tied in with the idea of a separate and independent subject or center of consciousness. Applying the modern concept of "person" without any modification to the doctrine of Trinity would leave us with three consciousnesses, three free wills, eventually three gods. The word *person*, therefore, is almost inevitably misunderstood today.

Where does that leave us? Can we simply reject the traditional formula first proposed by the Council of Alexandria (362), "one substance, three persons"? We cannot erase history, nor are we really in a position today to produce a better formula which could be universally intelligible, acceptable, and binding on the whole Church.

At least we can, with renewed determination, follow the pattern given from the beginning by the New Testament itself. We can speak of the Trinity always in the context of salvation history, using the names of Father, Son, and Holy Spirit, without forgetting that one God is spoken of throughout. We can also speak of *three distinct ways of God's being present in the history of salvation and three different ways of God's subsisting within the Godhead itself.*

The word *ways* has its strengths and weaknesses, to be sure. One of its strengths is that it can help us to see that the Persons are there as in relation to one another and that where the relationships are different, one from the other, we have put our finger, so to speak, on what constitutes difference in God. Father, Son, and Holy Spirit are one and the same God, but subsisting in different ways. It is only with respect to the ways of subsistence that the number three can be applied to God. A way of subsisting is *distinct* from another way of subsisting by its relation of opposition, and is *real* by virtue of its identity with the divine being. "He Who" subsists in such a way is truly God.

But there is an obvious risk in the use of the word *ways*. It is a short step indeed from that term to Modalism, which effectively denies the reality of the Trinity, economic or immanent. We have to be particularly attentive to the reminder of Bernard J. F. Lonergan that a subsistent is *that which is*, whereas a mode of being is *a way in which it is*. Thus, in God paternity is not a mode of being; it is God the Father. There are three in God to whom we can say "You" (*Divinarum Personarum Conceptionem Analogicam*, Rome: Gregorian University, 1957, pp. 172-175).

Finally, what of the so-called *psychological explanation* of the doctrine of the Trinity, the one proposed by Augustine and further developed by Thomas Aquinas? It uses the pattern of the human mind and an analysis of human consciousness in attempting to illustrate the two immanent processions of generation and spiration within the Godhead. Although it is not the official teaching of the Church, at least not directly, the approach can still be helpful. "It appears all the more legitimate in the light of a metaphysical anthropology which demonstrates that there are only two fundamental acts of spiritual existence, knowledge and love. The obvious thing is to regard these basic acts as paralleled in the two divine processions" (Karl Rahner, "Trinity," *The Concise Sacramentum Mundi*, p. 1764).

On the other hand, the psychological approach is not without its own difficulties. There is some measure of circular reasoning involved. The approach "postulates *from* the doctrine of the Trinity a model of human knowledge and love, which either remains questionable, or about which it is not clear that it can be more than a *model* of human knowledge precisely as *finite*. And this model it applies again to God. In other words, we are not told why in God knowledge and love demand a *processio ad modum operati* (as Word or as 'the beloved in the lover')" (Rahner, *The Trinity*, pp. 117–118). And without such a procession there is no real trinity of ways of subsistence.

What the mystery and doctrine of the Trinity mean, when all is said and done, is that the God who created us, who sustains us, who will judge us, and who will give us eternal life is not a God infinitely removed from us. On the contrary, our God is a God of absolute proximity, a God who is communicated truly in the flesh, in history, within our human family, and a God who is present in the spiritual depths of our existence as well as in the core of our unfolding human history, as the source of enlightenment and community.

That mystery and doctrine is, in its turn, the beginning, the end, *and* the center of all Christian theology.

SUMMARY

1.   The whole of *Christian theology* is trinitarian in origin and content. In *origin*, because theology itself is made possible by the self-communication of God the Father in the Word-made-flesh, and because our apprehension of God-in-Christ occurs only after we have been drawn by the Holy Spirit who dwells within our hearts and elevates our whole consciousness. In *content*, because every major Christian doctrine is an expression of the mystery and doctrine of the Trinity.

2.   Consideration of the Trinity might conceivably occur at the beginning of theology, as a preview, or at the end of theology, as a review and synthesis. Our *method* places the doctrine nearer to the center of the systematic presentation, since an understanding of the Trinity presupposes some understanding of human existence (theological anthropology), some notion of transcendence and of the process and signs by which the Transcendent is disclosed and/or discovered (revelation), and even some grasp of God's active and gracious presence in Jesus Christ (Christology and grace). On the other hand, certain mysteries and doctrines seem to presuppose so much the mystery and doctrine of the Trinity that they cannot easily be considered *before* the Trinity, namely, the mystery

of the Church, the sacraments, Christian existence, and, to a very large extent, Christology itself.

3.   In any event, there can be *no separation* between theological reflection on the one God and theological reflection on the triune God. The God of Christian theology is always and only the triune God.

4.   The mystery and doctrine of the Trinity is not foreshadowed in the *Old Testament*, but the elements for such a doctrine (e.g., the closeness and active presence of Yahweh among the people of Israel) are there as a kind of prelude to the Christian understanding of God as triune. At the very least, there is no inconsistency or contradiction between the two Testaments.

5.   But neither is the doctrine of the Trinity clearly in the *New Testament*. Again, certain elements are present: the special status and role of Jesus Christ, the Son of God, in particular. The New Testament does not specify the nature or the terms of the relationship between and among the Persons of the Trinity; indeed, it does not even use the word *person* in reference to the Father, Son, or Holy Spirit.

6.   The first questions posed *after the foundational period* of the New Testament were "How can there be one God, the Almighty, when Jesus Christ is also invested with divinity?" or, conversely, "How can Jesus be true God of true God if there is only one God?" Only later did the question of the divinity of the Holy Spirit arise.

7.   The *Greek Fathers* started with our experience of the triune God in salvation history (the economic Trinity), whereas the Latin Fathers, and especially Augustine, began with a more speculative analysis of the inner life of the Godhead, moving from nature or essence to Persons (the immanent Trinity).

8.   It was mainly through the achievement of the Greek Fathers that the principal conciliar formulations of trinitarian faith were constructed: Nicea, Constantinople, etc. *The councils* insisted that the Son is of the same substance (*homoousios*) with the Father, and is, therefore, an effective instrument of our redemption. The Holy Spirit, too, is divine, a separate *hypostasis* alongside the Father and the Son, without prejudice to the oneness of divinity itself.

9.   *Medieval Scholasticism*, especially as exemplified in Thomas Aquinas, adhered to the Augustinian approach, although there were certain "minority reports" being written, namely, by the Franciscan school represented by Richard of St. Victor, Alexander of Hales, and Bonaventure, who were closer to the approach of the Greek Fathers. Their contributions to trinitarian theology, however, did not attract a very wide constituency until recently.

10.   *Official teachings of the Church* on the Trinity have advanced the following principles: (1) The Trinity is an *absolute mystery*; i.e., it transcends our ordinary human capacity for understanding even after we know it as revealed; (2) God is triune: Father, Son, and Holy Spirit, coequal and coeternal, and yet each distinct one from the other, but not to the point where we have three gods; (3) the Father alone is unbegotten, begets or generates the Son, and sends forth or spirates the Holy Spirit (with or through the Son); (4) the Son is begotten by the Father, but not as a creature (Arianism); he is of the same substance as the Father, "true God of true God" (Nicea); (5) the Holy Spirit proceeds from the Father (and or through) the Son and has a distinct salvific mission in history: creating the community of faith (Church), forgiving sins, giving new life, etc.

11.   There are two *processions*, or missions, in God: generation and spiration; i.e., both the Son and the Holy Spirit are "sent."

12.   The processions, in turn, are the basis of the *relations* between and among the Persons or *hypostases* (which do not mean exactly the same, since *persons* are *rational hypostases*). There are four relations: paternity, filiation, active spiration, and passive spiration. But there are only three *subsistent relations*: paternity, filiation, and passive spiration. Active spiration is not really distinct from paternity or from filiation, since there is no opposition of relations between them.

13.   These subsistent relations are relatively opposed one to another, and thus are *hypostases* or Persons (again, the two terms are not exactly identical). The *hypostases* or Persons have names: Father, Son, and Holy Spirit.

14.   Although there are three Persons, there is only one divine nature or essence. Because of the unity of essence, there is a *mutual indwelling* of the Persons, i.e., of one in the other. This is also called *circumincession*.

15.   Such teachings as these are to be found throughout the history of the Church, particularly in the first fifteen centuries, but they are comprehensively proclaimed by the *Council of Florence* (1438–42).

16.   Despite this abundant corpus of official teachings on the mystery of the Trinity, many *fundamental difficulties* remain, especially the ambiguity that continues to revolve around the notion of "person," a term the New Testament does not use. The modern understanding of a person as an independent center or subject of consciousness does not apply to the Trinity. And yet we do not have a better term to replace it, and we cannot erase centuries of slow and painstaking debate and doctrinal formulations.

17.   A proper theological, not to say pastoral, understanding of the Trinity requires that we perceive the identity between the *economic Trinity* and the *immanent Trinity*. The God who is active on our behalf in salvation history is the triune God of the Godhead. It is not the immanent Trinity which is first revealed, but the economic Trinity. The constitution of the immanent Trinity is inferred from our experience of, and reflection upon, the functions of the economic Trinity.

18.   Since the notion of *"person"* continues to create ambiguity, confusion, even heresy at the rank-and-file level (*tritheism*, belief in three gods), and since we cannot simply abandon it, we should follow the pattern set by the New Testament and speak of the Trinity always in the context of salvation history. God deals with us in three distinct *ways* of being present to our history: As Father, as Son, and as Holy Spirit. There is a danger, of course, that an explanation of this sort might lapse into Modalism.

19.   The so-called *psychological analogy* first employed by Augustine also has its advantages and disadvantages, but, like the notion of "person," it cannot simply be set aside. It helps us see the basic parallel between the life of the Trinity, which is governed by the twin processes of truth and love, and our own lives, or at least the ideal expression of our own lives.

20.   *In the end*, the mystery and doctrine of the Trinity means that the God who created us, who sustains us, who will judge us, and who will give us eternal life is not infinitely removed from us, but is absolutely close to us, communicated in the flesh and present in our hearts, our consciousness, and our history as the source of enlightenment and community.

SUGGESTED READINGS

Bracken, Joseph. *What Are They Saying About the Trinity?* New York: Paulist Press, 1979.

Fortman, Edward J., ed. *The Triune God: A Historical Study of the Doctrine of the Trinity.* Philadelphia: Westminster Press, 1972.

Kelly, J. N. D. *Early Christian Creeds.* London: Longmans, Green, 1950.
——————. *Early Christian Doctrines.* New York: Harper & Row, 1965.

Lonergan, Bernard J. F. *The Way to Nicea: The Dialectical Development of Trinitarian Theology.* Philadelphia: Westminster Press, 1976.

Panikkar, Raimundo. *The Trinity and the Religious Experience of Man.* New York: Orbis Books, 1973.

Rahner, Karl. *A Rahner Reader*. Ed. Gerald A. McCool. New York: Seabury Press, 1975, pp. 132-144.
_____. *The Trinity*. New York: Herder & Herder, 1970.
Sloyan, Gerard. *The Three Persons in One God*. Englewood Cliffs, N.J.: Prentice-Hall, 1964.

PART THREE

JESUS CHRIST

JESUS CHRIST

INTRODUCTION

What is distinctively Christian about the Church's faith is its understanding of God as triune. But it is only because we first knew God in Jesus Christ that we came to know God as triune. Thus, it is equally true that the distinctively Christian element in Christian faith is the confession of the Lordship of Jesus. Christianity alone identifies Jesus of Nazareth with God. Jesus Christ is "true God of true God." He is of one substance with the Father.

A separate section on the mystery of Jesus Christ, therefore, requires little justification. Christian theology, not to say Catholic theology, focuses on him. Our understanding of, and response to, God is a function of our understanding of, and response to, Jesus Christ.

Why, then, is there not also a separate section on the Holy Spirit, if the Christian God is a triune God? First, there is no such separate "section," as it were, even in the New Testament, nor in the earliest tradition of the Church. The preoccupation of the New Testament is with God, the Almighty, and with Jesus Christ, who comes among us to manifest and to do the Father's will: to proclaim and practice and hasten the coming of the Kingdom of God. The Holy Spirit is never an object of that proclamation, whether of Jesus or of the Church. Rather, the Holy Spirit is the power through which that proclamation is uttered and fulfilled.

We do not have in this book a separate treatment of the Holy Spirit because the Holy Spirit is at issue in every major theological discussion: the divinization of humankind by grace, the renewing and reconciling presence of God in history, the mystery of the

Church, the celebration of the sacraments, the exercise of Christian witness. "The Holy Spirit cannot become a formula, a dogma apart," the Orthodox theologian Nikos Nissiotis writes. "Pneumatology is the heart of Christian theology, it touches all aspects of faith in Christ. It is a commentary on the acts of the revealed triune God, the life of the Church, and of the man who prays and is regenerated . . . orthodox pneumatology does not allow the doctrine of the Holy Spirit to become a separate chapter of dogmatic theology" (cited by Patrick Corcoran, *Irish Theological Quarterly,* vol. 39/3, July 1972, p. 277).

In this Part on Jesus Christ we examine first how he is understood, interpreted, and accepted today—whether as teacher, holy man, liberator, brother, etc.—and how he variously relates with contemporary culture (chapter 11).

The heart of the matter, of course, is the New Testament. We would know practically nothing about Jesus Christ (apart from the barest of biographical details) if it were not for the testimony of the Church preserved in the pages of the New Testament. And here we are confronted with the central problem of connecting the Jesus of history and the Christ of faith. Does the Church's testimony about Jesus conform with what Jesus thought, said, and did? What was the significance of his life and death? Did he rise from the dead (chapter 12)?

But the New Testament record was open to various interpretations, and the missionary needs of the early Church required it to communicate the Gospel across cultural lines. The supposedly straightforward, uncomplicated message of the Bible had to be reinterpreted, recast, reformulated. And it was: by the Fathers of the Church, by the early ecumenical councils, and by the theologians of the Middle Ages. The story of that process is not easily reviewed, but the Church's present and future understanding of the meaning and purpose of Jesus Christ is forever shaped by that story and by its dogmatic residue (chapter 13).

The discussion about the mystery of Jesus Christ has been, in a sense, reopened in the twentieth century, first because of the renewal of biblical studies and, secondly, because of a development in our understanding of the meaning of human existence and of human history. Both of these factors have generated a fresh outpouring of Christological writings, the first such outpouring since the medieval period. Who are the principal contributors? How do their contributions compare, one with another? How consistent are those contributions with the biblical and dogmatic traditions (chapter 14)?

Christology can be abstract unless it is always related to soteriology. In other words, we are ever concerned about the nature and person of Jesus Christ because we are ever concerned about his effectiveness in bringing about our salvation. If he is not truly God, then he could not *save* us. If he is not truly a human being, then he could not save *us*. If divinity and humanity are not united in a single person, then *he* could not save us. Certain practical questions help focus the central dogmatic issues: The questions of the virginal conception of Jesus and his sinlessness help focus the truth of his divinity, and the questions of his knowledge and sexuality help focus the truth of his humanity (chapter 15).

In the final accounting, how can we even begin to differentiate between Christologies which are consistent with the broad Catholic tradition and those which are not? The same fifteenth chapter proposes five theological criteria.

Chapter 16 elaborates upon one of those five criteria, namely, the principle that our Christological belief must correspond always with our worship. The "Christ of the Liturgy" is as much a norm of Christological orthodoxy as is the Christ of the New Testament, of the Fathers, of the councils, of medieval theology. The liturgy is Christology-as-worship-and-prayer.

Although the mystery of Jesus Christ is not the most fundamental doctrine of Christian faith (it is rooted, after all, in the mystery of the triune God), it is unquestionably at the heart of Christian faith. And so, too, is Part III in relation to the rest of the book.

· XI ·

CHRIST AND
CONTEMPORARY CULTURE

THE PROBLEM

We have said that what is distinctively Christian about the Church's faith is *the understanding of God as triune.* The God who created us and who sustains us, the God who will judge us and give us eternal life, is a God who has entered our history in the flesh and who continues to enter and dwell in our hearts and our minds as the principle of understanding and of love.

On the other hand, it is because we first knew God in the *Logos,* the Word that is Jesus Christ, that we eventually came also to know God as triune. So it is equally true that the distinctively Christian element in Christian faith is *the confession of the Lordship of Jesus.* Christianity alone identifies Jesus of Nazareth with God. Jesus Christ is "true God of true God." He is of the same substance as the Father.

But who is this Jesus whom we proclaim as Lord? How do we know him? How can we be sure that our picture of him is true to the facts? On what basis do we connect the Jesus of our prayers and devotions with the Jesus who lived in Palestine some two thousand years ago? Who is to say that we are really teaching and preaching as Jesus did? Does our present understanding of Christian faith accurately reflect the intentions and consciousness of the Lord himself? Is the Church truly faithful to the mission God has given it in Christ and in the Holy Spirit? Is Christianity as Christ meant it to be?

Such questions as these arise because of the gap between the so-called "Jesus of history" and the "Christ of faith." The distinction between the names "Jesus" and "Christ" is important. "Christ," after all, is not Jesus's last name. "Jesus" (literally, "Yahweh is salvation") is the name given him at birth.

Insofar as he lived at a certain time, in a certain place, with certain parents, was engaged in certain occupations, associated with certain persons, established a certain reputation among his contemporaries, and died a certain death, in a certain place, at a certain time, under certain circumstances, he, this "Jesus," is an *historical fact*.

But insofar as some of his contemporaries reacted to him in a particular way and estimated his significance in a particular fashion, and insofar as subsequent generations have readily affirmed with Paul that "God...reconciled us to himself through Christ" (2 Corinthians 5:18), this man "born of a woman" (Galatians 4:4), this "carpenter's son" (Matthew 13:55) bears *a meaning which transcends the historical fact* of his existence, although never disconnected from it. This "Jesus of Nazareth" is the "Christ" (literally, the "anointed one") who has been promised and whom we now accept in "faith."

Jesus, therefore, is a matter of historical record; *Christ* is a matter of meaning or of interpretation, an interpretation that we call "faith." To affirm the historicity of Jesus without affirming his Christhood is to take Jesus as a human being and no more, the greatness of his humanity notwithstanding. To affirm the Christhood, on the other hand, without identifying the historical Jesus with the Christ is to make of "Christ" a cosmic idea, an abstraction, a universal principle of growth and progress, a kind of theological yeast with no identity of its own.

Neither affirmation is true to the Christian faith. For Christians confess, as we shall see in some detail, the identity of Jesus with the Christ. Jesus *is* the Christ. He is indeed *Jesus Christ,* and he is "the same yesterday, today, and forever" (Hebrews 13:8).

But the Jesus Christ of the New Testament, of the creeds, of the dogmatic formulae, of the liturgy, and of the living faith of the whole Church is not always recognizable in the world about us, and sometimes not even in portions of the Church itself.

Too often the Christ of our personal faith bears little resemblance to the Jesus of history or to the Christ of the Church's faith. We make of Jesus Christ what *we* would like him to be for us. Consequently, he no longer challenges us from the outside to conform to him, but rather we project on him all that we are or would like to be. The affirmation of the Lordship of Jesus becomes, then, a form of *self*-affirmation.

JESUS CHRIST TODAY

There has been an extraordinary resurgence of interest in, even enthusiasm for, Jesus in recent years. He made the cover of *Time* magazine twice in one year (June 21 and October 25, 1971), at the high point of the so-called "Jesus movement." We had the "Jesus People," even "Jews for Jesus." He was celebrated on Broadway and in film: *Jesus Christ Superstar* and *Godspell*. Bumper stickers advertised his name: "Honk if you love Jesus," "Jesus is the answer," and "Jesus is Lord." The revival of Evangelical Christianity and the charismatic incursion into Roman Catholicism ran almost a parallel course to Jesus' sudden popularity in the "outside world."

But *which* Jesus was it who won the hearts of a new generation of young people and inspired the spiritual rebirth of young and middle-aged alike, including even a man destined to become president of the United States? And which Jesus was it who continued to be taught, and honored, and appealed to in the official churches? Which Jesus was preached from the pulpits? Which Jesus was the centerpiece of the catechisms and college textbooks? Which Jesus was the norm of conscience? Which Jesus set the example for a truly human, and therefore truly Christian, life?

One can detect at least five such Jesuses:

Jesus, Teacher: Gnosticism, insofar as it was a heretical exaggeration of the importance of knowledge (*gnosis*) for salvation, is not dead. There are still many in the Church who sincerely believe that orthodoxy is all that really counts in the end, and that, therefore, no greater threat to Christ exists in the world today than the internal "subversion" of the Church by dissident theologians. The primary duty of pastors (pope and bishops in particular) is to safeguard the faith and protect it from the impurities of so-called progressive thought. (We have already alluded to the confusion of "faith" with "theology" in chapter 2.)

Such views have several roots, of course. They reflect a particular ecclesiology, a particular understanding of God and of human existence, a particular notion of the redemption, and so forth. But they reflect as well a particular Christology, and that is what interests us here. Jesus Christ is perceived primarily as a *teacher*, as one who came among us, sent by the Father, in order to communicate certain truths about God and about ourselves that we must know if we are to achieve the ends for which we were created. We noted in the previous chapter how this mentality helped to marginalize the doctrine of the Trinity, as if it were some abstract concept which makes little or no real difference in our lives but which is set before us nonetheless as a test of our readiness and willingness to believe the word of God in Christ, "who can neither deceive nor be deceived" (from the "Act of Faith").

But the preceding attitude is an extreme one. It must not be allowed to obscure the fact that Jesus was indeed a *teacher*. This was a title, in fact, given him more frequently than any other. He was regarded as a teacher (Matthew 10:24; Luke 20:21; John 3:2). He gathered a group of disciples and acted as their rabbi, or teacher (Matthew 8:18-22; 21:1-11; 26:17-19; Mark 4:35-41; 11:1-11, e.g.). He is asked the type of questions a teacher would be asked (Matthew 22:36; Luke 10:25). His place for teaching was often the synagogue (Matthew 4:23; 9:35; 13:54; Mark 6:2; Luke 4:15,31; 6:6). He taught "with power" and as one having authority (Matthew 7:29; Mark 1:22; 11:18). His teaching is that of the one who sent him (John 7:16), and Jesus teaches whatever he himself was taught by the Father (John 8:28).

Not surprisingly, the early Church continued the ministry of teaching in fidelity to its charge from the Lord. Teachers appeared among the lists of officers in the Church (1 Corinthians 12:28; Ephesians 4:11), and teaching is regarded as part of the office of Apostles (1 Timothy 2:7; 2 Timothy 3:10) and of the bishop (2 Timothy 4:2). With the death of the last of the Apostles, the Church was particularly concerned that the apostolic traditions be preserved and that whatever was taught should be "sound doctrine" (1 Timothy 1:10; 2 Timothy 4:3; Titus 1:9, 2:1). Ultimately, the object of the Church's teaching, then as now, was the same as it was in Jesus' own teaching: the Kingdom of God (Mark 1:15). But after the resurrection of Christ, the Church increasingly saw Christ as the personification of the Kingdom, and so the Church's teaching centered more and more on Christ himself (Ephesians 4:21).

Jesus, Ruler, Judge, and King: Others have distorted the reality of Jesus by exaggerating his function as *ruler*, or shepherd, and as *judge*. How else explain why so many apparently sincere Christian leaders have adopted the life-styles of princes or of millionaires, have governed their communities in severe, authoritarian ways, and have gloried in the pomp and circumstance of ecclesiastical titles and ceremonies and public events? How else explain such institutionalized cruelties as the *Inquisition*, the imprisonment of *Galileo* (d. 1642), the suppression of the free access to the great works of literature and philosophy, the banishment of persons from their professional careers without due process, the harshness and rigidity of life in religious communities, the intricate ecclesiastical legal system of crimes and penalties? How else explain the bitterness of official denunciations of Protestants and others, and the literal insistence that no one can be saved outside the Catholic Church?

And yet Jesus was indeed a *ruler*, or shepherd, and a *judge*. But he is the shepherd who leaves the ninety-nine to search out for the one stray, and whose rejoicing over its recovery is beyond measure (Matthew 18:12-14; Luke 15:3-7). He is, in fact, the good shepherd (John 10:1-6,10-16) and the door of the sheepfold (10:7-9). He is concerned with the unity of the flock (an echo of Ezekiel 34:11-22).

The title of *shepherd* was applied to ministers of the Church as well. Pastors (etymologically "shepherds") are included on the lists of officers (Ephesians 4:11). The elders are addressed as shepherds of the flock (Acts of the Apostles 20:28; 1 Peter 5:2-4). Peter is given the distinctive ministry of shepherd (John 21:15-17).

Jesus is also accorded the title *king* in Matthew 2:2, where his royal character is the key to understanding the entire narrative, whose purpose is to present the true kingship of Jesus as free of external pomp. Jesus simply accepts the designation in his conversation with Pilate (Matthew 27:11; Mark 15:2; Luke 23:3). The longer version of the dialogue (John 18:33-39) makes even clearer the unworldly character of the kingship of Jesus. Indeed, the kingship of Jesus is mentioned only once in the post-resurrection period (1 Corinthians 15:24-26) and the reference there is eschatological. Jesus will be king only after the conquest of all his enemies.

The title of *judge* is also sparingly applied to Jesus. On the "day of wrath" Jesus will come to judge the living and the dead (2 Timothy 4:1). But Jesus' role as judge is at best paradoxical in John's Gospel. On the one hand, we are assured that God did not send his Son to judge the world but to save it (John 3:17), and Jesus himself says the same thing (John 12:47). Yet he also says that he has come into the world for judgment (John 9:39). Some biblical scholars explain the apparent discrepancy by noting that the *believer* is not judged, whereas the *unbeliever* is already judged by his or her very unbelief (3:18; 5:24). Jesus is the judge in the sense that he presents himself as the object of decision. He becomes the standard by which the world will, in a sense, judge itself.

Meanwhile, the disciples are warned that they themselves should not judge others (Matthew 7:1; Luke 6:37). Those who are merciless will be judged mercilessly (James 2:13).

Jesus, Holy Man of God: The Jesus of icons and holy cards, of songs and prayers and devotional literature, is often a Jesus almost totally removed from the ordinary currents of human life on this planet. This "holy man of God" is unmarried, because there is something inherently inferior about the married state (a "lawful remedy for concupiscence," the older moral theology textbooks conceded). Marriage is a less exalted state because there is something inherently evil about the flesh and in particular about genital expressions of love and affection. Pleasure, therefore, is to be kept in its place (how many "portraits" of Jesus have him smiling, not to say laughing?). To be virtuous is to act *against* one's natural inclinations and desires. "If it's not difficult, it's probably not virtuous," many assumed in the past. This attitude, of course, admits of degrees. For some Christians, the anti-pleasure, anti-flesh principle leads to prohibitions against alcohol, even against card-playing, for example.

Meanwhile, the more dignified, highly artistic representations of the Lord, as in the icons of Eastern Orthodox Christianity, tell also of an other-worldly Jesus, his expressionless facial features distorted to emphasize that his true home and his true interests are somewhere else. The gaze, untouched by even a hint of compassion, suggests a Being supremely uninterested in involving himself in this world, much less in changing its structures.

This is the Jesus, too, of the charismatic (the word in lower case to indicate a generic reference only, with no necessary application to adherents of the Catholic Charismatic Movement). He is totally consumed with the praise of God in word and song. He came among us for no other reason than to alert us to the presence and power of the Holy Spirit and to open our minds and our hearts totally to the God who heals and forgives, who affirms and confirms us in our individual existence.

Jesus is, to be sure, a *holy man of God*. But holiness is not the same as an other-worldliness which calls us to deny the radical goodness of the created order (see again chapters 5 and 7). Holiness is *wholeness*, according to the title of one of Josef Goldbrunner's works (*Holiness Is Wholeness*, Notre Dame: University of Notre Dame Press, 1964). The holy person is the one who is fully what God created that person to be, and who has indeed been re-created in the Holy Spirit. To be fully what God intends us to be is to live by the principle of the divine indwelling, to be open truly to the Transcendent, and to know and love by the light and power of that principle (see again chapter 5). Holiness, in its deepest biblical meaning, is simply the life of God. God alone is holy: "There is no Holy One like the Lord; there is no Rock like our God" (1 Samuel 2:2). God's name (which is equivalent to God's "person") is holy (Leviticus 20:3; 22:2; Ezekiel 20:39; 36:20). Persons, places, even seasons become holy by being touched with the divine presence (see, e.g., Deuteronomy 26:15; Exodus 3:5; 28:41; Psalm 46:5; Leviticus 25:12; Isaiah 65:5; Haggai 2:12).

Where the holiness of God is mentioned in the New Testament, the Old Testament roots are clear, as in the Lord's Prayer ("hallowed be your name"—Matthew 6:9; Luke 11:2) and in

1 John 2:20, for example. Jesus, too, is called the holy one of God (Mark 1:24; Luke 1:35; 4:34; John 6:69; Acts of the Apostles 3:14; Revelation 3:7) and the holy servant of God (Acts of the Apostles 4:27,30).

It is to the Church and its members that the term is more frequently applied. The Church is a temple holy to the Lord (Ephesians 2:21), made so by the indwelling of the Spirit (1 Corinthians 3:17). The principal effect and sign of Christian holiness, however, is a life lived according to Christian moral standards (2 Peter 3:11). Just as the holiness of Jesus was the principle of his life of servanthood (Mark 10:45), so the holiness of the Church and of the Christian is for the sake of Christian witness and service.

Jesus, Liberator: If the first three Christological types suggest a right-of-center or conservative understanding of Christian faith and mission, these last two reflect a left-of-center or liberal emphasis.

Given our new sensitivity to previously hidden or ignored pockets of injustice and oppression (see again chapter 3), the image of Jesus as instrument of liberation has become increasingly attractive. He is the one "who came into the world to preach the Gospel to the poor and liberate the oppressed" (Gustavo Gutierrez, Foreword to Hugo Assmann's *Practical Theology of Liberation*, London: Search Press, 1975, p. 11). He is indeed "the Liberator of the poor and the wretched of the land," and in that sense he may even be described as "black" (James Cone, *God of the Oppressed*, New York: Seabury Press, 1975, pp. 2, 133-137). For similar reasons and according to a similar theological method, Jesus is perceived as "red," "gay," or "feminist." Today, as in his own lifetime, Jesus is to be found in "bad company" (see Adolf Holl, *Jesus in Bad Company*, New York: Holt, Rinehart and Winston, 1973). But this is not to say that Jesus' whole life and work were that of a political revolutionary. His message of the Kingdom of God was directed not only against the existing order but against the Zealots as well, the political revolutionaries of his own day. "My kingdom does not belong to this world" (John 18:36).

That Jesus identified with the poor and the oppressed of his own day is without question, however. He himself belonged to the lower class and made it clear that wealth is an obstacle to entrance into the Kingdom of God (Matthew 19:16-30; Mark 10:17-31; Luke 18:18-30). He employs Isaiah 61:1 in responding to the Pharisees regarding his mission, a mission which includes preaching the good news to the poor (Matthew 11:5, Luke 4:18). He praises Zacchaeus for his generosity to the poor (Luke 19:1-10). Later Paul would propose that the wealthy should give away their superfluous goods so that some measure of equality might be established between themselves and the poor (2 Corinthians 8:14). And even if we cannot be absolutely certain that Jesus ascribed to himself the title "Suffering Servant of God" (with its roots in the Servant Songs of Deutero-Isaiah, chapters 40-55), it is clear that the early Church so interpreted his mission (Acts of the Apostles 3:13,26; 4:27,30). The words of the baptism of Jesus (Matthew 3:17; Mark 1:11; Luke 3:22) are almost an exact quotation from Isaiah 42:1. The various descriptions of the passion are probably a development of the idea of the Servant as well (Matthew 26:28; Mark 14:24; Luke 22:20). Jesus took the form of a slave on our behalf (Philippians 2:5-11). He touches lepers (Mark 1:40-41), feeds the hungry (Mark 6:34-44), converses frequently with women (Mark 7:24-30; John 4:4-30), has women in his company (Luke 8:1-3), cures on the Sabbath (Luke 13:10-17), defends an adulteress (John 8:1-11), condemns the hypocrisy of religious officials (Matthew 23:1-36), blesses those who are poor, hungry, mournful, persecuted, who seek peace (Matthew 5:1-12), places love of neighbor on par with the love of God (Mark 12:28-31), and insists that our attitude toward our neighbor in need will be the principal measure of judgment on the last day (Matthew 25:31-46).

Jesus, Our Brother: Others who are reluctant to acknowledge the Lordship of Jesus are satisfied to describe him as a kind of exemplary human being, one who inspires us to treat our fellow human beings as brothers and sisters. The great message of Christianity is summed up by Adolf Harnack as consisting of the fatherhood of God and the brotherhood of man. Jesus shows us what brotherhood is all about. This is the romanticized Jesus of *Jesus Christ Superstar* and *Godspell.* He is the symbol of joy and true life, a victimized figure who is nonetheless universally admired.

"He's a man—he's just a man. He's not a king—he's just the same as anyone I know" (*Jesus Christ Superstar*).

Brotherhood is important to the New Testament conception of the Christian life. That is undeniable. Christians are called brothers about one hundred and sixty times, and Jesus himself said that one who does the will of the Father is his (Jesus') own brother—and sister and mother (Matthew 12:50; Mark 3:35; Luke 8:31). But a Christology which goes no farther than that cannot be reconciled with the dogmatic development already outlined in the two preceding chapters. Such purely humanistic interpretations of Jesus recall a question the late Anglican Archbishop William Temple put to their adherents: "Why any man should have troubled to crucify the Christ of Liberal Protestantism has always been a mystery" (*Readings in St. John's Gospel*, New York: Macmillan, 1942, p. xxix).

CHRIST AND CULTURE

Each of these "Jesuses," when taken alone, represents a selective reading of the historical record. The principle of selection is an expression, in turn, of some cultural perspective. A given *culture* is the interlocking network of products which arises from the human activities of particular societies and communities: language, customs, ideas, beliefs, social organization, art, technology, values, and the like.

But Jesus, or at least our idea of Jesus, is not only a *reflection* of our cultural perspective. Jesus is also seen as having a *relationship* to culture, whether positive, negative, or some combination thereof. Protestant theologian H. Richard Niebuhr (d. 1962) identified five such relationships: Christ *against* culture; Christ *of* culture; Christ *above* culture; Christ and culture *in paradox*; and Christ as *transformer* of culture. The first two represent extreme views; the third, fourth, and fifth are variations on the mainstream, centrist position of the Church at large.

Christ Against Culture

Although it cannot simply be conceded that this was the original attitude of the Christian community toward the world, it surely was an answer which appeared very early in the history of the Church. The First Letter of John counsels the faithful against loving the world, for the world is under the power of evil, full of lies, hatred, murder, and lust. It is a dying world, destined to pass away (1:6, 2:8-9,11,15,17; 3:8,11-15; 5:4-5,19). The same negative orientation is to be found in the writings of Tertullian (*Apology* and *On Idolatry*), and later was significantly present in the monastic movement of the Catholic Church and in the sectarian movement within Protestantism (the Mennonites and the Quakers, for example).

The witness of radical Christianity is a perennial gift to the whole Church. Jesus alone is Lord. We cannot compromise our faith with the kingdoms of this world. On the other hand, the Christ-against-culture position denies in action what it affirms in word. The radical Christian uses the very language, thought-patterns, scientific understandings, sociological analyses, and so forth which are themselves expressions of culture. Even the writer of 1 John used the terms of the Gnostic philosophy to which he objected. Tertullian was a Roman to the core. And monasticism actually *contributed* to the advancement of culture. At the edges of the radical position, furthermore, is at least a touch of the Manichean heresy, which rejects the goodness of matter. But nature has been elevated by grace. God is present to the creation. Indeed, God took on human flesh.

The Christ of Culture

The opposite extreme is entirely comfortable with culture. There is no tension at all between Christ and the world. For those holding this view, Jesus may be a great educator, or philosopher, or reformer, or humanist. He comes not to challenge the world or to pronounce a judgment upon it but to bless and embrace it. In the earliest period this seemed to have been the position adopted by the *Judaizers*, i.e., those who sought to maintain loyalty to Christ

without abandoning any important element of their Jewish traditions, and by the *Gnostics*. In more recent times, the Christ-of-
culture approach is identified most closely with what Niebuhr
called "culture-Protestantism" of the nineteenth and early twentieth centuries, of Friedrich Schleiermacher, Albrecht Ritschl
(d. 1889), Harnack, and Walter Rauschenbusch (d. 1918), father of
the Social Gospel movement in American Protestantism. The
Kingdom of God for them was, for the most part, the realization of
human brotherhood in this world. We are all God's children. The
Lord calls us to accept and love one another.

There is much to be said about the Christ-of-culture view,
just as there is much to admire in the Christ-against-culture
stance. Earlier generations of non-Christians were not only
impressed with the constancy and uncompromising behavior of the
young Church; they were also attracted by the harmony of the
Christian message with the moral and religious philosophy of their
best teachers and by the agreement of Christian conduct with that
of their exemplary heroes. Furthermore, the word of God *is*
expressed in culturally diverse ways. The coherence of Christ
with culture is rooted in the incarnational principle itself. Jesus is
relevant to every time and place and people.

But the Christ-of-culture perspective is also too selective in
its reading of the New Testament. Jesus does in fact stand over
against the world, as the Christ-against-culture position convincingly argues. Sin is in the world—everywhere. Education alone
will not produce justice or goodness or peace. The oppressed, once
liberated from their oppression, too often become, in turn, the
oppressors. Jesus' kingdom is not of this world (John 18:36).

Christ Above Culture

This approach and the next two share the conviction that nature,
on which all culture is founded, is good and rightly ordered by the
Creator—indeed, that it has been re-created by Christ and the
Holy Spirit. These three positions also recognize the universality
and radical character of sin. Culture is possible because of grace,
i.e., God's presence; and grace has to be expressed sacramentally,
in cultural forms. Nonetheless, there are three variations within

this centrist point of view. We have *synthesists, dualists,* and *conversionists.*

The *synthesist* ("Christ above culture") confesses a Lord who is both of this world and of the other. Jesus is both God and a human being, one person with two natures, divine and human. As a human being, Jesus is very much *of* culture. As God, he is very much *above* culture. As a human being *and* God, he is at once *of* culture and *above* it.

This motif runs through the New Testament. Indeed, New Testament faith is a radically incarnational one. Christ insists, for example, that he has not come to abolish the Law and the Prophets, but to fulfill them (Matthew 5:17-19), that we should render to Caesar the things that are Caesar's and to God the things that are God's (Matthew 22:21). Justin Martyr and Clement of Alexandria were among the principal patristic synthesizers, but Thomas Aquinas and the Catholic theological tradition generally have been particularly strong representatives of this approach.

The position is attractive because it is consistent with our abiding human quest for achieving balance and for unity, a unity grounded in the unity of the Godhead itself. We shy away from single-minded, extreme positions. But some have worried that the synthesist view leads to a cultural conservatism. God is perceived by the synthesists to have been embodied very well in a particular culture; therefore, that culture (identified with "Christian civilization") should be preserved at all costs. But no culture is perfect. Does a synthesist approach take sufficient account of the radical evil which is everywhere present, or of the multiplicity of cultural ways in which the Lord can be expressed?

Christ and Culture in Paradox

The *dualist* view is identified especially with Paul and Luther. We dwell now in an "earthly tent," Paul reminds us. But when it is destroyed, as inevitably it will be, we shall have "a dwelling provided for us by God, a dwelling in the heavens, not made by hands but to last forever. We groan while we are here, even as we yearn to have our heavenly habitation envelop us" (2 Corinthians 5:1-2). For Luther there are two kingdoms, the one of God and the other of the world. God's kingdom is a kingdom of grace and mercy, but the kingdom of the world is a kingdom of wrath and severity. We cannot confuse the two, thereby putting wrath into God's kingdom or mercy into the world's, as the fanatics do. And yet the two kingdoms are closely related, and the Christian must affirm both in a single act of obedience to the one God of mercy and wrath, not as a divided soul with a double allegiance and duty. Living between time and eternity, between wrath and mercy, we find life at once tragic and joyful. There is no solution to this until the Kingdom of God comes in all its perfection at the end (see his *Treatise on Good Works*, for example). A twentieth-century variation on the Lutheran position has been expressed by Reinhold Niebuhr, especially in his *Moral Man and Immoral Society* (New York: Scribners, 1932).

The strengths of the dualist position are reasonably clear. Sin exists not only in the individual but in communities, in institutions, in laws. On the other hand, such dualism has also led Christians to a certain disdain for law and even toward the same kind of cultural conservatism we detected in the preceding view. The dualists seem to rest content with the quality of political and economic life. For the dualist, laws, institutions, the state are only restraining forces, without positive purpose and impact. All of our work in the temporal order, therefore, is transitory. However important cultural duties might be for us, the Christian's heart is simply not in them.

Christ the Transformer of Culture

This position emphasizes the participation of the Word in creation itself and of the Creator in the incarnation of the Son and in the redemption wrought through the Son's work. God brings order out of chaos in the act of creation, and Christ brings new order out of the chaos of sin in the act of redemption. History, therefore, is the dramatic interaction between God and humankind. It is the story of God's mighty deeds and of our response to them. We live "between the times." The future is already being realized in the present. The Kingdom of God is even now.

This *conversionist* motif is most clearly indicated in the Fourth Gospel, especially in its Prologue (1:1-18). "Yes, God so loved the world that he gave his only Son, that whoever believes in him may not die but may have eternal life. God did not send the Son into the world to condemn the world, but that the world might be saved through him" (3:16-17). John's sacramental vision, particularly his emphasis on the Eucharist and Baptism, stresses the conversion of ordinary elements and symbols into signs and instruments of God's redeeming and sanctifying presence. Christ is the one who transforms human actions. Indeed, when Christ is lifted up, he will draw all to himself (1:29; 3:14-17; 12:32,47).

The same conversionist motif can be found in Augustine's classic work, *The City of God*, and in his *Confessions*. Christ transforms culture in that he redirects, reinvigorates, and regenerates human life as expressed in human works which are at once perverted and corrupted by sin although of a radically good and holy nature. Whatever is is good. Jesus Christ has come to heal and to renew what sin has tarnished.

Calvin, unlike Luther and more like Augustine, also saw a positive role for social and political institutions. God's sovereignty must be made manifest in the whole network of human relationships, even in the public domain.

In the end, of course, there is no fundamental opposition between Christ and culture. The work of culture is the work of grace, and the power of grace is expressed in culture (as the *synthesists* hold). And yet we live as if in two worlds simultaneously: in *this* world, but not completely *of* it (as the *dualists* remind us). But if the world we live in is destined for the Kingdom of God, we are called to collaborate with God in its ongoing re-creation and renewal (as the *conversionist* position states). Meanwhile, the witness of the radicals helps to sharpen our sense that the Kingdom is not *of* this world, and the witness of the harmonizers or cultural Christians encourages us to commend the eternal message of Christ to those who might otherwise ignore it.

Who is the Christ of contemporary culture, then? He is all of these Christs, yet no one of them alone. But if he is to be the Christ of *history* and of Christian *faith* as well as the *contemporary* Christ, each of our modern versions of Jesus must be measured against the standards of the biblical texts and the Church's subsequent interpretations of those texts.

"One of the strange features of Christianity," George MacRae, Stillman Professor of Roman Catholic Studies at Harvard Divinity School, has observed, "is that its adherents are so often dissatisfied with the Jesus whom tradition has bequeathed to them. New theories about Jesus, new discoveries that present him in a different light, whatever their historical plausibility, never lack an eager reception among the curious. And it was always so—that is what we sometimes fail to recognize" (*Commonweal*, vol. 99, January 25, 1974, p. 417).

MacRae notes that Paul himself was frequently preoccupied with rejecting divergent images of Jesus and cites, by way of example, a passage in Second Corinthians:

> My fear is that, just as the serpent seduced Eve by his cunning, your thoughts may be corrupted and you may fall away from your sincere and complete devotion to Christ. I say this because, when someone comes preaching another Jesus than the one we preached, or when you receive a different spirit than the one you have received, or a gospel other than the gospel you accepted, you seem to endure it quite well. (11:3-4)

We move in the next chapter to a fuller discussion of those New Testament texts and of the Church's faith which they express.

SUMMARY

1. Christianity alone proclaims that Jesus of Nazareth is Lord, that he is "true God of true God." But even within the Christian community there are apparently widely divergent notions of Christ. Is the Christ of *faith* the same as the Jesus of *history*? Is the Christ of *our* faith the Christ of the Church's faith as well?

2. Popular views of Jesus Christ, both within and without the Church, range from one end of the theological spectrum to the other. Some see Jesus principally as a *teacher*, which he is, but as one principally concerned with the communication of doctrine and with its purity of expression. Others perceive Jesus as *ruler*, *judge*, and *king*, which he is,

but as one who lays down the law and who reigns over us enveloped in pomp and circumstance. Others know Jesus as the *holy man of God*, which he is, but it is a holiness that separates Christ from the world, that places him high on some pedestal removed from the everyday world of ordinary people. Still others understand Jesus as a *liberator* or revolutionary, which he is, but as one who is concerned primarily with overcoming economic and political exploitation and with renovating *this* world alone. Finally, there are those who can accept Jesus as no more, or no less, than their *brother*, a human being like us in all things. Jesus is our brother, to be sure, but he is also the Son of God, the Lord of history, the only one about whom it can be said that he is of the same substance as the Father, the Almighty.

3.   Whatever our concept of Jesus Christ, that Christ has some relationship, whether positive, negative, or some combination thereof, with the world around him. This is the problem of Christ and culture. Culture here is understood as the interlocking network of products which arises from the *human activities* of particular societies and communities: language, customs, beliefs, art, technology, social organizations, etc.

4.   Christ has been portrayed as standing entirely *against* culture. The world is evil, and we must keep our distance from it (monasticism, sectarianism, pacifism, e.g.). Although there is much that is true in this position, it tends to deny the goodness of creation as well as the inevitability of employing some cultural forms in the expression of the Word and the Kingdom of God.

5.   The Christ *of* culture is always at home wherever he finds himself. He is the fulfillment of our heart's desires and aspirations. He calls us to acknowledge God as our Father and all human beings as our brothers and sisters under God. Although this view does show the harmony that exists between the Gospel and human life, it neglects the prophetic and judgmental aspects of Christ's mission and pays too little heed to the universal presence of sin.

6.   Three other positions are generally part of the mainstream of the Church's attitude toward Christ and culture. The *synthesists* ("Christ above culture") stress the incarnational principle, namely, that Jesus is both God and a human being. As such, he is at once *above* culture and *of* it. The *dualists* ("Christ and culture in paradox") stress the fact that we live in two cities simultaneously and that complete synthesis can come only after death and the fullness of the Kingdom. The *conversionists* ("Christ the transformer of culture") emphasize the doctrines of creation and redemption. God did not send the Son to condemn the

world, which came forth from the divine hand in the first place, but to save it. When Christ is lifted up, he will draw all things to himself.

7. The work of culture is the work of grace, and the power of grace is expressed in culture (as the *synthesists* hold). And yet we live in this world of culture while not being completely of it (as the *dualists* declare). But this world is itself destined for the Kingdom of God, and we are called to facilitate its movement toward the Kingdom (as the *conversionists* insist). All the while, the radicals ("Christ against culture") remind us that the Kingdom ultimately is not of this world, and the harmonizers or cultural Christians ("Christ of culture") encourage us to commend the eternal message of Christ to those who might otherwise ignore it.

8. The Christ of contemporary culture is all of these Christs, yet no one of them alone.

SUGGESTED READINGS

Boff, Leonardo. *Jesus Christ Liberator: A Critical Christology for Our Time*. New York: Orbis Books, 1978.

Cullmann, Oscar. *Jesus and the Revolutionaries*. New York: Harper & Row, 1970.

Frei, Hans. *The Identity of Jesus Christ: The Hermeneutical Basis of Dogmatic Theology*. Philadelphia: Fortress Press, 1975.

McFadden, Thomas R., ed. *Does Jesus Make a Difference?* New York: Seabury Press, 1974.

Niebuhr, H. Richard. *Christ and Culture*. New York: Harper & Row, 1951.

O'Grady, John J. *Jesus, Lord and Christ*. New York: Paulist Press, 1972.

· XII ·

THE CHRIST OF THE NEW TESTAMENT

THE PROBLEM

Jesus of Nazareth really lived. No one questions that fact today. He was born at a certain time, in a certain place, of a certain family. He passed through various stages of human development just like anyone else: infancy, childhood, adolescence, young adulthood, adulthood. He had certain convictions, and he expressed them in a certain way, to certain audiences, at certain places. He engaged in certain activities, in certain ways, in certain company, in certain places. His words and deeds had a certain impact, on certain people, under certain circumstances. And he died at a certain time, in a certain manner, at a certain place, in the presence of certain people.

But if that were all there were to the matter, Jesus Christ would not be a problem, or indeed a matter of very great concern to us today. Indeed, he is called Jesus *Christ* and not simply Jesus *of Nazareth* because a certain meaning or interpretation was given the otherwise bare historical facts of his existence some two thousand years ago. It is clear, in fact, that a special value was placed on the life and death of Jesus of Nazareth even during the first century of Christianity, immediately after his death by crucifixion at the hands of the local Roman government and at the instigation of the local religious establishment.

To be specific: It was very early asserted that this Jesus of Nazareth, who "was crucified under Pontius Pilate, suffered and was buried," did not remain in the state of death but rose from the dead "on the third day." Furthermore, that he is now "seated at the right hand of the Father," and that "he shall come again in glory to judge the living and the dead" and that his Kingdom shall have "no end." This is so because Jesus is Lord; he is "true God from true God,...one in being with the Father."

The question arises: Was the Christ whom the Church confessed in faith, both within the New Testament and beyond it, the same Jesus of Nazareth whose sheer historical factity no one seriously challenges? In other words, *Did the primitive and post-biblical Church create a Christ who is divine from a Jesus who was purely human?* And what of Jesus himself? How did he estimate his own significance? Were the words and claims which the New Testament places on the lips of the carpenter's son really the words and claims of Jesus, or were they the words and claims of the Church read back into the life and ministry of Jesus? In other words, *What connection, if any, can we establish between the Church's evaluation of Jesus and Jesus' own evaluation of himself?*

It is, once again, *the problem of the Jesus of history and the Christ of faith.*

THE SOURCES AND THEIR INTERPRETATION
Non-Christian Sources

The few non-Christian sources for the life of Jesus provide us with very little information. They do confirm the argument, however, that from the earliest days it never occurred even to the bitterest enemies of Christianity that the historical existence of Jesus should be challenged. Tacitus (d. ca. 116) reported that Jesus was condemned to death by Pontius Pilate under Tiberius (*Annals* 15,4). Suetonius (d. ca. 120) wrote of a certain "Chrestus" who caused disturbances in Rome (*Claudius* 25,4). Pliny the Younger (d. ca. 110) acknowledged in a letter to Trajan that Christ was revered as a God (*Epistola* 10,96). Josephus the historian (d. ca. 93) referred to James as the brother of Jesus who is called the Christ (*Antiquities*, 20,200). The Talmud references and the apocryphal gospels (e.g., the Gospel of Thomas) likewise add nothing to our knowledge of Jesus. Again, at best this non-Christian material provides independent evidence for the actual existence of Jesus.

Christian Sources

New Testament

The most important source for the life of Jesus, therefore, remains the New Testament itself, and the four Gospels in particular. But when one dips into the Gospels, one finds that they do not present history as we generally understand that word today. In other words, they would not stand up alongside a lengthy obituary essay in the *New York Times* as a work of objective reporting and interpretation. They provide us instead with a testimony of faith. *Their purpose is not to reconstruct the life of Jesus in every chronologically accurate detail, but to illustrate the eternal significance of Jesus through selected examples of his preaching, his activities, and the impact of both upon his contemporaries.*

The Gospels were written by men of faith for men and women of faith. They are the product of subsequent reflection on the life of Jesus—a process that required anywhere from thirty-five to sixty years. They are complex documents because of their peculiar purpose, because of the diversity of their origin and the audiences to which they were initially addressed, and because of the various stages of development they passed through before reaching the form in which we have them.

There are at least *three stages of development* culminating in the actual writing of the Gospels: (1) the original words and deeds of Jesus; (2) the oral proclamation of the Apostles and disciples (catechesis, narratives, testimonies, hymns, doxologies, and prayers); and (3) the writings themselves. These are specified as such by the Instruction of the Pontifical Biblical Commission, *The Historical Truth of the Gospels*, 1964. (An excerpt is given in the Appendix. The full text and a commentary by Joseph Fitzmyer appear in *Theological Studies*, vol. 25, 1964, pp. 386-408.)

Depending upon one's point of view, one might expand the number of stages to five; for example: (1) the period of direct contact and communication between Jesus and the disciples and others; (2) the emergence of an oral tradition following the resurrection, a period in which there were no significant writings because the expectation of the Second Coming or return of Christ was intense and vivid; (3) the hardening of the oral tradition into the shape of accepted doctrine communicated through letters (Epistles), which were written for specific occasions and audiences and not for posterity; (4) the writing of the Gospels as soon as it became clear that the Lord was not about to return very soon, a period in which the first generation of Christians was dying out and a new generation, with no direct contact with, or memories of, Jesus was coming on the scene (much like the situation today when many young people have no personal recollection of a 1960s figure such as John F. Kennedy); (5) the completion of the New Testament canon (official collection of books accepted by the Church as inspired) with the composition of the pastoral Epistles (Timothy and Titus) and 2 Peter, a period in which the Church is newly conscious of itself as a society, still threatened from without and from within.

Development

How many stages of development there were is a matter of choice, but *the fact of development is beyond question today.* Indeed, we cannot easily overestimate the significance of the Pontifical Biblical Commission's Instruction of 1964 on the historicity of the Gospels. The Commission calmly and openly admits that we do not have in the written Gospels the words and deeds of Jesus as exactly and as completely as they were first uttered or performed, nor do we even have the full and exact record of what was communicated orally between the death and resurrection, on the one hand, and the actual composition of the Gospels, on the other. What we have, rather, is *the finally edited verson* given by the evangelists. This imposes upon us all the responsibility of trying to get behind and beyond the written Gospels, and to identify and sort out the various *levels of tradition* through which the evangelical process moved.

The *first layer* of tradition is made accessible through *historical criticism.* Historical criticism is a relatively late development in the history of Christian theology and of biblical interpretation. Until the Enlightenment of the eighteenth century it was generally assumed that the Gospels gave a clear and reliable account of the life of Jesus, that there was no discrepancy at all between the faith of the primitive Church and the facts upon which that faith was built. Herman Reimarus (d. 1768), a German professor of oriental languages, was the first to challenge this assumption with the rallying cry "Back from the Christ of dogma to the real Jesus." The immediate reaction to Reimarus' thesis was strongly negative. Many different versions of the "life of Jesus" appeared, as if in rebuttal of Reimarus. But the differences among the several "lives" of Jesus were glaringly obvious. As we pointed out in the preceding chapter, many authors portrayed Jesus as they would like him to have been rather than Jesus as the early Church knew him to be. The biographical confusion generated an attitude of fundamental skepticism about the whole project. Albert Schweitzer (d. 1965) slammed the door once and for all on Liberal efforts at reconstructing the life of Jesus with his own *The Quest of the Historical Jesus*, published right at the turn of the century. The historical Jesus, it now seemed, could not be recovered scientifically from the New Testament documents. But this, too, proved to be an over-reaction, and since Schweitzer's time there has, in fact, been a steady return of confidence in the scholar's and the Church's capacity to get behind the testimonies of faith and identify at least the basic historical foundation of Jesus' life and ministry.

The *second layer* of tradition is discovered through a method known as *form criticism*. This method was developed in Germany between the two world wars and was concerned primarily with the formation of the Gospel tradition which occurred through catechesis and liturgical expressions, roughly between 35 and 60 A.D. It is essentially a means of analyzing typical features of biblical texts (hymns, acclamations, confessions, sermons, instructional material, editorial remarks, descriptive narratives, sayings of Jesus, dialogues, Old Testament allusions and quotations, etc.) in order to relate them to their original "situation-in-life." It was the development of form criticism which brought out the fact that a long period of *oral* tradition preceded any writing of the New Testament.

The *third layer* of tradition is examined through the method of *redaction criticism*, whose origin is the most recent of all, i.e., the mid 1950s. Redaction criticism tries to discover the dominant ideas which governed the final editing of the Gospels as we have them today (e.g., What was the "peculiar purpose" of each evangelist mentioned by the Biblical Commission's 1964 Instruction?). Just as form criticism discloses the existence of an *oral* tradition prior to the formulation of the New Testament, so redaction criticism stresses the antecedent existence of *both* oral *and written* traditions from which the New Testament authors worked and which they creatively transformed to suit their particular theological and catechetical intentions.

Different Cultures

Furthermore, there are different cultures at work in the production of the New Testament, and these, in turn, generate distinctive theological viewpoints regarding the meaning of Jesus. These are the cultures of the Palestinian communities of Aramaic/Hebrew-speaking Jewish Christians, of the Syrian communities of Greek-speaking Jewish Christians, of the communities of Asia Minor and Greece with their Greek-speaking Gentile Christians, and finally of the particular communities influenced by major individual Christians like Paul and John. One might also classify these cultures more broadly as Palestinian, Jewish-Hellenistic, and Hellenistic-Gentile.

Only in the past century has biblical scholarship acquired the linguistic and historical data necessary for even recognizing such theological and cultural diversity within New Testament Christianity. Previous scholarship, for example, had known Aramaic, the language which Jesus apparently spoke. But the only forms of Aramaic which it had at its disposal came from several centuries before Jesus (Imperial Aramaic) or from several centuries after Jesus (Syriac and Talmudic Aramaic). "To reconstruct the language of Jesus from such evidence," Catholic biblical scholar Raymond Brown writes, "was not unlike trying to reconstruct Shakespearian English from Chaucer and the *New York Times*" (*Horizons*, vol. 1, 1974, p. 43). The situation improved over the past one hundred years through such relatively recent discoveries as the Dead Sea Scrolls in 1947. (For a good summary of their contents and significance, see John L. McKenzie, "Qumran Scrolls," *Dictionary of the Bible*, pp. 710-716.)

Sayings of Jesus

In spite of the plurality of stages, layers, forms, and so forth, biblical scholars have reached a consensus regarding criteria for establishing authentic sayings of the historical Jesus: (1) Sayings which contain Aramaicisms characteristic of the Palestine of Jesus' day are more likely to have their origin in Jesus. (2) The shorter or shortest of two or three different accounts of the same incident is probably the one closer or closest to the source, since authors tend to expand and explain. (3) Sayings or principles attributed to Jesus which are contrary to the developing traditions of the early Church are usually more authentic than those which clearly give support to current attitudes. (4) The same is true of elements in the message of Jesus which make a break with the accepted traditions and customs of Judaism. (5) Words and deeds which are attested to by many different sources probably have a strong historical basis. (6) Negatively, sayings which reflect the faith, practices, and situation of the post-resurrection Church cannot be taken always at face value.

Interpretations of the Sources

Until the eighteenth century, as we noted above, there was no New Testament problem. All Christians—Catholic, Anglican, Orthodox, and Protestant alike—assumed that the Christ of the New Testament and the Jesus of history were exactly one and the same. But once the assumption was challenged, Christians began dividing over the question of the relationship between the Christ of faith and the Jesus of history, i.e., between the Church's interpretation of Jesus and Jesus' own self-understanding.

Those positions move all the way from the conservative right, which posits a real relationship between Jesus' self-evaluation and the New Testament Church's Christology, to the liberal left, which denies any real relationship or continuity between the two. Those positions are also distinguished by their scholarly or non-scholarly bases of support. *Scholarly* conservatism and *scholarly* liberalism are expressed by reputable scholars who have produced a body of articles that meet the publishing standards of the professional biblical journals or whose books have been reviewed favorably in such journals. It is not enough, therefore, that a point of view be expressed and defended by someone holding a biblical degree or a teaching position in biblical studies. *Non-scholarly* conservatism and *non-scholarly* liberalism are the product of those who either hold no biblical degrees and/or no teaching position in biblical studies or who have not published a body of articles in serious professional journals or books which have been reviewed favorably in such journals. The distinction is important for making sense of such comments as "Scripture scholars are divided over this question," or "Not all Scripture scholars agree with this position," or "Scripture scholars tell us that...," or "Scripture scholars can't make up their minds about...."

What follows is a summary, with some modifications, of Catholic biblical scholar Raymond Brown's schematization of twentieth-century views on the Christology of the New Testament:

Non-scholarly Conservatism

This view *identifies* the Christology of the New Testament with Jesus' own self-evaluation. Even though the Gospels were written some thirty to sixty years after the ministry of Jesus, this conservative position maintains that there had been *no significant Christological development* in that time. Thus, when Jesus accepted Peter's confession that Jesus was indeed the Messiah, the Son of the living God (Matthew 16:13-20), that acceptance reflects the self-understanding of Jesus—despite the fact that Peter's confession and Jesus' reaction are very different in the *earlier* Gospel of Mark (8:27-30). And if in the Gospel of John, Jesus speaks as a pre-existent divine figure (8:58; 17:5), he must have actually spoken that way during his lifetime—despite the fact that there is no indication of this in the three synoptic Gospels.

This view was first held defensively (i.e., over against the views of the scholars of the major Protestant denominations) by Protestant fundamentalists and other less-than-fundamentalist

Christians, particularly in various main-line Reformation churches of the American South. Catholics generally also held this position, but not defensively. After the condemnations of Modernism there was strict supervision over Catholic biblical studies from 1910 until Pope Pius XII's encyclical *Divino Afflante Spiritu* in 1943. Before 1943, the non-scholarly conservative position was the only view taught, accepted, and preached in the Catholic Church; it was simply taken for granted. Once the principles of modern biblical criticism were approved by Rome and assimilated by Catholic scholars, however, some Catholics did become exceedingly defensive about the traditional approach.

In light of the fact that the Gospels do not provide a literal account of what Jesus said and did, and in light of the evidence for development in the production of the New Testament, the non-scholarly conservatives should have asked, "How much development?" Instead they asked, "How do we know that any of it is true?" And rather than risk the loss of faith itself, they simply rejected the whole network of scholarly premises, even those formally and explicitly endorsed by the pope in the encyclical of 1943 and by the Pontifical Biblical Commission's Instruction of 1964.

Non-scholarly Liberalism

As on a political spectrum (Stalin at the extreme left, Hitler at the extreme right), the extremes touch. If the non-scholarly conservative asked the wrong question ("How do I know any of it is true?"), so, too, did the non-scholarly liberal. The only difference is in the answers given. The conservative rejects the scholarship in order to "save" the Christ of faith. The non-scholarly liberal rejects the Christ of faith in order to "save" his or her favorite notion of the Jesus of history.

The non-scholarly liberal concludes that there is no continuity at all between the Christology of the New Testament and Jesus' self-evaluation. He was nothing more than an ordinary man, except that he was more brilliant, more charismatic, more of a revolutionary, or take your pick. It is not finally important that Jesus was or was not the Son of God. It is what he taught us about life that counts, and what he taught us is that we have to love one another.

Although non-scholarly liberalism began as a Protestant phenomenon, enjoying wide popularity during the early decades of this century before it was effectively challenged by scholars and by declining membership rolls, it has made a belated entrance into Catholicism as a reaction to the exaggerated dogmatism of the pre-Vatican II period.

Scholarly Liberalism

Scholarly liberalism, unlike its non-scholarly counterpart, does not dismiss the Christology of the New Testament as unimportant, nor does it deny that the New Testament writers claimed far more than that Christianity was a "way of life." On the other hand, scholarly liberalism shares with its non-scholarly cousin the conviction that the Christology of the New Testament is a mistaken evaluation of Jesus which does not stand in real continuity with the self-evaluation of Jesus. For the liberals, New Testament Christology is a *creation* of the early Church.

Unquestionably, modern biblical studies owe a great debt of gratitude to the previous work of the liberal scholars. They were the ones, after all, who first challenged the non-scholarly conservatism which dominated all Christian churches until the eighteenth century. It was the liberals who discerned developmental patterns in the New Testament and who laid the groundwork for many of our present principles of biblical interpretation. Perhaps the best example of this scholarly liberalism in terms of both method and content was Wilhelm Bousset (d. 1920), whose book *Kyrios Christos* was first published in German in 1913 and in English translation in 1970 (Nashville: Abingdon).

For the scholarly liberals the historical Jesus was a preacher of stark ethical demand who challenged the religious institutions and who cut through the false ideas of his time. If the early Church had not turned him into the heavenly Son of Man, the Lord and Judge of the world, or indeed the Son of God, his ideals and insights might otherwise have been lost. But now that the crutch of New Testament Christology is no longer necessary (Christ's place in history and in our collective memories is secure), it can be discarded.

Bultmannian Existentialism

World War I undercut the optimism of liberal theology, and of liberal biblical scholarship as well. The war created a need for a God who saves us in Jesus, rather than for a Jesus who taught us how to live and, in effect, to save ourselves. In theology the anti-liberal movement was headed by Karl Barth. In the area of biblical studies it was led by Rudolf Bultmann.

Some mistakenly place Bultmann in the liberal camp because so many of his views were regarded as radical when he first proposed them. Yet his New Testament theology is a rejection of pre-World War I liberalism. Without discarding the legitimate methodological achievements of liberalism, Bultmann nevertheless denied the liberal thesis that New Testament Christology was a creation of the early Church. That is not to say that Bultmann's own view is clear and unequivocal. Brown regards it "difficult to characterize exactly" and suggests that "in some of his writing at least he is agnostic about the self-evaluation of Jesus" (*Horizons* article, p. 45). But Bultmann definitely did not think that the Christology of the New Testament distorted the import of Jesus, as the liberals maintained. Rather, there is a *functional equivalence* between the Church's Christological proclamation and Jesus' own proclamation of the Kingdom.

It is in this functional equivalence that Bultmann's existentialist philosophy can be found at work (see chapter 4, where Bultmann's existentialist philosophy is mentioned in the context of various theologies of human existence). If we are to escape from the vicious circle of futile existence, it will only be through the saving action of God in Jesus. We are called upon to accept this action of God. Where Jesus preached the Kingdom, the Church preached Jesus. Functionally, this preaching was equivalent. Dispensing, therefore, with the Church's proclamation would be to dispense with the challenge that is at the core of Christianity, a challenge that is primarily based on what God has done for us, rather than what we can do for ourselves.

Moderate Conservatism

Just as Bultmann's position was somewhat to the right of the
scholarly liberals, so most contemporary biblical scholarship is
somewhat to the right of Bultmann. This does not ignore the fact
that Catholic scholarship has moved decidedly *to the left* since the
1940s, but it has moved "to the left" in relation to the non-
scholarly conservatism which controlled Catholic theology and
biblical studies beforehand.

This moderate conservatism posits a *discernible continuity*
between the self-evaluation of Jesus and the Christology of the
early Church. Nonetheless, there is some difference of opinion
within the moderate conservative group. On one side, there are
those for whom the Church's Christology is *explicit* in Jesus' self-
evaluation, and, on the other, those for whom the Church's Christology is only *implicit* in Jesus' self-understanding. Neither side,
however, holds that Jesus applied to himself or accepted the so-
called "higher" titles of later New Testament Christology, e.g.,
"Lord," "Son of God," or "God." Both sides regard the application of these titles to have been the result of later Christian
reflection on the mystery of Christ. Where the two sides differ,
therefore, is on the matter of the so-called "lower" titles that were
known to the Jews from the Old Testament or inter-testamental
writings—e.g., "Messiah," "Prophet," "Servant of God," or "Son
of Man."

The *explicit* school was popular in the 1950s and early 1960s
and is still respectable today. Among its adherents are such Protestant scholars as Oscar Cullmann, C. H. Dodd (d. 1973), Joachim
Jeremias, and Vincent Taylor (d. 1968). Most Roman Catholic
scholars writing on the subject in the 1960s were in the same
camp.

In the 1970s, however, in Protestant and Catholic writing
alike, the *implicit* school gained acceptance. According to this
approach, Jesus did not express his self-understanding in terms of
titles or accept titles attributed to him by others. Rather he conveyed what he was by speaking with unique authority and by
acting with unique power. This view of Jesus' attitude does not
necessarily detract from his greatness. If Jesus did not find the title
"Messiah" acceptable, for example, it may mean only that the title

simply did not match his uniqueness. The Church was able to call him "Messiah" successfully only after it reinterpreted the title to match Jesus' greatness. Thus, the ultimate tribute to Jesus may have been that every term or title in the theological vocabulary of Israel had to be reshaped by his followers to do justice to him, including even the title "God" itself. Even the Second Vatican Council, as early as 1965, anticipated this shift: "...Jesus perfected revelation by fulfilling it through His whole work of making Himself present and manifesting Himself: though His words and deeds, His signs and wonders, but especially through His death and glorious resurrection from the dead and final sending of the Spirit of truth" (*Dogmatic Constitution on Divine Revelation*, n. 4). Among the scholars holding to the *implicit* opinion are, on the Reformation side of the line, F. Hahn, Reginald Fuller, Norman Perrin (d. 1977), some of the post-Bultmannians in Germany, and Roman Catholic authors of the 1970s such as Bruce Vawter and Raymond Brown (it would seem).

Brown and others expect that for the rest of this century biblical scholarship will move back and forth between these two moderate conservative positions. But regardless of whether one detects explicit or implicit Christology in the self-evaluation of Jesus, the line of *continuity* between his self-understanding and the early Church's subsequent proclamation is more firmly secure than was ever thought possible earlier in the century.

(For a summary, see the chart on page 437.)

WHERE FROM HERE?
THE QUESTION OF METHOD

From this point we can proceed in one of two directions. We can adopt the more traditional approach and take up the life and teachings of Jesus, beginning with the Gospel accounts. Thereafter, we would present the early Church's estimation of Jesus. But there are problems with this alternative. The fact is that the New Testament contains no biography of Jesus written during his lifetime nor even shortly after his death. What we have, as noted earlier, are testimonies of faith, constituted from fragments of the oral and written traditions which developed after Jesus' death and resurrection. It is Jesus *as he was remembered* by the earliest Christians and *as he was experienced* in their communities of faith whom we meet in the Gospels.

A second course is open to us, one that *begins* with the faith of the Church as expressed in the New Testament and moves from there to the message, mission, and person of Jesus as the source of that faith. The faith of the Church is centered on the *resurrection* of Jesus from the dead. The *kerygma*, or proclamation, is by definition a testimony to the resurrection, the earliest witness to which is given in Paul's First Letter to the Corinthians (15:3-8), written sometime in the year 56 or 57. Paul is obviously incorporating a creedal formula that he had previously been taught:

> I handed on to you as of the greatest importance
>   what I myself received:
> that Christ died for our sins
>   in accordance with the Scriptures,
> and that he was buried,
> and that he was raised on the third day
>   in accordance with the Scriptures,
> and that he was seen by Cephas,
>   then by the Twelve.
> After that he was seen by five hundred brothers at
>   once, most of whom are still alive, although some
>   have fallen asleep.
> After that he was seen by James,
>   then by all the apostles.
> Last of all he was seen by me....

Paul explicitly states that he is drawing on tradition, and certain internal evidence suggests this—e.g., the stylized structure of the passage and the use of such terms as "the Twelve," which is not an expression he uses otherwise. Clearly, he had some ready-made text at hand. And this would have been an entirely normal practice in the composition of the various books of the New Testament. Authors like Paul would draw upon existing liturgical formulations, as Paul had done earlier in the same letter when he quoted from a traditional eucharistic prayer (1 Corinthians 11:23-26).

We begin, therefore, where the New Testament begins, not with the nativity scene in Bethlehem but with the Church's proclamation of the risen Christ.

THE RESURRECTION
Its Meaning and Importance

The resurrection has been understood poorly. We refer here not only to the question of its facticity (whether it was a bodily, historical happening) but to the question of its place and significance in the whole Christ-event. For Roman Catholic theology the resurrection has long been viewed as simply the strongest possible corroboration of Jesus' messianic claims. It had no importance in itself in the work of redemption. We were redeemed by the cross, and by the cross alone. This relatively narrow perception of the resurrection was not a peculiarly Catholic failing. Even so great a biblical scholar as C. H. Dodd lends unwitting support to such an approach in his book *The Founder of Christianity*, where the resurrection comes at the end, as "the sequel" to the whole story about Jesus. "Liberation Christology" has the same tendency, for reasons already suggested (e.g., Jon Sobrino, *Christology at the Crossroads: A Latin American Approach*, Maryknoll, N.Y.: Orbis Books, 1978).

Christian theology today, in keeping with the results of modern New Testament studies, more commonly understands the resurrection as central to, not simply confirmatory of, Christian faith, and as the beginning, not the end, of the story.

Three men died on crosses in occupied Palestine sometime during the fourth decade of the Christian era. The executions were relatively routine. And so, too, was the mode of execution. Without question the Roman authorities regarded all three as trouble-makers, disturbers of the Roman peace. Over the head of one of them, however, the Romans affixed a sign "The King of the Jews," obviously in a spirit of derision and contempt. If we could return to Calvary on that Good Friday, that is all we would have seen: three men being put to death by crucifixion. And yet one of the three, the one they called "King of the Jews," would not be swallowed up forever by his death. At some point soon after his death, his closest followers would become convinced that he had, in fact, risen from the dead and that he lived again in their midst in a new and more powerful way than before. On the basis of their experience of the resurrection, these disciples would see the life and death of Jesus in a whole new light. They would reinterpret everything that he had said and done, recalling and reconstructing it all to the best of their ability. The message of the New Testament was always the message of the resurrection:

> Men of Israel, listen to me [it is Peter who speaks]! Jesus the Nazorean was a man whom God sent to you with miracles, wonders, and signs as his credentials. These God worked through him in your midst, as you well know. He was delivered up by the set purpose and plan of God; you even made use of pagans to crucify and kill him. God freed him from death's bitter pangs, however, and raised him up again, for it was impossible that death should keep its hold on him....
>
> This is the Jesus God raised up, and we are his witnesses....
>
> Therefore let the whole house of Israel know beyond any doubt that God has made both Lord and Messiah this Jesus whom you crucified. (Acts of the Apostles 2:22-24,32,36)

Paul was even more explicit about the centrality and utterly crucial importance of the resurrection for Christian faith: "And if Christ has not been raised, our preaching is void of content and your faith is empty too" (1 Corinthians 15:14).

The ambiguity that surrounded the life and death of Jesus now disappears. Under the impact of the resurrection everything falls into place. For the first time the Apostles look upon the figure of Jesus with confidence and self-assurance. His relationship with the Father, the Almighty, is now clearer than ever before. Jesus is without doubt the Christ, the Anointed One, of God. He is the Son of Man, the Suffering Servant, the Son of God, the Lord, the Son of David, the Word. At first such titles as these were *functional*; i.e., they described what Jesus had done. Then they became *confessional*; i.e., they were used in prayer and worship. They specified what it meant to be a Christian, i.e., one who confesses that Jesus is Lord. And eventually the titles were to assume a *metaphysical* and *theological* character; i.e., they would become intellectual tools to probe the inner reality of Jesus Christ: his person, his natures, and their relationships.

It was because of the early Church's faith in the resurrection that it came to acknowledge the *divinity* of Jesus. And once the Church acknowledged the divinity of Jesus, it began laying the foundations for the doctrine of the *incarnation*, which sees Jesus as the Word made flesh (John 1:14). From the doctrine of the incarnation the Church was led ineluctably to the *preexistence* of Jesus (John 1:1; Philippians 2:5-9) and to the question of his relationship to the whole of *creation* and to the *history of salvation* (Colossians 1:15-20; Romans 8:19-22; Ephesians 1:9-10,22,23). He is indeed the "first fruits" (1 Corinthians 15:20) of the "new creation" (2 Corinthians 5:17), which is the *Kingdom of God.*

Varieties of Interpretation Within the New Testament

As noted earlier in this chapter, there are different cultures at work in the production of the New Testament, and these, in turn, generate distinctive theological viewpoints regarding the meaning of Jesus. In each case, however, it is the Easter experience which provides the foundation for Christology.

Palestinian Community

In the Palestinian community, the closest to the events of the life, death, and resurrection of Jesus, there is a keen sense of the *imminence* of the Second Coming of Jesus. Jesus is identified as the *Son of Man* (Acts of the Apostles 7:55-56), who will return in power and glory—an identification which has apparent roots in Jesus' own sayings about the Son of Man (Mark 8:38; Luke 12:8-10). The return of Jesus as the Son of Man is the final act of vindication for all that Jesus said and did during his lifetime. Indeed, this hope shaped the liturgy of the Palestinian Church. At the center of its eucharistic worship is the *Maranatha* prayer, "O Lord, come!" (1 Corinthians 16:22), "Come, Lord Jesus!" (Revelation 22:20).

More important and certainly more central to the Palestinian Christology was its confession of Jesus as *the Christ* (Acts 3:20), or the *Messiah* (literally, "the anointed"). And because Jesus is the Messiah, he is also seen as the *Son of David* (Revelation 3:7; 5:5) and the *Son of God* (Luke 1:32), who will appear at the Second Coming, or *Parousia.* This explains, too, why such stress is placed in Matthew and Luke on the genealogies (Matthew 1:1-17; Luke 3:23-38). It was necessary that Jesus be able to trace his ancestry all the way back to David, for it had to be a descendant of the house of David who would inaugurate the messianic era (Mark 11:10). The Son of God title, on the other hand, expressed the closeness between Jesus and God, but not necessarily his divinity, as many might think. In the Old Testament, for example, various individuals and groups are called sons of God (e.g., Exodus 4:22-23; Hosea 11:1; Isaiah 1:2; Jeremiah 3:19). Subsequently, the title came to have messianic significance, but it was not until the much later Hellenistic stage that the title signified divinity.

Among other titles applied to Jesus by the Palestinian community were *Prophet* (Acts of the Apostles 3:22-24) and *Servant* (3:26), fused as the Mosaic prophet-servant of Yahweh. But the *Christ* title remained the focal point for all the rest.

Jewish-Hellenistic Community

The Jewish-Hellenistic community, composed of Greek-speaking Jewish converts to Christianity, had to translate such Palestinian categories into intelligible Hellenistic ones. The delay of the *Parousia* seemed to require a major theological shift away from emphasis on the Second Coming of Jesus in the future to the *present exalted state* of Jesus. Thus, Jesus is the one who is *already* Lord (*Kyrios*) and Christ (Acts of the Apostles 2:36), for he is even now "exalted at God's right hand" (2:33). Indeed, that becomes the central confession of faith: "Jesus is Lord" (Acts of the Apostles 11:20; 16:31; Philippians 2:11). It is in the name of the "Lord Jesus" that Christians are baptized (Acts of the Apostles 8:16; 19:5). In using the title *Lord*, the Greek-speaking Jews were attributing divine status to Jesus, for it was a title employed in the Greek Old Testament (the *Septuagint*) to translate the Hebrew equivalent for Yahweh. And so the various Palestinian titles are recast in the light of this new and distinctive emphasis on the exaltation of Jesus: Christ, Son of Man, Son of David, Son of God (Acts of the Apostles 2:36; 11:17; Romans 1:3-4). At an even later stage, the Jewish-Hellenistic Church projects these titles back into the earthly life of Jesus as well.

Hellenistic-Gentile Community

The final stage of Christological development occurs within the Hellenistic-Gentile community, under the impact of the missionary activity of the Pauline and Johannine schools of theology. The Church now fully accommodates itself to the conceptual categories of the Greek world. The classic expression of this Christology is contained in the great hymn of Philippians 2:5-11, complete with the three-deckered Hellenistic cosmology: heaven, earth, and the underworld (v. 10). Correspondingly, there is a threefold division of Jesus' existence: his pre-existence (v. 6), his becoming flesh in the incarnation (vv. 7-8), and his exaltation following his death and resurrection (vv. 9-11). Variations on this threefold pattern can be found in Colossians 1:15-20 and the Prologue of John's Gospel (1:1-14).

Furthermore, what was only hinted at in the early stages of Jewish-Hellenistic Christology is fully developed in Hellenistic-Gentile Christology: The earthly life of Jesus is itself already an exalted form of existence, although veiled. In the synoptic Gospels we have evidence of this in the infancy narratives, the accounts of Jesus' baptism by John, and the Transfiguration (e.g., Luke 1:5—2:52; 3:21-22; 9:28-36). In John's Gospel, of course, this so-called "high Christology" is full-blown.

And there is a correlative reinterpretation of the titles as employed by the earlier Christologies. The *Son of Man* is portrayed as "the One who came down" from heaven (John 3:13), and when he ascends, it will be "to where he was before" (6:62). The title *Christ* becomes, for all practical purposes, a proper name for Jesus. *Son of God* takes on a higher meaning than it once enjoyed in the Old Testament, and *Lord* becomes entirely central. Thus, for the Hellenistic-Gentile Church God is even now present exercising lordship over the universe in and through Jesus Christ, who is the risen and exalted Lord.

Its Redemptive Effects

The resurrection is a saving event because it is not until Jesus has received the fullness of life which is properly his as Son of God and Son of Man that his redemptive work is complete. He is the firstborn of those who rise (Colossians 1:18). Jesus "was handed over to death for our sins and raised up for our justification" (Romans 4:25). Those of us who die and are buried with him will also rise with him to new life (6:3-11). He was in fact raised from the dead "so that we might bear fruit for God" (7:4). To be "in Christ" who is risen is to be "a new creation" (2 Corinthians 5:17). We have been born anew "unto hope...from the resurrection of Jesus Christ from the dead" (1 Peter 1:3). Indeed, the Spirit cannot be given until Jesus has been raised and glorified (John 7:39; 16:7), and the first thing the risen Lord does when he appears to the disciples behind locked doors is to breathe the Holy Spirit upon them (20:19-23). Our very bodies are given life through the Spirit which now possesses us (Romans 8:11).

The resurrection, therefore, is the principle of our own new being. The Father who raised Jesus will also raise us (2 Corinthians 4:14). Those who die with Christ will live with him (2 Timothy 2:11). Jesus is the resurrection and the life. Those who believe in him will be raised on the last day (John 11:25-26; 6:39-44,54). Nowhere is this theme more fully elaborated than in 1 Corinthians 15: "...if Christ was not raised, your faith is worthless. You are still in your sins, and those who have fallen asleep in Christ are the deadest of the dead" (vv. 17-18). But Christ was raised. And just as "death came through a man," so "the resurrection of the dead comes through a man also. Just as in Adam all die, so in Christ all will come to life again" (vv. 21-22).

Its Historicity

Did It Happen?

Something happened after the death of Jesus. The tomb was found empty on Easter morning, many claimed to have seen the risen Jesus, and many more were marvelously transformed by the event and its aftermath. Certainly from the very earliest days of Christianity, Jesus' followers were convinced that he had indeed been raised from the dead. The Pauline confession to which we referred earlier (1 Corinthians 15:3-8) has its origins at least as early as 35 A.D., the year of Paul's own conversion to Christ. The construction of these verses reflects an Aramaic or Hebrew background, which tends to confirm the hypothesis that it comes from a very primitive tradition indeed.

What Happened?

But the problem, of course, is that no one actually saw the resurrection. We have no eyewitnesses. To the extent that we know anything at all about it, we know it through its effects. Is it an historical event, therefore? The answer has to be "No" if by "historical" one means an event that could have been photographed as it was occurring or that a disinterested person could have observed happening. There is no indication in the New Testament record that the early Church believed the resurrection to have been in the very same category of history as the crucifixion, for example. Even the enemies of Jesus could see what was taking place on Calvary. On the contrary, Jesus is said to have entered an entirely new mode of life, a Spirit-filled existence in which he becomes the source of life for all humankind (2 Corinthians 3:17; 1 Corinthians 15:43). If Jesus had simply resumed the kind of bodily existence he had before his death, then he would not have been the risen Lord. On the contrary, for him there could be no return to the realm of ordinary space and time. His history was over. He had moved into the final and definitive state of existence and would never die again (unlike, for example, Lazarus whom Jesus had raised from the dead). And yet to concede that the resurrection was not an historical event in our ordinary sense of historical event (something open to scientific investigation and verifiable by neutral witnesses) does not mean that the resurrection was not a *real* event for Jesus with *historical implications* for others.

Behind the apostolic confession of faith in the risen Lord lies the experience of having witnessed him at some time and in some way. The disciples were convinced that they had indeed seen him, so that *for them* the appearances *are* historical. And it would have been very difficult from a purely psychological point of view to synchronize such a wide range of individual experiences of the risen Lord unless there was some basis in reality for them. Furthermore, the appearances are not to people in general, but to particular individuals, in particular places, at particular times.

Nonetheless, it would seem better to speak of the resurrection as *trans-historical* rather than *unhistorical*. The average person will translate *unhistorical* simply to mean that it never happened at all. It is trans-historical in the sense that it refers to an event that took place on the other side of death and, therefore, which lies beyond the confines of space and time. Similarly, the reality of the risen Lord is also a reality which transcends history as we know it. By the resurrection Jesus enters a completely new universe of being, the end-time of history, beyond the control of history and beyond the reach of historians.

To Whom Did It Happen?

Was the resurrection truly something that happened *to Jesus?* Some have argued that it did not happen to Jesus but to his disciples. In other words, the mystery of the resurrection means that the early Church and in particular the Apostles and disciples were suddenly enlightened regarding the meaning of Jesus' life and death. The resurrection was an evolution of their consciousness as they gradually began to understand what Jesus was all about, much as some Americans might have been inspired to work diligently in the cause of civil rights following the assassination of Martin Luther King, Jr. (d. 1968).

The question of the *bodiliness* of the resurrection, therefore, is a very important one. If it *was* a bodily occurrence, then it was something that *did* happen to Jesus, and not just to his disciples. It was a sovereign act of God the Father glorifying Jesus of Nazareth and making him the source of new life for all of us.

The bodily element is clear in the description of some of the post-resurrection appearances of Jesus to his disciples. The evangelists speak of touching (John 20:27), eating (Luke 24:41-43), and conversing (John 21:15-22). This drives home the underlying unity between the Jesus of history and the risen Lord. It also counteracts the Greek tendency to spiritualize everything, to make of the resurrection, therefore, an abstract, non-corporeal event. The physical emphasis also challenges certain Gnostic interpretations of Jesus that were already beginning to appear in the second half of the first century.

On the other hand, there had to be something radically different about Jesus' "bodiliness" following the resurrection. The resurrection, after all, was not the resuscitation of a corpse. The disciples, for example, sometimes did not recognize him as he stood before them (Luke 24:16; John 20:14; 21:4), and some even doubted that it was he (Matthew 28:17; Luke 24:41). The risen Jesus is portrayed as coming and going in a manner unlike that of any mortal body (Luke 24:31; John 20:19,26). Mark says explicitly that he appeared "in another form" (Mark 16:12). This contrary emphasis on the difference between Jesus' historical existence and his risen existence safeguards against a too-physical understanding of the resurrection, and stresses the Pauline teaching that Jesus underwent a marvelous *transformation* (1 Corinthians 15:42-44).

Therefore, in trying to determine what really happened and to whom, we have to avoid two extreme answers: one which denies all bodily reality to the resurrection and makes of it something that happened to the disciples alone; and the other which exaggerates the bodily character of the resurrection and makes of it an event that was equally available to the disinterested observer and to the person of faith. The first extreme can be called *subjectivist*; the second, *objectivist*.

The *subjectivist* has to ignore the accounts of the appearances and the empty tomb. He or she has to explain away the extraordinary change and conversion in the lives of a small group of ordinary men whose faith had just been shattered by the crucifixion, who had abandoned Jesus on Calvary, and who had apparently begun returning to their everyday lives. Suddenly, they begin to believe in the resurrection, go out and preach it, develop a whole new way of understanding human existence on the basis of it; then even lay down their lives for it. And what is the subjectivist to make, finally, of the whole network of doctrines developed by the Church in direct response to its faith in the resurrection: the doctrine of the Holy Spirit, the Church, the sacraments, eternal life? If the resurrection is not something that really happened to Jesus, then what foundation do the principal doctrines of Christianity have?

The *objectivist*, or fundamentalist, on the other hand, over-simplifies the New Testament and simply ignores the manner in which it was put together. He or she ignores the metaphorical character of New Testament language about the resurrection and the symbolic imagery used by Paul, who describes the risen Jesus in terms of "a spiritual body" (1 Corinthians 15:20,23). He or she also cannot make sense of the fact that even Jesus' closest disciples did not at first recognize the risen Lord when he appeared to them. Why not, if the resurrection was essentially the resuscitation of the corpse of Jesus?

Who Saw It Happen?

No one actually saw the resurrection happen, as we have already noted. But many claimed to have seen the risen Lord. The Gospels do not agree, however, regarding the places where Jesus *appeared after the resurrection*, nor regarding the persons to whom he appeared. (Compare Mark 16:1-8; Matthew 28; Luke 24; Mark 16:9-20; John 20; and John 21.)

It is better not to attempt an artificial harmonization of the accounts, but to accept the discrepancies as inevitable in view of the lateness of the reports, the nature of the events in question, and variations in authorship, audience, and theological purpose. In spite of these differences there is something *common* to all accounts of the appearances. *First*, those to whom he appears are in a state of depression or at least keen disappointment (Luke 24:21). *Secondly*, it is always Jesus who initiates the appearances

(John 20:19; Luke 24:15; Matthew 28:9,18). *Thirdly,* Jesus gives some form of greeting—e.g., "Peace be with you" (John 20:19; Matthew 28:9). *Fourthly,* a moment of recognition follows (John 21:7; 20:20; Matthew 28:9,17). And, *finally,* Jesus gives a word of command to go forth and make disciples (Matthew 28:19; John 20:21; 21:15-17; Luke 24:46-49).

Regarding the last item: Did Jesus actually speak during these appearances? Some Christians have thought, for example, that Jesus spent forty days after the resurrection instructing the Apostles in theology, ethics, and canon law. There is a self-contradictory character, for example, to the Lucan account of Paul's conversion experience on the road to Damascus (Acts 9:7 and 22:9). In one text the companions of Paul are reported to have heard the voice from heaven, but in the other they did not. Did the risen Lord communicate with the Apostles verbally, or did he communicate intuitively? It is a question that one cannot really answer with certitude. An increasing number of scholars, however, do doubt that the risen Jesus used words.

But some form of communication is said to have taken place. What was it? Raymond Brown's hypothesis, which is gaining favor among his colleagues, is as follows: After the crucifixion, the Twelve fled Jerusalem and made their way back to Galilee, thoroughly discouraged by recent events. If, in fact, they had heard of the empty tomb before leaving Jerusalem, their puzzlement and fright must have been only heightened all the more. As Peter returned to his fishing, Jesus appeared to him on the shores of the Sea of Tiberias (John 21:1-14), and faith in the resurrection was born. Subsequently, Jesus appeared to the rest of the Twelve, confirming perhaps the inchoate faith stirred by Peter's report. It was on the occasion of his appearance to the Apostles that he breathed the Holy Spirit upon them and commissioned them to proclaim that the Kingdom of God had come among them in a new and definitive way through what God had accomplished in Jesus.

The Apostles would gradually discover on their own that the proclamation of the Kingdom of God would involve bearing witness to the Lord in word and in deed, baptizing people and forgiving their sins, and forming a new community, a new Israel, the Church. By the time the Gospel narratives themselves were written, all this was already happening. Accordingly, certain words of

Jesus were incorporated into the actual commission, as if Jesus himself on that occasion had instructed them in detail.

One final point about the appearances: In the various accounts, the post-resurrectional confession is not "We have seen Jesus" but "We have seen the Lord" (John 20:18,25; 21:7; Luke 24:34). Since *Lord* is a "high" Christological evaluation of Jesus, the evangelists are telling us that the witnesses enjoyed not only the *sight* of Jesus but also and even primarily *insight*. They saw that Jesus had been transformed, that he was now in the realm of God (Acts of the Apostles 2:32,36). Thus, the appearances involve a sight that is revelatory, i.e., an experience of God within ordinary human experience.

Where Did It Happen?

Jesus was buried in a tomb owned by Joseph of Arimathea, "a distinguished member of the Sanhedrin" (Mark 15:43). Two days later the tomb was discovered to be empty. Those are the barest details.

Like reports of the appearances, the *empty tomb* accounts are full of inconsistencies and embellishments. (Compare Mark 16:1-8; Matthew 28; Luke 24; and John 20.) It is very curious indeed that in Mark's account the women flee the empty tomb out of fear and astonishment and "said nothing to anyone" about it (Mark 16:8). In Luke's account, when the women inform the Apostles, ". . . the story seemed like nonsense and they refused to believe them" (Luke 24:11), although Peter did get up and run out to the tomb to see for himself. But these indicate that *the fact of the empty tomb* proves nothing in itself. It simply raises questions like "What happened to Jesus' body? Did someone steal it? Did Jesus in fact rise from the dead?"

And yet an empty-tomb tradition did develop, and the nature of the evidence lends a high degree of probability to it. No author, for example, would have used female witnesses in a fabricated story, since women were simply not accepted at the time as witnesses. Furthermore, the early Jewish controversies about the resurrection all supposed that the tomb was empty. The arguments were over the question of how. Some charged that the disciples had stolen the body (Matthew 28:11-15; 27:64). Others said the gardener had taken it away (John 20:13-15). Indeed, if the tomb were still intact, it would have been impossible to propose the story in the first place.

What of the significance of the empty-tomb tradition? At best it is a secondary piece of evidence, second certainly to the appearances. *We do not make an act of faith in the empty tomb but in the resurrection.* There are plenty of empty tombs in the world. The publicity surrounding the King Tut exhibitions conducted throughout the United States in 1978-9 only dramatized that fact. He was one of the very few ancient figures whose tombs were discovered with the body and other artifacts still there. Does that mean all of the other Pharaohs rose from the dead?

The empty tomb was more important for the first Christians than it is for us today. For them it was yet another safeguard against the Gnostic denial of the bodiliness of Jesus and of his resurrection. In the actual genesis of faith in the resurrection, it was the appearances of the risen Lord that first brought the disciples to believe; this belief, in turn, made sense of the empty tomb. Having seen him, the Apostles now understood the reason why the tomb had been empty. He was raised and then appeared to them (1 Corinthians 15:4-5; Luke 24:34). The first Christians, therefore, proclaimed a bodily resurrection in the sense that they did not think that Jesus' body had corrupted in the tomb. On the other hand, that risen body was now a spiritual body and not simply a resuscitated corpse, as we noted earlier (1 Corinthians 15:42-44).

THE PASSION AND DEATH

Although the doctrine of the cross was not the earliest Christology to emerge from faith in the resurrection but was something developed only by degrees, it is inextricably linked with resurrection faith and is at the same time entirely central to the New Testament's evaluation of the life, message, and mission of Jesus. Already in the primitive creedal formula in 1 Corinthians 15:3-8, there is the confession of faith "that Christ died for our sins."

On the other hand, the connection between the crucifixion and the resurrection had not always been so explicitly drawn. The

great Christological hymn of Philippians 2:6-11 is one of the earliest attempts to make sense of the death of Jesus, not as Paul would
usually have it, i.e., "for our sins," but as the culmination of a life
of obedient humiliation within the human condition:

> Though he was in the form of God,
>> he did not deem equality with God
>> something to be grasped at.
>
> Rather, he emptied himself
>> and took the form of a slave,
>> being born in the likeness of men.
>
> He was known to be of human estate,
>> and it was thus that he humbled himself,
>> obediently accepting even death,
>> death on a cross!
>
> Because of this,
>> God highly exalted him
>> and bestowed on him the name
>> above every other name,
>
> So that at Jesus' name
>> every knee must bend
>> in the heavens, on the earth,
>> and under the earth,
>> and every tongue proclaim
>> to the glory of God the Father:
>> Jesus Christ is Lord!

However we finally interpret this text (regarding, for example, its origin, its proper punctuation, its structure, the Christological model upon which it is based), there is no question that it is a
very early Christology indeed (pre-56 or 57 A.D., when Paul wrote
to the Philippians), one that was inspired by the resurrection and
pieced together from various available images of Jesus. Yet it did
not attempt an interpretation of the death of Jesus, nor did it
concern itself with his historical existence. The words "death on a
cross" in verse 8c are not part of the original hymn but were added
by Paul or by a Pauline editor. The addition was consistent with a

growing trend within the early Church to work back from the resurrection experience to the death and life of the one who had been raised.

Indeed, his death makes sense only if the Gospel portrait of the historical Jesus is accepted as basically reliable. To suggest that he was executed because of his political attitudes and behavior toward the Roman government, whether as a Zealot or as a Zealot sympathizer, does not correspond with his preaching against violence and his almost-studied indifference to specifically political questions, and his central teaching about love for one's enemies. His problem was with the Jews, not with the Romans. That is how the Gospels present it, and that is how early Jewish antagonists of Christianity recalled it as well.

He was periodically locked in controversy with the Jewish men of power: the chief priests, the Pharisees, and their Scribes. Unfortunately, the portrayal of Jewish hostility to Jesus and of direct Jewish involvement in his condemnation and death has allowed many Christians down through the centuries to justify a virulent anti-Semitism ("Christ-killers" and all that). But the counter-reaction has also been unfortunate. In playing down Jewish complicity in the death of Jesus, even transferring it entirely to Roman shoulders, we remove the very basis for the Gospel traditions. In effect, the credibility of the event we seek to explain is undermined, perhaps destroyed completely. If Jesus has been remembered as he was, then his confrontation with the religious establishment was practically inevitable. But if that confrontation did not exist to the extent it is reported in the New Testament and with the effect it is also reported to have had, then the portrait of Jesus itself is open to question and to challenge.

Jesus functioned as a prophet greater than Moses. He claimed to forgive sin. He initiated a new form of table fellowship between God and humankind. He promised salvation. And he, of course, sharply criticized the religious situation as he found it in contemporary Israel. "The reason why the Jews were even more determined to kill him was that he not only was breaking the sabbath but, worse still, was speaking of God as his own Father, thereby making himself God's equal" (John 5:18). "He commits blasphemy!" they charged. "Who can forgive sins except God alone?" (Mark 2:7). When Jesus was asked by the high priest of the Sanhedrin whether or not he considered himself the Messiah, the Son of the Blessed One, Jesus answered, "I am; and you will see the Son of Man seated at the right hand of the Power and coming with clouds of heaven." With that the high priest tore his robes and said, "You have heard the blasphemy" (Mark 14:61-63).

But Jesus had been on a collision course from the beginning of his preaching ministry. He preached the Kingdom of God in a wholly new way, as a reality now "at hand" and demanding repentance and faith (Mark 1:15). "Do you think I have come to establish peace on the earth? I assure you, the contrary is true; I have come for division .... father will be split against son and son against father, mother against daughter and daughter against mother ..." (Luke 12:51-53; see also Matthew 10:34-36). He had to know, as many prophets before him knew, that his life was at stake because of his preaching.

But did he explicitly connect his death with our redemption? If he did, why did the earliest New Testament Christology not make the same connection? Presumably it would have done so if it had some basis for it in the sayings of Jesus. And yet eventually, within the New Testament, Jesus' death *is* interpreted in redemptive categories, as a work of atonement for our sins. Such a conviction evidently had to develop, not at once but over a period of time, as the life and death of Jesus continued to be contemplated in the light of the resurrection. But as we noted earlier, resurrection faith first inspired the Church to look forward to the Second Coming, not backward. Only later did it reverse direction and display greater interest in the actual historical existence of Jesus, an interest which produced the Gospels. But where the older Christologies of the Epistles worked out of contemporary thought patterns, the Gospels remained more or less faithful to Old Testament thinking. It was this kind of thinking which accommodated itself most readily to the notion of redemptive sacrifice.

The idea of *vicarious atonement,* i.e., the sufferings of an innocent person having redeeming value for the sins of others, was already well accepted in the Judaism of Jesus' day. The best-known expression of this concept occurs in the Servant songs of Deutero, or Second, Isaiah (42:1-4; 49:1-6; 50:4-9; 52:13—53:12), where the Servant, probably Israel itself, becomes an instrument of divine salvation through his/its passion and death. Jesus himself

is identified with the *Servant of the Lord* in the early Christian
proclamation (Acts of the Apostles 3:13,26; 4:27,30) and is taken
into the Gospel accounts themselves (Matthew 8:17; 12:18-21;
Luke 22:37). The Second Isaian imagery is clearly woven through
the passage of 1 Peter 2:22-25:

> He did no wrong; no deceit was found in
> his mouth.
>
> When he was insulted, he returned no
> insult.
> When he was made to suffer, he did not
> counter with threats.
> Instead, he delivered himself up to the One
> who judges justly.
>
> In his own body he brought your sins to the
> cross,
> so that all of us, dead to sin, could live in
> accord with God's will.
> By his wounds you were healed.
>
> At one time you were straying like sheep,
> but now you have returned to the Shepherd,
> the Guardian of your souls.

But the Servant role, at first eagerly attributed to Jesus, was
later abandoned as being too Jewish and, therefore, not readily
understandable within the Gentile world. Other, more flexible
Old Testament figures came to the surface, particularly the notion
of *ransom* and the associated idea of *redemption*. A Marcan saying
(10:45) is taken up by the Gospels (Matthew 20:28), with parallels
elsewhere (1 Timothy 2:6) to show that Jesus understood his own
mission as giving his life as a ransom for many.

In the New Testament world of commerce, a ransom was the
price that had to be paid to buy back a pawned object or to liberate
a slave. Thus, Christ is seen as the ransom given to liberate us all
from the slavery of sin. But it has been an extraordinary misunderstanding to view this act of ransoming in more than *metaphorical*
terms, as if it were some necessary payment demanded by God. On
the contrary, "the redemption wrought by Christ" is itself "the
gift of God" (Romans 3:24). We have no reason for supposing that

the New Testament intended to press the metaphor any farther than did the Old Testament.

We do not pay a ransom to God (Psalm 49:8); it is God who is our redeemer (Psalm 78:35; see also Psalm 19:14; Isaiah 63:5). The metaphor means that forgiveness of sin is not some casual or arbitrary act of God. Sin is truly a bondage leading to death. It "costs" God much to forgive and to deliver us from that bondage. In speaking of the blood of Christ as the "price" he had to pay, the New Testament is trying to emphasize that the risen Lord's life and death somehow served God's salvific purposes in history. *There is no exact "commercial" description of what actually occurred in Jesus' passion and death.*

What does it mean, therefore, to speak of Jesus as having become a "curse" for us, and as having shed his blood in *expiation* of our sins?

First, what does it *not* mean? It does *not* mean that Jesus was accursed of God like the *scapegoat* of the Old Testament (Leviticus 16:20-28), which was burdened with the sins of all the people and then driven away to die in the desert, the abode of the demons. Christ is never likened in New Testament Christology to the scapegoat of the Old Testament. It does *not* mean, therefore, that Jesus was marked out for death by the Father in expiation for offenses against the divine majesty, for neither is there any Old Testament model for such a notion.

What we have is an exercise in Pauline paradox (Galatians 3:13, with a quotation from Deuteronomy 21:22-23). Christ has brought us back from the "curse" of the Law by himself becoming a "curse" for us. As in the case of the word *ransom*, the usage here is *metaphorical*. He mixes proper and improper senses of the same word in order to make a point. The cross, which is "folly" to us, is the "wisdom" of God, who "saves those who believe through the absurdity of the preaching of the gospel" (1 Corinthians 1:20-21).

What of the blood sacrifices? When they were employed as a means of atonement, the death of the animal was entirely incidental. Blood in itself was regarded as a purifying and sacred element (Deuteronomy 12:23). Insofar as the shedding of Christ's blood is clearly associated with the establishment of a new covenant (Hebrews 9:12-14; Mark 14:24; Matthew 26:28; Luke 22:20), the allusion is always to the enactment of the Old Covenant on Sinai (Exodus 24); namely, the blood of a *peace offering*, not a sacrifice of expiation. It is not that God was so enraged by the world's sin that a price was to be exacted (the prevalent idea of God among the pagans), but that God "so loved the world that he gave his only Son . . ." (John 3:16).

In summary, the Church's faith in the saving power of Christ's death emerged from its initial faith in his resurrection, and not from any general sense of need for deliverance from sin or from some wide-ranging exploration of Old Testament texts. *Jesus' death assumes meaning within the context of his resurrection:* "Unless the grain of wheat falls to the earth and dies, it remains just a grain of wheat. But if it dies, it produces much fruit. The man who loves his life loses it, while the man who hates his life in this world preserves it to life eternal" (John 12:24-25).

THE LIFE AND MESSAGE OF JESUS
The Historical Situation

Basic introductions to the New Testament abound. The more one knows about and understands the social, economic, political, and religious situation at the time of Jesus, the more intelligently one will be able to interpret the New Testament's faith in him as well as the import and impact of Jesus' words and deeds upon his contemporaries. We can do no more here than outline that situation in the broadest of strokes. And that may not be particularly unfortunate. On the contrary, the late Protestant New Testament scholar Norman Perrin acknowledged that in his own experience as a teacher, students tend either to skip the introductory material on the Hellenistic, Roman, and Jewish "background" of the New Testament or to forget its content by the time they actually begin dealing with the texts themselves, just when the material is most necessary. So in his own book, *The New Testament: An Introduction*, to which I am greatly indebted for this last section of the chapter, Perrin places all this material at the end, in two appendices, and discusses the background materials when and where they are relevant to understanding the texts themselves.

Since 63 B.C. the Jews had been politically subject to Roman power. Although by present standards that power was exercised with some measure of tolerance for national and religious diversity, there was in Jesus' time a widespread expectation of a political messiah. The Jewish party known as the *Zealots* wanted to throw off the yoke of Roman domination, and by violent revolutionary means. Although some latter-day political leftists have tried to portray Jesus as a member of the Zealot party, there is no real evidence that he even took a stand on the political issues of his time. Indeed, the New Testament seldom mentions a political group hostile to him, with the exception of the discussion about taxation (e.g., Matthew 22:15-22). On the other hand, much attention is given his religious controversies with the Pharisees.

How closely Jesus is to be identified with the *Essenes* is a matter of dispute, although recent scholarship seems to suggest that the points of contact were substantially fewer than was thought soon after the Dead Sea Scrolls were discovered. The Essenes, or Qumran community, were a sect within Judaism which separated itself from regular commerce with the world and established hierarchically structured communities of salvation wherein members could follow the Law of God perfectly until the end of history. Jesus, on the other hand, addressed himself explicitly to the whole nation of Israel and not simply to this "remnant" within the nation.

The Jews of his day were exceedingly jealous of their religious and national traditions, and so, unlike their brothers and sisters living outside of Palestine, they tended, as least in Palestine, to resist the pervasive influence of Greek culture. Jesus, therefore, shows no sign of Hellenistic influence. He probably speaks in Aramaic. His parables are drawn from ordinary Jewish life; his theological arguments, from the Old Testament.

If it were not for the near universality of Hellenistic culture in this ancient world, Christianity might not have spread so rapidly and so widely. In most cities public instruction in the Greek language was available to anyone interested in acquiring it. And, of course, there was a real incentive to do so because people were needed to fill various positions in business and government. For a movement, therefore, that was composed primarily of "the world's lowborn and despised" (1 Corinthians 1:26-31), it was crucial to communicate its message in spoken and written form far beyond its own particular circle.

Life

We know relatively little about the actual life of Jesus. He was baptized by John the Baptist, and the beginning of his ministry in Galilee was in some way linked with that of the Baptist. His ministry centered on the proclamation of the Kingdom of God, with a sharp edge of challenge to it. His preaching was reinforced by an apparently deserved reputation as an exorcist (Mark 1:27; Luke 4:36). In a world that readily believed in the powers of good and evil, in demons and evil spirits, Jesus was able to help many who thought themselves to be possessed by such forces.

One of his fundamental concerns was to bring together a group of respondents to his proclamation of the Kingdom of God, regardless of their sex, status, or background. Central to the life of this group was sharing a common meal that celebrated their unity in their new relationship with God. Jesus, therefore, set himself and his group against the Jewish tendency to permit the fragmentation of the religious community and to engage rather freely in "excommunications" of certain undesirables. He spoke as one having great authority (Mark 1:22; John 7:46; Matthew 5:21-22). He forgave sins (Mark 2:10; Matthew 9:6; Luke 5:24). And he addressed God as Abba, or Father (Mark 10:36). These activities provoked severe opposition—an opposition which reached a climax during a Passover celebration in Jerusalem when he was arrested, tried by Jewish authorities on a charge of blasphemy, and by the Romans on a charge of sedition, and then crucified. Indeed, his decision to go up to Jerusalem and to end his Galilean ministry proved to be the major turning point. He definitively rejected a political mission, even though the hopes of some of his followers were still oriented in this direction to the very end (Luke 19:11; 24:21).

During his lifetime he had chosen from among his followers a small group of disciples who thereafter exhibited in their own activities something of his power and authority.

Message

Proclamation of the Kingdom of God

There is general agreement among New Testament scholars that four sayings concerning the Kingdom of God have very strong claims to authenticity: "This is the time of fulfillment. The reign of God is at hand!" (Mark 1:15); "But if it is by the finger of God that I cast out devils, then the reign of God is upon you" (Luke 11:20); "You cannot tell by careful watching when the reign of God will come. Neither is it a matter of reporting it is 'here' or 'there.' The reign of God is already in your midst" (Luke 17:20-21); and "From John the Baptizer's time until now the kingdom of God has suffered violence, and the violent take it by force" (Matthew 11:12). Nor is there any doubt at all that the proclamation of the Kingdom of God is at the very center of the message of Jesus.

To speak of the Kingdom of God is to speak of the exercise of divine power on our behalf. The Kingdom is an apocalyptic symbol referring to God's final act of redemption at the end of the world, and so it is a symbol filled with hope. God, acting as King, visits and redeems his people. This is the central theme of Jesus' preaching.

In the light of the four sayings listed above, there is obviously some tension between present and future in Jesus' understanding of the Kingdom. It is at once "in the midst of you" and "at hand"; i.e., it is imminent but still in the future. To the extent that the Kingdom is present, it comes about in the healings and exorcisms (Luke 11:20) and in the endurance of suffering (Matthew 11:12). On the other hand, Luke denies the possibility that the Kingdom comes about through any one experience (17:20-21), such as the prophet Daniel describes, for example (Daniel 11:3-35).

What, then, does Jesus mean when he says that the Kingdom is "in the midst of you"? If he is not speaking of the history of kings, wars, and persecutions, as Daniel was, then he is speaking of the history of the individual and of the individual's experience of reality. But, of course, individual reality is never divorced from its larger social and political context (which is the interpretation Bultmann's thoroughgoing existentialism gives), and so the power of God also realizes itself in our relationships with one another and in the many institutional expressions of those relationships.

The Parables

The following points seem to be agreed upon by modern New Testament scholars:

1. Jesus taught in parables, but the early Church translated them into *allegories*. In parables, the whole story counts as a totality; in allegories, each detail is important and has to be interpreted to detect its special meaning. Once the allegory has been deciphered, it can be set aside, for it has achieved its purpose. Not so with a parable, which keeps yielding new meanings. An example of allegory in the New Testament is the interpretation of the parable of the Sower in Mark 4:13-20.

2. Both the allegorizing of the parables and their placement and application within the Gospels are the work of the Church and the evangelists. To interpret a parable of Jesus, therefore, one must first reconstruct it in its original nonallegorical form and then interpret it as a parable in the context of the message of Jesus without reference to its place or function in the Gospels.

3. The fundamental element in a parable is the element of *metaphor*. The Kingdom of God, which is the unknown, is compared to something that is known. Thus, "The Kingdom of God is like . . ." (see, for example, Matthew 13:44-46).

4. There is in every parable, therefore, a *literal* point (what it means in itself) and a metaphorical point (what it refers to).

5. The purpose of a parable is normally *pedagogical*. But Jesus used parables not only for instruction but also for *proclamation*. An example is provided by the parable of the Good Samaritan (Luke 10:30-36). If the parable were merely exemplary, illustrating by way of example the principle of neighborliness, then it would have been more effective to have the hated Samaritan the injured man and the Israelite the one who gives aid. But the way Jesus tells it, the story in itself focuses attention not on the needs of the injured man but on the deed of the Samaritan, from whom no Jew would expect hospitality (see Luke 9:52-56). Thus, the para-

ble asks the listener to conceive the inconceivable: that the Samaritan is "good." The listener is thereby challenged to reexamine his or her most basic attitudes and values. The parable has become not instruction but *proclamation.*

The parable of the Unjust Steward (Luke 16:1-9) may be even more challenging, for Jesus commends a man who compounds his dishonesty (having cheated his master) by committing additional acts of dishonesty (cutting the debts owed his master so he will have friends after he loses his job). The point of the parable is to admit the presence of an order of reality that challenges all accepted norms of behavior and rules of human relationships. And that is how other parables function as well—i.e., by turning our worlds upside down and challenging us to reconsider our whole perspective on life (e.g., the Rich Man and Lazarus in Luke 16:19-31; the Pharisee and the Publican in Luke 18:10-14; and the Wedding Guest in Luke 14:7-11). That experience of sudden reversal is one experience of the inbreaking Kingdom of God.

But Jesus also used the parables for *instruction.* Examples are the Hidden Treasure and the Pearl (Matthew 13:44-46), the Tower Builder and the King Going to War (Luke 14:28-32), the Friend at Midnight (Luke 11:5-8), and the Unjust Judge (Luke 18:1-8).

The Proverbial Sayings

A proverb is a saying that gives insight into ordinary human situations—e.g., "No prophet is without honor except in his native place, among his own kindred, and in his own house" (Mark 6:4). Sometimes proverbs have an imperative ring to them—e.g., "Do not give what is holy to dogs or toss your pearls before swine. They will trample them under foot, at best, and perhaps even tear you to shreds" (Matthew 7:6). Some proverbs are formulated as questions—e.g., "Which of you by worrying can add a moment to his life-span?" (Matthew 6:27). In general, proverbs are affirmations of faith in God's rule over the world—i.e., faith in the Kingdom of God.

The most radical proverbial sayings of Jesus are the injunction to let the dead bury their own dead (Luke 9:60) and the command to turn the other cheek, to give away one's cloak (the only garment hiding sheer nakedness), and to walk the extra mile (Matthew 5:29-41). Again, they challenge the hearer not to radical obedience but to radical questioning. They jolt the hearer out of his or her routine existence and force him or her to see human existence in a new light. As such, proverbial sayings are a form of proclamation of the Kingdom of God.

Other proverbial sayings carry forward this technique. Jesus tells his listeners that the first will be last and the last first (Mark 10:31), that whoever would save his life must lose it (Mark 8:35), that it is easier for a camel to get through the eye of a needle than for a rich man to enter the Kingdom (Mark 10:23-25), and that the one who exalts himself will be humbled, and vice versa (Luke 14:11). Still other sayings highlight the element of *conflict*: A kingdom divided against itself cannot stand (Mark 3:24-26), and no one can plunder the house of a strong man without first binding him (Mark 3:27).

Finally, there are the *instructional* sayings: No one who puts his hand to the plough and looks back is fit for the Kingdom (Luke 9:62); entrance into the Kingdom is by a narrow gate (Matthew 7:13-14); nothing outside of a person is defiling; only what is inside defiles (Mark 7:15); one must receive the Kingdom like a child (Mark 10:15); and we must love our enemies if we are to be perfect (Matthew 5:44-48).

Always it is the Kingdom of God which is being proclaimed.

The Lord's Prayer

The Lucan version (11:2-4) is generally recognized as being close to the prayer which Jesus actually taught his disciples:

Father,
hallowed be your name,
your kingdom come.

Give us each day our daily bread.

Forgive us our sins
for we too forgive all who do us wrong;
and subject us not to the trial.

The simplicity and brevity of this prayer suggest a very special, intimate relationship between the petitioner and God. For the person who can pray the Lord's prayer, the Kingdom has already come. On the other hand, this prayer also asks that the Kingdom might yet come. It looks to the future as well as to the present, just as some of the parables challenge Jesus' hearers to look to the future (the Sower in Mark 4:3-9; the Mustard Seed in Mark 4:30-32; the Leaven in Matthew 13:33; and the Seed Growing of Itself in Mark 4:26-29).

It does not follow, however, that Jesus' conception of the future is the same as ours, namely, temporal and historical. On the contrary, Jesus rejected tendencies in first-century Judaism to exaggerate the importance of signs and wonders. Perhaps the future that Jesus spoke of is the future that emerges as the consummation of the present, the fulfillment of what is already available to those who respond to the challenge of his proclamation of the Kingdom of God.

FROM JESUS TO CHRIST

The one who proclaimed the Kingdom of God in his own lifetime became, after his death, the one *proclaimed*. The historical details of this transition are probably lost to us forever. What we have is what we began with in this chapter, namely, the early Church's testimony of faith in the risen Lord. All else in the New Testament flows from that—forward and backward alike.

SUMMARY

1.   No one questions that Jesus of Nazareth really lived. There is ample historical evidence of this. What is at issue is whether this same Jesus of history is also the Christ of faith proclaimed by the New Testament.

2.   The Gospels, however, do not provide us with the kind of biographical information which we are accustomed to receive from such "papers of record" as, for example, the *New York Times*.

3.   What we have in the Gospels, according not only to New Testament scholars but also according to the Pontifical Biblical Commis-

sion, is the finally edited version of the oral and written proclamation of the early Church regarding Jesus Christ. In order to reconstruct the process of development and come to a greater understanding of what the New Testament proclaims, we must employ *historical criticism* (What is the nature of documents we have in hand?), *form criticism* (What are the various units out of which the Gospels were put together?), and *redaction criticism* (What was the peculiar purpose of each evangelist?).

4.   Furthermore, the Gospels are products of different Christian communities with distinctive theological perspectives: *Palestinian, Jewish-Hellenistic,* and *Hellenistic-Gentile.* The first emphasized the imminence of the Second Coming of Jesus and his fulfillment of the role of the Christ, or the Messiah; the second shifted emphasis away from the future to the present exalted state of Jesus, who is now proclaimed as Lord; the third combines present and future with past, dividing Jesus' existence into pre-existence, the incarnation, and the exaltation.

5.   Until the eighteenth century there was no "New Testament problem." All Christians accepted the New Testament as an accurate and literal account of the life, teachings, ministry, death, and resurrection of Jesus. Ever since the assumption was challenged on the Protestant side by Reimarus and others, Christians have been divided across a broad spectrum of views, some scholarly and some non-scholarly.

6.   In *non-scholarly conservatism* the Christology of the New Testament is *identified* with Jesus' self-evaluation. Jesus knew and expressed from the beginning what the Church affirmed of him after the resurrection. It is a view held by Protestant fundamentalists and others, and was the common view of Roman Catholics before Pope Pius XII's encyclical on biblical studies, *Divino Afflante Spiritu* (1943).

7.   *Non-scholarly liberalism* concludes that there is *no continuity* at all between the Christ of faith and the Jesus of history. Once the fashion in Protestantism, it now enjoys some favor with Catholicism as well. Jesus is confessed as everything except what the New Testament confessed him to be.

8.   *Scholarly liberalism* insists that New Testament Christology is a *creation* of the early Church. The creative act was necessary at the time; otherwise, Jesus might have faded from memory. But since that is no longer possible, we can dispense with the theological overlay.

9.   *Bultmannian Existentialism* acknowledges a *functional equivalence* between the early Church's Christology and Jesus' own proclamation of the Kingdom. What the Church was proclaiming about Jesus is functionally the same as what Jesus was proclaiming about the Kingdom. The two proclamations made the same practical demands upon the hearers.

10. *Moderate Conservatism* posits a *discernible continuity* between the Christ of faith and Jesus' self-evaluation. One branch suggests that the Church's Christology was *explicit* in Jesus' self-understanding with regard to the so-called "lower" titles (e.g., Messiah, Prophet, Servant, Son of Man), while another indicates that such titles are at most *implicit* in Jesus' self-evaluation. That is, he conveyed what he was saying by speaking with unique authority and by acting with unique power. The explicit school was more popular in the 1950s and 1960s, although it is still respectable today, while the implicit school has tended to gain acceptance among Catholics and Protestants alike more recently.

11. One can proceed with a presentation of the Jesus of the New Testament in one of two ways: by the *traditional approach*, which views the resurrection as a kind of capstone of his whole ministry and mission; and by the *New Testament's own approach*, which is to begin with the resurrection and work forward and backward, viewing all that Jesus did and said in the light of the early Church's fundamental conviction of faith that he is indeed risen. This chapter follows the second approach.

12. The *resurrection* of Jesus from the dead is both the *starting-point* and the *center* of the early Church's faith in him as the Christ and Lord of history. This is evident in such primitive sources as the creedal formula in 1 Corinthians 15 and in the apostolic proclamation of Peter in the Acts of the Apostles 2.

13. In the light of the resurrection everything else falls into place and begins to make sense: Jesus' special relationship with the Father, Jesus' fulfillment of the hopes of Israel, the preaching of the Kingdom, the crucifixion, the empty tomb.

14. The interpretations and connections, however, differed from Christian community to Christian community. (See #4 above.)

15. The resurrection is perceived as a saving event in that it is the necessary step by which Jesus receives the *fullness of life* that he is destined to share with us. He is the *first-born of those who rise* (Colossians 1:18). To be "in Christ" is to be a "new creation" (2 Corinthians 5:17). Indeed, the Holy Spirit cannot be given until Jesus has been raised and glorified (John 7:39; 16:7). Jesus breathes the Spirit upon his disciples as soon as he first appears to them (20:19-23).

16. *Did it happen? Something* happened, we can be sure of that much. The tomb was found empty, many claimed to have seen the risen Jesus, and his followers were marvelously transformed. But there are *no eyewitnesses* to the actual event of the resurrection itself.

17. *What happened*, therefore? By modern scientific standards, the resurrection is not *historical*. It was not available to the disinterested

observer and the person of faith alike. But even by New Testament standards, neither is it an historical event in the sense that it involved simply the resuscitation of Jesus' corpse. That would not have been a saving event in that case. Jesus entered into an entirely *new mode of existence.* The fact that the disciples did not easily recognize him is significant. The resurrection was something *real, although trans-historical, for Jesus*; but it was something *real and historical* from the side of *the disciples*, so profoundly were they affected by it and by the appearances.

18.   *To whom did it happen?* Did it happen to Jesus, or did it happen to the disciples? The extreme liberal or *subjectivist* answer is that the resurrection, understood as a breach of the most fundamental laws of life and nature, could not have literally happened to Jesus. Therefore, it was something that happened to the disciples alone; i.e., it is the "miracle" of the sudden and wondrous transformation of the disciples as they reflected on the meaning of the life and death of Jesus. The extreme conservative or *objectivist* solution is that the resurrection was so literally real that a photographer could have captured the event on film had he or she been present. The *subjectivist* ignores the accounts of the appearances and the empty tomb, and has to explain away the whole network of doctrines which directly express the early Church's faith in the resurrection *of Jesus.* The *objectivist* has to treat the New Testament in fundamentalist categories, denying all that we know about it from historical, form, and redaction criticism, and ignoring Paul's teaching that Jesus rose with a "spiritual body," one not readily recognized even by some of his closest friends.

19.   *Who saw it happen?* No one. And yet many claimed to have seen Jesus *after* it happened. Those to whom he appeared were always in a state of depression or at least keen disappointment. Jesus always initiates the appearances. He gives some form of greeting—e.g., "Peace be with you." A moment of recognition follows. Then Jesus communicates some missionary command. The last, however, is not to be confused with formal, lengthy theological and canonical instruction, such as some of our earlier textbooks imagined. An increasing number of scholars, in fact, deny that Jesus actually spoke. Rather, they say, he communicated without the mediation of language—i.e., through direct mystical experience.

20.   *Where did it happen?* We know only that Jesus was buried in a tomb owned by Joseph of Arimathea and that two days later it was discovered to be empty. Like the accounts of the appearances, the accounts of the *empty tomb* are filled with inconsistencies. Nonetheless, all—even the earliest Jewish polemicists against Christianity—agree that the tomb was found empty. If it had not been empty, how could the

story of its empty status have been proposed in the first place without rebuttal? At best, however, the empty-tomb tradition is a *secondary piece of evidence*, secondary certainly to Jesus' appearances. We do not make an act of faith in the empty tomb. It is the early Church's faith in the resurrection, a faith generated by the appearances, which compelled it to take another look at the empty tomb and judge its significance. Although Jesus now enjoyed a spiritual body, his resurrection was indeed a *bodily* resurrection of some kind. The tomb *was* empty, after all.

21. Again, contrary to the impression given by some of our traditional textbooks and catechisms, the early Church did not at first focus on the redemptive significance of the *crucifixion* and then see the resurrection as simply Jesus' reward for suffering death or as the Father's way of proving Jesus' claims about himself. It was the other way around.

22. Did Jesus die "for our sins," or did he die because of his political views and activities? If one chooses the second possibility, the New Testament portrait of Jesus—and of the Jews of his time—no longer hangs together. He claimed to forgive sin. He initiated a new form of table fellowship. He promised salvation. And he sharply criticized the religious establishment of his day. In the end, the Jews rejected him and brought about his death because he *blasphemed* (Mark 14:61-63).

23. Did Jesus explicitly connect his death with our redemption? If so, why is that connection not made explicit in the New Testament? Eventually, however, the connection *is* made by the early Church as it contemplated the meaning and implications of the resurrection.

24. When the New Testament did develop a theology of the redemptive value of the cross, where did it derive its notion of *vicarious atonement*? The initial source is the Servant songs in Deutero-Isaiah, but that was later abandoned as being too Jewish. The notion of *ransom* came to the fore. But this, too, has been misunderstood, as if it were a commercial term alone. It is used *metaphorically* in the New Testament. Thus, it is not something we give to the Father or to anyone else in payment for our sins, nor even something Jesus is compelled to give to the Father or to anyone else on our behalf. Rather, it is something the *Father gives to us* (Romans 3:24).

25. Did Jesus die in *expiation* for our sins in any sense at all? Not in the sense of his becoming a scapegoat. The New Testament never likens him to that. The shedding of Christ's *blood* is not a sacrifice of expiation but, in the biblical sense, a *peace offering*. It was never necessary that the animal offered should die, but only that blood be shed as a sign of purification. So, too, with Christ. To say, on the other hand, that the Father somehow demanded the death of his Son in expiation for our sins

is to deny such fundamental principles as God's love for the world (John 3:16). Again, the redemptive value of the cross assumes meaning always in the light of the resurrection: "...unless the grain of wheat falls to the earth and dies..." (John 12:24-25).

26. The more one understands the social, economic, political, and religious *situation* at the time of Jesus, the more intelligently one will interpret the New Testament's faith in him as well as the import and impact of his words and deeds upon his contemporary world. Jesus was a Jew, but neither a Zealot nor an Essene. His parables are drawn from ordinary Jewish life, his theological arguments are rooted in the Old Testament, and his political interests are minimal.

27. We know very little about his actual *life*: He was baptized by John the Baptist, began his ministry in Galilee, and focused all his preaching and teaching on the Kingdom of God. He had a well-deserved reputation as an exorcist and healer, and attracted much attention because of it. He gathered a group of disciples around him, without regard for sex, status, or background, and celebrated their unity through the sharing of meals. He, therefore, set himself and his followers at odds with the more sectarian, excommunicating mentality and practice of contemporary Judaism. Opposition to him reached a climax during a Passover celebration in Jerusalem, when he was arrested, tried, and crucified.

28. His *message* centered on the *Kingdom of God*. He announced it as something "at hand" (Mark 1:15). The final redemptive power of God is already at work, realizing itself in the individual's experience of reality, in his or her relationships with other persons, and with social and political institutions, broadly understood.

29. Jesus' message was communicated principally through *parables, proverbial sayings*, and the *Lord's Prayer*. Always it is the Kingdom which is proclaimed and/or explained.

30. The one who proclaimed the Kingdom in his lifetime is himself proclaimed after his resurrection. God's final redemptive act has been exercised in and through the risen Lord. And so we end where we began: with the early Church's faith in the resurrection. All else in the New Testament flows forward from the resurrection to the exaltation of Christ and backward from the resurrection to the crucifixion, passion, ministry, early life, birth, and even pre-existence of Jesus. Faith in the resurrection is always at the center of the New Testament's witness to Jesus Christ.

SUGGESTED READINGS

Bornkamm, Gunther. *Jesus of Nazareth*. New York: Harper & Row, 1960.

Brown, Raymond. *The Virginal Conception and Bodily Resurrection of Jesus*. New York: Paulist Press, 1973.

——————. "'Who Do Men Say That I Am?'—Modern Scholarship on Gospel Christology." *Horizons. Vol. 1 (1974), pp. 35-50.*

Bultmann, Rudolf. *Jesus Christ and Mythology*. New York: Scribner, 1958.

Crossan, John D. *In Parables: The Challenge of the Historical Jesus*. New York: Harper & Row, 1973.

Dodd, Charles H. *The Founder of Christianity*. New York: Macmillan, 1970.

Fuller, Reginald. *The Foundations of New Testament Christology*. New York: Scribner, 1965.

Hengel, Martin. *Son of God*. Philadelphia: Fortress Press, 1976.

Lane, Dermot A. *The Reality of Jesus: An Essay in Christology*. New York: Paulist Press, 1975.

Neill, Stephen. *The Interpretation of the New Testament, 1861-1961*. London: Oxford University Press, 1964.

O'Collins, Gerald. *The Resurrection of Jesus*. Valley Forge: Judson Press, 1973.

Perrin, Norman. *The New Testament: An Introduction*. New York: Harcourt Brace Jovanovich, 1974.

Price, James. *Interpreting the New Testament*. 2d ed. New York: Holt, Rinehart & Winston, 1971.

Senior, Donald. *Jesus: A Gospel Portrait*. Dayton: Pflaum-Standard, 1975.

Sloyan, Gerard. *Jesus on Trial*. Philadelphia: Fortress Press, 1973.

Vawter, Bruce. *This Man Jesus: An Essay Toward a New Testament Christology*. New York: Doubleday, 1973.

TWENTIETH-CENTURY VIEWS ON THE CHRISTOLOGY OF THE NEW TESTAMENT

(A survey of opinions of the relationship between the evaluation of Jesus during his ministry and the christological evaluation of him in the NT writings composed some twenty to one hundred years later—from *Horizons*, vol. 1, 1974, p. 38.)

Non-Scholarly Liberalism	Scholarly Liberalism	Bultmannian Existentialism	Views Within The Domain Of Scholarship	Non-Scholarly Conservatism
			Scholarly Conservatism	
This view regards the christological question as unimportant, for Christianity is primarily concerned with how man should live. Jesus came to teach man a way of life centered on love. It was his followers who first gave any importance to evaluating him. Liberalism was popular in the Protestantism of the late 1800's and early 1900's. It has revived today in Catholicism as a reaction to the dogmatic strictness of the past.	(Early 1900's) Liberal scholars developed a scientific methodology for detecting precise states of growth in NT christology. They judged this growth to be a creation, distorting the historical Jesus. Christology was once necessary in order to preserve the memory of Jesus, but now modern scholarship can give us the historical Jesus without christology, which should be dispensed with. Exemplified in W. Bousset's *Kyrios Christos* (1913).	(1920's through the 1950's) A reaction to liberalism. He further refined the scientific methodology, but rejected the liberal judgment on the invalidity of christology. Bultmann is indefinite and even agnostic on how Jesus evaluated himself. But the NT christology is functionally equivalent to Jesus' message about the kingdom, since both are a demand to accept what God has done through Jesus. Christology cannot be dispensed with.	(1960's and 1970's) Most scholars today are less agnostic than Bultmann about the historical Jesus and admit a continuity between the evaluation of Jesus during the ministry and the evaluation of him in the NT. Yet they continue to use with refinement the methodology for detecting growth in NT christology. The dominating motif is development in continuity. A division exists as to whether to posit an explicit christology in the ministry of Jesus (he used or accepted some titles: Son of Man, Suffering Servant, Messiah) or an implicit christology (Jesus did not use or accept christological titles). Implicit Christology — Scholars such as Hahn, Fuller, Perrin; some post-Bultmannians; many Catholics of the 1970's. Explicit Christology — Scholars such as Cullmann, Jeremias, Dodd, Taylor; most Catholics of the 1960's.	A failure to allow any development from the ministry to the NT. This theory posits that Jesus was christologically evaluated during his ministry exactly as he is portrayed in the Gospels (which are literal accounts of the ministry). A view held defensively by fundamentalist Protestants. Also held by Catholics until Church changes in the approach to the Bible began to affect Gospel study in the 1960's.

· XIII ·

THE CHRIST OF THE FATHERS, THE COUNCILS, AND MEDIEVAL THEOLOGY

THE PROBLEM

Jesus is at the center of Christian faith. But not just the carpenter's son, Jesus of Nazareth; Christians confess that Jesus is the Christ, the Promised One of God, the risen Lord. An understanding of Jesus Christ, therefore, implies and/or presupposes some understanding of a dynamic God who is involved in our history, indeed of a God who became one of us in order that the whole world, first created through the Word, might be restored fully through the same Word-made-flesh. That is why the chapters on God and on the Trinity (9 and 10) preceded this one.

An understanding of Jesus Christ also implies and/or presupposes some understanding of what it means to be human, for we are a new creation in Christ. That is why the chapters on human existence (4 and 5) also preceded this one.

Christians confess that the one God—the God who created us, sustains us, and providentially guides us toward our eternal destiny in the Kingdom—identifies with us, accepts us, and redeems us in Jesus Christ. Jesus has this unique role in our salvation because he is at the same time divine and human. If he were not divine, by what power and authority does he redeem us from our sins? If he were not human, what does his redemptive work have to do with us or for us?

Soteriology ("the study of salvation") and Christology ("the study of Christ") are intimately connected, therefore. We inquire into the nature(s) and person of Jesus Christ because who he is *in himself* is the foundation of what he is *for us*. If he is not at once human and divine, how does he redeem us? But if he *is* at once human and divine, how is that union to be understood?

AN HISTORICAL AND THEOLOGICAL OVERVIEW

Development in the Church's understanding of faith occurred for various reasons: (1) the naturally inquisitive and probing impulse of the human mind; (2) the challenge of dissident opinions; and (3) the need to communicate the Christian message across cultural lines. Each of these factors was already at work even in the New Testament period. Christological development occurred as the early Church made contact with the wider Hellenistic world around it, and as the heresy of Gnosticism tested the limits of Christian orthodoxy. There was an acceleration of Christological development after the New Testament period as the Church extended its missionary outreach, and as the need increased to translate, clarify, and refine the inherited Jewish categories found in Sacred Scripture.

From the earliest stage of this theological development, the concept of Word, *Logos*, was at the center. For the *Jews*, the Word had been present and operative at creation (Genesis 1), in the utterances of the prophets, and in the Wisdom literature. For the *Greeks*, the Word was identified with reason and with the Truth of the philosophers. If for the Jews the Word was a form of God's presence in *history*, for the Greeks it was an all-pervasive principle of rationality within the *universe*. Christianity united and transformed these two understandings of the Word, as is evident in the Prologue of John's Gospel (1:1-18). By the second century the *Apologists* made the connection even more explicit. Jesus is the key to both history and the universe. The Christ-event is one of unlimited significance because through it the Word itself became flesh.

But exaggerations of the divinity or of the humanity of Jesus soon appeared within the Church itself. For the *Docetists* (from the Green verb, *dokein* = "to seem, to appear"), the body of Jesus only appeared to be real, and for the *Gnostics* it was at best incidental to our salvation. Over against these views, Ignatius of Antioch insisted that if Jesus was not fully human like us, then he could not have saved us. At the other extreme there were approaches which undermined the divinity in favor of the humanity of Jesus—e.g., the *Adoptionism* of the *Ebionites*, a Jewish-Christian sect. Such Fathers of the Church as Irenaeus argued that if Jesus is not "of God," then he could not have saved us. Note, again, that it is concern for our *salvation* which inspires these earliest rebuttals of Christological deviation.

Others attempted mediating positions—Tertullian, Origen, Paul of Samasota, Arius—but these proved unsatisfactory because they tended, in divergent ways to be sure, to make of Jesus something more than human but less than God. The Word is of one substance with the Father, but not of the same nature. Or the Word is within the Godhead, but lower in rank than the Father. Or the Word is a semi-divine creature. Such views fall under, or at least come close to, the general category of *Subordinationism*. It was at the Council of Nicea in 325 that Subordinationism of every kind was rejected. Jesus Christ is "true God of true God . . . begotten, not made."

In the aftermath of Nicea two major theological schools emerged: one in Alexandria, Egypt, and the other in Antioch, Syria. The *Alexandrian school* was interested principally in preserving the *divinity* of Jesus and focused on the *unity* of the humanity with the Word, while the *Antiochene school* was concerned principally with his *humanity* and so adopted a looser approach to the unity of the human and the divine. Thus, standard histories of Christology refer to the Alexandrian approach as *Logos-sarx* (literally, "Word-flesh"), and the Antiochene as *Logos-anthropos* (literally, "Word-human being"). The former stresses that *the Word* took on flesh; the latter, that the Word became *a human being*. As this theological and doctrinal history was to unfold, each school of thought would generate extremes. From the Alexandrian school there would be those like Apollinaris (d. 390) who would insist so strongly on the divinity of Jesus, i.e., on the unity of the humanity with the Word, that they would deny him a human soul. And from the Antiochene school there would be those like Nestorius (d. ca. 451) who would insist so strongly on the humanity of Jesus, regarding it as a separate and distinct personal entity, that they would deny that Mary was truly the Mother of God.

If one is to make any sense of the otherwise complicated and often confusing history of the controversies and the councils, one has to keep the tensions between these two schools always in mind. The mystery of Jesus Christ has to do with the way in which divinity and humanity come together in one and the same person. Stress the divinity too much, and you run the risk of supplanting his humanity. Stress the humanity too much, and you run the risk of denying his divinity. In either case, not only is orthodoxy lost, but our salvation in Christ as well.

That orthodoxy was first articulated and defended, not without ambiguity, by the Council of Nicea (325). As we noted above and in the earlier chapters on God and the Trinity, Nicea rejected every solution which made Jesus Christ anything less than divine. Next came the First Council of Constantinople (381), which condemned Apollinaris and, therefore, struck a doctrinal blow for Jesus' humanity. After that, the Council of Ephesus (431), which condemned Nestorius and reinforced the Church's conviction that the one person, Jesus, is "true God of true God" and that Mary, his mother, is not only the mother of Christ but the Mother of God as well (*Theotokos*). There followed the Council of Chalcedon (451), which balanced Nicea's "of one substance with the Father" with its own formula, "of one substance (being) with us as to the humanity, like unto us in all things but sin," thereby achieving some measure of synthesis between the Alexandrian and Antiochene schools. Still another doctrinal statement was provided by the Second Council of Constantinople (553), which to a great extent repeated the definition of Chalcedon, reiterating its condemnation of Nestorianism. Finally, there was the Third Council of Constantinople (680-681), which in fidelity to Chalcedon condemned *Monothelitism* (the view that in Jesus there is only *one will*, the *divine* will).

Since Constantinople III there has been no significant *doctrinal* development to this very day. What we have had are some refinements of concepts and terminology in the Scholastic period, but without the same concern for the soteriology as the New Testament and the Fathers and councils of the Church had. At the risk of oversimplifying, one might suggest that the medieval theologians were more interested in Jesus Christ as he is *in himself* (e.g., his consciousness, his knowledge, his freedom, his sinlessness, the mode of the divine-human union) than as he is *for us*, as our Savior. This same heavily speculative, not to say abstract, approach to Christology has governed the production of seminary textbooks and catechisms, and accounts in part for Christology's general lack of pastoral usefulness for preaching, religious education, social ministry, and spirituality.

For all practical purposes, it was not until the occasion of the fifteen hundredth anniversary of the Council of Chalcedon that Catholic theologians, in any concerted way, took a fresh look at their own doctrinal tradition. Not surprisingly, it was Karl Rahner who led the way with a highly influential article, "Chalcedon—End or Beginning?" (which appears in a still-untranslated work *Das Konzil von Chalkedon*, A. Grillmeier and H. Bacht, eds. Würzburg, 1954, 3 volumes). Rahner argued that every conciliar definition is *both* an end and a beginning: an *end* of one phase of a discussion and the settling of certain points of controversy, but the *beginning* of a whole new phase of questioning, leading to deeper insights. Doctrinal formulations must constantly be rethought, not because they are false or radically imperfect, but precisely because they are true and, as such, can yield further truth and shed new light on other, related matters. Indeed, doctrinal pronouncements remain alive only insofar as they are continually elucidated. Consistent with his own theological starting point (i.e., the human person as radically open to God), Rahner developed an understanding of the incarnation as the unique and supreme instance of the essential completion of human reality. Anthropology is fulfilled in Christology. (We shall return to his position, and several others', in the next chapter.)

THE THEOLOGICAL AND DOCTRINAL
DEVELOPMENT: PATRISTIC ERA
Before Nicea

The *earliest Christological heresies* came from opposite extremes: *Docetism* and *Gnosticism* on the right (denying the humanity of Jesus for the sake of the divinity) and *Adoptionism* on the left (denying the divinity of Jesus for the sake of his humanity). Neither extreme, perhaps because they were so obviously extreme, required any kind of official condemnation such as a general council of the Church might render. Certain of the early theologians and Fathers were quick to identify the fundamental errors in these positions, and especially their implications for our salvation.

"There is only one physician," Ignatius of Antioch wrote in his *Letter to the Ephesians*, "both carnal and spiritual, born and unborn. God became man, true life in death; sprung both from Mary and from God, first subject to suffering and then incapable of it—Jesus Christ our Lord" (n. 7). Ignatius hereby testifies to both the divinity and the humanity of Jesus united in a single person. Against the Docetists and Gnostics, he insists that Jesus is the son of Mary and is subject to suffering.

Later in the same epistle (nn. 18-19) Ignatius speaks of Jesus as the epiphany or manifestation of God. Jesus' purpose is "to mold 'the newness' (Romans 6:4) of eternal life." He is the Word who breaks God's silence in order to destroy death and bring new life. To accomplish this he was "really born and ate and drank, really persecuted by Pontius Pilate, really crucified and died . . . really rose from the dead" (*Letter to the Trallians*, nn. 9-11). If, however, all of this was "make-believe," then his saving work on our behalf is all for naught, and the Eucharist that we celebrate together is of no account (*Letter to the Smyrnaeans*, n. 7).

The Word, or *Logos*, concept is also central for *Justin* as he tries to show the connection between the Greek philosophers' pursuit of Truth and our common human quest for the fullness of life and for salvation. "The Christ who has appeared for us represents the *Logos* principle in its totality, that is both body and *Logos* and soul" (*Second Apology*, nn. 10,13). Only in him is the Word fully present. And yet that particular expression or embodiment of the Word is available in principle to all and for all, just as the Word already contains whatever truth is to be found apart from the particularity of the Christ-event and of Christian faith: "The truths which people in all lands have rightly spoken belong to us Christians. . . . Indeed, all writers, by means of the engrafted seed of the Word which was implanted in them, had a glimpse of the truth." The same approach is developed several decades later by Clement of Alexandria.

An early indication of what Scholastic theology calls the *communicatio idiomatum* is provided by Bishop Melito of Sardis (d. ca. 190), who testifies not only to the divinity and humanity of Jesus but also to their *mutuality*: ". . . he who suspended the earth is suspended; he who fixes the heavens in place is himself fixed in place; he who fastened all things is fastened to the wood; . . . God is murdered. . ." (*Homily on the Pasch*).

Since the "communication of the idioms" (the mutual predication of properties) is a matter of some importance in interpreting the later history of Christology, it might be appropriate to explain it now, where it first appears. Because there is only one person, Jesus Christ, who acts through two natures, one divine and one human, we may legitimately predicate, or affirm, of this one person attributes which are both human (e.g., the ability to suffer) and divine (e.g., unlimited knowledge). But even beyond that, one can also predicate of his humanity what is his by virtue of the divinity, and vice versa. Thus by the "communication of idioms," one can say that "Mary's son is all-knowing" or that "God was born of Mary." Rejection of the personal unity of Jesus led Nestorius, for example, to reject the "communication of idioms" with reference to Jesus' birth and the motherhood of Mary. The Council of Ephesus would insist that Mary is the Mother of God, and precisely on the theological principle that she gave birth not to a nature alone but to a person, a *divine* person. As a consequence of the union by which divinity and humanity are united in one person, we can predicate of the one person what is rooted in either nature.

The great third-century theologian Irenaeus carried forward the defense of Christological faith against the extremists. The balanced quality of his position is striking. Jesus was human and truly suffered, but he was also "our only true master. . . the Word of God." More to the point: "Had he not as a human being overcome our adversary, the enemy would not have been justly overcome. Again, had it not been God who bestowed salvation, we should not have it as a secure possession. And if we had not been united to God, we could not have become partakers of immortality. For the mediator between God and humankind had to bring both parties into friendship and concord through his kinship with both; both to present humankind to God, and make God known to humankind" (*Against Heresies* 3.18.6,7). Jesus Christ, therefore, *recapitulates* everything in himself, restoring all reality to fellowship and communion with God.

Irenaeus is well in advance of the formulation of a classic Christological principle, one to be fashioned and refined by Athanasius and Gregory of Nazianzus—namely, "What is not taken up (by the Word) is not healed; but what is united with God is also saved."

Subsequent efforts at preserving orthodoxy while opening new lines of communication with contemporary non-Christian philosophy led inevitably to some Christological ambiguity. If Jesus Christ was to be believable as the fullness of truth, then his identification with the world of ordinary intellectual experience had to be secure. Accordingly, such theologians as Origen, Tertullian, and Paul of Samasota struggled to find new formulations of the relationship between Jesus and God the Father, concerned as they were both about the intellectual skepticism of their colleagues outside the Church and about the Gnostic and Docetic tendencies of many of their brothers and sisters within the Church. And they were concerned as well with reconciling their faith in one God with their confession of Jesus as Lord. Accordingly, their language at times suggested a *Subordinationist* orientation, i.e., one that made the Son of God less than or "subordinate to" the Father.

Thus, Origen's *First Principles* speaks of the necessity for some "intermediate instrument" between God and flesh to make their union possible. And there is at least a hint of Nestorianism (the positing of two separate persons in Christ) in his *Commentary on John*, where he distinguishes perhaps too sharply between Christ as the Word and Christ as human, a distinction that is not overcome, according to Origen, until after the exaltation. So "spiritual" is Origen's approach that much of his Christology is open to misinterpretation. This will explain why the official Church reached back beyond Origen to Irenaeus to find theological grounding for its teachings on the unity of God and man in Jesus Christ.

Tertullian, on the other hand, anticipated by more than two centuries the Christological formulation of the Council of Chalcedon. In his *Against Praxeas* (n. 27) he insists that Jesus, who is truly God and truly human, is at the same time a single subject: "Jesus is one person, God and man." Such union does violence to neither the divinity nor to the humanity: "Flesh does not become spirit nor spirit flesh. . . ." Unfortunately, Tertullian's understanding of the redemptive significance of the incarnation is not so penetrating or balanced. True to his Roman legalistic spirit, he focused entirely on the cross as the price of our salvation. Jesus came into this world, taking on our humanity, for one purpose only: to suffer the death of the cross. There is no corresponding emphasis on the rest of Jesus' human life, nor on the significance of the Word's taking on our flesh. Jesus stands as our representative, therefore, in a juridical sense alone. It was this legalistic approach that would influence much of Western theology for centuries thereafter.

Paul of Samasota, perhaps in reaction to Origen's tendency to shake Jesus loose from his human roots, seems to have professed some kind of adoptionist Christology. The Father dwells in the human being Jesus, thereby making of him his son. Paul of Samasota's view was condemned by the Synod of Antioch, which declared in 268 that "the divine Word is in (Jesus) what the interior man is in us." But did the synod also mean that Jesus did not have a *human* soul? Precisely that implication would be drawn within the century, and it would create a storm of theological controversy and political conflict.

The Council of Nicea (325)

It was Arius (of whom we wrote in chapter 9) who carried these *Subordinationist* tendencies to their extreme. The Son is a creature, created in time by the Father and then used by the Father in the creation of the world. Thus, Christ was neither God nor a human being. Rather, he was less than God but more than a human being. He was a kind of composite intermediary being, but not the mediator spoken of by Irenaeus and others.

Against the Arian view, the Council of Nicea solemnly proclaimed the oneness in being ("consubstantiality") of the Son with the Father. He is "God from God, Light from Light, true God from true God, begotten, not made, one in being (*homoousios*) with the Father.... For us men and for our salvation He came down and became flesh, was made man, suffered, and rose again on the third day."

The First Council of Constantinople (381)

Its ambiguities still unresolved, the controversy generated by Paul of Samasota and by the Synod of Antioch's response to him surfaced again around 360, almost a century later. Apollinaris of Laodicea, a faithful supporter of Athanasius and a strong defender of the Council of Nicea, made the *denial of the human soul* in Jesus the very heart of his Christology. For Apollinaris the Word is the unique principle of the flesh of Jesus. If Christ also had a human soul, or mind, then the Word would have been *in* a man, as Paul of Samasota seemed to be saying, but the Word itself would not have been made flesh. "How can God become a human being without ceasing to be God except by taking the place of the mind in a human being?" Apollinaris asked.

As a reaction against perduring adoptionist tendencies in the Church, the position of Apollinaris was understandable. But it failed to safeguard the transcendence of the Word and the integrity of Jesus' human nature. And in failing to safeguard the latter in particular, it undermined the effect of Christ's saving activity on our behalf. Accordingly, the position had to be condemned, as it was, by the First Council of Constantinople in 381 and again the next year at a Council of Rome convened by Pope Damasus I (d. 384). The "heresy" of the "Apollinarists" was censured by name in Canon I of the former council's declarations, and in Canon VII of the latter's, the text of which follows: "We condemn those who say that the Word of God dwelling in human flesh took the place of the rational and spiritual soul, since the Son and the Word of God did not replace the rational and spiritual soul in His body but rather assumed our soul (i.e., a rational and spiritual one) without sin and saved it."

The Council of Ephesus (431)

The controversy which had broken out in Antioch around the year 360 saw the emergence of two distinct and opposed parties. The debate between them was of major moment because it would set the stage for, and shape the terms of, the landmark Christological definitions of both Ephesus and Chalcedon.

On the one side, there were those who regarded the unity of the Word and the human in Christ rather loosely and who were intent upon defending his full humanity. This was the Antiochene school, and Nestorianism was its extreme expression. On the other side, there were those who tended to exaggerate the unity of Christ to the point where, as in Apollinaris, the human soul was entirely supplanted. They were intent upon defending Christ's divinity. This was the Alexandrian school, and Monophysitism was its extreme expression.

Two of Apollinaris' opponents, Diodore of Tarsus (d. ca. 394) and Theodore of Mopsuestia (d. 428), launched their own counter-protest and proclaimed the complete fullness of the humanity of Jesus. But the aggressiveness of their disciple Nestorius (d. 451) provoked resistance from Cyril of Alexandria (d. 444), who, in turn, allowed himself to use Apollinarian expressions. The Council of Ephesus condemned Nestorius.

More specifically: Diodore of Tarsus, like almost every exponent of a heterodox or even heretical point of view, was not intent upon *denying* some aspect of Christological truth. He was concerned rather with *preserving* something which he feared to be in danger of denial from the other side, namely, the transcendence of the Word. Diodore, therefore, did not deliberately set out to divide the human Jesus from the divine Word, but that was the effect of his position that the human being Jesus was son of Mary in the flesh and of God *by grace*, whereas the Word is the Son of God (not of Mary) *by nature*: "The man born of Mary is son by grace; God the Word is Son by nature" (Syriac Fragments 31-32; cited in Carmody and Clarke, *Word and Redeemer*, p. 83).

Theodore, bishop of Mopsuestia, joined forces against the *Logos-sarx*, or Word-flesh, approach of the Alexandrians, namely, the view which emphasizes *the drawing of all that is of the flesh into the Word* (as against the Antiochene *Logos-anthropos*, or Word-human being, approach which emphasizes *the Word's becoming human*). It was important for Theodore, and for others of the *Logos-anthropos* school, that Jesus be an agent and model of our liberation from sin and death, and he could be such only to the extent that he was truly one of us and with us. "Therefore it was necessary," Theodore wrote in his *Catechetical Homilies*, "that he should assume not only the body but also the immortal and rational soul; and not only the death of the body . . . but also that of the soul, which is sin" (n. 5). And so the human being Jesus, body and soul, ascended into heaven beyond Satan's reach. We, too, ascend beyond Satan's power insofar as we participate in the death and resurrection of Jesus. Mary, therefore, *is* the Mother of God, but Theodore seemed to understand the title in a weakened sense, as Diodore had before him. The human being born of Mary is not identically God, but only has God (the Word) dwelling in him.

Nestorius, patriarch of Constantinople (until deposed by the Council of Ephesus in 431), carried these views to their extreme. He fully represented the Antiochene insistence on the *Logos-anthropos*, or Word-human being, approach. The Word really and truly *became human*. Accordingly, such expressions as "God has suffered" or "God was nursed at his mother's breast" were offensive to him. (See "communication of idioms," referred to earlier in this chapter.) They smacked of Arianism and of Apollinarianism, both of which in their own way rejected the full incarnation, or becoming flesh, of the Word.

For Nestorius there are two natures in Christ, one divine and the other human, and each has its own *personal* manifestation.

These, in turn, form a third "person of union." The Nestorian position demands, of course, a special understanding of the motherhood of Mary: "If anyone wishes to use this word *theotokos* (literally, "mother of God") with reference to the humanity which was born, joined to God the Word, and not with reference to the parent, we say that this word is not appropriate for her who gave birth, since a true mother should be of the same essence as what is born of her. . . none gives birth to one older than herself" (*Letter to Pope Celestine*, n. 2).

Cyril, bishop of Alexandria, brought the *Logos-sarx*, or Word-flesh, Christology to its peak in this controversy, as Nestorius had brought the opposite *Logos-anthropos*, or Word-human being, Christology to its own logical heights. As a bishop (and most of the participants were men in pastoral office, not academicians), Cyril was principally concerned with the effects of the debate on our understanding of salvation and, more immediately, of the Eucharist. If the divine and the human are not really and fully united in Jesus Christ but are, as Nestorius would have it, separate and divided, then the flesh of the Word could not be the life-giving instrument of our own divinization—neither in salvation history nor in Holy Communion. In an almost classic expression of the Alexandrian *Logos-sarx* approach, Cyril writes that "the flesh does not bring the Word down to its own level; for divinity can in no wise be diminished. Of itself the flesh is incapable of imparting life. . ." (*Commentary on John*, n. 4).

Cyril was to address three letters to Nestorius, the *second* of which (written in 430) the Council of Ephesus formally accepted as a statement of orthodox faith. Therein, Cyril explicitly disavowed any Apollinarian interpretation of his position. The Word truly became flesh through a real hypostatic union. The Word *is* truly human, and not merely *in* a human being. Therefore, Mary can be called the Mother of God, and not the Mother of Christ, because "It was not an ordinary man who was first born of the holy virgin, and upon whom afterwards the Word descended, but he himself, united to humanity from the womb, who is said to have undergone fleshly birth, as making his own the birth of his own flesh." Thus, we worship "one Christ and Lord," and not a "human being along with the Word." What was born of Mary was "his rationally animated body to which the Word was hypostatically united."

The Council of Ephesus, convened by the emperor Theodosius II (d. 450), was formally opened by Cyril on June 22, 431, before the arrival of the delegates from Rome, representing Pope Celestine (d. 432). Cyril's second letter to Nestorius was approved by the council Fathers. Nestorius' views were condemned, and Nestorius was deposed as patriarch of Constantinople. When the Roman delegation finally arrived, they ratified in the name of the pope what had already been decided and done.

Neither the council nor the pope's representatives, however, officially accepted the so-called twelve anathematizations, or condemnations, contained in Cyril's *third* letter to Nestorius. Nonetheless, the document was read to the council, and it created a great measure of dissatisfaction among the Eastern bishops, i.e., those close to the Antiochene school of thought. Some of Cyril's language, as we noted earlier, was at least suggestive of an Apollinarian approach, particularly his characterization of the union of the divine and the union in Christ as a "physical" one (third anathema). The council ended with the mutual excommunication of the two great patriarchs of the East, John of Antioch and Cyril of Alexandria.

At the invitation of the emperor Theodosius II, John of Antioch (d. 441) provided a profession of faith to which Cyril was able to subscribe in 433. It expressed better than Cyril had the reality of Christ's distinct human nature, and the distinction between the two natures united in one person. Pope Sixtus III (d. 440) congratulated both parties and by implication accepted the so-called *"Formula of Union"* (also known as the "Symbol of Union" and the "Edict of Union") between Cyril and the bishops of Antioch. It was chiefly through this formula that the Antiochene school made its contribution to the subsequent development of the Christological dogma at Chalcedon.

Because this formula is so important a bridge between Ephesus and Chalcedon, a relatively generous excerpt is reproduced here.

We confess therefore our Lord Jesus Christ, the only-begotten Son of God, perfect God and perfect human being composed of rational soul and body, begotten before all ages from the Father as to his divinity, and the same in the last days born of the Virgin Mary as to his humanity for us and for our salvation, consubstantial with the Father in divinity and consubstantial with us in humanity. For a union of two natures has taken place; hence we confess one Christ, one Son, one Lord. In accordance with this union without confusion, we profess the holy Virgin to be Mother of God (*theotokos*), for God the Word became flesh and was made human and from the moment of conception united to himself the temple he had taken from her.

As for the words of the gospels and of the apostles concerning the Lord, we know that theologians have considered some as common because they are said of the one person (*prosopon*), while they have distinguished others as applying to the two natures (*physeis*), reserving those which befit God to Christ in his divinity while assigning those which are lowly to Christ in his humanity.

The Council Of Chalcedon (451)

The *Formula of Union*, however well-intentioned and well-conceived, did not hold the parties permanently together. Cyril's successor as bishop of Alexandria, Dioscorus (d. 454), would interpret some of Cyril's ambiguous formulations too literally. In the heat of struggle against Nestorianism, he tended to understand the hypostatic union as something achieved at the level of nature (*physis*) rather than of person. Thus, the divine and the human come together in Christ in *one divine nature (Monophysitism)*. Eutyches (d. ca. 454), the aged head of a monastery in Constantinople, carried the position to an even greater extreme. Better known for his sanctity than for his theological scholarship, Eutyches denied that Christ was consubstantial with us. Christ's human nature was completely absorbed by the divine nature.

Eutyches was brought to trial and condemned at a synod in Constantinople in 448. Although temporarily rehabilitated by

Dioscorus, Eutyches was also subsequently condemned by Pope Leo the Great (d. 461), to whom he had appealed. In a letter (the *"Tome of Leo"*) addressed in June 449 to Flavian (d. 449), patriarch of Constantinople, the pope gave the clearest expression to date of the doctrine of the incarnation. In Christ there are two distinct natures united in one person: "For he who is truly God is the same who is also truly human and there is no deception in this unity in which the lowliness of a human being and the divine majesty coincide. . . . For each of the two natures performs the functions proper to it in communion with the other: the Word does what pertains to the Word and the flesh what pertains to the flesh."

With his Augustinian stress on Christ as Mediator and on the saving power of the miracles and mysteries of the life of Christ, the pope clearly linked Christology with soteriology. Because of the union of the divine and human natures in the one divine person, all of the activities of the human Jesus are rooted in, and spring from, the one divine person and are, therefore, of infinitely salvific value. And yet they also remain fully human actions and fully representative of the whole human community, for the Lord was "born with the complete and perfect nature of a true human being; he is complete in his nature and complete in ours."

But Pope Leo's letter did not settle the matter once and for all, at least not so far as Dioscorus and Eutyches were concerned. They exercised their considerable local influence and succeeded in having a synod convened at Ephesus in August of 449 at which, under very strong political pressure, the bishops approved Eutyches' doctrine and deposed two of his episcopal opponents. Pope Leo labeled the synod a "robbery" (*latrocinium*), and it is still known today as the "robber synod" of Ephesus. Its proceedings were condemned by a Roman synod which met the very next month. It also asked that the emperor, Theodosius II, convoke a general council in Italy. He refused. It was left to his successor, Marcion (d. 457), to summon the Council of Chalcedon in October, 451. With nearly six hundred bishops, including three papal legates and two representatives of Latin Africa, this was by far the largest and most important council of the early Church.

At the first sessions the legality of the "robber synod" of Ephesus was examined and found wanting. Eutyches' doctrine was once again rejected, and Dioscorus was condemned for his part in the synod and for his complicity in bringing such unwarranted pressure to bear on the bishops. But the Fathers of Chalcedon were not initially interested in drafting yet another confession of faith. They were satisfied with the formulations of Nicea (325), Constantinople (381), and the "Tome of Leo" (449). The emperor's representatives, however, insisted on something more. They prevailed. A commission of bishops drafted a schema, but it was so ambiguous about the union of natures in Christ that the papal legates rejected it and threatened to move the council back to Italy. The emperor's delegates sided with the pope's and ordered the bishops to face up to the issue. They would have to choose between Dioscorus and Pope Leo.

A new commission, whose members now also included the Roman delegates and the emperor's, composed a profession of faith which the council accepted. Borrowing freely from Cyril of Alexandria's second letter to Nestorius, the "Formula of Union," and the "Tome of Leo" (the reading of which had elicited cries of "Peter has spoken through the mouth of Leo"), the Chalcedonian symbol of faith repudiated *both* Nestorianism and Monophysitism.

The *Alexandrian* school had clearly triumphed in the central formula, "one and the same Lord Jesus Christ." It is the "one and the same Lord Jesus Christ" who appears and lives in the man Jesus of Nazareth. The *Arians* were once again repudiated for having seen in the incarnation the "proof" that the Son is not truly God; and so, too, were the *Nestorians*, who sacrificed the unity of Jesus Christ in order to "save" the complete humanity.

The *Antiochene* school also triumphed in the formula "the same truly God and truly man composed of rational soul and body...like unto us in all things but sin...." The Antiochenes had fought for these principles against the old *Docetism* and also against certain tendencies in the disciples of *Origen*. Jesus of Nazareth was truly one of us and of our human family, but through the hypostatic union he is, at the same time, the source of our redemption and sanctification.

The older Christologies of Irenaeus and Tertullian were also represented in the Chalcedonian definitions. It was Irenaeus who provided the formula "one and the same" and who insisted that "had it not been God who bestowed salvation, we should not have it as a secure possession. And if we had not been united to God, we could not have become partakers of immortality." And it was Tertullian's formula, one person in two natures, which the council took over and made its own, although without any detailed elaboration. The "person" is the "who" of the union, namely, the eternal Son of God. The "natures" are the "what" of the union. Accordingly, Jesus Christ is consubstantial with the Father and also substantially one with us.

The definition follows:

> Following therefore the holy Fathers, we unanimously teach and confess one and the same Son, our Lord Jesus Christ, the same perfect in divinity and perfect in humanity, the same truly God and truly man composed of rational soul and body, the same one in being (*homoousios*) with the Father as to divinity and one in being with us as to humanity, like unto us in all things but sin (cf. Hebrews 4:15). The same was begotten from the Father before the ages as to the divinity and in the latter days for us and for our salvation was born as to his humanity from Mary the Virgin Mother of God.

> We confess that one and the same Lord Jesus Christ, the only-begotten Son, must be acknowledged in two natures, without confusion or change, without division or separation. The distinction between the natures was never abolished by their union but rather the character proper to each of the two natures was preserved as they came together in one person (*prosopon*) and one hypostasis. He is not split or divided into two persons but he is one and the same only-begotten, God the Word, the Lord Jesus Christ, as formerly the prophets and later Jesus Christ himself have taught us about him and as has been handed down to us by the Symbol of the Fathers.

The Second Council of Constantinople (553)

The solemnity of the conciliar definition notwithstanding, some bishops in Syria and Egypt who were inclined to Monophysitism expressed concern that Chalcedon had contradicted Ephesus (the council that had condemned the opposite heresy of Nestorianism). In 519 some Monophysite monks sought from Pope Hormisdas (d. 523) approval of their own formula, "one of the three (Persons in the Trinity) has suffered in the flesh." They were not satisfied with the pope's response. Several years later the emperor Justinian (d. 565), himself sympathetic to the Monophysite cause, for political rather than theological reasons, asked Pope John II (d. 535) for papal approval of the formula. He gave it, more or less, in a letter to the Senate of Constantinople in 534, but he also reaffirmed the Church's rejection of *both* Nestorianism and Monophysitism.

The controversy continued. A so-called "neo-Chalcedonian" current developed, giving many the hope that somehow the Chalcedonian formula might be reconciled with Monophysitism. The current's supporters urged the condemnation of the first opponents of Monophysitism: Theodoret of Cyr (d. 466), Ibas of Edessa (d. 457), and Theodore of Mopsuestia (d. 428), Nestorius' teacher. All were accused of Nestorian tendencies, and their works were lumped together under the heading of *"Three Chapters."* Again, the emperor Justinian, concerned about the politically divisive effects of these disputes, asked a pope, this time Pope Vigilius (d. 555), to take a public stand against these three opponents of Monophysitism. At first the pope refused, insisting that the three were orthodox by Chalcedonian standards. Only after he had been taken by force to Constantinople in 548 did he issue the condemnation. The reaction in the West was severe. Relations between the emperor and the pope were broken off, and Vigilius published a strong anti-Monophysite profession of faith (552).

At Justinian's call the Second Council of Constantinople opened in May of 553, condemned the "Three Chapters," adopted vehemently anti-Nestorian positions, and embraced the newly popular Monophysite formula, "One of the three has suffered in the flesh." The Council never won acceptance in the West, nor did it achieve the union Justinian hoped for in the East. The pope did eventually approve it, but the doctrinal scope of that approval is not entirely clear. It seems to have been restricted to the three canons which were directly concerned with the "Three Chapters" of Theodoret, Ibas, and Theodore. To the extent that the council has any longer-term doctrinal significance for Catholic faith, its importance may consist simply in its reaffirmation of the earlier condemnations of Nestorianism. Otherwise, it is not an exceptionally bright moment in the conciliar history of the Church.

The Third Council of Constantinople (681)

By now Islam, a new and powerful threat to the unity of Christendom, had made its entrance upon the world scene. These internal theological divisions within the Church were a luxury it could now afford even less than before. A new emperor, Heraclius (d. 641), offered his support to Sergius (d. 638), patriarch of Constantinople, in the latter's attempts at some theological reconciliation. Unfortunately, Sergius only succeeded in producing yet another Christological deviation, this one called *Monothelitism* (one will), or *Monenergism* (one action). In one of those interesting cases of history where a pope seems to have come down on the side of a heretical position, Pope Honorius (d. 638) agreed with Sergius that the expression "one will" could be used, but then Sergius carried it one step further: If one will, then one nature. And so he was back to Monophysitism. It was inevitable that Monothelitism and its companion, Monenergism, would be condemned. The first conciliar blow against Monothelitism was delivered at a non-ecumenical Council of the Lateran (649), convoked by Pope Martin I (d. 655) and attended by one hundred and five bishops from Italy and Africa. The definitive thrust, however, came from the Third Council of Constantinople, convoked by the emperor Constantine IV (d. 685) with the consent of Pope Agatho (d. 681). The council accepted the doctrinal formulation which the pope had previously expressed in a letter to the emperor (March, 680), and it condemned Monothelitism and all of its supporters, even chastizing the late Pope Honorius for his unwitting approval of the heresy. One year later Pope Leo II (d. 683),

Pope Agatho's successor, formally approved the council's proceedings.

The definition follows:

> ...believing that one of the holy Trinity, who after the incarnation is our Lord Jesus Christ, is our true God, we say that his two natures shine forth in his one hypostasis. In it, throughout his entire human existence in the flesh, he made manifest his miracles and his sufferings, not in mere appearance but in reality. The difference of natures in that same and unique hypostasis is recognized by the fact that each of the two natures wills and performs what is proper to it in communion with the other. Thus, we confess two natural wills and actions concurring together for the salvation of the human race.

Subsequent Councils

Doctrinal development stopped at this point. To the extent that Christological dogma was touched upon by subsequent councils of the Church, it was always simply a matter of reiterating the teachings of one of these earlier councils—Nicea, Ephesus, and Chalcedon in particular. This is the case with the Fourth Lateran Council (1215) in its profession of faith; in the profession of faith given at the Second Council of Lyons (1274); in the *Decree for the Jacobites* at the Council of Florence (1442); in the *Decree on Justification* at the Council of Trent (1547); and in various papal encyclicals and decrees of Roman congregations in more recent years. As we shall see in Part IV, the Second Vatican Council focused its attention principally on the mystery of the Church, not on Christology. Vatican II's Christology, therefore, is to be inferred from its ecclesiology. All is fixed on the goal of unity. The Church is called to be a sign and instrument of unity: of the unity of humankind with God and of humankind within itself. This call to unity is grounded in the mystery of Christ and of the Kingdom of God. Just as Christ came to proclaim the Kingdom, to personify it, and to bring it about, so, too, the Church is summoned to carry forward Christ's mission for the sake of the Kingdom (see the

Dogmatic Constitution on the Church, n. 5, and the *Pastoral Constitution on the Church in the Modern World*, n. 45).

Synthesis

Against assorted Christological errors—especially Arianism, Nestorianism, and Monophysitism—the official teachings of the Church preserved an essential balance in its understanding of the mystery of Christ, at once God and a human being. The Word of God, who became human, suffered, died, and rose for our salvation, is truly God, of the same substance as the Father (*Nicea*). But he is also fully human, of one nature with us (*Constantinople I* and *Chalcedon*). In spite of the irreducible difference between his divine and his human natures, he is one and the same, the eternal Son of God, who as a human being is born of the Virgin Mary, the Mother of God (*Ephesus, Chalcedon,* and *Constantinople II*). Because he is a human being, he leads a truly human life in all things but sin: a life of truly human actions, of truly human freedom, of truly human consciousness (*Constantinople III*).

MEDIEVAL CHRISTOLOGY
Some Antecedents

Augustine

Augustine died in 430 and therefore had no direct role in any of the major Christological councils. And yet he remains, alongside Thomas Aquinas, as one of the most influential of all Christian theologians. For Augustine, Christ is the *Mediator* between God and humankind. He is the Word incarnate, a teacher of infinite knowledge and wisdom, who leads us to eternity through temporal realities. By identifying completely with our human condition, Jesus Christ shows us how to live and gives all of us hope for life without end. On the other hand, "...we would not be redeemed by the one mediator of God and man, the man Jesus Christ (1 Timothy 2:5), if he were not also God" (*Enchiridion*, n. 137). Christ, therefore, is the new head of the human race. We are predestined to glory through him, and we are joined to him even now as members of his Church.

Boethius

Boethius (d. 525) is the one generally credited with refining the meaning of the terms *person* and *nature* as they function in Christological discussion. It was his definition of *person* which carried over into medieval thought and which provided some verbal leverage for clarifying the preceding conciliar doctrines: "an individual substance of a rational nature." The definition was slightly modified by Thomas Aquinas (who spoke of an "incommunicable" substance as well) and especially by Richard of St. Victor (d. 1173), for whom person is "an incommunicable existence of an intellectual nature." Person, therefore, is the reality of a being which belongs to itself and is its own end. But personhood is never grasped as it is, directly. We are persons who act as persons and who come to the knowledge of our personhood only by reflecting on the meaning of what we do. But this is getting us into modern conceptions of "person," well beyond Boethius' pioneering efforts.

Anselm

Anselm of Canterbury's place in the history of Christology is insured by his distinctive *theory of satisfaction*. It is an understanding of redemption, however, which seems to distort rather than illuminate the meaning of Christ's mission, so far does it appear to be from the New Testament's theology of the cross and resurrection (see chapter 12).

According to Anselm's argument, as expressed in Book I of *Cur Deus Homo?* (*Why Did God Become Man?*), sin disturbed the order of the universe. Some compensation had to be offered to restore what had been disrupted. But we were simply not up to the task. The offense was against an infinite God, and we are finite. Only infinite satisfaction would do, and only God could provide it (chapter V). But not just God. It had to be one who is at once God and a human being, a God-man. This answered the question: Why did God become a human being? But it did not answer the question: Why did Jesus have to die?

Anselm proposed that satisfaction required more than the incarnation. Jesus had to do something which he as a human being was not otherwise bound to do. Because he was sinless, he was not bound to die. But he endured death nonetheless as a voluntary payment of the debt incurred by our sins, and so he satisfies for those sins (Chapters IX-XII).

Anselm's theory is to be understood against the background of the Germanic and early medieval feudal system. There is a bond of honor between feudal lord and vassal. Infringement of the lord's honor is tantamount to an assault upon the whole feudal system. A demand for satisfaction, therefore, is not for the sake of appeasing the lord's personal sense of honor but for the sake of restoring order to the "universe" (feudal system) in which, and therefore against which, the "sin" was committed. The feudal lord cannot simply overlook the offense, because the order of his whole economic and social world is at stake. So, too, with God (Chapters XIII-XV).

Aquinas would later modify Anselm's theory, arguing that it was *fitting* for God to act in that way, but it was not *necessary*, as Anselm had insisted (*Summa Theologica*, III, q. 1, a. 2). Thus altered, Anselm's theory entered the wider stream of medieval and then post-medieval theology. It was never made an official teaching of the Church, however. Over the years, many Catholics have incorrectly assumed it to be a matter of doctrine, if not even of dogma. Through Calvin and Luther, Protestants, too, ingested the theory in its more severe form (Christ died as our *substitute*, in punishment for sin).

Thomas Aquinas

Aquinas followed in the tradition of Augustine in formulating his own answer to the question at hand, "Why did God become a human being?" The incarnation occurred because ". . . it belongs to the essence of goodness to communicate itself to others . . . (and) to the essence of the highest goodness to communicate itself in the highest manner to the creature" (III, q. 1, a. 1). Thus, the incarnation deepens our faith in goodness, strengthens our hope, enkindles charity, sets us an example, divinizes us, turns us from evil, heightens our sense of human dignity, destroys our presumption about grace and salvation, removes our pride, and frees us from sin (q. 1, a. 2). Given the last effect, it was "fitting" that Jesus Christ serve as our Mediator between God and us since in him alone are God and humankind united.

Thomas turned his attention quickly, however, to the *mode of union*, and it is here, in question 2, that he defines and distinguishes the meanings of *nature* and *person*. *Nature* signifies *what* a thing is, as distinct from some other species of reality. *Person* signifies *who* it is, i.e., an individual substance of a rational nature (Boethius again). "If the human nature is not united to God the Word in person, it is not united to him at all; and thus belief in the incarnation is altogether done away with, and Christian faith wholly overturned" (q. 2, a. 2). He also insists, with Chalcedon, that the union is truly *hypostatic*, against those who would continue to argue that there are two hypostases in the incarnation, the one of God, the other of a human being, while there is but one person, Christ. "Person," Thomas notes, "only adds to hypostasis a determinate nature, i.e., rational" (q. 2, a. 3). To say otherwise is to lapse once more into Nestorianism, thereby destroying the unity of the God-human being and undermining his salvific work on our behalf.

The medieval discussion about the meaning of *person* would demand more effort and space than the purpose of this book requires or allows. It is sufficient simply to note that three discernible schools of opinion developed: The *Thomist* school, represented especially by the Dominican Banez (d. 1604); the *Scotist* school, represented by Duns Scotus himself (d. 1308); and a mediating *Jesuit* school, represented by Francis Suarez (d. 1617). The first insisted that Christ's human nature participates in the same act of existence by which the Word itself exists. The "act of human existence" is subtracted from it, without loss of human dignity. On the contrary, Christ's human nature receives an even higher dignity in being alive by the same principle of existence by which the

Word is alive. The second (Scotist) view preferred to define personality in a negative way, as an incapacity for dependence (conversely, a capacity for independence). In the hypostatic union the power of God brings to fulfillment this capacity for independence by fully orienting the human nature of Christ to God. Finally, the Suarezian position says, against the Thomists, that nothing is "subtracted" from the human nature of Christ. The two natures are joined by what Suarez called a created mode of union. Against the Scotists, Suarez argued that personality is a positive, not a negative, reality. It is an essentially necessary form in which a nature is manifested.

Three observations should be made about this discussion. (1) It showed how far medieval theology had veered from the historical, soteriological, and pastoral interest of New Testament and patristic thought in favor of an exceedingly speculative analysis of "how" the divine and the human are united in Jesus Christ. (2) The debate itself defies easy summarization, as the preceding paragraph shows. (3) Since the Church has never officially and finally defined its understanding of the mode of union, the matter is still open to debate. There is no one orthodox explanation, although there have been some unorthodox ones.

Much of the remainder of Thomas' Christology dwells on questions which have to do with the *inner makeup* of Christ: his intellect, his soul, the presence of grace, the virtues, his knowledge, his grasp of the Beatific Vision, his powers, his bodily integrity, his capacity for suffering, the unity of wills, his ability to merit, his subjection to the Father, and so forth. Principal exceptions, beyond the opening statement on the fittingness of the incarnation, are provided by the discussion of Christ's headship over the Church (q. 8), his role as Mediator (q. 26), and then the sequential treatment of the various mysteries of Christ's life, death, resurrection and exaltation (qq. 35-59). But these "exceptions" did not govern the Christologies of subsequent centuries. They remained focused on the so-called "constitutive" questions, i.e., Christ as he is *in himself* rather than *for us*. Christology and soteriology drew farther and farther apart.

Post-medieval Scholasticism

Catholic Christology from the medieval period to the middle of the twentieth century (specifically, the fifteen hundredth anniversary of the Chalcedonian definition) is really a history of commentaries on Thomas Aquinas' *Summa Theologica*, retaining all the while the *Summa's* basic structure. One can take up practically any Latin textbook from this vast period and find this verified. Thus, Charles Boyer, for many years professor at the Pontifical Gregorian University in Rome, the academic training ground of many Catholic bishops and theologians, patterned his own work almost exactly on the *Summa*. His *De Verbo Incarnato* discusses in sequence the fittingness of the incarnation, the mode of union, the two wills, and the redemptive work. Several other subsidiary questions appear almost exactly where Thomas himself treated them—e.g., the priesthood of Christ, the adorability of the humanity of Christ, the headship of Christ. On the other hand, Boyer, like many other post-medieval theologians, failed to carry forward some of Thomism's stronger biblical and patristic insights, especially the discussion of the mysteries of Christ's life and the more comprehensive understanding of the redemption. On the latter point, for example, Thomas does not completely limit Christ's saving work to the cross; Boyer and most others do. In this they reflect a Latin tradition which goes back even before the Middle Ages, to the time of Tertullian (d. 220). For them, the resurrection and exaltation are a *reward* for Christ's obedient death and a *proof* in support of his claims to divinity. As we saw in the last chapter, such a view brings us a considerable distance indeed from the theological perspective of the New Testament.

SUMMARY

1.   Development in the Church's understanding of Jesus Christ occurred for three reasons: (1) the naturally inquisitive and probing impulse of the human mind; (2) the challenge of dissident opinions; and (3) the need to communicate the Christian message across cultural lines.

2.   Distortions of the Church's Christological faith appeared at opposite ends of the theological spectrum. At the *extreme left* there were denials of the divinity in favor of the humanity (*Adoptionism*), and at the

extreme right there were denials of the humanity in favor of the divinity (*Gnosticism, Docetism*). These were opposed by such early Church Fathers as *Ignatius of Antioch, Justin, Melito of Sardis*, and *Irenaeus*. The connection between Christology (Christ in himself) and soteriology (Christ for us) is always firmly maintained by these Fathers. For Irenaeus, what is not taken up by the Word is not healed, and what is united to God is saved.

3.   Subsequent theological formulations, however, began to skirt the edges of orthodoxy. In their efforts to commend Christian faith to their philosophical contemporaries and, at the same time, to deal effectively with the Gnostic and Docetic threats from within the Church, some of the early Church theologians (*Origen*, in particular) came close to *Subordinationism*, making the Son of God less than, or subordinate to, the Father.

4.   It was *Arius*, however, who carried these tendencies to their logical conclusion. The Son is a *creature*, neither God nor a human being, but a composite intermediary being. Against the Arian view the *Council of Nicea* (325) defined the "consubstantiality" of the Son with the Father, insisting that the Son was "begotten, not made."

5.   Some pressed the Nicean definition too far in the other direction. *Apollinaris of Laodicea*, a member of the *Alexandrian school*, emphasized so much that the Word is the unique principle of the flesh of Jesus that Jesus was left with *no human soul* at all. Apollinarianism was condemned by the *First Council of Constantinople* (381). If the Word did not assume a human soul as well as a human body, then he did not save us in soul as well as in body.

6.   In the meantime, a theological approach opposite from Apollinaris' developed within the *Antiochene school*. Apollinaris had been concerned primarily with the *unity* of Christ's humanity with the Word. For *Diodore of Tarsus* and *Theodore of Mopsuestia*, however, Apollinaris' insistence on the unity of the Word with the humanity in effect suppressed the humanity altogether. The Antiochenes, therefore, preferred to regard the unity of Christ more loosely in order to protect the integrity of his humanity. Their position was carried forward, to an extreme, by *Nestorius*. There are two separate persons in Christ. Mary, therefore, is not the Mother of God (*theotokos*) but only the Mother of Christ, the human being. Nestorius was opposed by *Cyril of Alexandria* and then condemned by the *Council of Ephesus* (431).

7.   A *"Formula of Union"* was worked out after the Council of Ephesus between Cyril and some of the bishops of Antioch, who still were not satisfied with the results of the council nor with some of Cyril's

preconciliar expressions. But the "Formula" did not hold the parties together permanently. Indeed, Cyril's views were carried to their own extreme by *Eutyches*, a monk in Constantinople, who argued that Christ's human nature was completely absorbed by the divine nature so that we have not only one divine person but also one divine nature (*physis*). Thus, *Monophysitism*. The *Council of Chalcedon* (451) condemned Monophysitism and reaffirmed the condemnation of Nestorianism. The *Alexandrians* were satisfied with the council's formula, "one and the same Lord Jesus Christ," and the *Antiochenes* with the formula, "the same truly God and truly man composed of rational soul and body...like us in all things but sin...."

8.   Monophysitism continued, however, in Syria and Egypt, and charges and counter-charges were exchanged. Given the political as well as theological dimensions of the controversies, the situation was complicated by the intervention of the emperor, on the one side, and then by the pope, on the other. The *Second Council of Constantinople* (553) was convened by the emperor (and subsequently approved by the pope) to see if a pro-Monophysite "tilt" might contribute to political unity. It did not, and the council is of theological significance for us today only insofar as it repeated the earlier condemnations of Nestorianism.

9.   Monophysitism reappeared in the next century in slightly altered form. *Sergius*, patriarch of Constantinople, argued that there is only one divine will in Christ (*Monothelitism*). At first even the pope (*Honorius*) saw no problem with this, but then Sergius carried his position to *its* logical extreme: If only one will, then only one nature. Monothelitism was condemned at the *Third Council of Constantinople* (681).

10.   There has been no *doctrinal* development since Constantinople III. Subsequent councils have merely repeated the earlier conciliar definitions whenever they turned their attention to Christological issues: *Lateran IV* (1215), *Lyons II* (1274), *Florence* (1442), *Trent* (1547), and *Vatican II* (1962-1965).

11.   Subsequent *theological* development culminated in the medieval synthesis of *Thomas Aquinas*, which held sway in Catholic education until the middle of the twentieth century. That synthesis was rooted in the Patristic era generally, and in *Augustine* particularly. For Augustine, Christ is primarily our *Mediator* with God.

12.   Anselm of Canterbury is best known for his theory of satisfaction. Sin disrupted the balance of the universe, and at the same time imposed a debt upon the human race. Only a God-man could restore that balance and make adequate payment of that debt. Often misunderstood,

Anselm's theory entered the mainstream of medieval and post-medieval thought only after it was modified by Aquinas, who insisted that it was fitting but not necessary that God should have acted in that particular way.

13. *Aquinas'* own Christology reflected the concerns and preoccupations of medieval theology. Although he does speak of Christ's headship, his role as Mediator, the fittingness of the incarnation as a manifestation of divine goodness, and of the mysteries of Christ's life, the principal emphasis of Thomas' Christology is on the *inner makeup* of Jesus Christ: the union of natures with the one divine person, the knowledge of Christ, the operation of his wills, his powers, his consciousness, etc. The focus is on Christ as he is *in himself* rather than on Christ as he is *for us.*

14. Post-medieval Scholastic Christology follows that same pattern, but often without carrying forward some of Thomas' peculiar strengths, namely, his more comprehensive understanding of the redemption (to include the resurrection and exaltation) and his attention to the mysteries of Christ's life. By 1951, the fifteen hundredth anniversary of the Council of Chalcedon, the distance between the New Testament's Christological perspective and that of the Church's theologians was very considerable indeed.

SUGGESTED READINGS

Carmody, James, and Clarke, Thomas. *Word and Redeemer: Christology in the Fathers.* Glen Rock, N.J.: Paulist Press, 1966.

Hardy, E., and Richardson, C., eds. *Christology of the Later Fathers.* Library of Christian Classics, vol. 3. Philadelphia: Westminster Press, 1954.

Grillmeier, Aloys. *Christ in Christian Tradition: From the Apostolic Age to Chalcedon (451).* New York: Sheed & Ward, 1965.

Kelly, J. N. D. *Early Christian Doctrines.* New York: Harper & Row, 1960.

Neuner, J., and Dupuis, J., eds. "Jesus Christ the Savior." *The Christian Faith in the Doctrinal Documents of the Catholic Church.* Westminster, Md.: Christian Classics, 1975, pp. 135-190.

Smulders, Piet. *The Fathers in Christology: The Development of Christological Dogma from the Bible to the Great Councils.* De Pere, Wis.: St. Norbert Abbey Press, 1968.

· XIV ·

THE CHRIST OF
TWENTIETH-CENTURY
THEOLOGY

CATHOLIC CHRISTOLOGY BEFORE 1950

Catholic Christology from the time of Aquinas to the middle of the twentieth century remained essentially the same in structure and in content. The approach taken by the "Spanish Summa" (*Sacrae Theologiae Summa*, Madrid: Library of Christian Authors, 1953, vol. III) was typical of the textbooks in general use in Catholic seminaries and colleges throughout this period. The material was divided into two main parts: the mystery of the incarnation (Christ as he is in himself), and the redemptive work of Christ (Christ as he is for us). The two "Christs" are brought together by the sin of Adam. If Adam had not sinned, the Word would not have become flesh.

But the discussion immediately turned from the "fittingness" of the incarnation to a metaphysical analysis of the way in which the union of Word and flesh occurred and the conditions under which it was sustained. Herein, the treatment followed the conciliar teaching outlined in the previous chapter: The union occurs at the level of person, or hypostasis, not at the level of nature, and so forth. The residual medieval influence was particularly evident in the raising of various subsidiary questions—e.g., whether Christ could have been called a human being or the Christ while he lay in

the tomb between Good Friday and Easter Sunday; the reconciliation of the "sadness" of Christ with his sinlessness; the legitimacy
of devotion to the Sacred Heart.

The limitations of early twentieth-century Catholic Christology, however, were even more apparent in its treatment of the
redemption. The exposition was shaped by the medieval focus
upon *merit*, i.e., something which is or ought to be accepted by
another, for which the one accepting ought to give something in
return. By his passion Christ merited all the gifts of grace and of
glory for humankind. He rendered more-than-adequate reparation
for sin and, therefore, satisfied the "vindictive justice" of God.
The resurrection and exaltation of Christ were mentioned in
these Christologies, but their redemptive significance remained
unclear. Indeed, what Christ accomplished through his passion
was taken as fully sufficient for our salvation. A marked change in
this approach was signaled by the publication of Catholic scholar
Francis X. Durwell's *The Resurrection* (New York: Sheed & Ward,
1960). This book argued that the resurrection was the center, not
an adjunct, of Christ's redemptive work.

WHY THE CHANGE?

There is a pronounced difference between medieval Christology
and the Christology of the twentieth-century manuals, on the one
hand, and the Christologies of contemporary Catholicism
(Rahner, Küng, Schillebeeckx, Kasper, *et al.*), on the other. How
account for this? There are two principal reasons: (1) *the shift from
an uncritical to a critical reading of the New Testament;* and
(2) *the shift from a static to an evolutionary understanding of
human existence.* Both of these changes were, for the most part,
products of the major transformation of human consciousness connected more or less with the *Enlightenment* of the eighteenth
century. These developments, in turn, lay underneath the theological reexamination of the Council of Chalcedon, on the occasion of
its fifteen hundredth anniversary, to which reference was made in
the previous chapter.

There is no need here to retrace our steps. The significance of
the shift in the way we read the New Testament was explained in

the previous chapters. The shift in our understanding of human existence was described in Part I, chapters 3–5. Thus, the Jesus of the New Testament is neither the Jesus of traditional piety, based on a fundamentalist interpretation of the Bible, nor the Jesus of liberal revisionism, based on an anti-dogmatic, anti-supernatural, anti-transcendental interpretation of the biblical message and testimony. Since almost all Catholic Christologies before 1950 fell into the first category, these Christologies had to be reconstructed in the light of the biblical renewal.

And with few exceptions, before mid-century the Catholic theology of human existence was similarly untouched by the Enlightenment and its several products: the emergence of historical and political consciousness, and the corresponding development of processive and liberational modes of thinking. Thus, the Jesus of historically-minded Christian faith is neither the omniscient, omnipotent God-in-human-form of traditional piety, based on a static, classical concept of human existence, nor the flat, one-dimensional human being-with-the-aura-of-God of liberal piety. Catholic Christology assumed a new shape, therefore, as it assimilated the findings of twentieth-century New Testament scholarship, on the one hand, and of recent theological anthropology, on the other.

CURRENT AND RECENT CATHOLIC CHRISTOLOGY

Pre-note: The distinction between Christology "from above" and Christology "from below" must be clear at the outset because it recurs throughout this chapter.

Christology "from above" begins with the pre-existent Word of God in heaven, who "comes down" to earth to take on human flesh and to redeem us by dying on the cross, rising from the dead, and returning to enjoy an exalted state as Lord in heaven. This was the emphasis, as the reader may recall, of the Alexandrian School in the age of the great Christological controversies, as it was of the Fourth Gospel and of Paul.

Christology "from below" begins with the Jesus of history, a human being like us in all things except sin, who stands out from the rest of the human race by his proclamation of, and commitment to, the Kingdom of God. His life of dedicated service of others led him to the cross, from which point God raised him up and exalted him. This was the emphasis of the Antiochene School in the age of the Christological debates, as it was of the Synoptic Gospels.

Carried too far, a Christology "from above" becomes Monophysitism or Docetism: Jesus is not really human, but only appears to have taken on our human condition. Carried too far, a Christology "from below" becomes Nestorianism or Adoptionism: Jesus is not really divine, but fulfills a unique role in the history of the human race, calling attention to the demands of God's Kingdom among us.

Karl Rahner

Because he is the most important and most influential Catholic theologian of this century, Karl Rahner's Christology has to be taken with the greatest measure of seriousness. Although expressed in assorted articles in the various volumes of his *Theological Investigations*, the most comprehensive and systematic statement of Rahner's Christology is available in his *Foundations of Christian Faith* (New York: Seabury Press, 1978). The reader must be forewarned: The material is not easy to grasp. But its complexity does not diminish its importance.

Jesus Christ is what is specifically Christian about Christianity, Rahner insists at the outset. This is said without prejudice to the principle that someone who has no concrete, historical contact with the explicit preaching of the Church can nevertheless be justified and saved in virtue of the grace of Christ. The transcendental self-communication of God is available in principle to every person, as we noted in chapter 5. But for the Christian the process of divine self-communication reaches its goal and its climax in Jesus Christ. He or she alone is Christian who explicitly professes in faith and in Baptism that Jesus is the Christ, that he is the decisive and climactic moment in God's transcendental self-communication to humankind.

Contrary to the complaints of some of his critics, Rahner does not propose an ahistorical Christology. The basic and decisive point of departure for Christology, he argues, lies in an encounter with the historical Jesus of Nazareth, and hence in an "ascending Christology." On the other hand, he warns against placing too much emphasis on this approach. The idea of God coming into our history "from above" also has its power and significance. Both an ascending and a descending Christology have to be taken into account even if, in the light of modern evolutionary consciousness, our *starting point* is "from below" rather than "from above."

Rahner's notion of *evolution* is heavily influenced by Hegel. Matter and spirit, Rahner suggests, are intrinsically related to each other. They spring from the same creative act of God, and they have a single goal in the fullness of God's Kingdom. The world and its history are moving, i.e., are in evolution, toward a unity of matter and spirit, which Rahner (like Hegel) conceives as a *becoming* higher. The capacity for becoming something higher is called the capacity for "self-transcendence."

Since the free gift of God's grace, i.e., God's self-communication, was incorporated into the world from the beginning, the history of the world is really also the history of salvation. At the point (or points) where we realize that the direction of history is toward the Kingdom of God, we can speak of the experience of *revelation*. But whether we realize it or not, i.e., whether we are formally and explicitly religious, even Christian, or not, does not change what is in fact going on. God is always present to the world and to persons within the world as the principle of self-transcendence. We have the capacity to move beyond ourselves, to become something higher and better than we are, because "the Absolute Beyond" is already in our midst, summoning us forward toward the plenitude of the Kingdom.

There are, of course, other, relative causes at work in the world and in our individual histories. These, too, have to be taken into account when we strive to understand the course and direction of history. We have the human capacity to better ourselves by means of human resources already available to us. But even those mundane resources, or causes, are made possible in the first instance by God.

For Rahner, "The permanent beginning and the absolute guarantee that this ultimate self-transcendence, which is fundamentally unsurpassable, will succeed and has already begun is what we call the 'hypostatic union'" (p. 181). In other words, the unity of matter and spirit, which is what the movement of history achieves, reaches its climax in the union of Word and flesh in Jesus Christ. With the incarnation, history has entered its "final phase." The divinization of the world is underway but not yet complete. The further course of this phase and its final result remain "shrouded in mystery."

In light of the mystery of Jesus Christ, therefore, it is clear that the human person is neither purely matter (as the behaviorists believe) nor purely spirit (as the Platonists contend) but a single reality which comprehends both matter and spirit. Indeed, it is only in the human person that both of these elements can be experienced in their real essence and in their unity. The person is *spirit* insofar as he or she is conscious of himself or herself as one who lives in the presence of God and whose whole being is oriented toward God. The person is *matter* insofar as he or she is an individual whose concreteness as an individual is experienced as something inescapably given. Apart from matter the human person cannot experience the world, other persons, or even himself or herself. Indeed, apart from matter the human person cannot even experience the *spiritual* reality that is present in ourselves and in others. Thus, there is a fundamental *reciprocity* between matter and spirit. Together they constitute the world and human persons within the world.

On the other hand, there is an essential difference between matter and spirit. Influenced also by Teilhard de Chardin, Rahner argues that the whole historical process involves a movement from lower to higher, from the simple to the complex, from unconsciousness to consciousness, and from consciousness to self-consciousness. Everything is in a state of *becoming*, and becoming is a process of *self-transcendence*, and self-transcendence is possible because God is present to life as the principle of growth and development.

Human persons, therefore, are the self-transcendence of living matter. Apart from human persons, matter would never have achieved consciousness, much less self-consciousness. The history of the material world is thus intertwined with, even dependent upon, the history of humankind. Through humankind the material world reaches its goal by reaching beyond itself. Because we are not only observers of nature but a part of nature as' well, our history is also a history of the active transformation of the material world itself. It is through such free action, arising from the spiritual dimension of the human person, that both we and nature reach our single and common goal.

However, since we act in freedom, both the history of the material world and human history are in a state of guilt and trial. We can reject God's self-communication and refuse to enter this historical movement toward God. But our freedom always remains grounded in the reality of God. The religious person, and the Christian in particular, knows that the history of the world will find its fulfillment in spite of, as well as in and through, human freedom.

The human person, consequently, is not an accident of evolution but a necessary part of it. The world in fact becomes conscious of itself, of its essential unity, and of its purpose and goal by means of humankind. But this coming to consciousness is possible only because God is immediately present to reality in grace. In that sense, the end, or goal, of history is also its beginning. The history of the cosmos from the beginning is always and basically a history of the human spirit, a desire to become conscious of itself and of its ground, who is God.

It is from this *evolutionary perspective*, Rahner argues, that we must understand the place of Jesus Christ. The process of divine self-communication to the world and the process of our free acceptance of that self-communication of God reach a point in history which makes these acts, from God's side and ours, both irrevocable and irreversible. Since the goal of the whole historical movement is present to history from the beginning (as its *final cause*, the Scholastics would say), that event by which movement toward the goal of history becomes irrevocable and irreversible must also be part of that historical process from the beginning. Thus, all of history has a unity, and that unity is focused in the event of Jesus Christ.

Consequently, the doctrine of the hypostatic union is not a speculative doctrine alone. Jesus is truly a human being; i.e., he is truly part of the earth, truly a moment in this world's biological process of becoming, a human being in human history, for he was "born of a woman" (Galatians 4:4). He, too, has received God's self-communication, and he, too, accepts it and lives out that acceptance. That principle cannot be stressed too much. The Word *became flesh.* The Word did not simply draw near to flesh, and, therefore, affect the world indirectly, through affecting the spirit of the world, as the Gnostics contended. The Word takes hold of flesh and is expressed in its materiality. It is through the flesh that the Word is present to the world. Spirit and flesh are one in the Word-made-flesh.

Such an understanding of the incarnation, Rahner insists, in no way denies that God could also have created a world without an incarnation. In other words, God could have denied to the self-transcendence of matter that ultimate culmination which takes place in grace and incarnation. For every movement from a lower to a higher stage is always unexpected and unnecessary. Self-transcendence occurs as a kind of leap from one level to the next because it is only the presence of God to life which makes such leaps possible.

And that brings us to the other side of the doctrine of the incarnation. It is *God* who takes on flesh. But not in the sense that God simply enters our history from the outside, moves us a step further along the road to fulfillment, and then leaves us behind. Rather the incarnation is an intrinsic moment in the whole historical process by which grace is communicated to all persons. And because that divine self-communication occurs at a particular time and in a particular person, the self-communication becomes unconditional and irrevocable from God's side, and irrevocable and irreversible from our side, insofar as that divine self-communication is definitively accepted by a human being, Jesus Christ.

In Christ, the communication of grace is not only established *by* God; it *is* God. That which is offered is inseparable from the offerer. Here we have a human reality, Jesus of Nazareth, who belongs absolutely to God. And this is what the *hypostatic union* means: *God once-and-for-all, in a specific human individual, is communicated to us, and that communication is absolutely, unequivocally accepted.*

Because of the incarnation, God is in humankind and remains so for all eternity, and humankind is for all eternity the expression of the mystery of God because the *whole* human race has been assumed in the individual human reality of Jesus. For this reason Christology is the beginning and the end of anthropology. The finite is no longer in opposition to the infinite. Christ is a human being in the most radical way, and his humanity is the most autonomous and the most free not in spite of its being assumed, but because it has been assumed, because it has been created as God's self-expression. The humanity of Christ is not simply the "form" of God's appearance on earth. *God* ex-ists (literally, "stands out from") in Christ. The Church has consistently condemned every heretical attempt to say otherwise: whether Gnosticism, Docetism, Apollinarianism, Monophysitism, or Monothelitism.

Christian faith, therefore, is the acceptance of Jesus Christ as the *ultimate* word of God to humankind. But there are many who in effect have accepted Jesus Christ but do not *explicitly* acknowledge him as God's ultimate word. What of them? Anyone who fully accepts his or her own humanity and the humanity of others has at least *implicitly* accepted Christ because Christ is in all of us and God is in Christ. On the one hand, God accepts us and loves us in the neighbor. And, on the other hand, we accept and love God in the neighbor, as the parable of the Sheep and the Goats (Matthew 25) shows. Just as our love for our neighbor must always take some concrete form in the love of a specific individual, so must our love for God. "One who has no love for the brother he has seen cannot love the God he has not seen" (1 John 4:20).

For the same reason, a transcendental Christology (summarized above) requires that the self-communication of God occur in a particular, concrete individual, Jesus Christ. That is why Christology today begins "from below." It does not start by saying "God became a human being" but by saying that in Jesus God's merciful and absolute self-communication to the world is finally accomplished and made present to us. The incarnation must be historical because it must touch historical beings and the total actual history of the world. We can realize our humanity nowhere else except in history.

Jesus of Nazareth understood himself, however incompletely and gradually, to be this savior, and his resurrection established and manifested that he is such. He did not regard himself simply as another prophet, but he made our reaction to him decisive for our entrance into the Kingdom of God. Indeed, Jesus is himself the Kingdom.

Hans Küng

If Karl Rahner is the most important and most influential theologian in the Catholic Church today, Hans Küng is the best known and most controversial. His major Christological work, *On Being a Christian* (New York: Doubleday, 1976), was preceded by books on Church reform, papal infallibility, priesthood, and other practical topics. In *On Being a Christian* Küng shifts his attention from questions about the movement Jesus initiated to questions about Jesus himself.

The book is less philosophical and less speculative than Rahner's. Although Küng and Rahner share the same "from below" starting-point for their Christologies, Küng never ascends so far as Rahner, who establishes an eventual connection between the newer "from below" Christology and the traditional "from above" Christologies of the great councils of the Church and of the medieval theologians. Küng is also much less inclined to see the significance of Jesus in Rahner's larger historical and cosmic terms. Küng's Jesus is a man born to ordinary parents, with brothers and sisters, who grew up to become a wandering, uneducated Jewish layman, supremely indifferent to sacred traditions and institutions. Our knowledge of him comes from the earlier New Testament writings, Mark and the authentic letters of Paul, as interpreted by modern German scholarship.

Jesus addresses God as *Abba* (Father), organizes feasts in anticipation of the Kingdom of God, and makes the human person the center of biblical religion. He is condemned for blasphemy and put to death. His followers experience his "new life" as God's *representative* among us and as our representative before God. For

Küng, the various New Testament titles given to Jesus are only honorific. There is no pre-existence, no incarnation, and no redemption in any traditional sense of the words. Those doctrinal assertions which claim otherwise are the product of Greek speculation.

The main lines of the book's arguments are summarized in the form of twenty theses in a later work, *Signposts for the Future* (New York: Doubleday, 1978, pp. 2–40; see also *The Christian Challenge*, New York: Doubleday, 1979). The Christ of Christian faith, Küng argues, is no other than the historical Jesus of Nazareth (thesis #4). He was not interested in proclaiming himself. He was totally subordinated to God's cause, the Kingdom of God, the direct, unrestricted rule of God over the world. Jesus, therefore, preached the will of God as the one supreme norm of human action. And God's will is none other than humankind's total well-being (thesis #5). It was for the sake of our well-being that Jesus challenged and thereby relativized sacred institutions, law, and cult. In their place he preached love, even of one's enemies. He identified himself with the poor and the wretched of the earth, proclaiming all the while the forgiveness of God (thesis #6).

Because of his words and deeds, Jesus proved a divisive figure. Some hated and feared him; others showed him spontaneous trust and love. Jesus demanded of all a final decision: to direct one's life for God's cause or for our own. In claiming to be above Moses and the prophets and in forgiving sin, Jesus exposed himself to the charge of blasphemy (thesis #7). Indeed, Jesus so identified himself with God's cause that he even addressed God as Father (*Abba*), *his* Father. It became impossible to speak of Jesus without speaking of this God and Father, and it was difficult thereafter to speak of this God and Father without speaking of Jesus. "When it was a question of the *one true God*, the decision of faith was centered not on particular names and titles but on this *Jesus*" (p. 19). The way in which one came to terms with Jesus decided how one stood with God. Jesus acted and spoke in God's name, and for the sake of God he allowed himself to be slain (thesis #8).

Jesus did not simply accept his death. He actively provoked it. He appeared as the personification of sin and as the representative of all sinners. And the God with whom Jesus had identified himself throughout his public life did not identify with Jesus at the end. Jesus was "forsaken." Everything seemed to have been in vain (thesis #9). But Jesus' death was not the end. After his death his followers experienced him as alive. The death of Jesus, like the death of any one of us, is transition to God, retreat into God's hiddenness, into that domain which surpasses all imagination. It is significant, of course, that Küng describes the resurrection as primarily something that happened to the disciples: "...there remains the *unanimous testimony of the first believers,* who regarded their faith as based on something that really happened to them..." (p. 21; thesis #10).

Therefore, the cause of Jesus continued. His followers were convinced that he was still alive. He became the content of the Church's own proclamation (thesis #11). But, for Küng, it is not the resurrection which is at the heart of the Christian proclamation, but the crucifixion. It is the great distinctive reality which distinguishes this faith and its Lord from other religious and irreligious faiths and ideologies: the cross in the light of the resurrection, and the resurrection in the shadow of the cross (thesis #12). The crucifixion is "the permanent signature of the living Christ" (*On Being a Christian,* p. 400).

Walter Kasper

Walter Kasper has produced yet another Christology "from below" in his *Jesus the Christ* (New York: Paulist Press, 1976). According to his own introductory account, the book is indebted to the Catholic Tübingen School, and in particular to the Christological approaches of Karl Adam (d. 1966) and Joseph Geiselmann. Their theology focused on a study of the origins of Christianity in Jesus Christ which they knew were accessible only through biblical and ecclesiastical tradition. So, too, does Kasper begin there, with the New Testament, and with the historical Jesus who is proclaimed as the risen Christ.

Kasper develops what he calls an historically determined, universally responsible, and soteriologically determined Christology. It is *historically determined* in that it begins with, and is oriented to, the specific history and unique life and destiny of Jesus

Christ. It narrates the story of Jesus of Nazareth and asks: Who is he? What did he want? What was his message and mission? This means that Christology today must deal with problems of modern historical research: the quest for the historical Jesus, the quest for the origins of Easter faith, and the quest for the earliest Christological formulation of belief. These historical questions have to be answered if faith in Christ is to be taken seriously.

Christology must also be *universally responsible*, i.e., philosophically sophisticated. Christology inquires not just into this or that existent, but into existence in general. Christian faith claims that "the ultimate and most profound means of reality as a whole has been revealed only in Jesus Christ, in a unique and at the same time finally valid way" (p. 21). But such an understanding of Christ implies a specific understanding of reality. Thus, there can be no question of playing off an ontological or philosophical Christology (such as the Fathers and councils of the Church left us) against a non-ontological or functional Christology. We have to do both: to take seriously both the history and the deeper philosophical questions which the history provokes.

Finally, Christology must be *soteriologically determined*. Christology and soteriology form a whole. There are soteriological motives behind all the Christological pronouncements of the early Church. Both the defense of the true divinity and the defense of the true humanity were intended to protect the reality of the redemption. Kasper, therefore, rejects two extremes: the one which subordinates soteriology to Christology (as the medieval theologians did), and the other which reduces Christology entirely to soteriology, as the Reformers did and as Friedrich Schleiermacher did, arguing from the present experience of redemption back to the Redeemer, and making all Christological propositions an expression of Christian self-consciousness. Schleiermacher's influence, Kasper notes, can be seen in Tillich, Bultmann, and the Bultmannian school of thought. For Kasper, therefore, being and meaning are indissolubly joined. "What is believed can be known only in the exercise of belief. The exercise of belief, however, is meaningless if it is not directed to a something which is to be believed" (pp. 23-24).

The Jesus whom Kasper finally presents is the historical Jesus as mediated to us by conservative New Testament scholarship, in contrast, for example, to the more liberal exegesis upon which Küng relies. Jesus preached the Kingdom of God as "the coming to power in and through human beings of the self-communicating love of God" (p. 86). The Kingdom must be seen, therefore, "in the context of mankind's search for peace, freedom, justice and life" (p. 73). Through his miracles Jesus showed that in him "God was carrying out his plan, and that God acted in him for the salvation of mankind and the world" (p. 98). That preaching and activity include an "implicit Christology." Jesus went beyond the Law in his teaching. He made no distinction between his word and God's. And he summoned people to make a decision for or against him as the touchstone for their decision for or against the Kingdom of God. His summons to decision and his gathering of disciples underlined his authority and his (and his disciples') break with their past. Jesus, therefore, was reluctant to accept certain titles, not because they exceeded his own claims, but because he was more than those titles could express (p. 103). Jesus understood himself and functioned as our *representative*. He foresaw and accepted his death in that light, even though his disciples did not see the significance of his death until the resurrection.

Unlike Rahner, Kasper does not perceive the incarnation as an integral part of historical evolution. Whether the incarnation happened because of sin, or whether sin happened in order to make the incarnation possible, Kasper says is unanswerable. Whatever the case, the cross and resurrection of Jesus Christ are the climax of God's self-revelation for the salvation of the world. They are that "than which nothing greater can come to be" (p. 192). Insofar as he attempts an answer of his own, Kasper comes close to Anselm's. "The order of the universe (peace and reconciliation among men) is possible only if God himself becomes man, the man for others, and so establishes the beginning of a new human solidarity" (p. 225).

Kasper understands the hypostatic union, in the end, pneumatologically. The Father communicates himself in love to the Son. It is in the Spirit that this love can be communicated outside the Trinity. The Spirit is also involved in the reverse movement.

"The creature filled with God's Spirit becomes in freedom an historical figure through which the Son gives himself to the Father. In this all-consuming dedication to the point of death, the Spirit as it were becomes free; he is released from his particular historical figure, and consequently Jesus' death and resurrection mediate the coming of the Spirit (cf. John 16:7; 20:22). And thus Jesus Christ, who in the Spirit is in person the mediator between God and man, becomes in the Spirit the universal mediator of salvation" (p. 252).

Edward Schillebeeckx

Edward Schillebeeckx subtitles his 767-page book on *Jesus* "An Experiment in Christology" (New York: Seabury Press, 1979). And it is only the first, and shorter, of two volumes. The sequel treats of the Christ of Pauline and Johannine faith, whereas this one presents the historical figure we know as Jesus of Nazareth. So Schillebeeckx, too, constructs a Christology "from below." He is interested in discovering what is "peculiar, unique, about this person Jesus," for it was this Jesus who succeeded in touching off a religious movement that has become a world religion asserting that he, Jesus, is the revelation, in personal form, of God.

"Thus the question of his ultimate identity governs the whole of this enquiry," Schillebeeckx writes. "My purpose is to look for possible evidences in the picture of Jesus reconstructed by historical criticism. . . ." (p. 34). The volume confines itself, however, to the period of primitive Christianity, "a period that brings us closest to Jesus and is still very reticent over the matter of identifying Jesus of Nazareth, in whom followers of Jesus, after his death, found final and definitive salvation" (p. 35). The subtitle, therefore, is deliberate. The book is a prolegomenon. It clears the ground for the fuller argument.

The presentation is heavily exegetical. The aim is to discover the historical Jesus, and the historical Jesus is available to us only in the pages of the New Testament. Part I addresses the problem of how we get in touch with the historical Jesus. Schillebeeckx's alternative to other quests for the historical Jesus is to examine the actual movements (Christian communities) which Jesus set in motion, and especially their confessions of faith in him, all of which were based on some historical facet of Jesus' life and work.

Part II synthesizes what can be reconstructed: Jesus' message, the rejection, his death, and the response of his disciples after his death. The Easter experience is portrayed as one of receiving forgiveness and grace from a Jesus known to have died, and this experience of forgiveness, in turn, provided the basis for the disciples' coming back together again.

Part III describes and analyzes the growth of the early creeds, each of which was founded on some remembered experience of the historical Jesus. The various Christological titles were expanded and transformed by these historical memories. So we have here again a Christology "from below." It begins with "the encounter with and recollection of Jesus of Nazareth, the prophet of the near approach of God's rule and the praxis of the kingdom of God, who turns our human way of living upside down and thus is able to touch off some explosive situations..." (p. 570). But from the Council of Nicea onwards, Schillebeeckx contends, one particular Christological model ("from above"), the Johannine, developed as the norm of all reflection on Christ. Thus, the history of the Church has never done justice to the possibilities inherent in the Synoptic model, which he presents here.

Part IV of his book is an attempt at a beginning of such a Christology, developed out of a mixture of Thomism, existentialism, and some elements from linguistic philosophy. Here he underlines the universality of Jesus as the definitive salvation from God. Jesus is the parable of God and the paradigm of humanity, the one who realizes that human concerns and God's coincide and that we must realize that we are "of God" even when death seems to contradict this. "Through his historical self-giving, accepted by the Father, Jesus has shown us who God is: a *Deus humanissimus*" (p. 669). But precisely *how* the man Jesus can be for us at the same time the form and aspect of a divine Person, the Son, is in Schillebeeckx's view "a mystery theoretically unfathomable beyond this point."

What we affirm, however, is that what Jesus preached, what he lived and died for, the Kingdom of God, was in the end the person of Jesus Christ himself, the eschatological man, Jesus of

Nazareth, who is exalted to the presence of God and who of his plenitude sends us the Spirit of God, to open up "communication" among human beings. "Jesus' being as man is 'God translated' for us. His pro-existence as man is the sacrament among us of the pro-existence or self-giving of God's own being.... The unique universality lies, therefore, in Jesus' eschatological humanity, sacrament of God's universal love for human beings.... Jesus is the firstborn of the kingdom of God. The cause of God as the cause of man is personified in the very person of Jesus Christ" (p. 670). And this is the sole heart and center of Christianity. Jesus brought no new system or set of doctrines. Rather he came to put the Kingdom of God into practice. He had the wonderful freedom "to do a good deed" (Mark 3:4). In his dealings with people he liberated them and made them glad. He was a warm companion at table. His eating and drinking with his own and with outcasts brought freedom and salvation. He showed, in other words, that it *is* possible to put the Kingdom into practice in this world, in our history.

Jesus' unique universal significance is, in turn, historically mediated through the Church's own practice of the Kingdom: a work of service, carried out in faith, as we are led by the Spirit of Christ. "Thus it is in the power of Jesus' Spirit that the Church mediates the manner in which God is concerned with all human beings" (p. 672). And, thus, we are invited today to combine the theoretical theology with *orthopraxis* (literally, "right practice") i.e., "the practice of the kingdom of God, without which every theory and every story loses its credibility—certainly in a world calling in its impotence for justice and liberation" (p. 673).

James Mackey

Professor of Divinity at New College, Edinburgh, James Mackey sets out on a new quest of the historical Jesus, but without the presuppositions of those who engaged in earlier quests (*Jesus the Man and the Myth: A Contemporary Christology*, New York: Paulist Press, 1979). For Mackey, faith and history must be kept together, but the history we are concerned with is present-day history, not something recovered from the past. Indeed, we must be able to move from past history about Jesus to the present influence of Jesus in our historical experience. This he does by focusing on the experience of the spirit and power of Jesus which enables us, through its contagiousness, to continue in the faith of Jesus (pp. 188, 196, 259). It is Jesus' own faith in human existence as sheer gift from God, as belonging to God, and as binding us to God. In Jesus and in his faith we meet the one true God.

In search of the historical Jesus, Mackey begins with the most certain piece of evidence we have about him, namely, his death. But the fact of Jesus' death is overladen with theological interpretation, or myth. What do we know about his death apart from theology? That Jesus was put to death because he challenged the practices and institutions of Judaism and had tried to reform it. The myth grew up that Jesus not only died because of his political and religious confrontation but also because of our sins. This particular myth emerged from the conviction that Jesus was not finally contained by death, but that his power and his spirit lived on, enabling his disciples to overcome evil, to live in faith and love, and to defy death in a spirit of hope (p. 99). This experience of Jesus was at once "deep and infectious." That the experience was rooted in any particular, "objective" appearances of the risen Christ Mackey will not concede.

From the resurrection Mackey moves to the life and preaching of Jesus, both centered on the Kingdom of God, as the rediscovery of life as precious gift and absolute grace. The Kingdom of God is our experience of the contingency of life, of its giftedness, of the reality of God as Father. Jesus expressed this myth about God in his prayer, in his fellowship meals, and through his good works.

With Paul we see the movement of Jesus' own myth about the Kingdom of God to the Church's myth about Jesus. The full-grown myth about Jesus is given in the Nicene definition which states that Jesus is "one in being" with the Father. Such a doctrine is grounded, Mackey argues, in Jesus' own faith, namely, that God is immediately present as Father in everything around us, in the "very contingency of our existence" (p. 231). But the Nicene achievement became over-simplified with time, and people began speaking of the divinity of Jesus as if he were some kind of divine person or thing. The Council of Chalcedon, therefore, had to insist upon his humanity as well.

What is distinctive about Mackey's Christology is his choice of Jesus' own faith as its starting point. According to Mackey, Jesus was, before all else, a man of faith in God and in the giftedness of human existence. Christian faith is a sharing in the faith of Jesus. The symbol linking Jesus' faith with our own is the Kingdom of God.

The Kingdom, however, is very much a present-oriented reality for Mackey. The symbol refers to the reality of life-as-grace (gift), but without any real socio-political dimension. Nor is there any reversal of values in Jesus' preaching of the Kingdom. There is no apparent need for repentance and conversion in response to Jesus' proclamation (see our earlier discussion of these issues in chapter 12). There is no yet-to-be-realized future transformation of the cosmos and of the individual human being (topics to be discussed in chapter 29). Indeed Mackey professes impatience even with the word *eschatological*, calling it "the most abused word in contemporary theology, a kind of pseudo-verbal escape mechanism from all kinds of conceptual difficulty[;]. . .[it is] not easy to say what it means" (p. 287, n. 8). It is this uncertainty about eschatology that theological critics are most likely to fix upon.

Process Theologians

Teilhard de Chardin

Unlike the five major Catholic theologians just presented, Teilhard de Chardin (d. 1955) never produced a systematic Christology. Indeed, he was not primarily a theologian at all but a paleontologist and archaeologist. But because he was a convinced Christian and a priest, he felt a special need to reconcile somehow his work as a natural scientist with his faith and his vocation. He did this, as noted earlier in chapter 4, by placing Christ within an evolutionary framework.

Christ is both the bearer and the goal of the upward movement of the universe toward the divine. Christ is the Omega Point, the focus of union needed by the "noosphere" in order that the noosphere might achieve a creative breakthrough into a new and final state of complexity and convergence. All of history, therefore, is a movement toward Christ, and yet Christ is at the same time already present in the world. His presence gives all of reality a Christic dimension. The Church is that place where that Christification is explicitly understood and acknowledged. Insofar as the Church practices Christian charity, the Church injects the most active agent of hominization into the world. The world thereby becomes a commonwealth of persons united in selfless love.

This intimate link between Christ and the perfection of the universe Teilhard believed to be justifiable on New Testament grounds, specifically on the basis of the Fourth Gospel and the Epistles to the Colossians and the Ephesians. (For a fuller statement of Teilhard's Christology, see Christopher Mooney, *Teilhard de Chardin and the Mystery of Christ*, New York: Harper & Row, 1965.)

Teilhard's principal contribution to Christology is his insistence on an historically evolutionary framework for understanding the mystery of Christ. That Christology, however, is very much a Christology "from above," an approach more typical of the time in which he wrote. His influence on Karl Rahner has already been noted. He had an even more direct influence on Ansfried Hulsbosch, a Dutch Augustinian theologian.

Ansfried Hulsbosch

Hulsbosch's basic evolutionary position is expressed in his *God in Creation and Evolution* (New York: Sheed & Ward, 1965). A more formal expression of his Christology appeared the next year in a Dutch theological journal, *Tijdschrift voor Theologie* ("Jezus Christus, gekend als men, beleden as Zoon Gods"—"Jesus Christ, Known as Man, Confessed as the Son of God"—vol. 6, 1966, pp. 250-273; the article is summarized by Robert North in "Soul-Body Unity and Man-God Unity," *Theological Studies*, vol. 30, 1969, pp. 27-60).

Hulsbosch was principally concerned with accounting for the real unity of Christ. The traditional teaching, he argued, tends to leave us with the image of Christ divided into "two layers." A better way is offered by Teilhard's evolutionary perspective. The unity of Christ is an expression of the unity of the spiritual and the material in the human person. We are not composed of body and soul as if they were separate components of the human condition. We are absolutely indivisible subjects. So, too, Jesus is not man-plus-God but a divinized human being. Jesus is *known* as a human being and is *confessed* as the Son of God. This means that Jesus is God by being human in a special way; i.e., ". . . the divine nature of Jesus is relevant to the saving mystery only insofar as it alters and elevates the human nature. And whatever that is, it must be called a new mode of being man." To attribute divinity to a divine nature distinct from his human nature is just as alien to his truly unified being, therefore, as a separate spiritual soul would be alien to the human person's unity. Something would be brought in from the outside, making the person of Jesus "a juxtaposition of two realities."

Does this make Jesus a mere human being? Hulsbosch wants to avoid this conclusion. He insists that Jesus is a human being in a new and higher way. Through Jesus, humanity itself has been brought to a new threshold, and Jesus himself has crossed that threshold. He is "the image of God" (Colossians 1:15) in a unique and supreme way. He is in a very real sense the presence of God to human beings and to the entire cosmos, and hence divine. But his divinity is not in virtue of anything distinct from his humanity. It is there precisely in virtue of his humanity itself. What we have in Jesus is the "unfolding of the capabilities which lay latent within matter." He is not God who became a human being, but *a human being who became God.*

This is a Christology "from below" of a most radical kind, and yet very different from Küng's or Schillebeeckx's, for example. The latter two begin with, and focus fully upon, the historical Jesus as disclosed to us in the Gospels and the authentic Pauline letters. Hulsbosch, like Teilhard, focuses not upon the historical Jesus of Nazareth, the preacher and agent of the Kingdom of God, but upon the historical Christ, the yeast which makes history's evolution toward the Kingdom possible. The process Christologists are, in a sense, less historical than the others even though their stated intention is to propose a fully historical understanding of Christ and of salvation.

Piet Schoonenberg

Dutch Jesuit theologian Piet Schoonenberg follows a similar Christological course in his own contribution to the same special issue of the *Tijdschrift voor Theologie* and in his full-length *The Christ: A Study of the God-Man Relationship in the Whole of Creation and in Jesus Christ* (New York: Herder & Herder, 1971). We cannot point to anything divine in Jesus that is not realized in and from what is human. More deliberately than Hulsbosch, Schoonenberg confronts the question of the *pre-existence* of Christ. He argues that the Second Person of the Trinity is none other than the human person of Jesus, who came to exist at a specific moment in time. God is initially a single Person, therefore, but as history unfolds God becomes two Persons, and then three. Christ is God's ultimate revelation, however, and not simply a fortuitous climax to history. In him the fullness of what it is to be human is realized, just because the fullness of the Godhead dwells in him.

But as Schillebeeckx has pointed out, the idea of human transcendence is not so straightforward as might appear. It assumes that we know precisely what "humanness" is, so that starting from there we can come to realize what transcendental humanness is. According to Schillebeeckx, it is clearly true that God is revealed in humanity and that if we are to know Christ as God, we know this only out of his mode of being man. But it is also true, following Thomas Aquinas (III, q. 16, a. 11), that we encourage confusion when we say that "the man Jesus is God." Christ, insofar as he is human, has the grace of union, but one cannot say that Christ, *insofar as he is human*, is God. A more proper formula would be: Jesus Christ is the Son of God in humanity.

The most extreme statement of a process view of Christ thus far has come from outside the Roman Catholic tradition. Norman Pittenger, an Anglican theologian, concludes that Jesus is different from the rest of us in degree, not in kind. Jesus realized to an unsurpassed degree the possibilities open to us as human beings. Christ is divine only in the sense that the Love which is God is at work in and through him. If human beings have the capacity to live in love, it is Jesus Christ who fully actualizes that capacity. And so Christ and God are one with the other in Love. (See *Christology Reconsidered*, London: SCM Press, 1970.)

Liberation Theologians

Leonardo Boff

Another set of Christologies "from below" has emerged from the Latin American liberation school of theology. The most systematic effort thus far is offered by Leonardo Boff, a Brazilian Franciscan, in *Jesus Christ Liberator: A Critical Christology for Our Time* (Maryknoll, N.Y.: Orbis Books, 1978). Liberation Christology, he writes, stresses the historical Jesus over the Christ of faith. The historical Jesus, not the Christ of faith, speaks to our situation today. He did not present himself as the explanation of reality but as an urgent demand for the transformation of that reality (p. 279).

Accordingly, Jesus preached not himself but the Kingdom of God, which is "the realization of a utopia involving complete liberation, a liberation that is also structural and eschatological" (p. 280). The Kingdom is a reality that is at once present and still to be completed in the future. It is to the poor, the suffering, the hungry, and the persecuted that Jesus preaches, because it is they who must directly challenge the justice of the messianic king. Through Jesus, God has sided with them.

Everything about Jesus' words and deeds must be interpreted in this light. He was not merely a reformer but a liberator: "You have heard... but I tell you." He preaches a God to whom we have access not primarily through prayer and religious observance but through service to the poor, in whom God lies hidden and anonymous. Jesus establishes fellowship with society's outcasts (Matthew 11:19). He rejects wealth (Luke 19:9) and dominative power (Luke 22:25-28). Jesus' own praxis, in other words, establishes a new way of looking at God and at reality, i.e., through the prism of the struggle for liberation.

The conversion demanded by Jesus is not simply a change of convictions but a change of practice. And it is concerned not just with individuals but with social and political structures as well. "In the conditions of history, then, the kingdom of God does not come unless human beings accept it and enter into the whole process of conversion and liberation" (p. 287).

But Jesus chose to die rather than impose the Kingdom by violence. Indeed, he provoked his death by his call for conversion, his proclamation of a new image of God, his freedom from sacred traditions, his prophetic criticism of those in power. "His preaching and his outlook brought him close to the liberation project of the Zealots" (p. 289). On the other hand, he renounced the political messianism of the Zealots and their confidence in the use of force.

Through the resurrection the life that was hidden in Jesus was unveiled. The resurrection shows that it is not meaningless to die for another, that the murderer will not triumph over his victim. "Thanks to his resurrection, Jesus continues to exist among human beings, giving impetus to their struggle for liberation" (p. 291). Thereafter, to follow Jesus is to "follow through with his work and attain his fulfillment" (p. 292).

In effect, what we think of Christ, how we understand the meaning of the hypostatic union, the resurrection, and so forth is not primary. "Life is more important than reflection" (p. 157). Liberation Christology, therefore, is not so much a contribution to our understanding of the nature and mission of Jesus Christ as it is a way of understanding the meaning and demands of liberation. Liberation Christology has a prophetic, even messianic task, i.e., to move Christians outside Latin America to hear the painful cry of their oppressed brothers and sisters and to bring justice to those who fight to regain their freedom (p. 295).

Jon Sobrino

A Jesuit theologian from El Salvador, Jon Sobrino has produced a similarly comprehensive Christological statement in his *Christology at the Crossroads* (Maryknoll, N.Y.: Orbis Books, 1978). It is written from the same liberational framework and with the same "from below" starting-point: "If the *end* of Christology is to pro-fess that Jesus is the Christ, its *starting point* is the affirmation that this Christ is the Jesus of history" (p. xxi). And this means also giving priority to the praxis of Jesus over his own teaching and over the teaching of the New Testament theologians regarding Jesus' praxis. "Thus the New Testament will be viewed primarily as *history* and only secondarily as *doctrine* concerning the real nature of that history" (p. xxii).

Furthermore, Jesus' past can be recovered in the present only to the extent that it pushes us toward the future. The convergence of these three tenses occurs in the symbol of the Kingdom of God, and that is understood, in turn, in a trinitarian sense. It is the Father who is "the ultimate horizon of human existence and history" (p. xxiv), the Son who practices the Kingdom, and the Holy Spirit who makes possible life in accordance with the exam-ple of the Son. "Liberation theology is concentrated in Christology insofar as it reflects on Jesus himself as the way to liberation" (p. 37).

The emphasis remains functional; i.e., what is finally impor-tant is what Christ is for us, not what he is in himself. This functional emphasis runs the risk, to be sure, of collapsing com-pletely into functionalsim. Sobrino suggests, for example, that if at any point Christ ceased to be of interest to people or to serve as the path to salvation, he "would cease to be the revelation of what human beings are, and hence the revelation of who God is" (p. 388).

CURRENT AND RECENT PROTESTANT CHRISTOLOGY

Since the central interest of this book is in the Roman Catholic tradition, the description of current and recent Protestant (and Orthodox) Christologies will be abbreviated. Some general intro-ductory remarks, however, are in order: (1) The "from below" approach began at an earlier historical point for Protestants than for Catholics because Protestants were first to feel the impact of biblical criticism. Indeed, until the liberating encyclical of Pope

Pius XII, *Divino Afflante Spiritu* (1943), the field of biblical criticism was left almost entirely to Protestants. (2) Protestantism, in its very origins, has been a liberal rather than a conservative modification of historic Catholicism. The "Protestant principle" to which Paul Tillich referred in his book *The Protestant Era* (Chicago: University of Chicago Press, 1948) has rejected attempts to identify the divine with the finite, whether in sacraments, sacramentals, dogmas, or ministries. He called this attempted identification the temptation to idolatry. Some Protestants, not surprisingly, carried this principle to its logical extreme in Christology. For them, Jesus was a human being like us in all things, including sin, except that he was better than the rest of us. (3) Protestant Christology, however, is not unremittingly liberal. On the contrary, much of Protestant Christology in this century has been developed in reaction against the previous liberal, even reductionist, spirit of the nineteenth and early twentieth-century theology, just as much, indeed most, of present-day Catholic Christology has been developed in reaction against the ahistorical, metaphysical Christology "from above" which prevailed in the Catholic Church until the middle of this century.

Rudolf Bultmann (d. 1976)

The first sustained challenge to this thoroughly humanistic approach came in our century from Rudolf Bultmann, a German Lutheran. For Bultmann,"...we can know almost nothing concerning the life and personality of Jesus" (*Jesus and the Word*, New York: Scribners, 1958, p. 8). What we do know is what the early Church believed him to be, and, secondarily, that he actually existed and was crucified. At the center of Jesus' proclamation is the Kingdom of God, but not as a power outside of ourselves but as a power given to us to be authentically human in our existence. Jesus summons us to a decision to think deeply about our lives, to attend to the limit set to our lives by death, and to assume responsibility for our lives in view of our impending deaths.

Bultmann's *existentialist interpretation* does not commend itself to the more activist interpreters of Jesus Christ—the Latin American liberation school in particular—because it denies our capacity to get back to, much less reconstruct, the Jesus of history. But neither is Bultmann attractive to more conservative interpreters. For Bultmann, ". . . *faith in the resurrection is really the same thing as faith in the saving efficacy of the cross*" ("New Testament and Theology," in *Kerygma and Myth*, Hans Bartsch, ed., New York: Harper & Row, 1961, p. 41; author's italics). It is not something that happened to Jesus. It is something that happened to the disciples. It is also incorrect, according to Bultmann, to speak of Christ as divine. In Christ God speaks to the depths of the human person. The early councils of the Church, therefore, illegitimately Hellenized the primitive faith of the New Testament and turned from an existentialist to a metaphysical interpretation of the Christ-event.

Oscar Cullmann

At odds with Bultmann's approach is that of Oscar Cullmann, another German Lutheran. Where Bultmann placed little confidence in history, Cullmann placed almost total confidence there. What the New Testament presents is not primarily an existentialist interpretation of the Christ-event but a *salvation-history interpretation*. Unlike the Jewish and Greek conceptions of history, Christian historical understanding views history in linear rather than circular terms. History begins with creation and ends with the Second Coming (*parousia*). At the mid-point stands Jesus Christ. Over against the abiding temptation to Docetism, Cullmann insists that redemption occurs in time. It is not an abstraction. The redemptive events which culminate in Jesus Christ are historical events, and not just a mythological process of salvation, as Bultmann proposed. Jesus is the definitive revelation of God's redemptive love for humankind.

But if Cullmann's approach is different from, even opposed to, Bultmann's, so is it different from the more traditional ontological, metaphysical, "from above" approaches which have been common to Catholic theology since the medieval period. Cullmann offers a functional Christology in the sense that we discover who Jesus is by discovering what he has actually done for us in history. This was the approach of the New Testament, he argues. All of the titles of Christ, for example, are in virtue of what Christ does for us, rather than in virtue of what Christ is in himself. Each title signifies a specific function of Christ in salvation history. (See *Christ and Time*, Philadelphia: Westminster Press, 1964, rev. ed., and *The Christology of the New Testament*, Philadelphia: Westminster Press, 1963, rev. ed.)

Karl Barth (d. 1969)

The most direct rebuttal of Liberal Protestantism came from the Swiss Calvinist theologian Karl Barth. Over against both Liberalism and one of Liberalism's notable opponents, Rudolf Bultmann, Barth argued that our knowledge of God does not arise from our knowledge of the human condition but from revelation, i.e., from the Word of God given to us without predisposition, preunderstanding, or pre-anything else. There is only one God, the God of the Gospel, and that God can be known in only one way, through the Word which is Jesus Christ.

Theology, for Barth, is Christology. Christ tells us at once who God is and who we are. Christology frames our theology and our anthropology as well. Furthermore, the Jesus of history and the Christ of faith are one and the same. And the Christ as he is in himself is the same as the Christ as he is for us. He is the reconciling Christ. He is God for us. On the other hand, Jesus is "man totally and unreservedly as we are," uniting to himself and in himself all that is human. Although Barth's Christology tries to work both "from below" and "from above," the emphasis is clearly on the latter. (See *Church Dogmatics*, Edinburgh: T. & T. Clark, 1956, vol. IV/1; for a briefer summation of Barth's basic theological approach, see *Evangelical Theology: An Introduction*, New York: Doubleday, 1963.)

Paul Tillich (d. 1965)

A German Lutheran and an existentialist like Bultmann, Paul Tillich begins his Christology "from below" through an analysis of the human condition. We are beings marked by anxiety, faced as we are by the abiding threat of non-being. We are conscious of ourselves as alienated beings, as beings now separated from the ground of all being. It is a separation which implies an original union, a ruptured union which demands to be healed. This awareness leads us to seek "New Being," the Being who gives us "the courage to be." Christianity affirms that Jesus of Nazareth, who has been called the Christ, is the one who brings the new state of things, the New Being (see *Systematic Theology*, Chicago: University of Chicago Press, 1957, vol. 2, p. 97). What is significant about Jesus is "not that essential humanity includes the union of God and man (but) that in one personal life essential manhood has appeared under the conditions of existence without being conquered by them" (p. 94).

Tillich says that it makes no sense at all to speak of Jesus as divine. He argues that "the only thing God cannot do is to cease to be God. But that is just what the assertion that 'God has become man' means" (p. 94). The traditional teaching is to be discarded and replaced with "the assertion that in Jesus as the Christ the eternal unity of God and man has become historical reality" (p. 148). Indeed, there are Adoptionist overtones in Tillich's statement that essential God-manhood means that "there is one man in whom God *found* his image undistorted, and who stands for all mankind—the one, who for this reason, is called the Son or the Christ" (*The Eternal Now*, New York: Scribners, 1963, p. 76; my italics). For Tillich, Christ brings to all of us the hope that the existential anxiety and estrangement which characterizes and mars our situation can be healed and that unity with the ground of our being can be restored.

Dietrich Bonhoeffer (d. 1945)

Another German Lutheran theologian, influenced by Harnack on the left and Barth on the right in his years of academic formation, Dietrich Bonhoeffer marked out a course somewhere between their two approaches. He moved progressively through three phases of theological development: a liberal phase rudely shattered by the First World War, a confessional (Barthian) phase similarly undermined by the rise of Nazism in Germany, and an ecumenical phase prompted by the devastating experience of the Second World

War. Bonhoeffer never produced a formal, systematic Christology, but what we have of his Christology comes from class notes taken by his students in the second, confessional phase (see *Christ the Center*, New York: Harper & Row, 1966). Thus, Jesus is God for us (p. 107). God chose to come among us and to address us in weakness. He reconciled us with God through the crucifixion and rose for our justification. Christ is known to us today in the community of saints. He is present there *"pro me"* (for me). Christology and ecclesiology are, therefore, inseparable. Christ is really present only in the Church (*Communio Sanctorum*, New York: Harper & Row, 1964, p. 100). He is disclosed to us there as the new human being, or as new humanity itself (*Act and Being*, New York: Harper & Row, 1963, p. 121).

Jesus, and the God whom he reveals, is not at the borders of life where our human powers give out, but at its very center. And he is there only for others, as "the man for others." In fact, "His 'being there for others' is the experience of transcendence," i.e., the experience of God's transforming presence (*Letters and Papers from Prison*, New York: Macmillan, 1962, pp. 209-210).

With Bonhoeffer the emphasis within Protestant theology shifts once again to "the below" of human experience. But it is not simply a reproduction of the Liberal Protestant approach. He insists in *Christ the Center*, for example, that Jesus is important in what he does *for us* because of who he is *in himself.* Nor is it simply a slightly altered version of the "from below" existentialist analysis of Bultmann and Tillich. Bonhoeffer, on the contrary, laid the foundation for the development of the secular and radical theology of the 1960s. If Jesus is "the man for others," Christian existence must be existence for others, the Church must be a servant Church, and so forth. We meet this Jesus in one another. To use a Catholic phrase, Jesus is sacramentalized in the neighbor.

It is a theme that would be taken up by Bishop John Robinson, on the more conservative wing of secular theology (see *The New Reformation?*, Philadelphia: Westminster Press, 1965, and *The Human Face of God*, Philadelphia: Westminster Press, 1973), and by the so-called "death-of-God" theologians, on the more radical wing of the movement. Robinson would remain closer to the traditional Christology, although with a humanistic and then

Teilhardian leaning, while the "death-of-God" theologians, like Thomas Altizer and Paul Van Buren, would press the humanistic tilt all the way to the ground (see Altizer's *The Gospel of Christian Atheism*, Philadelphia: Westminster Press, 1966, and Van Buren's *The Secular Meaning of the Gospel*, New York: Macmillan, 1963). To believe in Christ is to stand at his side in the service of the neighbor.

Wolfhart Pannenberg

Still another German Lutheran, Wolfhart Pannenberg, provided one of the first modern systematic Christologies in his *Jesus: God and Man* (Philadelphia: Westminster Press, 1968). For several years, in fact, it was the only textbook available on the subject, even for Roman Catholic use. Following in the theological tradition of both Barth and Bonhoeffer, Pannenberg insisted that we can know God "only as he has been revealed in and through Jesus" (p. 19). We do not first know God and then come to a knowledge of Jesus as one with the God of Israel.

The God of Jesus Christ is a God who is revealed in and through *history*. But such revelation takes place not at the beginning of history but at its end. Jesus Christ is the end of history, and therefore it is only in the light of the revelation in Jesus Christ that everything that preceded him in the history of Israel assumes the character of revelation as well, "in the totality of events" (p. 388). Indeed, the end that stands before all of us has actually occurred already in Jesus Christ, in his death and resurrection. The latter is "the actual event of revelation" which establishes the divinity of Jesus and confirms God's self-revelation in him (p. 129).

The resurrection is, for Pannenberg, an utterly historical event. It is not something accessible only through the eyes of faith (p. 99). All of the biblical data regarding the resurrection (the empty tomb, the appearances, etc.) converge so that the assertion that Jesus really rose from the dead is to be presupposed until contrary evidence appears (p. 105). Significantly, Pannenberg pays almost no attention to the cross.

Using Hegelian categories (a practice, as we have seen, not at all uncommon among German theologians, Catholic and Protestant alike), Pannenberg locates the identity of Jesus with the Father in Jesus' *dedication* to the Father. And the Father is, in turn, dedicated to the Son (p. 332). Jesus' unity with the Father is not fully given at the incarnation, however. Rather, it is through the process of his life of dedication to the Father that Jesus' existence is integrated with the divine and his identity as Son of God becomes established (pp. 337, 344).

Pannenberg's Christology does not readily fit under either of our two working categories: "from above" or "from below." It may be more accurate to characterize his as a Christology "from ahead." It is an approach peculiar to Pannenberg, and no theologian of substance has taken it up since he first proposed it.

Jürgen Moltmann

A German Reformed theologian, Jürgen Moltmann is, among Protestant Christologists, closest to the perspective and interests of the Latin American liberation school. His position is expressed in his influential *Theology of Hope* (New York: Harper & Row, 1967) and, later, in *The Crucified God* (New York: Harper & Row, 1974). In the first book Moltmann's focus was, like Pannenberg's, on the resurrection. Influenced by the Marxist philospher Ernst Bloch, Moltmann concentrated on the themes of the future and of hope. Even though he left room for a prophetic role for Christian faith and for the Church (see his last chapter on "The Exodus Church"), Moltmann concluded that his approach was still abstract, bearing too little relationship to praxis. The Frankfurt School of social critical theory replaced Bloch as his philosophical inspiration. His thinking came to center on the cross of Jesus, shifting from hope in Christ's future to the following of the historical Jesus.

Christian existence is itself praxis. The following of the crucified God transforms us and our situation. If Christology is to be truly responsible, it must consider the psychic and political implications of its words, images, and symbols. It must be a political theology of the cross. The history of human suffering, focused on

Calvary, has to do in the end with justice. Human sympathy is insured only when the murderer does not finally triumph over the victim.

A central question posed by *The Crucified God* is "How can God himself be in one who has been forsaken by God?" (p. 190). His answer: "In the passion of the Son the Father himself suffers the pains of abandonment" (p. 192). The Good News of human hope and liberation is all contained in that proclamation. God is now inseparable from the Godforsaken of the earth. The Church, therefore, is called to identify in the same way with society's outcasts, the oppressed, the poor. "The glory of God," Moltmann insists, "does not shine on the crowns of the mighty, but on the face of the crucified Christ" (p. 327).

John B. Cobb

Methodist theologian and Whiteheadian, John B. Cobb, Jr., of the Southern California School of Theology at Claremont, California, acknowledges that his earlier Christological efforts were really exercises in Jesusology (*Christ in a Pluralistic Age*, Philadelphia: Westminster Press, 1975). Under the influence not only of process thought but of the writings of Pannenberg and Thomas Altizer, Cobb insists that "Christ" is not just Jesus but any incarnation of the Word of God. Christians, therefore, must be open to the possibility of "radical creative transformation" in light of the insights of other religious traditions. The Christian view must lose itself in other traditions in order to find itself.

The vision remains Whiteheadian from beginning to end. Christ is not so much a person as a process, although Christians name Christ only in "responsible relation" to Jesus. But "Christ" cannot name the process if the process leads to nothing. If there is no hope, then all that is said becomes pointless. The content of that hope is that we shall all transcend our separate individuality to enter "a fuller community with other people and with all things. In this community the tensions between self and Christ decline, and in a final consummation they would disappear. This is the movement of incarnation. Christ is the name of our hope" (p. 258).

A CONTEMPORARY ORTHODOX CHRISTOLOGY

Russian Orthodox theologian John Meyendorff provides a useful statement of Orthodox Christology in his *Christ in Eastern Christian Thought* (Washington: Corpus Books, 1969). It is his firm conviction that Byzantine Christological thought—far from being, as is sometime supposed, a crypto-Monophysitic, Hellenized form of Christianity—is in fact consistent with some of the most fundamental concerns in contemporary theology, the approach of Karl Rahner in particular. What has always been central to the whole Eastern patristic understanding of salvation is the principle that "Man is truly man when he participates in God's life. This participation...is not a supernatural gift, but the very core of man's nature" (p. viii). We must realize in ourselves the image and likeness of God, and this participation diminishes in no way our authentically human existence, energy, and will. And so it was with Jesus Christ.

By assuming humanity hypostatically, the *Logos* "becomes" what he was not before, and even "suffers in the flesh." This openness of God to the creature actually "modifies" God's personal existence. Such an understanding of the incarnation, according to Meyendorff, excludes all Docetism or Monophysitism, and it affirms that the salvation of humankind was a matter serious enough to bring the Son of God to the cross (p. 164). This, of course, represents a Christology "from above."

Meyendorff insists, however, that one can begin as well "from below." The notion of *participation* implies not only openness in the divine being but also a dynamic, open, teleological concept of the human. Since Gregory of Nyssa, the destiny of humankind is viewed, in Greek patristic thought, as an ascent in our knowledge of God through greater participation in the divine life itself. It is precisely at this point that post-Chalcedonian Byzantine Christology meets the modern Christological concerns. By basing Christological thinking on anthropology, as Rahner does, one is necessarily led to the other major conclusions of Greek patristics: The human being does not disappear in contact with God but, on the contrary, becomes more truly and more freely human, not only in the human being's similarity to God, but also in what makes the human being radically different from the Creator. "And this is the very meaning of the hypostatic union of divinity and humanity in Christ" (p. 165).

Nestorianism had argued the opposite, insisting on the idea of competition between, and mutual exclusion of, divinity and humanity. A proper understanding of Christ, Meyendorff continues, requires that we consider the *Logos* as the hypostasis, the "uniting unity" and the source of Christ's human existence. And this, in turn, challenges the traditional Scholastic notion of God's absolute immutability. God *became* human. A sound Christology, Meyendorff argues in concert with Rahner, implies "the return to the pre-Augustinian concept of God, where the three hypostases were seen first of all in their personal, irreducible functions, as Father-God, Son-Logos, and the Spirit of God, and not only as expressions of the unique immutable essence" (p. 166). The *being* of God, therefore, cannot simply be identified with the *essence* of God, as has been done in the West ever since Augustine.

Meyendorff is encouraged by the present movement in Western theology, represented in Rahner's work, because it implies not only a return to pre-Augustinian thought but also a return to the basic presuppositions of the Christological thought analyzed throughout Meyendorff's own book. This coincidence shows "the astonishing relevance, for our own time, of the patristic view of the Christian message.... The ecumenical significance of this discovery is incalculable" (p. 166).

SYNTHESIS

So broad and diverse a sampling of recent and current Christologies is not easily synthesized. They range all the way from the *Christomonism* (Christ *alone* manifests the presence and word of God) of Karl Barth to the bland universalism of Norman Pittenger, for whom Jesus Christ differs from the rest of humankind in degree only. On what basis, for example, does one categorize the various positions: (1) their understanding of the resurrection as an objective, or subjective, event? (2) their understanding of the divinity of Jesus? (3) their "from below," or "from above," or "from ahead" starting points? (4) their emphasis on the political implications of Jesus' preaching and practice? (5) their use of conservative, or liberal-to-radical, New Testament scholarship? (See Summary, n. 33.)

Taking all of these together and no one of them alone, certain relationships do begin to emerge. At the *far left* one might place the *process theologians* (Hulsbosch, Schoonenberg, and Pittenger—Teilhard himself is too complex for categorization, and so, too, perhaps is Cobb), Küng, Bultmann, Tillich, Altizer, and Van Buren. To their right, but still clearly *left-of-center* on the total spectrum, are Schillebeeckx, Mackey, the *liberation theologians* (Boff and Sobrino), Bonhoeffer, Robinson, and Moltmann. At the *center* is Rahner. Slightly to his right, Kasper, Cullmann, and Meyendorff. Further to the right, Pannenberg. Fully to the right, Barth.

Thus, none on the *far left* understands the resurrection in clearly objective as well as subjective terms. None unequivocally affirms the divinity of Jesus in the sense defined by the great Christological councils. All begin their Christologies "from below." The uniformity breaks down with items (4) and (5). Bultmann and Tillich do not emphasize the political dimensions of Jesus' preaching. On the contrary, Bultmann in particular resists a political interpretation of Jesus' preaching. Nor are political accents clearly discernible among the process Christologists. And some (e.g., the process theologians and the "death-of-God" theologians) do not employ any recent or current New Testament scholarship at all.

On the other hand, Barth and (to a lesser extent) Pannenberg offer a reasonably clear example of the *right-of-center* emphasis: The objectivity of the resurrection is affirmed; Jesus' divinity is accepted (although somewhat idiosyncratically in Pannenberg); the starting point is not "from below"; and conservative rather than radical New Testament scholarship is employed. One major divergence between Barth and Pannenberg, however, is on the matter of political implications. Pannenberg allows greater room for them in his understanding of the Kingdom of God than does Barth.

Rahner stands somewhere near the *center* in that he understands the resurrection in both objective and subjective categories, understands the divinity of Jesus in a way consistent with the councils but revised according to our modern evolutionary consciousness, reconciles his "from below" starting point with the abiding doctrinal concerns and principles of the "from above" Christologies, underlines the political implications of the Kingdom without exaggerating them or setting them off against other, non-political implications, and makes use of both conservative and liberal–to–radical New Testament scholarship, although here Rahner is more right-of-center than centrist.

But how does one even begin to evaluate such a wide array of theological positions? Legitimate diversities notwithstanding, some Christological views must be more (or less) consistent with the broad Catholic tradition than others. What should one look for in these various expressions of the mystery of Jesus Christ? The following principles should facilitate that critical process. A Christology which incorporates these principles is more consistent with the Catholic Christological tradition than is a Christology which overlooks or rejects one or several of them:

1.   Jesus Christ is what is specifically Christian about Christianity.

2.   He is the decisive and climactic moment in God's transcendent self-communication to humankind and of humankind's acceptance of God's self-communication. This "moment" is focused at the crucifixion and resurrection, which established and manifested the historic significance of Jesus Christ.

3.   The center of Jesus' preaching and the goal of all history is the Kingdom of God. The Kingdom is at once present and future.

4.   Our reaction to Jesus (conversion) and to his proclamation and practice of the Kingdom of God is decisive for our entrance into the Kingdom, for Jesus is the sacrament of God's universal love for human beings; and human beings (neighbors) are, in turn, the sacrament of Jesus' presence among us. Thus, love of God and love of neighbor are intimately linked.

5.   The Kingdom of God, therefore, has to do with the fulfillment of our humanity. *In that sense*, salvation is humanization, and humanization occurs through authentic liberation.

6. Christology and soteriology are inextricably connected. Jesus Christ as he is in himself is the same as Jesus Christ as he is for us. On the other hand, his *being-for-us* is rooted in his *being* (i.e., as Word of God made flesh).

SUMMARY

1. *Catholic Christology* from the time of Aquinas to the middle of the twentieth century remained essentially the same. It focused principally on the so-called ontological questions (i.e., Who is Christ *in himself*?) and only secondarily on the soteriological questions (i.e., Who is Christ *for us*?). But even in its treatment of the redemption, the discussion was limited to the crucifixion as the act by which our indebtedness to God for sin was fully satisfied. The resurrection and exaltation were seen as appendices rather than as constitutive elements of the redemption.

2. The *change* from the medieval approach to the so-called modern approach occurred for *two principal reasons:* (1) the shift from an uncritical to a critical reading of the New Testament; and (2) the shift from a static to an evolutionary understanding of human existence. Both of these changes were among the products of the eighteenth-century Enlightenment, which introduced an historically critical element in human reasoning and understanding. The spark which ignited the change for Catholic Christology was the occasion of the fifteen hundredth anniversary of the Council of Chalcedon.

3. *The principal Catholic Christologies today* are those produced by *Karl Rahner, Hans Küng, Walter Kasper,* and *Edward Schillebeeckx.* All four are generally consistent with the new approach of developing a Christology "from below," i.e., by starting with the Jesus of history rather than with the Word who became flesh ("from above"). Rahner and Kasper are generally more conservative in their Christologies than Küng and Schillebeeckx. Küng is the most liberal of the four. He stresses the humanity of Jesus more than the others do, and is least concerned with preserving the divinity.

4. *Karl Rahner,* the most influential of the four, calls his approach an *ascending* Christology. His point of departure is our encounter with the historical Jesus. On the other hand, he holds, there is also a *descending* course in Christology. The idea of God coming into our history "from above" also has power and significance. But in the light of modern evolutionary consciousness, the *starting point* is "from below."

5. Rahner's Christology is, of course, a function of his basic theological *method of transcendence.* The whole world is moving in evolution toward becoming something higher than it now is. It is called to self-

transcendence. Since the capacity for self-transcendence is rooted in the presence of God (grace, the self-communication of God), and since this presence has been there from the beginning, the history of the world is also the history of salvation.

6.   For Rahner the permanent beginning and absolute guarantee of this self-transcendence is the *hypostatic union*, where matter and spirit are climactically united in the union of Word and flesh in Jesus Christ. Ever since that union, *history is in its final phase*.

7.   But Christ does not exclude the possibility of *sin* or of short-term failure. *Human freedom* allows us to participate in the progressive transformation of the world, but it also allows us to reject God's self-communication and to refuse to enter the movement toward God.

8.   The world becomes conscious of itself through humankind, which alone unites matter and spirit in itself. The world moves forward toward its goal, *the Kingdom of God*, insofar as we actualize our capacity for self-transcendence. Thereby we become more than we are, and more than we could ever be if we were matter alone.

9.   From the beginning, *the whole evolutionary process is centered in Jesus Christ* as its final cause. The process towards the Kingdom becomes *irrevocable* and *irreversible* in him. The Word became flesh. The Word takes hold of the world by taking hold of flesh and materiality. Christ, because he is the Word-made-flesh, not only offers grace; he *is* grace. This is why the hypostatic union is not a purely speculative doctrine. *Jesus is the Kingdom which he proclaims*.

10.   *Hans Küng's* Jesus is not the cosmic figure of Rahner's Christology. He is an entirely ordinary historical figure who happened to say and do some extraordinary things and who made an extraordinary impact not only upon his contemporaries but upon much of the human race ever since.

11.   Küng's Jesus proclaims *the Kingdom*, but is not himself the Kingdom. Everything (laws, traditions, cult, etc.) is to be subordinated to the Kingdom, i.e., to human well-being. *Salvation is humanization*. Through his death, Jesus appeared as the personification of sin and as the *representative* of all sinners. After his death, his followers experienced him as alive (the resurrection). They felt a change in themselves.

12.   According to Küng, the cause of Jesus continued in the Church, which now proclaimed him, the crucified one, as the heart of the message about the Kingdom.

13.   *Walter Kasper's* Christology begins with the specific history of Jesus of Nazareth, but moves beyond that to philosophical reflection which history itself provokes. Finally, his Christology is *soteriologically determined*. The redemptive implications of what we believe about Jesus Christ are always uppermost in the minds of the New Testament writers,

the Fathers of the Church, and the ecumenical councils. On the other hand, soteriology is not the whole of Christology.

14.   Kasper *differs from Küng*, for example, in that Kasper follows a more conservative school of biblical interpretation and posits an implicit Christology in the thinking of Jesus. Jesus was reluctant to accept titles because he was greater than what those titles could express. Kasper, however, agrees with Küng in seeing Jesus as our *representative* before God.

15.   Kasper *disagrees with Rahner*, who perceives the incarnation as an integral part of historical evolution. Kasper adopts a position closer to *Anselm's*. Thus, God became man to restore order and balance to the universe.

16.   If there is anything distinctive about Kasper's Christology it is perhaps his *pneumatological* interpretation of the hypostatic union. It is the Holy Spirit who makes possible the movement of the Son outside the Trinity, and it is the Holy Spirit, released from the historical figure of Jesus after his death and resurrection, who makes possible the coming together of all humankind in saving unity.

17.   *Edward Schillebeeckx* argues that there are two ways of doing Christology: "from above" according to the Johannine model, or "from below" according to the Synoptic model. It is the latter which he presents in his book on *Jesus*. The historical Jesus is the parable of God and the paradigm of humanity. "His pro-existence as man is the sacrament among us of the pro-existence or self-giving of God's own being." He is "the sacrament of God's universal love for human beings. . . ."

18.   Jesus brought no new doctrine or religious system, according to Schillebeeckx. Rather he proclaimed and *practiced the Kingdom of God*. He showed that it is possible to put the Kingdom into practice. It is the Church which is called to mediate Christ's praxis of the Kingdom. The Church is led by the Spirit of Christ in doing this.

19.   *James Mackey* begins with Jesus' own faith in the Fatherhood of God and the giftedness of all human existence. The central symbol in Jesus' preaching (i.e., the Kingdom of God) means that life is graced. Christian faith is a sharing in Jesus' faith. To share Jesus' faith is to encounter the one true God who is immediately present to Jesus as to us.

20.   *Teilhard de Chardin, Ansfried Hulsbosch*, and *Piet Schoonenberg* share an evolutionary perspective. For *Teilhard*, all history is a movement toward Christ, the *Omega Point*, and yet Christ is also already present in and to the world, giving it a Christic (love-oriented) dimension. For *Hulsbosch*, Jesus is God by being human in a special way. He is *known* as a human being and *confessed* as God. He is not God who became a human being but a human being who became God. What we have in Jesus is the "unfolding of the capabilities which lay latent within

matter." *Schoonenberg*, finally, follows essentially the same approach but lays more emphasis on the question of Christ's pre-existence, which he rejects. The Second Person of the Trinity is none other than the human person of Jesus, who came into existence at a particular moment in time.

21. The Christology of the *Latin American liberation school* is represented in the work of *Leonardo Boff* and *Jon Sobrino*. Both stress the historical Jesus over the Christ of faith. Jesus preached not himself but the *Kingdom of God*, which is the realization of *complete liberation*. It is to the poor, the suffering, and the oppressed that he preaches, for these are the people who challenge the justice of God. Through Jesus, God has sided with them. The *conversion* he seeks is not only of convictions but of practice, and it is concerned not just with individuals but with social and political structures as well.

22. *Protestant Christology* has generally been more sympathetic to the "from below" approach and for a longer time because (1) biblical criticism developed first within Protestantism; and (2) Protestantism has characteristically been skeptical of identifying any human reality within the divine. On the other hand, much of twentieth-century Protestant Christology has been developed in reaction against extremely liberal or reductionist tendencies within Protestantism. On a relative scale, therefore, Protestant Christologies have been moving to the right, and Catholic Christologies to the left.

23. Thus, *Rudolf Bultmann* challenged Liberalism's assumption that we can know the historical Jesus with confidence. What the New Testament offers us is a philosophy of human existence. Bultmann's existentialist interpretation, focusing as it does on the private sphere of the individual person, puts him at odds also with the liberationist and political Christologies. Bultmann is also suspect on the right because of his refusal to accept the divinized Jesus of traditional theology.

24. *Oscar Cullmann*, to the right of Bultmann, makes salvation history the context for understanding Jesus Christ. He is the center of linear time and the definitive revelation of God. Cullmann prefers, however, a functional Christology (what Christ did for us) over an ontological Christology (what Christ was in himself). All of the New Testament titles applied to Jesus in a functional, not an ontological, way.

25. *Karl Barth* mounted the strongest and most direct assault upon Liberalism, opposing Bultmann at the same time. Jesus is the Word of God. All theology is Christology. There is no other point of access from and to God except through Jesus Christ.

26. *Paul Tillich* was for systematic Christology what Bultmann was for biblical Christology. Both offered an existentialist interpretation of the message and mission of Jesus. For Tillich, Christ is the "New

Being" who allows us to overcome the anxiety and estrangement which characterize human existence because he conquered both in his own life.

27. *Dietrich Bonhoeffer* marked a course somewhere between Liberalism and Barth. Jesus is the "man for others." He is Christ "for me." He exists for us today in and through the community of saints.

28. Bonhoeffer's "man for others" Christology laid the foundation for a more thoroughly secular interpretation of Jesus in the so-called secular theology of the 1960s: *Bishop John Robinson*, insisting that Jesus is to be discovered in the neighbor and that he shows us the "human face" of God; *Thomas Altizer* and *Paul Van Buren*, making Jesus the model and inspiration of our service of others.

29. *Wolfhart Pannenberg*, like Cullmann, emphasizes history as the vehicle of divine revelation. Revelation, however, takes place at the *end* of history, in Jesus Christ. It is only in the light of Christ that antecedent events become revelatory. Jesus' divinity is rooted in his complete dedication to the Father, and it is fully and finally established in the resurrection, which is a literally historical event. Pannenberg's Christology might appropriately be characterized as neither "from above" nor "from below" but rather "from ahead."

30. *Jürgen Moltmann* is, of all the modern Protestant Christologists, closest to the Latin American liberationist point of view. For him the cross is central and is a political event. Through the passion and death of Jesus, God actually suffers with us and identifies with the oppressed of the human race. It is only in the practice of the Kingdom of God that we truly follow the way of Christ, a practice which involves the same identification with the outcasts, the poor, and the persecuted of society.

31. *John Cobb* is difficult to categorize because he is influenced not only by the process thought of Whitehead but by Pannenberg and Altizer as well. The Christ is in Jesus, and yet not exclusively so. It is only in losing itself in other traditions that Christian faith can find itself. What Jesus represented and proclaimed is the common hope of all: full community with other people and with all things.

32. *John Meyendorff* is representative of Eastern Christian thought, with its historical emphasis on our participation in the divine life accomplished through the passion and death of Christ. Meyendorff insists that Karl Rahner's Christology, based as it is on an understanding of human existence as open to the transforming presence of God, is closest to the Orthodox way of understanding the mystery of Christ. Meyendorff and Rahner, in turn, reflect the pre-Augustinian thought of the Greek Fathers.

33. *Differences* among and between the preceding theologians can be determined on the basis of the following criteria: (1) What is their

understanding of the *resurrection?* Is the resurrection purely objective, purely subjective, or both? (2) How do they understand the *divinity* of Jesus? Is their understanding a literal appropriation of the councils, a rejection of the councils, or a critical reappropriation of the conciliar teaching? (3) What is their *starting point?* "From above"? "From below"? "From ahead"? (4) How do they understand the *political* implications of the Kingdom of God which Jesus preached? Is it totally political? Completely apolitical? Political within a larger context? (5) What kind of New Testament scholarship do they rely upon in constructing their understanding of Jesus Christ? Conservative? Liberal-to-radical? A broad cross-section?

34.   Contemporary Christologies which are consistent with the broad Catholic Christological tradition incorporate the following principles: (1) Jesus Christ is the specifically Christian element in Christianity; (2) he is the decisive moment in God's self-communication and of our definitive acceptance of God; (3) the Kingdom of God, at once present and future, is at the center of Jesus' preaching; (4) we make a decision for the Kingdom when we make our decision for Jesus Christ, the sacrament of God; and our decision for Jesus is linked, in turn, with our decision for the neighbor; (5) the Kingdom, therefore, has to do with humanization, and humanization, with liberation; and (6) Christology and soteriology are intimately connected: Jesus Christ-in-himself is Jesus Christ-for-us, and vice versa.

SUGGESTED READINGS

In addition to the titles already cited in this chapter:

Dulles, Avery. "Jesus as the Christ: Some Recent Protestant Positions." *Thought* 39 (1964), 359–379.

——————. "Contemporary Approaches to Christology: Analysis and Reflections." *Living Light* 13 (Spring 1976), 119-144.

Lane, Dermot A. *The Reality of Jesus: An Essay in Christology.* New York: Paulist Press, 1975.

May, William E. *Christ in Contemporary Thought.* Dayton: Pflaum, 1970.

O'Collins, Gerald. *What Are They Saying About Jesus?* New York: Paulist Press, 1977.

Schillebeeckx, Edward, and Van Iersel, Bas, eds. *Jesus Christ and Human Freedom.* New York: Herder & Herder, 1974.

· XV ·

SPECIAL QUESTIONS IN CHRISTOLOGY

This chapter addresses four specific questions in Christology: the *virginal conception* of Jesus, his *sinlessness*, his *knowledge*, and his *sexuality*. The first two underscore the *divinity* of Jesus Christ; the third and fourth, his *humanity*.

The chapter concludes with a list of criteria by which one might differentiate between Christologies which are consistent with the broad Catholic tradition and those which are not.

Section One: Special Questions

THE VIRGINAL CONCEPTION OF JESUS

The issue here is the belief that *Jesus was conceived in the womb of a virgin, Mary, without the intervention of a human father* (*virginitas ante partum*). The issue is *not* the related belief that Mary remained a virgin during the childbirth (*in partu*) and for the rest of her life (*post partum*). We shall be treating the question of Mary's *in partu* and *post partum* virginity in chapter 24. Our concern in the present chapter is Christological rather than Mariological.

There are five sub-questions to be considered: (1) Is the belief in the virginal conception of Jesus truly a belief of the New Testament Church? (2) Is that belief rooted in historical fact? I.e., was Jesus actually conceived without a human father? (3) Does the Church officially impose belief in the historicity of the virginal conception of Jesus? (4) Can New Testament scholarship and the official teaching of the Church be reconciled? (5) What does the belief finally mean in relation to Jesus Christ?

Is It a Belief of the New Testament Church?

Belief in the virginal conception of Jesus *is* to be found in the New Testament, and, given the nature of the New Testament, that belief was held by at least some Christian communities of the first century. The references are twofold: Matthew 1:18-25 and Luke 1:26-38, the so-called Infancy Narratives.

Matthew reports that Mary conceived before she and Joseph lived together, that "he had no relations with her at any time before she bore a son, whom he named Jesus" (v. 25). The child was conceived "through the power of the Holy Spirit" (v. 18). "All this happened," Matthew writes, "to fulfill what the Lord has said through the prophet: 'The virgin shall be with child and give birth to a son, and they shall call him Emmanuel' " (vv. 22-23).

No one questions the authenticity of the narrative. There is a difference of opinion on whether it is Matthew's own conviction that Jesus was virginally conceived, or whether Matthew was drawing upon a tradition which preceded him. The current weight of scholarship seems to be on the latter side. One major reason for saying so is that the other infancy account, Luke 1:26-38, also speaks of a virginal conception by the power of the Holy Spirit (v. 35). Since this is one of the few points on which they agree, scholars conclude that this tradition antedated both accounts. In fact, this tradition must have been old enough to have developed into narratives of very diverse character and to have circulated in different Christian communities.

The rest of the New Testament is silent about the virginal conception. Biblical exegetes, Catholic and Protestant alike, generally reject the hypothesis that implicit references to the virginal conception are given in Mark 6:3, John 1:13, 6:42, 7:42, and 8:41 (see Raymond E. Brown, *et al.*, eds., *Mary in the New Testament: A Collaborative Assessment by Protestant and Roman Catholic Scholars*, p. 289).

Is the Virginal Conception Historical?

This question cannot be answered with a clear "Yes" or a clear "No," at least not on the basis of scientifically controllable evidence from the New Testament.

The arguments *in favor* of historicity are twofold: (1) One searches in vain for exact parallels in non-Jewish religions, societies, and mythologies which might explain how early Christians happened upon the idea of a virginal conception without even a male deity or element to impregnate Mary, because apparent parallels (e.g., the births of Buddha, Krishna, the Pharaohs, *et al.*) all involved a divine male in some form or other. (2) There were rumors abroad that Jesus was conceived illegitimately. Matthew's account acknowledges this gossip, and it is implied also in Mark 6:3, where Jesus is referred to as the "son of Mary" —an unusual designation unless paternity is uncertain or unknown—and in John 8:41, where the Jews sneer, "*We* were not born illegitimate." In early Jewish polemics against the new Christian faith the charge persisted that Jesus was born of an adulterous union since he was obviously not the son of Joseph.

But the arguments *against* historicity are also strong. (1) If Joseph and Mary knew that their son had no human father but was conceived in truth by the Holy Spirit alone, why would they have kept this secret from Jesus? And if they had not kept the secret, why could he not have known and affirmed from the very beginning that he was the Messiah and the unique Son of God? Our consideration of the Christological development of the New Testament (chapter 12), however, disclosed a movement from a lower to a higher Christology within the New Testament period itself. Jesus may have had only an implicit Christology of his own. (2) The Infancy Narratives themselves, in both structure and content, suggest a non-historical rather than historical accounting of the conception of Jesus. The two basic stories are virtually irreconcilable; e.g., compare Matthew 2:14 with Luke 2:39. There is an artificiality in format—e.g., Matthew's genealogy with its three groupings of fourteen generations. There is folklore—e.g., the appearance of angels in dreams, guiding stars, treasures from the East. (3) The rest of the New Testament is completely silent about the virginal conception. (4) How could one have verified the historicity of the virginal conception in the first place? It would have been known to Mary and Joseph alone, and those to whom they told it.

The scales seem to tip in favor of the theory that the belief in the virginal conception of Jesus is the result of what is technically called a *theologoumenon*. A theologoumenon stands between a theological interpretation that is normative for faith (a doctrine or a dogma) and an historically verifiable affirmation. In other words, a theologoumenon is a non-normative, non-doctrinal theological interpretation that cannot be verified on the basis of historical evidence. In the case of the virginal conception of Jesus, the word *theologoumenon* means that the early Church, in the writings of Matthew and Luke, read back into the earthly origins of Jesus an historically unverifiable element that was designed to say something about the significance of Jesus for our salvation: Jesus did not *become* one with God as time went on; *Jesus was one with God from the moment of his conception.*

Does the Church Officially Teach the Historicity of the Virginal Conception?

Church creeds and doctrines presuppose the virginity of Mary but never unequivocally define it as an historical fact. For good reasons, therefore, one might reject the historicity of the virginal conception of Jesus without necessarily incurring the burden of heresy. Heresy, as we noted in chapter 2, is the denial of a dogma, i.e., a doctrine solemnly defined by the official Church.

Creedal and doctrinal references to the virginal conception ("born of the Virgin Mary") can be found in: (1) the Apostles' Creed (date uncertain); (2) the Nicene Creed (325); (3) the Nicene-Constantinopolitan Creed of the First Council of Constantinople (381); (4) the Athanasian Creed (end of fifth century); (5) the Fourth Lateran Council (1215); (6) the Second Council of Lyons (1274); and other less authoritative sources (for those references, see *The Christian Faith in the Doctrinal Documents of the Catholic Church*, J. Neuner and J. Dupuis, eds., Westminster, Md.: Christian Classics, 1975, p. 137).

Given the original setting and purpose of those creedal and doctrinal formulations, it is reasonable to conclude that their authors were *not* interested primarily in affirming the *historicity of the virginal conception* of Jesus. Rather, they were concerned with preserving the unity of the divine and the human in Jesus Christ. The Church was teaching, against the Gnostics, Docetists, Monophysites, and others, that Jesus was truly human, that he was truly born of a woman. And it was teaching, against the Adoptionists, the Nestorians, and others, that he was truly divine.

Nowhere, however, did the Church define the "how" of Jesus' conception. Clearly, his origin is in God, and the Holy Spirit is directly operative in his conception. But whether the Holy Spirit's involvement positively excluded the cooperation of Joseph is not *explicitly* defined.

One can assume, on the other hand, that the Fathers of the Church themselves believed the virginal conception to be historical. They simply presupposed it. And until the beginning of the nineteenth century the virginal conception of Jesus, even in this biological sense, was universally believed by Christians.

What happened to change that virtual unanimity of belief? The same factors which generated a change in our understanding of Jesus Christ and of Christian faith itself, namely, a newly critical way of reading the New Testament, and a newly evolutionary way of perceiving human existence and human history. Both of these developments are linked with that philosophical watershed known as the Enlightenment.

Can New Testament Scholarship and Official Church Teaching Be Reconciled?

There is no contradiction between the two. Even if it were clear that the official Church had explicitly defined the historicity of the virginal conception of Jesus, it would not follow that such a teaching is contradicted by biblical criticism. New Testament scholarship does not claim that the historicity of the virginal conception can be *disproved* exegetically. The exegetes conclude only that the arguments in favor of historicity are *dubious*.

Three additional points suggest themselves: (1) If the official Church *were* of a mind to make the biological element of Jesus' conception a matter of defined faith, it would have to give very serious weight indeed to the warnings raised even by Catholic exegetes. (2) In the beginning, the virginal conception of Jesus was denied only by those who opposed Christianity or who heretically understood the divine-human union in Jesus Christ. More recently, the virginal conception is questioned also by orthodox Christians, i.e., by Christians who accept the historic faith that Jesus Christ is "the same perfect in divinity and perfect in humanity, the same truly God and truly man..." (Council of Chalcedon). (3) This, in turn, suggests that belief in the virginal conception of Jesus as an historical fact is not essential to belief in his divinity. The Word could have become flesh *with* the cooperation of Joseph just as well as without it. Had Joseph been his human father, Jesus would have been no less divine.

What Is the Meaning of the Belief?

The virginal conception has been understood from the very beginning as a statement about Jesus first, and about Mary only secondarily. Through this belief, the Church intended to say that Jesus is from God, that he is unique, that in Christ the human race truly has a new beginning, that the salvation he brings transcends this world, and that God works through human instruments, often weak and humble instruments at that, to advance the course of saving history.

If in denying the historicity of the virginal conception, one is also denying such principles as these, then one has indeed moved outside the boundaries of the Christian, and certainly the Catholic, tradition.

THE SINLESSNESS OF JESUS

Belief in the sinlessness of Jesus Christ is a direct implication of belief in the hypostatic union, i.e., the belief that the human nature of Jesus Christ is perfectly united with the Second Person of the Trinity. The dogma of the hypostatic union, in turn, is a

product of the Church's reflection on the intimacy and communion between Jesus and the Father, to the extent that Jesus spoke
of God as his "Daddy" (*Abba*). Belief in the virginal conception of
Jesus establishes the basis of this intimacy in Jesus' origin. He is
from God, having been conceived by the power of the Holy Spirit.
It is in this context that the question of Jesus' sinlessness must be
answered.

There are five sub-questions to be considered here also: (1) Is
the belief in the sinlessness of Jesus Christ truly a belief of the New
Testament Church? (2) Is that belief rooted in historical fact? I.e.,
was Jesus actually without sin throughout his entire lifetime?
(3) Does the Church officially teach not only the sinlessness of
Christ but his impeccability as well? (4) Can our understanding of
the New Testament be reconciled with the official teaching of the
Church? (5) What does the belief in the sinlessness of Jesus Christ
mean?

Is It a Belief of the New Testament Church?

Belief in the sinlessness of Christ *is* rooted in the New Testament—more widely, in fact, than belief in the virginal conception.
The pertinent texts are John 8:46, 14:30; 2 Corinthians 5:21;
1 Peter 2:22; and Hebrews 4:15. Jesus declared that Satan had no
hold on him (John 14:30) and challenged his opponents to convict
him of sin if they could (John 8:46). Paul, in very early testimony,
proclaims that Jesus "did not know sin...that in him we might
become the very holiness of God" (2 Corinthians 5:21). "He did no
wrong," the author of 1 Peter writes (2:22). Finally, the Epistle to
the Hebrews commends Jesus Christ to us as our great high priest
"who was tempted in every way that we are, yet never sinned"
(4:15).

Significantly, nowhere is it asserted that Jesus could not have
sinned, that he was absolutely incapable of sin (*impeccabilitas*).
The New Testament declares that, in fact, Jesus did not sin
(*impeccantia*). Indeed, he was genuinely *tempted* to sin (Mark
1:12-13; Luke 4:2-13; Matthew 4:1-11). It was Scholastic Christology, on the contrary, which concluded to the impeccability of
Jesus. And since Scholastic Christology has prevailed in Catholic

teaching until the middle of the twentieth century, as we noted in the previous two chapters, the understanding of the sinlessness of Christ as impeccability has simply been taken for granted for the past five or six centuries.

Is That Belief Rooted in Historical Fact?

Did Jesus, in fact, never sin? It is a claim which is even more difficult to verify historically than the claim for the virginal conception. It is, for all practical purposes, impossible to verify. No one could have read into the mind and heart of Jesus to detect any sinful attitudes and wishes, even if he had them. And no one could have been with Jesus every moment of the day or night to notice his doing something sinful, even if he had committed a sinful act.

But neither do we have any evidence that Jesus *did* sin. Not even his gravest enemies could make the accusation, and even less make it stick. This is one of the most remarkable aspects of the belief in, and the claim of, the sinlessness of Christ. If the moral gap between Jesus' words and deeds had been apparent to anyone at all, it would have been brought to public attention, so threatening and so revolutionary was his message. Indeed, it would not have taken much to twist the Zacchaeus episode (Luke 19:1-10) into one of consorting with the oppressing class. Nor, as John A.T. Robinson has observed, "would most ministers today be able to survive three circumstantial (and, I believe, independent) reports that he had his feet (or head) kissed, scented and wiped with the hair of a woman, whether or not of doubtful repute" (*The Human Face of God*, p. 98; the references are to Mark 14:3-9; Luke 7:36-50; and John 12:1-8).

Does the Church Officially Teach the Impeccability of Jesus?

The official Church certainly teaches as much as the New Testament does, namely, that Jesus Christ was without sin. In fact, where the Church formulates its belief, it simply repeats biblical expressions, especially the Hebrews text. This is true in the following instances: (1) the Council of Chalcedon (451), which defines that Jesus Christ is "one in being with us as to the humanity, like unto us in all things but sin;" (2) the Lateran Council (649), "sin only being excepted;" and (3) the Eleventh Council of Toledo (675), "without sin."

The work of interpretation becomes difficult when moving to the Third Council of Constantinople (681), which condemned *Monothelitism* (in Christ there is only *one will*, and that divine). The council taught that there are two wills, the one human and the other divine, just as there are two natures. The human will, however, is "compliant, it does not resist or oppose but rather submits to the divine and almighty will." On the other hand, the same doctrinal formulation declares that the human will "has not been destroyed by being divinized. It has rather been preserved...."

Although one could reasonably infer from the teaching of Constantinople III that Jesus Christ was incapable of sin, that precise point is not explicitly made. Indeed, one could also reasonably argue that if Jesus were utterly incapable of sinning, his human will was not after all preserved. Rather, it would have become so "compliant" to the divine will as to be indistinguishable from it. But that is precisely the heresy of Monothelitism which the council condemned.

It seems better to conclude that *it is the clear and constant belief and teaching of the Church that Jesus Christ was perfect in his humanity, that he was so completely in union with the Father that he was in fact absolutely without sin.* It is not that Jesus Christ was absolutely *incapable* of sin, but rather that he was *able not to sin* and, in fact, *did not sin*.

Can the New Testament Witness Be Reconciled with the Official Church's Teaching?

This question, in the light of the preceding, answers itself. The New Testament does not enter the realm of theological speculation. There is no analysis of the operation of Jesus' human will, nor is there any philosophical reflection on the dynamics of human consciousness or of human freedom. But neither is there very much of this in the Church's doctrines, not to say dogmas. On the contrary, where the official Church formulates its teaching, it simply builds on the biblical testimony, relying in particular on the expression from the Epistle to the Hebrews, namely, that Jesus is completely like us in everything except sin. The text does not say—nor does the Church—that Jesus is different because sin is metaphysically impossible for him, but that he is different because, in fact, he was *without sin.*

What Does the Sinlessness of Jesus Christ Mean?

The fact that Jesus Christ is without sin makes him the supreme expression of communion between God and humankind. It is because he is utterly, completely, and perfectly holy in his very humanity that he is able to disclose the divine to us through that same humanity. Jesus Christ, the sinless one, shows us not only the human but the divine. He is "the reflection of the Father's glory, the exact representation of the Father's being" (Hebrews 1:3).

THE KNOWLEDGE OF JESUS

The question of the knowledge of Jesus is important for two reasons: (1) Many problems of New Testament interpretation cannot be solved if there is no possibility of development, even error, in the knowledge of Jesus (see again the discussion in chapter 12); and (2) Hebrews 4:15 and the Council of Chalcedon assert that Jesus is like us in all things "yet never sinned." How much like us is Jesus if he knew exactly what the future held for him, down to the finest detail? We face the future with wonder and hope, and sometimes with fear and dread. Jesus would have experienced none of these human emotions if he knew, with factual certitude, precisely what the Father had in store for him, and especially that the Father would raise him from the dead "on the third day."

At issue in the first two special questions were the origin of Jesus in God (the virginal conception) and the intimate communion of Jesus with God (the sinlessness of Jesus). Both italicize the *divinity* of Jesus Christ. At issue here, and in the next question, is the *humanity* of Jesus Christ. Is he really one with us—in all things except sin?

There are three sub-questions to be considered: (1) Does the New Testament attribute ignorance and even error to Jesus? (2) Does the official Church admit of ignorance and error in the mind of Jesus? (3) Can the New Testament record be reconciled with the official teaching of the Church?

Does the New Testament Attribute Ignorance and Even Error to Jesus?

Although there are indications in the New Testament that the early Church thought Jesus to be in possession of unlimited and infallible knowledge, the weight of the evidence seems to be on the other side.

Indications in Favor of Unlimited Knowledge

Given the development from a low (Jesus-as-human) to a high (Jesus-as-divine) Christology within the New Testament and within the Gospels themselves (e.g., from Mark to John), it is not surprising that the later New Testament material should have suppressed any suggestion of Jesus' ignorance. For example, Matthew 9:22 reports the same incident found in Mark 5:30-33, where a woman "afflicted with a hemorrhage for a dozen years" touched Jesus' garment and "healing power had gone out from him." In the earlier Marcan account, however, Jesus does not know who touched him. In Matthew's account, Jesus turns and immediately identifies the woman.

In John's report of the miracle of the loaves, Jesus asks Philip where they could find enough bread to feed such a "vast crowd" (John 6:5). But John quickly adds that Jesus already "knew well what he intended to do but he asked this to test Philip's response" (verse 6). Later in John 6:64 we are assured by the author of the Fourth Gospel that Jesus knew that some of his disciples would be unfaithful, and Judas in particular (6:71; 13:11).

All of the Gospels attribute to Jesus the ability to know what others are thinking (Mark 2:6-8; Mark 9:33-34; Luke 9:46-47; John

2:24-25; 16:19,30). But it is not always clear whether this reflects Jesus' own keen perception of human nature or whether it is really a form of superhuman knowledge.

Finally, there are several examples where Jesus is portrayed as having knowledge of events taking place somewhere else. In John 1:48-49 he knew that Nathanael had been under the fig tree. In Mark 11:2 he knew that there would be a colt at the entrance of a nearby village. In Mark 14:13-14 and Luke 22:10 Jesus sends two of his disciples to the city with the instruction that they would come upon a man carrying a water jar and that he would provide a room for them in which to celebrate the Passover feast. But the Old Testament prophets also were believed to have had this kind of knowledge. Thus, Ezekiel had visions of events in Jerusalem although he was still in Babylon (Ezekiel 8; see also 1 Samuel 10:1-8).

Indications Against Unlimited Knowledge

In Mark 5:30-33 (= Luke 8:45-47), to which we referred above, Jesus does not know who in the crowd touched his garment. In Luke 2:46 he asks questions of the teachers of the Law in the Temple. In Luke 2:52 he is described as having "progressed steadily in wisdom." Both these texts are significant because they are part of the Lucan Infancy Narrative, where Jesus is presented unequivocally as God's Son from the moment of his conception.

Even in the specifically religious realm Jesus is shown to have been ignorant about certain matters. He reflects the inadequate and sometimes erroneous biblical views of his contemporaries. He cites an Old Testament text which apparently does not exist (John 7:38). He is wrong about the identity of the high priest at the time David entered the house of God and ate the holy bread which only the priests were permitted to eat (Mark 2:26); it was Ahimelech (1 Samuel 21:1-6) and not Abiathar, as Jesus thought. He was in error, too, about the fact that Zechariah, son of Jehoiada, was killed in the Temple (2 Chronicles 24:20-22); it was not Zechariah son of Barachiah, as Jesus said (Matthew 23:35). And Jesus mistakenly attributed Psalm 110 to David, making it a messianic psalm besides (Mark 12:36), even though there was no expectation of a Messiah at the time it was composed.

Jesus also shared the primitive ideas of his contemporaries about demons, confusing demon possession with epilepsy and insanity (Mark 5:4, 9:17-18; Matthew 12:43-45; Luke 11:24-26). He drew upon the same limited religious concepts of his day to describe the afterlife and the end of the world (Mark 9:43-49; 13). There is nothing new, superhuman, or unique about such declarations. Jesus simply employed ideas and imagery that were already current.

We cannot even take at face value his foreknowledge and predictions of his passion, death, and resurrection (Mark 8:31; 9:31; 10:33-34; and parallels). Among other exegetical problems, one has to account for the exceedingly curious attitude of the disciples who, if they had really heard Jesus make such predictions, should not have been taken by such complete surprise by the crucifixion even when it was imminent; nor, of course, should they have been so totally unprepared for the resurrection (Luke 24:19-26).

Much the same can be said of Jesus' predictions of the destruction of the Temple at Jerusalem (Mark 13:2). He insisted, for example, that "not one stone will be left upon another." And yet they are still there, even today!

The biblical and theological discussions about Jesus' knowledge of the date of the Second Coming (*parousia*) cannot usefully be summarized here. But all those who favor a so-called maximalist position (namely, that Jesus knew everything, and everything about everything) have to contend with the stark assertion: "As to the exact day or hour, no one knows it, neither the angels in heaven nor even the Son, but only the Father" (Mark 13:32).

Did Jesus, finally, know himself to be the unique Son of God? It is true that Jesus spoke of God as his Father in such a way as to suggest a special, intimate relationship. But there is no incontrovertible proof that he claimed a unique sonship not open to other persons. "Why do you call me good?" he asks a man who kneels before him to inquire about everlasting life. "No one is good but God alone" (Mark 10:18). And when he teaches his disciples to pray, he instructs them, and all of us, to address God just as he addresses God, as "Our Father" (Luke 11:2). The Fourth Gospel, of course, clearly shows Jesus claiming to be the Son of God, but that book was written precisely to prove that point (20:31). It is difficult, to say the least, to find the historical basis for Jesus' explicit claim to unique Sonship.

The Firm Convictions of Jesus About the Kingdom

To suggest that Jesus did not have unlimited knowledge, that he was ignorant of many things and in error about others, is not to suggest at the same time that Jesus was a man without extraordinary intellectual strength and vision. On the contrary, Jesus displayed an exceedingly novel and courageous degree of *conviction* on the most central matter of all, the Kingdom of God. He was obviously convinced that the reign of God was active even now in his preaching, in his actions, and in his very person. He interpreted it with complete authority. Six times in the fifth chapter of Matthew he says to his disciples, "You have heard...," and follows each with the assertion, "What I say to you is...." He puts demands upon others. He forgives sins. He changes the Law of Moses. He violates the Sabbath ordinances. He offends against proprieties—e.g., by eating with sinners. He forbids divorce. He urges us to turn the other cheek, and so forth. All of this implies a unique conviction and, therefore, a unique human consciousness about himself and his relationship to God, a relationship without parallel in the lives of any of the Old Testament prophets. Moreover, there is no indication anywhere in the New Testament that Jesus only gradually developed this particular conviction. On the contrary, as he begins his public ministry, that conviction is at the heart of his proclamation (Mark 1:15).

Does the Official Church Admit
of Ignorance and Error in Jesus?

The gap between the New Testament and the official teaching of the Church is greater here than on the first two special questions, the virginal conception and the sinlessness of Jesus. On the other hand, the magisterial sources are less authoritative (nothing approaching an ecumenical council, for example), and their dependence upon the medieval synthesis is even more pronounced.

Medieval Christology had argued, on the basis of the hypostatic union, that no perfection is to be denied Jesus if it was at all possible for him to have had it. Therefore, he not only knew everything, but he knew everything about everything. He had *beatific* knowledge, i.e., God's knowledge of all things; *infused* knowledge, i.e., angelic knowledge requiring no learning effort; and *experimental* knowledge, i.e., what he inescapably encountered within the particularities of his earthly life. An extreme form of the medieval position was expressed by certain seventeenth-century commentators on Thomas Aquinas, known as the *Salmanticenses* (theologians associated with the University of Salamanca, in Spain). In their view, Jesus' knowledge was so unlimited that he could accurately be described as the greatest mathematician, the greatest doctor, the greatest painter, the greatest farmer, the greatest sailor, the greatest philosopher, and so forth.

Not all medieval theology was so narrowly focused. Thomas himself acknowledged that "if there had not been in the soul of Christ some other knowledge besides his divine knowledge, he would not have known anything. Divine knowledge cannot be an act of the human soul of Christ; it belongs to another nature" (*Summa Theologica* III, q. 9, a. 1). The official declarations of the post-medieval Church, however, have tended to carry forward the spirit, if not the letter, of the Salmanticenses rather than the frequently more-nuanced approach of Thomas.

In 1907 the Holy Office, under the direction of Pope Pius X, issued its anti-Modernist decree *Lamentabili*, in which it rejected certain contemporary assumptions about the knowledge and consciousness of Jesus, namely, that he was in error about "the proximity of the Messianic advent" and that his human knowledge was limited.

In 1918 the same Holy Office, this time under the direction of Pope Benedict XV, categorized certain propositions as being "unsafe" for teaching in Catholic seminaries and universities, namely, the opinion that Christ may not have had the beatific vision during his lifetime, that he would not have known "from the beginning...everything, past, present and future, that is to say everything which God knows with the 'knowledge of vision.'"

Finally, in 1943 Pope Pius XII declared in an encyclical letter on the Church as the Mystical Body of Christ (*Mystici Corporis*) that Jesus enjoyed the beatific vision "from the time He was received into the womb of the Mother of God." Consequently, "...the loving knowledge with which the divine Redeemer has pursued us from the first moment of His incarnation is such as completely to surpass all the searchings of the human mind."

There are also two pre-medieval pronouncements. The first comes from the *Constitutum* of Pope Vigilius (553), in which certain Nestorian propositions are condemned: "If anyone says that the one Jesus Christ who is both true Son of God and true Son of man did not know the future or the day of the Last Judgment and that He could know only as much as the divinity dwelling in Him as in another revealed to Him, *anathema sit.*"

The second comes from a letter of Pope Gregory the Great to Eulogius (d. 607), Patriarch of Alexandria, in which the pope commends the patriarch for his treatise against the *Agnoetes*, a sect which inverted the Monophysitism of the day by teaching that the divine nature was absorbed into the human. Resting their case on the passage in Mark's Gospel to which we referred above (13:32), the Agnoetes argued that Jesus was ignorant about the Day of Judgment. Gregory affirmed Eulogius' argument that the passage in question applied not to Christ as Head but to Christ as Body, i.e., Christ as Church. What Jesus knew *in* his human nature he did not know *from* his human nature. Because he is one in being with the Father, he has a knowledge which surpasses all others', including even that of the angels. Therefore, no ignorance was present in him, much less error.

Can We Reconcile the New Testament Record and the Teachings of the Church?

No; at least not *these* teachings. But then, what precisely are these teachings excluding, and what authority do they have?

The difficulty with answering the first of these two questions is compounded by the variety of theological universes which are operative in the New Testament, the medieval period, and in contemporary thought. On closer examination, the three universes are not mutually opposed. The medieval position is the "odd man out." The New Testament and modern theology are in closer harmony, one with another.

The teachings in question reflect certain assumptions about the meaning of knowledge which are deemed unacceptable today. The teachings assume, first, that God is not involved in human consciousness or in the growth of human knowledge except as a divine supplement. Thus, ordinary human beings (i.e., everyone except Jesus Christ) begin with absolutely nothing (*tabula rasa*) and proceed to accumulate knowledge experimentally, i.e., through human experience. Insofar as ordinary human beings know anything beyond what they can gather through experience, they receive it from God, as a revelation. Revelation, in this conception, is knowledge which is given over and above human knowledge. But we have already addressed in chapters 4 and 5 the problem of nature and grace, and in chapter 7 the question of revelation as such. The medieval approach to the problem of Jesus' knowledge is merely consistent with the medieval understanding of the relationship between nature and grace and of the meaning of revelation. Those same medieval conceptions of nature-and-grace and of revelation were immediately operative in the anti-Modernist documents and in *Mystici Corporis*.

The medieval understanding of Jesus' knowledge also reflects a pre-Enlightenment concept of history as something essentially static, as if history were simply the record of human actions in the world (e.g., comparable to a jet stream or the wake of a ship) rather than the evolutionary context in which human actions assume their meaning, significance, and direction (e.g., comparable to water as the element in which sea creatures live and develop). In the modern, as opposed to classical, understanding of history, an exact foreknowledge of all events (such as Christ is supposed to have had) would make truly free human action impossible. Human freedom is not simply the negative absence of contraints but the positive capacity to venture one's own future for something higher and greater. It involves risk-taking, trust, hope, fear, mystery.

Accordingly, to identify the human consciousness of Jesus with the divine consciousness, or to make Jesus' human consciousness something completely directed by the divine consciousness, is to relapse into Monophysitism. We might usefully distinguish, as these magisterial documents do not, between the *unreflexive consciousness* in the depths of Jesus' being and the *objectifying and verbalizing consciousness* which had a history and which fully shared in the human situation (concepts, ideas, etc.) of Jesus' time, encompassing processes of learning, surprising experiences, crises of self-identity, etc.

In his *unreflexive conciousness* Jesus was aware of himself as a subject in whom God was fully present and as one who was fully present in God. The *immediacy* of this contact with God was unique, based as it is on the hypostatic union, and it explains the extraordinary *conviction* with which Jesus proclaimed and practiced the Kingdom of God. Similarly, his sense that his own relationship with God is something *exemplary* for all other human beings generated the *conviction* that he was himself the personification of the Kingdom which he proclaimed and practiced.

In his *objectifying and verbalizing consciousness* Jesus understood and expressed *less* than the "content" of his unreflexive consciousness. In other words, Jesus, like the rest of us, knew more than he was capable of saying. Through dialogue with others he, like the rest of us, came to a fuller understanding of who he was and what or who he was for. He went to his death knowing at least that it was the fate of a prophet, and he accepted his death in the light of his conviction that God would vindicate what he had said, done, and been. Such a theological explanation does not at all deny that Jesus Christ was, in his very being and from the beginning, the Word made flesh, nor does it deny that through his death and resurrection he fully realized and achieved for us all that God intended to realize and achieve through him.

It is readily admitted that this theological explanation is not the one operative in the magisterial documents under consideration. But is this explanation positively excluded by those documents? And if so, what authority do these documents have?

The *Constitutum* of Pope Vigilius was directed specifically against Nestorian errors. Even if one were to grant *dogmatic* status to the *Constitutum*—and no one can—it does not explicitly exclude the position outlined above (proposed by Rahner, Schoonenberg, and others). The two Holy Office decrees of 1907 and 1918 also have to be interpreted carefully: The first rejected certain Modernist theses but contained no distinct censure of the view outlined above; the second simply called views like it "unsafe." *Mystici Corporis* raises the question of Jesus' knowledge almost in passing. The encyclical is not directed at contemporary Christological aberrations. Insofar as the passage is doctrinally pertinent, it applies more properly to the glorified Savior who now acts as the risen Head of the Body, which is the Church.

Even if one were to grant, however, that these documents do condemn the position advanced here, and by Rahner and other Catholic theologians elsewhere, one would still have to raise the question of the authoritative status of such condemnations. The reader is referred again to chapter 2, and is alerted as well to the ecclesiological discussion in Part IV of this book. It is sufficient here to note that, on a scale of authoritative value, decrees of Vatican congregations and even papal encyclicals fall well below infallible pronouncements of ecumenical councils. And one might, finally, make a reasonable case that they fall below the doctrinal pronouncements of an international synod of bishops or of a general council of the Church, i.e., one involving several national churches but not "the whole wide [Christian] world," which is the literal meaning of the word "ecumenical."

Moreover, the teaching authority of the Church—at whatever level of exercise—is "not above the word of God, but serves it . . ." (Vatican II, *Dogmatic Constitution on Divine Revelation*, n. 10). The word of God, as proclaimed in the New Testament and as interpreted in the light of present theological principles, calls into question the apparent intent of the magisterial pronouncements on this question of the knowledge of Jesus. Finally, this newer approach is not without precedent even in the patristic period. It was Cyril of Alexandria (d. 444), whose anti-Nestorian writings were officially adopted by the Council of Ephesus (431), who wrote of Jesus Christ: "We have admired his goodness in that for love of us he has not refused to descend to such a low position as to bear all that belongs to our nature, included in which is ignorance" (*Thesaurus on the Holy and Consubstantial Trinity*, thesis 22).

THE SEXUALITY OF JESUS

Here again the issue is the *humanity* of Jesus, but it is posed even more sharply than in the preceding question. Is he really like us in all things except sin, or is he so much an exception to the rule of human existence, indeed of *sexually* human existence, that he can scarcely be *one of us*, let alone the representative of *all of us*?

Our discussion will make its way through four sub-questions: (1) How does the New Testament portray the sexuality of Jesus? (2) How has the sexuality of Jesus been understood in the tradition and official teachings of the Church? (3) Can the New Testament record be reconciled with that tradition and those teachings? (4) Can our own contemporary understanding of sexuality be reconciled with either or both: the New Testament and the tradition, on the one hand, and teachings of the Church, on the other?

How Does the New Testament Portray the Sexuality of Jesus?

One is struck at once by the almost total silence of the New Testament about the sexuality of Jesus. The New Testament reports that he knew hunger and thirst. He even knew anger, as on the occasion of his driving the money-changers from the Temple (Mark 11:15-17). He was tempted to pride, idolatry, and the desire for power (Matthew 4:1-11). And he endured rejection, betrayal, physical abuse, and finally death itself. But nowhere is he sexually tempted, much less engaged in sexual activity. Was he, in fact, sexless? And if sexless, how was he fully human?

There are a few references to sexual morality which do convey something of Jesus' attitude toward sexuality: "You have heard the commandment, 'You shall not commit adultery.' What I say to you is: anyone who looks lustfully at a woman has already commited adultery with her in his thoughts" (Matthew 5:27-28).

He accentuates his point: "If your right eye is your trouble, gouge it out and throw it away. . . . if your right hand is your trouble, cut it off and throw it away. Better to lose part of your body than to have it all cast into Gehenna" (verses 29-30).

Jesus moves immediately from adultery to divorce: "What I say to you is: everyone who divorces his wife. . . forces her to commit adultery. The man who marries a divorced woman like-wise commits adultery" (verses 31-32). He also tells his audience that "when people rise from the dead, they neither marry nor are given in marriage but live like angels in heaven" (Matthew 22:30). (The meaning, force, and applicability of Jesus' ethical teaching will be examined more fully in Part V of the book, Christian Existence.)

On the other hand, the Gospels also present Jesus as a man known for his conviviality, his readiness to bless matrimonial unions, as one who even refers to the wedding feast as a symbol of the Kingdom of God (Matthew 22:1-14).

But how account for the obvious paucity of material on his sexuality? One plausible explanation is that Jesus deliberately wished to disassociate his proclamation of the Kingdom of God from the standard attitude toward human existence one finds in the other contemporary religions, where sex consistently played a large, if not even central, part. Some idealized sex as a sign of power that had to be replenished from on high; others condemned sex as a pollution to be purged from our lives. Jesus simply refused to sanction the religious status of sex. He is neither Dionysian nor anti-Dionysian.

Interpretations, beyond this one, vary widely. Hugh Montefiore, now an Anglican bishop, once suggested that Jesus may have had homosexual tendencies ("Jesus the Revelation of God," in *Christ for Us Today*, Norman Pittenger, ed., London: SCM Press, 1968, pp. 108-110). William Phipps, a Protestant theologian at Davis and Elkins College in West Virginia, has advanced the thesis that Jesus was married and that the post-resurrection encounter with Mary Magdalene can best be understood in light of his marital relationship with her (*Was Jesus Married?*, New York: Harper & Row, 1970). John 20:17 had been rendered by the Latin Vulgate as *"Noli me tangere"* ("Do not touch me"). The Greek,

"Me mou haptou," is much stronger: "Do not cling to me." The physical relations she had previously had with Jesus and which she desired to continue were no longer appropriate or possible in his risen life.

There are, however, at least three arguments against the suggestion that Jesus was married: (1) The Gospels say nothing at all about a marriage; (2) the anti-erotic bias of the New Testament churches came very early into Christianity, and it can be supposed that if Jesus had been married, that tendency would have been checked; and, most decisively, (3) when Paul invoked his right to marry a believing woman "like the rest of the apostles and the brothers of the Lord and Cephas" (1 Corinthians 9:5), why did he not appeal to Jesus' own marriage to support his argument?

How Has the Sexuality of Jesus Been Understood in the Tradition and Teachings of the Church?

In a word, poorly. The influence of idealistic Greek philosophy, and the thought of Plato in particular, has been profound. Plato's true philosopher does not concern himself with sexual pleasure (*Phaedo*, 64, 82). Sexual desire is referred to as a diseased aspect of the personality (*Republic*, 402-405). The well-balanced person is the one who sublimates his sexual energies in intellectual pursuits (*Republic*, 485). Aristotle is at least as negative. A woman, he noted, is "a mutilated male" (*On the Generation of Animals*, 737a). The male is by nature superior. He commands; the female obeys (*Politics* 1254b, 1260a).

This same spirit was carried forward into the patristic and medieval periods by such men as Gregory of Nyssa and Augustine, for whom the sexual impulse is a sin and a shame (*City of God*, 14:17-18). Indeed, the genital organs are indecent and dishonorable (*partes inhonestae*, Scholastic theology would call them). They are the bodily instruments for the transmission of Original Sin (*On Marriage and Concupiscence*, 1:13). The ideal society for Augustine was a society without passion, where male and female would join for reproduction not through the "eager desire of lust, but the normal exercise of the will" (*City of God*, 14:26). The highest ideal, therefore, is consecrated virginity.

Thomas Aquinas was more moderate, but his views were also influenced by Greek philosophy and Augustinianism. The celibate life is to be preferred, he argued, because it is "unseared by the heat of sexual desire" (*Summa Theologica* II-II, q. 152, a. 1). He quoted with approval Augustine's injunction that sexual contact proper to the married state pulls down the mind from its heights (q. 151, a. 3). Following Augustine's theory on Original Sin, Thomas also argued that Jesus had to be conceived virginally because sin is transmitted by the male seed (III, q. 31, a. 3). Aquinas' attitude toward women was similarly appalling by present standards: The woman is an entirely passive agent in the act of love, and is less than a man on nature's scale (I, q. 99, a. 2; II-II q. 26, a. 10; III, q. 32, a. 4). Comparably negative attitudes toward sexuality can be found in the major Protestant Reformers: Luther, Zwingli, and Calvin (see W. Phipps, *The Sexuality of Jesus*, New York: Harper & Row, 1973, pp. 95-104).

Not surprisingly, this same attitude found expression in religious art and a counter-reaction in secular *literature*. Mass-produced paintings, statues, and holy cards depicting Jesus in one form or another (the Infant of Prague, the Sacred Heart, e.g.) are unrelievedly sexless. It is an art style called *Kitsch*, something one instantly recognizes but cannot define. "*Kitsch* is weak, save in two respects," Bruno Brinkman, S.J., writes. "It encourages submission and obedience, and it is strong in repressing or infantilizing sex, which is different from sublimating it. It has been unmistakably powerful and popular. We must not forget that in religious houses such statues were for decades the object of regular private, if not community, *cultus* [worship]" ("The Humanity of Christ: Christ and Sexuality," *The Way*, vol. 15, 1975, p. 210). *Kitsch* expresses fear of the human body and of sexuality. It is patently Docetic in tendency. It preaches and teaches a Jesus who is not recognizably human.

This vehemently anti-sexual bias has brought forth a variety of reactions. The most celebrated is D. H. Lawrence's (d. 1930) short story "The Man Who Died" (reprinted in *Christian Faith and the Contemporary Arts*, Finley Eversole, ed., New York: Vintage Books, 1959). Lawrence makes Jesus' resurrection his awakening to sensual love. On the other side is Nikos Kazantzakis'

(d. 1957) *The Last Temptation* (New York: Simon and Schuster, 1960), in which Jesus' spiritual struggle, his final battle with Satan, is defined by his carnal desire for Mary Magdalene, even as he hangs on the cross. But Jesus is shaken out of his dream and overcomes the Devil's power: "The moment he cried ELI ELI and fainted, Temptation had captured him for a split second and led him astray. The joys, marriages and children were lies . . . illustrations sent by the Devil" (p. 496).

Just as Lawrence had read into Jesus' life his own exceedingly permissive approach to sexuality, so Kazantzakis had projected upon *his* Jesus a mixture of late Western asceticism and Buddhism.

And what of the *official teachings* of the Church? The Church is nearly as silent as the New Testament. The only direct reference is to be found in the documents of the Second Council of Constantinople (553), not one of the more authoritative of the Church's ecumenical councils, as we pointed out in chapter 13. A condemnation of Theodore of Mopsuestia is issued and is subsequently approved by Pope Vigilius. Among Theodore's allegedly *Nestorian* views is one which holds that "God the Word is one while Christ is another who, disturbed by the passions of the soul and the desires of the flesh, freed himself gradually from inferior inclinations. . . ." The issue at hand was not Jesus' sexuality, but the unity of the two natures in the one divine Word. In any case, it is not a *dogmatic* definition nor, as given there, is it even clearly a *doctrine* of the Church.

Can the New Testament and the Tradition and Teachings of the Church Be Reconciled?

On this precise point, i.e., whether or not Jesus had an active sexual life or was sexually tempted, there is no possibility of contradiction, since the New Testament says nothing about either. The larger question, i.e., whether the patristic and medieval traditions are fundamentally consistent with the whole of the New Testament message and of Christian faith, will be addressed by implication, at least, in the next section.

What Does Our Contemporary Christian Consciousness Disclose About Sexuality in General, and About Jesus' Sexuality in Particular?

It seems entirely consistent with Christian faith in the *humanity* of Jesus Christ that Jesus should have known sexual temptation. Temptation itself is no sin; therefore, it would not violate the previous principle that Jesus was indeed sinless. Moreover, the New Testament does explicitly acknowledge that Jesus was tempted by Satan in the areas of power and wordly acclaim. To accept a Jesus who is at once fully human and yet immune from sexual desires is to stretch not only one's imagination but also one's theological convictions about the incarnation and the fundamental goodness of creation, the human body, and human sexuality.

It would not necessarily follow, however, that Jesus, as a necessary expression of his humanity, actually did engage in sexual activities. Neither would it follow that sexual activity within marriage would have been inconsistent with Jesus' *divinity*. Although it is true of a small minority of the world's population, it is true nonetheless that there are well-integrated, courageous, forceful, responsible, and thoroughly dedicated human beings who do not marry. One has only to point to a random sample of such persons within the past few decades alone: Pope John XXIII, Dag Hammarskjold (d. 1961), Mother Teresa of Calcutta, Theodore Hesburgh, and many others.

But to think and speak of Jesus as if he—and they—were asexual, if not anti-sexual, not only does an injustice to God's creation of sexuality but may finally undermine the humanity of Jesus as well, and would thereby remove an indispensable basis for our redemption and salvation.

Sexuality is not to be understood in a biological sense alone. Even celibates are sexual beings. The sexual difference between a man and a woman is constitutive of human nature itself, and that constitutive dimension finds expression in the psychological as well as the physiological levels of human existence. Sexuality, therefore, is not something added on to a neutral human nature. It determines a person as man or as woman. The "human person" is neither man alone or woman alone. Man and woman together constitute what we mean by the human. The need for communication and complementarity is self-evident. In sexuality a man and a woman experience their individual insufficiency and their dependence upon each other. And each one depends not just on the other but on the other as his or her sexual complement.

Sexuality, even when fulfilled in marriage, still points beyond itself to its perfect fulfillment in God. In the "already" and the "not yet" experience of fulfillment in sexual union, we come to a certain understanding of the transcendental relationship we have with God. Jesus was fully a human being, with sexual desires and with an understanding of sexual struggle. But he subordinated (not "suppressed") the *genital* expression of that sexuality in order to leave himself completely free for the proclamation of the Kingdom of God. Freud called this "sublimation." It is not something negative, like "repression." On the contrary, it represents a change in the goal as well as the object of the powerful sexual drive, putting its enormous energies at the service of some other value. This happens when there has been a free choice by which this drive is accepted and redirected. In the absence of a consciously free decision, however, repression occurs and personal maturity is blocked. This leads, in turn, to false attitudes, compensations, and/or an exaggerated quest for power for its own sake. None of these effects of repression was ever attributed to Jesus. Jesus, the perfect human being, was a sexually integrated human being.

Section Two: Christological Criteria

What follows here is not offered as an easy way of indentifying unorthodox or even heretical understandings of Jesus Christ. Very few deficient Christologies are expressed so unequivocally as, e.g., "I begin with the premise that it makes no sense at all to speak of Jesus of Nazareth as divine." At the serious academic and scholarly levels, even views which may be *reductively* unorthodox are first proposed as bona fide efforts to explain real difficulties in the mystery of Christ. That could undoubtedly have been said of each of the theologians of the first seven centuries who, in the end, found their explanations condemned by one or more of the great Christological councils.

On the other hand, there *is* an objective and objectifiable Christian and Catholic tradition. It is carried forward in the New Testament, in the dogmatic formulations of the ecumenical councils, the theological writings of the Fathers and doctors of the Church, the doctrinal assertions of other, non-ecumenical councils and of popes, and in the Church's liturgy. In listing criteria by which to differentiate between Christologies which are consistent with this broad tradition from those which are not, I do not suggest that the content of that tradition is always readily identified and understood. But the opposite impression also has to be checked, namely, that, when it comes to expressing our faith in Jesus Christ, one Christian's ideas are as good as another's, that we somehow begin afresh in each generation, taking or leaving what history bequeaths to us or what the Church universal proclaims, celebrates, and teaches today.

1. The Catholic Christological tradition, *synthesized at the Council of Chalcedon (451)*, has *three principal dogmatic components:* (1) *Jesus is divine;* (2) *Jesus is human;* and (3) *the divine and the human are united in one person, Jesus Christ.*

   a. These principles are *not* purely metaphysical. They are primarily *soteriological.* If Jesus is not *at once* divine *and* human, then he did not save us. Both the divinity and the humanity are fully operative and effective in the redemption because they are indeed *united* in one person.

   Christological explanations which explicitly or implicitly deny any of these three principles are inconsistent with the Catholic tradition. *Examples:* (1) "Jesus was not an ordinary human being, to be sure. He was the greatest of human beings. He achieved the highest *degree* of humanity." (2) "Jesus could not have been tainted in the least by ignorance, error, or, dare we say it, sexual appetites. That would be demeaning to the Son of God present in the human body of Jesus." (3) "Jesus is the Christ, to be sure. But there are other expressions of 'the Christ' as well.

Indeed, 'the Christ' is a cosmic process carrying the world toward its final perfection, and Jesus is one of his/its principal carriers and instruments."

b.   The need for constant reinterpretation notwithstanding, no Christological interpretation can prescind from the objective data of this tradition in its biblical, dogmatic, doctrinal, theological, and liturgical expressions.

On the other hand, any such reinterpretation must be initiated and sustained by the most serious biblical, theological, and historical scholarship. Idiosyncratic interpretations, without any recognizable connection with, or even awareness of, the scholarly discussions are to be rejected.

2.   *The object of Christian faith is not Christology, i.e., the dogmatic or even the biblical formulae, but Jesus himself. There is no radical separation, therefore, between the Jesus of history and the Christ of faith.*

This criterion is an elaboration of the third dogmatic component listed above, namely, that the divine and the human are united in one person, Jesus Christ. No processive or evolutionary Christology is consistent with the Catholic tradition which breaks the unique and definitive connection between Jesus of Nazareth and the Christ of the cosmos. This principle does not, on the other hand, exclude evolutionary or processive Christologies. Karl Rahner's Christology is one which reflects an evolutionary perspective, yet, by the standards proposed here, his is eminently consistent with the Catholic tradition.

3.   *Jesus' life, death, and resurrection are redemptive. However they are finally explained, no explanation is consistent with the Catholic tradition if the explanation makes them merely exemplary or inspiring, or if it so divorces them from the human situation that they are simply divine disruptions of physical and natural laws.*

This criterion is an elaboration of the first two dogmatic components given in criterion #1 above, namely, that Jesus is divine *and* human. A merely exemplary or motivational explanation effectively denies the first dogmatic principle; a purely interventionist explanation effectively denies the second. No explanation, from whatever side of the theological spectrum, is consistent with the Catholic tradition if the *redemptive* significance of the life, death, and resurrection of Jesus is simply ignored. Thus, the resurrection is not simply a proof of Jesus' divinity or a reward from the Father.

4. *Christological explanations which contradict the central affirmations of the Church's liturgy are in violation of the long-standing theological norm: "The rule of prayer is the rule of belief" ("Lex orandi, lex credendi").*

The applicability of this criterion to Christology will be explored in the next chapter. For the moment it is sufficient to note its probable origin in the *Indiculus*, composed sometime between 435 and 442 by Prosper of Aquitaine (d. 460), a disciple of Augustine. The axiom is cited throughout the history of the Church, and in such recent documents as Pope Pius XII's encyclical on the Sacred Litury, *Mediator Dei* (1947). Pope Pius XI attributes the formula to Pope Celestine I (d. 432). In any case, it goes back at least to the early fifth century.

5. *Christological explanations which deny or are completely silent about the social implications of Jesus Christ's saving work misunderstand or supplant what was central to Jesus' proclamation and practice, namely, the Kingdom of God.*

Although this principle was not central to the conciliar debates of the first seven centuries, it is a clear implication of Jesus' preaching and activity on behalf of the reign of God. It also follows from the second major criterion above.

We addressed ourselves already to this issue in chapter 12, and will return to it again and again throughout the rest of the book: in the discussion of the Church's mission, of Christian existence, and, in chapter 29, of the Kingdom of God as such.

SUMMARY

1. The chapter addresses four specific questions as a way of elaborating upon the Christological discussion contained in chapters 12-14; it also offers a list of theological criteria by which Christologies which are consistent with the broad Catholic tradition can be differentiated from those which are not.

2.   The *virginal conception of Jesus* refers to the belief that *Jesus was conceived in the womb of a virgin, Mary, without the intervention of a human father (virginitas ante partum)*. It does *not* refer to the virginity of Mary during or after the birth of Jesus (*in partu* or *post partum*).

3.   Belief in the virginal conception of Jesus *is* to be found in the *New Testament*, specifically in the Infancy Narratives of Matthew and Luke. The rest of the New Testament is silent about it.

4.   It cannot be determined, on the basis of the New Testament evidence, whether the virginal conception of Jesus was an *historical fact*. There are exegetical arguments for and against its historicity, with the scales perhaps tipping in favor of the negative side. Belief in the virginal conception, therefore, may have been a *theologoumenon*, i.e., a theological belief that is read back into the historical life of Jesus in order to make a point of faith: *Jesus was one with God from the moment of his conception.*

5.   The *official Church* presupposes the virginity of Mary ("born of the Virgin Mary"). Given the original setting and purpose of the creedal and doctrinal affirmations, however, it is reasonable to conclude that the Church was not interested primarily in the *historicity* of the virginal conception but in *preserving the unity of the divine and the human in Jesus Christ*. Belief in the historicity of the virginal conception, however, remained universal within the Church at least until the Enlightenment.

6.   Rejection of the historicity of the virginal conception does not necessarily imply rejection of the *divinity* of Jesus Christ. *The Word could also have become flesh with the human cooperation of Joseph.*

7.   Belief in the virginal conception, apart now from the question of historicity, means that Jesus is from God, that Jesus is unique, that in him the human race has had a new beginning, that the salvation he brings transcends this world, and that God works through the weakness and even powerlessness of human instruments to advance the course of salvation history. If in denying the historicity of the virginal conception one also denies one or more of these principles, then one has effectively moved outside the Christian, and certainly the Catholic, tradition.

8.   Because Jesus Christ is believed to be "from God," he is also believed to be *without sin.*

9.   Belief in the *sinlessness* of Jesus is rooted in the *New Testament*, and especially in Hebrews 4:15. The New Testament affirms only that Jesus was without sin (*impeccantia*), not that he was absolutely incapable of sin (*impeccabilitas*).

10.   The sinlessness of Christ cannot be *historically verified* because no one could have read the thoughts and heart of Jesus nor observed him in his every waking moment. But neither do we have any historical evidence or even accusations that Jesus *did* sin, and this is remarkable in view of Jesus' extremely controversial and threatening public image.

11.   The *official Church* teaches at least as much as the New Testament; namely, that Jesus was de facto without sin. It would appear that *Constantinople III* (681) also taught that Jesus was incapable of sin, but that point is not explicitly formulated. In any case, such teaching would rest on the assumption that Jesus' human will was effectively absorbed or absolutely directed by the divine will. But this was precisely what the council was trying to combat (*Monothelitism*). The official teaching of the Church, it seems better to conclude, is that Jesus Christ was perfect in his humanity and so completely in union with the Father that he was absolutely without sin. Not that he was incapable of sin, but that he was able not to sin and, in fact, did not sin.

12.   The belief in the sinlessness of Jesus underscores the more fundamental belief that he is the *supreme expression of communion between God and humankind*, that he is "the reflection of the Father's glory, the exact representation of the Father's being" (Hebrews 1:3).

13.   The question of Jesus' *knowledge* is important because, unless we can admit to ignorance and perhaps even error in Jesus, certain problems of New Testament interpretation cannot be solved. Secondly, a Jesus who knows all things, and everything about all things, is not apparently the same human Jesus who the Council of Chalcedon confessed is like us in all things except sin.

14.   On the basis of the *New Testament* evidence alone, one finds arguments on both sides of the question. Some texts, reflecting a later, higher Christology, attribute unlimited knowledge to Jesus, while many other texts, reflecting an earlier, lower Christology, reveal both ignorance and error in Jesus. The weight of the evidence however, seems to favor those who are prepared to accept ignorance and error in Jesus, even with regard to his messianic consciousness and his understanding of himself as the *unique* Son of God.

15.   In any case, Jesus displayed a novel and courageous degree of *conviction* about the Kingdom of God, seeing his preaching, his actions, and his very person as signs and instruments of its inbreaking. He spoke with unprecedented *authority*. He put *demands* on others. He *forgave sins*. He *changed the Law of Moses*, and so forth. Indeed, he *began* his

public ministry with this conviction already in place, so to speak (Mark 1:15).

16. The *medieval tradition* and the *twentieth-century decrees of the Holy Office* clearly favor the "unlimited knowledge" side of the argument, but this tradition and these teachings reflect a particular understanding of knowledge, of revelation, of history, and of the relationship between nature and grace. In the light of our *modern understanding* of these philosophical and theological issues, Jesus would not have been a free human being, and therefore would not have really been one like us in all things except sin, if he knew exactly what lay ahead for him.

17. We might usefully distinguish between (a) Jesus' *unreflexive consciousness* which was the source of his unshakable conviction about his role in the coming of the reign of God—in other words, his unarticulated, not-yet-objectified sense of himself as a distinct subject with a uniquely intimate relationship with God—and (b) his *objectifying and verbalizing consciousness* which gradually reached the level of clear and precise self-understanding and expression, especially through dialogue with other people.

18. The few *doctrinal pronouncements* which have addressed the issue of Jesus' knowledge, of course, support the view that Jesus did have unlimited knowledge. But the preceding explanation was not current at the time of these magisterial formulations, nor is it exactly clear which Modernist understandings were condemned, and to what extent they were condemned. In any case, none of these ecclesiastical documents has *dogmatic* status.

19. The issue of Jesus' humanity is posed even more sharply by the question of his *sexuality*. If Jesus was sexless, how was he human?

20. The *New Testament* is silent about the matter. It reports other basic human emotions (anger, hunger, temptations to power, etc.) but affords no indications of sexual desires or sexual activities. Is it perhaps because Jesus did not want his proclamation of the Kingdom of God confused with other contemporary religious attitudes? Other religions accorded religious status to sexuality, either exaggerating its importance or fundamentally rejecting its goodness.

21. The *tradition* of the Church on this question has been influenced, in a decidedly negative way, by Greek and especially *Platonic* philosophy, as mediated by *Augustine* and other Fathers. Sexuality is evil. Indeed, it is the means through which Original Sin is transmitted. This same negative attitude toward sexuality in general, and toward women in particular, was carried forward in popular art and spirituality and, in

turn, evoked strong counter-reactions among secular artists such as D. H. Lawrence.

22.   The *official Church* is nearly as silent as the New Testament on Jesus' sexuality. *Constantinople II* (553) alone refers to the matter, but it is in the context of its anti-Nestorian thrust. The issue was not directly the sexuality of Jesus but the unity of the two natures in the one divine Word. In any case, the formulation is not a *dogmatic* definition, nor is it even clearly a *doctrinal* pronouncement.

23.   In conclusion, it would seem entirely consistent with Christian faith in the *humanity* of Jesus to believe that he knew *sexual desires and sexual temptations*. The contrary view seems to undermine his full humanity in all things except sin. Temptation and desires are not in themselves sinful.

24.   One need not, on the other hand, attribute *overt genital sexual activity* to Jesus on the grounds that his humanity could not have been fulfilled without it. Sexuality has to do with more than the biological. It has to do with the way we are, with the way we understand ourselves as male or female, and with the way we relate to the other, male or female, to complement our humanity. Even Freud acknowledged the importance of *sublimation*, as distinguished from *repression*. Sublimation involves a free acceptance of our sexual drives and a free redirection of those drives for other values. Repression, on the other hand, leads to false attitudes, compensatory behavior, and inordinate quests for power over others. Jesus was never accused of any of these traits. He was a sexually integrated man.

25.   The following *criteria* may be helpful in differentiating between Christologies which are consistent with the broad Catholic tradition and those which are not.

(1)   The Catholic Christological tradition, synthesized at the Council of Chalcedon (451), has three principal dogmatic components: (1) *Jesus is divine*; (2) *Jesus is human*; and (3) *the divine and the human are united in one person, Jesus Christ.*

(1-a)   These principles are primarily *soteriological*; i.e., unless the one Jesus is at once human and divine, we are not saved.

(1-b)   The need for *constant reinterpretation* notwithstanding, no Christological interpretation can ignore the *objective data* of this tradition, as appropriated and understood by modern scholarship.

(2)   *The object of Christian faith* is not Christology, i.e., the dogmatic or even the biblical formulae, but *Jesus himself.* There is *no radical separation*, therefore, *between the Jesus of history and the Christ of faith.*

(3) *Jesus' life, death, and resurrection are redemptive.* However they are finally explained, no explanation is consistent with the
Catholic tradition if it makes them merely exemplary or inspiring, or if it
so divorces them from the human situation that they are simply divine
disruptions of physical and natural laws.

(4) Christological explanations which contradict the central
affirmations of the Church's *liturgy* are in violation of the longstanding
theological norm: *"The rule of prayer is the rule of belief" (Lex orandi,
lex credendi).*

(5) Christological explanations which deny or are completely
silent about the *social implications* of Jesus Christ's saving work misunderstand or supplant what was central to Jesus' proclamation and practice, namely, the *Kingdom of God.*

SUGGESTED READINGS

Brinkman, Bruno. "The Humanity of Christ: Christ and Sexuality." *The
    Way* 15 (1975), 209–224.
Brown, Raymond E. "How Much Did Jesus Know?" *Jesus, God and
    Man: Modern Biblical Reflections.* Milwaukee: Bruce, 1967, pp.
    39–105.
——————. et al., eds. *Mary in the New Testament: A Collaborative
    Assessment by Protestant and Roman Catholic Scholars.* New York:
    Paulist Press, 1978.
——————. *The Virginal Conception and Bodily Resurrection of
    Jesus.* New York: Paulist Press, 1973, pp. 21–68.
Driver, Thomas F. "Sexuality and Jesus." *New Theology No. 3.* Eds.
    Martin Marty and Dean Peerman. New York: Macmillan, 1966, pp.
    118–132.
Malatesta, Edward, ed. *Jesus in Christian Devotion and Contemplation.*
    St. Meinrad, Ind.: Abbey Press, 1974.
Phipps, William E. *The Sexuality of Jesus: Theological and Literary
    Perspectives.* New York: Harper & Row, 1973.
Rahner, Karl. "Dogmatic Reflections on the Knowledge and Self-Con-
    sciousness of Christ." *Theological Investigations.* Baltimore: Heli-
    con, 1966, vol. 5, pp. 193–215.
Robinson, John A. T. *The Human Face of God.* Philadelphia: Westmin-
    ster Press, 1973, pp. 1–98.
Schoonenberg, Piet. *The Christ: A Study of the God-Man Relationship in
    the Whole of Creation and in Jesus Christ.* New York: Herder &
    Herder, 1971, pp. 104–152.

· XVI ·

THE CHRIST OF THE LITURGY

This chapter is by way of an appendix to the preceding Christological reflections (chapters 11-15). More specifically, it provides a fuller exposition of the fourth criterion given at the end of the previous chapter, namely, that Christological explanations which contradict the central affirmations of the Church's liturgy are in violation of the longstanding theological axiom: "The rule of prayer is the rule of belief" (*Lex orandi, lex credendi*).

The *thesis* of this chapter is that *the eucharistic and other sacramental rites* of the Catholic Church, especially as they have been revised by decree of the Second Vatican Council and Pope Paul VI, *at once express and confirm the major Christological principles* which have been set forth thus far, namely, the centrality of the *resurrection* of Jesus to redemption; the centrality of the *Kingdom of God* within the message and mission of Jesus; the centrality of the same Kingdom of God for the *Church's* message, mission, and hope within the *history of salvation*; and the empowerment of the Church by the *Holy Spirit* to carry forward that mission in history *until the Lord returns*.

This chapter has a limited purpose and scope. It does not attempt to do in advance the work of chapters 21 and 22, on the sacraments. It proposes only to show that the Christology of the Church's liturgy is consistent with the main Christological principles of contemporary Catholic theology, and to suggest that contemporary Christology, in turn, has shaped and guided the revision process mandated by Vatican II.

Accordingly, the chapter examines the prayers used in the seven sacraments of the Church, beginning with the new Rite of Christian Initiation (Baptism, Confirmation, and Eucharist). Because the Eucharist is the supreme Christian sacrament, special attention is given to it: the introductory rite, the service of the word, the canons, or Eucharistic Prayers, and the Communion rite. The chapter then moves to the sacraments of Penance, Marriage, Holy Order (the latter consisting of diaconate, priesthood, and episcopate), and the Anointing of the Sick. The focus of interest in each instance is the specifically Christological content of the various prayers and sacramental formulae.

The liturgy, after all, is Christology as worship and prayer; Christology, in turn, is worship and prayer as theological and doctrinal formulation. Indeed the very word *orthodoxy* means, in the Greek, "right praise," and the Church's historic Christological creeds are, for the most part, liturgical formulae or are derived therefrom.

THE SACRAMENTS OF CHRISTIAN INITIATION
Baptism

First Stage: Rite of Becoming Catechumens

Although "God enlightens every person who comes into the world," the celebrant reminds the candidate for Baptism, "you are called to walk by the light of Christ and to trust in his wisdom. He asks you to submit yourself to him more and more and to believe in him with all your heart. This is the way of faith on which Christ will lovingly guide you to eternal life. Are you ready to enter on this path today under the leadership of Christ?" The candidate responds, "I am."

The celebrant then turns to the candidate's sponsors and to the entire assembly and asks if they are "ready to help (him/her) come to know and follow Christ." Faith in him, in other words, is never a purely individual matter. The Church mediates Christian faith.

There follows a brief rite of *exorcism* in which the celebrant lightly breathes toward the face of the candidate and says:

"Breathe your Spirit, Lord, and drive out the spirits of evil: command them to depart, for your kingdom is drawing near." From the very beginning, the candidate's attention is focused on what was in fact central to Jesus' own preaching and mission: the coming Kingdom of God. (See chapter 12.)

The primitive biblical and patristic *distinction* between God, the Almighty (*Pantokrator*), and Jesus, the Christ ("anointed") of God, is preserved in an optional rite in which the candidate renounces non-Christian worship and spirits or magical arts: "With the help of God and in response to his call, you have indicated your intention to worship and serve God alone and his Christ." And immediately thereafter: "Do you reject every power which sets itself up in opposition to God and his Christ?" (See chapter 13.)

Then the sponsors are asked to assure the celebrant that the candidate has indeed "chosen Christ as Lord and wishes to serve him alone." The candidate and sponsors come forward, and the celebrant makes the sign of the cross on the candidate's forehead: "Receive the cross on your forehead: by this sign of love (or: of his triumph) Christ will be your strength. Learn now to know and follow him."

There follows the signing of the various senses and parts of the body: ears, eyes, lips, breast, shoulders, each accompanied by an appropriate formula: "May you hear the voice of the Lord"; "May you see with the light of God"; "May you respond to the word of God"; "May Christ dwell in your heart by faith"; and "May you accept the sweet yoke of Christ." And then the general blessing: "I sign you in the name of the Father, and of the Son, and of the Holy Spirit: may you live for ever and ever."

Then the celebrant prays that the candidate may be kept safe by the "power" of the cross of Christ. An optional form of the prayer is even more soteriologically comprehensive: "Almighty God, you have given life to your people by the death *and resurrection* of your Son . . ." (italics mine).

A service of the Word follows: readings, homily, and presentation of the Gospels. Then the sponsors and the whole assembly pray that "God the Father reveal his Christ to (him/her) more and more with every passing day," and that, with the support of the community, the candidate may be "found ready, in due time, to receive the new birth of baptism and life from the Holy Spirit." The ceremony concludes with the prayer that those "who have listened to the word in this community be renewed by its power and come to reflect the image of Christ who lives and reigns for ever and ever. Amen."

During the course of the catechumenate minor *exorcisms* are celebrated to show the candidate the true nature of the spiritual life as a battle between flesh and spirit, and to underline both the importance of self-denial in order to gain the blessings of the Kingdom of God and the continuing need of God's help. "Even when (we) sinned against you, you did not abandon (us), but in love and wisdom you chose to save (us) by the coming of your Son as man." And again: "Lord Jesus Christ, when ascending and preaching from the hillside you led your followers from the path of sin and made known to them the way of happiness of the Kingdom. . . . May they work for peace among men and joyfully endure persecution. May they come to share in your Kingdom and in the forgiveness you promised them."

Second Stage: Rite of Election or Enrollment of Names

The celebrant extends his hands over the candidate(s) and prays: "God our Father, you created the human race that you might also be the One who makes it ever new. Count these adopted children as sons and daughters reborn to your new covenant. Make them children of the promise. Although they cannot reach eternal life by their own nature, they may come to share it by the power of your love. We ask this through Christ our Lord. Amen." The close connection between Christology and Christian anthropology is evident. Our humanity is good because it comes from the creative act of God. We are all alive by a principle which transcends us. The presence of God in us enters into the very definition of what it means to be human (see chapter 5). Through the redemptive work of Jesus Christ the goodness of our humanity is reconfirmed. We are renewed. Evident, too, is the priority of God's work over our own in the coming of the Kingdom: "Keep them faithful to their calling, help them *to be built into* the Kingdom of your Son..."(italics mine)

In a later rite of exorcism, the *uniqueness* of Jesus is attested to in the words: "Lord Jesus, you are the fountain we thirst for, you are the teacher we seek; you alone are the Holy One." And again: "Lord Jesus, you are the true light that enlightens all men." And again: "Father of eternal life, you are a God, not of the dead, but of the living: you sent your Son to proclaim the good news of life, to rescue men from the kingdom of death and to lead them to resurrection. Free these chosen people from the power of the evil spirit who brings death. May they receive new life from Christ and bear witness to his resurrection."

The *miracles* of Jesus are portrayed for what they are: not interruptions of the laws of nature in order to overwhelm, but signs given in order to teach. "Lord Jesus, you raised Lazarus from death as a sign that you had come to give men life in fullest measure." (See chapters 9 and 12.)

A profession of faith follows in which the candidate confesses faith in "Jesus Christ, his only Son, our Lord. He was conceived by the power of the Holy Spirit and born of the Virgin Mary. He suffered under Pontius Pilate, was crucified, died, and was buried. He descended to the dead. On the third day he rose again. He ascended into heaven, and is seated at the right hand of the Father. He will come again to judge the living and the dead."

Third Stage: Celebration of the Sacrament

The celebrant blesses the baptismal water with these words: "We ask you, Father, with your Son to send the Holy Spirit upon the water of this font. May all who are buried with Christ in the death of baptism rise also with him to newness of life." There follow a renunciation of Satan, an anointing, a profession of faith, and then the actual rite of Bapitsm "in the name of the Father, and of the Son, and of the Holy Spirit." A post-baptismal anointing is accompanied by the prayer: "As Christ was anointed Priest, Prophet, and King, so may you live always as a member of his body, sharing everlasting life." Then the new Christian is clothed in a white garment to symbolize his or her having become "a new creation," clothed in Christ.

Confirmation

Baptism is completed through the rite of Confirmation, in which the Church prays in a special way that the Spirit might be poured forth upon the new Christians "to strengthen them with his abundant gifts and anoint them to be more like Christ his Son." The candidates are called "to witness to his grace by [their] manner of life."

Eucharist

Christology-as-worship is most fully expressed, of course, in the Eucharist. Here more than anywhere else in the Church's liturgical and devotional life, the Church's perception of Jesus Christ is expressed in a manner at once comprehensive and precise.

Introductory Rites

The third penitential rite is filled with explicit Christological references: "You were sent to heal the contrite"; "You came to call sinners"; "You plead for us at the right hand of the Father"; "You came to reconcile us to one another and to the Father"; "You heal the wounds of sin and division"; "You raise the dead to life in the Spirit"; "You bring pardon and peace to the sinner"; "You bring light to those in darkness"; "You raise us to new life"; "You forgive us our sins"; "You feed us with your body and blood"; "You healed the sick." Jesus is a healer of spiritual *and* bodily sickness. He brings truth that enlightens the mind. He gives us himself in the Eucharist. And through all of these activities, he reconciles us with God the Father (see chapter 12).

In the "Glory to God" (*Gloria*) the Church prays: "Lord Jesus Christ, only Son of the Father, Lord God, Lamb of God, you take away the sin of the world: have mercy on us; you are seated at the right hand of the Father: receive our prayer. For you alone are the Holy One, you alone are the Lord, you alone are the Most High,

Jesus Christ, with the Holy Spirit, in the glory of God the Father. Amen." The reconciling work of Christ, therefore, continues. Even now he pleads for us "at the right hand of the Father." The Jesus of history, the Nazarene who died on the cross, is our living Lord.

Liturgy of the Word

Herein there are readings from both Testaments. The selections from the New Testament, of course, are regularly focused on Jesus Christ, but since they are not the same from Eucharist to Eucharist, they cannot be cited here. What is constant on Sundays and major feasts is the "Profession of Faith," or Nicaeo-Constantinopolitan Creed, to which reference has been made several times already: "We believe in one Lord, Jesus Christ, the only Son of God, eternally begotten of the Father, God from God, Light from Light, true God from true God, begotten, not made, one in Being with the Father. Through him all things were made. For us men and for our salvation he came down from heaven: by the power of the Holy Spirit he was born of the Virgin Mary, and became man. For our sake he was crucified under Pontius Pilate; he suffered, died, and was buried. On the third day he rose again in fulfillment of the Scriptures; he ascended into heaven and is seated at the right hand of the Father. He will come again in glory to judge the living and the dead, and his kingdom will have no end." We have here, of course, a summary of the Church's historic faith in Jesus Christ. This summary is the fruit of centuries of controversy and doctrinal clarification (see chapter 13).

Liturgy of the Eucharist

As the celebrant pours wine and a little water into the chalice, he prays: "By the mystery of this water and wine may we come to share in the divinity of Christ, who humbled himself to share in our humanity." The Christological perspective here is "from above," but it is also decidedly incarnational. Jesus is truly one with us.

The *prefaces* of the Eucharistic Prayer, or canon, also vary from season to season. The regular weekday preface, however, expresses its Christology with commendable leanness: "With love we celebrate his death. With living faith we proclaim his resurrection. With unwavering hope we await his return in glory." Jesus Christ is situated at the center of salvation history. He alters its course by his death; he renews it by his resurrection; and he will bring it to perfection at the Second Coming.

Eucharistic Prayer I sounds the purpose of the Mass from the very beginning. It is an act of "praise and thanksgiving (of the Father) through Jesus Christ (his) Son." The consecratory prayer cites the words of Jesus in which he speaks of "the blood of the new and everlasting covenant" which is shed for all for the forgiveness of sins. The memorial acclamations which immediately follow the consecration declare that "Christ has died, Christ is risen, Christ will come again"; "Dying you destroyed our death, rising you restored our life. Lord Jesus, come in glory"; "Lord, by your cross and resurrection you have set us free. You are the Savior of the world." And all four Eucharistic Prayers conclude with the words: "Through him, with him, in him, in the unity of the Holy Spirit, all glory and honor is yours, almighty Father, for ever and ever. Amen." The trinitarian dimension remains central always (see chapters 9 and 10). The reconciling work for which the Son is sent is completed by the Holy Spirit.

Eucharistic Prayer II has its own *preface* which speaks of Jesus Christ as "the Word through whom you [the Father] made the universe, the Savior you sent to redeem us. By the power of the Holy Spirit he took flesh and was born of the Virgin Mary. For our sake he opened his arms on the cross; he put an end to death and revealed the resurrection. In this he fulfilled your will and won for you a holy people." The consecratory prayer is introduced with the words "Before he was given up to death, a death he freely accepted...."

Eucharistic Prayer III begins with the words "All life, all holiness comes from you [the Father] through your Son, Jesus Christ our Lord, by the working of the Holy Spirit." After the consecration, the Church calls "to mind the death your Son endured for our salvation, his glorious resurrection and ascension into heaven," and expresses its readiness "to greet him when he comes again." We pray that the Father will look with favor on the

Church's offering "and see the Victim whose death has reconciled us to yourself." Finally, we express the "hope to enjoy for ever the vision of your glory, through Christ our Lord, from whom all good things come."

Eucharistic Prayer IV acknowledges the goodness and mercy of the Father in not abandoning us to the power of death. "Father, you so loved the world that in the fullness of time you sent your only Son to be our Savior. He was conceived through the power of the Holy Spirit, and born of the Virgin Mary, a man like us in all things but sin. To the poor he proclaimed the good news of salvation, to prisoners, freedom, and to those in sorrow, joy. In fulfillment of your will he gave himself up to death; but by rising from the dead, he destroyed death and restored life. And that we might live no longer for ourselves but for him, he sent the Holy Spirit from you, Father, as his first gift to those who believe, to complete his work on earth and bring us the fullness of grace." And, as in all the Eucharistic Prayers, there is a recalling (*anamnesis*) of the redemptive work of Christ on our behalf, through his death, resurrection, exaltation, and coming again in glory. But this Eucharistic Prayer, more than the other three, underlines the redemptive significance of Jesus' earthly ministry *before* the crucifixion: his proclamation of the good news to the poor and the oppressed (see chapters 11 and 12).

Communion Rite

The Communion rite begins with the Lord's Prayer, and that, in turn, is introduced with such formulae as "Jesus taught us to call God our Father, and so we have the courage to say . . ." or "Let us pray for the coming of the kingdom as Jesus taught us. . . ." Afterwards, we pray to the Father to "Keep us free from sin and protect us from all anxiety as we wait in joyful hope for the coming of our Savior, Jesus Christ." We pray also *directly to Christ*, asking him to "look not on our sins, but on the faith of your Church, and grant us the peace and unity of your kingdom, where you live for ever and ever. Amen." Jesus Christ is not only our brother but our Lord as well. We pray not only with him but *to* him.

The eucharistic bread is broken, and the community prays: "Lamb of God, you take away the sins of the world, have mercy on us." Then the celebrant prays privately before Communion: "Lord Jesus Christ, Son of the living God, by the will of the Father and the work of the Holy Spirit your death brought life to the world." As the celebrant raises the host before the general distribution of Communion, he proclaims: "This is the Lamb of God who takes away the sins of the world." Again, Jesus' life and ministry, indeed his place in history, make no sense apart from the forgiveness of sins and the reconciliation of God and humankind.

THE OTHER SACRAMENTS
Penance

After the penitent's confession of sins, he or she makes an act of contrition which concludes with "Our Savior Jesus Christ suffered and died for us. In his name, my God, have mercy." Then the priest extends his hands over the penitent's head and pronounces the absolution: "God, the Father of mercies, through the death and resurrection of his Son has reconciled the world to himself and sent the Holy Spirit among us for the forgiveness of sins; through the ministry of the Church may God give you pardon and peace, and I absolve you from your sins in the name of the Father, and of the Son, and of the Holy Spirit."

One of the suggested prayers to be recited by a deacon or other minister within a public rite of reconciliation (to be followed by individual confession and absolution) focuses on the earthly life of Jesus, in keeping with the more recent "from below" Christologies (see chapter 15): "You were sent with good news for the poor and healing for the contrite"; "You came to call sinners, not the just"; "You forgave the many sins of the woman who showed you great love"; "You did not shun the company of outcasts and sinners"; "You carried back to the fold the sheep that had strayed"; "You did not condemn the woman taken in adultery, but sent her away in peace"; "You called Zacchaeus to repentance and a new life"; "You promised Paradise to the repentant thief." Each prayer is followed by the response "Lord, be merciful to me, a sinner" or simply "Lord, have mercy."

The entire public rite is concluded with a common prayer: "You sent your Son into the world to destroy sin and death by his passion, and to restore life and joy by his resurrection. . . . You have shown us your mercy and made us a new creation in the likeness of your Son."

Marriage

The Nuptial Blessing, recited after the Lord's Prayer of the Mass, refers to the newly wedded man and woman as "married in Christ." The marriage "symbolizes the marriage of Christ and his Church." Otherwise the distinctively Christological content of this sacrament is meagre.

Holy Order

Ordination of Deacons

In the instruction at the beginning of the rite, the bishop reminds the candidates that they are to be "ministers of Jesus Christ who was recognized among his disciples as the one who served." In the course of the examination of the candidate, the bishop asks if the new deacon will shape his way of life "according to the example of Christ." In the prayer of consecration itself, through which (in connection with the imposition of hands) the diaconate is conferred, the bishop speaks of Jesus Christ as the Father's Word, power, and wisdom. The deacons are to be "steadfast in Christ. Just as your own Son came not to be served but to give himself in service to others, may these deacons imitate him on earth and reign with him in heaven." Jesus Christ is at once Lord and *servant*.

Ordination of Priests

In the opening instruction by the bishop, he refers to Jesus Christ as "our high priest. . . sent by the Father," who, in turn, "sent the Apostles into the world so that through them and their successors, the bishops, he might continue forever his work as Teacher, Priest and Pastor." It is Christ's ministry "to make his own body, the

Church, grow into the people of God, a holy temple." Although priests are called to a ministry of instruction, it is always "in the name of Christ who is the chief Teacher." (See chapter 11.) The mystery of the death and resurrection of Jesus Christ is to provide the pattern for the priest's own ministry. All that the priest does as a priest, he does in the name of Christ and to carry on the work of Christ, who is "Head of the Church and its Pastor." The priest is to lead the faithful together like a unified family "through Christ and in the Holy Spirit to God the Father." Finally, the priest is always to "remember the example of the good shepherd who came to serve rather than to be served, to seek out and save what had gone astray."

In the course of the Examination, the bishop asks if the candidate is "resolved to unite [himself] more closely every day to Christ the first priest who offered himself for us to the Father as a perfect sacrifice." The consecratory prayer itself is only tangentially Christological. The bishop prays that "the gospel may reach the farthest parts of the earth, and [that] all nations, gathered together in Christ, may become one holy people of God."

As the newly ordained priest's hands are anointed, the bishop refers to Christ's own anointing by the Father through the power of the Holy Spirit. While the new priest is being invested in stole and chasuble, Psalm 100 may be sung, with the antiphon "Christ the Lord, a priest for ever according to the order of Melchisedech, offered bread and wine." Christ's redemptive and reconciling work on our behalf is a *priestly* work.

Ordination of a Bishop

The principal consecrator addresses the clergy, people, and bishop-elect on the duties of a bishop, and uses words to this effect: "Our Lord Jesus Christ, who was sent by the Father to redeem the human race, sent in turn twelve apostles into the world." The Apostles selected helpers for themselves and "passed on to them the gift of the Holy Spirit they had received from Christ." The Lord Jesus Christ is called "high priest for ever," one "present among you." This same Christ continues to proclaim the word of God and to unfold the mysteries of faith through the ministry of the bishop, and he adds to his Body and incorporates new members into it in the paternal functions of the bishop. Finally, through the bishop's wisdom and prudence Christ guides the Church in its earthly pilgrimage toward eternal happiness. (For a more detailed statement on the relationship between Christ and the Church, see chapters 17 and 20.)

The principal consecrator recalls the example of Christ himself. A bishop, like Christ, must serve rather than rule. "Such is the counsel of the Master that the most important should behave as if he were the least, and the leader as if he were the one who serves." (For a contrast, see chapter 11 on the image of Jesus as ruler, judge, and king.) The grace that the priest draws upon for the people has its source in the "the overflowing holiness of Christ." Christ is the good Shepherd "who knows his sheep and is always known by them and who did not hesitate to lay down his life for his sheep." The instruction refers, finally, to Christ's triple office of Teacher, Priest, and Pastor.

In the Examination the bishop-elect is also asked if he is resolved "to show kindness and compassion in the name of the Lord to the poor and to strangers and to all who are in need" and to be a good shepherd and "seek out the sheep who stray and to gather them into the fold of the Lord."

In the consecratory prayer all the bishops present, their hands joined, pray that "the perfect Spirit" who was given to Jesus Christ should flow out upon the bishop-elect.

Anointing of the Sick

As the priest enters the sickroom, he addresses those present in these or similar words: "We have come together in the name of our Lord Jesus Christ, who restored the sick to health, and who himself suffered much for our sake." He says a prayer of thanksgiving over the holy oil: "Praise to you, almighty God and Father. You sent your son to live among us and bring us salvation. Praise to you, Lord Jesus Christ, the Father's only Son. You humbled yourself to share in our humanity, and you desired to cure all illnesses." And then, as the priest anoints the sick person, he says, "May the Lord who frees you from sin save you and raise you up." An alternate prayer after the anointing reads: "Lord Jesus Christ, you shared in our human nature to heal the sick and save all mankind."

After the giving of Communion, the rite concludes with this prayer: "Father, your son, Jesus Christ, is our way, our truth and our life. Our brother (sister) entrusts himself (herself) to you with full confidence in all your promises. Refresh him (her) with the body and blood of your Son and lead him (her) to your kingdom in peace. We ask this through Christ our Lord. Amen." Finally, the priest imparts a blessing in the name of "the Father, and the Son, and the Holy Spirit."

SUMMARY

1.   The eucharistic and other sacramental rites of the Catholic Church at once express and confirm the major Christological principles: the redemptive significance of the death and resurrection, the centrality of the Kingdom of God in Jesus' preaching and in our own mission and hope, the centrality of Jesus Christ to all of salvation history.

2.   Christian initiation occurs over the course of three sacraments: Baptism, Confirmation, and the Eucharist. In *Baptism*—and in the catechumate rites leading up to it—Christ is "the light" for our way to eternal life: He is our leader and example for Christian existence; by the power of the Holy Spirit, he drives out the spirits of evil and makes the Kingdom draw nearer; he is the Christ of God, the Almighty; his death and resurrection are the source of our life from God; he does not abandon us even when we sin, but offers us the peace and forgiveness of the Kingdom.

3.   Christ is our teacher (prophet), priest, and king; he alone is the Holy One, the true light that enlightens all; he proclaims the good news of life to rescue us from the kingdom of death and lead us to the resurrection; his miracles, especially the raising of Lazarus, are signs that he had come to give us life in the fullest measure.

4.   *Confirmation* completes the baptismal rite. The Church prays that, through the working of the Holy Spirit, the new Christian might be strengthened to be more like Christ, the Son of God, through the witness of his or her life.

5.   Christology-as-worship is most fully expresed in the *Eucharist*.

6.   The *third penitential rite* speaks of Christ healing the contrite, calling sinners, pleading for us at the right hand of God, reconciling us to

the Father, healing the wounds of sin and division, raising the dead to life in the Holy Spirit, bringing pardon and peace, forgiving sins, healing the sick. The *Gloria* continues these themes and addresses Christ as "alone...the Holy One,...the Lord,...the Most High."

7.   *The Nicaeo-Constantinopolitan Creed* encapsulates the whole conciliar tradition, which culminates eventually in the dogmatic decrees of the Council of Chalcedon. Jesus Christ is the eternal Son of God, begotten, not made, who became a human being for our salvation and who accomplished that salvation through his passion, death, and resurrection. He will come again in glory, and his kingdom will have no end.

8.   *Eucharistic Prayer I* emphasizes that the Mass is an act of praise and thanksgiving to the Father *through* Jesus Christ, that we have a new and everlasting covenant in his blood, which was shed for the forgiveness of sins.

9.   *Eucharistic Prayer II* has its own *preface* which speaks of Christ as the Word through whom the Father made the universe and the Savior he sent to redeem us. He put an end to death and revealed the resurrection, and so won for the Father a holy people. Indeed, he freely accepted the death by which he conquered sin and death.

10.   *Eucharistic Prayer III* begins with "All life, all holiness comes from [the Father] through [the] Son, Jesus Christ our Lord, by the working of the Holy Spirit." It asks, after the consecration, that the Father will look upon the Church's offering and "see the Victim whose death has reconciled us" to the Father. Finally, it expresses hope that we shall enjoy the vision of his glory, through Christ.

11.   *Eucharistic Prayer IV* explicitly employs the text from Hebrews 4:15 and the Council of Chalcedon which says that Jesus was like us in all things except sin. It puts Christ's saving work in an historical context and refers more directly than the other Eucharistic Prayers to Jesus' earthly ministry of proclaiming the good news to the poor, freedom to prisoners, joy to those in sorrow. By rising from the dead, he destroyed death and restored life, and then sent us the Holy Spirit to complete his work on earth and to bring us the fullness of grace.

12.   In all of the Eucharistic Prayers there are the *memorial acclamations* following the consecration which declare that Christ died, rose, and will return; that he destroyed death through *his* death and restored life through his resurrection; that he set us free by both; and that he is the Savior of the world.

13.   In each of the Eucharistic Prayers there is also the *anamnesis*, or recalling, of what Christ did to accomplish our redemption: He died, rose, was exalted, and will come again.

14.   Finally, all of the Eucharistic Prayers end with the words "Through him, with him, in him, in the unity of the Holy Spirit, all glory and honor is yours, almighty Father, for ever and ever. Amen."

15.   The *Communion Rite* begins with the Lord's Prayer, and that, in turn, is introduced by formulae which recall that Jesus taught us to address God as Father, to pray for the coming of the Kingdom, to forgive sins against us. Christ keeps us free from sin and anxiety now, and he will come again in a final act of salvation. His death brought life to the world, we are reminded as Communion is about to be distributed.

16.   The same themes are sounded in the sacrament of *Penance*: Christ suffered, died, and rose for our salvation, and sends the Holy Spirit for the forgiveness of sins. One of the suggested prayers for a public celebration of Penance underlines the earthly ministry of Jesus: his concern for the poor, the outcasts, sinners.

17.   *Marriage* establishes a union "in Christ" akin to the union of Christ and the Church.

18.   *Holy Order* is conferred at three ministerial levels: the diaconate, the priesthood (or presbyterate), and the episcopacy. In all, the example of Christ who came to serve, and not to be served, is held up as a model.

19.   In the ordination to the *priesthood*, the priesthood of Christ himself is emphasized. He is teacher, priest, and pastor. He is also head of the Church. He seeks to unify the whole human family in the Holy Spirit. The same themes are reiterated in the ordination of a *bishop*.

20.   The sacrament of the *Anointing of the Sick* highlights Jesus' concern for healing of body as well as of soul, and recalls that he suffered much for our sake. Indeed, he shared our human nature in order to heal the sick and save all humankind, that all might be led to the Kingdom.

SUGGESTED READINGS

The Rites of the Catholic Church as Revised by Decree of the Second Vatican Ecumenical Council and Published by Authority of Pope Paul VI. New York: Pueblo Publishing Co., 1976.

The Roman Missal: Revised by Decree of the Second Vatican Council and Published by Authority of Pope Paul VI. Washington: National Conference of Catholic Bishops, 1970.

The Roman Pontifical: Revised by Decree of the Second Vatican Council and Published by Authority of Pope Paul VI. Washington: National Conference of Catholic Bishops, 1973.

APPENDIX

The Creed of the Council of Constantinople (381) (The council of Constantinople was convened to reaffirm the faith of the council of Nicea, of 325. Though not itself promulgated by the council of Constantinople, this creed soon acquired greater authority than even the Nicene Creed. Since the seventh century it has been known as the *Nicene-Constantinopolitan Creed.)*

> We believe in one God,
>   the Father, the Almighty,
>   maker of heaven and earth,
>   of all that is seen and unseen.
> We believe in one Lord, Jesus Christ,
>   the only Son of God,
>   eternally begotten of the Father,
>   God from God, Light from Light,
>   true God from true God,
>   begotten, not made, one in Being with the Father.
>   Through him all things were made.
>   For us men and for our salvation
>   he came down from heaven:
>   by the power of the Holy Spirit
>   he was born of the Virgin Mary, and became man.
>   For our sake he was crucified under Pontius Pilate;
>   he suffered, died, and was buried.
>   On the third day he rose again
>   in fulfillment of the Scriptures;
>   he ascended into heaven
>   and is seated at the right hand of the Father.
>   He will come again in glory to judge the living and the
>   dead,
>   and his kingdom will have no end.
> We believe in the Holy Spirit, the Lord, the giver of life,
>   who proceeds from the Father and the Son.
>   With the Father and the Son he is worshiped and
>   glorified.
>   He has spoken through the Prophets.
> We believe in one holy catholic and apostolic Church.
> We acknowledge one baptism for the forgiveness of sins.
> We look for the resurrection of the dead,
>   and the life of the world to come. Amen.

Instruction on the Historical Truth of the Gospels, Pontifical Biblical Commission, April 21, 1964. (Excerpt. Full text in the *Catholic Biblical Quarterly,* vol. 26, July 1964, pp. 305-312.)

1. The Catholic exegete, under the guidance of the Church, must turn to account all the resources for the understanding of the sacred text which have been put at his disposal by previous interpreters, especially the holy Fathers and Doctors of the Church, whose labors it is for him to take up and to carry on. In order to bring out with fullest clarity the enduring truth and authority of the Gospels he must, whilst carefully observing the rules of rational and of Catholic hermeneutics, make skillful use of the new aids to exegesis, especially those which the historical method, taken in its widest sense, has provided; that method, namely, which minutely investigates sources, determining their nature and bearing, and availing itself of the findings of textual criticism, literary criticism, and linguistic studies. The interpreter must be alert to the reminder given him by Pope Pius XII of happy memory when he charged him "to make judicious inquiry as to how far the form of expression or the type of literature adopted by the sacred writer may help towards the true and genuine interpretation, and to remain convinced that this part of his task cannot be neglected without great detriment to Catholic exegesis."[5] In this reminder Pius XII of happy memory is laying down a general rule of hermeneutics, one by whose help the books both of the Old Testament and of the New are to be explained, since the sacred writers when composing them followed the way of thinking and of writing current amongst their contemporaries. In a word, the exegete must make use of every means which will help him to reach a deeper understanding of the character of the gospel testimony, of the religious life of the first churches, and of the significance and force of the apostolic tradition.

In appropriate cases the interpreter is free to seek out what sound elements there are in "the Method of Form-history," and these he can duly make use of to gain a fuller understanding of the Gospels. He must be circumspect in doing so, however, because the method in question is often found alloyed with principles of a philosophical or theological nature which are quite inadmissible, and which not infrequently vitiate both the method itself and the conclusions arrived at regarding literary questions. For certain exponents of this method, led astray by rationalistic prejudices, refuse to admit that there exists a supernatural order, or that a personal God intervenes in the world by revelation properly so called, or that miracles and prophecies are possible and have actually occurred. There are others who have as their starting-point a wrong notion of faith, taking it that faith is indifferent to historical truth, and is

indeed incompatible with it. Others practically deny *a priori* the historical value and character of the documents of revelation. Others finally
there are who on the one hand underestimate the authority which the
Apostles had as witnesses of Christ, and the office and influence which
they wielded in the primitive community, whilst on the other hand they
overestimate the creative capacity of the community itself. All these
aberrations are not only opposed to Catholic doctrine, but are also devoid
of any scientific foundation, and are foreign to the genuine principles of
the historical method.

2. In order to determine correctly the trustworthiness of what is
transmitted in the Gospels, the interpreter must take careful note of the
three stages of tradition by which the teaching and the life of Jesus have
come down to us.

Christ our Lord attached to Himself certain chosen disciples[6] who
had followed Him from the beginning,[7] who had seen His works and had
heard His words, and thus were qualified to become witnesses of His life
and teaching.[8] Our Lord, when expounding His teaching by word of
mouth, observed the methods of reasoning and of exposition which were
in common use at the time; in this way He accommodated Himself to the
mentality of His hearers, and ensured that His teachings would be deeply
impressed on their minds and would be easily retained in memory by His
disciples. These latter grasped correctly the idea that the miracles and
other events of the life of Jesus were things purposely performed or
arranged by Him in such a way that men would thereby be led to believe
in Christ and to accept by faith the doctrine of salvation.

The Apostles, bearing testimony to Jesus,[9] proclaimed first and foremost the death and resurrection of the Lord, faithfully recounting His
life and words[10] and, as regards the manner of their preaching, taking
into account the circumstances of their hearers.[11] After Jesus had risen
from the dead, and when His divinity was clearly perceived,[12] the faith of
the disciples, far from blotting out the remembrance of the events that
had happened, rather consolidated it, since their faith was based on what
Jesus had done and taught.[13] Nor was Jesus transformed into a "mythi-
cal" personage, and His teaching distorted, by reason of the worship
which the disciples now paid Him, revering Him as Lord and Son of God.
Yet it need not be denied that the Apostles, when handing on to their
hearers the things which in actual fact the Lord had said and done, did so
in the light of that fuller understanding which they enjoyed as a result of
being schooled by the glorious things accomplished in Christ,[14] and of
being illumined by the Spirit of Truth.[15] Thus it came about that, just as
Jesus Himself after His resurrection had "interpreted to them"[16] both the
words of the Old Testament and the words which He Himself had
spoken,[17] so now they in their turn interpreted His words and deeds

according to the needs of their hearers. "Devoting (themselves) to the ministry of the word,"[18] they made use, as they preached, of such various forms of speech as were adapted to their own purposes and to the mentality of their hearers; for it was "to Greek and barbarian, to learned and simple,"[19] that they had a duty to discharge.[20] These varied ways of speaking which the heralds of Christ made use of in proclaiming Him must be distinguished one from the other and carefully appraised: catecheses, narratives, testimonies, hymns, doxologies, prayers and any other such literary forms as were customarily employed in Sacred Scripture and by people of that time.

The sacred authors, for the benefit of the churches, took this earliest body of instruction, which had been handed on orally at first and then in writing—for many soon set their hands to "drawing up a narrative"[21] of matters concerning the Lord Jesus—and set it down in the four Gospels. In doing this each of them followed a method suitable to the special purpose which he had in view. They selected certain things out of the many which had been handed on; some they synthesized, some they explained with an eye to the situation of the churches, painstakingly using every means of bringing home to their readers the solid truth of the things in which they had been instructed.[22] For, out of the material which they had received, the sacred authors selected especially those items which were adapted to the varied circumstances of the faithful as well as to the end which they themselves wished to attain; these they recounted in a manner consonant with those circumstances and with that end. And since the meaning of a statement depends, amongst other things, on the place which it has in a given sequence, the Evangelists, in handing on the words or the deeds of our Savior, explained them for the advantage of their readers by respectively setting them, one Evangelist in one context, another in another. For this reason the exegete must ask himself what the Evangelist intended by recounting a saying or a fact in a certain way, or by placing it in a certain context. For the truth of the narrative is not affected in the slightest by the fact that the Evangelists report the sayings or the doings of our Lord in a different order,[23] and that they use different words to express what He said, not keeping to the very letter, but nevertheless preserving the sense.[24] For, as St. Augustine says: "Where it is a question only of those matters whose order in the narrative may be indifferently this or that without in any way taking from the truth and authority of the Gospel, it is probable enough that each Evangelist believed he should narrate them in that same order in which God was pleased to suggest them to his recollection. The Holy Spirit distributes His gifts to each one according as He wills;[25] therefore, too, for the sake of those Books which were to be set so high at the very summit of authority, He undoubtedly guided and controlled the minds of the holy writers in their recollection of what they were to write; but as to why, in doing so, He should have permitted them, one to follow this order in his narrative, another to follow that—that is a question whose answer may possibly be found with God's help, if one seeks it out with reverent care."[26]

Unless the exegete, then, pays attention to all those factors which have a bearing on the origin and the composition of the Gospels, and makes due use of the acceptable findings of modern research, he will fail in his duty of ascertaining what the intentions of the sacred writers were, and what it is that they have actually said. The results of recent study have made it clear that the teachings and the life of Jesus were not simply recounted for the mere purpose of being kept in remembrance, but were "preached" in such a way as to furnish the Church with the foundation on which to build up faith and morals. It follows that the interpreter who subjects the testimony of the Evangelists to persevering scrutiny will be in a position to shed further light on the enduring theological value of the Gospels, and to throw into clearest relief the vital importance of the Church's interpretation.

[5] *Divino afflante Spiritu; EB* 560.
[6] Cf. *Mc.* 3,14; *Lc.* 6,13.
[7] Cf. *Lc.* 1,2; *Act.* 1,21-22.
[8] Cf. *Lc.* 24,48; *Jn.* 15,27; *Act.* 1,8; 10,39; 13,31.
[9] Cf. *Lc.* 24, 44-48; *Act.* 2,32; 3,15; 5,30-32.
[10] Cf. *Act.* 10,36-41.
[11] Cf. *Act.* 13,16-41 with *Act.* 17,22-31.
[12] *Act.* 2,36; *Jn.* 20,28.
[18] *Act* 2,22; 10,37-39.
[14] *Jn.* 2,22; 12,16; 11,51-52; cf. 14,26; 16,12-13; 7,39.
[15] Cf. *Jn.* 14,26; 16,13.
[16] *Lc.* 24,27.
[17] Cf. *Lc.* 24,44-45; *Act.* 1,3.
[18] *Act.* 6,4.
[19] *Rom.* 1,14.
[20] *1 Cor.* 9,19-23.
[21] Cf. *Lc.* 1,1.
[22] Cf. *Lc.* 1,4.
[23] Cf. St. John Chrys., *In Mat. Hom.* I,3; *PG* 57,16,17.
[24] Cf. St August., *De consensu Evang.* 2,12,28; *PL* 34, 1090-1091.
[25] *I Cor.* 12,11.
[26] *De consensu Evang.,* 2, 21, 51 s.; *PL* 34,1102.

*Declaration in Defense of the Catholic Doctrine on the Church Against
Certain Errors of the Present Day (Mysterium Ecclesiae),* Congregation
for the Doctrine of the Faith, June 24, 1973. (Excerpt. Full text in
Origins: NC Documentary Service, vol. 3, July 19, 1973, pp. 97,99,100.)

The transmission of divine Revelation by the Church encounters
difficulties of various kinds. These arise from the fact that the hidden
mysteries of God 'by their nature so far transcend the human intellect
that even if they are revealed to us and accepted by faith, they remain
concealed by the veil of faith itself and are as it were wrapped in
darkness'. Difficulties arise also from the historical condition that affects
the expression of Revelation.

With regard to this historical condition, it must first be observed
that the meaning of the pronouncements of faith depend partly upon the
expressive power of the language used at a certain point in time and in
particular circumstances. Moreover, it sometimes happens that some
dogmatic truth is first expressed incompletely (but not falsely), and at a
later date, when considered in a broader context of faith or human
knowledge, it receives a fuller and more perfect expression. In addition,
when the Church makes new pronouncements she intends to confirm or
clarify what is in some way contained in Sacred Scripture or in previous
expressions of Tradition; but at the same time she usually has the intention of solving certain questions or removing certain errors. All these
things have to be taken into account in order that these pronouncements
may be properly interpreted. Finally, even though the truths which the
Church intends to teach through her dogmatic formulas are distinct from
the changeable conceptions of a given epoch and can be expressed without them, nevertheless it can sometimes happen that these truths may be
enunciated by the Sacred Magisterium in terms that bear traces of such
conceptions.

In view of the above, it must be stated that the dogmatic formulas of
the Church's Magisterium were from the very beginning suitable for
communicating revealed truth, and that as they are they remain for ever
suitable for communicating this truth to those who interpret them correctly. It does not however follow that every one of these formulas has
always been or will always be so to the same extent. For this reason
theologians seek to define exactly the intention of teaching proper to the
various formulas, and in carrying out this work they are of considerable
assistance to the living Magisterium of the Church, to which they remain
subordinated. For this reason also it oftens happens that ancient dogmatic formulas and others closely connected with them remain living
and fruitful in the habitual usage of the Church, but with suitable
expository and explanatory additions that maintain and clarify their

original meaning. In addition, it has sometimes happened that in this habitual usage of the Church certain of these formulas gave way to new expressions which, proposed and approved by the Sacred Magisterium, presented more clearly or more completely the same meaning.

As for the meaning of dogmatic formulas, this remains ever true and constant in the Church, even when it is expressed with greater clarity or [is] more developed. The faithful therefore must shun the opinion, first, that dogmatic formulas (or some category of them) cannot signify truth in a determinate way, but can only offer changeable approximations to it, which to a certain extent distort or alter it; secondly, that these formulas signify the truth only in an indeterminate way, this truth being like a goal that is constantly being sought by means of such approximations. Those who hold such an opinion do not avoid dogmatic relativism and they corrupt the concept of the Church's infallibility relative to the truth to be taught or held in a determinate way.

•••

"A Courageous Worldwide Theology," an address by Karl Rahner, S.J., at John Carroll University, Cleveland, Ohio, April 6, 1979, on the occasion of receiving an honorary degree marking his seventy-fifth birthday. (Excerpt. Full text in *National Jesuit News,* vol. 8, June 1979, p. 10.)

It is my preference that both the tribute and my thanks be directed toward the contemporary theology in its entirety—that theology shaped in the last 30 years and recognized somewhat officially by the Second Vatican Council.

Of course, I have in mind an orthodox Catholic theology. That goes without saying. A theology which would not be obedient and docile under the word of God as it is proclaimed in the Church would not be Catholic theology. But I am envisaging a Catholic theology that is courageous and does not shun relative and restricted conflicts with Church authorities. I am thinking of a theology which can no longer be uniform in a neoscholastic approach.

I call that time of uniformity the "Pius epoch," but that era of the Popes who bore the name "Pius" has after all come to an end. I envisage a theology which is in dialogue with its time and lives courageously with it and in it.

This is all the more possible because it is characteristic of this time to be at a critical distance from itself, something *God makes possible.* It is a special grace to this age to be able now to have a critical distance from ourselves given us from the Cross of Christ.

From this more critical distance, I envisage a theology which in the Church at large must be the theology of a worldwide Church. That means a theology which does not only recite its own medieval history, but one that can listen to the wisdom of the East, to the longing for freedom in Latin America, and also to the sound of African drums.

I envisage a systematic theology that is an inner unity and what Trinitarian theologians call *perichoresis* (literally a dancing around together) of fundamental and dogmatic theology. I envisage a theology that enables human beings of our time to have a real grasp on the message of freedom and redemption, a theology that courageously abandons external stanchions of seemingly self-evident truths and things, something which does not stem necessarily from what is Christian, but rather from the changing historical situation structured by its intellectual and social elements.

I envisage a theology that does not only move along the numbers in our familiar friend "Denzinger" interpreting old ecclesiastical pronouncements, but a theology which breaks new ground for *new* pronouncements of the Church.

It would be a theology which takes seriously the hierarchy of truths, a theology which lives by the ecumenical hope that baptized Christians should be able to communicate in that which they all live in their faith. Such a communication should be possible without losing sight of the multiplicity of charisms of life and thought.

I envisage a theology which comprehends itself as an interpretation of the reality which through grace is present in every human being; a reality which is not only given to man by external indoctrination.

It would be a theology through which this reality would find itself, and which would not pride itself upon its clear concepts but would force them to open over and over again into the incomprehensibility of God himself. Such a theology would not secretly seek to understand itself as *the* theoretical underpinning of a life of middle-class ethics supervised by God.

One could continue in this vein for long. But my purpose is not to degrade the old theology, whose grateful children we are and remain. It has been rather to hint from afar that our time calls also us theologians sleeping under the broom tree of orthodoxy like Elijah in old days: *Surge, grandis tibi restat via*—Arise, a long journey lies ahead of you.

GLOSSARY

(The purpose of this glossary is *not* to provide new information or greater precision. Each term has already been explained, and in most cases defined, in the text itself. The reader should consult the Index of Subjects for such references. The glossary is provided instead as a convenience to the reader, as a quick memory-refresher and time-saver.)

ADOPTIONISM   General term for views which look upon Jesus Christ as the purely human, "adopted" son of God.

AGNOSTICISM   The suspension of belief regarding the reality of God.

ALEXANDRIA, SCHOOL OF   Theological and catechetical center in Egypt, from the end of the second century, which emphasized the divinity of Christ. (Principal representatives: Clement, Origen.)

ANATHEMA   An official condemnation by the Church of a doctrinal or moral position.

ANNULMENT   An official declaration by the Church that a presumed marriage never really existed in the first place—e.g., because the couple was psychologically incapable of making a permanent commitment.

ANTHROPOLOGY, THEOLOGICAL   The meaning of human existence in light of God, Christ, redemption, etc.

ANTICHRIST   The embodiment of all historical forces hostile to God.

ANTINOMIANISM   An attitude which rejects any and every law as the basis of Christian conduct.

ANTIOCH, SCHOOL OF   Theological and catechetical center in Syria, from the end of the second century, which emphasized the humanity of Jesus. (Principal representatives: Arius, Theodore of Mopsuestia, John Chrysostom.)

APOCALYPTICISM   A comprehensive name for a style of thought and writing associated with the later period of the Old Testament (e.g., Daniel), the period between the two Testaments, and the New Testament itself. Emphasis is on visions, signs, and predictions of future events brought about entirely by divine power, beyond history.

APOKATASTASIS The belief, associated especially with Origen, that every human being will eventually be saved.

APOLOGETICS. That part of theology which tries to show the reasonableness of Christian faith.

APOSTLE A missionary or messenger of the Church in the New Testament period. The term is not coextensive with *the Twelve* (see below).

APOSTOLIC SUCCESSION In the wider sense, the process by which the whole Church continues, and is faithful to, the word, the witness, and the service of the Apostles. In the stricter sense, the legitimation of the bishops' office and authority by their valid derivation from the Apostles.

ARIANISM The heresy, condemned by the council of Nicea (325), which made the Son of God the highest of creatures, greater than we but less than God.

ASCETICISM Exercises undertaken to live the Gospel more faithfully, especially in light of the cross of Christ and the sacrificial nature of his whole life.

ASSUMPTION Dogma defined in 1950 by Pope Pius XII that the body of the Blessed Virgin Mary was taken directly to heaven after her life on earth had ended.

ATHEISM The denial of the reality of God.

ATONEMENT The act of healing the breach between God and humankind opened by sin. Usually associated with the crucifixion of Christ.

AUTHENTICITY OF CHURCH TEACHINGS A quality of teachings which have authority because they are issued by persons holding a canonically recognized teaching office in the Church.

AUTHENTICITY OF SACRED SCRIPTURE A quality of the various books of the Bible by which they are recognized to have been produced by the individuals or communities with whom the Church associates these writings.

BAIANISM Unorthodox sixteenth-century view which held that after Original Sin everything we do is sinful. We have no real freedom of choice.

BAPTISM OF DESIRE The process by which individuals are said to merit eternal life because of their good will, even though, through no fault of their own, they have not been baptized with water.

BASILEIA   The Greek word for "Kingdom (of God)."

BEATIFIC VISION   Our final union with God in heaven.

BELIEF   Any expression of faith. Not all beliefs are *doctrines* or *dogmas* (see below).

CANON   A list which seves as a "measure" or standard.

CANON LAW   The code of Church laws promulgated in 1918. More generally, any official code, or listing, of Church laws.

CANON OF SCRIPTURE   The official list of inspired books of the Bible, solemnly defined by the Council of Trent (1546).

CANONICAL FORM   The requirement of the Catholic Church that every Catholic be married in the presence of a priest and two witnesses, unless specifically dispensed.

CASUISTRY   An approach to the solution of moral problems which reduces theology to canon law, i.e., to a solver of "cases" ("Is it sinful? If so, how seriously?").

CATECHESIS   The process of "echoing" the Gospel, of introducing young people or adult converts to the main elements of the Christian faith.

CATECHISM   A handbook for catechesis. Usually in question-and-answer form.

CATECHUMEN   One who is undergoing catechesis.

CATECHUMENATE   The formal stage of preparation for entrance into the Church.

CHALCEDON   The city in Asia Minor where in 451 the fourth ecumenical council was held in which it was defined that Jesus Christ is true God and true man, and that his divine and human natures are united in one divine person, without confusion, change, division, or separation.

CHARACTER, MORAL   That which gives orientation, direction, and shape to our lives. The cluster of virtues which make a person what he or she is.

CHARACTER, SACRAMENTAL   The permanent effect of three sacraments: Baptism, Confirmation, and Holy Order. (Hence, these sacraments are never conferred more than once.)

CHARISM   A gift of the Holy Spirit—e.g., wisdom.

CHARISMATIC   One who manifests and is attentive to the gifts of the Holy Spirit.

CHRISTOCENTRISM Seeing all reality, and therefore all of theology, in light of Jesus Christ.

CHRISTOLOGY The theological study of Jesus Christ: natures, person, ministry, consciousness, etc. Christology "from above" starts with the Word of God (*Logos*) in heaven and views Jesus as the Word who has come down to earth for our salvation (John and Paul). Christology "from below" starts with the Jesus of history and shows how his earthly life is significant for our salvation (the Synoptics).

CHRISTOMONISM Seeing all reality, and doing all theology, only in light of Jesus Christ, so that there is no revelation or salvation apart from Christ and apart from explicit faith in him.

CIRCUMINCESSION The presence, or indwelling, of the three divine Persons in one another. The Son and the Holy Spirit are present in the Father, and the Father in the Son and the Holy Spirit. The Father and the Son are present in the Holy Spirit, and the Holy Spirit in the Father and the Son. And so forth. Known also as *perichoresis.*

CLASSICISM The philosophical world view which holds that reality (truth) is essentially static, unchanging, and unaffected by history. Such truth can readily be captured in propositions or statements whose meaning is fixed and clear from century to century.

COGNITIVE Pertaining to knowledge. A theological approach is said to be "cognitive" if it emphasizes knowledge, the intellect, principles rather than emotions, imagination, the will, the subject, the situation, and circumstances.

COLLEGIALITY The principle that the Church is a community (college) of local churches which together make up the Church universal. In practice, collegiality introduces a mode of decision-making in the Church which emphasizes coresponsibility not only between the pope and the bishops but also among all communities and groups within the Body of Christ.

COMMUNICATIO IDIOMATUM The "communication of properties" between the divine and human natures of Jesus Christ because both natures are united in one divine Person, without confusion. The properties of both natures can and must be applied to, or predicated of, the one divine person; e.g., "The Word of God was crucified."

COMMUNICATIO IN SACRIS Literally, "communication in sacred things." It refers to Catholic and non-Catholic Christians sharing in the Eucharist by receiving Holy Communion in one or another's liturgy.

COMMUNION OF SAINTS   The whole community of believers in Christ, living and dead. Those on earth are called the *Church Militant*. Those in purgatory are the *Church Suffering*. Those in heaven are the *Church Triumphant*.

CONCILIARISM   The medieval movement which viewed an ecumenical council as superior in authority to the pope.

CONCUPISCENCE   Natural "desires," impulses, or instincts of the human person which move the person toward something morally good or morally evil even before he or she has begun any moral reflection about it.

CONSCIENCE   The experience of ourselves as moral agents, as persons responsible for our actions. Decisions are made in light of who we think we are and are called to become.

CONSERVATISM, BIBLICAL   The tendency to take the accounts of Sacred Scripture at face value—e.g., Jesus really understood himself to be the Messiah and the Son of God right from the beginning of his life and ministry.

CONSERVATISM, THEOLOGICAL   The tendency to adhere to the literal meaning of the official teachings of the Church and to emphasize their decisive authority in matters under discussion among theologians.

CONSUBSTANTIATION   The Reformation view that the bread and wine remain along with the body and blood of Christ after the eucharistic consecration ("This is my body. . . . This is my blood. . . ."). It is distinguished from *transubstantiation* (see below).

CONTEMPLATION   Conscious attention to the presence of God in the depths of oneself, in others, and in the world. A form of prayer.

CONTEMPLATIVE   Generally, one whose life is governed by the spirit and practice of contemplation. Specifically, a member of a monastic community.

CONVENIENCE, ARGUMENT FROM   A method of reaching theological conclusions not on the basis of sources (Bible, doctrines, etc.) but on the basis of the seeming appropriateness of a particular conclusion. The usual form of such an argument is: It is fitting that God should have done so; God had the power to do so; therefore, God must have done so. Especially applicable to *Mariology* (see below).

CONVERSION   The fundamental change of heart (*metanoia*) by which a person accepts Jesus as the Christ and orients his or her whole life around Christ and the Kingdom of God which he proclaimed.

COREDEMPTRIX   A title sometimes given to the Blessed Virgin Mary to emphasize her cooperative role in the redemption of the human race by Christ.

COUNCIL   An official church assembly. It is *ecumenical*, or *general*, if it draws representatives from the "whole wide world." It is *regional* if it draws representatives from various dioceses in a particular region of the world or of a particular nation. It is *local* if it involves only a particular diocese, or local church.

COUNTER-REFORMATION   The Catholic response to the Protestant Reformation of the sixteenth century. At the center was the *Council of Trent* and its reform of doctrine, liturgy, and law.

COVENANT   The bond, contract, or "testament" between God and Israel in the Old Testament, established with Noah, Abraham, Moses, and David, and between God and the whole human community in the New Testament, established by the blood of Christ.

COVENANTAL   Pertaining to the close bond of love and friendship between God and ourselves.

CREED   An official profession of faith, usually promulgated by a council of the Church and used in the Church's liturgy.

CRITICISM, FORM   A method of biblical study employed to uncover the second layer of tradition in the composition of the Gospels, namely, the oral proclamation of the Apostles and the disciples (catechesis, narratives, hymns, prayers, etc.).

CRITICISM, HISTORICAL   A method of biblical study employed to uncover the first layer of tradition in the composition of the Gospels, namely, the original words and deeds of Jesus. It asks, "How can we know the historical Jesus?"

CRITICISM, REDACTION   A method of biblical study employed to uncover the third layer of tradition in the composition of the Gospels, namely, the writings themselves. It tries to identify the dominant ideas which governed the final editing of the texts as we have them today.

DECALOGUE   The Ten Commandments.

DEISM A view of God which looks upon God as a divine "watch-maker." Once the world has been created, God no longer takes an active part in its course. Rejected by Vatican I (1869).

DEMYTHOLOGIZATION A method of New Testament interpretation originated by Rudolf Bultmann. It seeks to get back to the original message of Jesus by stripping away all irrelevant stories (myths) about Jesus' divine powers and his comings and goings between heaven and earth.

DEONTOLOGICAL Pertaining to a way of doing moral theology which emphasizes duty and obligation (*deontos*) in relation to law.

DEPOSIT OF FAITH The "content" of Christian faith given by Christ and the Apostles and preserved as a treasury by the Church ever since.

DESCENT INTO HELL The item in the Apostles' Creed which refers to the time between the crucifixion and the resurrection when Jesus was "among the dead." It does not refer to hell as a state of eternal punishment for sin, but rather to *Sheol* (see below).

DIACONATE The ministry of, and state of being, a deacon of the Church, i.e., an ordained assistant to the bishop or the *presbyter* (see below).

DIALECTICAL Pertaining to a way of understanding reality by noting and keeping in balance seemingly opposite values—e.g., God is wholly Other, but God is also one with us in Christ; the Bible is the Word of God, but it is also the product of human effort; we are sinners, but we are also graced and redeemed.

DISCERNMENT The process, associated with the virtue of prudence, by which we try to decide what God wills us to do in these particular circumstances and for the future.

DISCIPLE A follower of Christ. One who literally "learns from" Christ. All Apostles were disciples, but not all disciples were *Apostles* (see above).

DISPENSATION An action of the official Church by which an individual or individuals are exempted from an ecclesiastical law, temporarily or permanently.

DOCETIC Pertaining to a theological attitude which tends to deny the reality of the material and the bodily in creation, redemption, and salvation.

DOCETISM A view which held that Christ only "seemed" to have a human body.

DOCTRINE   An official teaching of the Church.

DOCTRINE, DEVELOPMENT OF   The process by which official teachings are revised in accordance with changes in historical circumstances and understanding.

DOGMA   A doctrine which is promulgated with the highest authority and solemnity. Its denial is a *heresy* (see below). Every dogma is a doctrine, but not every doctrine is a dogma.

DOGMATIC THEOLOGY   Systematic reflection on the Christian faith as that faith has been articulated by the official Church.

DONATISM   A North African movement of the fourth century which held that Baptism had to be administered a second time to those who had left the Church and then returned. Opposed strongly by Augustine.

DOUBLE EFFECT, PRINCIPLE OF   The principle which holds that an evil effect can be permitted so long as it is not directly intended, is not the means of achieving a good effect, and is not out of proportion to the good effect.

DUALISM   The general theological view that all reality is composed of, and arises from, two distinct, absolutely independent, antagonistic, and co-equal principles: Good and Evil.

ECCLESIAL   Pertaining to the Church as a mystery, i.e., as the Body of Christ and the Temple of the Holy Spirit, as distinguished from *ecclesiastical*, which pertains to the Church as an institution.

ECCLESIOLOGY   The theological study of the Church.

ECUMENICAL   Pertaining to a theological attitude which is attentive to the experience and critical reflections of other churches and traditions.

ECUMENISM   The movement which seeks to achieve unity of Christians within the Church and ultimately of all humankind throughout the "whole wide world" (the literal meaning of the word).

ENCYCLICAL   A letter written by the pope and "circulated" throughout the whole Church and even the whole world beyond the Church.

ENLIGHTENMENT   The eighteenth-century philosophical movement which exalted freedom of inquiry and freedom in decision-making. A *post-Enlightenment* mentality criticizes the Enlightenment for its "uncritical" celebration of reason and its failure to attend to the imagination and the larger social context of our ideas.

EPHESUS   A city in Asia Minor where the third ecumenical council was held in 431. It condemned *Nestorianism* (see below) and held that Mary is truly the Mother of God (*theotokos*).

EPISCOPACY   The highest level of the sacrament of Holy Order. Those who are ordained to the episcopacy are called "bishops." The word is derived from *episkopos*, meaning "overseer."

EPISCOPATE   The body of bishops.

ESCHATOLOGICAL   Pertaining to a theological attitude which sees all reality in light of the coming Kingdom of God.

ESCHATOLOGY   Literally, "the study of the last things." That area of theology which focuses on the Kingdom of God, judgment, heaven, hell, purgatory, the resurrection of the body, and the Second Coming of Christ.

EUCHARIST   Literally, a "thanksgiving." The common name for the Mass, or Lord's Supper.

EVANGELICAL   Pertaining to the Gospel and to a theological approach which emphasizes the preaching of Jesus and the biblical expression of that preaching.

EVANGELIZATION   The proclamation of the Gospel.

EX OPERE OPERANTIS   "From the work of the worker." A phrase explaining how a *sacramental* (see below) achieves its effect: not only by the prayer of the Church but also, and necessarily, by the faith and disposition of the recipient and minister.

EX OPERE OPERATO   "From the work done." A phrase explaining how a sacrament achieves its effect: not because of the faith of the recipient and/or the worthiness of the minister but because of the power of Christ who acts within and through it.

EXCOMMUNICATION   The expulsion of an individual from the Church, more particularly from the Eucharist.

EXEGESIS   The scientific interpretation of the texts of Sacred Scripture.

EXISTENTIALIST THEOLOGY   An approach to theology which emphasizes the value of the individual person, the primacy of conscience, and the importance of freedom and authenticity in decision-making.

EXPIATION   See *atonement*.

EXTRA ECCLESIAM NULLA SALUS   "Outside the Church no salvation." The belief that unless one is somehow related to the

Church, that person cannot be saved. The meaning of the formula has been disputed. Father Leonard Feeney, S.J., of Boston, was condemned by the Vatican in 1949 for an extreme interpretation of the principle.

EXTREME UNCTION   The former name for the sacrament of the Anointing of the Sick.

FAITH   Personal knowledge of God. Christian faith is personal knowledge of God as disclosed in Jesus Christ.

FAITH DEVELOPMENT   The process by which faith advances progressively through various stages of human growth—e.g., from an adolescent's desire to win approval to a mature adult's commitment to values apart from self-interest.

FATHERS OF THE CHURCH   Writers of Christian antiquity who had a major impact on the doctrinal tradition of the Church. The period of the Fathers is said to have ended by the mid-eighth century.

FIDEISM   The nineteenth-century view that faith has no rational content at all. Conviction is rooted in the heart, not the mind.

FIDES FIDUCIALIS   Luther's notion of faith as "trust." This view was rejected by the Council Trent (1547) because it seemed to deny any objective content to faith.

FILIOQUE   Literally, "and from the Son." This word was added to the Creed of Nicea-Constantinople at the end of the seventh century, contending that the Holy Spirit proceeds from the Father and the Son as from a single principle. It was opposed by the Greek Church, which preferred the term *"per Filium"* to emphasize the primacy of God the Father in the work of salvation.

FLORENCE   An ecumenical council, held in this Italian city in 1439, which not only tried to heal the East-West schism but also defined the seven sacraments.

FUNDAMENTAL OPTION   The radical orientation of one's whole life toward or away from God. Akin to conversion. Our destiny is determined by this fundamental "choice" and not by individual acts, unless those acts are such that our basic relationship with God is fully engaged.

FUNDAMENTAL THEOLOGY   That area of theology which deals with the most basic introductory questions: e.g., revelation, faith, authority, the ways of knowing God, the nature and task of theology itself.

GALLICANISM   A form of national *conciliarism* (see above) peculiar to France (Gaul), and implicitly rejected by the First Vatican Council (1869-1870).

GAUDIUM ET SPES   Vatican II's *Pastoral Constitution on the Church in the Modern World.*

GNOSTIC   Pertaining to a theological attitude which exaggerates the role of knowledge (*gnosis*) in salvation and which insists that such saving knowledge is available to only a select few.

GNOSTICISM   The earliest of Christian heresies, first refuted in the Fourth Gospel. Besides stressing the role of saving knowledge, it also denied the goodness of creation and of the material order.

GOSPEL   The "good news" proclaimed by Jesus Christ and thereafter by the Apostles and the Church. The Gospel is interpreted and recorded in the four Gospels of Matthew, Mark, Luke, and John.

GRACE   The presence of God.

GRACE, ACTUAL   The presence of God given as a power to guide particular human actions.

GRACE, CREATED   The presence of God in particular persons, manifested in virtues, in gifts of the Holy Spirit, etc.

GRACE, SANCTIFYING   The abiding presence of God in the human person.

GRACE, UNCREATED   God. The uncreated Word of God in Jesus Christ. The Holy Spirit.

HEILSGESCHICHTE   See *salvation history.*

HELLENISM   Theological and philosophical movements dictated and shaped by Greek culture, where the emphasis is on the realm of ideas and universal principles rather than on the world of the concrete and the changeable.

HELLENIZATION OF DOGMA   The progressive introduction of Greek categories in the formulation and interpretation of the Christian faith. They are often distinguished from biblical categories of faith.

HERESY   Literally, a "choice." It is the denial of a *dogma* (see above).

HERMENEUTICS   The science of interpretation; the body of principles which governs the interpretation of any statement or text.

HIERARCHICAL Pertaining to a theological mentality which emphasizes the role of ecclesiastical officers in the life and teaching of the Church.

HIERARCHY Literally, "rule by priests." It is the body of ordained ministers in the Church: pope, bishops, priests, and deacons.

HISTORICAL CONSCIOUSNESS A theological and philosophical mentality which is attentive to the impact of history on human thought and action and which, therefore, takes into account the concrete and the changeable. Distinguished from *classicism* (see above).

HISTORICITY That fundamental human condition by which we are set in time and shaped by the movement of history.

HISTORY The movement of the world toward the final Kingdom of God under the impact of God's grace and the shaping influence of human freedom.

HOMOIOUSIOS Literally, "of a *similar* substance." This term was proposed by Eusebius of Caesarea, who thought it was closer to the teaching of Sacred Scripture, namely, that the Son is *like* the Father. It is simply a different emphasis and approach and is not regarded as unorthodox if correctly understood.

HOMOOUSIOS Literally, "of the *same* substance." Used in the teaching of the early Christological councils, especially Nicea (325), to affirm that the Father and the *Logos* (see below) are of the same substance, or nature. Therefore, Jesus is truly divine.

HORIZON A philosophical term meaning the range, or context, of one's view of reality and, therefore, the spectrum of questions one is prepared to ask about human existence, the world, meaning, etc.

HUMANAE VITAE The 1968 encyclical of Pope Paul VI in which he condemned as immoral all artificial means of regulating births.

HUMANIZATION The process by which the world and its history, through heightened consciousness and freedom, become progressively truer to their vocation and closer to their final destiny in the Kingdom of God.

HYLOMORPHISM A medieval Scholastic notion which regarded all reality as composed of matter and form. The notion was applied to the theology of the Eucharist, grace, the human person, and the sacraments in general; e.g., the *matter* of a sacrament is what is used (water in Baptism), the *form* of a sacrament is the words and gestures (pouring the water and saying the baptismal formula); or, the body is the *matter* of the human person, the soul is the *form*.

HYPOSTATIC UNION   The word *hypostasis* refers to the person of the *Logos* (see below). The hypostatic union is the permanent union of divine and human natures in the one divine Person of the Word in Jesus Christ (see *Chalcedon* above).

ICONOCLASM   Literally, "the destroying of images." The negative attitude toward images (*icons*) and their veneration. An iconoclastic controversy raged in the East during the eighth and ninth centuries.

IDEALISM   The philosophical attitude which identifies reality with ideas. It is distinguished from *realism* (see below).

IDOLATRY   The worship of idols. The term applies to any tendency to equate something finite with the infinite (God).

IMMACULATE CONCEPTION   The dogma defined by Pope Pius IX in 1854 which holds that the Blessed Virgin Mary was free from sin from the very first moment of her existence. This is not to be confused with the *virgin birth* (see below).

IMPECCABILITAS   The attribute of Jesus Christ by which he is incapable of sinning.

IMPECCANTIA   The sinlessness of Jesus. Even if Jesus Christ were capable of sinning, in fact he did not sin.

INCARNATION   The process by which the Word of God became flesh. (See also *hypostatic union.*)

INDIFFERENTISM   A theological attitude which holds that one religion is as good, or as bad, as another.

INDISSOLUBILITY   The quality of permanence (literally "unbreakability") which applies to marriage.

INDULGENCE   The partial or full remission of the penalties still due to sins which have already been forgiven.

INERRANCY   The immunity of Sacred Scripture from fundamental error about God and the things of God.

INFALLIBILITY   Literally, "immunity from error." The charism by which the Church is protected from fundamental error in matters of faith and morals. It can be exercised by the pope and by an ecumenical council.

INFRALAPSARIAN   Pertaining to the period of history after the "fall" of Adam.

INITIATION, CHRISTIAN   The total liturgical and catechetical process of becoming a Christian through Baptism, Confirmation, and Eucharist.

INITIUM FIDEI   Literally, the "beginning of faith." The grace of God is necessary for the whole process of faith, from beginning to end. There is no point at which the movement of, and toward, faith is possible without the impulse of divine grace.

INSPIRATION, BIBLICAL   The guidance of the Holy Spirit in the writing of Sacred Scripture. More generally, inspiration refers to the guidance of the Holy Spirit over the whole Church.

INTEGRALISM   A theological attitude, prevalent especially in France in the nineteenth and twentieth centuries, which insists that everything must become formally and explicitly Christian before it is good. Literally, nothing is "whole" (integral) unless and until it is brought within the orbit of the Church.

INTENTIONALITY   A philosophical and theological term which refers to the purposive character of human decision-making and behavior.

INTERCOMMUNION   See *communicatio in sacris* (above).

INTERNAL FORUM   The realm of conscience and/or of the sacrament of Penance. A decision reached in the "internal forum" is known only to God, the individual, and the confessor or spiritual director.

IURE DIVINO   Literally, "by divine law." The term refers to institutions (e.g., sacraments) which are said to exist by the explicit will of God, as articulated by Christ and/or the Church. Hence, they are not subject to abolition or substantial tampering by the Church or other human agents.

JANSENISM   A seventeenth- and eighteenth-century movement in Europe, especially France, which stressed moral austerity, the evil of the human body and of human desires, and an elitist notion of salvation (Jesus died for a few).

JANSENISTIC   Pertaining to a moral attitude which displays a negative appreciation of the bodily and a fear of the sexual. It passed from France to Ireland and then to the United States of America in the late nineteenth and early twentieth centuries.

JESUS OF HISTORY/CHRIST OF FAITH   Refers to the distinction between Jesus as he actually was (and whom we can never fully know on the basis of historical evidence) and Jesus as he was understood and interpreted by the Church after the resurrection (namely, as the Christ).

JOHANNINE   Pertaining to the writings of the New Testament attributed to John, the Evangelist and the "beloved disciple," or at least to those influenced by him. These are the Fourth Gospel, the three epistles, and the Book of Revelation. They present a high Christology ("from above") and emphasize the law of love and the work of the Spirit.

JURIDICAL   Pertaining to a theological attitude which stresses the importance of law in the formation and exercise of Christian life.

JUSTIFICATION   The event by which God, acting in Jesus Christ, makes us holy (just) in the divine sight. The immediate effect of justification is *sanctification* (see below). The ultimate effect is *salvation* (see below). The foundation of justification is the *redemption* (see below).

KENOSIS   A biblical term (Philippians 2: 5-11) which refers to the "self-emptying" of Christ. He did not cling to his divinity but became obedient even unto death.

KERYGMA   The "message" of the Gospel. That which was originally proclaimed.

KERYGMATIC THEOLOGY   A theology which adheres closely to the literal meaning and emphasis of the biblical message (see also *evangelical*).

KINGDOM OF GOD   The reign, or rule, of God. It is the presence of God in the heart, in groups, in the world at large, renewing and reconciling all things. It is both a process ("reign of God") and the reality towards which the process is moving ("Kingdom of God").

KOINONIA   Community, or fellowship, produced by the Holy Spirit.

LAST THINGS   Death, judgment, heaven, hell, purgatory, Second Coming of Christ, resurrection of the body, and the fulfillment of the Kingdom of God.

LAW   In the Old Testament: the Ten Commandments, the Torah, and other norms of conduct, founded in the *Covenant* (see above). In the New Testament: the law of the Gospel, fulfilled in the commandment of love of God and love of neighbor.

xlvii

LAXISM   A moral attitude which tries to find ways of getting around Christian obligations and which always resolves the doubt in favor of exemption, even when good reasons are not present.

LEGALISM   A moral attitude which identifies morality with the literal observance of laws, even if the spirit of the law requires something more or different.

LEX ORANDI, LEX CREDENDI   "The law of praying is the law of believing." Christian belief is expressed in Christian worship. Christian worship is, in turn, a norm of faith.

LIBERALISM, BIBLICAL   The tendency to reduce the content of the Bible to its most natural meaning; e.g., Jesus had no idea that he was the Messiah or the Son of God.

LIBERALISM, THEOLOGICAL   The tendency to place a rational or humanistic interpretation on all dogmas and doctrines so that they are devoid of supernatural content. The word is sometimes used in Catholic circles to describe those who assume a critical attitude toward the teaching authority of the Church or toward traditional doctrines of the faith.

LIBERATION THEOLOGY   A type of theology which emphasizes the motif of liberation in both Old and New Testaments and which reinterprets all doctrines in terms of that motif. Forms of liberation theology include: Latin American, black, and feminist.

LITURGY   The official public worship of the Church, especially the Eucharist and the sacraments.

LOGOS   The Word of God, the Second Person of the Trinity, who became flesh in the *incarnation* (see above).

LUMEN GENTIUM   Vatican II's *Dogmatic Constitution on the Church.*

LUMEN GLORIAE   "The light of glory." That power by which we are enabled to "see God face to face" in heaven. (See also *beatific vision.*)

MACEDONIANISM   A fourth-century heresy which denied the divinity of the Holy Spirit. It was condemned by the Council of Constantinople (381).

MAGISTERIUM   The teaching authority of the Church, which belongs to some by reason of office (pope and bishops) and to others by reason of scholarly competence (theologians). The term also applies to the body of teachers.

MANICHAEISM   A blend of *dualism* and *Gnosticism* (see above for both terms), which began in the mid-third century and did not finally die out until the fourteenth.

MARIOLOGY   The theological study of the Blessed Virgin Mary in terms of her role in the Church and in our redemption.

MARTYR   Literally, a "witness." One who is put to death because of his or her faith in Jesus Christ.

MASS   The Eucharist, or Lord's Supper.

MATER ET MAGISTRA   The 1961 encyclical of Pope John XXIII on social justice.

MEDIATION   The theological principle that God is available to us and acts upon us through secondary causes: persons, places, events, things, nature, history.

MEDIEVAL   Pertaining to the period known as the Middle Ages, the beginning of which some place as early as the seventh century and the end as late as the sixteenth. The high Middle Ages are the twelfth and thirteenth centuries, which are sometimes mistakenly identified with the origins of Catholicism itself.

MERIT   Spiritual "credit" earned with God for having performed some good action.

METANOIA   See *conversion*.

METHOD   A regular and recurrent pattern of operations. A fundamental way of doing theology. Thus, an historical method treats every question from the point of view of its development from its origins to the present time.

MINISTRY   Literally, a "service." Any service publicly designated by the Church to assist in the fulfillment of its mission.

MIRACLE   An unusual event by which God makes a special impact on history. A special manifestation of the presence and power of God.

MISSION OF THE CHURCH   That for which the Church has been "sent"; i.e., its purpose: to proclaim the Gospel in word, in sacrament, in witness, and in service.

MIXED MARRIAGE   A marriage between a Catholic and one who is not a Catholic.

MODALISM   A general theological approach to the Trinity which sees the three Persons as three different modes of the one God's operations (creation, incarnation, and sanctification).

xlix

MODERNISM   An early-twentieth-century movement in Catholicism condemned by Pope Pius X because it seemed to deny the permanence of dogmas and tended to reduce all doctrines to their rational or humanistic components. (See also *liberalism, theological.*)

MODERNITY   A frame of mind induced by technology, and especially by the innovations effected by advances in communications and transportation. The modern mentality is characterized by its stress on the necessity of making choices from among a relatively large number of possibilities and, therefore, of consulting as wide a spectrum of views as possible. (See also *pluralism.*)

MONASTICISM   A style of Christian life, begun in the third century as a flight to the desert to avoid persecution and later to protest the newly privileged status of the Church; it emphasizes life-in-community, common prayer, silence, and contemplation.

MONOGENISM   The view that the whole human race is descended from a single couple, Adam and Eve. It is distinguished from *polygenism.*

MONOPHYSITISM   The teaching, condemned by the Council of Chalcedon (451), that the human nature of Christ was totally absorbed by the divine nature. As an expression of the *Alexandrian School* (see above), it emphasized the divinity of Christ.

MONOTHEISM   The belief in one God. It is distinguished from *polytheism.*

MONOTHELITISM   The view, rejected by the Third Council of Constantinople (681), that there is only one will in Christ, the divine will. This is also known as *Monenergism.*

MONTANISM   A second-century charismatic belief which stressed the imminent end of the world and imposed an austere morality in preparation for the event. Tertullian was its best-known adherent.

MORAL THEOLOGY   That branch of theology which attends to the individual and social implications of the Gospel, and which draws normative inferences for the conduct of the Church and its individual members.

MORTAL SIN   So fundamental a rejection of the Gospel and/or the will of God that it merits eternal punishment. Thus, the adjective "mortal."

MYSTERIUM ECCLESIAE   The 1973 declaration of the Congregation for the Doctrine of the Faith on infallibility and on the development of doctrine. The document is especially significant because it acknowledges the historicity of doctrinal and dogmatic statements.

MYSTERY   A reality imbued with the hidden presence of God. The term is most akin to the word *sacrament*. It also refers to the plan of God for our salvation, as worked out historically in Christ.

MYSTICISM   A human's experience of God. Christian mysticism is the experiencing of God in Jesus Christ in light of the Holy Spirit.

NATURAL LAW   The whole order of reality which, by the will of God, defines us as human persons and contributes to human development. For the Greeks, it was a "given" of reality; for the Romans, it was something to be discovered and reshaped through common sense and intelligence.

NATURE   The human condition apart from grace, but with the radical capacity to receive grace. ("Pure" nature, i.e., without the capacity for grace, does not exist.)

NEO-ORTHODOXY   The early-twentieth-century movement within Protestantism (especially Karl Barth) which sought to return to the basic principles of Reformation theology: the primacy of the Word of God, e.g.

NEOPLATONISM   The final stage of ancient Greek philosophy which strongly influenced certain Christian thinkers, especially Origen and Augustine. It stressed the reality of God as *Logos*, of finite beings as participants in the *Logos*, and as always in movement back to their source in God. Negatively, it tended to underestimate the goodness of the material order and the importance of the individual person.

NESTORIANISM   The teaching, condemned by the council of Ephesus (431), that posited two separate persons in Jesus Christ, the one human and the other divine. Therefore, Mary was the mother of the human Jesus only. As an expression of the *Antioch School* of theology (see above), it emphasized the humanity of Christ.

NICEA   The city in Asia Minor where in 325 the first ecumenical council was held to condemn *Arianism* (see above).

NOMINALISM   A medieval philosophical view which denied the reality of universal principles. Emphasis was always on the individual person, situation, or term, and on its uniqueness.

ORDAINED MINISTRY   A *ministry* (see above) conferred by the imposition of hands: diaconate, presbyterate (priesthood), and the episcopate.

ORDINATION   A sacramental act, usually involving a laying on of hands by a bishop, through which an individual is admitted to the diaconate, the presbyterate (priesthood), or the episcopate.

ORIGENISM   A tendency in Eastern theology of the third through fifth centuries which emphasized the necessity and eternity of the world and of souls and which looked upon matter as a consequence of sin.

ORIGINAL JUSTICE   The state in which the first human beings were thought to have existed before Original Sin.

ORIGINAL SIN   The state in which all human beings are now born. It is a situation or condition in which the possibility of sin becomes instead a probability because grace is not at our disposal in the manner and to the degree that God intended.

ORTHODOXY   Literally, "right praise." Consistency with the faith of the Church as embodied in Sacred Scripture, the Fathers, official teachings, and the liturgy.

PACEM IN TERRIS   The 1963 encyclical of Pope John XXIII on social justice and international development.

PARABLE   A story which makes a theological point through the use of metaphors.

PAROUSIA   The Second Coming of Christ at the end of history.

PARTHENOGENESIS   See *virgin birth.*

PASTORAL   Pertaining to the actual life of the Church, especially at the parish and diocesan levels.

PATRISTIC   Pertaining to the *Fathers of the Church* (see above).

PAULINE   Pertaining to the writings of the New Testament attributed to Paul. They are known as Epistles, or letters: Romans, 1 and 2 Corinthians, Galatians, etc.

PAULINE PRIVILEGE   Based on 1 Corinthians 7:10-16, the principle which allows a convert to the Church to remarry if his or her unbaptized spouse does not also become a Christian.

PELAGIAN   Pertaining to a theological attitude which exaggerates the role of human effort in moral life.

PELAGIANISM   A heresy with roots in the fifth century which declared that salvation is possible through human effort alone, without grace.

PENTATEUCH   The first five books of the Old Testament: Genesis, Exodus, Leviticus, Numbers, and Deuteronomy. Also known as the *Torah*, or the *Law* (see above).

PERICHORESIS   See *circumincession*.

PERSON   An existing being with the capacity for consciousness and freedom. In the Trinity, the word "person" is used analogically; i.e., Father, Son, and Holy Spirit are "like" human persons, but there are not three separate Gods, only different relationships within the Godhead and different ways in which the one God acts outside the Godhead itself. (See also *subject*.)

PERSONALISM   A theological and philosophical view which stresses the importance of the individual human being, or person, in reaching moral decisions.

PETRINE MINISTRY, OFFICE   The service rendered the Church by the pope. The papacy. Both ministry and office attend to the universal Church's need for unity in life and mission.

PETRINE PRIVILEGE   Also known as the "Privilege of the Faith." It allows the pope to dissolve a marriage between a Christian and a non-Christian when the Christian wishes to marry another Christian or the non-Christian wishes to become a Catholic and remarry.

PHENOMENOLOGY   A philosophical and theological view which begins with, and emphasizes, observable realities (phenomena) rather than general principles.

PHILOSOPHY   The branch of knowledge concerned with the ultimate meaning of reality, but it does not assume responsibility (as *theology* does) for articulating that meaning in terms of particular religious traditions. Closely related to, and sometimes indistinguishable from, theology itself.

PIETISM   A seventeenth- and eighteenth-century movement within German Lutheranism which stressed the interior life, the experience of conversion, and personal devotion to Jesus.

PIETISTIC   Pertaining to a spiritual or moral attitude which stresses personal devotion at the expense of sound biblical, theological, and doctrinal principles.

PLURALISM   The inevitable variety of human experiences and of expressions. The "discovery" of pluralism is a modern phenomenon brought about especially by advances in communications and in transportation.

PNEUMA   The Greek word for "spirit." It refers to the spiritual principle in human existence, opposed to the flesh (*sarx*).

PNEUMATOLOGICAL   Pertaining to the Holy Spirit.

POLITICAL THEOLOGY   A type of theology which stresses the relationship between Christian faith and the socio-political order or, more generally, between theory and practice.

POLYTHEISM   Belief in many gods.

POSITIVISM   A philosophical and theological view which not only begins with observable realities, as does the *phenomenological* approach (see *phenomenology* above), but insists that reality consists *only* of the concrete, the visible, and the particular. In theology it leads to reflection on God not in terms of the totality of reality but in terms of the understanding of God as given in certain sources—e.g., the Bible, the teachings of the Church.

POTENTIA OBEDIENTIALIS   The fundamental human capacity for grace.

PRAXIS   Reflective action. Reflection which is the fruit of one's concrete experience and situation. Action which is the expression of such reflection. Not identical, therefore, simply with "practice." A central term in *liberation theology* (see above).

PREDESTINATION   The eternal decree of God regarding the destination, or final goal, of all reality and especially of humankind.

PREDESTINATIONISM   The Calvinist doctrine that God decides, independently of a person's exercise of freedom and manifestation of good will, who will be saved and who will be damned. The latter decree is also known as *antecedent negative reprobation*.

PRESBYTER   A priest of the second "order"—i.e., less than a bishop but more than a deacon. A priest.

PRESBYTERATE   The body of priests.

PRIMACY   The authority which the pope has over the whole Church.

PROBABILISM   The moral principle which holds that one can safely follow a theological opinion if it is proposed by someone having sufficient theological authority and standing. *Equiprobabilism* requires that the more lenient opinion be at least as strong as the stricter opinion. *Probabiliorism* requires that the more lenient opinion be stronger than the stricter opinion.

PROCESS THEOLOGY   A type of theology which emphasizes the movement, dynamism, changeability, and relativity of God, of history, and of all reality. Closely linked on the Catholic side with the writings of Teilhard de Chardin; on the Protestant side, with Alfred North Whitehead.

PROPHECY   Literally, a "speaking on behalf (of God)." More specifically, the proclamation of a word and the doing of a deed on behalf of the Kingdom of God.

PROTOLOGY   The "study of the first things" (creation, Original Justice, Original Sin).

PROVIDENCE   God's abiding guidance of the whole created order toward the final Kingdom.

PURGATORY   The state of purification and/or maturation which one may need to enter after death and before the *beatific vision* (see above).

QUIETISM   A seventeenth-century movement in France which held that we can do nothing at all for our salvation and that the way of Christian spirituality is a way of inwardness, of resignation, and of complete passivity.

RATIONALISM   The philosophical view which holds that nothing can be accepted as true unless it can be proved by reason alone.

RATIONALISTIC   Pertaining to a philosophical and theological approach which exaggerates the powers of human reason to know truth and even God to the point where revelation is denied.

REALISM   A philosophical view which emphasizes the objectivity of things, apart from the person thinking about them. *Naive* realism assumes that things are exactly what they seem to be ("Just take a look"). *Critical* realism insists that all reality is "mediated by meaning"—i.e., the real is what we *judge* to be true, on the basis of our experience.

REAL PRESENCE   The sacramental presence of Christ in the Eucharist.

REDEMPTION   The act by which we are literally "bought back" into the grace of God by the work of Jesus Christ. See also *soteriology*.

REIGN OF GOD   The more active, or dynamic, expression for the Kingdom of God (see above). It is the Kingdom as it is now in process.

lv

RELIC An object regarded as worthy of veneration because of its connection with a saint—e.g., a piece of bone.

RELIGION The external, social, institutionalized expression of our faith in God.

RELIGIOUS Pertaining to an attitude of seeing all reality in light of the presence and action of God, and of responding to God's presence and action with reverence, gratitude, and appropriate moral behavior.

RELIGIOUS CONGREGATION, ORDER An organized group of Christians who have taken vows to live in community and to observe the evangelical counsels of poverty, chastity, and obedience.

RELIGIOUS EDUCATION That field which comes into existence at the point of intersection between theology and education. It is concerned with interpreting and directing human experience in light of the conviction that God is present to that experience, that Jesus Christ is the sacrament of God's presence in the world, and that the Church is the primary place where the presence of God in Christ is acknowledged, celebrated, and lived out.

RES ET SACRAMENTUM Literally, "the reality and the sign." In sacramental theology, it refers to the lasting effect of a sacrament—e.g., the Real Presence of Christ in the Eucharist.

RES TANTUM Literally, "the reality alone." In sacramental theology, it refers to the immediate effect of a sacrament, namely, grace.

REVELATION God's self-disclosure (literally, "unveiling") to humankind through creation, events, persons, and especially Jesus Christ.

REVIVISCENCE The revival of grace from a *character* sacrament (see above) received in *mortal sin* (see above). If a person receives a character sacrament in the state of mortal sin, the grace of that sacrament is not given. But that grace "revives" and is applied to the individual as soon as contrition blots out the sin.

RIGHT A power that we have to do things which are necessary for achieving the end or purpose for which we are destined as rational and free persons.

RIGHTEOUSNESS The state of being just in the sight of God.

SABELLIANISM A third- and fourth-century heresy which held that God is three only in relation to the world. There is no trinity of Persons *within* the godhead. A form of *Modalism* (see above).

SACRAMENT   In general, any visible sign of God's invisible presence. Specifically, a sign through which the Church manifests its faith and communicates the saving reality (grace) of God which is present in the Church and in the signs themselves. In Catholic doctrine there are Baptism, Confirmation, Eucharist, Penance, Marriage, Holy Order, and the Anointing of the Sick.

SACRAMENTAL   A grace-bearing sign which does not so fully express the nature of the Church and which, according to Catholic doctrine, does not carry the guarantee of grace associated with the seven sacraments—e.g., holy water, the palm branches used on Palm Sunday, a crucifix.

SACRAMENTALITY, PRINCIPLE OF   The fundamentally Catholic notion that all reality is potentially and in fact the bearer of God's presence and the instrument of divine action on our behalf. Closely related to the principle of *mediation* (see above).

SACRAMENTUM TANTUM   Literally, "the sign alone." In sacramental theology, it is a rite or sacred action—e.g., the pouring of the water and the recitation of the formula "I baptize you...."

SALVATION   From the Latin word *salus*, meaning "health." It is the goal and end-product of creation, the incarnation, the redemption, conversion, justification, and sanctification. To be saved is to be fully and permanently united with God and with one another in God.

SALVATION-HISTORY   History perceived as the arena in which God progressively brings humankind toward the Kingdom. Salvation-history begins with creation, ends with the Second Coming of Christ, and has its midpoint in Jesus Christ. Such a view of history is associated with Luke in the New Testament and with Oscar Cullmann in modern theology.

SANCTIFICATION   The state of holiness by reason of the presence of God within oneself. It is not to be confused with *justification* (see above), which is the act or process by which we are made holy, or just, in God's sight.

SANCTIFYING GRACE   See *grace*.

SARX   The Greek word for "flesh." It is the body apart from the spirit, and even opposed to it.

SATAN   Literally, "the evil one." The personification of evil. The one in whom all evil is focused.

lvii

SCHISM   A breach of Church unity which occurs when a whole group or community separates itself from the rest of the Body of Christ. In Catholic theology, this happens when communion with the pope is broken.

SCHOLASTIC   Pertaining to a general approach to the doing of theology which derives its style from the medieval "schools." Such theology is deductive, abstract, doctrinal, and *classicist* (see above).

SCHOLASTICISM   A theological and philosophical movement in the Middle Ages attached to certain "schools" (thus, the term "scholastic") and emphasizing the interpretation of texts, especially of other theologians and philosophers rather than of the Bible and the Fathers of the Church.

SEMI-PELAGIANISM   The heresy, condemned by the Second Council of Orange (527), which held that the beginning of faith (*initium fidei*) is made independently of God's grace but that thereafter the grace of God is necessary for salvation.

SENSUS FIDELIUM   Literally, "the sense of the faithful." It is one of the norms of theological truth, namely, the actual belief of Christians down through the centuries.

SHEOL   The Old Testament name for the "underworld" inhabited by all the dead. Not to be confused with hell, which is a state of eternal alienation from God because of sin.

SIMONY   The buying and selling of spiritual goods.

SIMUL JUSTUS ET PECCATOR   Literally, "at the same time just and sinner." A formula made famous by Martin Luther to make the point that even though we have been declared just by God because of Christ, we are still as corrupt as ever inside. Catholic doctrine insists that *justification* leads to *sanctification* (see above).

SIN   Any deliberate infidelity to the will of God. It can be individual or social. The condition that makes sin possible, not to say probable, is *Original Sin* (see above). Sins which reverse our *fundamental option* (see above) for God, are *mortal sins*. Sins which reflect poorly on our commitment to God but which do not reverse our course toward God are *serious sins*. Less serious sins are *venial sins*. Below those in gravity are *imperfections*.

SOCIAL DOCTRINE   The body of official teachings, developed since Pope Leo XIII in 1891, which identify the implications of the Gospel in matters pertaining to social justice, peace, and human rights.

SOCIALIZATION A process by which nations and humankind in general are becoming increasingly interdependent. Emphasized by Pope John XXIII's social encyclicals, *Mater et Magistra* (1961) and *Pacem in Terris* (1963).

SOLA FIDE Literally, "by faith alone." The Protestant principle that we are saved by faith alone, not by good works. Catholic doctrine insists that faith must issue in good works and that good works are saving insofar as they are expressions of faith.

SOLA GRATIA Literally, "by grace alone." The Protestant principle that we are saved by grace alone, i.e., by God's action and not at all by our own. Catholic doctrine insists that God requires our free cooperation although it is God alone who makes that cooperation possible.

SOLA SCRIPTURA Literally, "by Scripture alone." The Protestant principle that the Word of God is given to us in the Bible alone and not in the official teachings of the Church. Catholic doctrine insists that the Bible itself is the Church's book—i.e., that the authority of the Church has determined which books are inspired and, therefore, *canonical* (see above). Furthermore, all official teachings are subject to the authority of the Word of God as contained in the Bible.

SOMA The Greek word for "body." But in contradistinction to *sarx* (see above), *soma* stands for the whole person: flesh and spirit together.

SOTERIOLOGY Literally, "the study of salvation." It is that area of theology which focuses on the passion, death, resurrection, and exaltation of Christ insofar as they bring about our salvation.

SPIRITUAL Pertaining to an attitude and style which reflect an attentiveness to the presence and action of God within us and in the world around us.

SPIRITUALITY Our way of being *religious* (see above). *Christian* spirituality is the cultivation of a style of life consistent with the presence of the Spirit of the Risen Christ within us and with our status as members of the Body of Christ.

SUBJECT The human *person* (see above) insofar as the person is conscious, interrelates with others, and freely determines who and what he or she will become.

SUBJECTIVE Pertaining to a philosophical and theological attitude which emphasizes the values of individual consciousness and freedom.

SUBORDINATIONISM   A second- and third-century heresy which held that the Son and the Holy Spirit are less than the Father because they proceed from the Father. Therefore, the Son and the Spirit are not fully divine.

SUBSIDIARITY   A principle in Catholic social doctrine which holds that nothing should be done by a higher agency which can be done as well, or better, by a lower agency.

SUMMA THEOLOGICA   The major work of systematic theology done by Thomas Aquinas.

SUPERNATURAL   Pertaining to that which exceeds the power and capacity of human nature apart from the grace of God.

"SUPERNATURAL EXISTENTIAL"   A term used by Karl Rahner, meaning our radical capacity for God. It is the permanent modification of the human person, in the depths of one's being, by which the person is transformed from within and oriented toward God. It is not grace itself, but God's offer of grace.

SYMBOL   A sign which embodies what it signifies. Close to the meaning of *sacrament* (see above). Therefore, it is not an arbitrary sign, but a sign that is intimately connected with what it signifies.

SYNOD   An official assembly of the Church at the international, national, regional, provincial, or diocesan level.

SYNOPTICS   The first three Gospels, Matthew, Mark, and Luke, so called because when they are read side by side (synoptically), certain parallels in structure and content readily emerge.

SYSTEMATIC THEOLOGY   That theology which tries to see the Christian tradition as a whole, by understanding the whole in terms of the interrelationships among all its parts, and each part in terms of its relationships to other parts and to the whole.

TELEOLOGICAL   Pertaining to a way of doing moral theology which emphasizes the end (*telos*), or purpose, of human existence.

THEOLOGY   The ordered effort to bring our experience of God to the level of intelligent expression. It is "faith seeking understanding" (Anselm).

THEOTOKOS   Literally, "the Bearer of God." The title given to Mary at the Council of Ephesus (431), which taught that there is one divine person in Jesus Christ, not two as the Nestorians argued. Therefore, Mary is truly the "Mother of God" and not only the mother of the human Jesus.

THOMISM   An approach to theology derived from Thomas Aquinas. It is based on *critical realism* (see above under *realism*) and follows a strongly *systematic* method (see above). It is not to be confused with *Scholasticism* (see above).

TRADITION   Both the process of "handing on" the faith and that which has been handed on. Tradition (upper-case) includes Scripture, the essential doctrines of the Church, the major writings and teachings of the Fathers, the liturgical life of the Church, and the living and lived faith of the whole Church down through the centuries. Tradition (upper-case) is not to be confused with tradition (lower-case), which includes customs, institutions, practices which are simply usual ways of thinking about, and giving expression to, the Christian faith.

TRADITIONALISM   The nineteenth-century opinion, rejected by Vatican I, that reason can know nothing at all about religious truth because such knowledge comes only through the revelation that has been "handed down" to us. As a modern term, it refers to the attitude of those Catholics who are opposed to the reforms of Vatican II and who wish the Church would return to its traditional pre-Vatican II ways.

TRANSCENDENTAL   Pertaining to that which is above and beyond the ordinary, the concrete, the tangible—i.e., to God.

TRANSCENDENTAL THOMISM   That twentieth-century approach to theology which is rooted in the principle that God is already present to life as a principle that renders all life open to becoming something more than it is already.

TRANSUBSTANTIATION   The official Catholic teaching, given by the Council of Trent, that the substance of the bread and the wine are changed into the substance of Christ's body and blood at the Eucharist, so that nothing of the bread and wine remains except what is accidental—e.g., taste, shape, weight. This teaching is distinguished from *consubstantiation* (see above).

TRENT   The Italian city in which the nineteenth ecumenical council was held from 1545 to 1563, and hence the council itself. This council was the Catholic Church's principal response to the Protestant Reformation. It defined the canon of Sacred Scripture, Original Sin, grace, justification, the seven sacraments, etc. Trent was the primary influence on Catholic life until the pontificate of John XXIII (1958-1963).

TRINITARIAN   Pertaining to a theological emphasis which views all doctrines in light of the creative activity of the Father, the redemptive work of the Son, and the reconciling action of the Holy Spirit.

TRINITY, ECONOMIC   The reality of the Trinity insofar as the triune God is active and manifested in the world and its history: the Father as creator, the Son as redeemer, the Spirit as reconciler. Refers, therefore, to the exterior activity of the Trinity in history.

TRINITY, IMMANENT   The reality of the Trinity insofar as the three Persons are different not in terms of their different work on our behalf but in terms of their different relationships, one to another; e.g., the Father is unbegotten, the Son is begotten. Refers, therefore, to the inner life of the Trinity.

TRITHEISM   Belief in three gods. An exaggeration of the doctrine of the Trinity.

TWELVE, THE   The twelve men directly called by Jesus to carry his message of the Kingdom of God to the world. All of the Twelve were apostles, but not all apostles were among the original Twelve.

TYPE   A person in whom the qualities of a greater or later reality are somehow "typified" or anticipated—e.g., Mary as a "type" of the Church, and Moses as a "type" of Christ.

ULTRAMONTANISM   Literally, "beyond the mountains" (the Alps). It is a form of rigid *traditionalism* (see above) developed in France, distrustful of theological reflection, and excessively loyal to the Holy See "beyond the mountains."

VATICAN   The territory politically operated and controlled by the papacy, and the site of the twentieth (1869-1870) and twenty-first (1962-1965) ecumenical councils. *Vatican I* addressed itself to the questions of reason and faith, on the one hand, and papal primacy and papal infallibility, on the other. *Vatican II* opened the Church to more of its own members, to other Christians, and to the whole world.

VENIAL SIN   A less serious infidelity to the will of God, sufficient to diminish one's Christian character (see *character, moral*) but not to reverse one's fundamental orientation toward God.

VIATICUM   Literally, "on the way with you." The last sacrament, i.e., the final reception of Holy Communion before death.

VIRGIN BIRTH The belief that Jesus became a human being without the cooperation of a human father. This is not to be confused with the *Immaculate Conception* (see above).

VIRGINAL CONCEPTION The belief that Jesus was conceived in the womb of Mary without the cooperation of a human father.

VIRGINITY OF MARY The belief that Mary was a virgin throughout her life, including the time when she conceived and brought forth Jesus, her Son.

VIRTUE The power to realize moral good and to do it joyfully and with perseverance in spite of obstacles. *Theological* virtues are those which have been *infused* by God: faith, hope, and charity. The *moral* virtues—prudence, justice, temperance, and fortitude—are those which have to be *acquired* through cooperation with God's grace and which, in turn, are the linchpins (*cardinal* virtues) of other, lesser virtues.

VOLUNTARISM A theological and philosophical view which exaggerates the place and function of the human will in the attainment of truth as well as moral good. It is the opposite of *rationalism*.

VULGATE The name given since the thirteenth century to the Latin translation of the Bible done by St. Jerome.

WORLD The totality of created reality. Insofar as the world is shaped and directed by human consciousness and human freedom under the grace of God, the world is identical with *history* (see above).

YAHWEH The Old Testament name for God.

INDEX OF PERSONAL NAMES

INDEX OF SUBJECTS

This index should be used in conjunction with the Table of Contents, Index of Personal Names, and Glossary.

Corporal works of mercy, 991
Corporate personality, 163, 593, 596
Counter-Reformation, 635-8
Covenant: 203-4, 264, 588-9, 594-5,
  912, 915-16, 981; and faith, 31,
  32; and creation, 159; and Jesus
  Christ, 159; and Judasim, 272;
  and Last Supper, 758; and
  spirituality, 1058-9
Creation: goodness of, 135, 136, 225,
  1064; and revelation, 206;
  doctrine of, 224-8; and
  incarnation, 386; and
  marriage, 788
Creaturehood, 151
"Credo of the People of God," 352,
  1142, 1144, 1151
Critical realism, 1178, 1179,
  1182, 1183
Crucifixion: 405-6, 479-80, 486; and
  resurrection, 417-18; and
  redemption, 420, 540-1, 556; and
  spirituality, 1077
Crusades, 621, 1114, 1146, 1175
Culture, 382
Curia, Roman, 619, 630, 635,
  661, 680
Cursillo Movement, 1079

Deaconesses, 849-51, 852, 853
Deacons, 557, 800, 804, 850
Dead Sea Scrolls, 396-7, 424
Death: 117-18, 123, 137, 166, 167,
  193, 194, 974, 1060, 1103,
  1135-8; and Original Sin, 163,
  1136; Hebrew concept, 1135;
  medieval notions, 1136
"Death-of-God" theology, 60, 94,
  315, 317, 498-9
Declaration on Christian Education,
  683
*Declaration on the Relationship of
  the Church to Non-Christian
  Religions,* 273, 275, 678
Declaration on Religious Freedom,
  664, 667-8, 706, 1003
Decree on the Apostolate of the Laity,
  679-80
*Decree on the Appropriate Renewal
  of Religious Life,* 682

*Decree on the Bishops' Pastoral Office
  in the Church,* 680
*Decree on the Church's Missionary
  Activity,* 679
Decree on Eastern Catholic Churches,
  680
Decree on Ecumenism, 675, 677,
  678, 856
*Decree on the Instruments of Social
  Communication,* 683
*Decree on the Ministry and Life of
  Priests,* 681
Decree on Priestly Formation, 681-2
Deism, 257, 304, 325
Demonology, 1153-4
Deontology, 941, 942
Deposit of faith, 213, 220
"Descent into hell," 1152
Despair, 965, 973
Detachment, 1065, 1068, 1071, 1081
Deterrence, policy of, 1041-2
Devil. *See* Satan
Devotio Moderna, 1065
Devotions, 1063, 1069
Diaconate, 744, 807, 846, 850
Dialectics, 84, 312, 1063
Dialogue Mass, 666, 762
Diaspora Church, 662
Dictatus Papae, 619, 660
Didache, 750, 802, 803
Diocese, 680-1, 685, 801, 810, 832
Disarmament, 1039, 1041
Discernment, 980-1, 1062, 1088-90
Disciples, 577
Discipleship, 919, 1110
Dispensation, 709, 794, 1180
Dissent, 71-72
Distributive justice, 985, 1046, 1047,
  1048, 1049
Divine law, 781, 830
Divinization, 152, 155, 156, 165
Divino Afflante Spiritu, 56, 399, 494,
  646, 647
Divorce, 533, 616, 789, 925
Divorce and remarriage, 794, 797
Docetism, 440-1, 444, 446, 455, 472,
  477, 495, 502, 517, 535, 611,
  870, 871
Doctrinal theology, 58